M000166658

20

SAVITRI

A LEGEND AND A SYMBOL

Sri Aurobindo

SAVITRI

A LEGEND AND A SYMBOL

LOTUS LIGHT PUBLICATIONS
Box 325, Twin Lakes, WI 53181
USA

First edition 1950-51
First American edition 1995

This edition is published and distributed in the United States by Lotus
Light Publications, Box 325, Twin Lakes, WI 53181 by arrangement
with Sri Aurobindo Ashram Trust, Publication Department,
Pondicherry 605002 India.

ISBN 0-941524-80-9
Library of Congress Catalog Card #94-72970

Printed at Sri Aurobindo Ashram Press
Pondicherry, India

Printed in India.

Publisher's Note

This edition of *Savitri*, the first to be published in America, is textually the same as the fourth, critically revised edition published in India in 1993. This edition is the result of a systematic comparison of the previous text with the manuscripts. Sri Aurobindo's letters on the poem are included at the end.

Contents

CONTENTS

Book Three

THE BOOK OF THE DIVINE MOTHER

CONTENTS

PART TWO

Book Four

THE BOOK OF BIRTH AND QUEST

Book Five

THE BOOK OF LOVE

Book Six

THE BOOK OF FATE

CONTENTS

CONTENTS

Author's Note

The tale of Satyavan and Savitri is recited in the Mahabharata as a story of conjugal love conquering death. But this legend is, as shown by many features of the human tale, one of the many symbolic myths of the Vedic cycle. Satyavan is the soul carrying the divine truth of being within itself but descended into the grip of death and ignorance; Savitri is the Divine Word, daughter of the Sun, goddess of the supreme Truth who comes down and is born to save; Aswapati, the Lord of the Horse, her human father, is the Lord of Tapasya, the concentrated energy of spiritual endeavour that helps us to rise from the mortal to the immortal planes; Dyumatsena, Lord of the Shining Hosts, father of Satyavan, is the Divine Mind here fallen blind, losing its celestial kingdom of vision, and through that loss its kingdom of glory. Still this is not a mere allegory, the characters are not personified qualities, but incarnations or emanations of living and conscious Forces with whom we can enter into concrete touch and they take human bodies in order to help man and show him the way from his mortal state to a divine consciousness and immortal life.

SRI AUROBINDO

PART ONE

BOOKS I-III

BOOK ONE

The Book of Beginnings

Canto One

The Symbol Dawn

IT WAS the hour before the Gods awake.
Across the path of the divine Event
The huge foreboding mind of Night, alone
In her unlit temple of eternity,
Lay stretched immobile upon Silence' marge.
Almost one felt, opaque, impenetrable,
In the sombre symbol of her eyeless muse
The abysm of the unbodied Infinite;
A fathomless zero occupied the world.
A power of fallen boundless self awake
Between the first and the last Nothingness,
Recalling the tenebrous womb from which it came,
Turned from the insoluble mystery of birth
And the tardy process of mortality
And longed to reach its end in vacant Nought.
As in a dark beginning of all things,
A mute featureless semblance of the Unknown
Repeating for ever the unconscious act,
Prolonging for ever the unseeing will,
Cradled the cosmic drowse of ignorant Force
Whose moved creative slumber kindles the suns
And carries our lives in its somnambulist whirl.
Athwart the vain enormous trance of Space,
Its formless stupor without mind or life,
A shadow spinning through a soulless Void,
Thrown back once more into unthinking dreams,
Earth wheeled abandoned in the hollow gulfs
Forgetful of her spirit and her fate.
The impassive skies were neutral, empty, still.
Then something in the inscrutable darkness stirred;
A nameless movement, an unthought Idea

Insistent, dissatisfied, without an aim,
Something that wished but knew not how to be,
Teased the Inconscient to wake Ignorance.
A throe that came and left a quivering trace,
Gave room for an old tired want unfilled,
At peace in its subconscient moonless cave
To raise its head and look for absent light,
Straining closed eyes of vanished memory,
Like one who searches for a bygone self
And only meets the corpse of his desire.
It was as though even in this Nought's profound,
Even in this ultimate dissolution's core,
There lurked an unremembering entity,
Survivor of a slain and buried past
Condemned to resume the effort and the pang,
Reviving in another frustrate world.
An unshaped consciousness desired light
And a blank prescience yearned towards distant change.
As if a childlike finger laid on a cheek
Reminded of the endless need in things
The heedless Mother of the universe,
An infant longing clutched the sombre Vast.
Insensibly somewhere a breach began:
A long lone line of hesitating hue
Like a vague smile tempting a desert heart
Troubled the far rim of life's obscure sleep.
Arrived from the other side of boundlessness
An eye of deity peered through the dumb deeps;
A scout in a reconnaissance from the sun,
It seemed amid a heavy cosmic rest,
The torpor of a sick and weary world,
To seek for a spirit sole and desolate
Too fallen to recollect forgotten bliss.
Intervening in a mindless universe,
Its message crept through the reluctant hush
Calling the adventure of consciousness and joy

And, conquering Nature's disillusioned breast,
Compelled renewed consent to see and feel.
A thought was sown in the unsounded Void,
A sense was born within the darkness' depths,
A memory quivered in the heart of Time
As if a soul long dead were moved to live:
But the oblivion that succeeds the fall,
Had blotted the crowded tablets of the past,
And all that was destroyed must be rebuilt
And old experience laboured out once more.
All can be done if the god-touch is there.
A hope stole in that hardly dared to be
Amid the Night's forlorn indifference.
As if solicited in an alien world
With timid and hazardous instinctive grace,
Orphaned and driven out to seek a home,
An errant marvel with no place to live,
Into a far-off nook of heaven there came
A slow miraculous gesture's dim appeal.
The persistent thrill of a transfiguring touch
Persuaded the inert black quietude
And beauty and wonder disturbed the fields of God.
A wandering hand of pale enchanted light
That glowed along a fading moment's brink,
Fixed with gold panel and opalescent hinge
A gate of dreams ajar on mystery's verge.
One lucent corner windowing hidden things
Forced the world's blind immensity to sight.
The darkness failed and slipped like a falling cloak
From the reclining body of a god.
Then through the pallid rift that seemed at first
Hardly enough for a trickle from the suns,
Outpoured the revelation and the flame.
The brief perpetual sign recurred above.
A glamour from unreached transcendences
Iridescent with the glory of the Unseen,

A message from the unknown immortal Light
Ablaze upon creation's quivering edge,
Dawn built her aura of magnificent hues
And buried its seed of grandeur in the hours.
An instant's visitor the godhead shone.
On life's thin border awhile the Vision stood
And bent over earth's pondering forehead curve.
Interpreting a recondite beauty and bliss
In colour's hieroglyphs of mystic sense,
It wrote the lines of a significant myth
Telling of a greatness of spiritual dawns,
A brilliant code penned with the sky for page.
Almost that day the epiphany was disclosed
Of which our thoughts and hopes are signal flares;
A lonely splendour from the invisible goal
Almost was flung on the opaque Inane.
Once more a tread perturbed the vacant Vasts;
Infinity's centre, a Face of rapturous calm
Parted the eternal lids that open heaven;
A Form from far beatitudes seemed to near.
Ambassadress twixt eternity and change,
The omniscient Goddess leaned across the breadths
That wrap the fated journeyings of the stars
And saw the spaces ready for her feet.
Once she half looked behind for her veiled sun,
Then, thoughtful, went to her immortal work.
Earth felt the Imperishable's passage close:
The waking ear of Nature heard her steps
And wideness turned to her its limitless eye,
And, scattered on sealed depths, her luminous smile
Kindled to fire the silence of the worlds.
All grew a consecration and a rite.
Air was a vibrant link between earth and heaven;
The wide-winged hymn of a great priestly wind
Arose and failed upon the altar hills;
The high boughs prayed in a revealing sky.

Here where our half-lit ignorance skirts the gulfs
On the dumb bosom of the ambiguous earth,
Here where one knows not even the step in front
And Truth has her throne on the shadowy back of doubt,
On this anguished and precarious field of toil
Outspread beneath some large indifferent gaze,
Impartial witness of our joy and bale,
Our prostrate soil bore the awakening ray.
Here too the vision and prophetic gleam
Lit into miracles common meaningless shapes;
Then the divine afflatus, spent, withdrew,
Unwanted, fading from the mortal's range.
A sacred yearning lingered in its trace,
The worship of a Presence and a Power
Too perfect to be held by death-bound hearts,
The prescience of a marvellous birth to come.
Only a little the god-light can stay:
Spiritual beauty illumining human sight
Lines with its passion and mystery Matter's mask
And squanders eternity on a beat of Time.
As when a soul draws near the sill of birth,
Adjoining mortal time to Timelessness,
A spark of deity lost in Matter's crypt
Its lustre vanishes in the inconscient planes,
That transitory glow of magic fire
So now dissolved in bright accustomed air.
The message ceased and waned the messenger.
The single Call, the uncompanioned Power,
Drew back into some far-off secret world
The hue and marvel of the supernal beam:
She looked no more on our mortality.
The excess of beauty natural to god-kind
Could not uphold its claim on time-born eyes;
Too mystic-real for space-tenancy
Her body of glory was expunged from heaven:
The rarity and wonder lived no more.

There was the common light of earthly day.
Affranchised from the respite of fatigue
Once more the rumour of the speed of Life
Pursued the cycles of her blinded quest.
All sprang to their unvarying daily acts;
The thousand peoples of the soil and tree
Obeyed the unforeseeing instant's urge,
And, leader here with his uncertain mind,
Alone who stares at the future's covered face,
Man lifted up the burden of his fate.

And Savitri too awoke among these tribes
That hastened to join the brilliant Summoner's chant
And, lured by the beauty of the apparent ways,
Acclaimed their portion of ephemeral joy.
Akin to the eternity whence she came,
No part she took in this small happiness;
A mighty stranger in the human field,
The embodied Guest within made no response.
The call that wakes the leap of human mind,
Its chequered eager motion of pursuit,
Its fluttering-hued illusion of desire,
Visited her heart like a sweet alien note.
Time's message of brief light was not for her.
In her there was the anguish of the gods
Imprisoned in our transient human mould,
The deathless conquered by the death of things.
A vaster Nature's joy had once been hers,
But long could keep not its gold heavenly hue
Or stand upon this brittle earthly base.
A narrow movement on Time's deep abysm,
Life's fragile littleness denied the power,
The proud and conscious wideness and the bliss
She had brought with her into the human form,
The calm delight that weds one soul to all,
The key to the flaming doors of ecstasy.

Earth's grain that needs the sap of pleasure and tears
Rejected the undying rapture's boon:
Offered to the daughter of infinity
Her passion-flower of love and doom she gave.
In vain now seemed the splendid sacrifice.
A prodigal of her rich divinity,
Her self and all she was she had lent to men,
Hoping her greater being to implant
And in their body's lives acclimatise
That heaven might native grow on mortal soil.
Hard is it to persuade earth-nature's change;
Mortality bears ill the eternal's touch:
It fears the pure divine intolerance
Of that assault of ether and of fire;
It murmurs at its sorrowless happiness,
Almost with hate repels the light it brings;
It trembles at its naked power of Truth
And the might and sweetness of its absolute Voice.
Inflicting on the heights the abysm's law,
It sullies with its mire heaven's messengers:
Its thorns of fallen nature are the defence
It turns against the saviour hands of Grace;
It meets the sons of God with death and pain.
A glory of lightnings traversing the earth-scene,
Their sun-thoughts fading, darkened by ignorant minds,
Their work betrayed, their good to evil turned,
The cross their payment for the crown they gave,
Only they leave behind a splendid Name.
A fire has come and touched men's hearts and gone;
A few have caught flame and risen to greater life.
Too unlike the world she came to help and save,
Her greatness weighed upon its ignorant breast
And from its dim chasms welled a dire return,
A portion of its sorrow, struggle, fall.
To live with grief, to confront death on her road,—
The mortal's lot became the Immortal's share.

Thus trapped in the gin of earthly destinies,
Awaiting her ordeal's hour abode,
Outcast from her inborn felicity,
Accepting life's obscure terrestrial robe,
Hiding herself even from those she loved,
The godhead greater by a human fate.
A dark foreknowledge separated her
From all of whom she was the star and stay;
Too great to impart the peril and the pain,
In her torn depths she kept the grief to come.
As one who watching over men left blind
Takes up the load of an unwitting race,
Harbouring a foe whom with her heart she must feed,
Unknown her act, unknown the doom she faced,
Unhelped she must foresee and dread and dare.
The long-foreknown and fatal morn was here
Bringing a noon that seemed like every noon.
For Nature walks upon her mighty way
Unheeding when she breaks a soul, a life;
Leaving her slain behind she travels on:
Man only marks and God's all-seeing eyes.
Even in this moment of her soul's despair,
In its grim rendezvous with death and fear,
No cry broke from her lips, no call for aid;
She told the secret of her woe to none:
Calm was her face and courage kept her mute.
Yet only her outward self suffered and strove;
Even her humanity was half divine:
Her spirit opened to the Spirit in all,
Her nature felt all Nature as its own.
Apart, living within, all lives she bore;
Aloof, she carried in herself the world:
Her dread was one with the great cosmic dread,
Her strength was founded on the cosmic mights;
The universal Mother's love was hers.
Against the evil at life's afflicted roots,

Her own calamity its private sign,
Of her pangs she made a mystic poignant sword.
A solitary mind, a world-wide heart,
To the lone Immortal's unshared work she rose.
At first life grieved not in her burdened breast:
On the lap of earth's original somnolence
Inert, released into forgetfulness,
Prone it reposed, unconscious on mind's verge,
Obtuse and tranquil like the stone and star.
In a deep cleft of silence twixt two realms
She lay remote from grief, unsawn by care,
Nothing recalling of the sorrow here.
Then a slow faint remembrance shadowlike moved,
And sighing she laid her hand upon her bosom
And recognised the close and lingering ache,
Deep, quiet, old, made natural to its place,
But knew not why it was there nor whence it came.
The Power that kindles mind was still withdrawn:
Heavy, unwilling were life's servitors
Like workers with no wages of delight;
Sullen, the torch of sense refused to burn;
The unassisted brain found not its past.
Only a vague earth-nature held the frame.
But now she stirred, her life shared the cosmic load.
At the summons of her body's voiceless call
Her strong far-winging spirit travelled back,
Back to the yoke of ignorance and fate,
Back to the labour and stress of mortal days,
Lighting a pathway through strange symbol dreams
Across the ebbing of the seas of sleep.
Her house of Nature felt an unseen sway,
Illumined swiftly were life's darkened rooms,
And memory's casements opened on the hours
And the tired feet of thought approached her doors.
All came back to her: Earth and Love and Doom,
The ancient disputants, encircled her

Like giant figures wrestling in the night:
The godheads from the dim Inconscient born
Awoke to struggle and the pang divine,
And in the shadow of her flaming heart,
At the sombre centre of the dire debate,
A guardian of the unconsoled abyss
Inheriting the long agony of the globe,
A stone-still figure of high and godlike Pain
Stared into Space with fixed regardless eyes
That saw grief's timeless depths but not life's goal.
Afflicted by his harsh divinity,
Bound to his throne, he waited unappeased
The daily oblation of her unwept tears.
All the fierce question of man's hours relived.
The sacrifice of suffering and desire
Earth offers to the immortal Ecstasy
Began again beneath the eternal Hand.
Awake she endured the moments' serried march
And looked on this green smiling dangerous world,
And heard the ignorant cry of living things.
Amid the trivial sounds, the unchanging scene
Her soul arose confronting Time and Fate.
Immobile in herself, she gathered force.
This was the day when Satyavan must die.

END OF CANTO ONE

Canto Two

The Issue

AWHILE, withdrawn in secret fields of thought,
Her mind moved in a many-imaged past
That lived again and saw its end approach:
Dying, it lived imperishably in her;
Transient and vanishing from transient eyes,
Invisible, a fateful ghost of self,
It bore the future on its phantom breast.
Along the fleeting event's far-backward trail
Regressed the stream of the insistent hours,
And on the bank of the mysterious flood
Peopled with well-loved forms now seen no more
And the subtle images of things that were,
Her witness spirit stood reviewing Time.
All that she once had hoped and dreamed and been,
Flew past her eagle-winged through memory's skies.
As in a many-hued flaming inner dawn,
Her life's broad highways and its sweet bypaths
Lay mapped to her sun-clear recording view,
From the bright country of her childhood's days
And the blue mountains of her soaring youth
And the paradise groves and peacock wings of Love
To joy clutched under the silent shadow of doom
In a last turn where heaven raced with hell.
Twelve passionate months led in a day of fate.
An absolute supernatural darkness falls
On man sometimes when he draws near to God:
An hour arrives when fail all Nature's means;
Forced out from the protecting Ignorance
And flung back on his naked primal need,
He at length must cast from him his surface soul
And be the ungarbed entity within:

That hour had fallen now on Savitri.
A point she had reached where life must be in vain
Or, in her unborn element awake,
Her will must cancel her body's destiny.
For only the unborn spirit's timeless power
Can lift the yoke imposed by birth in Time.
Only the Self that builds this figure of self
Can rase the fixed interminable line
That joins these changing names, these numberless lives,
These new oblivious personalities
And keeps still lurking in our conscious acts
The trail of old forgotten thoughts and deeds,
Disown the legacy of our buried selves,
The burdensome heirship to our vanished forms
Accepted blindly by the body and soul.
An episode in an unremembered tale,
Its beginning lost, its motive and plot concealed,
A once living story has prepared and made
Our present fate, child of past energies.
The fixity of the cosmic sequences
Fastened with hidden inevitable links
She must disrupt, dislodge by her soul's force
Her past, a block on the Immortal's road,
Make a rased ground and shape anew her fate.
A colloquy of the original Gods
Meeting upon the borders of the unknown,
Her soul's debate with embodied Nothingness
Must be wrestled out on a dangerous dim background:
Her being must confront its formless Cause,
Against the universe weigh its single self.
On the bare peak where Self is alone with Nought
And life has no sense and love no place to stand,
She must plead her case upon extinction's verge,
In the world's death-cave uphold life's helpless claim
And vindicate her right to be and love.
Altered must be Nature's harsh economy;

Acquittance she must win from her past's bond,
An old account of suffering exhaust,
Strike out from Time the soul's long compound debt
And the heavy servitudes of the Karmic Gods,
The slow revenge of unforgiving Law
And the deep need of universal pain
And hard sacrifice and tragic consequence.
Out of a timeless barrier she must break,
Penetrate with her thinking depths the Void's monstrous hush,
Look into the lonely eyes of immortal Death
And with her nude spirit measure the Infinite's night.
The great and dolorous moment now was close.
A mailed battalion marching to its doom,
The last long days went by with heavy tramp,
Long but too soon to pass, too near the end.
Alone amid the many faces loved,
Aware among unknowing happy hearts,
Her armoured spirit kept watch upon the hours
Listening for a foreseen tremendous step
In the closed beauty of the inhuman wilds.
A combatant in silent dreadful lists,
The world unknowing, for the world she stood:
No helper had she save the Strength within;
There was no witness of terrestrial eyes;
The Gods above and Nature sole below
Were the spectators of that mighty strife.
Around her were the austere sky-pointing hills,
And the green murmurous broad deep-thoughted woods
Muttered incessantly their muffled spell.
A dense magnificent coloured self-wrapped life
Draped in the leaves' vivid emerald monotone
And set with chequered sunbeams and blithe flowers
Immured her destiny's secluded scene.
There had she grown to the stature of her spirit:
The genius of titanic silences
Steeping her soul in its wide loneliness

Had shown to her her self's bare reality
And mated her with her environment.
Its solitude greatened her human hours
With a background of the eternal and unique.
A force of spare direct necessity
Reduced the heavy framework of man's days
And his overburdening mass of outward needs
To a first thin strip of simple animal wants,
And the mighty wildness of the primitive earth
And the brooding multitude of patient trees
And the musing sapphire leisure of the sky
And the solemn weight of the slowly-passing months
Had left in her deep room for thought and God.
There was her drama's radiant prologue lived.
A spot for the eternal's tread on earth
Set in the cloistral yearning of the woods
And watched by the aspiration of the peaks
Appeared through an aureate opening in Time,
Where stillness listening felt the unspoken word
And the hours forgot to pass towards grief and change.
Here with the suddenness divine advents have,
Repeating the marvel of the first descent,
Changing to rapture the dull earthly round,
Love came to her hiding the shadow, Death.
Well might he find in her his perfect shrine.
Since first the earth-being's heavenward growth began,
Through all the long ordeal of the race,
Never a rarer creature bore his shaft,
That burning test of the godhead in our parts,
A lightning from the heights on our abyss.
All in her pointed to a nobler kind.
Near to earth's wideness, intimate with heaven,
Exalted and swift her young large-visioned spirit
Voyaging through worlds of splendour and of calm
Overflew the ways of Thought to unborn things.
Ardent was her self-poised unstumbling will;

Her mind, a sea of white sincerity,
Passionate in flow, had not one turbid wave.
As in a mystic and dynamic dance
A priestess of immaculate ecstasies
Inspired and ruled from Truth's revealing vault
Moves in some prophet cavern of the gods,
A heart of silence in the hands of joy
Inhabited with rich creative beats
A body like a parable of dawn
That seemed a niche for veiled divinity
Or golden temple-door to things beyond.
Immortal rhythms swayed in her time-born steps;
Her look, her smile awoke celestial sense
Even in earth-stuff, and their intense delight
Poured a supernal beauty on men's lives.
A wide self-giving was her native act;
A magnanimity as of sea or sky
Enveloped with its greatness all that came
And gave a sense as of a greatened world:
Her kindly care was a sweet temperate sun,
Her high passion a blue heaven's equipoise.
As might a soul fly like a hunted bird,
Escaping with tired wings from a world of storms,
And a quiet reach like a remembered breast,
In a haven of safety and splendid soft repose
One could drink life back in streams of honey-fire,
Recover the lost habit of happiness,
Feel her bright nature's glorious ambience,
And preen joy in her warmth and colour's rule.
A deep of compassion, a hushed sanctuary,
Her inward help unbarred a gate in heaven;
Love in her was wider than the universe,
The whole world could take refuge in her single heart.
The great unsatisfied godhead here could dwell:
Vacant of the dwarf self's imprisoned air,
Her mood could harbour his sublimer breath

Spiritual that can make all things divine.
For even her gulfs were secrecies of light.
At once she was the stillness and the word,
A continent of self-diffusing peace,
An ocean of untrembling virgin fire;
The strength, the silence of the gods were hers.
In her he found a vastness like his own,
His high warm subtle ether he refound
And moved in her as in his natural home.
In her he met his own eternity.

Till then no mournful line had barred this ray.
On the frail breast of this precarious earth,
Since her orbed sight in its breath-fastened house,
Opening in sympathy with happier stars
Where life is not exposed to sorrowful change,
Remembered beauty death-claimed lids ignore
And wondered at this world of fragile forms
Carried on canvas-strips of shimmering Time,
The impunity of unborn Mights was hers.
Although she leaned to bear the human load,
Her walk kept still the measures of the gods.
Earth's breath had failed to stain that brilliant glass:
Unsmeared with the dust of our mortal atmosphere
It still reflected heaven's spiritual joy.
Almost they saw who lived within her light
Her playmate in the sempiternal spheres
Descended from its unattainable realms
In her attracting advent's luminous wake,
The white-fire dragon-bird of endless bliss
Drifting with burning wings above her days:
Heaven's tranquil shield guarded the missioned child.
A glowing orbit was her early term,
Years like gold raiment of the gods that pass;
Her youth sat throned in calm felicity.
But joy cannot endure until the end:

There is a darkness in terrestrial things
That will not suffer long too glad a note.
On her too closed the inescapable Hand:
The armed Immortal bore the snare of Time.
One dealt with her who meets the burdened great.
Assigner of the ordeal and the path
Who chooses in this holocaust of the soul
Death, fall and sorrow as the spirit's goads,
The dubious godhead with his torch of pain
Lit up the chasm of the unfinished world
And called her to fill with her vast self the abyss.
August and pitiless in his calm outlook,
Heightening the Eternal's dreadful strategy,
He measured the difficulty with the might
And dug more deep the gulf that all must cross.
Assailing her divinest elements,
He made her heart kin to the striving human heart
And forced her strength to its appointed road.
For this she had accepted mortal breath;
To wrestle with the Shadow she had come
And must confront the riddle of man's birth
And life's brief struggle in dumb Matter's night.
Whether to bear with Ignorance and death
Or hew the ways of Immortality,
To win or lose the godlike game for man,
Was her soul's issue thrown with Destiny's dice.
But not to submit and suffer was she born;
To lead, to deliver was her glorious part.
Here was no fabric of terrestrial make
Fit for a day's use by busy careless Powers.
An image fluttering on the screen of Fate,
Half-animated for a passing show,
Or a castaway on the ocean of Desire
Flung to the eddies in a ruthless sport
And tossed along the gulfs of Circumstance,
A creature born to bend beneath the yoke,

A chattel and a plaything of Time's lords,
Or one more pawn who comes destined to be pushed
One slow move forward on a measureless board
In the chess-play of the earth-soul with Doom, —
Such is the human figure drawn by Time.
A conscious frame was here, a self-born Force.
In this enigma of the dusk of God,
This slow and strange uneasy compromise
Of limiting Nature with a limitless Soul,
Where all must move between an ordered Chance
And an uncaring blind Necessity,
Too high the fire spiritual dare not blaze.
If once it met the intense original Flame,
An answering touch might shatter all measures made
And earth sink down with the weight of the Infinite.
A gaol is this immense material world:
Across each road stands armed a stone-eyed Law,
At every gate the huge dim sentinels pace.
A grey tribunal of the Ignorance,
An Inquisition of the priests of Night
In judgment sit on the adventurer soul,
And the dual tables and the Karmic norm
Restrain the Titan in us and the God:
Pain with its lash, joy with its silver bribe
Guard the Wheel's circling immobility.
A bond is put on the high-climbing mind,
A seal on the too large wide-open heart;
Death stays the journeying discoverer, Life.
Thus is the throne of the Inconscient safe
While the tardy coilings of the aeons pass
And the Animal browses in the sacred fence
And the gold Hawk can cross the skies no more.
But one stood up and lit the limitless flame.
Arraigned by the dark Power that hates all bliss
In the dire court where life must pay for joy,
Sentenced by the mechanic justicer

To the afflicting penalty of man's hopes,
Her head she bowed not to the stark decree
Baring her helpless heart to destiny's stroke.
So bows and must the mind-born will in man
Obedient to the statutes fixed of old,
Admitting without appeal the nether gods.
In her the superhuman cast its seed.
Inapt to fold its mighty wings of dream
Her spirit refused to hug the common soil,
Or, finding all life's golden meanings robbed,
Compound with earth, struck from the starry list,
Or quench with black despair the God-given light.
Accustomed to the eternal and the true,
Her being conscious of its divine founts
Asked not from mortal frailty pain's relief,
Patched not with failure bargain or compromise.
A work she had to do, a word to speak:
Writing the unfinished story of her soul
In thoughts and actions graved in Nature's book,
She accepted not to close the luminous page,
Cancel her commerce with eternity,
Or set a signature of weak assent
To the brute balance of the world's exchange.
A force in her that toiled since earth was made,
Accomplishing in life the great world-plan,
Pursuing after death immortal aims,
Repugned to admit frustration's barren role,
Forfeit the meaning of her birth in Time,
Obey the government of the casual fact
Or yield her high destiny up to passing Chance.
In her own self she found her high recourse;
She matched with the iron law her sovereign right:
Her single will opposed the cosmic rule.
To stay the wheels of Doom this greatness rose.
At the Unseen's knock upon her hidden gates
Her strength made greater by the lightning's touch

Awoke from slumber in her heart's recess.
It bore the stroke of That which kills and saves.
Across the awful march no eye can see,
Barring its dreadful route no will can change,
She faced the engines of the universe;
A heart stood in the way of the driving wheels:
Its giant workings paused in front of a mind,
Its stark conventions met the flame of a soul.
A magic leverage suddenly is caught
That moves the veiled Ineffable's timeless will:
A prayer, a master act, a king idea
Can link man's strength to a transcendent Force.
Then miracle is made the common rule,
One mighty deed can change the course of things;
A lonely thought becomes omnipotent.
All now seems Nature's massed machinery;
An endless servitude to material rule
And long determination's rigid chain,
Her firm and changeless habits aping Law,
Her empire of unconscious deft device
Annul the claim of man's free human will.
He too is a machine amid machines;
A piston brain pumps out the shapes of thought,
A beating heart cuts out emotion's modes;
An insentient energy fabricates a soul.
Or the figure of the world reveals the signs
Of a tied Chance repeating her old steps
In circles around Matter's binding-posts.
A random series of inept events
To which reason lends illusive sense, is here,
Or the empiric Life's instinctive search,
Or a vast ignorant mind's colossal work.
But wisdom comes, and vision grows within:
Then Nature's instrument crowns himself her king;
He feels his witnessing self and conscious power;
His soul steps back and sees the Light supreme.

A Godhead stands behind the brute machine.
This truth broke in in a triumph of fire;
A victory was won for God in man,
The deity revealed its hidden face.
The great World-Mother now in her arose:
A living choice reversed fate's cold dead turn,
Affirmed the spirit's tread on Circumstance,
Pressed back the senseless dire revolving Wheel
And stopped the mute march of Necessity.
A flaming warrior from the eternal peaks
Empowered to force the door denied and closed
Smote from Death's visage its dumb absolute
And burst the bounds of consciousness and Time.

END OF CANTO TWO

The Yoga of the King:
The Yoga of the Soul's Release

A WORLD'S desire compelled her mortal birth.
One in the front of the immemorial quest,
Protagonist of the mysterious play
In which the Unknown pursues himself through forms
And limits his eternity by the hours
And the blind Void struggles to live and see,
A thinker and toiler in the ideal's air,
Brought down to earth's dumb need her radiant power.
His was a spirit that stooped from larger spheres
Into our province of ephemeral sight,
A colonist from immortality.
A pointing beam on earth's uncertain roads,
His birth held up a symbol and a sign;
His human self like a translucent cloak
Covered the All-Wise who leads the unseeing world.
Affiliated to cosmic Space and Time
And paying here God's debt to earth and man
A greater sonship was his divine right.
Although consenting to mortal ignorance,
His knowledge shared the Light ineffable.
A strength of the original Permanence
Entangled in the moment and its flow,
He kept the vision of the Vasts behind:
A power was in him from the Unknowable.
An archivist of the symbols of the Beyond,
A treasurer of superhuman dreams,
He bore the stamp of mighty memories
And shed their grandiose ray on human life.
His days were a long growth to the Supreme.
A skyward being nourishing its roots

On sustenance from occult spiritual founts
Climbed through white rays to meet an unseen Sun.
His soul lived as eternity's delegate,
His mind was like a fire assailing heaven,
His will a hunter in the trails of light.
An ocean impulse lifted every breath;
Each action left the footprints of a god,
Each moment was a beat of puissant wings.
The little plot of our mortality
Touched by this tenant from the heights became
A playground of the living Infinite.
This bodily appearance is not all;
The form deceives, the person is a mask;
Hid deep in man celestial powers can dwell.
His fragile ship conveys through the sea of years
An incognito of the Imperishable.
A spirit that is a flame of God abides,
A fiery portion of the Wonderful,
Artist of his own beauty and delight,
Immortal in our mortal poverty.
This sculptor of the forms of the Infinite,
This screened unrecognised Inhabitant,
Initiate of his own veiled mysteries,
Hides in a small dumb seed his cosmic thought.
In the mute strength of the occult Idea
Determining predestined shape and act,
Passenger from life to life, from scale to scale,
Changing his imaged self from form to form,
He regards the icon growing by his gaze
And in the worm foresees the coming god.
At last the traveller in the paths of Time
Arrives on the frontiers of eternity.
In the transient symbol of humanity draped,
He feels his substance of undying self
And loses his kinship to mortality.
A beam of the Eternal smites his heart,

His thought stretches into infinitude;
All in him turns to spirit vastnesses.
His soul breaks out to join the Oversoul,
His life is oceaned by that superlife.
He has drunk from the breasts of the Mother of the worlds;
A topless Supernature fills his frame:
She adopts his spirit's everlasting ground
As the security of her changing world
And shapes the figure of her unborn mights.
Immortally she conceives herself in him,
In the creature the unveiled Creatrix works:
Her face is seen through his face, her eyes through his eyes;
Her being is his through a vast identity.
Then is revealed in man the overt Divine.
A static Oneness and dynamic Power
Descend in him, the integral Godhead's seals;
His soul and body take that splendid stamp.
A long dim preparation is man's life,
A circle of toil and hope and war and peace
Tracked out by Life on Matter's obscure ground.
In his climb to a peak no feet have ever trod,
He seeks through a penumbra shot with flame
A veiled reality half-known, ever missed,
A search for something or someone never found,
Cult of an ideal never made real here,
An endless spiral of ascent and fall
Until at last is reached the giant point
Through which his Glory shines for whom we were made
And we break into the infinity of God.
Across our nature's border line we escape
Into Supernature's arc of living light.
This now was witnessed in that son of Force;
In him that high transition laid its base.
Original and supernal Immanence
Of which all Nature's process is the art,
The cosmic Worker set his secret hand

To turn this frail mud-engine to heaven-use.
A Presence wrought behind the ambiguous screen:
It beat his soil to bear a Titan's weight,
Refining half-hewn blocks of natural strength
It built his soul into a statued god.
The Craftsman of the magic stuff of self
Who labours at his high and difficult plan
In the wide workshop of the wonderful world,
Modelled in inward Time his rhythmic parts.
Then came the abrupt transcendent miracle:
The masked immaculate Grandeur could outline,
At travail in the occult womb of life,
His dreamed magnificence of things to be.
A crown of the architecture of the worlds,
A mystery of married Earth and Heaven
Annexed divinity to the mortal scheme.
A Seer was born, a shining Guest of Time.
For him mind's limiting firmament ceased above.
In the griffin forefront of the Night and Day
A gap was rent in the all-concealing vault;
The conscious ends of being went rolling back:
The landmarks of the little person fell,
The island ego joined its continent.
Overpassed was this world of rigid limiting forms:
Life's barriers opened into the Unknown.
Abolished were conception's covenants
And, striking off subjection's rigorous clause,
Annulled the soul's treaty with Nature's nescience.
All the grey inhibitions were torn off
And broken the intellect's hard and lustrous lid;
Truth unpartitioned found immense sky-room;
An empyrean vision saw and knew;
The bounded mind became a boundless light,
The finite self mated with infinity.
His march now soared into an eagle's flight.
Out of apprenticeship to Ignorance

Wisdom upraised him to her master craft
And made him an archmason of the soul,
A builder of the Immortal's secret house,
An aspirant to supernal Timelessness:
Freedom and empire called to him from on high;
Above mind's twilight and life's star-led night
There gleamed the dawn of a spiritual day.

As so he grew into his larger self,
Humanity framed his movements less and less;
A greater being saw a greater world.
A fearless will for knowledge dared to erase
The lines of safety Reason draws that bar
Mind's soar, soul's dive into the Infinite.
Even his first steps broke our small earth-bounds
And loitered in a vaster freer air.
In hands sustained by a transfiguring Might
He caught up lightly like a giant's bow
Left slumbering in a sealed and secret cave
The powers that sleep unused in man within.
He made of miracle a normal act
And turned to a common part of divine works,
Magnificently natural at this height,
Efforts that would shatter the strength of mortal hearts,
Pursued in a royalty of mighty ease
Aims too sublime for Nature's daily will:
The gifts of the spirit crowding came to him;
They were his life's pattern and his privilege.
A pure perception lent its lucent joy:
Its intimate vision waited not to think;
It enveloped all Nature in a single glance,
It looked into the very self of things;
Deceived no more by form he saw the soul.
In beings it knew what lurked to them unknown;
It seized the idea in mind, the wish in the heart;
It plucked out from grey folds of secrecy

The motives which from their own sight men hide.
He felt the beating life in other men
Invade him with their happiness and their grief;
Their love, their anger, their unspoken hopes
Entered in currents or in pouring waves
Into the immobile ocean of his calm.
He heard the inspired sound of his own thoughts
Re-echoed in the vault of other minds;
The world's thought-streams travelled into his ken;
His inner self grew near to others' selves
And bore a kinship's weight, a common tie,
Yet stood untouched, king of itself, alone.
A magical accord quickened and attuned
To ethereal symphonies the old earthy strings;
It raised the servitors of mind and life
To be happy partners in the soul's response,
Tissue and nerve were turned to sensitive chords,
Records of lustre and ecstasy; it made
The body's means the spirit's acolytes.
A heavenlier function with a finer mode
Lit with its grace man's outward earthliness;
The soul's experience of its deeper sheaths
No more slept drugged by Matter's dominance.
In the dead wall closing us from wider self,
Into a secrecy of apparent sleep,
The mystic tract beyond our waking thoughts,
A door parted, built in by Matter's force,
Releasing things unseized by earthly sense:
A world unseen, unknown by outward mind
Appeared in the silent spaces of the soul.
He sat in secret chambers looking out
Into the luminous countries of the unborn
Where all things dreamed by the mind are seen and true
And all that the life longs for is drawn close.
He saw the Perfect in their starry homes
Wearing the glory of a deathless form,

Lain in the arms of the Eternal's peace,
Rapt in the heart-beats of God-ecstasy.
He lived in the mystic space where thought is born
And will is nursed by an ethereal Power
And fed on the white milk of the Eternal's strengths
Till it grows into the likeness of a god.
In the Witness's occult rooms with mind-built walls
On hidden interiors, lurking passages
Opened the windows of the inner sight.
He owned the house of undivided Time.
Lifting the heavy curtain of the flesh
He stood upon a threshold serpent-watched,
And peered into gleaming endless corridors,
Silent and listening in the silent heart
For the coming of the new and the unknown.
He gazed across the empty stillnesses
And heard the footsteps of the undreamed Idea
In the far avenues of the Beyond.
He heard the secret Voice, the Word that knows,
And saw the secret face that is our own.
The inner planes uncovered their crystal doors;
Strange powers and influences touched his life.
A vision came of higher realms than ours,
A consciousness of brighter fields and skies,
Of beings less circumscribed than brief-lived men
And subtler bodies than these passing frames,
Objects too fine for our material grasp,
Acts vibrant with a superhuman light
And movements pushed by a superconscient force,
And joys that never flowed through mortal limbs,
And lovelier scenes than earth's and happier lives.
A consciousness of beauty and of bliss,
A knowledge which became what it perceived,
Replaced the separated sense and heart
And drew all Nature into its embrace.
The mind leaned out to meet the hidden worlds:

Air glowed and teemed with marvellous shapes and hues,
In the nostrils quivered celestial fragrances,
On the tongue lingered the honey of paradise.
A channel of universal harmony,
Hearing was a stream of magic audience,
A bed for occult sounds earth cannot hear.
Out of a covert tract of slumber self
The voice came of a truth submerged, unknown
That flows beneath the cosmic surfaces,
Only mid an omniscient silence heard,
Held by intuitive heart and secret sense.
It caught the burden of secrecies sealed and dumb,
It voiced the unfulfilled demand of earth
And the song of promise of unrealised heavens
And all that hides in an omnipotent Sleep.
In the unceasing drama carried by Time
On its long listening flood that bears the world's
Insoluble doubt on a pilgrimage without goal,
A laughter of sleepless pleasure foamed and spumed
And murmurings of desire that cannot die:
A cry came of the world's delight to be,
The grandeur and greatness of its will to live,
Recall of the soul's adventure into space,
A traveller through the magic centuries
And being's labour in Matter's universe,
Its search for the mystic meaning of its birth
And joy of high spiritual response,
Its throb of satisfaction and content
In all the sweetness of the gifts of life,
Its large breath and pulse and thrill of hope and fear,
Its taste of pangs and tears and ecstasy,
Its rapture's poignant beat of sudden bliss,
The sob of its passion and unending pain.
The murmur and whisper of the unheard sounds
Which crowd around our hearts but find no window
To enter, swelled into a canticle

Of all that suffers to be still unknown
And all that labours vainly to be born
And all the sweetness none will ever taste
And all the beauty that will never be.
Inaudible to our deaf mortal ears
The wide world-rhythms wove their stupendous chant
To which life strives to fit our rhyme-beats here,
Melting our limits in the illimitable,
Tuning the finite to infinity.
A low muttering rose from the subconscient caves,
The stammer of the primal ignorance;
Answer to that inarticulate questioning,
There stooped with lightning neck and thunder's wings
A radiant hymn to the Inexpressible
And the anthem of the superconscient light.
All was revealed there none can here express;
Vision and dream were fables spoken by truth
Or symbols more veridical than fact,
Or were truths enforced by supernatural seals.
Immortal eyes approached and looked in his,
And beings of many kingdoms neared and spoke:
The ever-living whom we name as dead
Could leave their glory beyond death and birth
To utter the wisdom which exceeds all phrase:
The kings of evil and the kings of good,
Appellants at the reason's judgment seat,
Proclaimed the gospel of their opposites,
And all believed themselves spokesmen of God:
The gods of light and titans of the dark
Battled for his soul as for a costly prize.
In every hour loosed from the quiver of Time
There rose a song of new discovery,
A bow-twang's hum of young experiment.
Each day was a spiritual romance,
As if he was born into a bright new world;
Adventure leaped an unexpected friend,

And danger brought a keen sweet tang of joy;
Each happening was a deep experience.
There were high encounters, epic colloquies,
And counsels came couched in celestial speech,
And honeyed pleadings breathed from occult lips
To help the heart to yield to rapture's call,
And sweet temptations stole from beauty's realms
And sudden ecstasies from a world of bliss.
It was a region of wonder and delight.
All now his bright clairaudience could receive;
A contact thrilled of mighty unknown things.
Awakened to new unearthly closenesses,
The touch replied to subtle infinities,
And with a silver cry of opening gates
Sight's lightnings leaped into the invisible.
Ever his consciousness and vision grew;
They took an ampler sweep, a loftier flight;
He passed the border marked for Matter's rule
And passed the zone where thought replaces life.
Out of this world of signs suddenly he came
Into a silent self where world was not
And looked beyond into a nameless vast.
These symbol figures lost their right to live,
All tokens dropped our sense can recognise;
There the heart beat no more at body's touch,
There the eyes gazed no more on beauty's shape.
In rare and lucent intervals of hush
Into a signless region he could soar
Packed with the deep contents of formlessness
Where world was into a single being rapt
And all was known by the light of identity
And Spirit was its own self-evidence.
The Supreme's gaze looked out through human eyes
And saw all things and creatures as itself
And knew all thought and word as its own voice.
There unity is too close for search and clasp

And love is a yearning of the One for the One,
And beauty is a sweet difference of the Same
And oneness is the soul of multitude.
There all the truths unite in a single Truth,
And all ideas rejoin Reality.
There knowing herself by her own termless self,
Wisdom supernal, wordless, absolute
Sat uncompanioned in the eternal Calm,
All-seeing, motionless, sovereign and alone.
There knowledge needs not words to embody Idea;
Idea, seeking a house in boundlessness,
Weary of its homeless immortality,
Asks not in thought's carved brilliant cell to rest
Whose single window's clipped outlook on things
Sees only a little arc of God's vast sky.
The boundless with the boundless there consorts;
While there, one can be wider than the world;
While there, one is one's own infinity.
His centre was no more in earthly mind;
A power of seeing silence filled his limbs:
Caught by a voiceless white epiphany
Into a vision that surpasses forms,
Into a living that surpasses life,
He neared the still consciousness sustaining all.
The voice that only by speech can move the mind
Became a silent knowledge in the soul;
The strength that only in action feels its truth
Was lodged now in a mute omnipotent peace.
A leisure in the labour of the worlds,
A pause in the joy and anguish of the search
Restored the stress of Nature to God's calm.
A vast unanimity ended life's debate.
The war of thoughts that fathers the universe,
The clash of forces struggling to prevail
In the tremendous shock that lights a star
As in the building of a grain of dust,

The grooves that turn their dumb ellipse in space
Ploughed by the seeking of the world's desire,
The long regurgitations of Time's flood,
The torment edging the dire force of lust
That wakes kinetic in earth's dullard slime
And carves a personality out of mud,
The sorrow by which Nature's hunger is fed,
The oestrus which creates with fire of pain,
The fate that punishes virtue with defeat,
The tragedy that destroys long happiness,
The weeping of Love, the quarrel of the Gods,
Ceased in a truth which lives in its own light.
His soul stood free, a witness and a king.
Absorbed no more in the moment-ridden flux
Where mind incessantly drifts as on a raft
Hurried from phenomenon to phenomenon,
He abode at rest in indivisible Time.
As if a story long written but acted now,
In his present he held his future and his past,
Felt in the seconds the uncounted years
And saw the hours like dots upon a page.
An aspect of the unknown Reality
Altered the meaning of the cosmic scene.
This huge material universe became
A small result of a stupendous force:
Overtaking the moment the eternal Ray
Illumined That which never yet was made.
Thought lay down in a mighty voicelessness;
The toiling Thinker widened and grew still,
Wisdom transcendent touched his quivering heart:
His soul could sail beyond thought's luminous bar;
Mind screened no more the shoreless infinite.
Across a void retreating sky he glimpsed
Through a last glimmer and drift of vanishing stars
The superconscient realms of motionless Peace
Where judgment ceases and the word is mute

And the Unconceived lies pathless and alone.
There came not form or any mounting voice;
There only were Silence and the Absolute.
Out of that stillness mind new-born arose
And woke to truths once inexpressible,
And forms appeared, dumbly significant,
A seeing thought, a self-revealing voice.
He knew the source from which his spirit came:
Movement was married to the immobile Vast;
He plunged his roots into the Infinite,
He based his life upon eternity.

Only awhile at first these heavenlier states,
These large wide-poised upliftings could endure.
The high and luminous tension breaks too soon,
The body's stone stillness and the life's hushed trance,
The breathless might and calm of silent mind;
Or slowly they fail as sets a golden day.
The restless nether members tire of peace;
A nostalgia of old little works and joys,
A need to call back small familiar selves,
To tread the accustomed and inferior way,
The need to rest in a natural pose of fall,
As a child who learns to walk can walk not long,
Replace the titan will for ever to climb,
On the heart's altar dim the sacred fire.
An old pull of subconscious cords renews;
It draws the unwilling spirit from the heights,
Or a dull gravitation drags us down
To the blind driven inertia of our base.
This too the supreme Diplomat can use,
He makes our fall a means for greater rise.
For into ignorant Nature's gusty field,
Into the half-ordered chaos of mortal life
The formless Power, the Self of eternal light
Follow in the shadow of the spirit's descent;

The twin duality for ever one
Chooses its home mid the tumults of the sense.
He comes unseen into our darker parts
And, curtained by the darkness, does his work,
A subtle and all-knowing guest and guide,
Till they too feel the need and will to change.
All here must learn to obey a higher law,
Our body's cells must hold the Immortal's flame.
Else would the spirit reach alone its source
Leaving a half-saved world to its dubious fate.
Nature would ever labour unredeemed;
Our earth would ever spin unhelped in Space,
And this immense creation's purpose fail
Till at last the frustrate universe sank undone.
Even his godlike strength to rise must fall:
His greater consciousness withdrew behind;
Dim and eclipsed, his human outside strove
To feel again the old sublimities,
Bring the high saving touch, the ethereal flame,
Call back to its dire need the divine Force.
Always the power poured back like sudden rain,
Or slowly in his breast a presence grew;
It clambered back to some remembered height
Or soared above the peak from which it fell.
Each time he rose there was a larger poise,
A dwelling on a higher spirit plane;
The Light remained in him a longer space.
In this oscillation between earth and heaven,
In this ineffable communion's climb
There grew in him as grows a waxing moon
The glory of the integer of his soul.
A union of the Real with the unique,
A gaze of the Alone from every face,
The presence of the Eternal in the hours
Widening the mortal mind's half-look on things,
Bridging the gap between man's force and Fate

Made whole the fragment-being we are here.
At last was won a firm spiritual poise,
A constant lodging in the Eternal's realm,
A safety in the Silence and the Ray,
A settlement in the Immutable.
His heights of being lived in the still Self;
His mind could rest on a supernal ground
And look down on the magic and the play
Where the God-child lies on the lap of Night and Dawn
And the Everlasting puts on Time's disguise.
To the still heights and to the troubled depths
His equal spirit gave its vast assent:
A poised serenity of tranquil strength,
A wide unshaken look on Time's unrest
Faced all experience with unaltered peace.
Indifferent to the sorrow and delight,
Untempted by the marvel and the call,
Immobile it beheld the flux of things,
Calm and apart supported all that is:
His spirit's stillness helped the toiling world.
Inspired by silence and the closed eyes' sight
His force could work with a new luminous art
On the crude material from which all is made
And the refusal of Inertia's mass
And the grey front of the world's Ignorance
And nescient Matter and the huge error of life.
As a sculptor chisels a deity out of stone
He slowly chipped off the dark envelope,
Line of defence of Nature's ignorance,
The illusion and mystery of the Inconscient
In whose black pall the Eternal wraps his head
That he may act unknown in cosmic Time.
A splendour of self-creation from the peaks,
A transfiguration in the mystic depths,
A happier cosmic working could begin
And fashion the world-shape in him anew,

God found in Nature, Nature fulfilled in God.
Already in him was seen that task of Power:
Life made its home on the high tops of self;
His soul, mind, heart became a single sun;
Only life's lower reaches remained dim.
But there too, in the uncertain shadow of life,
There was a labour and a fiery breath;
The ambiguous cowled celestial puissance worked
Watched by the inner Witness's moveless peace.
Even on the struggling Nature left below
Strong periods of illumination came:
Lightnings of glory after glory burned,
Experience was a tale of blaze and fire,
Air rippled round the argosies of the Gods,
Strange riches sailed to him from the Unseen;
Splendours of insight filled the blank of thought,
Knowledge spoke to the inconscient stillnesses,
Rivers poured down of bliss and luminous force,
Visits of beauty, storm-sweeps of delight
Rained from the all-powerful Mystery above.
Thence stooped the eagles of Omniscience.
A dense veil was rent, a mighty whisper heard;
Repeated in the privacy of his soul,
A wisdom-cry from rapt transcendences
Sang on the mountains of an unseen world;
The voices that an inner listening hears
Conveyed to him their prophet utterances,
And flame-wrapped outbursts of the immortal Word
And flashes of an occult revealing Light
Approached him from the unreachable Secrecy.
An inspired Knowledge sat enthroned within
Whose seconds illumined more than reason's years:
An ictus of revealing lustre fell
As if a pointing accent upon Truth,
And like a sky-flare showing all the ground
A swift intuitive discernment shone.

One glance could separate the true and false,
Or raise its rapid torch-fire in the dark
To check the claimants crowding through mind's gates
Covered by the forged signatures of the gods,
Detect the magic bride in her disguise
Or scan the apparent face of thought and life.

Oft inspiration with her lightning feet,
A sudden messenger from the all-seeing tops,
Traversed the soundless corridors of his mind
Bringing her rhythmic sense of hidden things.
A music spoke transcending mortal speech.
As if from a golden phial of the All-Bliss,
A joy of light, a joy of sudden sight,
A rapture of the thrilled undying Word
Poured into his heart as into an empty cup,
A repetition of God's first delight
Creating in a young and virgin Time.
In a brief moment caught, a little space,
All-Knowledge packed into great wordless thoughts
Lodged in the expectant stillness of his depths
A crystal of the ultimate Absolute,
A portion of the inexpressible Truth
Revealed by silence to the silent soul.
The intense creatrix in his stillness wrought;
Her power fallen speechless grew more intimate;
She looked upon the seen and the unforeseen,
Unguessed domains she made her native field.
All-vision gathered into a single ray,
As when the eyes stare at an invisible point
Till through the intensity of one luminous spot
An apocalypse of a world of images
Enters into the kingdom of the seer.
A great nude arm of splendour suddenly rose;
It rent the gauze opaque of Nescience:
Her lifted finger's keen unthinkable tip

Bared with a stab of flame the closed Beyond.
An eye awake in voiceless heights of trance,
A mind plucking at the unimaginable,
Overleaping with a sole and perilous bound
The high black wall hiding superconscience,
She broke in with inspired speech for scythe
And plundered the Unknowable's vast estate.
A gleaner of infinitesimal grains of Truth,
A sheaf-binder of infinite experience,
She pierced the guarded mysteries of World-Force
And her magic methods wrapped in a thousand veils;
Or she gathered the lost secrets dropped by Time
In the dust and crannies of his mounting route
Mid old forsaken dreams of hastening Mind
And buried remnants of forgotten space.
A traveller between summit and abyss,
She joined the distant ends, the viewless deeps,
Or streaked along the roads of Heaven and Hell
Pursuing all knowledge like a questing hound.
A reporter and scribe of hidden wisdom talk,
Her shining minutes of celestial speech,
Passed through the masked office of the occult mind,
Transmitting gave to prophet and to seer
The inspired body of the mystic Truth.
A recorder of the inquiry of the gods,
Spokesman of the silent seeings of the Supreme,
She brought immortal words to mortal men.
Above the reason's brilliant slender curve,
Released like radiant air dimming a moon,
Broad spaces of a vision without line
Or limit swam into his spirit's ken.
Oceans of being met his voyaging soul
Calling to infinite discovery;
Timeless domains of joy and absolute power
Stretched out surrounded by the eternal hush;
The ways that lead to endless happiness

Ran like dream-smiles through meditating vasts:
Disclosed stood up in a gold moment's blaze
White sun-steppes in the pathless Infinite.
Along a naked curve in bourneless Self
The points that run through the closed heart of things
Shadowed the indeterminable line
That carries the Everlasting through the years.
The magician order of the cosmic Mind
Coercing the freedom of infinity
With the stark array of Nature's symbol facts
And life's incessant signals of event,
Transmuted chance recurrences into laws,
A chaos of signs into a universe.
Out of the rich wonders and the intricate whorls
Of the spirit's dance with Matter as its mask
The balance of the world's design grew clear,
Its symmetry of self-arranged effects
Managed in the deep perspectives of the soul,
And the realism of its illusive art,
Its logic of infinite intelligence,
Its magic of a changing eternity.
A glimpse was caught of things for ever unknown:
The letters stood out of the unmoving Word:
In the immutable nameless Origin
Was seen emerging as from fathomless seas
The trail of the Ideas that made the world,
And, sown in the black earth of Nature's trance,
The seed of the Spirit's blind and huge desire
From which the tree of cosmos was conceived
And spread its magic arms through a dream of space.
Immense realities took on a shape:
There looked out from the shadow of the Unknown
The bodiless Namelessness that saw God born
And tries to gain from the mortal's mind and soul
A deathless body and a divine name.
The immobile lips, the great surreal wings,

The visage masked by superconscient Sleep,
The eyes with their closed lids that see all things,
Appeared of the Architect who builds in trance.
The original Desire born in the Void
Peered out; he saw the hope that never sleeps,
The feet that run behind a fleeting fate,
The ineffable meaning of the endless dream.
Hardly for a moment glimpsed viewless to Mind,
As if a torch held by a power of God,
The radiant world of the everlasting Truth
Glimmered like a faint star bordering the night
Above the golden Overmind's shimmering ridge.
Even were caught as through a cunning veil
The smile of love that sanctions the long game,
The calm indulgence and maternal breasts
Of Wisdom suckling the child-laughter of Chance,
Silence, the nurse of the Almighty's power,
The omniscient hush, womb of the immortal Word,
And of the Timeless the still brooding face,
And the creative eye of Eternity.
The inspiring goddess entered a mortal's breast,
Made there her study of divining thought
And sanctuary of prophetic speech
And sat upon the tripod seat of mind:
All was made wide above, all lit below.
In darkness' core she dug out wells of light,
On the undiscovered depths imposed a form,
Lent a vibrant cry to the unuttered vasts,
And through great shoreless, voiceless, starless breadths
Bore earthward fragments of revealing thought
Hewn from the silence of the Ineffable.
A Voice in the heart uttered the unspoken Name,
A dream of seeking Thought wandering through Space
Entered the invisible and forbidden house:
The treasure was found of a supernal Day.
In the deep subconscient glowed her jewel-lamp;

Lifted, it showed the riches of the Cave
Where, by the miser traffickers of sense
Unused, guarded beneath Night's dragon paws,
In folds of velvet darkness draped they sleep
Whose priceless value could have saved the world.
A darkness carrying morning in its breast
Looked for the eternal wide returning gleam,
Waiting the advent of a larger ray
And rescue of the lost herds of the Sun.
In a splendid extravagance of the waste of God
Dropped carelessly in creation's spendthrift work,
Left in the chantiers of the bottomless world
And stolen by the robbers of the Deep,
The golden shekels of the Eternal lie,
Hoarded from touch and view and thought's desire,
Locked in blind antres of the ignorant flood,
Lest men should find them and be even as Gods.
A vision lightened on the viewless heights,
A wisdom illumined from the voiceless depths:
A deeper interpretation greatened Truth,
A grand reversal of the Night and Day;
All the world's values changed heightening life's aim;
A wiser word, a larger thought came in
Than what the slow labour of human mind can bring,
A secret sense awoke that could perceive
A Presence and a Greatness everywhere.
The universe was not now this senseless whirl
Borne round inert on an immense machine;
It cast away its grandiose lifeless front,
A mechanism no more or work of Chance,
But a living movement of the body of God.
A spirit hid in forces and in forms
Was the spectator of the mobile scene:
The beauty and the ceaseless miracle
Let in a glow of the Unmanifest:
The formless Everlasting moved in it

Seeking its own perfect form in souls and things.
Life kept no more a dull and meaningless shape.
In the struggle and upheaval of the world
He saw the labour of a godhead's birth.
A secret knowledge masked as Ignorance;
Fate covered with an unseen necessity
The game of chance of an omnipotent Will.
A glory and a rapture and a charm,
The All-Blissful sat unknown within the heart;
Earth's pains were the ransom of its prisoned delight.
A glad communion tinged the passing hours;
The days were travellers on a destined road,
The nights companions of his musing spirit.
A heavenly impetus quickened all his breast;
The trudge of Time changed to a splendid march;
The divine Dwarf towered to unconquered worlds,
Earth grew too narrow for his victory.
Once only registering the heavy tread
Of a blind Power on human littleness,
Life now became a sure approach to God,
Existence a divine experiment
And cosmos the soul's opportunity.
The world was a conception and a birth
Of Spirit in Matter into living forms,
And Nature bore the Immortal in her womb,
That she might climb through him to eternal life.
His being lay down in bright immobile peace
And bathed in wells of pure spiritual light;
It wandered in wide fields of wisdom-self
Lit by the rays of an everlasting sun.
Even his body's subtle self within
Could raise the earthly parts towards higher things
And feel on it the breath of heavenlier air.
Already it journeyed towards divinity:
Upbuoyed upon winged winds of rapid joy,
Upheld to a Light it could not always hold,

It left mind's distance from the Truth supreme
And lost life's incapacity for bliss.
All now suppressed in us began to emerge.

Thus came his soul's release from Ignorance,
His mind and body's first spiritual change.
A wide God-knowledge poured down from above,
A new world-knowledge broadened from within:
His daily thoughts looked up to the True and One,
His commonest doings welled from an inner Light.
Awakened to the lines that Nature hides,
Attuned to her movements that exceed our ken,
He grew one with a covert universe.
His grasp surprised her mightiest energies' springs;
He spoke with the unknown Guardians of the worlds,
Forms he descried our mortal eyes see not.
His wide eyes bodied viewless entities,
He saw the cosmic forces at their work
And felt the occult impulse behind man's will.
Time's secrets were to him an oft-read book;
The records of the future and the past
Outlined their excerpts on the etheric page.
One and harmonious by the Maker's skill,
The human in him paced with the divine;
His acts betrayed not the interior flame.
This forged the greatness of his front to earth.
A genius heightened in his body's cells
That knew the meaning of his fate-hedged works
Akin to the march of unaccomplished Powers
Beyond life's arc in spirit's immensities.
Apart he lived in his mind's solitude,
A demigod shaping the lives of men:
One soul's ambition lifted up the race;
A Power worked, but none knew whence it came.
The universal strengths were linked with his;
Filling earth's smallness with their boundless breadths,

He drew the energies that transmute an age.
Immeasurable by the common look,
He made great dreams a mould for coming things
And cast his deeds like bronze to front the years.
His walk through Time outstripped the human stride.
Lonely his days and splendid like the sun's.

END OF CANTO THREE

Canto Four

The Secret Knowledge

ON A height he stood that looked towards greater heights.
Our early approaches to the Infinite
Are sunrise splendours on a marvellous verge
While lingers yet unseen the glorious sun.
What now we see is a shadow of what must come.
The earth's uplook to a remote Unknown
Is a preface only of the epic climb
Of human soul from its flat earthly state
To the discovery of a greater self
And the far gleam of an eternal Light.
This world is a beginning and a base
Where Life and Mind erect their structured dreams;
An unborn Power must build reality.
A deathbound littleness is not all we are:
Immortal our forgotten vastnesses
Await discovery in our summit selves;
Unmeasured breadths and depths of being are ours.
Akin to the ineffable Secrecy,
Mystic, eternal in unrealised Time,
Neighbours of Heaven are Nature's altitudes.
To these high-peaked dominions sealed to our search,
Too far from surface Nature's postal routes,
Too lofty for our mortal lives to breathe,
Deep in us a forgotten kinship points
And a faint voice of ecstasy and prayer
Calls to those lucent lost immensities.
Even when we fail to look into our souls
Or lie embedded in earthly consciousness,
Still have we parts that grow towards the light,
Yet are there luminous tracts and heavens serene
And Eldorados of splendour and ecstasy

And temples to the godhead none can see.
A shapeless memory lingers in us still
And sometimes, when our sight is turned within,
Earth's ignorant veil is lifted from our eyes;
There is a short miraculous escape.
This narrow fringe of clamped experience
We leave behind meted to us as life,
Our little walks, our insufficient reach.
Our souls can visit in great lonely hours
Still regions of imperishable Light,
All-seeing eagle-peaks of silent Power
And moon-flame oceans of swift fathomless Bliss
And calm immensities of spirit space.
In the unfolding process of the Self
Sometimes the inexpressible Mystery
Elects a human vessel of descent.
A breath comes down from a supernal air,
A Presence is born, a guiding Light awakes,
A stillness falls upon the instruments:
Fixed, motionless like a marble monument,
Stone-calm, the body is a pedestal
Supporting a figure of eternal Peace.
Or a revealing Force sweeps blazing in;
Out of some vast superior continent
Knowledge breaks through trailing its radiant seas,
And Nature trembles with the power, the flame.
A greater Personality sometimes
Possesses us which yet we know is ours:
Or we adore the Master of our souls.
Then the small bodily ego thins and falls;
No more insisting on its separate self,
Losing the punctilio of its separate birth,
It leaves us one with Nature and with God.
In moments when the inner lamps are lit
And the life's cherished guests are left outside,
Our spirit sits alone and speaks to its gulfs.

A wider consciousness opens then its doors;
Invading from spiritual silences
A ray of the timeless Glory stoops awhile
To commune with our seized illumined clay
And leaves its huge white stamp upon our lives.
In the oblivious field of mortal mind,
Revealed to the closed prophet eyes of trance
Or in some deep internal solitude
Witnessed by a strange immaterial sense,
The signals of eternity appear.
The truth mind could not know unveils its face,
We hear what mortal ears have never heard,
We feel what earthly sense has never felt,
We love what common hearts repel and dread;
Our minds hush to a bright Omniscient;
A Voice calls from the chambers of the soul;
We meet the ecstasy of the Godhead's touch
In golden privacies of immortal fire.
These signs are native to a larger self
That lives within us by ourselves unseen;
Only sometimes a holier influence comes,
A tide of mightier surgings bears our lives
And a diviner Presence moves the soul;
Or through the earthly coverings something breaks,
A grace and beauty of spiritual light,
The murmuring tongue of a celestial fire.
Ourself and a high stranger whom we feel,
It is and acts unseen as if it were not;
It follows the line of sempiternal birth,
Yet seems to perish with its mortal frame.
Assured of the Apocalypse to be,
It reckons not the moments and the hours;
Great, patient, calm it sees the centuries pass,
Awaiting the slow miracle of our change
In the sure deliberate process of world-force
And the long march of all-revealing Time.

It is the origin and the master-clue,
A silence overhead, an inner voice,
A living image seated in the heart,
An unwalled wideness and a fathomless point,
The truth of all these cryptic shows in Space,
The Real towards which our strivings move,
The secret grandiose meaning of our lives.
A treasure of honey in the combs of God,
A Splendour burning in a tenebrous cloak,
It is our glory of the flame of God,
Our golden fountain of the world's delight,
An immortality cowled in the cape of death,
The shape of our unborn divinity.
It guards for us our fate in depths within
Where sleeps the eternal seed of transient things.
Always we bear in us a magic key
Concealed in life's hermetic envelope.
A burning Witness in the sanctuary
Regards through Time and the blind walls of Form;
A timeless Light is in his hidden eyes;
He sees the secret things no words can speak
And knows the goal of the unconscious world
And the heart of the mystery of the journeying years.

But all is screened, subliminal, mystical;
It needs the intuitive heart, the inward turn,
It needs the power of a spiritual gaze.
Else to our waking mind's small moment look
A goalless voyage seems our dubious course
Some Chance has settled or hazarded some Will,
Or a Necessity without aim or cause
Unwillingly compelled to emerge and be.
In this dense field where nothing is plain or sure,
Our very being seems to us questionable,
Our life a vague experiment, the soul
A flickering light in a strange ignorant world,

The earth a brute mechanic accident,
A net of death in which by chance we live.
All we have learned appears a doubtful guess,
The achievement done a passage or a phase
Whose farther end is hidden from our sight,
A chance happening or a fortuitous fate.
Out of the unknown we move to the unknown.
Ever surround our brief existence here
Grey shadows of unanswered questionings;
The dark Inconscient's signless mysteries
Stand up unsolved behind Fate's starting-line.
An aspiration in the Night's profound,
Seed of a perishing body and half-lit mind,
Uplifts its lonely tongue of conscious fire
Towards an undying Light for ever lost;
Only it hears, sole echo of its call,
The dim reply in man's unknowing heart
And meets, not understanding why it came
Or for what reason is the suffering here,
God's sanction to the paradox of life
And the riddle of the Immortal's birth in Time.
Along a path of aeons serpentine
In the coiled blackness of her nescient course
The Earth-Goddess toils across the sands of Time.
A Being is in her whom she hopes to know,
A Word speaks to her heart she cannot hear,
A Fate compels whose form she cannot see.
In her unconscious orbit through the Void
Out of her mindless depths she strives to rise,
A perilous life her gain, a struggling joy;
A Thought that can conceive but hardly knows
Arises slowly in her and creates
The idea, the speech that labels more than it lights;
A trembling gladness that is less than bliss
Invades from all this beauty that must die.
Alarmed by the sorrow dragging at her feet

And conscious of the high things not yet won,
Ever she nurses in her sleepless breast
An inward urge that takes from her rest and peace.
Ignorant and weary and invincible,
She seeks through the soul's war and quivering pain
The pure perfection her marred nature needs,
A breath of Godhead on her stone and mire.
A faith she craves that can survive defeat,
The sweetness of a love that knows not death,
The radiance of a truth for ever sure.
A light grows in her, she assumes a voice,
Her state she learns to read and the act she has done,
But the one needed truth eludes her grasp,
Herself and all of which she is the sign.
An inarticulate whisper drives her steps
Of which she feels the force but not the sense;
A few rare intimations come as guides,
Immense divining flashes cleave her brain,
And sometimes in her hours of dream and muse
The truth that she has missed looks out on her
As if far off and yet within her soul.
A change comes near that flees from her surmise
And, ever postponed, compels attempt and hope,
Yet seems too great for mortal hope to dare.
A vision meets her of supernal Powers
That draw her as if mighty kinsmen lost
Approaching with estranged great luminous gaze.
Then is she moved to all that she is not
And stretches arms to what was never hers.
Outstretching arms to the unconscious Void,
Passionate she prays to invisible forms of Gods
Soliciting from dumb Fate and toiling Time
What most she needs, what most exceeds her scope,
A Mind unvisited by illusion's gleams,
A Will expressive of soul's deity,
A Strength not forced to stumble by its speed,

A Joy that drags not sorrow as its shade.
For these she yearns and feels them destined hers:
Heaven's privilege she claims as her own right.
Just is her claim the all-witnessing Gods approve,
Clear in a greater light than reason owns:
Our intuitions are its title-deeds;
Our souls accept what our blind thoughts refuse.
Earth's winged chimaeras are Truth's steeds in Heaven,
The impossible God's sign of things to be.
But few can look beyond the present state
Or overleap this matted hedge of sense.
All that transpires on earth and all beyond
Are parts of an illimitable plan
The One keeps in his heart and knows alone.
Our outward happenings have their seed within,
And even this random Fate that imitates Chance,
This mass of unintelligible results,
Are the dumb graph of truths that work unseen:
The laws of the Unknown create the known.
The events that shape the appearance of our lives
Are a cipher of subliminal quiverings
Which rarely we surprise or vaguely feel,
Are an outcome of suppressed realities
That hardly rise into material day:
They are born from the spirit's sun of hidden powers
Digging a tunnel through emergency.
But who shall pierce into the cryptic gulf
And learn what deep necessity of the soul
Determined casual deed and consequence?
Absorbed in a routine of daily acts,
Our eyes are fixed on an external scene;
We hear the crash of the wheels of Circumstance
And wonder at the hidden cause of things.
Yet a foreseeing Knowledge might be ours,
If we could take our spirit's stand within,
If we could hear the muffled daemon voice.

Too seldom is the shadow of what must come
Cast in an instant on the secret sense
Which feels the shock of the invisible,
And seldom in the few who answer give
The mighty process of the cosmic Will
Communicates its image to our sight,
Identifying the world's mind with ours.
Our range is fixed within the crowded arc
Of what we observe and touch and thought can guess
And rarely dawns the light of the Unknown
Waking in us the prophet and the seer.
The outward and the immediate are our field,
The dead past is our background and support;
Mind keeps the soul prisoner, we are slaves to our acts;
We cannot free our gaze to reach wisdom's sun.
Inheritor of the brief animal mind,
Man, still a child in Nature's mighty hands,
In the succession of the moments lives;
To a changing present is his narrow right;
His memory stares back at a phantom past,
The future flees before him as he moves;
He sees imagined garments, not a face.
Armed with a limited precarious strength,
He saves his fruits of work from adverse chance.
A struggling ignorance is his wisdom's mate:
He waits to see the consequence of his acts,
He waits to weigh the certitude of his thoughts,
He knows not what he shall achieve or when;
He knows not whether at last he shall survive,
Or end like the mastodon and the sloth
And perish from the earth where he was king.
He is ignorant of the meaning of his life,
He is ignorant of his high and splendid fate.
Only the Immortals on their deathless heights
Dwelling beyond the walls of Time and Space,
Masters of living, free from the bonds of Thought,

Who are overseers of Fate and Chance and Will
And experts of the theorem of world-need,
Can see the Idea, the Might that change Time's course,
Come maned with light from undiscovered worlds,
Hear, while the world toils on with its deep blind heart,
The galloping hooves of the unforeseen event,
Bearing the superhuman Rider, near
And, impassive to earth's din and startled cry,
Return to the silence of the hills of God;
As lightning leaps, as thunder sweeps, they pass
And leave their mark on the trampled breast of Life.
Above the world the world-creators stand,
In the phenomenon see its mystic source.
These heed not the deceiving outward play,
They turn not to the moment's busy tramp,
But listen with the still patience of the Unborn
For the slow footsteps of far Destiny
Approaching through huge distances of Time,
Unmarked by the eye that sees effect and cause,
Unheard mid the clamour of the human plane.
Attentive to an unseen Truth they seize
A sound as of invisible augur wings,
Voices of an unplumbed significance,
Mutterings that brood in the core of Matter's sleep.
In the heart's profound audition they can catch
The murmurs lost by Life's uncaring ear,
A prophet-speech in Thought's omniscient trance.
Above the illusion of the hopes that pass,
Behind the appearance and the overt act,
Behind this clock-work Chance and vague surmise,
Amid the wrestle of force, the trampling feet,
Across the cries of anguish and of joy,
Across the triumph, fighting and despair,
They watch the Bliss for which earth's heart has cried
On the long road which cannot see its end
Winding undetected through the sceptic days

And to meet it guide the unheedful moving world.
Thus will the masked Transcendent mount his throne.
When darkness deepens strangling the earth's breast
And man's corporeal mind is the only lamp,
As a thief's in the night shall be the covert tread
Of one who steps unseen into his house.
A Voice ill-heard shall speak, the soul obey,
A Power into mind's inner chamber steal,
A charm and sweetness open life's closed doors
And beauty conquer the resisting world,
The Truth-Light capture Nature by surprise,
A stealth of God compel the heart to bliss
And earth grow unexpectedly divine.
In Matter shall be lit the spirit's glow,
In body and body kindled the sacred birth;
Night shall awake to the anthem of the stars,
The days become a happy pilgrim march,
Our will a force of the Eternal's power,
And thought the rays of a spiritual sun.
A few shall see what none yet understands;
God shall grow up while the wise men talk and sleep;
For man shall not know the coming till its hour
And belief shall be not till the work is done.

A Consciousness that knows not its own truth,
A vagrant hunter of misleading dawns,
Between the being's dark and luminous ends
Moves here in a half-light that seems the whole:
An interregnum in Reality
Cuts off the integral Thought, the total Power;
It circles or stands in a vague interspace,
Doubtful of its beginning and its close,
Or runs upon a road that has no end;
Far from the original Dusk, the final Flame
In some huge void Inconscience it lives,
Like a thought persisting in a wide emptiness.

As if an unintelligible phrase
Suggested a million renderings to the Mind,
It lends a purport to a random world.
A conjecture leaning upon doubtful proofs,
A message misunderstood, a thought confused
Missing its aim is all that it can speak
Or a fragment of the universal word.
It leaves two giant letters void of sense
While without sanction turns the middle sign
Carrying an enigmatic universe,
As if a present without future or past
Repeating the same revolution's whirl
Turned on its axis in its own Inane.
Thus is the meaning of creation veiled;
For without context reads the cosmic page:
Its signs stare at us like an unknown script,
As if appeared screened by a foreign tongue
Or code of splendour signs without a key
A portion of a parable sublime.
It wears to the perishable creature's eyes
The grandeur of a useless miracle;
Wasting itself that it may last awhile,
A river that can never find its sea,
It runs through life and death on an edge of Time;
A fire in the Night is its mighty action's blaze.
This is our deepest need to join once more
What now is parted, opposite and twain,
Remote in sovereign spheres that never meet
Or fronting like far poles of Night and Day.
We must fill the immense lacuna we have made,
Re-wed the closed finite's lonely consonant
With the open vowels of Infinity,
A hyphen must connect Matter and Mind,
The narrow isthmus of the ascending soul:
We must renew the secret bond in things,
Our hearts recall the lost divine Idea,

Reconstitute the perfect word, unite
The Alpha and the Omega in one sound;
Then shall the Spirit and Nature be at one.
Two are the ends of the mysterious plan.
In the wide signless ether of the Self,
In the unchanging Silence white and nude,
Aloof, resplendent like gold dazzling suns
Veiled by the ray no mortal eye can bear,
The Spirit's bare and absolute potencies
Burn in the solitude of the thoughts of God.
A rapture and a radiance and a hush,
Delivered from the approach of wounded hearts,
Denied to the Idea that looks at grief,
Remote from the Force that cries out in its pain,
In his inalienable bliss they live.
Immaculate in self-knowledge and self-power,
Calm they repose on the eternal Will.
Only his law they count and him obey;
They have no goal to reach, no aim to serve.
Implacable in their timeless purity,
All barter or bribe of worship they refuse;
Unmoved by cry of revolt and ignorant prayer
They reckon not our virtue and our sin;
They bend not to the voices that implore,
They hold no traffic with error and its reign;
They are guardians of the silence of the Truth,
They are keepers of the immutable decree.
A deep surrender is their source of might,
A still identity their way to know,
Motionless is their action like a sleep.
At peace, regarding the trouble beneath the stars,
Deathless, watching the works of Death and Chance,
Immobile, seeing the millenniums pass,
Untouched while the long map of Fate unrolls,
They look on our struggle with impartial eyes,
And yet without them cosmos could not be.

Impervious to desire and doom and hope,
Their station of inviolable might
Moveless upholds the world's enormous task,
Its ignorance is by their knowledge lit,
Its yearning lasts by their indifference.
As the height draws the low ever to climb,
As the breadths draw the small to adventure vast,
Their aloofness drives man to surpass himself.
Our passion heaves to wed the Eternal's calm,
Our dwarf-search mind to meet the Omniscient's light,
Our helpless hearts to enshrine the Omnipotent's force.
Acquiescing in the wisdom that made hell
And the harsh utility of death and tears,
Acquiescing in the gradual steps of Time,
Careless they seem of the grief that stings the world's heart,
Careless of the pain that rends its body and life;
Above joy and sorrow is that grandeur's walk:
They have no portion in the good that dies,
Mute, pure, they share not in the evil done;
Else might their strength be marred and could not save.
Alive to the truth that dwells in God's extremes,
Awake to a motion of all-seeing Force,
The slow outcome of the long ambiguous years
And the unexpected good from woeful deeds,
The immortal sees not as we vainly see.
He looks on hidden aspects and screened powers,
He knows the law and natural line of things.
Undriven by a brief life's will to act,
Unharassed by the spur of pity and fear,
He makes no haste to untie the cosmic knot
Or the world's torn jarring heart to reconcile.
In Time he waits for the Eternal's hour.
Yet a spiritual secret aid is there;
While a tardy Evolution's coils wind on
And Nature hews her way through adamant
A divine intervention thrones above.

Alive in a dead rotating universe
We whirl not here upon a casual globe
Abandoned to a task beyond our force;
Even through the tangled anarchy called Fate
And through the bitterness of death and fall
An outstretched Hand is felt upon our lives.
It is near us in unnumbered bodies and births;
In its unslackening grasp it keeps for us safe
The one inevitable supreme result
No will can take away and no doom change,
The crown of conscious Immortality,
The godhead promised to our struggling souls
When first man's heart dared death and suffered life.
One who has shaped this world is ever its lord:
Our errors are his steps upon the way;
He works through the fierce vicissitudes of our lives,
He works through the hard breath of battle and toil,
He works through our sins and sorrows and our tears,
His knowledge overrules our nescience;
Whatever the appearance we must bear,
Whatever our strong ills and present fate,
When nothing we can see but drift and bale,
A mighty Guidance leads us still through all.
After we have served this great divided world
God's bliss and oneness are our inborn right.
A date is fixed in the calendar of the Unknown,
An anniversary of the Birth sublime:
Our soul shall justify its chequered walk,
All will come near that now is naught or far.
These calm and distant Mights shall act at last.
Immovably ready for their destined task,
The ever-wise compassionate Brilliances
Await the sound of the Incarnate's voice
To leap and bridge the chasms of Ignorance
And heal the hollow yearning gulfs of Life
And fill the abyss that is the universe.

Here meanwhile at the Spirit's opposite pole
In the mystery of the deeps that God has built
For his abode below the Thinker's sight,
In this compromise of a stark absolute Truth
With the Light that dwells near the dark end of things,
In this tragi-comedy of divine disguise,
This long far seeking for joy ever near,
In the grandiose dream of which the world is made,
In this gold dome on a black dragon base,
The conscious Force that acts in Nature's breast,
A dark-robed labourer in the cosmic scheme
Carrying clay images of unborn gods,
Executrix of the inevitable Idea
Hampered, enveloped by the hoops of Fate,
Patient trustee of slow eternal Time,
Absolves from hour to hour her secret charge.
All she foresees in masked imperative depths;
The dumb intention of the unconscious gulfs
Answers to a will that sees upon the heights,
And the evolving Word's first syllable
Ponderous, brute-sensed, contains its luminous close,
Privy to a summit victory's vast descent
And the portent of the soul's immense uprise.

All here where each thing seems its lonely self
Are figures of the sole transcendent One:
Only by him they are, his breath is their life;
An unseen Presence moulds the oblivious clay.
A playmate in the mighty Mother's game,
One came upon the dubious whirling globe
To hide from her pursuit in force and form.
A secret spirit in the Inconscient's sleep,
A shapeless Energy, a voiceless Word,
He was here before the elements could emerge,
Before there was light of mind or life could breathe.
Accomplice of her cosmic huge pretence,

His semblances he turns to real shapes
And makes the symbol equal with the truth:
He gives to his timeless thoughts a form in Time.
He is the substance, he the self of things;
She has forged from him her works of skill and might:
She wraps him in the magic of her moods
And makes of his myriad truths her countless dreams.
The Master of being has come down to her,
An immortal child born in the fugitive years.
In objects wrought, in the persons she conceives,
Dreaming she chases her idea of him,
And catches here a look and there a gest:
Ever he repeats in them his ceaseless births.
He is the Maker and the world he made,
He is the vision and he is the Seer;
He is himself the actor and the act,
He is himself the knower and the known,
He is himself the dreamer and the dream.
There are Two who are One and play in many worlds;
In Knowledge and Ignorance they have spoken and met
And light and darkness are their eyes' interchange;
Our pleasure and pain are their wrestle and embrace,
Our deeds, our hopes are intimate to their tale;
They are married secretly in our thought and life.
The universe is an endless masquerade:
For nothing here is utterly what it seems;
It is a dream-fact vision of a truth
Which but for the dream would not be wholly true,
A phenomenon stands out significant
Against dim backgrounds of eternity;
We accept its face and pass by all it means;
A part is seen, we take it for the whole.
Thus have they made their play with us for roles:
Author and actor with himself as scene,
He moves there as the Soul, as Nature she.
Here on the earth where we must fill our parts,

We know not how shall run the drama's course;
Our uttered sentences veil in their thought.
Her mighty plan she holds back from our sight:
She has concealed her glory and her bliss
And disguised the Love and Wisdom in her heart;
Of all the marvel and beauty that are hers,
Only a darkened little we can feel.
He too wears a diminished godhead here;
He has forsaken his omnipotence,
His calm he has foregone and infinity.
He knows her only, he has forgotten himself;
To her he abandons all to make her great.
He hopes in her to find himself anew,
Incarnate, wedding his infinity's peace
To her creative passion's ecstasy.
Although possessor of the earth and heavens,
He leaves to her the cosmic management
And watches all, the Witness of her scene.
A supernumerary on her stage,
He speaks no words or hides behind the wings.
He takes birth in her world, waits on her will,
Divines her enigmatic gesture's sense,
The fluctuating chance turns of her mood,
Works out her meanings she seems not to know
And serves her secret purpose in long Time.
As one too great for him he worships her;
He adores her as his regent of desire,
He yields to her as the mover of his will,
He burns the incense of his nights and days
Offering his life, a splendour of sacrifice.
A rapt solicitor for her love and grace,
His bliss in her to him is his whole world:
He grows through her in all his being's powers;
He reads by her God's hidden aim in things.
Or, a courtier in her countless retinue,
Content to be with her and feel her near

He makes the most of the little that she gives
And all she does drapes with his own delight.
A glance can make his whole day wonderful,
A word from her lips with happiness wings the hours.
He leans on her for all he does and is:
He builds on her largesses his proud fortunate days
And trails his peacock-plumaged joy of life
And suns in the glory of her passing smile.
In a thousand ways he serves her royal needs;
He makes the hours pivot around her will,
Makes all reflect her whims; all is their play:
This whole wide world is only he and she.

    This is the knot that ties together the stars:
The Two who are one are the secret of all power,
The Two who are one are the might and right in things.
His soul, silent, supports the world and her,
His acts are her commandment's registers.
Happy, inert, he lies beneath her feet:
His breast he offers for her cosmic dance
Of which our lives are the quivering theatre,
And none could bear but for his strength within,
Yet none would leave because of his delight.
His works, his thoughts have been devised by her,
His being is a mirror vast of hers:
Active, inspired by her he speaks and moves;
His deeds obey her heart's unspoken demands:
Passive, he bears the impacts of the world
As if her touches shaping his soul and life:
His journey through the days is her sun-march;
He runs upon her roads; hers is his course.
A witness and student of her joy and dole,
A partner in her evil and her good,
He has consented to her passionate ways,
He is driven by her sweet and dreadful force.
His sanctioning name initials all her works;

His silence is his signature to her deeds;
In the execution of her drama's scheme,
In her fancies of the moment and its mood,
In the march of this obvious ordinary world
Where all is deep and strange to the eyes that see
And Nature's common forms are marvel-wefts,
She through his witness sight and motion of might
Unrolls the material of her cosmic Act,
Her happenings that exalt and smite the soul,
Her force that moves, her powers that save and slay,
Her Word that in the silence speaks to our hearts,
Her silence that transcends the summit Word,
Her heights and depths to which our spirit moves,
Her events that weave the texture of our lives
And all by which we find or lose ourselves,
Things sweet and bitter, magnificent and mean,
Things terrible and beautiful and divine.
Her empire in the cosmos she has built,
He is governed by her subtle and mighty laws.
His consciousness is a babe upon her knees,
His being a field of her vast experiment,
Her endless space is the playground of his thoughts;
She binds to knowledge of the shapes of Time
And the creative error of limiting mind
And chance that wears the rigid face of fate
And her sport of death and pain and Nescience,
His changed and struggling immortality.
His soul is a subtle atom in a mass,
His substance a material for her works.
His spirit survives amid the death of things,
He climbs to eternity through being's gaps,
He is carried by her from Night to deathless Light.
This grand surrender is his free-will's gift,
His pure transcendent force submits to hers.
In the mystery of her cosmic ignorance,
In the insoluble riddle of her play,

A creature made of perishable stuff,
In the pattern she has set for him he moves,
He thinks with her thoughts, with her trouble his bosom heaves;
He seems the thing that she would have him seem,
He is whatever her artist will can make.
Although she drives him on her fancy's roads,
At play with him as with her child or slave,
To freedom and the Eternal's mastery
And immortality's stand above the world,
She moves her seeming puppet of an hour.
Even in his mortal session in body's house,
An aimless traveller between birth and death,
Ephemeral dreaming of immortality,
To reign she spurs him. He takes up her powers;
He has harnessed her to the yoke of her own law.
His face of human thought puts on a crown.
Held in her leash, bound to her veiled caprice,
He studies her ways if so he may prevail
Even for an hour and she work out his will;
He makes of her his moment passion's serf:
To obey she feigns, she follows her creature's lead:
For him she was made, lives only for his use.
But conquering her, then is he most her slave;
He is her dependent, all his means are hers;
Nothing without her he can, she rules him still.
At last he wakes to a memory of Self:
He sees within the face of deity,
The Godhead breaks out through the human mould:
Her highest heights she unmasks and is his mate.
Till then he is a plaything in her game;
Her seeming regent, yet her fancy's toy,
A living robot moved by her energy's springs,
He acts as in the movements of a dream,
An automaton stepping in the grooves of Fate,
He stumbles on driven by her whip of Force:
His thought labours, a bullock in Time's fields;

His will he thinks his own, is shaped in her forge.
Obedient to World-Nature's dumb control,
Driven by his own formidable Power,
His chosen partner in a titan game,
Her will he has made the master of his fate,
Her whim the dispenser of his pleasure and pain;
He has sold himself into her regal power
For any blow or boon that she may choose:
Even in what is suffering to our sense,
He feels the sweetness of her mastering touch,
In all experience meets her blissful hands;
On his heart he bears the happiness of her tread
And the surprise of her arrival's joy
In each event and every moment's chance.
All she can do is marvellous in his sight:
He revels in her, a swimmer in her sea,
A tireless amateur of her world-delight,
He rejoices in her every thought and act
And gives consent to all that she can wish;
Whatever she desires he wills to be:
The Spirit, the innumerable One,
He has left behind his lone eternity,
He is an endless birth in endless Time,
Her finite's multitude in an infinite Space.

   The master of existence lurks in us
And plays at hide-and-seek with his own Force;
In Nature's instrument loiters secret God.
The Immanent lives in man as in his house;
He has made the universe his pastime's field,
A vast gymnasium of his works of might.
All-knowing he accepts our darkened state,
Divine, wears shapes of animal or man;
Eternal, he assents to Fate and Time,
Immortal, dallies with mortality.
The All-Conscious ventured into Ignorance,

The All-Blissful bore to be insensible.
Incarnate in a world of strife and pain,
He puts on joy and sorrow like a robe
And drinks experience like a strengthening wine.
He whose transcendence rules the pregnant Vasts,
Prescient now dwells in our subliminal depths,
A luminous individual Power, alone.
The Absolute, the Perfect, the Alone
Has called out of the Silence his mute Force
Where she lay in the featureless and formless hush
Guarding from Time by her immobile sleep
The ineffable puissance of his solitude.
The Absolute, the Perfect, the Alone
Has entered with his silence into space:
He has fashioned these countless persons of one self;
He has built a million figures of his power;
He lives in all, who lived in his Vast alone;
Space is himself and Time is only he.
The Absolute, the Perfect, the Immune,
One who is in us as our secret self,
Our mask of imperfection has assumed,
He has made this tenement of flesh his own,
His image in the human measure cast
That to his divine measure we might rise;
Then in a figure of divinity
The Maker shall recast us and impose
A plan of godhead on the mortal's mould
Lifting our finite minds to his infinite,
Touching the moment with eternity.
This transfiguration is earth's due to heaven:
A mutual debt binds man to the Supreme:
His nature we must put on as he put ours;
We are sons of God and must be even as he:
His human portion, we must grow divine.
Our life is a paradox with God for key.

But meanwhile all is a shadow cast by a dream
And to the musing and immobile spirit
Life and himself don the aspect of a myth,
The burden of a long unmeaning tale.
For the key is hid and by the Inconscient kept;
The secret God beneath the threshold dwells.
In a body obscuring the immortal Spirit
A nameless Resident vesting unseen powers
With Matter's shapes and motives beyond thought
And the hazard of an unguessed consequence,
An omnipotent indiscernible Influence,
He sits, unfelt by the form in which he lives
And veils his knowledge by the groping mind.
A wanderer in a world his thoughts have made,
He turns in a chiaroscuro of error and truth
To find a wisdom that on high is his.
As one forgetting he searches for himself;
As if he had lost an inner light he seeks:
As a sojourner lingering amid alien scenes
He journeys to a home he knows no more.
His own self's truth he seeks who is the Truth;
He is the Player who became the play,
He is the Thinker who became the thought;
He is the many who was the silent One.
In the symbol figures of the cosmic Force
And in her living and inanimate signs
And in her complex tracery of events
He explores the ceaseless miracle of himself,
Till the thousandfold enigma has been solved
In the single light of an all-witnessing Soul.
    This was his compact with his mighty mate,
For love of her and joined to her for ever
To follow the course of Time's eternity,
Amid magic dramas of her sudden moods
And the surprises of her masked Idea
And the vicissitudes of her vast caprice.

Two seem his goals, yet ever are they one
And gaze at each other over bourneless Time;
Spirit and Matter are their end and source.
A seeker of hidden meanings in life's forms,
Of the great Mother's wide uncharted will
And the rude enigma of her terrestrial ways
He is the explorer and the mariner
On a secret inner ocean without bourne:
He is the adventurer and cosmologist
Of a magic earth's obscure geography.
In her material order's fixed design
Where all seems sure and, even when changed, the same,
Even though the end is left for ever unknown
And ever unstable is life's shifting flow,
His paths are found for him by silent fate;
As stations in the ages' weltering flood
Firm lands appear that tempt and stay awhile,
Then new horizons lure the mind's advance.
There comes no close to the finite's boundlessness,
There is no last certitude in which thought can pause
And no terminus to the soul's experience.
A limit, a farness never wholly reached,
An unattained perfection calls to him
From distant boundaries in the Unseen:
A long beginning only has been made.

This is the sailor on the flow of Time,
This is World-Matter's slow discoverer,
Who, launched into this small corporeal birth,
Has learned his craft in tiny bays of self,
But dares at last unplumbed infinitudes,
A voyager upon eternity's seas.
In his world-adventure's crude initial start
Behold him ignorant of his godhead's force,
Timid initiate of its vast design.
An expert captain of a fragile craft,

A trafficker in small impermanent wares,
At first he hugs the shore and shuns the breadths,
Dares not to affront the far-off perilous main.
He in a petty coastal traffic plies,
His pay doled out from port to neighbour port,
Content with his safe round's unchanging course,
He hazards not the new and the unseen.
But now he hears the sound of larger seas.
A widening world calls him to distant scenes
And journeyings in a larger vision's arc
And peoples unknown and still unvisited shores.
On a commissioned keel his merchant hull
Serves the world's commerce in the riches of Time
Severing the foam of a great land-locked sea
To reach unknown harbour lights in distant climes
And open markets for life's opulent arts,
Rich bales, carved statuettes, hued canvases,
And jewelled toys brought for an infant's play
And perishable products of hard toil
And transient splendours won and lost by the days.
Or passing through a gate of pillar-rocks,
Venturing not yet to cross oceans unnamed
And journey into a dream of distances
He travels close to unfamiliar coasts
And finds new haven in storm-troubled isles,
Or, guided by a sure compass in his thought,
He plunges through a bright haze that hides the stars,
Steering on the trade-routes of Ignorance.
His prow pushes towards undiscovered shores,
He chances on unimagined continents:
A seeker of the islands of the Blest,
He leaves the last lands, crosses the ultimate seas,
He turns to eternal things his symbol quest;
Life changes for him its time-constructed scenes,
Its images veiling infinity.
Earth's borders recede and the terrestrial air

Hangs round him no longer its translucent veil.
He has crossed the limit of mortal thought and hope,
He has reached the world's end and stares beyond;
The eyes of mortal body plunge their gaze
Into Eyes that look upon eternity.
A greater world Time's traveller must explore.
At last he hears a chanting on the heights
And the far speaks and the unknown grows near:
He crosses the boundaries of the unseen
And passes over the edge of mortal sight
To a new vision of himself and things.
He is a spirit in an unfinished world
That knows him not and cannot know itself:
The surface symbol of his goalless quest
Takes deeper meanings to his inner view;
His is a search of darkness for the light,
Of mortal life for immortality.
In the vessel of an earthly embodiment
Over the narrow rails of limiting sense
He looks out on the magic waves of Time
Where mind like a moon illumines the world's dark.
There is limned ever retreating from the eyes,
As if in a tenuous misty dream-light drawn,
The outline of a dim mysterious shore.
A sailor on the Inconscient's fathomless sea,
He voyages through a starry world of thought
On Matter's deck to a spiritual sun.
Across the noise and multitudinous cry,
Across the rapt unknowable silences,
Through a strange mid-world under supernal skies,
Beyond earth's longitudes and latitudes,
His goal is fixed outside all present maps.
But none learns whither through the unknown he sails
Or what secret mission the great Mother gave.
In the hidden strength of her omnipotent Will,
Driven by her breath across life's tossing deep,

Through the thunder's roar and through the windless hush,
Through fog and mist where nothing more is seen,
He carries her sealed orders in his breast.
Late will he know, opening the mystic script,
Whether to a blank port in the Unseen
He goes or, armed with her fiat, to discover
A new mind and body in the city of God
And enshrine the Immortal in his glory's house
And make the finite one with Infinity.
Across the salt waste of the endless years
Her ocean winds impel his errant boat,
The cosmic waters plashing as he goes,
A rumour around him and danger and a call.
Always he follows in her force's wake.
He sails through life and death and other life,
He travels on through waking and through sleep.
A power is on him from her occult force
That ties him to his own creation's fate,
And never can the mighty Traveller rest
And never can the mystic voyage cease
Till the nescient dusk is lifted from man's soul
And the morns of God have overtaken his night.
As long as Nature lasts, he too is there,
For this is sure that he and she are one;
Even when he sleeps, he keeps her on his breast:
Whoever leaves her, he will not depart
To repose without her in the Unknowable.
There is a truth to know, a work to do;
Her play is real; a Mystery he fulfils:
There is a plan in the Mother's deep world-whim,
A purpose in her vast and random game.
This ever she meant since the first dawn of life,
This constant will she covered with her sport,
To evoke a Person in the impersonal Void,
With the Truth-Light strike earth's massive roots of trance,
Wake a dumb self in the inconscient depths

And raise a lost Power from its python sleep
That the eyes of the Timeless might look out from Time
And the world manifest the unveiled Divine.
For this he left his white infinity
And laid on the spirit the burden of the flesh,
That Godhead's seed might flower in mindless Space.

END OF CANTO FOUR

The Yoga of the King:
The Yoga of the Spirit's Freedom and Greatness

THIS knowledge first he had of time-born men.
Admitted through a curtain of bright mind
That hangs between our thoughts and absolute sight,
He found the occult cave, the mystic door
Near to the well of vision in the soul,
And entered where the Wings of Glory brood
In the silent space where all is for ever known.
Indifferent to doubt and to belief,
Avid of the naked real's single shock
He shore the cord of mind that ties the earth-heart
And cast away the yoke of Matter's law.
The body's rules bound not the spirit's powers:
When life had stopped its beats, death broke not in;
He dared to live when breath and thought were still.
Thus could he step into that magic place
Which few can even glimpse with hurried glance
Lifted for a moment from mind's laboured works
And the poverty of Nature's earthly sight.
All that the Gods have learned is there self-known.
There in a hidden chamber closed and mute
Are kept the record graphs of the cosmic scribe,
And there the tables of the sacred Law,
There is the Book of Being's index page;
The text and glossary of the Vedic truth
Are there; the rhythms and metres of the stars
Significant of the movements of our fate:
The symbol powers of number and of form,
And the secret code of the history of the world
And Nature's correspondence with the soul
Are written in the mystic heart of Life.

In the glow of the spirit's room of memories
He could recover the luminous marginal notes
Dotting with light the crabbed ambiguous scroll,
Rescue the preamble and the saving clause
Of the dark Agreement by which all is ruled
That rises from material Nature's sleep
To clothe the Everlasting in new shapes.
He could re-read now and interpret new
Its strange symbol letters, scattered abstruse signs,
Resolve its oracle and its paradox,
Its riddling phrases and its blindfold terms,
The deep oxymoron of its truth's repliques,
And recognise as a just necessity
Its hard conditions for the mighty work, —
Nature's impossible Herculean toil
Only her warlock-wisecraft could enforce,
Its law of the opposition of the gods,
Its list of inseparable contraries.
The dumb great Mother in her cosmic trance
Exploiting for creation's joy and pain
Infinity's sanction to the birth of form,
Accepts indomitably to execute
The will to know in an inconscient world,
The will to live under a reign of death,
The thirst for rapture in a heart of flesh,
And works out through the appearance of a soul
By a miraculous birth in plasm and gas
The mystery of God's covenant with the Night.
Once more was heard in the still cosmic Mind
The Eternal's promise to his labouring Force
Inducing the world-passion to begin,
The cry of birth into mortality
And the opening verse of the tragedy of Time.
Out of the depths the world's buried secret rose;
He read the original ukase kept back
In the locked archives of the spirit's crypt,

And saw the signature and fiery seal
Of Wisdom on the dim Power's hooded work
Who builds in Ignorance the steps of Light.
A sleeping deity opened deathless eyes:
He saw the unshaped thought in soulless forms,
Knew Matter pregnant with spiritual sense,
Mind dare the study of the Unknowable,
Life its gestation of the Golden Child.
In the light flooding thought's blank vacancy,
Interpreting the universe by soul signs
He read from within the text of the without:
The riddle grew plain and lost its catch obscure.
A larger lustre lit the mighty page.
A purpose mingled with the whims of Time,
A meaning met the stumbling pace of Chance
And Fate revealed a chain of seeing Will;
A conscious wideness filled the old dumb Space.
In the Void he saw throned the Omniscience supreme.

    A Will, a hope immense now seized his heart,
And to discern the superhuman's form
He raised his eyes to unseen spiritual heights,
Aspiring to bring down a greater world.
The glory he had glimpsed must be his home.
A brighter heavenlier sun must soon illume
This dusk room with its dark internal stair,
The infant soul in its small nursery school
Mid objects meant for a lesson hardly learned
Outgrow its early grammar of intellect
And its imitation of Earth-Nature's art,
Its earthly dialect to God-language change,
In living symbols study Reality
And learn the logic of the Infinite.
The Ideal must be Nature's common truth,
The body illumined with the indwelling God,
The heart and mind feel one with all that is,

A conscious soul live in a conscious world.
As through a mist a sovereign peak is seen,
The greatness of the eternal Spirit appeared,
Exiled in a fragmented universe
Amid half-semblances of diviner things.
These now could serve no more his regal turn;
The Immortal's pride refused the doom to live
A miser of the scanty bargain made
Between our littleness and bounded hopes
And the compassionate Infinitudes.
His height repelled the lowness of earth's state:
A wideness discontented with its frame
Resiled from poor assent to Nature's terms,
The harsh contract spurned and the diminished lease.
Only beginnings are accomplished here;
Our base's Matter seems alone complete,
An absolute machine without a soul.
Or all seems a misfit of half ideas,
Or we saddle with the vice of earthly form
A hurried imperfect glimpse of heavenly things,
Guesses and travesties of celestial types.
Here chaos sorts itself into a world,
A brief formation drifting in the void:
Apings of knowledge, unfinished arcs of power,
Flamings of beauty into earthly shapes,
Love's broken reflexes of unity
Swim, fragment-mirrorings of a floating sun.
A packed assemblage of crude tentative lives
Are pieced into a tessellated whole.
There is no perfect answer to our hopes;
There are blind voiceless doors that have no key;
Thought climbs in vain and brings a borrowed light,
Cheated by counterfeits sold to us in life's mart,
Our hearts clutch at a forfeited heavenly bliss.
There is provender for the mind's satiety,
There are thrills of the flesh, but not the soul's desire.

Here even the highest rapture Time can give
Is a mimicry of ungrasped beatitudes,
A mutilated statue of ecstasy,
A wounded happiness that cannot live,
A brief felicity of mind or sense
Thrown by the World-Power to her body-slave,
Or a simulacrum of enforced delight
In the seraglios of Ignorance.
For all we have acquired soon loses worth,
An old disvalued credit in Time's bank,
Imperfection's cheque drawn on the Inconscient.
An inconsequence dogs every effort made,
And chaos waits on every cosmos formed:
In each success a seed of failure lurks.
He saw the doubtfulness of all things here,
The incertitude of man's proud confident thought,
The transience of the achievements of his force.
A thinking being in an unthinking world,
An island in the sea of the Unknown,
He is a smallness trying to be great,
An animal with some instincts of a god,
His life a story too common to be told,
His deeds a number summing up to nought,
His consciousness a torch lit to be quenched,
His hope a star above a cradle and grave.
And yet a greater destiny may be his,
For the eternal Spirit is his truth.
He can re-create himself and all around
And fashion new the world in which he lives:
He, ignorant, is the Knower beyond Time,
He is the Self above Nature, above Fate.

    His soul retired from all that he had done.
Hushed was the futile din of human toil,
Forsaken wheeled the circle of the days;
In distance sank the crowded tramp of life.

The Silence was his sole companion left.
Impassive he lived immune from earthly hopes,
A figure in the ineffable Witness' shrine
Pacing the vast cathedral of his thoughts
Under its arches dim with infinity
And heavenward brooding of invisible wings.
A call was on him from intangible heights;
Indifferent to the little outpost Mind,
He dwelt in the wideness of the Eternal's reign.
His being now exceeded thinkable Space,
His boundless thought was neighbour to cosmic sight:
A universal light was in his eyes,
A golden influx flowed through heart and brain;
A Force came down into his mortal limbs,
A current from eternal seas of Bliss;
He felt the invasion and the nameless joy.
Aware of his occult omnipotent Source,
Allured by the omniscient Ecstasy,
A living centre of the Illimitable
Widened to equate with the world's circumference,
He turned to his immense spiritual fate.
Abandoned on a canvas of torn air,
A picture lost in far and fading streaks,
The earth-nature's summits sank below his feet:
He climbed to meet the infinite more above.
The Immobile's ocean-silence saw him pass,
An arrow leaping through eternity
Suddenly shot from the tense bow of Time,
A ray returning to its parent sun.
Opponent of that glory of escape,
The black Inconscient swung its dragon tail
Lashing a slumbrous Infinite by its force
Into the deep obscurities of form:
Death lay beneath him like a gate of sleep.
One-pointed to the immaculate Delight,
Questing for God as for a splendid prey,

He mounted burning like a cone of fire.
To a few is given that godlike rare release.
One among many thousands never touched,
Engrossed in the external world's design,
Is chosen by a secret witness Eye
And driven by a pointing hand of Light
Across his soul's unmapped immensitudes.
A pilgrim of the everlasting Truth,
Our measures cannot hold his measureless mind;
He has turned from the voices of the narrow realm
And left the little lane of human Time.
In the hushed precincts of a vaster plan
He treads the vestibules of the Unseen,
Or listens following a bodiless Guide
To a lonely cry in boundless vacancy.
All the deep cosmic murmur falling still,
He lives in the hush before the world was born,
His soul left naked to the timeless One.
Far from compulsion of created things
Thought and its shadowy idols disappear,
The moulds of form and person are undone:
The ineffable Wideness knows him for its own.
A lone forerunner of the Godward earth,
Among the symbols of yet unshaped things
Watched by closed eyes, mute faces of the Unborn,
He journeys to meet the Incommunicable,
Hearing the echo of his single steps
In the eternal courts of Solitude.
A nameless Marvel fills the motionless hours.
His spirit mingles with eternity's heart
And bears the silence of the Infinite.

In a divine retreat from mortal thought,
In a prodigious gesture of soul-sight,
His being towered into pathless heights,
Naked of its vesture of humanity.

As thus it rose, to meet him bare and pure
A strong Descent leaped down. A Might, a Flame,
A Beauty half-visible with deathless eyes,
A violent Ecstasy, a Sweetness dire,
Enveloped him with its stupendous limbs
And penetrated nerve and heart and brain
That thrilled and fainted with the epiphany:
His nature shuddered in the Unknown's grasp.
In a moment shorter than death, longer than Time,
By a Power more ruthless than Love, happier than Heaven,
Taken sovereignly into eternal arms,
Haled and coerced by a stark absolute bliss,
In a whirlwind circuit of delight and force
Hurried into unimaginable depths,
Upborne into immeasurable heights,
It was torn out from its mortality
And underwent a new and bourneless change.
An Omniscient knowing without sight or thought,
An indecipherable Omnipotence,
A mystic Form that could contain the worlds,
Yet make one human breast its passionate shrine,
Drew him out of his seeking loneliness
Into the magnitudes of God's embrace.
As when a timeless Eye annuls the hours
Abolishing the agent and the act,
So now his spirit shone out wide, blank, pure:
His wakened mind became an empty slate
On which the Universal and Sole could write.
All that represses our fallen consciousness
Was taken from him like a forgotten load:
A fire that seemed the body of a god
Consumed the limiting figures of the past
And made large room for a new self to live.
Eternity's contact broke the moulds of sense.
A greater Force than the earthly held his limbs,
Huge workings bared his undiscovered sheaths,

Strange energies wrought and screened tremendous hands
Unwound the triple cord of mind and freed
The heavenly wideness of a Godhead's gaze.
As through a dress the wearer's shape is seen,
There reached through forms to the hidden absolute
A cosmic feeling and transcendent sight.
Increased and heightened were the instruments.
Illusion lost her aggrandising lens;
As from her failing hand the measures fell,
Atomic looked the things that loomed so large.
The little ego's ring could join no more;
In the enormous spaces of the self
The body now seemed only a wandering shell,
His mind the many-frescoed outer court
Of an imperishable Inhabitant:
His spirit breathed a superhuman air.
The imprisoned deity rent its magic fence.
As with a sound of thunder and of seas,
Vast barriers crashed around the huge escape.
Immutably coeval with the world,
Circle and end of every hope and toil
Inexorably drawn round thought and act,
The fixed immovable peripheries
Effaced themselves beneath the Incarnate's tread.
The dire velamen and the bottomless crypt
Between which life and thought for ever move,
Forbidden still to cross the dim dread bounds,
The guardian darknesses mute and formidable,
Empowered to circumscribe the wingless spirit
In the boundaries of Mind and Ignorance,
Protecting no more a dual eternity
Vanished rescinding their enormous role:
Once figure of creation's vain ellipse,
The expanding zero lost its giant curve.
The old adamantine vetoes stood no more:
Overpowered were earth and Nature's obsolete rule;

The python coils of the restricting Law
Could not restrain the swift arisen God:
Abolished were the scripts of destiny.
There was no small death-hunted creature more,
No fragile form of being to preserve
From an all-swallowing Immensity.
The great hammer-beats of a pent-up world-heart
Burst open the narrow dams that keep us safe
Against the forces of the universe.
The soul and cosmos faced as equal powers.
A boundless being in a measureless Time
Invaded Nature with the infinite;
He saw unpathed, unwalled, his titan scope.

All was uncovered to his sealless eye.
A secret Nature stripped of her defence,
Once in a dreaded half-light formidable,
Overtaken in her mighty privacy
Lay bare to the burning splendour of his will.
In shadowy chambers lit by a strange sun
And opening hardly to hid mystic keys
Her perilous arcanes and hooded Powers
Confessed the advent of a mastering Mind
And bore the compulsion of a time-born gaze.
Incalculable in their wizard modes,
Immediate and invincible in the act,
Her secret strengths native to greater worlds
Lifted above our needy limited scope,
The occult privilege of demigods
And the sure power-pattern of her cryptic signs,
Her diagrams of geometric force,
Her potencies of marvel-fraught design
Courted employment by an earth-nursed might.
A conscious Nature's quick machinery
Armed with a latent splendour of miracle
The prophet-passion of a seeing Mind,

And the lightning bareness of a free soul-force.
All once impossible deemed could now become
A natural limb of possibility,
A new domain of normalcy supreme.
An almighty occultist erects in Space
This seeming outward world which tricks the sense;
He weaves his hidden threads of consciousness,
He builds bodies for his shapeless energy;
Out of the unformed and vacant Vast he has made
His sorcery of solid images,
His magic of formative number and design,
The fixed irrational links none can annul,
This criss-cross tangle of invisible laws;
His infallible rules, his covered processes,
Achieve unerringly an inexplicable
Creation where our error carves dead frames
Of knowledge for a living ignorance.
In her mystery's moods divorced from the Maker's laws
She too as sovereignly creates her field,
Her will shaping the undetermined vasts,
Making a finite of infinity;
She too can make an order of her caprice,
As if her rash superb wagered to outvie
The veiled Creator's cosmic secrecies.
The rapid footsteps of her fantasy,
Amid whose falls wonders like flowers rise,
Are surer than reason, defter than device
And swifter than Imagination's wings.
All she new-fashions by the thought and word,
Compels all substance by her wand of Mind.
Mind is a mediator divinity:
Its powers can undo all Nature's work:
Mind can suspend or change earth's concrete law.
Affranchised from earth-habit's drowsy seal
The leaden grip of Matter it can break;
Indifferent to the angry stare of Death,

It can immortalise a moment's work:
A simple fiat of its thinking force,
The casual pressure of its slight assent
Can liberate the Energy dumb and pent
Within its chambers of mysterious trance:
It makes the body's sleep a puissant arm,
Holds still the breath, the beatings of the heart,
While the unseen is found, the impossible done,
Communicates without means the unspoken thought;
It moves events by its bare silent will,
Acts at a distance without hands or feet.
This giant Ignorance, this dwarfish Life
It can illumine with a prophet sight,
Invoke the bacchic rapture, the Fury's goad,
In our body arouse the demon or the god,
Call in the Omniscient and Omnipotent,
Awake a forgotten Almightiness within.
In its own plane a shining emperor,
Even in this rigid realm, Mind can be king:
The logic of its demigod Idea
In the leap of a transitional moment brings
Surprises of creation never achieved
Even by Matter's strange unconscious skill.
All's miracle here and can by miracle change.
This is that secret Nature's edge of might.
On the margin of great immaterial planes,
In kingdoms of an untrammelled glory of force,
Where Mind is master of the life and form
And soul fulfils its thoughts by its own power,
She meditates upon mighty words and looks
On the unseen links that join the parted spheres.
Thence to the initiate who observes her laws
She brings the light of her mysterious realms:
Here where he stands, his feet on a prostrate world,
His mind no more cast into Matter's mould,
Over their bounds in spurts of splendid strength

She carries their magician processes
And the formulas of their stupendous speech,
Till heaven and hell become purveyors to earth
And the universe the slave of mortal will.
A mediatrix with veiled and nameless gods
Whose alien will touches our human life,
Imitating the World-Magician's ways
She invents for her self-bound free-will its grooves
And feigns for magic's freaks a binding cause.
All worlds she makes the partners of her deeds,
Accomplices of her mighty violence,
Her daring leaps into the impossible:
From every source she has taken her cunning means,
She draws from the free-love marriage of the planes
Elements for her creation's tour-de-force:
A wonder-weft of knowledge incalculable,
A compendium of divine invention's feats
She has combined to make the unreal true
Or liberate suppressed reality:
In her unhedged Circean wonderland
Pell-mell she shepherds her occult mightinesses;
Her mnemonics of the craft of the Infinite,
Jets of the screened subliminal's caprice,
Tags of the gramarye of Inconscience,
Freedom of a sovereign Truth without a law,
Thoughts that were born in the immortals' world,
Oracles that break out from behind the shrine,
Warnings from the daemonic inner voice
And peeps and lightning-leaps of prophecy
And intimations to the inner ear,
Abrupt interventions stark and absolute
And the Superconscient's unaccountable acts,
Have woven her balanced web of miracles
And the weird technique of her tremendous art.
This bizarre kingdom passed into his charge.
As one resisting more the more she loves,

Her great possessions and her power and lore
She gave, compelled, with a reluctant joy;
Herself she gave for rapture and for use.
Absolved from aberrations in deep ways,
The ends she recovered for which she was made:
She turned against the evil she had helped
Her engined wrath, her invisible means to slay;
Her dangerous moods and arbitrary force
She surrendered to the service of the soul
And the control of a spiritual will.
A greater despot tamed her despotism.
Assailed, surprised in the fortress of her self,
Conquered by her own unexpected king,
Fulfilled and ransomed by her servitude,
She yielded in a vanquished ecstasy,
Her sealed hermetic wisdom forced from her,
Fragments of the mystery of omnipotence.

    A border sovereign is the occult Force.
A threshold guardian of the earth-scene's Beyond,
She has canalised the outbreaks of the Gods
And cut through vistas of intuitive sight
A long road of shimmering discoveries.
The worlds of a marvellous Unknown were near,
Behind her an ineffable Presence stood:
Her reign received their mystic influences,
Their lion-forces crouched beneath her feet;
The future sleeps unknown behind their doors.
Abysms infernal gaped round the soul's steps
And called to its mounting vision peaks divine:
An endless climb and adventure of the Idea
There tirelessly tempted the explorer mind
And countless voices visited the charmed ear;
A million figures passed and were seen no more.
This was a forefront of God's thousandfold house,
Beginnings of the half-screened Invisible.

A magic porch of entry glimmering
Quivered in a penumbra of screened Light,
A court of the mystical traffic of the worlds,
A balcony and miraculous façade.
Above her lightened high immensities;
All the unknown looked out from boundlessness:
It lodged upon an edge of hourless Time,
Gazing out of some everlasting Now,
Its shadows gleaming with the birth of gods,
Its bodies signalling the Bodiless,
Its foreheads glowing with the Oversoul,
Its forms projected from the Unknowable,
Its eyes dreaming of the Ineffable,
Its faces staring into eternity.
Life in him learned its huge subconscient rear;
The little fronts unlocked to the unseen Vasts:
Her gulfs stood nude, her far transcendences
Flamed in transparencies of crowded light.

    A giant order was discovered here
Of which the tassel and extended fringe
Are the scant stuff of our material lives.
This overt universe whose figures hide
The secrets merged in superconscient light,
Wrote clear the letters of its glowing code:
A map of subtle signs surpassing thought
Was hung upon a wall of inmost mind.
Illumining the world's concrete images
Into significant symbols by its gloss,
It offered to the intuitive exegete
Its reflex of the eternal Mystery.
Ascending and descending twixt life's poles
The seried kingdoms of the graded Law
Plunged from the Everlasting into Time,
Then glad of a glory of multitudinous mind
And rich with life's adventure and delight

And packed with the beauty of Matter's shapes and hues
Climbed back from Time into undying Self,
Up a golden ladder carrying the soul,
Tying with diamond threads the Spirit's extremes.
In this drop from consciousness to consciousness
Each leaned on the occult Inconscient's power,
The fountain of its needed Ignorance,
Archmason of the limits by which it lives.
In this soar from consciousness to consciousness
Each lifted tops to That from which it came,
Origin of all that it had ever been
And home of all that it could still become.
An organ scale of the Eternal's acts,
Mounting to their climax in an endless Calm,
Paces of the many-visaged Wonderful,
Predestined stadia of the evolving Way,
Measures of the stature of the growing soul,
They interpreted existence to itself
And, mediating twixt the heights and deeps,
United the veiled married opposites
And linked creation to the Ineffable.
A last high world was seen where all worlds meet;
In its summit gleam where Night is not nor Sleep,
The light began of the Trinity supreme.
All there discovered what it seeks for here.
It freed the finite into boundlessness
And rose into its own eternities.
The Inconscient found its heart of consciousness,
The idea and feeling groping in Ignorance
At last clutched passionately the body of Truth,
The music born in Matter's silences
Plucked nude out of the Ineffable's fathomlessness
The meaning it had held but could not voice;
The perfect rhythm now only sometimes dreamed
An answer brought to the torn earth's hungry need
Rending the night that had concealed the Unknown,

Giving to her her lost forgotten soul.
A grand solution closed the long impasse
In which the heights of mortal effort end.
A reconciling Wisdom looked on life;
It took the striving undertones of mind
And took the confused refrain of human hopes
And made of them a sweet and happy call;
It lifted from an underground of pain
The inarticulate murmur of our lives
And found for it a sense illimitable.
A mighty oneness its perpetual theme,
It caught the soul's faint scattered utterances,
Read hardly twixt our lines of rigid thought
Or mid this drowse and coma on Matter's breast
Heard like disjointed mutterings in sleep;
It grouped the golden links that they had lost
And showed to them their divine unity,
Saving from the error of divided self
The deep spiritual cry in all that is.
All the great Words that toiled to express the One
Were lifted into an absoluteness of light,
An ever-burning Revelation's fire
And the immortality of the eternal Voice.
There was no quarrel more of truth with truth;
The endless chapter of their differences
Retold in light by an omniscient Scribe
Travelled through difference towards unity,
Mind's winding search lost every tinge of doubt
Led to its end by an all-seeing speech
That garbed the initial and original thought
With the finality of an ultimate phrase:
United were Time's creative mood and tense
To the style and syntax of Identity.
A paean swelled from the lost musing deeps;
An anthem pealed to the triune ecstasies,
A cry of the moments to the Immortal's bliss.

As if the strophes of a cosmic ode,
A hierarchy of climbing harmonies
Peopled with voices and with visages
Aspired in a crescendo of the Gods
From Matter's abysses to the Spirit's peaks.
Above were the Immortal's changeless seats,
White chambers of dalliance with eternity
And the stupendous gates of the Alone.
Across the unfolding of the seas of self
Appeared the deathless countries of the One.
A many-miracled Consciousness unrolled
Vast aim and process and unfettered norms,
A larger Nature's great familiar roads.
Affranchised from the net of earthly sense
Calm continents of potency were glimpsed;
Homelands of beauty shut to human eyes,
Half-seen at first through wonder's gleaming lids,
Surprised the vision with felicity;
Sunbelts of knowledge, moonbelts of delight
Stretched out in an ecstasy of widenesses
Beyond our indigent corporeal range.
There he could enter, there awhile abide.
A voyager upon uncharted routes
Fronting the viewless danger of the Unknown,
Adventuring across enormous realms,
He broke into another Space and Time.

END OF CANTO FIVE
End of Book One

BOOK TWO

The Book of the Traveller of the Worlds

Canto One

The World-Stair

ALONE he moved watched by the infinity
Around him and the Unknowable above.
All could be seen that shuns the mortal eye,
All could be known the mind has never grasped;
All could be done no mortal will can dare.
A limitless movement filled a limitless peace.
In a profound existence beyond earth's
Parent or kin to our ideas and dreams
Where Space is a vast experiment of the soul,
In an immaterial substance linked to ours
In a deep oneness of all things that are,
The universe of the Unknown arose.
A self-creation without end or pause
Revealed the grandeurs of the Infinite:
It flung into the hazards of its play
A million moods, a myriad energies,
The world-shapes that are fancies of its Truth
And the formulas of the freedom of its Force.
It poured into the Ever-stable's flux
A bacchic rapture and revel of Ideas,
A passion and motion of everlastingness.
There rose unborn into the Unchanging's surge
Thoughts that abide in their deathless consequence,
Words that immortal last though fallen mute,
Acts that brought out from Silence its dumb sense,
Lines that convey the inexpressible.
The Eternal's stillness saw in unmoved joy
His universal Power at work display
In plots of pain and dramas of delight
The wonder and beauty of her will to be.
All, even pain, was the soul's pleasure here;

Here all experience was a single plan,
The thousandfold expression of the One.
All came at once into his single view;
Nothing escaped his vast intuitive sight,
Nothing drew near he could not feel as kin:
He was one spirit with that immensity.
Images in a supernal consciousness
Embodying the Unborn who never dies,
The structured visions of the cosmic Self
Alive with the touch of being's eternity
Looked at him like form-bound spiritual thoughts
Figuring the movements of the Ineffable.
Aspects of being donned world-outline; forms
That open moving doors on things divine,
Became familiar to his hourly sight;
The symbols of the Spirit's reality,
The living bodies of the Bodiless
Grew near to him, his daily associates.
The exhaustless seeings of the unsleeping Mind,
Letterings of its contact with the invisible,
Surrounded him with countless pointing signs;
The voices of a thousand realms of Life
Missioned to him her mighty messages.
The heaven-hints that invade our earthly lives,
The dire imaginations dreamed by Hell,
Which if enacted and experienced here
Our dulled capacity soon would cease to feel
Or our mortal frailty could not long endure,
Were set in their sublime proportions there.
There lived out in their self-born atmosphere,
They resumed their topless pitch and native power;
Their fortifying stress upon the soul
Bit deep into the ground of consciousness
The passion and purity of their extremes,
The absoluteness of their single cry
And the sovereign sweetness or violent poetry

Of their beautiful or terrible delight.
All thought can know or widest sight perceive
And all that thought and sight can never know,
All things occult and rare, remote and strange
Were near to heart's contact, felt by spirit-sense.
Asking for entry at his nature's gates
They crowded the widened spaces of his mind,
His self-discovery's flaming witnesses,
Offering their marvel and their multitude.
These now became new portions of himself,
The figures of his spirit's greater life,
The moving scenery of his large time-walk
Or the embroidered tissue of his sense:
These took the place of intimate human things
And moved as close companions of his thoughts,
Or were his soul's natural environment.
Tireless the heart's adventure of delight,
Endless the kingdoms of the Spirit's bliss,
Unnumbered tones struck from one harmony's strings;
Each to its wide-winged universal poise,
Its fathomless feeling of the All in one,
Brought notes of some perfection yet unseen,
Its single retreat into Truth's secrecies,
Its happy sidelight on the Infinite.
All was found there the Unique has dreamed and made
Tinging with ceaseless rapture and surprise
And an opulent beauty of passionate difference
The recurring beat that moments God in Time.
Only was missing the sole timeless Word
That carries eternity in its lonely sound,
The Idea self-luminous key to all ideas,
The integer of the Spirit's perfect sum
That equates the unequal All to the equal One,
The single sign interpreting every sign,
The absolute index to the Absolute.

There walled apart by its own innerness
In a mystical barrage of dynamic light
He saw a lone immense high-curved world-pile
Erect like a mountain-chariot of the Gods
Motionless under an inscrutable sky.
As if from Matter's plinth and viewless base
To a top as viewless, a carved sea of worlds
Climbing with foam-maned waves to the Supreme
Ascended towards breadths immeasurable;
It hoped to soar into the Ineffable's reign:
A hundred levels raised it to the Unknown.
So it towered up to heights intangible
And disappeared in the hushed conscious Vast
As climbs a storeyed temple-tower to heaven
Built by the aspiring soul of man to live
Near to his dream of the Invisible.
Infinity calls to it as it dreams and climbs;
Its spire touches the apex of the world;
Mounting into great voiceless stillnesses
It marries the earth to screened eternities.
Amid the many systems of the One
Made by an interpreting creative joy
Alone it points us to our journey back
Out of our long self-loss in Nature's deeps;
Planted on earth it holds in it all realms:
It is a brief compendium of the Vast.
This was the single stair to being's goal.
A summary of the stages of the spirit,
Its copy of the cosmic hierarchies
Refashioned in our secret air of self
A subtle pattern of the universe.
It is within, below, without, above.
Acting upon this visible Nature's scheme
It wakens our earth-matter's heavy doze
To think and feel and to react to joy;
It models in us our diviner parts,

Lifts mortal mind into a greater air,
Makes yearn this life of flesh to intangible aims,
Links the body's death with immortality's call:
Out of the swoon of the Inconscience
It labours towards a superconscient Light.
If earth were all and this were not in her,
Thought could not be nor life-delight's response:
Only material forms could then be her guests
Driven by an inanimate world-force.
Earth by this golden superfluity
Bore thinking man and more than man shall bear;
This higher scheme of being is our cause
And holds the key to our ascending fate;
It calls out of our dense mortality
The conscious spirit nursed in Matter's house.
The living symbol of these conscious planes,
Its influences and godheads of the unseen,
Its unthought logic of Reality's acts
Arisen from the unspoken truth in things,
Have fixed our inner life's slow-scaled degrees.
Its steps are paces of the soul's return
From the deep adventure of material birth,
A ladder of delivering ascent
And rungs that Nature climbs to deity.
Once in the vigil of a deathless gaze
These grades had marked her giant downward plunge,
The wide and prone leap of a godhead's fall.
Our life is a holocaust of the Supreme.
The great World-Mother by her sacrifice
Has made her soul the body of our state;
Accepting sorrow and unconsciousness
Divinity's lapse from its own splendours wove
The many-patterned ground of all we are.
An idol of self is our mortality.
Our earth is a fragment and a residue;
Her power is packed with the stuff of greater worlds

And steeped in their colour-lustres dimmed by her drowse;
An atavism of higher births is hers,
Her sleep is stirred by their buried memories
Recalling the lost spheres from which they fell.
Unsatisfied forces in her bosom move;
They are partners of her greater growing fate
And her return to immortality;
They consent to share her doom of birth and death;
They kindle partial gleams of the All and drive
Her blind laborious spirit to compose
A meagre image of the mighty Whole.
The calm and luminous Intimacy within
Approves her work and guides the unseeing Power.
His vast design accepts a puny start.
An attempt, a drawing half-done is the world's life;
Its lines doubt their concealed significance,
Its curves join not their high intended close.
Yet some first image of greatness trembles there,
And when the ambiguous crowded parts have met
The many-toned unity to which they moved,
The Artist's joy shall laugh at reason's rules;
The divine intention suddenly shall be seen,
The end vindicate intuition's sure technique.
A graph shall be of many meeting worlds,
A cube and union-crystal of the gods;
A Mind shall think behind Nature's mindless mask,
A conscious Vast fill the old dumb brute Space.
This faint and fluid sketch of soul called man
Shall stand out on the background of long Time
A glowing epitome of eternity,
A little point reveal the infinitudes.
A Mystery's process is the universe.
At first was laid a strange anomalous base,
A void, a cipher of some secret Whole,
Where zero held infinity in its sum
And All and Nothing were a single term,

An eternal negative, a matrix Nought:
Into its forms the Child is ever born
Who lives for ever in the vasts of God.
A slow reversal's movement then took place:
A gas belched out from some invisible Fire,
Of its dense rings were formed these million stars;
Upon earth's new-born soil God's tread was heard.
Across the thick smoke of earth's ignorance
A Mind began to see and look at forms
And groped for knowledge in the nescient Night:
Caught in a blind stone-grip Force worked its plan
And made in sleep this huge mechanical world,
That Matter might grow conscious of its soul
And like a busy midwife the life-power
Deliver the zero carrier of the All.
Because eternal eyes turned on earth's gulfs
The lucent clarity of a pure regard
And saw a shadow of the Unknowable
Mirrored in the Inconscient's boundless sleep,
Creation's search for self began its stir.
A spirit dreamed in the crude cosmic whirl,
Mind flowed unknowing in the sap of life
And Matter's breasts suckled the divine Idea.
A miracle of the Absolute was born;
Infinity put on a finite soul,
All ocean lived within a wandering drop,
A time-made body housed the Illimitable.
To live this Mystery out our souls came here.

A Seer within who knows the ordered plan
Concealed behind our momentary steps,
Inspires our ascent to viewless heights
As once the abysmal leap to earth and life.
His call had reached the Traveller in Time.
Apart in an unfathomed loneliness,
He travelled in his mute and single strength

Bearing the burden of the world's desire.
A formless Stillness called, a nameless Light.
Above him was the white immobile Ray,
Around him the eternal Silences.
No term was fixed to the high-pitched attempt;
World after world disclosed its guarded powers,
Heaven after heaven its deep beatitudes,
But still the invisible Magnet drew his soul.
A figure sole on Nature's giant stair,
He mounted towards an indiscernible end
On the bare summit of created things.

END OF CANTO ONE

Canto Two

The Kingdom of Subtle Matter

IN THE impalpable field of secret self,
This little outer being's vast support
Parted from vision by earth's solid fence,
He came into a magic crystal air
And found a life that lived not by the flesh,
A light that made visible immaterial things.
A fine degree in wonder's hierarchy,
The kingdom of subtle Matter's faery craft
Outlined against a sky of vivid hues,
Leaping out of a splendour-trance and haze,
The wizard revelation of its front.
A world of lovelier forms lies near to ours,
Where, undisguised by earth's deforming sight,
All shapes are beautiful and all things true.
In that lucent ambience mystically clear
The eyes were doors to a celestial sense,
Hearing was music and the touch a charm,
And the heart drew a deeper breath of power.
There dwell earth-nature's shining origins:
The perfect plans on which she moulds her works,
The distant outcomes of her travailing force,
Repose in a framework of established fate.
Attempted vainly now or won in vain,
Already were mapped and scheduled there the time
And figure of her future sovereignties
In the sumptuous lineaments traced by desire.
The golden issue of mind's labyrinth plots,
The riches unfound or still uncaught by our lives,
Unsullied by the attaint of mortal thought
Abide in that pellucid atmosphere.
Our vague beginnings are overtaken there,

Our middle terms sketched out in prescient lines,
Our finished ends anticipated live.
This brilliant roof of our descending plane,
Intercepting the free boon of heaven's air,
Admits small inrushes of a mighty breath
Or fragrant circuits through gold lattices;
It shields our ceiling of terrestrial mind
From deathless suns and the streaming of God's rain,
Yet canalises a strange irised glow,
And bright dews drip from the Immortal's sky.
A passage for the Powers that move our days,
Occult behind this grosser Nature's walls,
A gossamer marriage-hall of Mind with Form
Is hidden by a tapestry of dreams;
Heaven's meanings steal through it as through a veil,
Its inner sight sustains this outer scene.
A finer consciousness with happier lines,
It has a tact our touch cannot attain,
A purity of sense we never feel;
Its intercession with the eternal Ray
Inspires our transient earth's brief-lived attempts
At beauty and the perfect shape of things.
In rooms of the young divinity of power
And early play of the eternal Child
The embodiments of his outwinging thoughts
Laved in a bright everlasting wonder's tints
And lulled by whispers of that lucid air
Take dream-hued rest like birds on timeless trees
Before they dive to float on earth-time's sea.
All that here seems has lovelier semblance there.
Whatever our hearts conceive, our heads create,
Some high original beauty forfeiting,
Thence exiled here consents to an earthly tinge.
Whatever is here of visible charm and grace
Finds there its faultless and immortal lines;
All that is beautiful here is there divine.

Figures are there undreamed by mortal mind:
Bodies that have no earthly counterpart
Traverse the inner eye's illumined trance
And ravish the heart with their celestial tread
Persuading heaven to inhabit that wonder sphere.
The future's marvels wander in its gulfs;
Things old and new are fashioned in those depths:
A carnival of beauty crowds the heights
In that magic kingdom of ideal sight.
In its antechambers of splendid privacy
Matter and soul in conscious union meet
Like lovers in a lonely secret place:
In the clasp of a passion not yet unfortunate
They join their strength and sweetness and delight
And mingling make the high and low worlds one.
Intruder from the formless Infinite
Daring to break into the Inconscient's reign,
The spirit's leap towards body touches ground.
As yet unwrapped in earthly lineaments,
Already it wears outlasting death and birth,
Convincing the abyss by heavenly form,
A covering of its immortality
Alive to the lustre of the wearer's rank,
Fit to endure the rub of Change and Time.
A tissue mixed of the soul's radiant light
And Matter's substance of sign-burdened Force, —
Imagined vainly in our mind's thin air
An abstract phantasm mould of mental make, —
It feels what earthly bodies cannot feel
And is more real than this grosser frame.
After the falling of mortality's cloak
Lightened is its weight to heighten its ascent;
Refined to the touch of finer environments
It drops old patterned palls of denser stuff,
Cancels the grip of earth's descending pull
And bears the soul from world to higher world,

Till in the naked ether of the peaks
The spirit's simplicity alone is left,
The eternal being's first transparent robe.
But when it must come back to its mortal load
And the hard ensemble of earth's experience,
Then its return resumes that heavier dress.
For long before earth's solid vest was forged
By the technique of the atomic Void,
A lucent envelope of self-disguise
Was woven round the secret spirit in things.
The subtle realms from those bright sheaths are made.
This wonder-world with all its radiant boon
Of vision and inviolate happiness,
Only for expression cares and perfect form;
Fair on its peaks, it has dangerous nether planes;
Its light draws towards the verge of Nature's lapse;
It lends beauty to the terror of the gulfs
And fascinating eyes to perilous Gods,
Invests with grace the demon and the snake.
Its trance imposes earth's inconscience,
Immortal it weaves for us death's sombre robe
And authorises our mortality.
This medium serves a greater Consciousness:
A vessel of its concealed autocracy,
It is the subtle ground of Matter's worlds,
It is the immutable in their mutable forms,
In the folds of its creative memory
It guards the deathless type of perishing things:
Its lowered potencies found our fallen strengths;
Its thought invents our reasoned ignorance;
Its sense fathers our body's reflexes.
Our secret breath of untried mightier force,
The lurking sun of an instant's inner sight,
Its fine suggestions are a covert fount
For our iridescent rich imaginings
Touching things common with transfiguring hues

Till even earth's mud grows rich and warm with the skies
And a glory gleams from the soul's decadence.
Its knowledge is our error's starting-point;
Its beauty dons our mud-mask ugliness,
Its artist good begins our evil's tale.
A heaven of creative truths above,
A cosmos of harmonious dreams between,
A chaos of dissolving forms below,
It plunges lost in our inconscient base.
Out of its fall our denser Matter came.

   Thus taken was God's plunge into the Night.
This fallen world became a nurse of souls
Inhabited by concealed divinity.
A Being woke and lived in the meaningless void,
A world-wide Nescience strove towards life and thought,
A Consciousness plucked out from mindless sleep.
All here is driven by an insentient will.
Thus fallen, inconscient, frustrate, dense, inert,
Sunk into inanimate and torpid drowse
Earth lay, a drudge of sleep, forced to create
By a subconscient yearning memory
Left from a happiness dead before she was born,
An alien wonder on her senseless breast.
This mire must harbour the orchid and the rose,
From her blind unwilling substance must emerge
A beauty that belongs to happier spheres.
This is the destiny bequeathed to her,
As if a slain god left a golden trust
To a blind force and an imprisoned soul.
An immortal godhead's perishable parts
She must reconstitute from fragments lost,
Reword from a document complete elsewhere
Her doubtful title to her divine Name.
A residue her sole inheritance,
All things she carries in her shapeless dust.

Her giant energy tied to petty forms
In the slow tentative motion of her power
With only frail blunt instruments for use,
She has accepted as her nature's need
And given to man as his stupendous work
A labour to the gods impossible.
A life living hardly in a field of death
Its portion claims of immortality;
A brute half-conscious body serves as means
A mind that must recover a knowledge lost
Held in stone grip by the world's inconscience,
And wearing still these countless knots of Law
A spirit bound stand up as Nature's king.
    A mighty kinship is this daring's cause.
All we attempt in this imperfect world,
Looks forward or looks back beyond Time's gloss
To its pure idea and firm inviolate type
In an absolute creation's flawless skill.
To seize the absolute in shapes that pass,
To fix the eternal's touch in time-made things,
This is the law of all perfection here.
A fragment here is caught of heaven's design;
Else could we never hope for greater life
And ecstasy and glory could not be.
Even in the littleness of our mortal state,
Even in this prison-house of outer form,
A brilliant passage for the infallible Flame
Is driven through gross walls of nerve and brain,
A Splendour presses or a Power breaks through,
Earth's great dull barrier is removed awhile,
The inconscient seal is lifted from our eyes
And we grow vessels of creative might.
The enthusiasm of a divine surprise
Pervades our life, a mystic stir is felt,
A joyful anguish trembles in our limbs;
A dream of beauty dances through the heart,

A thought from the eternal Mind draws near,
Intimations cast from the Invisible
Awaking from Infinity's sleep come down,
Symbols of That which never yet was made.
But soon the inert flesh responds no more,
Then sinks the sacred orgy of delight,
The blaze of passion and the tide of power
Are taken from us and, though a glowing form
Abides astonishing earth, imagined supreme,
Too little of what was meant has left a trace.
Earth's eyes half-see, her forces half-create;
Her rarest works are copies of heaven's art.
A radiance of a golden artifice,
A masterpiece of inspired device and rule,
Her forms hide what they house and only mime
The unseized miracle of self-born shapes
That live for ever in the Eternal's gaze.
Here in a difficult half-finished world
Is a slow toiling of unconscious Powers;
Here is man's ignorant divining mind,
His genius born from an inconscient soil.
To copy on earth's copies is his art.
For when he strives for things surpassing earth,
Too rude the workman's tools, too crude his stuff,
And hardly with his heart's blood he achieves
His transient house of the divine Idea,
His figure of a Time-inn for the Unborn.
Our being thrills with high far memories
And would bring down their dateless meanings here,
But, too divine for earthly Nature's scheme,
Beyond our reach the eternal marvels blaze.
Absolute they dwell, unborn, immutable,
Immaculate in the Spirit's deathless air,
Immortal in a world of motionless Time
And an unchanging muse of deep self-space.
Only when we have climbed above ourselves,

A line of the Transcendent meets our road
And joins us to the timeless and the true;
It brings to us the inevitable word,
The godlike act, the thoughts that never die.
A ripple of light and glory wraps the brain,
And travelling down the moment's vanishing route
The figures of eternity arrive.
As the mind's visitors or the heart's guests
They espouse our mortal brevity awhile,
Or seldom in some rare delivering glimpse
Are caught by our vision's delicate surmise.
Although beginnings only and first attempts,
These glimmerings point to the secret of our birth
And the hidden miracle of our destiny.
What we are there and here on earth shall be
Is imaged in a contact and a call.
As yet earth's imperfection is our sphere,
Our nature's glass shows not our real self;
That greatness still abides held back within.
Earth's doubting future hides our heritage:
The Light now distant shall grow native here,
The Strength that visits us our comrade power;
The Ineffable shall find a secret voice,
The Imperishable burn through Matter's screen
Making this mortal body godhead's robe.
The Spirit's greatness is our timeless source
And it shall be our crown in endless Time.
A vast Unknown is round us and within;
All things are wrapped in the dynamic One:
A subtle link of union joins all life.
Thus all creation is a single chain:
We are not left alone in a closed scheme
Between a driving of inconscient Force
And an incommunicable Absolute.
Our life is a spur in a sublime soul-range,
Our being looks beyond its walls of mind

And it communicates with greater worlds;
There are brighter earths and wider heavens than ours.
There **are** realms where Being broods in its own depths;
It **feels in** its immense dynamic core
Its nameless, unformed, unborn potencies
Cry for expression in the unshaped Vast:
Ineffable beyond Ignorance and death,
The images of its everlasting Truth
Look out from a chamber of its self-rapt soul:
As if to its own inner witness gaze
The Spirit holds up its mirrored self and works,
The power and passion of its timeless heart,
The figures of its formless ecstasy,
The grandeurs of its multitudinous might.
Thence comes the mystic substance of our souls
Into the prodigy of our nature's birth,
There is the unfallen height of all we are
And dateless fount of all we hope to be.
On every plane the hieratic Power,
Initiate of unspoken verities,
Dreams to transcribe and make a part of life
In its own native style and living tongue
Some trait of the perfection of the Unborn,
Some vision seen in the omniscient Light,
Some far tone of the immortal rhapsodist Voice,
Some rapture of the all-creating Bliss,
Some form and plan of the Beauty unutterable.
Worlds are there nearer to those absolute realms,
Where the response to Truth is swift and sure
And spirit is not hampered by its frame
And hearts by sharp division seized and rent
And delight and beauty are inhabitants
And love and sweetness are the law of life.
A finer substance in a subtler mould
Embodies the divinity earth but dreams;
Its strength can overtake joy's running feet;

Overleaping the fixed hurdles set by Time,
The rapid net of an intuitive clasp
Captures the fugitive happiness we desire.
A Nature lifted by a larger breath,
Plastic and passive to the all-shaping Fire,
Answers the flaming Godhead's casual touch:
Immune from our inertia of response
It hears the word to which our hearts are deaf,
Adopts the seeing of immortal eyes
And, traveller on the roads of line and hue,
Pursues the spirit of beauty to its home.
Thus we draw near to the All-Wonderful
Following his rapture in things as sign and guide;
Beauty is his footprint showing us where he has passed,
Love is his heart-beats' rhythm in mortal breasts,
Happiness the smile on his adorable face.
A communion of spiritual entities,
A genius of creative Immanence,
Makes all creation deeply intimate:
A fourth dimension of aesthetic sense
Where all is in ourselves, ourselves in all,
To the cosmic wideness re-aligns our souls.
A kindling rapture joins the seer and seen;
The craftsman and the craft grown inly one
Achieve perfection by the magic throb
And passion of their close identity.
All that we slowly piece from gathered parts,
Or by long labour stumblingly evolve,
Is there self-born by its eternal right.
In us too the intuitive Fire can burn;
An agent Light, it is coiled in our folded hearts,
On the celestial levels is its home:
Descending, it can bring those heavens here.
But rarely burns the flame nor burns for long;
The joy it calls from those diviner heights
Brings brief magnificent reminiscences

And high splendid glimpses of interpreting thought,
But not the utter vision and delight.
A veil is kept, something is still held back,
Lest, captives of the beauty and the joy,
Our souls forget to the Highest to aspire.

In that fair subtle realm behind our own
The form is all, and physical gods are kings.
The inspiring Light plays in fine boundaries;
A faultless beauty comes by Nature's grace;
There liberty is perfection's guarantee:
Although the absolute Image lacks, the Word
Incarnate, the sheer spiritual ecstasy,
All is a miracle of symmetric charm,
A fantasy of perfect line and rule.
There all feel satisfied in themselves and whole,
A rich completeness is by limit made,
Marvel in an utter littleness abounds,
An intricate rapture riots in a small space:
Each rhythm is kin to its environment,
Each line is perfect and inevitable,
Each object faultlessly built for charm and use.
All is enamoured of its own delight.
Intact it lives of its perfection sure
In a heaven-pleased self-glad immunity;
Content to be, it has need of nothing more.
Here was not futile effort's broken heart:
Exempt from the ordeal and the test,
Empty of opposition and of pain,
It was a world that could not fear nor grieve.
It had no grace of error or defeat,
It had no room for fault, no power to fail.
Out of some packed self-bliss it drew at once
Its form-discoveries of the mute Idea
And the miracle of its rhythmic thoughts and acts,
Its clear technique of firm and rounded lives,

Its gracious people of inanimate shapes
And glory of breathing bodies like our own.
Amazed, his senses ravished with delight,
He moved in a divine, yet kindred world
Admiring marvellous forms so near to ours
Yet perfect like the playthings of a god,
Deathless in the aspect of mortality.
In their narrow and exclusive absolutes
The finite's ranked supremacies throned abide;
It dreams not ever of what might have been;
Only in boundaries can this absolute live.
In a supremeness bound to its own plan
Where all was finished and no widths were left,
No space for shadows of the immeasurable,
No room for the incalculable's surprise,
A captive of its own beauty and ecstasy,
In a magic circle wrought the enchanted Might.
The spirit stood back effaced behind its frame.
Admired for the bright finality of its lines
A blue horizon limited the soul;
Thought moved in luminous facilities,
The outer ideal's shallows its swim-range:
Life in its boundaries lingered satisfied
With the small happiness of the body's acts.
Assigned as Force to a bound corner-Mind,
Attached to the safe paucity of her room,
She did her little works and played and slept
And thought not of a greater work undone.
Forgetful of her violent vast desires,
Forgetful of the heights to which she rose,
Her walk was fixed within a radiant groove.
The beautiful body of a soul at ease,
Like one who laughs in sweet and sunlit groves,
Childlike she swung in her gold cradle of joy.
The spaces' call reached not her charmed abode,
She had no wings for wide and dangerous flight,

She faced no peril of sky or of abyss,
She knew no vistas and no mighty dreams,
No yearning for her lost infinitudes.
A perfect picture in a perfect frame,
This faery artistry could not keep his will:
Only a moment's fine release it gave;
A careless hour was spent in a slight bliss.
Our spirit tires of being's surfaces,
Transcended is the splendour of the form;
It turns to hidden powers and deeper states.
So now he looked beyond for greater light.
His soul's peak-climb abandoning in its rear
This brilliant courtyard of the House of Days,
He left that fine material Paradise.
His destiny lay beyond in larger Space.

END OF CANTO TWO

Canto Three

The Glory and the Fall of Life

AN UNEVEN broad ascent now lured his feet.
Answering a greater Nature's troubled call
He crossed the limits of embodied Mind
And entered wide obscure disputed fields
Where all was doubt and change and nothing sure,
A world of search and toil without repose.
As one who meets the face of the Unknown,
A questioner with none to give reply,
Attracted to a problem never solved,
Always uncertain of the ground he trod,
Always drawn on to an inconstant goal
He travelled through a land peopled by doubts
In shifting confines on a quaking base.
In front he saw a boundary ever unreached
And thought himself at each step nearer now, —
A far retreating horizon of mirage.
A vagrancy was there that brooked no home,
A journey of countless paths without a close.
Nothing he found to satisfy his heart;
A tireless wandering sought and could not cease.
There life is the manifest Incalculable,
A movement of unquiet seas, a long
And venturous leap of spirit into Space,
A vexed disturbance in the eternal Calm,
An impulse and passion of the Infinite.
Assuming whatever shape her fancy wills,
Escaped from the restraint of settled forms
She has left the safety of the tried and known.
Unshepherded by the fear that walks through Time,
Undaunted by Fate that dogs and Chance that springs,
She accepts disaster as a common risk;

Careless of suffering, heedless of sin and fall,
She wrestles with danger and discovery
In the unexplored expanses of the soul.
To be seemed only a long experiment,
The hazard of a seeking ignorant Force
That tries all truths and, finding none supreme,
Moves on unsatisfied, unsure of its end.
As saw some inner mind, so life was shaped:
From thought to thought she passed, from phase to phase,
Tortured by her own powers or proud and blest,
Now master of herself, now toy and slave.
A huge inconsequence was her action's law,
As if all possibility must be drained,
And anguish and bliss were pastimes of the heart.
In a gallop of thunder-hooved vicissitudes
She swept through the race-fields of Circumstance,
Or, swaying, she tossed between her heights and deeps,
Uplifted or broken on Time's inconstant wheel.
Amid a tedious crawl of drab desires
She writhed, a worm mid worms in Nature's mud,
Then, Titan-statured, took all earth for food,
Ambitioned the seas for robe, for crown the stars
And shouting strode from peak to giant peak,
Clamouring for worlds to conquer and to rule.
Then, wantonly enamoured of Sorrow's face,
She plunged into the anguish of the depths
And, wallowing, clung to her own misery.
In dolorous converse with her squandered self
She wrote the account of all that she had lost,
Or sat with grief as with an ancient friend.
A romp of violent raptures soon was spent,
Or she lingered tied to an inadequate joy
Missing the turns of fate, missing life's goal.
A scene was planned for all her numberless moods
Where each could be the law and way of life,
But none could offer a pure felicity;

Only a flickering zest they left behind
Or the fierce lust that brings a dead fatigue.
Amid her swift untold variety
Something remained dissatisfied, ever the same
And in the new saw only a face of the old,
For every hour repeated all the rest
And every change prolonged the same unease.
A spirit of her self and aim unsure,
Tired soon of too much joy and happiness,
She needs the spur of pleasure and of pain
And the native taste of suffering and unrest:
She strains for an end that never can she win.
A perverse savour haunts her thirsting lips:
For the grief she weeps which came from her own choice,
For the pleasure yearns that racked with wounds her breast;
Aspiring to heaven she turns her steps towards hell.
Chance she has chosen and danger for playfellows;
Fate's dreadful swing she has taken for cradle and seat.
Yet pure and bright from the Timeless was her birth,
A lost world-rapture lingers in her eyes,
Her moods are faces of the Infinite:
Beauty and happiness are her native right,
And endless Bliss is her eternal home.

    This now revealed its antique face of joy,
A sudden disclosure to the heart of grief
Tempting it to endure and long and hope.
Even in changing worlds bereft of peace,
In an air racked with sorrow and with fear
And while his feet trod on a soil unsafe,
He saw the image of a happier state.
In an architecture of hieratic Space
Circling and mounting towards creation's tops,
At a blue height which never was too high
For warm communion between body and soul,
As far as heaven, as near as thought and hope,

Glimmered the kingdom of a griefless life.
Above him in a new celestial vault
Other than the heavens beheld by mortal eyes,
As on a fretted ceiling of the gods,
An archipelago of laughter and fire,
Swam stars apart in a rippled sea of sky.
Towered spirals, magic rings of vivid hue
And gleaming spheres of strange felicity
Floated through distance like a symbol world.
On the trouble and the toil they could not share,
On the unhappiness they could not aid,
Impervious to life's suffering, struggle, grief,
Untarnished by its anger, gloom and hate,
Unmoved, untouched, looked down great visioned planes
Blissful for ever in their timeless right.
Absorbed in their own beauty and content,
Of their immortal gladness they live sure.
Apart in their self-glory plunged, remote
Burning they swam in a vague lucent haze,
An everlasting refuge of dream-light,
A nebula of the splendours of the gods
Made from the musings of eternity.
Almost unbelievable by human faith,
Hardly they seemed the stuff of things that are.
As through a magic television's glass
Outlined to some magnifying inner eye
They shone like images thrown from a far scene
Too high and glad for mortal lids to seize.
But near and real to the longing heart
And to the body's passionate thought and sense
Are the hidden kingdoms of beatitude.
In some close unattained realm which yet we feel,
Immune from the harsh clutch of Death and Time,
Escaping the search of sorrow and desire,
In bright enchanted safe peripheries
For ever wallowing in bliss they lie.

In dream and trance and muse before our eyes,
Across a subtle vision's inner field,
Wide rapturous landscapes fleeting from the sight,
The figures of the perfect kingdom pass
And behind them leave a shining memory's trail.
Imagined scenes or great eternal worlds,
Dream-caught or sensed, they touch our hearts with their depths;
Unreal-seeming, yet more real than life,
Happier than happiness, truer than things true,
If dreams these were or captured images,
Dream's truth made false earth's vain realities.
In a swift eternal moment fixed there live
Or ever recalled come back to longing eyes
Calm heavens of imperishable Light,
Illumined continents of violet peace,
Oceans and rivers of the mirth of God
And griefless countries under purple suns.

   This, once a star of bright remote idea
Or imagination's comet trail of dream,
Took now a close shape of reality.
The gulf between dream-truth, earth-fact was crossed,
The wonder-worlds of life were dreams no more;
His vision made all they unveiled its own:
Their scenes, their happenings met his eyes and heart
And smote them with pure loveliness and bliss.
A breathless summit region drew his gaze
Whose boundaries jutted into a sky of Self
And dipped towards a strange ethereal base.
The quintessence glowed of Life's supreme delight.
On a spiritual and mysterious peak
Only a miracle's high transfiguring line
Divided life from the formless Infinite
And sheltered Time against eternity.
Out of that formless stuff Time mints his shapes;
The Eternal's quiet holds the cosmic act:

The protean images of the World-Force
Have drawn the strength to be, the will to last
From a deep ocean of dynamic peace.
Inverting the spirit's apex towards life,
She spends the plastic liberties of the One
To cast in acts the dreams of her caprice,
His wisdom's call steadies her careless feet,
He props her dance upon a rigid base,
His timeless still immutability
Must standardise her creation's miracle.
Out of the Void's unseeing energies
Inventing the scene of a concrete universe,
By his thought she has fixed its paces, in its blind acts
She sees by flashes of his all-knowing Light.
At her will the inscrutable Supermind leans down
To guide her force that feels but cannot know,
Its breath of power controls her restless seas
And life obeys the governing Idea.
At her will, led by a luminous Immanence
The hazardous experimenting Mind
Pushes its way through obscure possibles
Mid chance formations of an unknowing world.
Our human ignorance moves towards the Truth
That Nescience may become omniscient,
Transmuted instincts shape to divine thoughts,
Thoughts house infallible immortal sight
And Nature climb towards God's identity.
The Master of the worlds self-made her slave
Is the executor of her fantasies:
She has canalised the seas of omnipotence;
She has limited by her laws the Illimitable.
The Immortal bound himself to do her works;
He labours at the tasks her Ignorance sets,
Hidden in the cape of our mortality.
The worlds, the forms her goddess fancy makes
Have lost their origin on unseen heights:

Even severed, straying from their timeless source,
Even deformed, obscure, accursed and fallen, —
Since even fall has its perverted joy
And nothing she leaves out that serves delight, —
These too can to the peaks revert or here
Cut out the sentence of the spirit's fall,
Recover their forfeited divinity.
At once caught in an eternal vision's sweep
He saw her pride and splendour of highborn zones
And her regions crouching in the nether deeps.
Above was a monarchy of unfallen self,
Beneath was the gloomy trance of the abyss,
An opposite pole or dim antipodes.
There were vasts of the glory of life's absolutes:
All laughed in a safe immortality
And an eternal childhood of the soul
Before darkness came and pain and grief were born
Where all could dare to be themselves and one
And Wisdom played in sinless innocence
With naked Freedom in Truth's happy sun.
There were worlds of her laughter and dreadful irony,
There were fields of her taste of toil and strife and tears;
Her head lay on the breast of amorous Death,
Sleep imitated awhile extinction's peace.
The light of God she has parted from his dark
To test the savour of bare opposites.
Here mingling in man's heart their tones and hues
Have woven his being's mutable design,
His life a forward-rippling stream in Time,
His nature's constant fixed mobility,
His soul a moving picture's changeful film,
His cosmos-chaos of personality.
The grand creatrix with her cryptic touch
Has turned to pathos and power being's self-dream,
Made a passion-play of its fathomless mystery.

But here were worlds lifted half-way to heaven.
The Veil was there but not the Shadowy Wall;
In forms not too remote from human grasp
Some passion of the inviolate purity
Broke through, a ray of the original Bliss.
Heaven's joys might have been earth's if earth were pure.
There could have reached our divinised sense and heart
Some natural felicity's bright extreme,
Some thrill of Supernature's absolutes:
All strengths could laugh and sport on earth's hard roads
And never feel her cruel edge of pain,
All love could play and nowhere Nature's shame.
But she has stabled her dreams in Matter's courts
And still her doors are barred to things supreme.
These worlds could feel God's breath visiting their tops;
Some glimmer of the Transcendent's hem was there.
Across the white aeonic silences
Immortal figures of embodied joy
Traversed wide spaces near to eternity's sleep.
Pure mystic voices in beatitude's hush
Appealed to Love's immaculate sweetnesses,
Calling his honeyed touch to thrill the worlds,
His blissful hands to seize on Nature's limbs,
His sweet intolerant might of union
To take all beings into his saviour arms,
Drawing to his pity the rebel and the waif
To force on them the happiness they refuse.
A chant hymeneal to the unseen Divine,
A flaming rhapsody of white desire
Lured an immortal music into the heart
And woke the slumbering ear of ecstasy.
A purer, fierier sense had there its home,
A burning urge no earthly limbs can hold;
One drew a large unburdened spacious breath
And the heart sped from beat to rapturous beat.
The voice of Time sang of the Immortal's joy;

An inspiration and a lyric cry,
The moments came with ecstasy on their wings;
Beauty unimaginable moved heaven-bare
Absolved from boundaries in the vasts of dream;
The cry of the Birds of Wonder called from the skies
To the deathless people of the shores of Light.
Creation leaped straight from the hands of God;
Marvel and rapture wandered in the ways.
Only to be was a supreme delight,
Life was a happy laughter of the soul
And Joy was king with Love for minister.
The spirit's luminousness was bodied there.
Life's contraries were lovers or natural friends
And her extremes keen edges of harmony:
Indulgence with a tender purity came
And nursed the god on her maternal breast:
There none was weak, so falsehood could not live;
Ignorance was a thin shade protecting light,
Imagination the free-will of Truth,
Pleasure a candidate for heaven's fire;
The intellect was Beauty's worshipper,
Strength was the slave of calm spiritual law,
Power laid its head upon the breasts of Bliss.
There were summit-glories inconceivable,
Autonomies of Wisdom's still self-rule
And high dependencies of her virgin sun,
Illumined theocracies of the seeing soul
Throned in the power of the Transcendent's ray.
A vision of grandeurs, a dream of magnitudes
In sun-bright kingdoms moved with regal gait:
Assemblies, crowded senates of the gods,
Life's puissances reigned on seats of marble will,
High dominations and autocracies
And laurelled strengths and armed imperative mights.
All objects there were great and beautiful,
All beings wore a royal stamp of power.

There sat the oligarchies of natural Law,
Proud violent heads served one calm monarch brow:
All the soul's postures donned divinity.
There met the ardent mutual intimacies
Of mastery's joy and the joy of servitude
Imposed by Love on Love's heart that obeys
And Love's body held beneath a rapturous yoke.
All was a game of meeting kinglinesses.
For worship lifts the worshipper's bowed strength
Close to the god's pride and bliss his soul adores:
The ruler there is one with all he rules;
To him who serves with a free equal heart
Obedience is his princely training's school,
His nobility's coronet and privilege,
His faith is a high nature's idiom,
His service a spiritual sovereignty.
There were realms where Knowledge joined creative Power
In her high home and made her all his own:
The grand Illuminate seized her gleaming limbs
And filled them with the passion of his ray
Till all her body was its transparent house
And all her soul a counterpart of his soul.
Apotheosised, transfigured by wisdom's touch,
Her days became a luminous sacrifice;
An immortal moth in happy and endless fire,
She burned in his sweet intolerable blaze.
A captive Life wedded her conqueror.
In his wide sky she built her world anew;
She gave to mind's calm pace the motor's speed,
To thinking a need to live what the soul saw,
To living an impetus to know and see.
His splendour grasped her, her puissance to him clung;
She crowned the Idea a king in purple robes,
Put her magic serpent sceptre in Thought's grip,
Made forms his inward vision's rhythmic shapes
And her acts the living body of his will.

A flaming thunder, a creator flash,
His victor Light rode on her deathless Force;
A centaur's mighty gallop bore the god.
Life throned with mind, a double majesty.
Worlds were there of a happiness great and grave
And action tinged with dream, laughter with thought,
And passion there could wait for its desire
Until it heard the near approach of God.
Worlds were there of a childlike mirth and joy;
A carefree youthfulness of mind and heart
Found in the body a heavenly instrument;
It lit an aureate halo round desire
And freed the deified animal in the limbs
To divine gambols of love and beauty and bliss.
On a radiant soil that gazed at heaven's smile
A swift life-impulse stinted not nor stopped:
It knew not how to tire; happy were its tears.
There work was play and play the only work,
The tasks of heaven a game of godlike might:
A celestial bacchanal for ever pure,
Unstayed by faintness as in mortal frames
Life was an eternity of rapture's moods:
Age never came, care never lined the face.
Imposing on the safety of the stars
A race and laughter of immortal strengths,
The nude god-children in their play-fields ran
Smiting the winds with splendour and with speed;
Of storm and sun they made companions,
Sported with the white mane of tossing seas,
Slew distance trampled to death under their wheels
And wrestled in the arenas of their force.
Imperious in their radiance like the suns
They kindled heaven with the glory of their limbs
Flung like a divine largess to the world.
A spell to force the heart to stark delight,
They carried the pride and mastery of their charm

As if Life's banner on the roads of Space.
Ideas were luminous comrades of the soul;
Mind played with speech, cast javelins of thought,
But needed not these instruments' toil to know;
Knowledge was Nature's pastime like the rest.
Investitured with the fresh heart's bright ray,
An early God-instinct's child inheritors,
Tenants of the perpetuity of Time
Still thrilling with the first creation's bliss,
They steeped existence in their youth of soul.
An exquisite and vehement tyranny,
The strong compulsion of their will to joy
Poured smiling streams of happiness through the world.
There reigned a breath of high immune content,
A fortunate gait of days in tranquil air,
A flood of universal love and peace.
A sovereignty of tireless sweetness lived
Like a song of pleasure on the lips of Time.
A large spontaneous order freed the will,
A sun-frank winging of the soul to bliss,
The breadth and greatness of the unfettered act
And the swift fire-heart's golden liberty.
There was no falsehood of soul-severance,
There came no crookedness of thought or word
To rob creation of its native truth;
All was sincerity and natural force.
There freedom was sole rule and highest law.
In a happy series climbed or plunged these worlds:
In realms of curious beauty and surprise,
In fields of grandeur and of titan power,
Life played at ease with her immense desires.
A thousand Edens she could build nor pause;
No bound was set to her greatness and to her grace
And to her heavenly variety.
Awake with a cry and stir of numberless souls,
Arisen from the breast of some deep Infinite,

Smiling like a new-born child at love and hope,
In her nature housing the Immortal's power,
In her bosom bearing the eternal Will,
No guide she needed but her luminous heart:
No fall debased the godhead of her steps,
No alien Night had come to blind her eyes.
There was no use for grudging ring or fence;
Each act was a perfection and a joy.
Abandoned to her rapid fancy's moods
And the rich coloured riot of her mind,
Initiate of divine and mighty dreams,
Magician builder of unnumbered forms
Exploring the measures of the rhythms of God,
At will she wove her wizard wonder-dance,
A Dionysian goddess of delight,
A Bacchant of creative ecstasy.

   This world of bliss he saw and felt its call,
But found no way to enter into its joy;
Across the conscious gulf there was no bridge.
A darker air encircled still his soul
Tied to an image of unquiet life.
In spite of yearning mind and longing sense,
To a sad Thought by grey experience formed
And a vision dimmed by care and sorrow and sleep
All this seemed only a bright desirable dream
Conceived in a longing distance by the heart
Of one who walks in the shadow of earth-pain.
Although he once had felt the Eternal's clasp,
Too near to suffering worlds his nature lived,
And where he stood were entrances of Night.
Hardly, too close beset by the world's care,
Can the dense mould in which we have been made
Return sheer joy to joy, pure light to light.
For its tormented will to think and live
First to a mingled pain and pleasure woke

And still it keeps the habit of its birth:
A dire duality is our way to be.
In the crude beginnings of this mortal world
Life was not nor mind's play nor heart's desire.
When earth was built in the unconscious Void
And nothing was save a material scene,
Identified with sea and sky and stone
Her young gods yearned for the release of souls
Asleep in objects, vague, inanimate.
In that desolate grandeur, in that beauty bare,
In the deaf stillness, mid the unheeded sounds,
Heavy was the uncommunicated load
Of Godhead in a world that had no needs;
For none was there to feel or to receive.
This solid mass which brooked no throb of sense
Could not contain their vast creative urge:
Immersed no more in Matter's harmony,
The Spirit lost its statuesque repose.
In the uncaring trance it groped for sight,
Passioned for the movements of a conscious heart,
Famishing for speech and thought and joy and love,
In the dumb insensitive wheeling day and night
Hungered for the beat of yearning and response.
The poised inconscience shaken with a touch,
The intuitive Silence trembling with a name,
They cried to Life to invade the senseless mould
And in brute forms awake divinity.
A voice was heard on the mute rolling globe,
A murmur moaned in the unlistening Void.
A being seemed to breathe where once was none:
Something pent up in dead insentient depths,
Denied conscious existence, lost to joy,
Turned as if one asleep since dateless time.
Aware of its own buried reality,
Remembering its forgotten self and right,
It yearned to know, to aspire, to enjoy, to live.

Life heard the call and left her native light.
Overflowing from her bright magnificent plane
On the rigid coil and sprawl of mortal Space,
Here too the gracious great-winged Angel poured
Her splendour and her swiftness and her bliss,
Hoping to fill a fair new world with joy.
As comes a goddess to a mortal's breast
And fills his days with her celestial clasp,
She stooped to make her home in transient shapes;
In Matter's womb she cast the Immortal's fire,
In the unfeeling Vast woke thought and hope,
Smote with her charm and beauty flesh and nerve
And forced delight on earth's insensible frame.
Alive and clad with trees and herbs and flowers
Earth's great brown body smiled towards the skies,
Azure replied to azure in the sea's laugh;
New sentient creatures filled the unseen depths,
Life's glory and swiftness ran in the beauty of beasts,
Man dared and thought and met with his soul the world.
But while the magic breath was on its way,
Before her gifts could reach our prisoned hearts,
A dark ambiguous Presence questioned all.
The secret Will that robes itself with Night
And offers to spirit the ordeal of the flesh,
Imposed a mystic mask of death and pain.
Interned now in the slow and suffering years
Sojourns the winged and wonderful wayfarer
And can no more recall her happier state,
But must obey the inert Inconscient's law,
Insensible foundation of a world
In which blind limits are on beauty laid
And sorrow and joy as struggling comrades live.
A dim and dreadful muteness fell on her:
Abolished was her subtle mighty spirit
And slain her boon of child-god happiness,
And all her glory into littleness turned

And all her sweetness into a maimed desire.
To feed death with her works is here life's doom.
So veiled was her immortality that she seemed,
Inflicting consciousness on unconscious things,
An episode in an eternal death,
A myth of being that must for ever cease.
Such was the evil mystery of her change.

END OF CANTO THREE

Canto Four

The Kingdoms of the Little Life

A QUIVERING trepidant uncertain world
Born from that dolorous meeting and eclipse
Appeared in the emptiness where her feet had trod,
A quick obscurity, a seeking stir.
There was a writhing of half-conscious force
Hardly awakened from the Inconscient's sleep,
Tied to an instinct-driven Ignorance,
To find itself and find its hold on things.
Inheritor of poverty and loss,
Assailed by memories that fled when seized,
Haunted by a forgotten uplifting hope,
It strove with a blindness as of groping hands
To fill the aching and disastrous gap
Between earth-pain and the bliss from which Life fell.
A world that ever seeks for something missed,
Hunts for the joy that earth has failed to keep.
Too near to our gates its unappeased unrest
For peace to live on the inert solid globe:
It has joined its hunger to the hunger of earth,
It has given the law of craving to our lives,
It has made our spirit's need a fathomless gulf.
An Influence entered mortal night and day,
A shadow overcast the time-born race;
In the troubled stream where leaps a blind heart-pulse
And the nerve-beat of feeling wakes in sense
Dividing Matter's sleep from conscious Mind,
There strayed a call that knew not why it came.
A Power beyond earth's scope has touched the earth;
The repose that might have been can be no more;
A formless yearning passions in man's heart,
A cry is in his blood for happier things:

Else could he roam on a free sunlit soil
With the childlike pain-forgetting mind of beasts
Or live happy, unmoved, like flowers and trees.
The Might that came upon the earth to bless,
Has stayed on earth to suffer and aspire.
The infant laugh that rang through time is hushed:
Man's natural joy of life is overcast
And sorrow is his nurse of destiny.
The animal's thoughtless joy is left behind,
Care and reflection burden his daily walk;
He has risen to greatness and to discontent,
He is awake to the Invisible.
Insatiate seeker, he has all to learn:
He has exhausted now life's surface acts,
His being's hidden realms remain to explore.
He becomes a mind, he becomes a spirit and self;
In his fragile tenement he grows Nature's lord.
In him Matter wakes from its long obscure trance,
In him earth feels the Godhead drawing near.
An eyeless Power that sees no more its aim,
A restless hungry energy of Will,
Life cast her seed in the body's indolent mould;
It woke from happy torpor a blind Force
Compelling it to sense and seek and feel.
In the enormous labour of the Void
Perturbing with her dreams the vast routine
And dead roll of a slumbering universe
The mighty prisoner struggled for release.
Alive with her yearning woke the inert cell,
In the heart she kindled a fire of passion and need,
Amid the deep calm of inanimate things
Arose her great voice of toil and prayer and strife.
A groping consciousness in a voiceless world,
A guideless sense was given her for her road;
Thought was withheld and nothing now she knew,
But all the unknown was hers to feel and clasp.

Obeying the push of unborn things towards birth
Out of her seal of insentient life she broke:
In her substance of unthinking mute soul-strength
That cannot utter what its depths divine,
Awoke a blind necessity to know.
The chain that bound her she made her instrument;
Instinct was hers, the chrysalis of Truth,
And effort and growth and striving nescience.
Inflicting on the body desire and hope,
Imposing on inconscience consciousness,
She brought into Matter's dull tenacity
Her anguished claim to her lost sovereign right,
Her tireless search, her vexed uneasy heart,
Her wandering unsure steps, her cry for change.
Adorer of a joy without a name,
In her obscure cathedral of delight
To dim dwarf gods she offers secret rites.
But vain unending is the sacrifice,
The priest an ignorant mage who only makes
Futile mutations in the altar's plan
And casts blind hopes into a powerless flame.
A burden of transient gains weighs down her steps
And hardly under that load can she advance;
But the hours cry to her, she travels on
Passing from thought to thought, from want to want;
Her greatest progress is a deepened need.
Matter dissatisfies, she turns to Mind;
She conquers earth, her field, then claims the heavens.
Insensible, breaking the work she has done
The stumbling ages over her labour pass,
But still no great transforming light came down
And no revealing rapture touched her fall.
Only a glimmer sometimes splits mind's sky
Justifying the ambiguous providence
That makes of night a path to unknown dawns
Or a dark clue to some diviner state.

In Nescience began her mighty task,
In Ignorance she pursues the unfinished work,
For knowledge gropes, but meets not Wisdom's face.
Ascending slowly with unconscious steps,
A foundling of the Gods she wanders here
Like a child-soul left near the gates of Hell
Fumbling through fog in search of Paradise.

In this slow ascension he must follow her pace
Even from her faint and dim subconscious start:
So only can earth's last salvation come.
For so only could he know the obscure cause
Of all that holds us back and baffles God
In the jail-delivery of the imprisoned soul.
Along swift paths of fall through dangerous gates
He chanced into a grey obscurity
Teeming with instincts from the mindless gulfs
That pushed to wear a form and win a place.
Life here was intimate with Death and Night
And ate Death's food that she might breathe awhile;
She was their inmate and adopted waif.
Accepting subconscience, in dumb darkness' reign
A sojourner, she hoped not any more.
There far away from Truth and luminous thought
He saw the original seat, the separate birth
Of the dethroned, deformed and suffering Power.
An unhappy face of falsity made true,
A contradiction of our divine birth,
Indifferent to beauty and to light,
Parading she flaunted her animal disgrace
Unhelped by camouflage, brutal and bare,
An authentic image recognised and signed
Of her outcast force exiled from heaven and hope,
Fallen, glorying in the vileness of her state,
The grovel of a strength once half divine,
The graceless squalor of her beast desires,

The staring visage of her ignorance,
The naked body of her poverty.
Here first she crawled out from her cabin of mud
Where she had lain inconscient, rigid, mute:
Its narrowness and torpor held her still,
A darkness clung to her uneffaced by Light.
There neared no touch redeeming from above:
The upward look was alien to her sight,
Forgotten the fearless godhead of her walk;
Renounced was the glory and felicity,
The adventure in the dangerous fields of Time:
Hardly she availed, wallowing, to bear and live.

A wide unquiet mist of seeking Space,
A rayless region swallowed in vague swathes,
That seemed, unnamed, unbodied and unhoused,
A swaddled visionless and formless mind,
Asked for a body to translate its soul.
Its prayer denied, it fumbled after thought.
As yet not powered to think, hardly to live,
It opened into a weird and pigmy world
Where this unhappy magic had its source.
On dim confines where Life and Matter meet
He wandered among things half-seen, half-guessed,
Pursued by ungrasped beginnings and lost ends.
There life was born but died before it could live.
There was no solid ground, no constant drift;
Only some flame of mindless Will had power.
Himself was dim to himself, half-felt, obscure,
As if in a struggle of the Void to be.
In strange domains where all was living sense
But mastering thought was not nor cause nor rule,
Only a crude child-heart cried for toys of bliss,
Mind flickered, a disordered infant glow,
And random shapeless energies drove towards form
And took each wisp-fire for a guiding sun.

This blindfold force could place no thinking step;
Asking for light she followed darkness' clue.
An inconscient Power groped towards consciousness,
Matter smitten by Matter glimmered to sense,
Blind contacts, slow reactions beat out sparks
Of instinct from a cloaked subliminal bed,
Sensations crowded, dumb substitutes for thought,
Perception answered Nature's wakening blows
But still was a mechanical response,
A jerk, a leap, a start in Nature's dream,
And rude unchastened impulses jostling ran
Heedless of every motion but their own
And, darkling, clashed with darker than themselves,
Free in a world of settled anarchy.
The need to exist, the instinct to survive
Engrossed the tense precarious moment's will
And an unseeing desire felt out for food.
The gusts of Nature were the only law,
Force wrestled with force, but no result remained:
Only were achieved a nescient grasp and drive
And feelings and instincts knowing not their source,
Sense-pleasures and sense-pangs soon caught, soon lost,
And the brute motion of unthinking lives.
It was a vain unnecessary world
Whose will to be brought poor and sad results
And meaningless suffering and a grey unease.
Nothing seemed worth the labour to become.

But judged not so his spirit's wakened eye.
As shines a solitary witness star
That burns apart, Light's lonely sentinel,
In the drift and teeming of a mindless Night,
A single thinker in an aimless world
Awaiting some tremendous dawn of God,
He saw the purpose in the works of Time.
Even in that aimlessness a work was done

Pregnant with magic will and change divine.
The first writhings of the cosmic serpent Force
Uncoiled from the mystic ring of Matter's trance;
It raised its head in the warm air of life.
It could not cast off yet Night's stiffening sleep
Or wear as yet mind's wonder-flecks and streaks,
Put on its jewelled hood the crown of soul
Or stand erect in the blaze of spirit's sun.
As yet were only seen foulness and force,
The secret crawl of consciousness to light
Through a fertile slime of lust and battening sense,
Beneath the body's crust of thickened self
A tardy fervent working in the dark,
The turbid yeast of Nature's passionate change,
Ferment of the soul's creation out of mire.
A heavenly process donned this grey disguise,
A fallen ignorance in its covert night
Laboured to achieve its dumb unseemly work,
A camouflage of the Inconscient's need
To release the glory of God in Nature's mud.
His sight, spiritual in embodying orbs,
Could pierce through the grey phosphorescent haze
And scan the secrets of the shifting flux
That animates these mute and solid cells
And leads the thought and longing of the flesh
And the keen lust and hunger of its will.
This too he tracked along its hidden stream
And traced its acts to a miraculous fount.
A mystic Presence none can probe nor rule,
Creator of this game of ray and shade
In this sweet and bitter paradoxical life,
Asks from the body the soul's intimacies
And by the swift vibration of a nerve
Links its mechanic throbs to light and love.
It summons the spirit's sleeping memories
Up from subconscient depths beneath Time's foam;

Oblivious of their flame of happy truth,
Arriving with heavy eyes that hardly see,
They come disguised as feelings and desires,
Like weeds upon the surface float awhile
And rise and sink on a somnambulist tide.
Impure, degraded though her motions are,
Always a heaven-truth broods in life's deeps;
In her obscurest members burns that fire.
A touch of God's rapture in creation's acts,
A lost remembrance of felicity
Lurks still in the dumb roots of death and birth,
The world's senseless beauty mirrors God's delight.
That rapture's smile is secret everywhere;
It flows in the wind's breath, in the tree's sap,
Its hued magnificence blooms in leaves and flowers.
When life broke through its half-drowse in the plant
That feels and suffers but cannot move or cry,
In beast and in winged bird and thinking man
It made of the heart's rhythm its music's beat;
It forced the unconscious tissues to awake
And ask for happiness and earn the pang
And thrill with pleasure and laughter of brief delight,
And quiver with pain and crave for ecstasy.
Imperative, voiceless, ill-understood,
Too far from light, too close to being's core,
Born strangely in Time from the eternal Bliss,
It presses on heart's core and vibrant nerve;
Its sharp self-seeking tears our consciousness;
Our pain and pleasure have that sting for cause:
Instinct with it, but blind to its true joy
The soul's desire leaps out towards passing things.
All Nature's longing drive none can resist,
Comes surging through the blood and quickened sense;
An ecstasy of the infinite is her cause.
It turns in us to finite loves and lusts,
The will to conquer and have, to seize and keep,

To enlarge life's room and scope and pleasure's range,
To battle and overcome and make one's own,
The hope to mix one's joy with others' joy,
A yearning to possess and be possessed,
To enjoy and be enjoyed, to feel, to live.
Here was its early brief attempt to be,
Its rapid end of momentary delight
Whose stamp of failure haunts all ignorant life.
Inflicting still its habit on the cells
The phantom of a dark and evil start
Ghostlike pursues all that we dream and do.
Although on earth are firm established lives,
A working of habit or a sense of law,
A steady repetition in the flux,
Yet are its roots of will ever the same;
These passions are the stuff of which we are made.
This was the first cry of the awaking world.
It clings around us still and clamps the god.
Even when reason is born and soul takes form,
In beast and reptile and in thinking man
It lasts and is the fount of all their life.
This too was needed that breath and living might be.
The spirit in a finite ignorant world
Must rescue so its prisoned consciousness
Forced out in little jets at quivering points
From the Inconscient's sealed infinitude.
Then slowly it gathers mass, looks up at Light.
This Nature lives tied to her origin,
A clutch of nether force is on her still;
Out of unconscious depths her instincts leap;
A neighbour is her life to insentient Nought.
Under this law an ignorant world was made.
    In the enigma of the darkened Vasts,
In the passion and self-loss of the Infinite
When all was plunged in the negating Void,
Non-Being's night could never have been saved

If Being had not plunged into the dark
Carrying with it its triple mystic cross.
Invoking in world-time the timeless truth,
Bliss changed to sorrow, knowledge made ignorant,
God's force turned into a child's helplessness
Can bring down heaven by their sacrifice.
A contradiction founds the base of life:
The eternal, the divine Reality
Has faced itself with its own contraries;
Being became the Void and Conscious-Force
Nescience and walk of a blind Energy
And Ecstasy took the figure of world-pain.
In a mysterious dispensation's law
A Wisdom that prepares its far-off ends
Planned so to start her slow aeonic game.
A blindfold search and wrestle and fumbling clasp
Of a half-seen Nature and a hidden Soul,
A game of hide-and-seek in twilit rooms,
A play of love and hate and fear and hope
Continues in the nursery of mind
Its hard and heavy romp of self-born twins.
At last the struggling Energy can emerge
And meet the voiceless Being in wider fields;
Then can they see and speak and, breast to breast,
In a larger consciousness, a clearer light,
The Two embrace and strive and each know each
Regarding closer now the playmate's face.
Even in these formless coilings he could feel
Matter's response to an infant stir of soul.
In Nature he saw the mighty Spirit concealed,
Watched the weak birth of a tremendous Force,
Pursued the riddle of Godhead's tentative pace,
Heard the faint rhythms of a great unborn Muse.

Then came a fierier breath of waking Life,
And there arose from the dim gulf of things

The strange creations of a thinking sense,
Existences half-real and half-dream.
A life was there that hoped not to survive:
Beings were born who perished without trace,
Events that were a formless drama's limbs
And actions driven by a blind creature will.
A seeking Power found out its road to form,
Patterns were built of love and joy and pain
And symbol figures for the moods of Life.
An insect hedonism fluttered and crawled
And basked in a sunlit Nature's surface thrills,
And dragon raptures, python agonies
Crawled in the marsh and mire and licked the sun.
Huge armoured strengths shook a frail quaking ground,
Great puissant creatures with a dwarfish brain,
And pigmy tribes imposed their small life-drift.
In a dwarf model of humanity
Nature now launched the extreme experience
And master-point of her design's caprice,
Luminous result of her half-conscious climb
On rungs twixt her sublimities and grotesques
To massive from infinitesimal shapes,
To a subtle balancing of body and soul,
To an order of intelligent littleness.
Around him in the moment-beats of Time
The kingdom of the animal self arose,
Where deed is all and mind is still half-born
And the heart obeys a dumb unseen control.
The Force that works by the light of Ignorance,
Her animal experiment began,
Crowding with conscious creatures her world-scheme;
But to the outward only were they alive,
Only they replied to touches and surfaces
And to the prick of need that drove their lives.
A body that knew not its own soul within,
There lived and longed, had wrath and joy and grief;

A mind was there that met the objective world
As if a stranger or enemy at its door:
Its thoughts were kneaded by the shocks of sense;
It captured not the spirit in the form,
It entered not the heart of what it saw;
It looked not for the power behind the act,
It studied not the hidden motive in things
Nor strove to find the meaning of it all.
Beings were there who wore a human form;
Absorbed they lived in the passion of the scene,
But knew not who they were or why they lived:
Content to breathe, to feel, to sense, to act,
Life had for them no aim save Nature's joy
And the stimulus and delight of outer things;
Identified with the spirit's outward shell,
They worked for the body's wants, they craved no more.
The veiled spectator watching from their depths
Fixed not his inward eye upon himself
Nor turned to find the author of the plot,
He saw the drama only and the stage.
There was no brooding stress of deeper sense,
The burden of reflection was not borne:
Mind looked on Nature with unknowing eyes,
Adored her boons and feared her monstrous strokes.
It pondered not on the magic of her laws,
It thirsted not for the secret wells of Truth,
But made a register of crowding facts
And strung sensations on a vivid thread:
It hunted and it fled and sniffed the winds,
Or slothed inert in sunshine and soft air:
It sought the engrossing contacts of the world,
But only to feed the surface sense with bliss.
These felt life's quiver in the outward touch,
They could not feel behind the touch the soul.
To guard their form of self from Nature's harm,
To enjoy and to survive was all their care.

The narrow horizon of their days was filled
With things and creatures that could help and hurt:
The world's values hung upon their little self.
Isolated, cramped in the vast unknown,
To save their small lives from surrounding Death
They made a tiny circle of defence
Against the siege of the huge universe:
They preyed upon the world and were its prey,
But never dreamed to conquer and be free.
Obeying the World-Power's hints and firm taboos
A scanty part they drew from her rich store;
There was no conscious code and no life-plan:
The patterns of thinking of a little group
Fixed a traditional behaviour's law.
Ignorant of soul save as a wraith within,
Tied to a mechanism of unchanging lives
And to a dull usual sense and feeling's beat,
They turned in grooves of animal desire.
In walls of stone fenced round they worked and warred,
Did by a banded selfishness a small good
Or wrought a dreadful wrong and cruel pain
On sentient lives and thought they did no ill.
Ardent from the sack of happy peaceful homes
And gorged with slaughter, plunder, rape and fire,
They made of human selves their helpless prey,
A drove of captives led to lifelong woe,
Or torture a spectacle made and holiday,
Mocking or thrilled by their torn victims' pangs;
Admiring themselves as titans and as gods
Proudly they sang their high and glorious deeds
And praised their victory and their splendid force.
An animal in the instinctive herd
Pushed by life impulses, forced by common needs,
Each in his own kind saw his ego's glass;
All served the aim and action of the pack.
Those like himself, by blood or custom kin,

To him were parts of his life, his adjunct selves,
His personal nebula's constituent stars,
Satellite companions of his solar I.
A master of his life's environment,
A leader of a huddled human mass
Herding for safety on a dangerous earth,
He gathered them round him as if minor Powers
To make a common front against the world,
Or, weak and sole on an indifferent earth,
As a fortress for his undefended heart,
Or else to heal his body's loneliness.
In others than his kind he sensed a foe,
An alien unlike force to shun and fear,
A stranger and adversary to hate and slay.
Or he lived as lives the solitary brute;
At war with all he bore his single fate.
Absorbed in the present act, the fleeting days,
None thought to look beyond the hour's gains,
Or dreamed to make this earth a fairer world,
Or felt some touch divine surprise his heart.
The gladness that the fugitive moment gave,
The desire grasped, the bliss, the experience won,
Movement and speed and strength were joy enough
And bodily longings shared and quarrel and play,
And tears and laughter and the need called love.
In war and clasp these life-wants joined the All-Life,
Wrestlings of a divided unity
Inflicting mutual grief and happiness
In ignorance of the Self for ever one.
Arming its creatures with delight and hope
A half-awakened Nescience struggled there
To know by sight and touch the outside of things.
Instinct was formed; in memory's crowded sleep
The past lived on as in a bottomless sea:
Inverting into half-thought the quickened sense
She felt around for truth with fumbling hands,

Clutched to her the little she could reach and seize
And put aside in her subconscient cave.
So must the dim being grow in light and force
And rise to his higher destiny at last,
Look up to God and round at the universe,
And learn by failure and progress by fall
And battle with environment and doom,
By suffering discover his deep soul
And by possession grow to his own vasts.
Half-way she stopped and found her path no more.
Still nothing was achieved but to begin,
Yet finished seemed the circle of her force.
Only she had beaten out sparks of ignorance;
Only the life could think and not the mind,
Only the sense could feel and not the soul.
Only was lit some heat of the flame of Life,
Some joy to be, some rapturous leaps of sense.
All was an impetus of half-conscious Force,
A spirit sprawling drowned in dense life-foam,
A vague self grasping at the shape of things.
Behind all moved seeking for vessels to hold
A first raw vintage of the grapes of God,
On earth's mud a spilth of the supernal Bliss,
Intoxicating the stupefied soul and mind
A heady wine of rapture dark and crude,
Dim, uncast yet into spiritual form,
Obscure inhabitant of the world's blind core,
An unborn godhead's will, a mute Desire.

A third creation now revealed its face.
A mould of body's early mind was made.
A glint of light kindled the obscure World-Force;
It dowered a driven world with the seeing Idea
And armed the act with thought's dynamic point:
A small thinking being watched the works of Time.
A difficult evolution from below

Called a masked intervention from above;
Else this great, blind inconscient universe
Could never have disclosed its hidden mind,
Or even in blinkers worked in beast and man
The Intelligence that devised the cosmic scheme.
At first he saw a dim obscure mind-power
Moving concealed by Matter and dumb life.
A current thin, it streamed in life's vast flow
Tossing and drifting under a drifting sky
Amid the surge and glimmering tremulous wash,
Released in splash of sense and feeling's waves.
In the deep midst of an insentient world
Its huddled waves and foam of consciousness ran
Pressing and eddying through a narrow strait,
Carrying experience in its crowded pace.
It flowed emerging into upper light
From the deep pool of its subliminal birth
To reach some high existence still unknown.
There was no thinking self, aim there was none:
All was unorganised stress and seekings vague.
Only to the unstable surface rose
Sensations, stabs and edges of desire
And passion's leaps and brief emotion's cries,
A casual colloquy of flesh with flesh,
A murmur of heart to longing wordless heart,
Glimmerings of knowledge with no shape of thought
And jets of subconscious will or hunger's pulls.
All was dim sparkle on a foaming top:
It whirled around a drifting shadow-self
On an inconscient flood of Force in Time.
Then came the pressure of a seeing Power
That drew all into a dancing turbid mass
Circling around a single luminous point,
Centre of reference in a conscious field,
Figure of a unitary Light within.
It lit the impulse of the half-sentient flood,

Even an illusion gave of fixity
As if a sea could serve as a firm soil.
That strange observing Power imposed its sight.
It forced on flux a limit and a shape,
It gave its stream a lower narrow bank,
Drew lines to snare the spirit's formlessness.
It fashioned the life-mind of bird and beast,
The answer of the reptile and the fish,
The primitive pattern of the thoughts of man.
A finite movement of the Infinite
Came winging its way through a wide air of Time;
A march of knowledge moved in Nescience
And guarded in the form a separate soul.
Its right to be immortal it reserved,
But built a wall against the siege of death
And threw a hook to clutch eternity.
A thinking entity appeared in Space.
A little ordered world broke into view
Where being had prison-room for act and sight,
A floor to walk, a clear but scanty range.
An instrument-personality was born,
And a restricted clamped intelligence
Consented to confine in narrow bounds
Its seeking; it tied the thought to visible things,
Prohibiting the adventure of the Unseen
And the soul's tread through unknown infinities.
A reflex reason, Nature-habit's glass
Illumined life to know and fix its field,
Accept a dangerous ignorant brevity
And the inconclusive purpose of its walk
And profit by the hour's precarious chance
In the allotted boundaries of its fate.
A little joy and knowledge satisfied
This little being tied into a knot
And hung on a bulge of its environment,
A little curve cut off in measureless Space,

A little span of life in all vast Time.
A thought was there that planned, a will that strove,
But for small aims within a narrow scope,
Wasting unmeasured toil on transient things.
It knew itself a creature of the mud;
It asked no larger law, no loftier aim;
It had no inward look, no upward gaze.
A backward scholar on logic's rickety bench
Indoctrinated by the erring sense,
It took appearance for the face of God,
For casual lights the marching of the suns,
For heaven a starry strip of doubtful blue;
Aspects of being feigned to be the whole.
There was a voice of busy interchange,
A market-place of trivial thoughts and acts:
A life soon spent, a mind the body's slave
Here seemed the brilliant crown of Nature's work,
And tiny egos took the world as means
To sate awhile dwarf lusts and brief desires,
In a death-closed passage saw life's start and end
As though a blind alley were creation's sign,
As if for this the soul had coveted birth
In the wonderland of a self-creating world
And the opportunities of cosmic Space.
This creature passionate only to survive,
Fettered to puny thoughts with no wide range
And to the body's needs and pangs and joys,
This fire growing by its fuel's death,
Increased by what it seized and made its own:
It gathered and grew and gave itself to none.
Only it hoped for greatness in its den
And pleasure and victory in small fields of power
And conquest of life-room for self and kin,
An animal limited by its feeding-space.
It knew not the Immortal in its house;
It had no greater deeper cause to live.

In limits only it was powerful;
Acute to capture truth for outward use,
Its knowledge was the body's instrument;
Absorbed in the little works of its prison-house
It turned around the same unchanging points
In the same circle of interest and desire,
But thought itself the master of its jail.
Although for action, not for wisdom made,
Thought was its apex — or its gutter's rim:
It saw an image of the external world
And saw its surface self, but knew no more.
Out of a slow confused embroiled self-search
Mind grew to a clarity cut out, precise,
A gleam enclosed in a stone ignorance.
In this bound thinking's narrow leadership
Tied to the soil, inspired by common things,
Attached to a confined familiar world,
Amid the multitude of her motived plots,
Her changing actors and her million masks,
Life was a play monotonously the same.
There were no vast perspectives of the spirit,
No swift invasions of unknown delight,
No golden distances of wide release.
This petty state resembled our human days
But fixed to eternity of changeless type,
A moment's movement doomed to last through Time.
Existence bridge-like spanned the inconscient gulfs,
A half-illumined building in a mist,
Which from a void of Form arose to sight
And jutted out into a void of Soul.
A little light in a great darkness born,
Life knew not where it went nor whence it came.
Around all floated still the nescient haze.

END OF CANTO FOUR

Canto Five

The Godheads of the Little Life

A FIXED and narrow power with rigid forms,
He saw the empire of the little life,
An unhappy corner in eternity.
It lived upon the margin of the Idea
Protected by Ignorance as in a shell.
Then, hoping to learn the secret of this world
He peered across its scanty fringe of sight,
To disengage from its surface-clear obscurity
The Force that moved it and the Idea that made,
Imposing smallness on the Infinite,
The ruling spirit of its littleness,
The divine law that gave it right to be,
Its claim on Nature and its need in Time.
He plunged his gaze into the siege of mist
That held this ill-lit straitened continent
Ringed with the skies and seas of ignorance
And kept it safe from Truth and Self and Light.
As when a searchlight stabs the Night's blind breast
And dwellings and trees and figures of men appear
As if revealed to an eye in Nothingness,
All lurking things were torn out of their veils
And held up in his vision's sun-white blaze.
A busy restless uncouth populace
Teemed in their dusky unnoted thousands there.
In a mist of secrecy wrapping the world-scene
The little deities of Time's nether act
Who work remote from Heaven's controlling eye,
Plotted, unknown to the creatures whom they move,
The small conspiracies of this petty reign
Amused with the small contrivings, the brief hopes
And little eager steps and little ways

And reptile wallowings in the dark and dust,
And the crouch and ignominy of creeping life.
A trepidant and motley multitude,
A strange pell-mell of magic artisans,
Was seen moulding the plastic clay of life,
An elfin brood, an elemental kind.
Astonished by the unaccustomed glow,
As if immanent in the shadows started up
Imps with wry limbs and carved beast visages,
Sprite-prompters goblin-wizened or faery-small,
And genii fairer but unsouled and poor
And fallen beings, their heavenly portion lost,
And errant divinities trapped in Time's dust.
Ignorant and dangerous wills but armed with power,
Half-animal, half-god their mood, their shape.
Out of the greyness of a dim background
Their whispers come, an inarticulate force,
Awake in mind an echoing thought or word,
To their sting of impulse the heart's sanction draw,
And in that little Nature do their work
And fill its powers and creatures with unease.
Its seed of joy they curse with sorrow's fruit,
Put out with error's breath its scanty lights
And turn its surface truths to falsehood's ends,
Its small emotions spur, its passions drive
To the abyss or through the bog and mire:
Or else with a goad of hard dry lusts they prick,
While jogs on devious ways that nowhere lead
Life's cart finding no issue from ignorance.
To sport with good and evil is their law;
Luring to failure and meaningless success,
All models they corrupt, all measures cheat,
Make knowledge a poison, virtue a pattern dull
And lead the endless cycles of desire
Through semblances of sad or happy chance
To an inescapable fatality.

All by their influence is enacted there.
Nor there alone is their empire or their role:
Wherever are soulless minds and guideless lives
And in a small body self is all that counts,
Wherever love and light and largeness lack,
These crooked fashioners take up their task.
To all half-conscious worlds they extend their reign.
Here too these godlings drive our human hearts,
Our nature's twilight is their lurking-place:
Here too the darkened primitive heart obeys
The veiled suggestions of a hidden Mind
That dogs our knowledge with misleading light
And stands between us and the Truth that saves.
It speaks to us with the voices of the Night:
Our darkened lives to greater darkness move;
Our seekings listen to calamitous hopes.
A structure of unseeing thoughts is built
And reason used by an irrational Force.
This earth is not alone our teacher and nurse;
The powers of all the worlds have entrance here.
In their own fields they follow the wheel of law
And cherish the safety of a settled type;
On earth out of their changeless orbit thrown
Their law is kept, lost their fixed form of things.
Into a creative chaos they are cast
Where all asks order but is driven by Chance;
Strangers to earth-nature, they must learn earth's ways,
Aliens or opposites, they must unite:
They work and battle and with pain agree:
These join, those part, all parts and joins anew,
But never can we know and truly live
Till all have found their divine harmony.
Our life's uncertain way winds circling on,
Our mind's unquiet search asks always light,
Till they have learned their secret in their source,
In the light of the Timeless and its spaceless home,

In the joy of the Eternal sole and one.
But now the Light supreme is far away:
Our conscious life obeys the Inconscient's laws;
To ignorant purposes and blind desires
Our hearts are moved by an ambiguous force;
Even our mind's conquests wear a battered crown.
A slowly changing order binds our will.
This is our doom until our souls are free.
A mighty Hand then rolls mind's firmaments back,
Infinity takes up the finite's acts
And Nature steps into the eternal Light.
Then only ends this dream of nether life.

At the outset of this enigmatic world
Which seems at once an enormous brute machine
And a slow unmasking of the spirit in things,
In this revolving chamber without walls
In which God sits impassive everywhere
As if unknown to himself and by us unseen
In a miracle of inconscient secrecy,
Yet is all here his action and his will.
In this whirl and sprawl through infinite vacancy
The Spirit became Matter and lay in the whirl,
A body sleeping without sense or soul.
A mass phenomenon of visible shapes
Supported by the silence of the Void
Appeared in the eternal Consciousness
And seemed an outward and insensible world.
There was none there to see and none to feel;
Only the miraculous Inconscient,
A subtle wizard skilled, was at its task.
Inventing ways for magical results,
Managing creation's marvellous device,
Marking mechanically dumb wisdom's points,
Using the unthought inevitable Idea,
It did the works of God's intelligence

Or wrought the will of some supreme Unknown.
Still consciousness was hidden in Nature's womb,
Unfelt was the Bliss whose rapture dreamed the worlds.
Being was an inert substance driven by Force.
At first was only an etheric Space:
Its huge vibrations circled round and round
Housing some unconceived initiative:
Upheld by a supreme original Breath
Expansion and contraction's mystic act
Created touch and friction in the void,
Into abstract emptiness brought clash and clasp:
Parent of an expanding universe
In a matrix of disintegrating force,
By spending it conserved an endless sum.
On the hearth of Space it kindled a viewless Fire
That, scattering worlds as one might scatter seeds,
Whirled out the luminous order of the stars.
An ocean of electric Energy
Formlessly formed its strange wave-particles
Constructing by their dance this solid scheme,
Its mightiness in the atom shut to rest;
Masses were forged or feigned and visible shapes;
Light flung the photon's swift revealing spark
And showed, in the minuteness of its flash
Imaged, this cosmos of apparent things.
Thus has been made this real impossible world,
An obvious miracle or convincing show.
Or so it seems to man's audacious mind
Who seats his thought as the arbiter of truth,
His personal vision as impersonal fact,
As witnesses of an objective world
His erring sense and his instruments' artifice.
Thus must he work life's tangible riddle out
In a doubtful light, by error seize on Truth
And slowly part the visage and the veil.
Or else, forlorn of faith in mind and sense,

His knowledge a bright body of ignorance,
He sees in all things strangely fashioned here
The unwelcome jest of a deceiving Force,
A parable of Maya and her might.
This vast perpetual motion caught and held
In the mysterious and unchanging change
Of the persistent movement we call Time
And ever renewing its recurrent beat,
These mobile rounds that stereotype a flux,
These static objects in the cosmic dance
That are but Energy's self-repeating whorls
Prolonged by the spirit of the brooding Void,
Awaited life and sense and waking Mind.
A little the Dreamer changed his pose of stone.
But when the Inconscient's scrupulous work was done
And Chance coerced by fixed immutable laws,
A scene was set for Nature's conscious play.
Then stirred the Spirit's mute immobile sleep;
The Force concealed broke dumbly, slowly out.
A dream of living woke in Matter's heart,
A will to live moved the Inconscient's dust,
A freak of living startled vacant Time,
Ephemeral in a blank eternity,
Infinitesimal in a dead Infinite.
A subtler breath quickened dead Matter's forms;
The world's set rhythm changed to a conscious cry;
A serpent Power twinned the insensible Force.
Islands of living dotted lifeless Space
And germs of living formed in formless air.
A Life was born that followed Matter's law,
Ignorant of the motives of its steps;
Ever inconstant, yet for ever the same,
It repeated the paradox that gave it birth:
Its restless and unstable stabilities
Recurred incessantly in the flow of Time
And purposeful movements in unthinking forms

Betrayed the heavings of an imprisoned Will.
Waking and sleep lay locked in mutual arms;
Helpless and indistinct came pleasure and pain
Trembling with the first faint thrills of a World-Soul.
A strength of life that could not cry or move,
Yet broke into beauty signing some deep delight:
An inarticulate sensibility,
Throbs of the heart of an unknowing world,
Ran through its somnolent torpor and there stirred
A vague uncertain thrill, a wandering beat,
A dim unclosing as of secret eyes.
Infant self-feeling grew and birth was born.
A godhead woke but lay with dreaming limbs;
Her house refused to open its sealed doors.
Insentient to our eyes that only see
The form, the act and not the imprisoned God,
Life hid in her pulse occult of growth and power
A consciousness with mute stifled beats of sense,
A mind suppressed that knew not yet of thought,
An inert spirit that could only be.
At first she raised no voice, no motion dared:
Charged with world-power, instinct with living force,
Only she clung with her roots to the safe earth,
Thrilled dumbly to the shocks of ray and breeze
And put out tendril fingers of desire;
The strength in her yearning for sun and light
Felt not the embrace that made her breathe and live;
Absorbed she dreamed content with beauty and hue.
At last the charmed Immensity looked forth:
Astir, vibrant, hungering, she groped for mind;
Then slowly sense quivered and thought peered out;
She forced the reluctant mould to grow aware.
The magic was chiselled of a conscious form;
·Its tranced vibrations rhythmed a quick response,
And luminous stirrings prompted brain and nerve,
Awoke in Matter spirit's identity

And in a body lit the miracle
Of the heart's love and the soul's witness gaze.
Impelled by an unseen Will there could break out
Fragments of some vast impulse to become
And vivid glimpses of a secret self,
And the doubtful seeds and force of shapes to be
Awoke from the inconscient swoon of things.
An animal creation crept and ran
And flew and called between the earth and sky,
Hunted by death but hoping still to live
And glad to breathe if only for a while.
Then man was moulded from the original brute.
A thinking mind had come to lift life's moods,
The keen-edged tool of a Nature mixed and vague,
An intelligence half-witness, half-machine.
This seeming driver of her wheel of works
Missioned to motive and record her drift
And fix its law on her inconstant powers,
This master-spring of a delicate enginery,
Aspired to enlighten its user and refine
Lifting to a vision of the indwelling Power
The absorbed mechanic's crude initiative:
He raised his eyes; Heaven-light mirrored a Face.
Amazed at the works wrought in her mystic sleep,
She looked upon the world that she had made:
Wondering now seized the great automaton;
She paused to understand her self and aim,
Pondering she learned to act by conscious rule,
A visioned measure guided her rhythmic steps;
Thought bordered her instincts with a frame of will
And lit with the idea her blinded urge.
On her mass of impulses, her reflex acts,
On the Inconscient's pushed or guided drift
And mystery of unthinking accurate steps
She stuck the specious image of a self,
A living idol of disfigured spirit;

On Matter's acts she imposed a patterned law;
She made a thinking body from chemic cells
And moulded a being out of a driven force.
To be what she was not inflamed her hope:
She turned her dream towards some high Unknown;
A breath was felt below of One supreme.
An opening looked up to spheres above
And coloured shadows limned on mortal ground
The passing figures of immortal things;
A quick celestial flash could sometimes come:
The illumined soul-ray fell on heart and flesh
And touched with semblances of ideal light
The stuff of which our earthly dreams are made.
A fragile human love that could not last,
Ego's moth-wings to lift the seraph soul,
Appeared, a surface glamour of brief date
Extinguished by a scanty breath of Time;
Joy that forgot mortality for a while
Came, a rare visitor who left betimes,
And made all things seem beautiful for an hour,
Hopes that soon fade to drab realities
And passions that crumble to ashes while they blaze
Kindled the common earth with their brief flame.
A creature insignificant and small
Visited, uplifted by an unknown Power,
Man laboured on his little patch of earth
For means to last, to enjoy, to suffer and die.
A spirit that perished not with the body and breath
Was there like a shadow of the Unmanifest
And stood behind the little personal form
But claimed not yet this earthly embodiment.
Assenting to Nature's long slow-moving toil,
Watching the works of his own Ignorance,
Unknown, unfelt the mighty Witness lives
And nothing shows the Glory that is here.
A Wisdom governing the mystic world,

A Silence listening to the cry of Life,
It sees the hurrying crowd of moments stream
Towards the still greatness of a distant hour.

   This huge world unintelligibly turns
In the shadow of a mused Inconscience;
It hides a key to inner meanings missed,
It locks in our hearts a voice we cannot hear.
An enigmatic labour of the spirit,
An exact machine of which none knows the use,
An art and ingenuity without sense,
This minute elaborate orchestrated life
For ever plays its motiveless symphonies.
The mind learns and knows not, turning its back to truth;
It studies surface laws by surface thought,
Life's steps surveys and Nature's process sees,
Not seeing for what she acts or why we live;
It marks her tireless care of just device,
Her patient intricacy of fine detail,
The ingenious spirit's brave inventive plan
In her great futile mass of endless works,
Adds purposeful figures to her purposeless sum,
Its gabled storeys piles, its climbing roofs
On the close-carved foundations she has laid,
Imagined citadels reared in mythic air
Or mounts a stair of dream to a mystic moon:
Transient creations point and hit the sky:
A world-conjecture's scheme is laboured out
On the dim floor of mind's incertitude,
Or painfully built a fragmentary whole.
Impenetrable, a mystery recondite
Is the vast plan of which we are a part;
Its harmonies are discords to our view
Because we know not the great theme they serve.
Inscrutable work the cosmic agencies.
Only the fringe of a wide surge we see;

Our instruments have not that greater light,
Our will tunes not with the eternal Will,
Our heart's sight is too blind and passionate.
Impotent to share in Nature's mystic tact,
Inapt to feel the pulse and core of things,
Our reason cannot sound life's mighty sea
And only counts its waves and scans its foam;
It knows not whence these motions touch and pass,
It sees not whither sweeps the hurrying flood:
Only it strives to canalise its powers
And hopes to turn its course to human ends:
But all its means come from the Inconscient's store.
Unseen here act dim huge world-energies
And only trickles and currents are our share.
Our mind lives far off from the authentic Light
Catching at little fragments of the Truth
In a small corner of infinity,
Our lives are inlets of an ocean's force.
Our conscious movements have sealed origins
But with those shadowy seats no converse hold;
No understanding binds our comrade parts;
Our acts emerge from a crypt our minds ignore.
Our deepest depths are ignorant of themselves;
Even our body is a mystery shop;
As our earth's roots lurk screened below our earth,
So lie unseen our roots of mind and life.
Our springs are kept close hid beneath, within;
Our souls are moved by powers behind the wall.
In the subterranean reaches of the spirit
A puissance acts and recks not what it means;
Using unthinking monitors and scribes,
It is the cause of what we think and feel.
The troglodytes of the subconscious Mind,
Ill-trained slow stammering interpreters
Only of their small task's routine aware
And busy with the record in our cells,

Concealed in the subliminal secrecies
Mid an obscure occult machinery,
Capture the mystic Morse whose measured lilt
Transmits the messages of the cosmic Force.
A whisper falls into life's inner ear
And echoes from the dun subconscient caves,
Speech leaps, thought quivers, the heart vibrates, the will
Answers and tissue and nerve obey the call.
Our lives translate these subtle intimacies;
All is the commerce of a secret Power.
  A thinking puppet is the mind of life:
Its choice is the work of elemental strengths
That know not their own birth and end and cause
And glimpse not the immense intent they serve.
In this nether life of man drab-hued and dull,
Yet filled with poignant small ignoble things,
The conscious Doll is pushed a hundred ways
And feels the push but not the hands that drive.
For none can see the masked ironic troupe
To whom our figure-selves are marionettes,
Our deeds unwitting movements in their grasp,
Our passionate strife an entertainment's scene.
Ignorant themselves of their own fount of strength
They play their part in the enormous whole.
Agents of darkness imitating light,
Spirits obscure and moving things obscure,
Unwillingly they serve a mightier Power.
Ananke's engines organising Chance,
Channels perverse of a stupendous Will,
Tools of the Unknown who use us as their tools,
Invested with power in Nature's nether state,
Into the actions mortals think their own
They bring the incoherencies of Fate,
Or make a doom of Time's slipshod caprice
And toss the lives of men from hand to hand
In an inconsequent and devious game.

Against all higher truth their stuff rebels;
Only to Titan force their will lies prone.
Inordinate their hold on human hearts,
In all our nature's turns they intervene.
Insignificant architects of low-built lives
And engineers of interest and desire,
Out of crude earthiness and muddy thrills
And coarse reactions of material nerve
They build our huddled structures of self-will
And the ill-lighted mansions of our thought,
Or with the ego's factories and marts
Surround the beautiful temple of the soul.
Artists minute of the hues of littleness,
They set the mosaic of our comedy
Or plan the trivial tragedy of our days,
Arrange the deed, combine the circumstance
And the fantasia of the moods costume.
These unwise prompters of man's ignorant heart
And tutors of his stumbling speech and will,
Movers of petty wraths and lusts and hates
And changeful thoughts and shallow emotion's starts,
These slight illusion-makers with their masks,
Painters of the decor of a dull-hued stage
And nimble scene-shifters of the human play,
Ever are busy with this ill-lit scene.
Ourselves incapable to build our fate
Only as actors speak and strut our parts
Until the piece is done and we pass off
Into a brighter Time and subtler Space.
Thus they inflict their little pigmy law
And curb the mounting slow uprise of man,
Then his too scanty walk with death they close.

This is the ephemeral creature's daily life.
As long as the human animal is lord
And a dense nether nature screens the soul,

As long as intellect's outward-gazing sight
Serves earthy interest and creature joys,
An incurable littleness pursues his days.
Ever since consciousness was born on earth,
Life is the same in insect, ape and man,
Its stuff unchanged, its way the common route.
If new designs, if richer details grow
And thought is added and more tangled cares,
If little by little it wears a brighter face,
Still even in man the plot is mean and poor.
A gross content prolongs his fallen state;
His small successes are failures of the soul,
His little pleasures punctuate frequent griefs:
Hardship and toil are the heavy price he pays
For the right to live and his last wages death.
An inertia sunk towards inconscience,
A sleep that imitates death is his repose.
A puny splendour of creative force
Is made his spur to fragile human works
Which yet outlast their brief creator's breath.
He dreams sometimes of the revels of the gods
And sees the Dionysian gesture pass,—
A leonine greatness that would tear his soul
If through his failing limbs and fainting heart
The sweet and joyful mighty madness swept:
Trivial amusements stimulate and waste
The energy given to him to grow and be.
His little hour is spent in little things.
A brief companionship with many jars,
A little love and jealousy and hate,
A touch of friendship mid indifferent crowds
Draw his heart-plan on life's diminutive map.
If something great awakes, too frail his pitch
To reveal its zenith tension of delight,
His thought to eternise its ephemeral soar,
Art's brilliant gleam is a pastime for his eyes,

A thrill that smites the nerves is music's spell.
Amidst his harassed toil and welter of cares,
Pressed by the labour of his crowding thoughts,
He draws sometimes around his aching brow
Nature's calm mighty hands to heal his life-pain.
He is saved by her silence from his rack of self;
In her tranquil beauty is his purest bliss.
A new life dawns, he looks out from vistas wide;
The Spirit's breath moves him but soon retires:
His strength was not made to hold that puissant guest.
All dulls down to convention and routine
Or a fierce excitement brings him vivid joys:
His days are tinged with the red hue of strife
And lust's hot glare and passion's crimson stain;
Battle and murder are his tribal game.
Time has he none to turn his eyes within
And look for his lost self and his dead soul.
His motion on too short an axis wheels;
He cannot soar but creeps on his long road
Or if, impatient of the trudge of Time,
He would make a splendid haste on Fate's slow road,
His heart that runs soon pants and tires and sinks;
Or he walks ever on and finds no end.
Hardly a few can climb to greater life.
All tunes to a low scale and conscious pitch.
His knowledge dwells in the house of Ignorance;
His force nears not even once the Omnipotent,
Rare are his visits of heavenly ecstasy.
The bliss which sleeps in things and tries to wake,
Breaks out in him in a small joy of life:
This scanty grace is his persistent stay;
It lightens the burden of his many ills
And reconciles him to his little world.
He is satisfied with his common average kind;
Tomorrow's hopes and his old rounds of thought,
His old familiar interests and desires

He has made into a thick and narrowing hedge
Defending his small life from the Invisible;
His being's kinship to infinity
He has shut away from him into inmost self,
Fenced off the greatnesses of hidden God.
His being was formed to play a trivial part
In a little drama on a petty stage;
In a narrow plot he has pitched his tent of life
Beneath the wide gaze of the starry Vast.
He is the crown of all that has been done:
Thus is creation's labour justified;
This is the world's result, Nature's last poise!
And if this were all and nothing more were meant,
If what now seems were the whole of what must be,
If this were not a stade through which we pass
On our road from Matter to eternal Self,
To the Light that made the worlds, the Cause of things,
Well might interpret our mind's limited view
Existence as an accident in Time,
Illusion or phenomenon or freak,
The paradox of a creative Thought
Which moves between unreal opposites,
Inanimate Force struggling to feel and know,
Matter that chanced to read itself by Mind,
Inconscience monstrously engendering soul.
At times all looks unreal and remote:
We seem to live in a fiction of our thoughts
Pieced from sensation's fanciful traveller's tale,
Or caught on the film of the recording brain,
A figment or circumstance in cosmic sleep.
A somnambulist walking under the moon,
An image of ego treads through an ignorant dream
Counting the moments of a spectral Time.
In a false perspective of effect and cause,
Trusting to a specious prospect of world-space,
It drifts incessantly from scene to scene,

Whither it knows not, to what fabulous verge.
All here is dreamed or doubtfully exists,
But who the dreamer is and whence he looks
Is still unknown or only a shadowy guess.
Or the world is real but ourselves too small,
Insufficient for the mightiness of our stage.
A thin life-curve crosses the titan whirl
Of the orbit of a soulless universe,
And in the belly of the sparse rolling mass
A mind looks out from a small casual globe
And wonders what itself and all things are.
And yet to some interned subjective sight
That strangely has formed in Matter's sightless stuff,
A pointillage minute of little self
Takes figure as world-being's conscious base.
Such is our scene in the half-light below.
This is the sign of Matter's infinite,
This the weird purport of the picture shown
To Science the giantess, measurer of her field,
As she pores on the record of her close survey
And mathematises her huge external world,
To Reason bound within the circle of sense,
Or in Thought's broad impalpable Exchange
A speculator in tenuous vast ideas,
Abstractions in the void her currency
We know not with what firm values for its base.
Only religion in this bankruptcy
Presents its dubious riches to our hearts
Or signs unprovisioned cheques on the Beyond:
Our poverty shall there have its revenge.
Our spirits depart discarding a futile life
Into the blank unknown or with them take
Death's passport into immortality.

Yet was this only a provisional scheme,
A false appearance sketched by limiting sense,

Mind's insufficient self-discovery,
An early attempt, a first experiment.
This was a toy to amuse the infant earth;
But knowledge ends not in these surface powers
That live upon a ledge in the Ignorance
And dare not look into the dangerous depths
Or to stare upward measuring the Unknown.
There is a deeper seeing from within
And, when we have left these small purlieus of mind,
A greater vision meets us on the heights
In the luminous wideness of the spirit's gaze.
At last there wakes in us a witness Soul
That looks at truths unseen and scans the Unknown;
Then all assumes a new and marvellous face:
The world quivers with a God-light at its core,
In Time's deep heart high purposes move and live,
Life's borders crumble and join infinity.
This broad, confused, yet rigid scheme becomes
A magnificent imbroglio of the Gods,
A game, a work ambiguously divine.
Our seekings are short-lived experiments
Made by a wordless and inscrutable Power
Testing its issues from inconscient Night
To meet its luminous self of Truth and Bliss.
It peers at the Real through the apparent form;
It labours in our mortal mind and sense;
Amid the figures of the Ignorance,
In the symbol pictures drawn by word and thought,
It seeks the truth to which all figures point;
It looks for the source of Light with vision's lamp;
It works to find the Doer of all works,
The unfelt Self within who is the guide,
The unknown Self above who is the goal.
All is not here a blinded Nature's task:
A Word, a Wisdom watches us from on high,
A Witness sanctioning her will and works,

An Eye unseen in the unseeing vast;
There is an Influence from a Light above,
There are thoughts remote and sealed eternities;
A mystic motive drives the stars and suns.
In this passage from a deaf unknowing Force
To struggling consciousness and transient breath
A mighty Supernature waits on Time.
The world is other than we now think and see,
Our lives a deeper mystery than we have dreamed;
Our minds are starters in the race to God,
Our souls deputed selves of the Supreme.
Across the cosmic field through narrow lanes
Asking a scanty dole from Fortune's hands
And garbed in beggar's robes there walks the One.
Even in the theatre of these small lives
Behind the act a secret sweetness breathes,
An urge of miniature divinity.
A mystic passion from the wells of God
Flows through the guarded spaces of the soul;
A force that helps supports the suffering earth,
An unseen nearness and a hidden joy.
There are muffled throbs of laughter's undertones,
The murmur of an occult happiness,
An exultation in the depths of sleep,
A heart of bliss within a world of pain.
An Infant nursed on Nature's covert breast,
An Infant playing in the magic woods,
Fluting to rapture by the spirit's streams,
Awaits the hour when we shall turn to his call.
In this investiture of fleshly life
A soul that is a spark of God survives
And sometimes it breaks through the sordid screen
And kindles a fire that makes us half-divine.
In our body's cells there sits a hidden Power
That sees the unseen and plans eternity,
Our smallest parts have room for deepest needs;

There too the golden Messengers can come:
A door is cut in the mud wall of self;
Across the lowly threshold with bowed heads
Angels of ecstasy and self-giving pass,
And lodged in an inner sanctuary of dream
The makers of the image of deity live.
Pity is there and fire-winged sacrifice,
And flashes of sympathy and tenderness
Cast heaven-lights from the heart's secluded shrine.
A work is done in the deep silences;
A glory and wonder of spiritual sense,
A laughter in beauty's everlasting space
Transforming world-experience into joy,
Inhabit the mystery of the untouched gulfs;
Lulled by Time's beats eternity sleeps in us.
In the sealed hermetic heart, the happy core,
Unmoved behind this outer shape of death
The eternal Entity prepares within
Its matter of divine felicity,
Its reign of heavenly phenomenon.
Even in our sceptic mind of ignorance
A foresight comes of some immense release,
Our will lifts towards it slow and shaping hands.
Each part in us desires its absolute.
Our thoughts covet the everlasting Light,
Our strength derives from an omnipotent Force,
And since from a veiled God-joy the worlds were made
And since eternal Beauty asks for form
Even here where all is made of being's dust,
Our hearts are captured by ensnaring shapes,
Our very senses blindly seek for bliss.
Our error crucifies Reality
To force its birth and divine body here,
Compelling, incarnate in a human form
And breathing in limbs that one can touch and clasp,
Its Knowledge to rescue an ancient Ignorance,

Its saviour light the inconscient universe.
And when that greater Self comes sea-like down
To fill this image of our transience,
All shall be captured by delight, transformed:
In waves of undreamed ecstasy shall roll
Our mind and life and sense and laugh in a light
Other than this hard limited human day,
The body's tissues thrill apotheosised,
Its cells sustain bright metamorphosis.
This little being of Time, this shadow soul,
This living dwarf-figurehead of darkened spirit
Out of its traffic in petty dreams shall rise.
Its shape of person and its ego-face
Divested of this mortal travesty,
Like a clay troll kneaded into a god
New-made in the image of the eternal Guest,
It shall be caught to the breast of a white Force
And, flaming with the paradisal touch
In a rose-fire of sweet spiritual grace,
In the red passion of its infinite change,
Quiver, awake, and shudder with ecstasy.
As if reversing a deformation's spell,
Released from the black magic of the Night,
Renouncing servitude to the dim Abyss,
It shall learn at last who lived within unseen,
And seized with marvel in the adoring heart
To the enthroned Child-Godhead kneel aware,
Trembling with beauty and delight and love.
But first the spirit's ascent we must achieve
Out of the chasm from which our nature rose.
The soul must soar sovereign above the form
And climb to summits beyond mind's half-sleep;
Our hearts we must inform with heavenly strength,
Surprise the animal with the occult god.
Then kindling the gold tongue of sacrifice,
Calling the powers of a bright hemisphere,

We shall shed the discredit of our mortal state,
Make the abysm a road for Heaven's descent,
Acquaint our depths with the supernal Ray
And cleave the darkness with the mystic Fire.

　　Adventuring once more in the natal mist
Across the dangerous haze, the pregnant stir,
He through the astral chaos shore a way
Mid the grey faces of its demon gods,
Questioned by whispers of its flickering ghosts,
Besieged by sorceries of its fluent force.
As one who walks unguided through strange fields
Tending he knows not where nor with what hope,
He trod a soil that failed beneath his feet
And journeyed in stone strength to a fugitive end.
His trail behind him was a vanishing line
Of glimmering points in a vague immensity;
A bodiless murmur travelled at his side
In the wounded gloom complaining against light.
A huge obstruction its immobile heart,
The watching opacity multiplied as he moved
Its hostile mass of dead and staring eyes;
The darkness glimmered like a dying torch.
Around him an extinguished phantom glow
Peopled with shadowy and misleading shapes
The vague Inconscient's dark and measureless cave.
His only sunlight was his spirit's flame.

END OF CANTO FIVE

Canto Six

The Kingdoms and Godheads of the Greater Life

As ONE who between dim receding walls
Towards the far gleam of a tunnel's mouth,
Hoping for light, walks now with freer pace
And feels approach a breath of wider air,
So he escaped from that grey anarchy.
Into an ineffectual world he came,
A purposeless region of arrested birth
Where being from non-being fled and dared
To live but had no strength long to abide.
Above there gleamed a pondering brow of sky
Tormented, crossed by wings of doubtful haze
Adventuring with a voice of roaming winds
And crying for a direction in the void
Like blind souls looking for the selves they lost
And wandering through unfamiliar worlds;
Wings of vague questioning met the query of Space.
After denial dawned a dubious hope,
A hope of self and form and leave to live
And the birth of that which never yet could be,
And joy of the mind's hazard, the heart's choice,
Grace of the unknown and hands of sudden surprise
And a touch of sure delight in unsure things:
To a strange uncertain tract his journey came
Where consciousness played with unconscious self
And birth was an attempt or episode.
A charm drew near that could not keep its spell,
An eager Power that could not find its way,
A Chance that chose a strange arithmetic
But could not bind with it the forms it made,
A multitude that could not guard its sum
Which less than zero grew and more than one.

Arriving at a large and shadowy sense
That cared not to define its fleeting drift,
Life laboured in a strange and mythic air
Denuded of her sweet magnificent suns.
In worlds imagined, never yet made true,
A lingering glimmer on creation's verge,
One strayed and dreamed and never stopped to achieve:
To achieve would have destroyed that magic Space.
The marvels of a twilight wonderland
Full of a beauty strangely, vainly made,
A surge of fanciful realities,
Dim tokens of a Splendour sealed above,
Awoke the passion of the eyes' desire,
Compelled belief on the enamoured thought
And drew the heart but led it to no goal.
A magic flowed as if of moving scenes
That kept awhile their fugitive delicacy
Of sparing lines limned by an abstract art
In a rare scanted light with faint dream-brush
On a silver background of incertitude.
An infant glow of heavens near to morn,
A fire intense conceived but never lit,
Caressed the air with ardent hints of day.
The perfect longing for imperfection's charm,
The illumined caught by the snare of Ignorance,
Ethereal creatures drawn by body's lure
To that region of promise, beating invisible wings,
Came hungry for the joy of finite life
But too divine to tread created soil
And share the fate of perishable things.
The Children of the unembodied Gleam
Arisen from a formless thought in the soul
And chased by an imperishable desire,
Traversed the field of the pursuing gaze.
A Will that unpersisting failed, worked there:
Life was a search but finding never came.

There nothing satisfied, but all allured,
Things seemed to be that never wholly are,
Images were seen that looked like living acts
And symbols hid the sense they claimed to show,
Pale dreams grew real to the dreamer's eyes.
The souls came there that vainly strive for birth,
And spirits entrapped might wander through all time,
Yet never find the truth by which they live.
All ran like hopes that hunt a lurking chance;
Nothing was solid, nothing felt complete:
All was unsafe, miraculous and half-true.
It seemed a realm of lives that had no base.

Then dawned a greater seeking, broadened sky,
A journey under wings of brooding Force.
First came the kingdom of the morning star:
A twilight beauty trembled under its spear
And the throb of promise of a wider Life.
Then slowly rose a great and doubting sun
And in its light she made of self a world.
A spirit was there that sought for its own deep self,
Yet was content with fragments pushed in front
And parts of living that belied the whole
But, pieced together, might one day be true.
Yet something seemed to be achieved at last.
A growing volume of the will-to-be,
A text of living and a graph of force,
A script of acts, a song of conscious forms
Burdened with meanings fugitive from thought's grasp
And crowded with undertones of life's rhythmic cry,
Could write itself on the hearts of living things.
In an outbreak of the might of secret Spirit,
In Life and Matter's answer of delight,
Some face of deathless beauty could be caught
That gave immortality to a moment's joy,
Some word that could incarnate highest Truth

Leaped out from a chance tension of the soul,
Some hue of the Absolute could fall on life,
Some glory of knowledge and intuitive sight,
Some passion of the rapturous heart of Love.
A hierophant of the bodiless Secrecy
Interned in an unseen spiritual sheath,
The Will that pushes sense beyond its scope
To feel the light and joy intangible,
Half found its way into the Ineffable's peace,
Half captured a sealed sweetness of desire
That yearned from a bosom of mysterious Bliss,
Half manifested veiled Reality.
A soul not wrapped into its cloak of mind
Could glimpse the true sense of a world of forms;
Illumined by a vision in the thought,
Upbuoyed by the heart's understanding flame,
It could hold in the conscious ether of the spirit
The divinity of a symbol universe.
　　This realm inspires us with our vaster hopes;
Its forces have made landings on our globe,
Its signs have traced their pattern in our lives:
It lends a sovereign movement to our fate,
Its errant waves motive our life's high surge.
All that we seek for is prefigured there
And all we have not known nor ever sought
Which yet one day must be born in human hearts
That the Timeless may fulfil itself in things.
Incarnate in the mystery of the days,
Eternal in an unclosed Infinite,
A mounting endless possibility
Climbs high upon a topless ladder of dream
For ever in the Being's conscious trance.
All on that ladder mounts to an unseen end.
An Energy of perpetual transience makes
The journey from which no return is sure,
The pilgrimage of Nature to the Unknown.

As if in her ascent to her lost source
She hoped to unroll all that could ever be,
Her high procession moves from stage to stage,
A progress leap from sight to greater sight,
A process march from form to ampler form,
A caravan of the inexhaustible
Formations of a boundless Thought and Force.
Her timeless Power that lay once on the lap
Of a beginningless and endless Calm,
Now severed from the Spirit's immortal bliss,
Erects the type of all the joys she has lost;
Compelling transient substance into shape,
She hopes by the creative act's release
To o'erleap sometimes the gulf she cannot fill,
To heal awhile the wound of severance,
Escape from the moment's prison of littleness
And meet the Eternal's wide sublimities
In the uncertain time-field portioned here.
Almost she nears what never can be attained;
She shuts eternity into an hour
And fills a little soul with the Infinite;
The Immobile leans to the magic of her call;
She stands on a shore in the Illimitable,
Perceives the formless Dweller in all forms
And feels around her infinity's embrace.
Her task no ending knows; she serves no aim
But labours driven by a nameless Will
That came from some unknowable formless Vast.
This is her secret and impossible task
To catch the boundless in a net of birth,
To cast the spirit into physical form,
To lend speech and thought to the Ineffable;
She is pushed to reveal the ever Unmanifest.
Yet by her skill the impossible has been done:
She follows her sublime irrational plan,
Invents devices of her magic art

To find new bodies for the Infinite
And images of the Unimaginable;
She has lured the Eternal into the arms of Time.
Even now herself she knows not what she has done.
For all is wrought beneath a baffling mask:
A semblance other than its hidden truth
The aspect wears of an illusion's trick,
A feigned time-driven unreality,
The unfinished creation of a changing soul
In a body changing with the inhabitant.
Insignificant her means, infinite her work;
On a great field of shapeless consciousness
In little finite strokes of mind and sense
An endless Truth she endlessly unfolds;
A timeless mystery works out in Time.
The greatness she has dreamed her acts have missed,
Her labour is a passion and a pain,
A rapture and pang, her glory and her curse;
And yet she cannot choose but labours on;
Her mighty heart forbids her to desist.
As long as the world lasts her failure lives
Astonishing and foiling Reason's gaze,
A folly and a beauty unspeakable,
A superb madness of the will to live,
A daring, a delirium of delight.
This is her being's law, its sole resource;
She sates, though satisfaction never comes,
Her hungry will to lavish everywhere
Her many-imaged fictions of the Self
And thousand fashions of one Reality.
A world she made touched by truth's fleeing hem,
A world cast into a dream of what it seeks,
An icon of truth, a conscious mystery's shape.
It lingered not like the earth-mind hemmed in
In solid barriers of apparent fact;
It dared to trust the dream-mind and the soul.

A hunter of spiritual verities
Still only thought or guessed or held by faith,
It seized in imagination and confined
A painted bird of paradise in a cage.
This greater life is enamoured of the Unseen;
It calls to some highest Light beyond its reach,
It can feel the Silence that absolves the soul;
It feels a saviour touch, a ray divine:
Beauty and good and truth its godheads are.
It is near to heavenlier heavens than earth's eyes see,
A direr darkness than man's life can bear:
It has kinship with the demon and the god.
A strange enthusiasm has moved its heart;
It hungers for heights, it passions for the supreme.
It hunts for the perfect word, the perfect shape,
It leaps to the summit thought, the summit light.
For by the form the Formless is brought close
And all perfection fringes the Absolute.
A child of heaven who never saw his home,
Its impetus meets the eternal at a point:
It can only near and touch, it cannot hold;
It can only strain towards some bright extreme:
Its greatness is to seek and to create.
    On every plane, this Greatness must create.
On earth, in heaven, in hell she is the same;
Of every fate she takes her mighty part.
A guardian of the fire that lights the suns,
She triumphs in her glory and her might:
Opposed, oppressed she bears God's urge to be born:
The spirit survives upon non-being's ground,
World-force outlasts world-disillusion's shock:
Dumb, she is still the Word, inert the Power.
Here fallen, a slave of death and ignorance,
To things deathless she is driven to aspire
And moved to know even the Unknowable.
Even nescient, null, her sleep creates a world.

When most unseen, most mightily she works;
Housed in the atom, buried in the clod,
Her quick creative passion cannot cease.
Inconscience is her long gigantic pause,
Her cosmic swoon is a stupendous phase:
Time-born, she hides her immortality;
In death, her bed, she waits the hour to rise.
Even with the Light denied that sent her forth
And the hope dead she needed for her task,
Even when her brightest stars are quenched in Night,
Nourished by hardship and calamity
And with pain for her body's handmaid, masseuse, nurse,
Her tortured invisible spirit continues still
To toil though in darkness, to create though with pangs;
She carries crucified God upon her breast.
In chill insentient depths where joy is none,
Immured, oppressed by the resisting Void
Where nothing moves and nothing can become,
Still she remembers, still invokes the skill
The Wonder-worker gave her at her birth,
Imparts to drowsy formlessness a shape,
Reveals a world where nothing was before.
In realms confined to a prone circle of death,
To a dark eternity of Ignorance,
A quiver in an inert inconscient mass,
Or imprisoned in immobilised whorls of Force,
By Matter's blind compulsion deaf and mute
She refuses motionless in the dust to sleep.
Then, for her rebel waking's punishment
Given only hard mechanic Circumstance
As the enginery of her magic craft,
She fashions godlike marvels out of mud;
In the plasm she sets her dumb immortal urge,
Helps the live tissue to think, the closed sense to feel,
Flashes through the frail nerves poignant messages,
In a heart of flesh miraculously loves,

To brute bodies gives a soul, a will, a voice.
Ever she summons as by a sorcerer's wand
Beings and shapes and scenes innumerable,
Torch-bearers of her pomps through Time and Space.
This world is her long journey through the night,
The suns and planets lamps to light her road,
Our reason is the confidante of her thoughts,
Our senses are her vibrant witnesses.
There drawing her signs from things half true, half false,
She labours to replace by realised dreams
The memory of her lost eternity.
   These are her deeds in this huge world-ignorance:
Till the veil is lifted, till the night is dead,
In light or dark she keeps her tireless search;
Time is her road of endless pilgrimage.
One mighty passion motives all her works.
Her eternal Lover is her action's cause;
For him she leaped forth from the unseen Vasts
To move here in a stark unconscious world.
Its acts are her commerce with her hidden Guest,
His moods she takes for her heart's passionate moulds;
In beauty she treasures the sunlight of his smile.
Ashamed of her rich cosmic poverty,
She cajoles with her small gifts his mightiness,
Holds with her scenes his look's fidelity
And woos his large-eyed wandering thoughts to dwell
In figures of her million-impulsed Force.
Only to attract her veiled companion
And keep him close to her breast in her world-cloak
Lest from her arms he turn to his formless peace,
Is her heart's business and her clinging care.
Yet when he is most near, she feels him far.
For contradiction is her nature's law.
Although she is ever in him and he in her,
As if unaware of the eternal tie,
Her will is to shut God into her works

And keep him as her cherished prisoner
That never they may part again in Time.
A sumptuous chamber of the spirit's sleep
At first she made, a deep interior room,
Where he slumbers as if a forgotten guest.
But now she turns to break the oblivious spell,
Awakes the sleeper on the sculptured couch;
She finds again the Presence in the form
And in the light that wakes with him recovers
A meaning in the hurry and trudge of Time,
And through this mind that once obscured the soul
Passes a glint of unseen deity.
Across a luminous dream of spirit-space
She builds creation like a rainbow bridge
Between the original Silence and the Void.
A net is made of the mobile universe;
She weaves a snare for the conscious Infinite.
A knowledge is with her that conceals its steps
And seems a mute omnipotent Ignorance.
A might is with her that makes wonders true;
The incredible is her stuff of common fact.
Her purposes, her workings riddles prove;
Examined, they grow other than they were,
Explained, they seem yet more inexplicable.
Even in our world a mystery has reigned
Earth's cunning screen of trivial plainness hides;
Her larger levels are of sorceries made.
There the enigma shows its splendid prism,
There is no deep disguise of commonness;
Occult, profound comes all experience,
Marvel is ever new, miracle divine.
There is a screened burden, a mysterious touch,
There is a secrecy of hidden sense.
Although no earthen mask weighs on her face,
Into herself she flees from her own sight.
All forms are tokens of some veiled idea

Whose covert purpose lurks from mind's pursuit,
Yet is a womb of sovereign consequence.
There every thought and feeling is an act,
And every act a symbol and a sign,
And every symbol hides a living power.
A universe she builds from truths and myths,
But what she needed most she cannot build;
All shown is a figure or copy of the Truth,
But the Real veils from her its mystic face.
All else she finds, there lacks eternity;
All is sought out, but missed the Infinite.

A consciousness lit by a Truth above
Was felt; it saw the light but not the Truth:
It caught the Idea and built from it a world;
It made an Image there and called it God.
Yet something true and inward harboured there.
The beings of that world of greater life,
Tenants of a larger air and freer space,
Live not by the body or in outward things:
A deeper living was their seat of self.
In that intense domain of intimacy
Objects dwell as companions of the soul;
The body's actions are a minor script,
The surface rendering of a life within.
All forces are Life's retinue in that world
And thought and body as her handmaids move.
The universal widenesses give her room:
All feel the cosmic movement in their acts
And are the instruments of her cosmic might.
Or their own self they make their universe.
In all who have risen to a greater Life,
A voice of unborn things whispers to the ear,
To their eyes visited by some high sunlight
Aspiration shows the image of a crown:
To work out a seed that she has thrown within,

To achieve her power in them her creatures live.
Each is a greatness growing towards the heights
Or from his inner centre oceans out;
In circling ripples of concentric power
They swallow, glutted, their environment.
Even of that largeness many a cabin make;
In narrower breadths and briefer vistas pent
They live content with some small greatness won.
To rule the little empire of themselves,
To be a figure in their private world
And make the milieu's joys and griefs their own
And satisfy their life-motives and life-wants
Is charge enough and office for this strength,
A steward of the Person and his fate.
This was transition-line and starting-point,
A first immigration into heavenliness,
For all who cross into that brilliant sphere:
These are the kinsmen of our earthly race;
This region borders on our mortal state.
  This wider world our greater movements gives,
Its strong formations build our growing selves;
Its creatures are our brighter replicas,
Complete the types we only initiate
And are securely what we strive to be.
As if thought-out eternal characters,
Entire, not pulled as we by contrary tides,
They follow the unseen leader in the heart,
Their lives obey the inner nature's law.
There is kept grandeur's store, the hero's mould;
The soul is the watchful builder of its fate;
None is a spirit indifferent and inert;
They choose their side, they see the god they adore.
A battle is joined between the true and false,
A pilgrimage sets out to the divine Light.
For even Ignorance there aspires to know
And shines with the lustre of a distant star;

There is a knowledge in the heart of sleep
And Nature comes to them as a conscious force.
An ideal is their leader and their king:
Aspiring to the monarchy of the sun
They call in Truth for their high government,
Hold her incarnate in their daily acts
And fill their thoughts with her inspired voice
And shape their lives into her breathing form,
Till in her sun-gold godhead they too share.
Or to the truth of Darkness they subscribe;
Whether for Heaven or Hell they must wage war:
Warriors of Good, they serve a shining cause
Or are Evil's soldiers in the pay of Sin.
For evil and good an equal tenure keep
Wherever Knowledge is Ignorance's twin.
All powers of Life towards their godhead tend
In the wideness and the daring of that air,
Each builds its temple and expands its cult,
And Sin too there is a divinity.
Affirming the beauty and splendour of her law
She claims life as her natural domain,
Assumes the world's throne or dons the papal robe:
Her worshippers proclaim her sacred right.
A red-tiaraed Falsehood they revere,
Worship the shadow of a crooked God,
Admit the black Idea that twists the brain
Or lie with the harlot Power that slays the soul.
A mastering virtue statuesques the pose,
Or a Titan passion goads to a proud unrest:
At Wisdom's altar they are kings and priests
Or their life a sacrifice to an idol of Power.
Or Beauty shines on them like a wandering star;
Too far to reach, passionate they follow her light;
In Art and life they catch the All-Beautiful's ray
And make the world their radiant treasure house:
Even common figures are with marvel robed;

A charm and greatness locked in every hour
Awakes the joy which sleeps in all things made.
A mighty victory or a mighty fall,
A throne in heaven or a pit in hell,
The dual Energy they have justified
And marked their souls with her tremendous seal:
Whatever Fate may do to them they have earned;
Something they have done, something they have been, they live.
There Matter is soul's result and not its cause.
In a contrary balance to earth's truth of things
The gross weighs less, the subtle counts for more;
On inner values hangs the outer plan.
As quivers with the thought the expressive word,
As yearns the act with the passion of the soul
This world's apparent sensible design
Looks vibrant back to some interior might.
A Mind not limited by external sense
Gave figures to the spirit's imponderables,
The world's impacts without channels registered
And turned into the body's concrete thrill
The vivid workings of a bodiless Force;
Powers here subliminal that act unseen
Or in ambush crouch waiting behind the wall
Came out in front uncovering their face.
The occult grew there overt, the obvious kept
A covert turn and shouldered the unknown;
The unseen was felt and jostled visible shapes.
In the communion of two meeting minds
Thought looked at thought and had no need of speech;
Emotion clasped emotion in two hearts,
They felt each other's thrill in the flesh and nerves
Or melted each in each and grew immense
As when two houses burn and fire joins fire:
Hate grappled hate and love broke in on love,
Will wrestled with will on mind's invisible ground;
Others' sensations passing through like waves

Left quivering the subtle body's frame,
Their anger rushed galloping in brute attack,
A charge of trampling hooves on shaken soil;
One felt another's grief invade the breast,
Another's joy exulting ran through the blood:
Hearts could draw close through distance, voices near
That spoke upon the shore of alien seas.
There beat a throb of living interchange:
Being felt being even when afar
And consciousness replied to consciousness.
And yet the ultimate oneness was not there.
There was a separateness of soul from soul:
An inner wall of silence could be built,
An armour of conscious might protect and shield;
The being could be closed in and solitary;
One could remain apart in self, alone.
Identity was not yet nor union's peace.
All was imperfect still, half-known, half-done:
The miracle of Inconscience overpassed,
The miracle of the Superconscient still,
Unknown, self-wrapped, unfelt, unknowable,
Looked down on them, origin of all they were.
As forms they came of the formless Infinite,
As names lived of a nameless Eternity.
The beginning and the end were there occult;
A middle term worked unexplained, abrupt:
They were words that spoke to a vast wordless Truth,
They were figures crowding an unfinished sum.
None truly knew himself or knew the world
Or the Reality living there enshrined:
Only they knew what Mind could take and build
Out of the secret Supermind's huge store.
A darkness under them, a bright Void above,
Uncertain they lived in a great climbing Space;
By mysteries they explained a Mystery,
A riddling answer met the riddle of things.

As he moved in this ether of ambiguous life,
Himself was soon a riddle to himself;
As symbols he saw all and sought their sense.

   Across the leaping springs of death and birth
And over shifting borders of soul-change,
A hunter on the spirit's creative track,
He followed in life's fine and mighty trails
Pursuing her sealed formidable delight
In a perilous adventure without close.
At first no aim appeared in those large steps:
Only the wide source he saw of all things here
Looking towards a wider source beyond.
For as she drew away from earthly lines,
A tenser drag was felt from the Unknown,
A higher context of delivering thought
Drove her towards marvel and discovery;
There came a high release from pettier cares,
A mightier image of desire and hope,
A vaster formula, a greater scene.
Ever she circled towards some far-off Light:
Her signs still covered more than they revealed;
But tied to some immediate sight and will
They lost their purport in the joy of use,
Till stripped of their infinite meaning they became
A cipher gleaming with unreal sense.
Armed with a magical and haunted bow
She aimed at a target kept invisible
And ever deemed remote though always near.
As one who spells illumined characters,
The key-book of a crabbed magician text,
He scanned her subtle tangled weird designs
And the screened difficult theorem of her clues,
Traced in the monstrous sands of desert Time
The thread beginnings of her titan works,
Watched her charade of action for some hint,

Read the Nō-gestures of her silhouettes,
And strove to capture in their burdened drift
The dance-fantasia of her sequences
Escaping into rhythmic mystery,
A glimmer of fugitive feet on fleeing soil.
In the labyrinth pattern of her thoughts and hopes
And the byways of her intimate desires,
In the complex corners crowded with her dreams
And rounds crossed by an intrigue of irrelevant rounds,
A wanderer straying amid fugitive scenes,
He lost its signs and chased each failing guess.
Ever he met key-words, ignorant of their key.
A sun that dazzled its own eye of sight,
A luminous enigma's brilliant hood
Lit the dense purple barrier of thought's sky:
A dim large trance showed to the night her stars.
As if sitting near an open window's gap,
He read by lightning-flash on crowding flash
Chapters of her metaphysical romance
Of the soul's search for lost Reality
And her fictions drawn from spirit's authentic fact,
Her caprices and conceits and meanings locked,
Her rash unseizable freaks and mysteried turns.
The magnificent wrappings of her secrecy
That fold her desirable body out of sight,
The strange significant forms woven on her robe,
Her meaningful outlines of the souls of things
He saw, her false transparencies of thought-hue,
Her rich brocades with imaged fancies sewn
And mutable masks and broideries of disguise.
A thousand baffling faces of the Truth
Looked at him from her forms with unknown eyes
And wordless mouths unrecognisable,
Spoke from the figures of her masquerade,
Or peered from the recondite magnificence
And subtle splendour of her draperies.

In sudden scintillations of the Unknown,
Inexpressive sounds became veridical,
Ideas that seemed unmeaning flashed out truth;
Voices that came from unseen waiting worlds
Uttered the syllables of the Unmanifest
To clothe the body of the mystic Word,
And wizard diagrams of the occult Law
Sealed some precise unreadable harmony,
Or used hue and figure to reconstitute
The herald blazon of Time's secret things.
In her green wildernesses and lurking depths,
In her thickets of joy where danger clasps delight,
He glimpsed the hidden wings of her songster hopes,
A glimmer of blue and gold and scarlet fire.
In her covert lanes, bordering her chance field-paths
And by her singing rivulets and calm lakes
He found the glow of her golden fruits of bliss
And the beauty of her flowers of dream and muse.
As if a miracle of heart's change by joy
He watched in the alchemist radiance of her suns
The crimson outburst of one secular flower
On the tree-of-sacrifice of spiritual love.
In the sleepy splendour of her noons he saw,
A perpetual repetition through the hours,
Thought's dance of dragonflies on mystery's stream
That skim but never test its murmurs' race,
And heard the laughter of her rose desires
Running as if to escape from longed-for hands,
Jingling sweet anklet-bells of fantasy.
Amidst live symbols of her occult power
He moved and felt them as close real forms:
In that life more concrete than the lives of men
Throbbed heart-beats of the hidden reality:
Embodied was there what we but think and feel,
Self-framed what here takes outward borrowed shapes.
A comrade of Silence on her austere heights

Accepted by her mighty loneliness,
He stood with her on meditating peaks
Where life and being are a sacrament
Offered to the Reality beyond,
And saw her loose into infinity
Her hooded eagles of significance,
Messengers of Thought to the Unknowable.
Identified in soul-vision and soul-sense,
Entering into her depths as into a house,
All he became that she was or longed to be,
He thought with her thoughts and journeyed with her steps,
Lived with her breath and scanned all with her eyes
That so he might learn the secret of her soul.
A witness overmastered by his scene,
He admired her splendid front of pomp and play
And the marvels of her rich and delicate craft,
And thrilled to the insistence of her cry;
Impassioned he bore the sorceries of her might,
Felt laid on him her abrupt mysterious will,
Her hands that knead fate in their violent grasp,
Her touch that moves, her powers that seize and drive.
But this too he saw, her soul that wept within,
Her seekings vain that clutch at fleeing truth,
Her hopes whose sombre gaze mates with despair,
The passion that possessed her longing limbs,
The trouble and rapture of her yearning breasts,
Her mind that toils unsatisfied with its fruits,
Her heart that captures not the one Beloved.
Always he met a veiled and seeking Force,
An exiled goddess building mimic heavens,
A Sphinx whose eyes look up to a hidden Sun.

    Ever he felt near a spirit in her forms:
Its passive presence was her nature's strength;
This sole is real in apparent things,
Even upon earth the spirit is life's key,

But her solid outsides nowhere bear its trace.
Its stamp on her acts is undiscoverable.
A pathos of lost heights is its appeal.
Only sometimes is caught a shadowy line
That seems a hint of veiled reality.
Life stared at him with vague confused outlines
Offering a picture the eyes could not keep,
A story that was yet not written there.
As in a fragmentary half-lost design
Life's meanings fled from the pursuing eye.
Life's visage hides life's real self from sight;
Life's secret sense is written within, above.
The thought that gives it sense lives far beyond;
It is not seen in its half-finished design.
In vain we hope to read the baffling signs
Or find the word of the half-played charade.
Only in that greater life a cryptic thought
Is found, is hinted some interpreting word
That makes the earth-myth a tale intelligible.
Something was seen at last that looked like truth.
In a half-lit air of hazardous mystery
The eye that looks at the dark half of truth
Made out an image mid a vivid blur
And peering through a mist of subtle tints
He saw a half-blind chained divinity
Bewildered by the world in which he moved,
Yet conscious of some light prompting his soul.
Attracted to strange far-off shimmerings,
Led by the fluting of a distant Player
He sought his way amid life's laughter and call
And the index chaos of her myriad steps
Towards some total deep infinitude.
Around crowded the forest of her signs:
At hazard he read by arrow-leaps of Thought
That hit the mark by guess or luminous chance,
Her changing coloured road-lights of idea

And her signals of uncertain swift event,
The hieroglyphs of her symbol pageantries
And her landmarks in the tangled paths of Time.
In her mazes of approach and of retreat
To every side she draws him and repels,
But drawn too near escapes from his embrace;
All ways she leads him but no way is sure.
Allured by the many-toned marvel of her chant,
Attracted by the witchcraft of her moods
And moved by her casual touch to joy and grief,
He loses himself in her but wins her not.
A fugitive paradise smiles at him from her eyes:
He dreams of her beauty made for ever his,
He dreams of his mastery her limbs shall bear,
He dreams of the magic of her breasts of bliss.
In her illumined script, her fanciful
Translation of God's pure original text,
He thinks to read the Scripture Wonderful,
Hieratic key to unknown beatitudes.
But the Word of Life is hidden in its script,
The chant of Life has lost its divine note.
Unseen, a captive in a house of sound,
The spirit lost in the splendour of a dream
Listens to a thousand-voiced illusion's ode.
A delicate weft of sorcery steals the heart
Or a fiery magic tints her tones and hues,
Yet they but wake a thrill of transient grace;
A vagrant march struck by the wanderer Time,
They call to a brief unsatisfied delight
Or wallow in ravishments of mind and sense,
But miss the luminous answer of the soul.
A blind heart-throb that reaches joy through tears,
A yearning towards peaks for ever unreached,
An ecstasy of unfulfilled desire
Track the last heavenward climbings of her voice.
Transmuted are past suffering's memories

Into an old sadness's sweet escaping trail:
Turned are her tears to gems of diamond pain,
Her sorrow into a magic crown of song.
Brief are her snatches of felicity
That touch the surface, then escape or die:
A lost remembrance echoes in her depths,
A deathless longing is hers, a veiled self's call;
A prisoner in the mortal's limiting world,
A spirit wounded by life sobs in her breast;
A cherished suffering is her deepest cry.
A wanderer on forlorn despairing routes,
Along the roads of sound a frustrate voice
Forsaken cries to a forgotten bliss.
Astray in the echo caverns of Desire,
It guards the phantoms of a soul's dead hopes
And keeps alive the voice of perished things
Or lingers upon sweet and errant notes
Hunting for pleasure in the heart of pain.
A fateful hand has touched the cosmic chords
And the intrusion of a troubled strain
Covers the inner music's hidden key
That guides unheard the surface cadences.
Yet is it joy to live and to create
And joy to love and labour though all fails,
And joy to seek though all we find deceives
And all on which we lean betrays our trust;
Yet something in its depths was worth the pain,
A passionate memory haunts with ecstasy's fire.
Even grief has joy hidden beneath its roots:
For nothing is truly vain the One has made:
In our defeated hearts God's strength survives
And victory's star still lights our desperate road;
Our death is made a passage to new worlds.
This to Life's music gives its anthem swell.
To all she lends the glory of her voice;
Heaven's raptures whisper to her heart and pass,

Earth's transient yearnings cry from her lips and fade.
Alone the God-given hymn escapes her art
That came with her from her spiritual home
But stopped half-way and failed, a silent word
Awake in some deep pause of waiting worlds,
A murmur suspended in eternity's hush:
But no breath comes from the supernal peace:
A sumptuous interlude occupies the ear
And the heart listens and the soul consents;
An evanescent music it repeats
Wasting on transience Time's eternity.
A tremolo of the voices of the hours
Oblivious screens the high intended theme
The self-embodying spirit came to play
On the vast clavichord of Nature-Force.
Only a mighty murmur here and there
Of the eternal Word, the blissful Voice
Or Beauty's touch transfiguring heart and sense,
A wandering splendour and a mystic cry,
Recalls the strength and sweetness heard no more.

Here is the gap, here stops or sinks life's force;
This deficit paupers the magician's skill:
This want makes all the rest seem thin and bare.
A half-sight draws the horizon of her acts:
Her depths remember what she came to do,
But the mind has forgotten or the heart mistakes:
In Nature's endless lines is lost the God.
In knowledge to sum up omniscience,
In action to erect the Omnipotent,
To create her Creator here was her heart's conceit,
To invade the cosmic scene with utter God.
Toiling to transform the still far Absolute
Into an all-fulfilling epiphany,
Into an utterance of the Ineffable,
She would bring the glory here of the Absolute's force,

Change poise into creation's rhythmic swing,
Marry with a sky of calm a sea of bliss.
A fire to call eternity into Time,
Make body's joy as vivid as the soul's,
Earth she would lift to neighbourhood with heaven,
Labours life to equate with the Supreme
And reconcile the Eternal and the Abyss.
Her pragmatism of the transcendent Truth
Fills silence with the voices of the gods,
But in the cry the single Voice is lost.
For Nature's vision climbs beyond her acts.
A life of gods in heaven she sees above,
A demigod emerging from an ape
Is all she can in our mortal element.
Here the half-god, the half-titan are her peak:
This greater life wavers twixt earth and sky.
A poignant paradox pursues her dreams:
Her hooded energy moves an ignorant world
To look for a joy her own strong clasp puts off:
In her embrace it cannot turn to its source.
Immense her power, endless her act's vast drive,
Astray is its significance and lost.
Although she carries in her secret breast
The law and journeying curve of all things born
Her knowledge partial seems, her purpose small;
On a soil of yearning tread her sumptuous hours.
A leaden Nescience weighs the wings of Thought,
Her power oppresses the being with its garbs,
Her actions prison its immortal gaze.
A sense of limit haunts her masteries
And nowhere is assured content or peace:
For all the depth and beauty of her work
A wisdom lacks that sets the spirit free.
An old and faded charm had now her face
And palled for him her quick and curious lore;
His wide soul asked a deeper joy than hers.

Out of her daedal lines he sought escape;
But neither gate of horn nor ivory
He found nor postern of spiritual sight,
There was no issue from that dreamlike space.
Our being must move eternally through Time;
Death helps us not, vain is the hope to cease;
A secret Will compels us to endure.
Our life's repose is in the Infinite;
It cannot end, its end is Life supreme.
Death is a passage, not the goal of our walk:
Some ancient deep impulsion labours on:
Our souls are dragged as with a hidden leash,
Carried from birth to birth, from world to world,
Our acts prolong after the body's fall
The old perpetual journey without pause.
No silent peak is found where Time can rest.
This was a magic stream that reached no sea.
However far he went, wherever turned,
The wheel of works ran with him and outstripped;
Always a farther task was left to do.
A beat of action and a cry of search
For ever grew in that unquiet world;
A busy murmur filled the heart of Time.
All was contrivance and unceasing stir.
A hundred ways to live were tried in vain:
A sameness that assumed a thousand forms
Strove to escape from its long monotone
And made new things that soon were like the old.
A curious decoration lured the eye
And novel values furbished ancient themes
To cheat the mind with the idea of change.
A different picture that was still the same
Appeared upon the cosmic vague background.
Only another labyrinthine house
Of creatures and their doings and events,
A city of the traffic of bound souls,

A market of creation and her wares,
Was offered to the labouring mind and heart.
A circuit ending where it first began
Is dubbed the forward and eternal march
Of progress on perfection's unknown road.
Each final scheme leads to a sequel plan.
Yet every new departure seems the last,
Inspired evangel, theory's ultimate peak,
Proclaiming a panacea for all Time's ills
Or carrying thought in its ultimate zenith flight
And trumpeting supreme discovery;
Each brief idea, a structure perishable,
Publishes the immortality of its rule,
Its claim to be the perfect form of things,
Truth's last epitome, Time's golden best.
But nothing has been achieved of infinite worth:
A world made ever anew, never complete,
Piled always half-attempts on lost attempts
And saw a fragment as the eternal Whole.
In the aimless mounting total of things done
Existence seemed a vain necessity's act,
A wrestle of eternal opposites
In a clasped antagonism's close-locked embrace,
A play without denouement or idea,
A hunger march of lives without a goal,
Or, written on a bare blackboard of Space,
A futile and recurring sum of souls,
A hope that failed, a light that never shone,
The labour of an unaccomplished Force
Tied to its acts in a dim eternity.
There is no end or none can yet be seen:
Although defeated, life must struggle on;
Always she sees a crown she cannot grasp;
Her eyes are fixed beyond her fallen state.
There quivers still within her breast and ours
A glory that was once and is no more,

Or there calls to us from some unfulfilled beyond
A greatness yet unreached by the halting world.
In a memory behind our mortal sense
A dream persists of larger happier air
Breathing around free hearts of joy and love,
Forgotten by us, immortal in lost Time.
A ghost of bliss pursues her haunted depths;
For she remembers still, though now so far,
Her realm of golden ease and glad desire
And the beauty and strength and happiness that were hers
In the sweetness of her glowing paradise,
In her kingdom of immortal ecstasy
Half-way between God's silence and the Abyss.
This knowledge in our hidden parts we keep;
Awake to a vague mystery's appeal,
We meet a deep unseen Reality
Far truer than the world's face of present truth:
We are chased by a self we cannot now recall
And moved by a Spirit we must still become.
As one who has lost the kingdom of his soul,
We look back to some god-phase of our birth
Other than this imperfect creature here
And hope in this or a diviner world
To recover yet from Heaven's patient guard
What by our mind's forgetfulness we miss,
Our being's natural felicity,
Our heart's delight we have exchanged for grief,
The body's thrill we bartered for mere pain,
The bliss for which our mortal nature yearns
As yearns an obscure moth to blazing Light.
Our life is a march to a victory never won.
This wave of being longing for delight,
This eager turmoil of unsatisfied strengths,
These long far files of forward-striving hopes
Lift worshipping eyes to the blue Void called heaven
Looking for the golden Hand that never came,

The advent for which all creation waits,
The beautiful visage of Eternity
That shall appear upon the roads of Time.
Yet still to ourselves we say rekindling faith,
"Oh, surely one day he shall come to our cry,
One day he shall create our life anew
And utter the magic formula of peace
And bring perfection to the scheme of things.
One day he shall descend to life and earth,
Leaving the secrecy of the eternal doors,
Into a world that cries to him for help,
And bring the truth that sets the spirit free,
The joy that is the baptism of the soul,
The strength that is the outstretched arm of Love.
One day he shall lift his beauty's dreadful veil,
Impose delight on the world's beating heart
And bare his secret body of light and bliss."
But now we strain to reach an unknown goal:
There is no end of seeking and of birth,
There is no end of dying and return;
The life that wins its aim asks greater aims,
The life that fails and dies must live again;
Till it has found itself it cannot cease.
All must be done for which life and death were made.
But who shall say that even then is rest?
Or there repose and action are the same
In the deep breast of God's supreme delight.
In a high state where ignorance is no more,
Each movement is a wave of peace and bliss,
Repose God's motionless creative force,
Action a ripple in the Infinite
And birth a gesture of Eternity.
A sun of transfiguration still can shine
And Night can bare its core of mystic light;
The self-cancelling, self-afflicting paradox
Into a self-luminous mystery might change,

The imbroglio into a joyful miracle.
Then God could be visible here, here take a shape;
Disclosed would be the spirit's identity;
Life would reveal her true immortal face.
But now a termless labour is her fate:
In its recurrent decimal of events
Birth, death are a ceaseless iteration's points;
The old question-mark margins each finished page,
Each volume of her effort's history.
A limping Yes through the aeons journeys still
Accompanied by an eternal No.
All seems in vain, yet endless is the game.
Impassive turns the ever-circling Wheel,
Life has no issue, death brings no release.
A prisoner of itself the being lives
And keeps its futile immortality;
Extinction is denied, its sole escape.
An error of the gods has made the world.
Or indifferent the Eternal watches Time.

END OF CANTO SIX

Canto Seven

The Descent into Night

A MIND absolved from life, made calm to know,
A heart divorced from the blindness and the pang,
The seal of tears, the bond of ignorance,
He turned to find that wide world-failure's cause.
Away he looked from Nature's visible face
And sent his gaze into the viewless Vast,
The formidable unknown Infinity,
Asleep behind the endless coil of things,
That carries the universe in its timeless breadths
And the ripples of its being are our lives.
The worlds are built by its unconscious Breath
And Matter and Mind are its figures or its powers,
Our waking thoughts the output of its dreams.
The veil was rent that covers Nature's depths:
He saw the fount of the world's lasting pain
And the mouth of the black pit of Ignorance;
The evil guarded at the roots of life
Raised up its head and looked into his eyes.
On a dim bank where dies subjective Space,
From a stark ridge overlooking all that is,
A tenebrous awakened Nescience,
Her wide blank eyes wondering at Time and Form,
Stared at the inventions of the living Void
And the Abyss whence our beginnings rose.
Behind appeared a grey carved mask of Night
Watching the birth of all created things.
A hidden Puissance conscious of its force,
A vague and lurking Presence everywhere,
A contrary Doom that threatens all things made,
A Death figuring as the dark seed of life,
Seemed to engender and to slay the world.

Then from the sombre mystery of the gulfs
And from the hollow bosom of the Mask
Something crept forth that seemed a shapeless Thought.
A fatal Influence upon creatures stole
Whose lethal touch pursued the immortal spirit,
On life was laid the haunting finger of death
And overcast with error, grief and pain
The soul's native will for truth and joy and light.
A deformation coiled that claimed to be
The being's very turn, Nature's true drive.
A hostile and perverting Mind at work
In every corner ensconced of conscious life
Corrupted Truth with her own formulas;
Interceptor of the listening of the soul,
Afflicting knowledge with the hue of doubt
It captured the oracles of the occult gods,
Effaced the signposts of Life's pilgrimage,
Cancelled the firm rock-edicts graved by Time,
And on the foundations of the cosmic Law
Erected its bronze pylons of misrule.
Even Light and Love by that cloaked danger's spell
Turned from the brilliant nature of the gods
To fallen angels and misleading suns,
Became themselves a danger and a charm,
A perverse sweetness, heaven-born malefice:
Its power could deform divinest things.
A wind of sorrow breathed upon the world;
All thought with falsehood was besieged, all act
Stamped with defect or with frustration's sign,
All high attempt with failure or vain success,
But none could know the reason of his fall.
The grey Mask whispered and, though no sound was heard,
Yet in the ignorant heart a seed was sown
That bore black fruit of suffering, death and bale.
Out of the chill steppes of a bleak Unseen
Invisible, wearing the Night's grey mask,

Arrived the shadowy dreadful messengers,
Invaders from a dangerous world of power,
Ambassadors of evil's absolute.
In silence the inaudible voices spoke,
Hands that none saw planted the fatal grain,
No form was seen, yet a dire work was done,
An iron decree in crooked uncials written
Imposed a law of sin and adverse fate.
Life looked at him with changed and sombre eyes:
Her beauty he saw and the yearning heart in things
That with a little happiness is content,
Answering to a small ray of truth or love;
He saw her gold sunlight and her far blue sky,
Her green of leaves and hue and scent of flowers
And the charm of children and the love of friends
And the beauty of women and kindly hearts of men,
But saw too the dreadful Powers that drive her moods
And the anguish she has strewn upon her ways,
Fate waiting on the unseen steps of men
And her evil and sorrow and last gift of death.
A breath of disillusion and decadence
Corrupting watched for Life's maturity
And made to rot the full grain of the soul:
Progress became a purveyor of Death.
A world that clung to the law of a slain Light
Cherished the putrid corpses of dead truths,
Hailed twisted forms as things free, new and true,
Beauty from ugliness and evil drank
Feeling themselves guests at a banquet of the gods
And tasted corruption like a high-spiced food.
A darkness settled on the heavy air;
It hunted the bright smile from Nature's lips
And slew the native confidence in her heart
And put fear's crooked look into her eyes.
The lust that warps the spirit's natural good
Replaced by a manufactured virtue and vice

The frank spontaneous impulse of the soul:
Afflicting Nature with the dual's lie,
Their twin values whetted a forbidden zest,
Made evil a relief from spurious good,
The ego battened on righteousness and sin
And each became an instrument of Hell.
In rejected heaps by a monotonous road
The old simple delights were left to lie
On the wasteland of life's descent to Night.
All glory of life was dimmed, tarnished with doubt;
All beauty ended in an aging face;
All power was dubbed a tyranny cursed by God
And Truth a fiction needed by the mind:
The chase of joy was now a tired hunt;
All knowledge was left a questioning Ignorance.

As from a womb obscure he saw emerge
The body and visage of a dark Unseen
Hidden behind the fair outsides of life.
Its dangerous commerce is our suffering's cause.
Its breath is a subtle poison in men's hearts;
All evil starts from that ambiguous face.
A peril haunted now the common air;
The world grew full of menacing Energies,
And wherever turned for help or hope his eyes,
In field and house, in street and camp and mart
He met the prowl and stealthy come and go
Of armed disquieting bodied Influences.
A march of goddess figures dark and nude
Alarmed the air with grandiose unease;
Appalling footsteps drew invisibly near,
Shapes that were threats invaded the dream-light,
And ominous beings passed him on the road
Whose very gaze was a calamity:
A charm and sweetness sudden and formidable,
Faces that raised alluring lips and eyes

Approached him armed with beauty like a snare,
But hid a fatal meaning in each line
And could in a moment dangerously change.
But he alone discerned that screened attack.
A veil upon the inner vision lay,
A force was there that hid its dreadful steps;
All was belied, yet thought itself the truth;
All were beset but knew not of the siege:
For none could see the authors of their fall.
    Aware of some dark wisdom still withheld
That was the seal and warrant of this strength,
He followed the track of dim tremendous steps
Returning to the night from which they came.
A tract he reached unbuilt and owned by none:
There all could enter but none stay for long.
It was a no man's land of evil air,
A crowded neighbourhood without one home,
A borderland between the world and hell.
There unreality was Nature's lord:
It was a space where nothing could be true,
For nothing was what it had claimed to be:
A high appearance wrapped a specious void.
Yet nothing would confess its own pretence
Even to itself in the ambiguous heart:
A vast deception was the law of things;
Only by that deception they could live.
An unsubstantial Nihil guaranteed
The falsehood of the forms this Nature took
And made them seem awhile to be and live.
A borrowed magic drew them from the Void;
They took a shape and stuff that was not theirs
And showed a colour that they could not keep,
Mirrors to a phantasm of reality.
Each rainbow brilliance was a splendid lie;
A beauty unreal graced a glamour face.
Nothing could be relied on to remain:

Joy nurtured tears and good an evil proved,
But never out of evil one plucked good:
Love ended early in hate, delight killed with pain,
Truth into falsity grew and death ruled life.
A Power that laughed at the mischiefs of the world,
An irony that joined the world's contraries
And flung them into each other's arms to strive,
Put a sardonic rictus on God's face.
Aloof, its influence entered everywhere
And left a cloven hoof-mark on the breast;
A twisted heart and a strange sombre smile
Mocked at the sinister comedy of life.
Announcing the advent of a perilous Form
An ominous tread softened its dire footfall
That none might understand or be on guard;
None heard until a dreadful grasp was close.
Or else all augured a divine approach,
An air of prophecy felt, a heavenly hope,
Listened for a gospel, watched for a new star.
The Fiend was visible but cloaked in light;
He seemed a helping angel from the skies:
He armed untruth with Scripture and the Law;
He deceived with wisdom, with virtue slew the soul
And led to perdition by the heavenward path.
A lavish sense he gave of power and joy,
And, when arose the warning from within,
He reassured the ear with dulcet tones
Or took the mind captive in its own net;
His rigorous logic made the false seem true.
Amazing the elect with holy lore
He spoke as with the very voice of God.
The air was full of treachery and ruse;
Truth-speaking was a stratagem in that place;
Ambush lurked in a smile and peril made
Safety its cover, trust its entry's gate:
Falsehood came laughing with the eyes of truth;

Each friend might turn an enemy or spy,
The hand one clasped ensleeved a dagger's stab
And an embrace could be Doom's iron cage.
Agony and danger stalked their trembling prey
And softly spoke as to a timid friend:
Attack sprang suddenly vehement and unseen;
Fear leaped upon the heart at every turn
And cried out with an anguished dreadful voice;
It called for one to save but none came near.
All warily walked, for death was ever close;
Yet caution seemed a vain expense of care,
For all that guarded proved a deadly net,
And when after long suspense salvation came
And brought a glad relief disarming strength,
It served as a smiling passage to worse fate.
There was no truce and no safe place to rest;
One dared not slumber or put off one's arms:
It was a world of battle and surprise.
All who were there lived for themselves alone;
All warred against all, but with a common hate
Turned on the mind that sought some higher good;
Truth was exiled lest she should dare to speak
And hurt the heart of darkness with her light
Or bring her pride of knowledge to blaspheme
The settled anarchy of established things.

Then the scene changed, but kept its dreadful core:
Altering its form the life remained the same.
A capital was there without a State:
It had no ruler, only groups that strove.
He saw a city of ancient Ignorance
Founded upon a soil that knew not Light.
There each in his own darkness walked alone:
Only they agreed to differ in Evil's paths,
To live in their own way for their own selves
Or to enforce a common lie and wrong;

There Ego was lord upon his peacock seat
And Falsehood sat by him, his mate and queen:
The world turned to them as Heaven to Truth and God.
Injustice justified by firm decrees
The sovereign weights of Error's legalised trade,
But all the weights were false and none the same;
Ever she watched with her balance and a sword,
Lest any sacrilegious word expose
The sanctified formulas of her old misrule.
In high professions wrapped self-will walked wide
And licence stalked prating of order and right:
There was no altar raised to Liberty;
True freedom was abhorred and hunted down:
Harmony and tolerance nowhere could be seen;
Each group proclaimed its dire and naked Law.
A frame of ethics knobbed with scriptural rules
Or a theory passionately believed and praised
A table seemed of high Heaven's sacred code.
A formal practice mailed and iron-shod
Gave to a rude and ruthless warrior kind
Drawn from the savage bowels of the earth
A proud stern poise of harsh nobility,
A civic posture rigid and formidable.
But all their private acts belied the pose:
Power and utility were their Truth and Right,
An eagle rapacity clawed its coveted good,
Beaks pecked and talons tore all weaker prey.
In their sweet secrecy of pleasant sins
Nature they obeyed and not a moralist God.
Inconscient traders in bundles of contraries,
They did what in others they would persecute;
When their eyes looked upon their fellow's vice,
An indignation flamed, a virtuous wrath;
Oblivious of their own deep-hid offence,
Moblike they stoned a neighbour caught in sin.
A pragmatist judge within passed false decrees,

Posed worst iniquities on equity's base,
Reasoned ill actions just, sanctioned the scale
Of the merchant ego's interest and desire.
Thus was a balance kept, the world could live.
A zealot fervour pushed their ruthless cults,
All faith not theirs bled scourged as heresy;
They questioned, captived, tortured, burned or smote
And forced the soul to abandon right or die.
Amid her clashing creeds and warring sects
Religion sat upon a blood-stained throne.
A hundred tyrannies oppressed and slew
And founded unity upon fraud and force.
Only what seemed was prized as real there:
The ideal was a cynic ridicule's butt;
Hooted by the crowd, mocked by enlightened wits,
Spiritual seeking wandered outcasted, —
A dreamer's self-deceiving web of thought
Or mad chimaera deemed or hypocrite's fake,
Its passionate instinct trailed through minds obscure
Lost in the circuits of the Ignorance.
A lie was there the truth and truth a lie.
Here must the traveller of the upward Way —
For daring Hell's kingdoms winds the heavenly route —
Pause or pass slowly through that perilous space,
A prayer upon his lips and the great Name.
If probed not all discernment's keen spear-point,
He might stumble into falsity's endless net.
Over his shoulder often he must look back
Like one who feels on his neck an enemy's breath;
Else stealing up behind a treasonous blow
Might prostrate cast and pin to unholy soil,
Pierced through his back by Evil's poignant stake.
So might one fall on the Eternal's road
Forfeiting the spirit's lonely chance in Time
And no news of him reach the waiting gods,
Marked "missing" in the register of souls,

His name the index of a failing hope,
The position of a dead remembered star.
Only were safe who kept God in their hearts:
Courage their armour, faith their sword, they must walk,
The hand ready to smite, the eye to scout,
Casting a javelin regard in front,
Heroes and soldiers of the army of Light.
Hardly even so, the grisly danger past,
Released into a calmer purer air,
They dared at length to breathe and smile once more.
Once more they moved beneath a real sun.
Though Hell claimed rule, the spirit still had power.
This No-man's-land he passed without debate;
Him the heights missioned, him the Abyss desired:
None stood across his way, no voice forbade.
For swift and easy is the downward path,
And now towards the Night was turned his face.

A greater darkness waited, a worse reign,
If worse can be where all is evil's extreme;
Yet to the cloaked the uncloaked is naked worst.
There God and Truth and the supernal Light
Had never been or else had power no more.
As when one slips in a deep moment's trance
Over mind's border into another world,
He crossed a boundary whose stealthy trace
Eye could not see but only the soul feel.
Into an armoured fierce domain he came
And saw himself wandering like a lost soul
Amid grimed walls and savage slums of Night.
Around him crowded grey and squalid huts
Neighbouring proud palaces of perverted Power,
Inhuman quarters and demoniac wards.
A pride in evil hugged its wretchedness;
A misery haunting splendour pressed those fell
Dun suburbs of the cities of dream-life.

There Life displayed to the spectator soul
The shadow depths of her strange miracle.
A strong and fallen goddess without hope,
Obscured, deformed by some dire Gorgon spell,
As might a harlot empress in a bouge,
Nude, unashamed, exulting she upraised
Her evil face of perilous beauty and charm
And, drawing panic to a shuddering kiss
Twixt the magnificence of her fatal breasts,
Allured to their abyss the spirit's fall.
Across his field of sight she multiplied
As on a scenic film or moving plate
The implacable splendour of her nightmare pomps.
On the dark background of a soulless world
She staged between a lurid light and shade
Her dramas of the sorrow of the depths
Written on the agonised nerves of living things:
Epics of horror and grim majesty,
Wry statues spat and stiffened in life's mud,
A glut of hideous forms and hideous deeds
Paralysed pity in the hardened breast.
In booths of sin and night-repairs of vice
Styled infamies of the body's concupiscence
And sordid imaginations etched in flesh,
Turned lust into a decorative art:
Abusing Nature's gift her pervert skill
Immortalised the sown grain of living death,
In a mud goblet poured the bacchic wine,
To a satyr gave the thyrsus of a god.
Impure, sadistic, with grimacing mouths,
Grey foul inventions gruesome and macabre
Came televisioned from the gulfs of Night.
Her craft ingenious in monstrosity,
Impatient of all natural shape and poise,
A gape of nude exaggerated lines,
Gave caricature a stark reality,

And art-parades of weird distorted forms,
And gargoyle masques obscene and terrible
Trampled to tormented postures the torn sense.
An inexorable evil's worshipper,
She made vileness great and sublimated filth;
A dragon power of reptile energies
And strange epiphanies of grovelling Force
And serpent grandeurs couching in the mire
Drew adoration to a gleam of slime.
All Nature pulled out of her frame and base
Was twisted into an unnatural pose:
Repulsion stimulated inert desire;
Agony was made a red-spiced food for bliss,
Hatred was trusted with the work of lust
And torture took the form of an embrace;
A ritual anguish consecrated death;
Worship was offered to the Undivine.
A new aesthesis of Inferno's art
That trained the mind to love what the soul hates,
Imposed allegiance on the quivering nerves
And forced the unwilling body to vibrate.
Too sweet and too harmonious to excite
In this regime that soiled the being's core,
Beauty was banned, the heart's feeling dulled to sleep
And cherished in their place sensation's thrills;
The world was probed for jets of sense-appeal.
Here cold material intellect was the judge
And needed sensual prick and jog and lash
That its hard dryness and dead nerves might feel
Some passion and power and acrid point of life.
A new philosophy theorised evil's rights,
Gloried in the shimmering rot of decadence,
Or gave to a python Force persuasive speech
And armed with knowledge the primaeval brute.
Over life and Matter only brooding bowed,
Mind changed to the image of a rampant beast;

It scrambled into the pit to dig for truth
And lighted its search with the subconscient's flares.
Thence bubbling rose sullying the upper air,
The filth and festering secrets of the Abyss:
This it called positive fact and real life.
This now composed the fetid atmosphere.
A wild-beast passion crept from secret Night
To watch its prey with fascinating eyes:
Around him like a fire with sputtering tongues
There lolled and laughed a bestial ecstasy;
The air was packed with longings brute and fierce;
Crowding and stinging in a monstrous swarm
Pressed with a noxious hum into his mind
Thoughts that could poison Nature's heavenliest breath,
Forcing reluctant lids assailed the sight
Acts that revealed the mystery of Hell.
All that was there was on this pattern made.

A race possessed inhabited those parts.
A force demoniac lurking in man's depths
That heaves suppressed by the heart's human law,
Awed by the calm and sovereign eyes of Thought,
Can in a fire and earthquake of the soul
Arise and, calling to its native night,
Overthrow the reason, occupy the life
And stamp its hoof on Nature's shaking ground:
This was for them their being's flaming core.
A mighty energy, a monster god,
Hard to the strong, implacable to the weak,
It stared at the harsh unpitying world it made
With the stony eyelids of its fixed idea.
Its heart was drunk with a dire hunger's wine,
In others' suffering felt a thrilled delight
And of death and ruin the grandiose music heard.
To have power, to be master, was sole virtue and good:
It claimed the whole world for Evil's living room,

Its party's grim totalitarian reign
The cruel destiny of breathing things.
All on one plan was shaped and standardised
Under a dark dictatorship's breathless weight.
In street and house, in councils and in courts
Beings he met who looked like living men
And climbed in speech upon high wings of thought
But harboured all that is subhuman, vile
And lower than the lowest reptile's crawl.
The reason meant for nearness to the gods
And uplift to heavenly scale by the touch of mind
Only enhanced by its enlightening ray
Their inborn nature's wry monstrosity.
Often, a familiar visage studying
Joyfully encountered at some dangerous turn,
Hoping to recognise a look of light,
His vision warned by the spirit's inward eye
Discovered suddenly Hell's trademark there,
Or saw with the inner sense that cannot err,
In the semblance of a fair or virile form
The demon and the goblin and the ghoul.
An insolence reigned of cold stone-hearted strength
Mighty, obeyed, approved by the Titan's law,
The huge laughter of a giant cruelty
And fierce glad deeds of ogre violence.
In that wide cynic den of thinking beasts
One looked in vain for a trace of pity or love;
There was no touch of sweetness anywhere,
But only Force and its acolytes, greed and hate:
There was no help for suffering, none to save,
None dared resist or speak a noble word.
Armed with the aegis of tyrannic Power,
Signing the edicts of her dreadful rule
And using blood and torture as a seal,
Darkness proclaimed her slogans to the world.
A servile blinkered silence hushed the mind

Or only it repeated lessons taught,
While mitred, holding the good shepherd's staff,
Falsehood enthroned on awed and prostrate hearts
The cults and creeds that organise living death
And slay the soul on the altar of a lie.
All were deceived or served their own deceit;
Truth in that stifling atmosphere could not live.
There wretchedness believed in its own joy
And fear and weakness hugged their abject depths;
All that is low and sordid-thoughted, base,
All that is drab and poor and miserable,
Breathed in a lax content its natural air
And felt no yearning of divine release:
Arrogant, gibing at more luminous states
The people of the gulfs despised the sun.
A barriered autarchy excluded light;
Fixed in its will to be its own grey self,
It vaunted its norm unique and splendid type:
It soothed its hunger with a plunderer's dream;
Flaunting its cross of servitude like a crown,
It clung to its dismal harsh autonomy.
A bull-throat bellowed with its brazen tongue;
Its hard and shameless clamour filling Space
And threatening all who dared to listen to truth
Claimed the monopoly of the battered ear;
A deafened acquiescence gave its vote,
And braggart dogmas shouted in the night
Kept for the fallen soul once deemed a god
The pride of its abysmal absolute.

A lone discoverer in these menacing realms
Guarded like termite cities from the sun,
Oppressed mid crowd and tramp and noise and flare,
Passing from dusk to deeper dangerous dusk,
He wrestled with powers that snatched from mind its light
And smote from him their clinging influences.

Soon he emerged in a dim wall-less space.
For now the peopled tracts were left behind;
He walked between wide banks of failing eve.
Around him grew a gaunt spiritual blank,
A threatening waste, a sinister loneliness
That left mind bare to an unseen assault,
An empty page on which all that willed could write
Stark monstrous messages without control.
A travelling dot on downward roads of Dusk
Mid barren fields and barns and straggling huts
And a few crooked and phantasmal trees,
He faced a sense of death and conscious void.
But still a hostile Life unseen was there
Whose deathlike poise resisting light and truth
Made living a bleak gap in nullity.
He heard the grisly voices that deny;
Assailed by thoughts that swarmed like spectral hordes,
A prey to the staring phantoms of the gloom
And terror approaching with its lethal mouth,
Driven by a strange will down ever down,
The sky above a communiqué of Doom,
He strove to shield his spirit from despair,
But felt the horror of the growing Night
And the Abyss rising to claim his soul.
Then ceased the abodes of creatures and their forms
And solitude wrapped him in its voiceless folds.
All vanished suddenly like a thought expunged;
His spirit became an empty listening gulf
Void of the dead illusion of a world:
Nothing was left, not even an evil face.
He was alone with the grey python Night.
A dense and nameless Nothing conscious, mute,
Which seemed alive but without body or mind,
Lusted all beings to annihilate
That it might be for ever nude and sole.
As in a shapeless beast's intangible jaws,

Gripped, strangled by that lusting viscous blot,
Attracted to some black and giant mouth
And swallowing throat and a huge belly of doom,
His being from its own vision disappeared
Drawn towards depths that hungered for its fall.
A formless void oppressed his struggling brain,
A darkness grim and cold benumbed his flesh,
A whispered grey suggestion chilled his heart;
Haled by a serpent-force from its warm home
And dragged to extinction in bleak vacancy
Life clung to its seat with cords of gasping breath;
Lapped was his body by a tenebrous tongue.
Existence smothered travailed to survive;
Hope strangled perished in his empty soul,
Belief and memory abolished died
And all that helps the spirit in its course.
There crawled through every tense and aching nerve
Leaving behind its poignant quaking trail
A nameless and unutterable fear.
As a sea nears a victim bound and still,
The approach alarmed his mind for ever dumb
Of an implacable eternity
Of pain inhuman and intolerable.
This he must bear, his hope of heaven estranged;
He must ever exist without extinction's peace
In a slow suffering Time and tortured Space,
An anguished nothingness his endless state.
A lifeless vacancy was now his breast,
And in the place where once was luminous thought,
Only remained like a pale motionless ghost
An incapacity for faith and hope
And the dread conviction of a vanquished soul
Immortal still but with its godhead lost,
Self lost and God and touch of happier worlds.
But he endured, stilled the vain terror, bore
The smothering coils of agony and affright;

Then peace returned and the soul's sovereign gaze.
To the blank horror a calm Light replied:
Immutable, undying and unborn,
Mighty and mute the Godhead in him woke
And faced the pain and danger of the world.
He mastered the tides of Nature with a look:
He met with his bare spirit naked Hell.

END OF CANTO SEVEN

The World of Falsehood, the Mother of Evil and the Sons of Darkness

THEN could he see the hidden heart of Night:
The labour of its stark unconsciousness
Revealed the endless terrible Inane.
A spiritless blank Infinity was there;
A Nature that denied the eternal Truth
In the vain braggart freedom of its thought
Hoped to abolish God and reign alone.
There was no sovereign Guest, no witness Light;
Unhelped it would create its own bleak world.
Its large blind eyes looked out on demon acts,
Its deaf ears heard the untruth its dumb lips spoke;
Its huge misguided fancy took vast shapes,
Its mindless sentience quivered with fierce conceits;
Engendering a brute principle of life
Evil and pain begot a monstrous soul.
The Anarchs of the formless depths arose,
Great Titan beings and demoniac powers,
World-egos racked with lust and thought and will,
Vast minds and lives without a spirit within:
Impatient architects of error's house,
Leaders of the cosmic ignorance and unrest
And sponsors of sorrow and mortality
Embodied the dark Ideas of the Abyss.
A shadow substance into emptiness came,
Dim forms were born in the unthinking Void
And eddies met and made an adverse Space
In whose black folds Being imagined Hell.
His eyes piercing the triple-plated gloom
Identified their sight with its blind stare:
Accustomed to the unnatural dark, they saw

Unreality made real and conscious Night.
A violent, fierce and formidable world,
An ancient womb of huge calamitous dreams,
Coiled like a larva in the obscurity
That keeps it from the spear-points of Heaven's stars.
It was the gate of a false Infinite,
An eternity of disastrous absolutes,
An immense negation of spiritual things.
All once self-luminous in the spirit's sphere
Turned now into their own dark contraries:
Being collapsed into a pointless void
That yet was a zero parent of the worlds;
Inconscience swallowing up the cosmic Mind
Produced a universe from its lethal sleep;
Bliss into black coma fallen, insensible,
Coiled back to itself and God's eternal joy
Through a false poignant figure of grief and pain
Still dolorously nailed upon a cross
Fixed in the soil of a dumb insentient world
Where birth was a pang and death an agony,
Lest all too soon should change again to bliss.
Thought sat, a priestess of Perversity,
On her black tripod of the triune Snake
Reading by opposite signs the eternal script,
A sorceress reversing life's God-frame.
In darkling aisles with evil eyes for lamps
And fatal voices chanting from the apse,
In strange infernal dim basilicas
Intoning the magic of the unholy Word,
The ominous profound Initiate
Performed the ritual of her Mysteries.
There suffering was Nature's daily food
Alluring to the anguished heart and flesh,
And torture was the formula of delight,
Pain mimicked the celestial ecstasy.
There Good, a faithless gardener of God,

Watered with virtue the world's upas-tree
And, careful of the outward word and act,
Engrafted his hypocrite blooms on native ill.
All high things served their nether opposite:
The forms of Gods sustained a demon cult;
Heaven's face became a mask and snare of Hell.
There in the heart of vain phenomenon,
In an enormous action's writhen core
He saw a Shape illimitable and vague
Sitting on Death who swallows all things born.
A chill fixed face with dire and motionless eyes,
Her dreadful trident in her shadowy hand
Outstretched, she pierced all creatures with one fate.

When nothing was save Matter without soul
And a spiritless hollow was the heart of Time,
Then Life first touched the insensible Abyss;
Awaking the stark Void to hope and grief
Her pallid beam smote the unfathomed Night
In which God hid himself from his own view.
In all things she sought their slumbering mystic truth,
The unspoken Word that inspires unconscious forms;
She groped in his deeps for an invisible Law,
Fumbled in the dim subconscient for his mind
And strove to find a way for spirit to be.
But from the Night another answer came.
A seed was in that nether matrix cast,
A dumb unprobed husk of perverted truth,
A cell of an insentient infinite.
A monstrous birth prepared its cosmic form
In Nature's titan embryo, Ignorance.
Then in a fatal and stupendous hour
Something that sprang from the stark Inconscient's sleep
Unwillingly begotten by the mute Void,
Lifted its ominous head against the stars;
Overshadowing earth with its huge body of Doom

It chilled the heavens with the menace of a face.
A nameless Power, a shadowy Will arose
Immense and alien to our universe.
In the inconceivable Purpose none can gauge
A vast Non-Being robed itself with shape,
The boundless Nescience of the unconscious depths
Covered eternity with nothingness.
A seeking Mind replaced the seeing Soul:
Life grew into a huge and hungry death,
The Spirit's bliss was changed to cosmic pain.
Assuring God's self-cowled neutrality
A mighty opposition conquered Space.
A sovereign ruling falsehood, death and grief,
It pressed its fierce hegemony on the earth;
Disharmonising the original style
Of the architecture of her fate's design,
It falsified the primal cosmic Will
And bound to struggle and dread vicissitudes
The long slow process of the patient Power.
Implanting error in the stuff of things
It made an Ignorance of the all-wise Law;
It baffled the sure touch of life's hid sense,
Kept dumb the intuitive guide in Matter's sleep,
Deformed the insect's instinct and the brute's,
Disfigured man's thought-born humanity.
A shadow fell across the simple Ray:
Obscured was the Truth-light in the cavern heart
That burns unwitnessed in the altar crypt
Behind the still velamen's secrecy
Companioning the Godhead of the shrine.
Thus was the dire antagonist Energy born
Who mimes the eternal Mother's mighty shape
And mocks her luminous infinity
With a grey distorted silhouette in the Night.
Arresting the passion of the climbing soul,
She forced on life a slow and faltering pace;

Her hand's deflecting and retarding weight
Is laid on the mystic evolution's curve:
The tortuous line of her deceiving mind
The Gods see not and man is impotent;
Oppressing the God-spark within the soul
She forces back to the beast the human fall.
Yet in her formidable instinctive mind
She feels the One grow in the heart of Time
And sees the Immortal shine through the human mould.
Alarmed for her rule and full of fear and rage
She prowls around each light that gleams through the dark
Casting its ray from the spirit's lonely tent,
Hoping to enter with fierce stealthy tread
And in the cradle slay the divine Child.
Incalculable are her strength and ruse;
Her touch is a fascination and a death;
She kills her victim with his own delight;
Even Good she makes a hook to drag to Hell.
For her the world runs to its agony.
Often the pilgrim on the Eternal's road
Ill-lit from clouds by the pale moon of Mind,
Or in devious byways wandering alone,
Or lost in deserts where no path is seen,
Falls overpowered by her lion leap,
A conquered captive under her dreadful paws.
Intoxicated by a burning breath
And amorous grown of a destroying mouth,
Once a companion of the sacred Fire,
The mortal perishes to God and Light,
An Adversary governs heart and brain,
A Nature hostile to the Mother-Force.
The self of life yields up its instruments
To Titan and demoniac agencies
That aggrandise earth-nature and disframe:
A cowled fifth-columnist is now thought's guide;
His subtle defeatist murmur slays the faith

And, lodged in the breast or whispering from outside,
A lying inspiration fell and dark
A new order substitutes for the divine.
A silence falls upon the spirit's heights,
From the veiled sanctuary the God retires,
Empty and cold is the chamber of the Bride;
The golden Nimbus now is seen no more,
No longer burns the white spiritual ray
And hushed for ever is the secret Voice.
Then by the Angel of the Vigil Tower
A name is struck from the recording book;
A flame that sang in Heaven sinks quenched and mute;
In ruin ends the epic of a soul.
This is the tragedy of the inner death
When forfeited is the divine element
And only a mind and body live to die.

For terrible agencies the Spirit allows
And there are subtle and enormous Powers
That shield themselves with the covering Ignorance.
Offspring of the gulfs, agents of the shadowy Force,
Haters of light, intolerant of peace,
Aping to the thought the shining Friend and Guide,
Opposing in the heart the eternal Will,
They veil the occult uplifting Harmonist.
His wisdom's oracles are made our bonds;
The doors of God they have locked with keys of creed
And shut out by the Law his tireless Grace.
Along all Nature's lines they have set their posts
And intercept the caravans of Light;
Wherever the Gods act, they intervene.
A yoke is laid upon the world's dim heart;
Masked are its beats from the supernal Bliss,
And the closed peripheries of brilliant Mind
Block the fine entries of celestial Fire.
Always the dark Adventurers seem to win;

Nature they fill with evil's institutes,
Turn into defeats the victories of Truth,
Proclaim as falsehoods the eternal laws,
And load the dice of Doom with wizard lies;
The world's shrines they have occupied, usurped its thrones.
In scorn of the dwindling chances of the Gods
They claim creation as their conquered fief
And crown themselves the iron Lords of Time.
Adepts of the illusion and the mask,
The artificers of Nature's fall and pain
Have built their altars of triumphant Night
In the clay temple of terrestrial life.
In the vacant precincts of the sacred Fire,
In front of the reredos in the mystic rite
Facing the dim velamen none can pierce,
Intones his solemn hymn the mitred priest
Invoking their dreadful presence in his breast:
Attributing to them the awful Name
He chants the syllables of the magic text
And summons the unseen communion's act,
While twixt the incense and the muttered prayer
All the fierce bale with which the world is racked
Is mixed in the foaming chalice of man's heart
And poured to them like sacramental wine.
Assuming names divine they guide and rule.
Opponents of the Highest they have come
Out of their world of soulless thought and power
To serve by enmity the cosmic scheme.
Night is their refuge and strategic base.
Against the sword of Flame, the luminous Eye,
Bastioned they live in massive forts of gloom,
Calm and secure in sunless privacy:
No wandering ray of Heaven can enter there.
Armoured, protected by their lethal masks,
As in a studio of creative Death
The giant sons of Darkness sit and plan

The drama of the earth, their tragic stage.
All who would raise the fallen world must come
Under the dangerous arches of their power;
For even the radiant children of the gods
To darken their privilege is and dreadful right.
None can reach heaven who has not passed through hell.

This too the traveller of the worlds must dare.
A warrior in the dateless duel's strife,
He entered into dumb despairing Night
Challenging the darkness with his luminous soul.
Alarming with his steps the threshold gloom
He came into a fierce and dolorous realm
Peopled by souls who never had tasted bliss;
Ignorant like men born blind who know not light,
They could equate worst ill with highest good,
Virtue was to their eyes a face of sin
And evil and misery were their natural state.
A dire administration's penal code
Making of grief and pain the common law,
Decreeing universal joylessness
Had changed life into a stoic sacrament
And torture into a daily festival.
An act was passed to chastise happiness;
Laughter and pleasure were banned as deadly sins:
A questionless mind was ranked as wise content,
A dull heart's silent apathy as peace:
Sleep was not there, torpor was the sole rest,
Death came but neither respite gave nor end;
Always the soul lived on and suffered more.
Ever he deeper probed that kingdom of pain;
Around him grew the terror of a world
Of agony followed by worse agony,
And in the terror a great wicked joy
Glad of one's own and others' calamity.
There thought and life were a long punishment,

The breath a burden and all hope a scourge,
The body a field of torment, a massed unease;
Repose was a waiting between pang and pang.
This was the law of things none dreamed to change:
A hard sombre heart, a harsh unsmiling mind
Rejected happiness like a cloying sweet;
Tranquillity was a tedium and ennui:
Only by suffering life grew colourful;
It needed the spice of pain, the salt of tears.
If one could cease to be, all would be well;
Else only fierce sensations gave some zest:
A fury of jealousy burning the gnawed heart,
The sting of murderous spite and hate and lust,
The whisper that lures to the pit and treachery's stroke
Threw vivid spots on the dull aching hours.
To watch the drama of infelicity,
The writhing of creatures under the harrow of doom
And sorrow's tragic gaze into the night
And horror and the hammering heart of fear
Were the ingredients in Time's heavy cup
That pleased and helped to enjoy its bitter taste.
Of such fierce stuff was made up life's long hell:
These were the threads of the dark spider's-web
In which the soul was caught, quivering and rapt;
This was religion, this was Nature's rule.
In a fell chapel of iniquity
To worship a black pitiless image of Power
Kneeling one must cross hard-hearted stony courts,
A pavement like a floor of evil fate.
Each stone was a keen edge of ruthless force
And glued with the chilled blood from tortured breasts;
The dry gnarled trees stood up like dying men
Stiffened into a pose of agony,
And from each window peered an ominous priest
Chanting Te Deums for slaughter's crowning grace,
Uprooted cities, blasted human homes,
Burned writhen bodies, the bombshell's massacre.

"Our enemies are fallen, are fallen," they sang,
"All who once stayed our will are smitten and dead;
How great we are, how merciful art Thou."
Thus thought they to reach God's impassive throne
And Him command whom all their acts opposed,
Magnifying their deeds to touch his skies,
And make him an accomplice of their crimes.
There no relenting pity could have place,
But ruthless strength and iron moods had sway,
A dateless sovereignty of terror and gloom:
This took the figure of a darkened God
Revered by the racked wretchedness he had made,
Who held in thrall a miserable world,
And helpless hearts nailed to unceasing woe
Adored the feet that trampled them into mire.
It was a world of sorrow and of hate,
Sorrow with hatred for its lonely joy,
Hatred with others' sorrow as its feast;
A bitter rictus curled the suffering mouth;
A tragic cruelty saw its ominous chance.
Hate was the black archangel of that realm;
It glowed, a sombre jewel in the heart
Burning the soul with its malignant rays,
And wallowed in its fell abysm of might.
These passions even objects seemed to exude,—
For mind overflowed into the inanimate
That answered with the wickedness it received,—
Against their users used malignant powers,
Hurt without hands and strangely, suddenly slew,
Appointed as instruments of an unseen doom.
Or they made themselves a fateful prison wall
Where men condemned wake through the creeping hours
Counted by the tollings of an ominous bell.
An evil environment worsened evil souls:
All things were conscious there and all perverse.
In this infernal realm he dared to press
Even into its deepest pit and darkest core,

Perturbed its tenebrous base, dared to contest
Its ancient privileged right and absolute force:
In Night he plunged to know her dreadful heart,
In Hell he sought the root and cause of Hell.
Its anguished gulfs opened in his own breast;
He listened to clamours of its crowded pain,
The heart-beats of its fatal loneliness.
Above was a chill deaf eternity.
In vague tremendous passages of Doom
He heard the goblin Voice that guides to slay,
And faced the enchantments of the demon Sign,
And traversed the ambush of the opponent Snake.
In menacing tracts, in tortured solitudes
Companionless he roamed through desolate ways
Where the red Wolf waits by the fordless stream
And Death's black eagles scream to the precipice,
And met the hounds of bale who hunt men's hearts
Baying across the veldts of Destiny,
In footless battlefields of the Abyss
Fought shadowy combats in mute eyeless depths,
Assaults of Hell endured and Titan strokes
And bore the fierce inner wounds that are slow to heal.
A prisoner of a hooded magic Force,
Captured and trailed in Falsehood's lethal net
And often strangled in the noose of grief,
Or cast in the grim morass of swallowing doubt,
Or shut into pits of error and despair,
He drank her poison draughts till none was left.
In a world where neither hope nor joy could come
The ordeal he suffered of evil's absolute reign,
Yet kept intact his spirit's radiant truth.
Incapable of motion or of force,
In Matter's blank denial gaoled and blind,
Pinned to the black inertia of our base
He treasured between his hands his flickering soul.
His being ventured into mindless Void,
Intolerant gulfs that knew not thought nor sense;

Thought ceased, sense failed, his soul still saw and knew.
In atomic parcellings of the Infinite
Near to the dumb beginnings of lost Self,
He felt the curious small futility
Of the creation of material things.
Or, stifled in the Inconscient's hollow dusk,
He sounded the mystery dark and bottomless
Of the enormous and unmeaning deeps
Whence struggling life in a dead universe rose.
There in the stark identity lost by mind
He felt the sealed sense of the insensible world
And a mute wisdom in the unknowing Night.
Into the abysmal secrecy he came
Where darkness peers from her mattress, grey and nude,
And stood on the last locked subconscient's floor
Where Being slept unconscious of its thoughts
And built the world not knowing what it built.
There waiting its hour the future lay unknown,
There is the record of the vanished stars.
There in the slumber of the cosmic Will
He saw the secret key of Nature's change.
A light was with him, an invisible hand
Was laid upon the error and the pain
Till it became a quivering ecstasy,
The shock of sweetness of an arm's embrace.
He saw in Night the Eternal's shadowy veil,
Knew death for a cellar of the house of life,
In destruction felt creation's hasty pace,
Knew loss as the price of a celestial gain
And hell as a short cut to heaven's gates.
Then in Illusion's occult factory
And in the Inconscient's magic printing-house
Torn were the formats of the primal Night
And shattered the stereotypes of Ignorance.
Alive, breathing a deep spiritual breath,
Nature expunged her stiff mechanical code
And the articles of the bound soul's contract,

Falsehood gave back to Truth her tortured shape.
Annulled were the tables of the law of Pain,
And in their place grew luminous characters.
The skilful Penman's unseen finger wrote
His swift intuitive calligraphy;
Earth's forms were made his divine documents,
The wisdom embodied mind could not reveal,
Inconscience chased from the world's voiceless breast;
Transfigured were the fixed schemes of reasoning Thought.
Arousing consciousness in things inert,
He imposed upon dark atom and dumb mass
The diamond script of the Imperishable,
Inscribed on the dim heart of fallen things
A paean-song of the free Infinite
And the Name, foundation of eternity,
And traced on the awake exultant cells
In the ideographs of the Ineffable
The lyric of the love that waits through Time
And the mystic volume of the Book of Bliss
And the message of the superconscient Fire.
Then life beat pure in the corporeal frame;
The infernal Gleam died and could slay no more.
Hell split across its huge abrupt façade
As if a magic building were undone,
Night opened and vanished like a gulf of dream.
Into being's gap scooped out as empty Space
In which she had filled the place of absent God,
There poured a wide intimate and blissful Dawn;
Healed were all things that Time's torn heart had made
And sorrow could live no more in Nature's breast:
Division ceased to be, for God was there.
The soul lit the conscious body with its ray,
Matter and spirit mingled and were one.

END OF CANTO EIGHT

Canto Nine

The Paradise of the Life-Gods

AROUND him shone a great felicitous Day.
A lustre of some rapturous Infinite,
It held in the splendour of its golden laugh
Regions of the heart's happiness set free,
Intoxicated with the wine of God,
Immersed in light, perpetually divine.
A favourite and intimate of the Gods
Obeying the divine command to joy,
It was the sovereign of its own delight
And master of the kingdoms of its force.
Assured of the bliss for which all forms were made,
Unmoved by fear and grief and the shocks of Fate
And unalarmed by the breath of fleeting Time
And unbesieged by adverse circumstance,
It breathed in a sweet secure unguarded ease
Free from our body's frailty inviting death,
Far from our danger-zone of stumbling Will.
It needed not to curb its passionate beats;
Thrilled by the clasp of the warm satisfied sense
And the swift wonder-rush and flame and cry
Of the life-impulses' red magnificent race,
It lived in a jewel-rhythm of the laughter of God
And lay on the breast of universal love.
Immune the unfettered Spirit of Delight
Pastured his gleaming sun-herds and moon-flocks
Along the lyric speed of griefless streams
In fragrance of the unearthly asphodel.
A silence of felicity wrapped the heavens,
A careless radiance smiled upon the heights;
A murmur of inarticulate ravishment
Trembled in the winds and touched the enchanted soil;

Incessant in the arms of ecstasy
Repeating its sweet involuntary note
A sob of rapture flowed along the hours.
Advancing under an arch of glory and peace,
Traveller on plateau and on musing ridge,
As one who sees in the World-Magician's glass
A miracled imagery of soul-scapes flee
He traversed scenes of an immortal joy
And gazed into abysms of beauty and bliss.
Around him was a light of conscious suns
And a brooding gladness of great symbol things;
To meet him crowded plains of brilliant calm,
Mountains and violet valleys of the Blest,
Deep glens of joy and crooning waterfalls
And woods of quivering purple solitude;
Below him lay like gleaming jewelled thoughts
Rapt dreaming cities of Gandharva kings.
Across the vibrant secrecies of Space
A dim and happy music sweetly stole,
Smitten by unseen hands he heard heart-close
The harps' cry of the heavenly minstrels pass,
And voices of unearthly melody
Chanted the glory of eternal love
In the white-blue-moonbeam air of Paradise.
A summit and core of all that marvellous world,
Apart stood high Elysian nameless hills,
Burning like sunsets in a trance of eve.
As if to some new unsearched profundity,
Into a joyful stillness plunged their base;
Their slopes through a hurry of laughter and voices sank,
Crossed by a throng of singing rivulets,
Adoring blue heaven with their happy hymn,
Down into woods of shadowy secrecy:
Lifted into wide voiceless mystery
Their peaks climbed towards a greatness beyond life.
The shining Edens of the vital gods

Received him in their deathless harmonies.
All things were perfect there that flower in Time;
Beauty was there creation's native mould,
Peace was a thrilled voluptuous purity.
There Love fulfilled her gold and roseate dreams
And Strength her crowned and mighty reveries;
Desire climbed up, a swift omnipotent flame,
And Pleasure had the stature of the gods;
Dream walked along the highways of the stars;
Sweet common things turned into miracles:
Overtaken by the spirit's sudden spell,
Smitten by a divine passion's alchemy,
Pain's self compelled transformed to potent joy
Curing the antithesis twixt heaven and hell.
All life's high visions are embodied there,
Her wandering hopes achieved, her aureate combs
Caught by the honey-eater's darting tongue,
Her burning guesses changed to ecstasied truths,
Her mighty pantings stilled in deathless calm
And liberated her immense desires.
In that paradise of perfect heart and sense
No lower note could break the endless charm
Of her sweetness ardent and immaculate;
Her steps are sure of their intuitive fall.
After the anguish of the soul's long strife
At length were found calm and celestial rest
And, lapped in a magic flood of sorrowless hours,
Healed were his warrior nature's wounded limbs
In the encircling arms of Energies
That brooked no stain and feared not their own bliss.
In scenes forbidden to our pallid sense
Amid miraculous scents and wonder-hues
He met the forms that divinise the sight,
To music that can immortalise the mind
And make the heart wide as infinity
Listened, and captured the inaudible

Cadences that awake the occult ear:
Out of the ineffable hush it hears them come
Trembling with the beauty of a wordless speech,
And thoughts too great and deep to find a voice,
Thoughts whose desire new-makes the universe.
A scale of sense that climbed with fiery feet
To heights of unimagined happiness,
Recast his being's aura in joy-glow,
His body glimmered like a skiey shell;
His gates to the world were swept with seas of light.
His earth, dowered with celestial competence,
Harboured a power that needed now no more
To cross the closed customs-line of mind and flesh
And smuggle godhead into humanity.
It shrank no more from the supreme demand
Of an untired capacity for bliss,
A might that could explore its own infinite
And beauty and passion and the depths' reply
Nor feared the swoon of glad identity
Where spirit and flesh in inner ecstasy join
Annulling the quarrel between self and shape.
It drew from sight and sound spiritual power,
Made sense a road to reach the intangible:
It thrilled with the supernal influences
That build the substance of life's deeper soul.
Earth-nature stood reborn, comrade of heaven.
A fit companion of the timeless Kings,
Equalled with the godheads of the living Suns,
He mixed in the radiant pastimes of the Unborn,
Heard whispers of the Player never seen
And listened to his voice that steals the heart
And draws it to the breast of God's desire,
And felt its honey of felicity
Flow through his veins like the rivers of Paradise,
Made body a nectar-cup of the Absolute.
In sudden moments of revealing flame,

In passionate responses half-unveiled
He reached the rim of ecstasies unknown;
A touch supreme surprised his hurrying heart,
The clasp was remembered of the Wonderful,
And hints leaped down of white beatitudes.
Eternity drew close disguised as Love
And laid its hand upon the body of Time.
A little gift comes from the Immensitudes,
But measureless to life its gain of joy;
All the untold Beyond is mirrored there.
A giant drop of the Bliss unknowable
Overwhelmed his limbs and round his soul became
A fiery ocean of felicity;
He foundered drowned in sweet and burning vasts:
The dire delight that could shatter mortal flesh,
The rapture that the gods sustain he bore.
Immortal pleasure cleansed him in its waves
And turned his strength into undying power.
Immortality captured Time and carried Life.

END OF CANTO NINE

The Kingdoms and Godheads of the Little Mind

THIS too must now be overpassed and left,
As all must be until the Highest is gained
In whom the world and self grow true and one:
Till That is reached our journeying cannot cease.
Always a nameless goal beckons beyond,
Always ascends the zigzag of the gods
And upward points the spirit's climbing Fire.
This breath of hundred-hued felicity
And its pure heightened figure of Time's joy,
Tossed upon waves of flawless happiness,
Hammered into single beats of ecstasy,
This fraction of the spirit's integer
Caught into a passionate greatness of extremes,
This limited being lifted to zenith bliss,
Happy to enjoy one touch of things supreme,
Packed into its sealed small infinity,
Its endless time-made world outfacing Time,
A little output of God's vast delight.
The moments stretched towards the eternal Now,
The hours discovered immortality,
But, satisfied with their sublime contents,
On peaks they ceased whose tops half-way to Heaven
Pointed to an apex they could never mount,
To a grandeur in whose air they could not live.
Inviting to their high and exquisite sphere,
To their secure and fine extremities
This creature who hugs his limits to feel safe,
These heights declined a greater adventure's call.
A glory and sweetness of satisfied desire
Tied up the spirit to golden posts of bliss.
It could not house the wideness of a soul

Which needed all infinity for its home.
A memory soft as grass and faint as sleep,
The beauty and call receding sank behind
Like a sweet song heard fading far away
Upon the long high road to Timelessness.
Above was an ardent white tranquillity.
A musing spirit looked out on the worlds
And like a brilliant clambering of skies
Passing through clarity to an unseen Light
Large lucent realms of Mind from stillness shone.
But first he met a silver-grey expanse
Where Day and Night had wedded and were one:
It was a tract of dim and shifting rays
Parting Life's sentient flow from Thought's self-poise.
A coalition of uncertainties
There exercised uneasy government
On a ground reserved for doubt and reasoned guess,
A rendezvous of Knowledge with Ignorance.
At its low extremity held difficult sway
A mind that hardly saw and slowly found;
Its nature to our earthly nature close
And kin to our precarious mortal thought
That looks from soil to sky and sky to soil
But knows not the below nor the beyond,
It only sensed itself and outward things.
This was the first means of our slow ascent
From the half-conscience of the animal soul
Living in a crowded press of shape-events
In a realm it cannot understand nor change;
Only it sees and acts in a given scene
And feels and joys and sorrows for a while.
The ideas that drive the obscure embodied spirit
Along the roads of suffering and desire
In a world that struggles to discover Truth,
Found here their power to be and Nature-force.
Here are devised the forms of an ignorant life

That sees the empiric fact as settled law,
Labours for the hour and not for eternity
And trades its gains to meet the moment's call:
The slow process of a material mind
Which serves the body it should rule and use
And needs to lean upon an erring sense,
Was born in that luminous obscurity.
Advancing tardily from a limping start,
Crutching hypothesis on argument,
Throning its theories as certitudes,
It reasons from the half-known to the unknown,
Ever constructing its frail house of thought,
Ever undoing the web that it has spun.
A twilight sage whose shadow seems to him self,
Moving from minute to brief minute lives;
A king dependent on his satellites
Signs the decrees of ignorant ministers,
A judge in half-possession of his proofs,
A voice clamant of uncertainty's postulates,
An architect of knowledge, not its source.
This powerful bondslave of his instruments
Thinks his low station Nature's highest top,
Oblivious of his share in all things made
And haughtily humble in his own conceit
Believes himself a spawn of Matter's mud
And takes his own creations for his cause.
To eternal light and knowledge meant to rise,
Up from man's bare beginning is our climb;
Out of earth's heavy smallness we must break,
We must search our nature with spiritual fire:
An insect crawl preludes our glorious flight;
Our human state cradles the future god,
Our mortal frailty an immortal force.
     At the glow-worm top of these pale glimmer-realms
Where dawn-sheen gambolled with the native dusk
And helped the Day to grow and Night to fail,

Escaping over a wide and shimmering bridge,
He came into a realm of early Light
And the regency of a half-risen sun.
Out of its rays our mind's full orb was born.
Appointed by the Spirit of the Worlds
To mediate with the unknowing depths,
A prototypal deft Intelligence
Half-poised on equal wings of thought and doubt
Toiled ceaselessly twixt being's hidden ends.
A Secrecy breathed in life's moving act;
A covert nurse of Nature's miracles,
It shaped life's wonders out of Matter's mud:
It cut the pattern of the shapes of things,
It pitched mind's tent in the vague ignorant Vast.
A master Magician of measure and device
Has made an eternity from recurring forms
And to the wandering spectator thought
Assigned a seat on the inconscient stage.
On earth by the will of this Arch-Intelligence
A bodiless energy put on Matter's robe;
Proton and photon served the imager Eye
To change things subtle into a physical world
And the invisible appeared as shape
And the impalpable was felt as mass:
Magic of percept joined with concept's art
And lent to each object an interpreting name:
Idea was disguised in a body's artistry,
And by a strange atomic law's mystique
A frame was made in which the sense could put
Its symbol picture of the universe.
Even a greater miracle was done.
The mediating light linked body's power,
The sleep and dreaming of the tree and plant,
The animal's vibrant sense, the thought in man,
To the effulgence of a Ray above.
Its skill endorsing Matter's right to think

Cut sentient passages for the mind of flesh
And found a means for Nescience to know.
Offering its little squares and cubes of word
As figured substitutes for reality,
A mummified mnemonic alphabet,
It helped the unseeing Force to read her works.
A buried consciousness arose in her
And now she dreams herself human and awake.
But all was still a mobile Ignorance;
Still Knowledge could not come and firmly grasp
This huge invention seen as a universe.
A specialist of logic's hard machine
Imposed its rigid artifice on the soul;
An aide of the inventor intellect,
It cut Truth into manageable bits
That each might have his ration of thought-food,
Then new-built Truth's slain body by its art:
A robot exact and serviceable and false
Displaced the spirit's finer view of things:
A polished engine did the work of a god.
None the true body found, its soul seemed dead:
None had the inner look which sees Truth's whole;
All glorified the glittering substitute.
Then from the secret heights a wave swept down,
A brilliant chaos of rebel light arose;
It looked above and saw the dazzling peaks,
It looked within and woke the sleeping god.
Imagination called her shining squads
That venture into undiscovered scenes
Where all the marvels lurk none yet has known:
Lifting her beautiful and miraculous head,
She conspired with inspiration's sister brood
To fill thought's skies with glimmering nebulae.
A bright Error fringed the mystery-altar's frieze;
Darkness grew nurse to wisdom's occult sun,
Myth suckled knowledge with her lustrous milk;

The infant passed from dim to radiant breasts.
Thus worked the Power upon the growing world;
Its subtle craft withheld the full-orbed blaze,
Cherished the soul's childhood and on fictions fed
Far richer in their sweet and nectarous sap
Nourishing its immature divinity
Than the staple or dry straw of Reason's tilth,
Its heaped fodder of innumerable facts,
Plebeian fare on which today we thrive.
Thus streamed down from the realm of early Light
Ethereal thinkings into Matter's world;
Its gold-horned herds trooped into earth's cave-heart.
Its morning rays illume our twilight's eyes,
Its young formations move the mind of earth
To labour and to dream and new-create,
To feel beauty's touch and know the world and self:
The Golden Child began to think and see.

In those bright realms are Mind's first forward steps.
Ignorant of all but eager to know all,
Its curious slow enquiry there begins;
Ever its searching grasps at shapes around,
Ever it hopes to find out greater things.
Ardent and golden-gleamed with sunrise fires,
Alert it lives upon invention's verge.
Yet all it does is on an infant's scale,
As if the cosmos were a nursery game,
Mind, life the playthings of a Titan's babe.
As one it works who builds a mimic fort
Miraculously stable for a while,
Made of the sands upon a bank of Time
Mid an occult eternity's shoreless sea.
A small keen instrument the great Puissance chose,
An arduous pastime passionately pursues;
To teach the Ignorance is her difficult charge,
Her thought starts from an original nescient Void

And what she teaches she herself must learn
Arousing knowledge from its sleepy lair.
For knowledge comes not to us as a guest
Called into our chamber from the outer world;
A friend and inmate of our secret self,
It hid behind our minds and fell asleep
And slowly wakes beneath the blows of life;
The mighty daemon lies unshaped within,
To evoke, to give it form is Nature's task.
All was a chaos of the true and false,
Mind sought amid deep mists of Nescience;
It looked within itself but saw not God.
A material interim diplomacy
Denied the Truth that transient truths might live
And hid the Deity in creed and guess
That the World-Ignorance might grow slowly wise.
This was the imbroglio made by sovereign Mind
Looking from a gleam-ridge into the Night
In her first tamperings with Inconscience:
Its alien dusk baffles her luminous eyes;
Her rapid hands must learn a cautious zeal;
Only a slow advance the earth can bear.
Yet was her strength unlike the unseeing earth's
Compelled to handle makeshift instruments
Invented by the life-force and the flesh.
Earth all perceives through doubtful images,
All she conceives in hazardous jets of sight,
Small lights kindled by touches of groping thought.
Incapable of the soul's direct inlook
She sees by spasms and solders knowledge-scrap,
Makes Truth the slave-girl of her indigence,
Expelling Nature's mystic unity
Cuts into quantum and mass the moving All;
She takes for measuring-rod her ignorance.
In her own domain a pontiff and a seer,
That greater Power with her half-risen sun

Wrought within limits but possessed her field;
She knew by a privilege of thinking force
And claimed an infant sovereignty of sight.
In her eyes however darkly fringed was lit
The Archangel's gaze who knows inspired his acts
And shapes a world in its far-seeing flame.
In her own realm she stumbles not nor fails,
But moves in boundaries of subtle power
Across which mind can step towards the sun.
A candidate for a higher suzerainty,
A passage she cut through from Night to Light,
And searched for an ungrasped Omniscience.

A dwarf three-bodied trinity was her serf.
First, smallest of the three, but strong of limb,
A low-brow with a square and heavy jowl,
A pigmy Thought needing to live in bounds
For ever stooped to hammer fact and form.
Absorbed and cabined in external sight,
It takes its stand on Nature's solid base.
A technician admirable, a thinker crude,
A riveter of Life to habit's grooves,
Obedient to gross Matter's tyranny,
A prisoner of the moulds in which it works,
It binds itself by what itself creates.
A slave of a fixed mass of absolute rules,
It sees as Law the habits of the world,
It sees as Truth the habits of the mind.
In its realm of concrete images and events
Turning in a worn circle of ideas
And ever repeating old familiar acts,
It lives content with the common and the known.
It loves the old ground that was its dwelling-place:
Abhorring change as an audacious sin,
Distrustful of each new discovery
Only it advances step by careful step

And fears as if a deadly abyss the unknown.
A prudent treasurer of its ignorance,
It shrinks from adventure, blinks at glorious hope,
Preferring a safe foothold upon things
To the dangerous joy of wideness and of height.
The world's slow impressions on its labouring mind,
Tardy imprints almost indelible,
Increase their value by their poverty;
The old sure memories are its capital stock:
Only what sense can grasp seems absolute:
External fact it figures as sole truth,
Wisdom identifies with the earthward look,
And things long known and actions always done
Are to its clinging hold a balustrade
Of safety on the perilous stair of Time.
Heaven's trust to it are the established ancient ways,
Immutable laws man has no right to change,
A sacred legacy from the great dead past
Or the one road that God has made for life,
A firm shape of Nature never to be changed,
Part of the huge routine of the universe.
A smile from the Preserver of the Worlds
Sent down of old this guardian Mind to earth
That all might stand in their fixed changeless type
And from their secular posture never move.
One sees it circling faithful to its task,
Tireless in an assigned tradition's round;
In decayed and crumbling offices of Time
It keeps close guard in front of custom's wall,
Or in an ancient Night's dim environs
It dozes on a little courtyard's stones
And barks at every unfamiliar light
As at a foe who would break up its home,
A watch-dog of the spirit's sense-railed house
Against intruders from the Invisible,
Nourished on scraps of life and Matter's bones

In its kennel of objective certitude.
And yet behind it stands a cosmic might:
A measured Greatness keeps its vaster plan,
A fathomless sameness rhythms the tread of life;
The stars' changeless orbits furrow inert Space,
A million species follow one mute Law.
A huge inertness is the world's defence,
Even in change is treasured changelessness;
Into inertia revolution sinks,
In a new dress the old resumes its role;
The Energy acts, the stable is its seal:
On Shiva's breast is stayed the enormous dance.
    A fiery spirit came, next of the three.
A hunchback rider of the red Wild-Ass,
A rash Intelligence leaped down lion-maned
From the great mystic Flame that rings the worlds
And with its dire edge eats at being's heart.
Thence sprang the burning vision of Desire.
A thousand shapes it wore, took numberless names:
A need of multitude and uncertainty
Pricks it for ever to pursue the One
On countless roads across the vasts of Time
Through circuits of unending difference.
It burns all breasts with an ambiguous fire.
A radiance gleaming on a murky stream,
It flamed towards heaven, then sank, engulfed, towards hell;
It climbed to drag down Truth into the mire
And used for muddy ends its brilliant Force;
A huge chameleon gold and blue and red
Turning to black and grey and lurid brown,
Hungry it stared from a mottled bough of life
To snap up insect joys, its favourite food,
The dingy sustenance of a sumptuous frame
Nursing the splendid passion of its hues.
A snake of flame with a dull cloud for tail,
Followed by a dream-brood of glittering thoughts,

A lifted head with many-tinged flickering crests,
It licked at knowledge with a smoky tongue.
A whirlpool sucking in an empty air,
It based on vacancy stupendous claims,
In Nothingness born to Nothingness returned,
Yet all the time unwittingly it drove
Towards the hidden Something that is All.
Ardent to find, incapable to retain,
A brilliant instability was its mark,
To err its inborn trend, its native cue.
At once to an unreflecting credence prone,
It thought all true that flattered its own hopes;
It cherished golden nothings born of wish,
It snatched at the unreal for provender.
In darkness it discovered luminous shapes;
Peering into a shadow-hung half-light
It saw hued images scrawled on Fancy's cave;
Or it swept in circles through conjecture's night
And caught in imagination's camera
Bright scenes of promise held by transient flares,
Fixed in life's air the feet of hurrying dreams,
Kept prints of passing Forms and hooded Powers
And flash-images of half-seen verities.
An eager spring to seize and to possess
Unguided by reason or the seeing soul
Was its first natural motion and its last,
It squandered life's force to achieve the impossible:
It scorned the straight road and ran on wandering curves
And left what it had won for untried things;
It saw unrealised aims as instant fate
And chose the precipice for its leap to heaven.
Adventure its system in the gamble of life,
It took fortuitous gains as safe results;
Error discouraged not its confident view
Ignorant of the deep law of being's ways
And failure could not slow its fiery clutch;

One chance made true warranted all the rest.
Attempt, not victory, was the charm of life.
An uncertain winner of uncertain stakes,
Instinct its dam and the life-mind its sire,
It ran its race and came in first or last.
Yet were its works nor small and vain nor null;
It nursed a portion of infinity's strength
And could create the high things its fancy willed;
Its passion caught what calm intelligence missed.
Insight of impulse laid its leaping grasp
On heavens high Thought had hidden in dazzling mist,
Caught glimmers that revealed a lurking sun:
It probed the void and found a treasure there.
A half-intuition purpled in its sense;
It threw the lightning's fork and hit the unseen.
It saw in the dark and vaguely blinked in the light,
Ignorance was its field, the unknown its prize.
　Of all these Powers the greatest was the last.
Arriving late from a far plane of thought
Into a packed irrational world of Chance
Where all was grossly felt and blindly done,
Yet the haphazard seemed the inevitable,
Came Reason, the squat godhead artisan,
To her narrow house upon a ridge in Time.
Adept of clear contrivance and design,
A pensive face and close and peering eyes,
She took her firm and irremovable seat,
The strongest, wisest of the troll-like Three.
Armed with her lens and measuring-rod and probe,
She looked upon an object universe
And the multitudes that in it live and die
And the body of Space and the fleeing soul of Time,
And took the earth and stars into her hands
To try what she could make of these strange things.
In her strong purposeful laborious mind,
Inventing her scheme-lines of reality

And the geometric curves of her time-plan,
She multiplied her slow half-cuts at Truth:
Impatient of enigma and the unknown,
Intolerant of the lawless and the unique,
Imposing reflection on the march of Force,
Imposing clarity on the unfathomable,
She strove to reduce to rules the mystic world.
Nothing she knew but all things hoped to know.
In dark inconscient realms once void of thought,
Missioned by a supreme Intelligence
To throw its ray upon the obscure Vast,
An imperfect light leading an erring mass
By the power of sense and the idea and word,
She ferrets out Nature's process, substance, cause.
All life to harmonise by thought's control,
She with the huge imbroglio struggles still;
Ignorant of all but her own seeking mind
To save the world from Ignorance she came.
A sovereign worker through the centuries
Observing and remoulding all that is,
Confident she took up her stupendous charge.
There the low bent and mighty figure sits
Bowed under the arc-lamps of her factory home
Amid the clatter and ringing of her tools.
A rigorous stare in her creative eyes
Coercing the plastic stuff of cosmic Mind,
She sets the hard inventions of her brain
In a pattern of eternal fixity:
Indifferent to the cosmic dumb demand,
Unconscious of too close realities,
Of the unspoken thought, the voiceless heart,
She leans to forge her credos and iron codes
And metal structures to imprison life
And mechanic models of all things that are.
For the world seen she weaves a world conceived:
She spins in stiff but unsubstantial lines

Her gossamer word-webs of abstract thought,
Her segment systems of the Infinite,
Her theodicies and cosmogonic charts
And myths by which she explains the inexplicable.
At will she spaces in thin air of mind
Like maps in the school-house of intellect hung,
Forcing wide Truth into a narrow scheme,
Her numberless warring strict philosophies;
Out of Nature's body of phenomenon
She carves with Thought's keen edge in rigid lines,
Like rails for the World-Magician's power to run,
Her sciences precise and absolute.
On the huge bare walls of human nescience
Written round Nature's deep dumb hieroglyphs
She pens in clear demotic characters
The vast encyclopaedia of her thoughts;
An algebra of her mathematics' signs,
Her numbers and unerring formulas
She builds to clinch her summary of things.
On all sides runs as if in a cosmic mosque
Tracing the scriptural verses of her laws
The daedal of her patterned arabesques,
Art of her wisdom, artifice of her lore.
This art, this artifice are her only stock.
In her high works of pure intelligence,
In her withdrawal from the senses' trap,
There comes no breaking of the walls of mind,
There leaps no rending flash of absolute power,
There dawns no light of heavenly certitude.
A million faces wears her knowledge here
And every face is turbaned with a doubt.
All now is questioned, all reduced to nought.
Once monumental in their massive craft
Her old great mythic writings disappear
And into their place start strict ephemeral signs;
This constant change spells progress to her eyes:

Her thought is an endless march without a goal.
There is no summit on which she can stand
And see in a single glance the Infinite's whole.
  An inconclusive play is Reason's toil.
Each strong idea can use her as its tool;
Accepting every brief she pleads her case.
Open to every thought, she cannot know.
The eternal Advocate seated as judge
Armours in logic's invulnerable mail
A thousand combatants for Truth's veiled throne
And sets on a high horse-back of argument
To tilt for ever with a wordy lance
In a mock tournament where none can win.
Assaying thought's values with her rigid tests
Balanced she sits on wide and empty air,
Aloof and pure in her impartial poise.
Absolute her judgments seem but none is sure;
Time cancels all her verdicts in appeal.
Although like sunbeams to our glow-worm mind
Her knowledge feigns to fall from a clear heaven,
Its rays are a lantern's lustres in the Night;
She throws a glittering robe on Ignorance.
But now is lost her ancient sovereign claim
To rule mind's high realm in her absolute right,
Bind thought with logic's forged infallible chain
Or see truth nude in a bright abstract haze.
A master and slave of stark phenomenon,
She travels on the roads of erring sight
Or looks upon a set mechanical world
Constructed for her by her instruments.
A bullock yoked in the cart of proven fact,
She drags huge knowledge-bales through Matter's dust
To reach utility's immense bazaar.
Apprentice she has grown to her old drudge;
An aided sense is her seeking's arbiter.
This now she uses as the assayer's stone.

As if she knew not facts are husks of truth,
The husks she keeps, the kernel throws aside.
An ancient wisdom fades into the past,
The ages' faith becomes an idle tale,
God passes out of the awakened thought,
An old discarded dream needed no more:
Only she seeks mechanic Nature's keys.
Interpreting stone-laws inevitable
She digs into Matter's hard concealing soil,
To unearth the processes of all things done.
A loaded huge self-worked machine appears
To her eye's eager and admiring stare,
An intricate and meaningless enginery
Of ordered fateful and unfailing Chance:
Ingenious and meticulous and minute,
Its brute unconscious accurate device
Unrolls an unerring march, maps a sure road;
It plans without thinking, acts without a will,
A million purposes serves with purpose none
And builds a rational world without a mind.
It has no mover, no maker, no idea:
Its vast self-action toils without a cause;
A lifeless Energy irresistibly driven,
Death's head on the body of Necessity,
Engenders life and fathers consciousness,
Then wonders why all was and whence it came.
Our thoughts are parts of the immense machine,
Our ponderings but a freak of Matter's law,
The mystic's lore was a fancy or a blind;
Of soul or spirit we have now no need:
Matter is the admirable Reality,
The patent unescapable miracle,
The hard truth of things, simple, eternal, sole.
A suicidal rash expenditure
Creating the world by a mystery of self-loss
Has poured its scattered works on empty Space;

Late shall the self-disintegrating Force
Contract the immense expansion it has made:
Then ends this mighty and unmeaning toil,
The Void is left bare, vacant as before.
Thus vindicated, crowned, the grand new Thought
Explained the world and mastered all its laws,
Touched the dumb roots, woke veiled tremendous powers;
It bound to service the unconscious djinns
That sleep unused in Matter's ignorant trance.
All was precise, rigid, indubitable.
But when on Matter's rock of ages based
A whole stood up firm and clear-cut and safe,
All staggered back into a sea of doubt;
This solid scheme melted in endless flux:
She had met the formless Power inventor of forms;
Suddenly she stumbled upon things unseen:
A lightning from the undiscovered Truth
Startled her eyes with its perplexing glare
And dug a gulf between the Real and Known
Till all her knowledge seemed an ignorance.
Once more the world was made a wonder-web,
A magic's process in a magical space,
An unintelligible miracle's depths
Whose source is lost in the Ineffable.
Once more we face the blank Unknowable.
In a crash of values, in a huge doom-crack,
In the sputter and scatter of her breaking work
She lost her clear conserved constructed world.
A quantum dance remained, a sprawl of chance
In Energy's stupendous tripping whirl:
A ceaseless motion in the unbounded Void
Invented forms without a thought or aim:
Necessity and Cause were shapeless ghosts;
Matter was an incident in being's flow,
Law but a clock-work habit of blind force.
Ideals, ethics, systems had no base

And soon collapsed or without sanction lived;
All grew a chaos, a heave and clash and strife.
Ideas warring and fierce leaped upon life;
A hard compression held down anarchy
And liberty was only a phantom's name:
Creation and destruction waltzed inarmed
On the bosom of a torn and quaking earth;
All reeled into a world of Kali's dance.
Thus tumbled, sinking, sprawling in the Void,
Clutching for props, a soil on which to stand,
She only saw a thin atomic Vast,
The rare-point sparse substratum universe
On which floats a solid world's phenomenal face.
Alone a process of events was there
And Nature's plastic and protean change
And, strong by death to slay or to create,
The riven invisible atom's omnipotent force.
One chance remained that here might be a power
To liberate man from the old inadequate means
And leave him sovereign of the earthly scene.
For Reason then might grasp the original Force
To drive her car upon the roads of Time.
All then might serve the need of the thinking race,
An absolute State found order's absolute,
To a standardised perfection cut all things,
In society build a just exact machine.
Then science and reason careless of the soul
Could iron out a tranquil uniform world,
Aeonic seekings glut with outward truths
And a single-patterned thinking force on mind,
Inflicting Matter's logic on Spirit's dreams
A reasonable animal make of man
And a symmetrical fabric of his life.
This would be Nature's peak on an obscure globe,
The grand result of the long ages' toil,
Earth's evolution crowned, her mission done.

So might it be if the spirit fell asleep;
Man then might rest content and live in peace,
Master of Nature who once her bondslave worked,
The world's disorder hardening into Law, —
If Life's dire heart arose not in revolt,
If God within could find no greater plan.
But many-visaged is the cosmic Soul;
A touch can alter the fixed front of Fate.
A sudden turn can come, a road appear.
A greater Mind may see a greater Truth,
Or we may find when all the rest has failed
Hid in ourselves the key of perfect change.
Ascending from the soil where creep our days,
Earth's consciousness may marry with the Sun,
Our mortal life ride on the spirit's wings,
Our finite thoughts commune with the Infinite.
　　In the bright kingdoms of the rising Sun
All is a birth into a power of light:
All here deformed guards there its happy shape,
Here all is mixed and marred, there pure and whole;
Yet each is a passing step, a moment's phase.
Awake to a greater Truth beyond her acts,
The mediatrix sat and saw her works
And felt the marvel in them and the force
But knew the power behind the face of Time:
She did the task, obeyed the knowledge given,
Her deep heart yearned towards great ideal things
And from the light looked out to wider light:
A brilliant hedge drawn round her narrowed her power;
Faithful to her limited sphere she toiled, but knew
Its highest, widest seeing was a half-search,
Its mightiest acts a passage or a stage.
For not by Reason was creation made
And not by Reason can the Truth be seen
Which through the veils of thought, the screens of sense
Hardly the spirit's vision can descry

Dimmed by the imperfection of its means:
The little Mind is tied to little things:
Its sense is but the spirit's outward touch,
Half-waked in a world of dark Inconscience;
It feels out for its beings and its forms
Like one left fumbling in the ignorant Night.
In this small mould of infant mind and sense
Desire is a child-heart's cry crying for bliss,
Our reason only a toys' artificer,
A rule-maker in a strange stumbling game.
But she her dwarf aides knew whose confident sight
A bounded prospect took for the far goal.
The world she has made is an interim report
Of a traveller towards the half-found truth in things
Moving twixt nescience and nescience.
For nothing is known while aught remains concealed;
The Truth is known only when all is seen.
Attracted by the All that is the One,
She yearns towards a higher light than hers;
Hid by her cults and creeds she has glimpsed God's face:
She knows she has but found a form, a robe,
But ever she hopes to see him in her heart
And feel the body of his reality.
As yet a mask is there and not a brow,
Although sometimes two hidden eyes appear:
Reason cannot tear off that glimmering mask,
Her efforts only make it glimmer more;
In packets she ties up the Indivisible;
Finding her hands too small to hold vast Truth
She breaks up knowledge into alien parts
Or peers through cloud-rack for a vanished sun:
She sees, not understanding what she has seen,
Through the locked visages of finite things
The myriad aspects of infinity.
One day the Face must burn out through the mask.
Our ignorance is Wisdom's chrysalis,

Our error weds new knowledge on its way,
Its darkness is a blackened knot of light;
Thought dances hand in hand with Nescience
On the grey road that winds towards the Sun.
Even while her fingers fumble at the knots
Which bind them to their strange companionship,
Into the moments of their married strife
Sometimes break flashes of the enlightening Fire.
Even now great thoughts are here that walk alone:
Armed they have come with the infallible word
In an investiture of intuitive light
That is a sanction from the eyes of God;
Announcers of a distant Truth they flame
Arriving from the rim of eternity.
A fire shall come out of the infinitudes,
A greater Gnosis shall regard the world
Crossing out of some far omniscience
On lustrous seas from the still rapt Alone
To illumine the deep heart of self and things.
A timeless knowledge it shall bring to Mind,
Its aim to life, to Ignorance its close.

Above in a high breathless stratosphere,
Overshadowing the dwarfish trinity,
Lived, aspirants to a limitless Beyond,
Captives of Space, walled by the limiting heavens,
In the unceasing circuit of the hours
Yearning for the straight paths of eternity,
And from their high station looked down on this world
Two sun-gaze Daemons witnessing all that is.
A power to uplift the laggard world,
Imperious rode a huge high-winged Life-Thought
Unwont to tread the firm unchanging soil:
Accustomed to a blue infinity,
It planed in sunlit sky and starlit air;
It saw afar the unreached Immortal's home

And heard afar the voices of the Gods.
Iconoclast and shatterer of Time's forts,
Overleaping limit and exceeding norm,
It lit the thoughts that glow through the centuries
And moved to acts of superhuman force.
As far as its self-winged air-planes could fly,
Visiting the future in great brilliant raids
It reconnoitred vistas of dream-fate.
Apt to conceive, unable to attain,
It drew its concept-maps and vision-plans
Too large for the architecture of mortal Space.
Beyond in wideness where no footing is,
An imagist of bodiless Ideas,
Impassive to the cry of life and sense,
A pure Thought-Mind surveyed the cosmic act.
Archangel of a white transcending realm,
It saw the world from solitary heights
Luminous in a remote and empty air.

END OF CANTO TEN

Canto Eleven

The Kingdoms and Godheads of the Greater Mind

THERE ceased the limits of the labouring Power.
But being and creation cease not there.
For Thought transcends the circles of mortal mind,
It is greater than its earthly instrument:
The godhead crammed into mind's narrow space
Escapes on every side into some vast
That is a passage to infinity.
It moves eternal in the spirit's field,
A runner towards the far spiritual light,
A child and servant of the spirit's force.
But mind too falls back from a nameless peak.
His being stretched beyond the sight of Thought.
For the spirit is eternal and unmade
And not by thinking was its greatness born,
And not by thinking can its knowledge come.
It knows itself and in itself it lives,
It moves where no thought is nor any form.
Its feet are steadied upon finite things,
Its wings can dare to cross the Infinite.
Arriving into his ken a wonder space
Of great and marvellous meetings called his steps,
Where Thought leaned on a Vision beyond thought
And shaped a world from the Unthinkable.
On peaks imagination cannot tread,
In the horizons of a tireless sight,
Under a blue veil of eternity
The splendours of ideal Mind were seen
Outstretched across the boundaries of things known.
Origin of the little that we are,
Instinct with the endless more that we must be,
A prop of all that human strength enacts,

Creator of hopes by earth unrealised,
It spreads beyond the expanding universe;
It wings beyond the boundaries of Dream,
It overtops the ceiling of life's soar.
Awake in a luminous sphere unbound by Thought,
Exposed to omniscient immensities,
It casts on our world its great crowned influences,
Its speed that outstrips the ambling of the hours,
Its force that strides invincibly through Time,
Its mights that bridge the gulf twixt man and God,
Its lights that combat Ignorance and Death.
In its vast ambit of ideal Space
Where beauty and mightiness walk hand in hand,
The Spirit's truths take form as living Gods
And each can build a world in its own right.
In an air which doubt and error cannot mark
With the stigmata of their deformity,
In communion with the musing privacy
Of a truth that sees in an unerring light
Where the sight falters not nor wanders thought,
Exempt from our world's exorbitant tax of tears,
Dreaming its luminous creations gaze
On the Ideas that people eternity.
In a sun-blaze of joy and absolute power
Above the Masters of the Ideal throne
In sessions of secure felicity,
In regions of illumined certitude.
Far are those realms from our labour and yearning and call,
Perfection's reign and hallowed sanctuary
Closed to the uncertain thoughts of human mind,
Remote from the turbid tread of mortal life.
But since our secret selves are next of kin,
A breath of unattained divinity
Visits the imperfect earth on which we toil;
Across a gleaming ether's golden laugh
A light falls on our vexed unsatisfied lives,

A thought comes down from the ideal worlds
And moves us to new-model even here
Some image of their greatness and appeal
And wonder beyond the ken of mortal hope.
Amid the heavy sameness of the days
And contradicted by the human law,
A faith in things that are not and must be
Lives comrade of this world's delight and pain,
The child of the secret soul's forbidden desire
Born of its amour with eternity.
Our spirits break free from their environment;
The future brings its face of miracle near,
Its godhead looks at us with present eyes;
Acts deemed impossible grow natural;
We feel the hero's immortality;
The courage and the strength death cannot touch
Awake in limbs that are mortal, hearts that fail;
We move by the rapid impulse of a will
That scorns the tardy trudge of mortal time.
These promptings come not from an alien sphere:
Ourselves are citizens of that mother State,
Adventurers, we have colonised Matter's night.
But now our rights are barred, our passports void;
We live self-exiled from our heavenlier home.
An errant ray from the immortal Mind
Accepted the earth's blindness and became
Our human thought, servant of Ignorance.
An exile, labourer on this unsure globe
Captured and driven in Life's nescient grasp,
Hampered by obscure cell and treacherous nerve,
It dreams of happier states and nobler powers,
The natural privilege of unfallen gods,
Recalling still its old lost sovereignty.
Amidst earth's mist and fog and mud and stone
It still remembers its exalted sphere
And the high city of its splendid birth.

A memory steals in from lost heavens of Truth,
A wide release comes near, a Glory calls,
A might looks out, an estranged felicity.
In glamorous passages of half-veiled light
Wandering, a brilliant shadow of itself,
This quick uncertain leader of blind gods,
This tender of small lamps, this minister serf
Hired by a mind and body for earth-use
Forgets its work mid crude realities;
It recovers its renounced imperial right,
It wears once more a purple robe of thought
And knows itself the Ideal's seer and king,
Communicant and prophet of the Unborn,
Heir to delight and immortality.
All things are real that here are only dreams,
In our unknown depths sleeps their reserve of truth,
On our unreached heights they reign and come to us
In thought and muse trailing their robes of light.
But our dwarf will and cold pragmatic sense
Admit not the celestial visitants:
Awaiting us on the Ideal's peaks
Or guarded in our secret self unseen
Yet flashed sometimes across the awakened soul,
Hide from our lives their greatness, beauty, power.
Our present feels sometimes their regal touch,
Our future strives towards their luminous thrones:
Out of spiritual secrecy they gaze,
Immortal footfalls in mind's corridors sound:
Our souls can climb into the shining planes,
The breadths from which they came can be our home.
His privilege regained of shadowless sight
The Thinker entered the immortals' air
And drank again his pure and mighty source.
Immutable in rhythmic calm and joy
He saw, sovereignly free in limitless light,
The unfallen planes, the thought-created worlds

Where Knowledge is the leader of the act
And Matter is of thinking substance made,
Feeling, a heaven-bird poised on dreaming wings,
Answers Truth's call as to a parent's voice,
Form luminous leaps from the all-shaping beam
And Will is a conscious chariot of the Gods,
And Life, a splendour stream of musing Force,
Carries the voices of the mystic Suns.
A happiness it brings of whispered truth;
There runs in its flow honeying the bosom of Space
A laughter from the immortal heart of Bliss,
And the unfathomed Joy of timelessness,
The sound of Wisdom's murmur in the Unknown
And the breath of an unseen Infinity.
In gleaming clarities of amethyst air
The chainless and omnipotent Spirit of Mind
Brooded on the blue lotus of the Idea.
A gold supernal sun of timeless Truth
Poured down the mystery of the eternal Ray
Through a silence quivering with the word of Light
On an endless ocean of discovery.
Far-off he saw the joining hemispheres.
On meditation's mounting edge of trance
Great stairs of thought climbed up to unborn heights
Where Time's last ridges touch eternity's skies
And Nature speaks to the spirit's absolute.

A triple realm of ordered thought came first,
A small beginning of immense ascent:
Above were bright ethereal skies of mind,
A packed and endless soar as if sky pressed sky
Buttressed against the Void on bastioned light;
The highest strove to neighbour eternity,
The largest widened into the infinite.
But though immortal, mighty and divine,
The first realms were close and kin to human mind;

Their deities shape our greater thinking's roads,
A fragment of their puissance can be ours:
These breadths were not too broad for our souls to range,
These heights were not too high for human hope.
A triple flight led to this triple world.
Although abrupt for common strengths to tread,
Its upward slope looks down on our earth-poise:
On a slant not too precipitously steep
One could turn back travelling deep descending lines
To commune with the mortal's universe.
The mighty wardens of the ascending stair
Who intercede with the all-creating Word,
There waited for the pilgrim heaven-bound soul;
Holding the thousand keys of the Beyond
They proffered their knowledge to the climbing mind
And filled the life with Thought's immensities.
The prophet hierophants of the occult Law,
The flame-bright hierarchs of the divine Truth,
Interpreters between man's mind and God's,
They bring the immortal fire to mortal men.
Iridescent, bodying the invisible,
The guardians of the Eternal's bright degrees
Fronted the Sun in radiant phalanxes.
Afar they seemed a symbol imagery,
Illumined originals of the shadowy script
In which our sight transcribes the ideal Ráy,
Or icons figuring a mystic Truth,
But, nearer, Gods and living Presences.
A march of friezes marked the lowest steps;
Fantastically ornate and richly small,
They had room for the whole meaning of a world,
Symbols minute of its perfection's joy,
Strange beasts that were Nature's forces made alive
And, wakened to the wonder of his role,
Man grown an image undefaced of God
And objects the fine coin of Beauty's reign;

But wide the terrains were those levels serve.
In front of the ascending epiphany
World-Time's enjoyers, favourites of World-Bliss,
The Masters of things actual, lords of the hours,
Playmates of youthful Nature and child God,
Creators of Matter by hid stress of Mind
Whose subtle thoughts support unconscious Life
And guide the fantasy of brute events,
Stood there, a race of young keen-visioned gods,
King-children born on Wisdom's early plane,
Taught in her school world-making's mystic play.
Archmasons of the eternal Thaumaturge,
Moulders and measurers of fragmented Space,
They have made their plan of the concealed and known
A dwelling-house for the invisible king.
Obeying the Eternal's deep command
They have built in the material front of things
This wide world-kindergarten of young souls
Where the infant spirit learns through mind and sense
To read the letters of the cosmic script
And study the body of the cosmic self
And search for the secret meaning of the whole.
To all that Spirit conceives they give a mould;
Persuading Nature into visible moods
They lend a finite shape to infinite things.
Each power that leaps from the Unmanifest
Leaving the largeness of the Eternal's peace
They seized and held by their precisian eye
And made a figurante in the cosmic dance.
Its free caprice they bound by rhythmic laws
And compelled to accept its posture and its line
In the wizardry of an ordered universe.
The All-containing was contained in form,
Oneness was carved into units measurable,
The limitless built into a cosmic sum:
Unending Space was beaten into a curve,

Indivisible Time into small minutes cut,
The infinitesimal massed to keep secure
The mystery of the Formless cast into form.
Invincibly their craft devised for use
The magic of sequent number and sign's spell,
Design's miraculous potency was caught
Laden with beauty and significance
And by the determining mandate of their gaze
Figure and quality equating joined
In an inextricable identity.
On each event they stamped its curves of law
And its trust and charge of burdened circumstance;
A free and divine incident no more
At each moment willed or adventure of the soul,
It lengthened a fate-bound mysterious chain,
A line foreseen of an immutable plan,
One step more in Necessity's long march.
A term was set for every eager Power
Restraining its will to monopolise the world,
A groove of bronze prescribed for force and act
And shown to each moment its appointed place
Forewilled inalterably in the spiral
Huge Time-loop fugitive from eternity.
Inevitable their thoughts like links of Fate
Imposed on the leap and lightning race of mind
And on the frail fortuitous flux of life
And on the liberty of atomic things
Immutable cause and adamant consequence.
Idea gave up the plastic infinity
To which it was born and now traced out instead
Small separate steps of chain-work in a plot:
Immortal once, now tied to birth and end,
Torn from its immediacy of errorless sight,
Knowledge was rebuilt from cells of inference
Into a fixed body flasque and perishable;
Thus bound it grew, but could not last and broke

And to a new thinking's body left its place.
A cage for the Infinite's great-eyed seraphim Thoughts
Was closed with a criss-cross of world-laws for bars
And hedged into a curt horizon's arc
The irised vision of the Ineffable.
A timeless Spirit was made the slave of the hours;
The Unbound was cast into a prison of birth
To make a world that Mind could grasp and rule.
On an earth which looked towards a thousand suns,
That the created might grow Nature's lord
And Matter's depths be illumined with a soul
They tied to date and norm and finite scope
The million-mysteried movement of the One.
   Above stood ranked a subtle archangel race
With larger lids and looks that searched the unseen.
A light of liberating knowledge shone
Across the gulfs of silence in their eyes;
They lived in the mind and knew truth from within;
A sight withdrawn in the concentrated heart
Could pierce behind the screen of Time's results
And the rigid cast and shape of visible things.
All that escaped conception's narrow noose
Vision descried and gripped; their seeing thoughts
Filled in the blanks left by the seeking sense.
High architects of possibility
And engineers of the impossible,
Mathematicians of the infinitudes
And theoricians of unknowable truths,
They formulate enigma's postulates
And join the unknown to the apparent worlds.
Acolytes they wait upon the timeless Power,
The cycle of her works investigate;
Passing her fence of wordless privacy
Their mind could penetrate her occult mind
And draw the diagram of her secret thoughts;
They read the codes and ciphers she had sealed,

Copies they made of all her guarded plans,
For every turn of her mysterious course
Assigned a reason and unchanging rule.
The unseen grew visible to student eyes,
Explained was the immense Inconscient's scheme,
Audacious lines were traced upon the Void;
The Infinite was reduced to square and cube.
Arranging symbol and significance,
Tracing the curve of a transcendent Power,
They framed the cabbala of the cosmic Law,
The balancing line discovered of Life's technique
And structured her magic and her mystery.
Imposing schemes of knowledge on the Vast
They clamped to syllogisms of finite thought
The free logic of an infinite Consciousness,
Grammared the hidden rhythms of Nature's dance,
Critiqued the plot of the drama of the worlds,
Made figure and number a key to all that is:
The psycho-analysis of cosmic Self
Was traced, its secrets hunted down, and read
The unknown pathology of the Unique.
Assessed was the system of the probable,
The hazard of fleeing possibilities,
To account for the Actual's unaccountable sum,
Necessity's logarithmic tables drawn,
Cast into a scheme the triple act of the One.
Unveiled, the abrupt invisible multitude
Of forces whirling from the hands of Chance
Seemed to obey some vast imperative:
Their tangled motives worked out unity.
A wisdom read their mind to themselves unknown,
Their anarchy rammed into a formula
And from their giant randomness of Force,
Following the habit of their million paths,
Distinguishing each faintest line and stroke
Of a concealed unalterable design,

Out of the chaos of the Invisible's moods
Derived the calculus of Destiny.
In its bright pride of universal lore
Mind's knowledge overtopped the Omniscient's power:
The Eternal's winging eagle puissances
Surprised in their untracked empyrean
Stooped from their gyres to obey the beck of Thought:
Each mysteried God forced to revealing form,
Assigned his settled moves in Nature's game,
Zigzagged at the gesture of a chess-player Will
Across the chequerboard of cosmic Fate.
In the wide sequence of Necessity's steps
Predicted, every act and thought of God,
Its values weighed by the accountant Mind,
Checked in his mathematised omnipotence,
Lost its divine aspect of miracle
And was a figure in a cosmic sum.
The mighty Mother's whims and lightning moods
Arisen from her all-wise unruled delight
In the freedom of her sweet and passionate breast,
Robbed of their wonder were chained to a cause and aim;
An idol of bronze replaced her mystic shape
That captures the movements of the cosmic vasts,
In the sketch precise of an ideal face
Forgotten was her eyelashes' dream-print
Carrying on their curve infinity's dreams,
Lost the alluring marvel of her eyes;
The surging wave-throbs of her vast sea-heart
They bound to a theorem of ordered beats:
Her deep designs which from herself she had veiled
Bowed self-revealed in their confessional.
For the birth and death of the worlds they fixed a date,
The diameter of infinity was drawn,
Measured the distant arc of the unseen heights
And visualised the plumbless viewless depths,
Till all seemed known that in all time could be.

All was coerced by number, name and form;
Nothing was left untold, incalculable.
Yet was their wisdom circled with a nought:
Truths they could find and hold but not the one Truth:
The Highest was to them unknowable.
By knowing too much they missed the whole to be known:
The fathomless heart of the world was left unguessed
And the Transcendent kept its secrecy.
   In a sublimer and more daring soar
To the wide summit of the triple stairs
Bare steps climbed up like flaming rocks of gold
Burning their way to a pure absolute sky.
August and few the sovereign Kings of Thought
Have made of Space their wide all-seeing gaze
Surveying the enormous work of Time:
A breadth of all-containing Consciousness
Supported Being in a still embrace.
Intercessors with a luminous Unseen,
They capt in the long passage to the world
The imperatives of the creator Self
Obeyed by unknowing earth, by conscious heaven;
Their thoughts are partners in its vast control.
A great all-ruling Consciousness is there
And Mind unwitting serves a higher Power;
It is a channel, not the source of all.
The cosmos is no accident in Time;
There is a meaning in each play of Chance,
There is a freedom in each face of Fate.
A Wisdom knows and guides the mysteried world;
A Truth-gaze shapes its beings and events;
A Word self-born upon creation's heights,
Voice of the Eternal in the temporal spheres,
Prophet of the seeings of the Absolute,
Sows the Idea's significance in Form
And from that seed the growths of Time arise.
On peaks beyond our ken the All-Wisdom sits:

A single and infallible look comes down,
A silent touch from the supernal's air
Awakes to ignorant knowledge in its acts
The secret power in the inconscient depths,
Compelling the blinded Godhead to emerge,
Determining Necessity's nude dance
As she passes through the circuit of the hours
And vanishes from the chase of finite eyes
Down circling vistas of aeonic Time.
The unseizable forces of the cosmic whirl
Bear in their bacchant limbs the fixity
Of an original foresight that is Fate.
Even Nature's ignorance is Truth's instrument;
Our struggling ego cannot change her course:
Yet is it a conscious power that moves in us,
A seed-idea is parent of our acts
And destiny the unrecognised child of Will.
Infallibly by Truth's directing gaze
All creatures here their secret self disclose,
Forced to become what in themselves they hide.
For He who Is grows manifest in the years
And the slow Godhead shut within the cell
Climbs from the plasm to immortality.
But hidden, but denied to mortal grasp,
Mystic, ineffable is the spirit's truth,
Unspoken, caught only by the spirit's eye.
When naked of ego and mind it hears the Voice;
It looks through light to ever greater light
And sees Eternity ensphering Life.
This greater Truth is foreign to our thoughts;
Where a free Wisdom works, they seek for a rule;
Or we only see a tripping game of Chance
Or a labour in chains forced by bound Nature's law,
An absolutism of dumb unthinking Power.
Audacious in their sense of God-born strength
These dared to grasp with their thought Truth's absolute;

By an abstract purity of godless sight,
By a percept nude, intolerant of forms,
They brought to Mind what Mind could never reach
And hoped to conquer Truth's supernal base.
A stripped imperative of conceptual phrase
Architectonic and inevitable
Translated the unthinkable into thought:
A silver-winged fire of naked subtle sense,
An ear of mind withdrawn from the outward's rhymes
Discovered the seed-sounds of the eternal Word,
The rhythm and music heard that built the worlds,
And seized in things the bodiless Will to be.
The Illimitable they measured with number's rods
And traced the last formula of limited things,
In transparent systems bodied termless truths,
The Timeless made accountable to Time
And valued the incommensurable Supreme.
To park and hedge the ungrasped infinitudes
They erected absolute walls of thought and speech
And made a vacuum to hold the One.
In their sight they drove towards an empty peak,
A mighty space of cold and sunlit air.
To unify their task, excluding life
Which cannot bear the nakedness of the Vast,
They made a cipher of a multitude,
In negation found the meaning of the All
And in nothingness the absolute positive.
A single law simplessed the cosmic theme,
Compressing Nature into a formula;
Their titan labour made all knowledge one,
A mental algebra of the Spirit's ways,
An abstract of the living Divinity.
Here the mind's wisdom stopped; it felt complete;
For nothing more was left to think or know:
In a spiritual zero it sat throned
And took its vast silence for the Ineffable.

This was the play of the bright gods of Thought.
Attracting into time the timeless Light,
Imprisoning eternity in the hours,
This they have planned, to snare the feet of Truth
In an aureate net of concept and of phrase
And keep her captive for the thinker's joy
In his little world built of immortal dreams:
There must she dwell mured in the human mind,
An empress prisoner in her subject's house,
Adored and pure and still on his heart's throne,
His splendid property cherished and apart
In the wall of silence of his secret muse,
Immaculate in white virginity,
The same for ever and for ever one,
His worshipped changeless Goddess through all time.
Or else, a faithful consort of his mind
Assenting to his nature and his will,
She sanctions and inspires his words and acts
Prolonging their resonance through the listening years,
Companion and recorder of his march
Crossing a brilliant tract of thought and life
Carved out of the eternity of Time.
A witness to his high triumphant star,
Her godhead servitor to a crowned Idea,
He shall dominate by her a prostrate world;
A warrant for his deeds and his beliefs,
She attests his right divine to lead and rule.
Or as a lover clasps his one beloved,
Godhead of his life's worship and desire,
Icon of his heart's sole idolatry,
She now is his and must live for him alone:
She has invaded him with her sudden bliss,
An exhaustless marvel in his happy grasp,
An allurement, a caught ravishing miracle.
Her now he claims after long rapt pursuit,
The one joy of his body and his soul:

Inescapable is her divine appeal,
Her immense possession an undying thrill,
An intoxication and an ecstasy:
The passion of her self-revealing moods,
A heavenly glory and variety,
Makes ever new her body to his eyes,
Or else repeats the first enchantment's touch,
The luminous rapture of her mystic breasts
And beautiful vibrant limbs a living field
Of throbbing new discovery without end.
A new beginning flowers in word and laugh,
A new charm brings back the old extreme delight:
He is lost in her, she is his heaven here.
Truth smiled upon the gracious golden game.
Out of her hushed eternal spaces leaned
The great and boundless Goddess feigned to yield
The sunlit sweetness of her secrecies.
Incarnating her beauty in his clasp
She gave for a brief kiss her immortal lips
And drew to her bosom one glorified mortal head:
She made earth her home, for whom heaven was too small.
In a human breast her occult presence lived;
He carved from his own self his figure of her:
She shaped her body to a mind's embrace.
Into thought's narrow limits she has come;
Her greatness she has suffered to be pressed
Into the little cabin of the Idea,
The closed room of a lonely thinker's grasp:
She has lowered her heights to the stature of our souls
And dazzled our lids with her celestial gaze.
Thus each is satisfied with his high gain
And thinks himself beyond mortality blest,
A king of truth upon his separate throne.
To her possessor in the field of Time
A single splendour caught from her glory seems
The one true light, her beauty's glowing whole.

But thought nor word can seize eternal Truth:
The whole world lives in a lonely ray of her sun.
In our thinking's close and narrow lamp-lit house
The vanity of our shut mortal mind
Dreams that the chains of thought have made her ours;
But only we play with our own brilliant bonds;
Tying her down, it is ourselves we tie.
In our hypnosis by one luminous point
We see not what small figure of her we hold;
We feel not her inspiring boundlessness,
We share not her immortal liberty.
Thus is it even with the seer and sage;
For still the human limits the divine:
Out of our thoughts we must leap up to sight,
Breathe her divine illimitable air,
Her simple vast supremacy confess,
Dare to surrender to her absolute.
Then the Unmanifest reflects his form
In the still mind as in a living glass;
The timeless Ray descends into our hearts
And we are rapt into eternity.
For Truth is wider, greater than her forms.
A thousand icons they have made of her
And find her in the idols they adore;
But she remains herself and infinite.

END OF CANTO ELEVEN

The Heavens of the Ideal

ALWAYS the Ideal beckoned from afar.
Awakened by the touch of the Unseen,
Deserting the boundary of things achieved,
Aspired the strong discoverer, tireless Thought,
Revealing at each step a luminous world.
It left known summits for the unknown peaks:
Impassioned, it sought the lone unrealised Truth,
It longed for the Light that knows not death and birth.
Each stage of the soul's remote ascent was built
Into a constant heaven felt always here.
At each pace of the journey marvellous
A new degree of wonder and of bliss,
A new rung formed in Being's mighty stair,
A great wide step trembling with jewelled fire
As if a burning spirit quivered there
Upholding with his flame the immortal hope,
As if a radiant God had given his soul
That he might feel the tread of pilgrim feet
Mounting in haste to the Eternal's house.
At either end of each effulgent stair
The heavens of the ideal Mind were seen
In a blue lucency of dreaming Space
Like strips of brilliant sky clinging to the moon.
On one side glimmered hue on floating hue,
A glory of sunrise breaking on the soul,
In a tremulous rapture of the heart's insight
And the spontaneous bliss that beauty gives,
The lovely kingdoms of the deathless Rose.
Above the spirit cased in mortal sense
Are superconscious realms of heavenly peace,
Below, the Inconscient's sullen dim abyss,

Between, behind our life, the deathless Rose.
Across the covert air the spirit breathes,
A body of the cosmic beauty and joy
Unseen, unguessed by the blind suffering world,
Climbing from Nature's deep surrendered heart
It blooms for ever at the feet of God,
Fed by life's sacrificial mysteries.
Here too its bud is born in human breasts;
Then by a touch, a presence or a voice
The world is turned into a temple ground
And all discloses the unknown Beloved.
In an outburst of heavenly joy and ease
Life yields to the divinity within
And gives the rapture-offering of its all,
And the soul opens to felicity.
A bliss is felt that never can wholly cease,
A sudden mystery of secret Grace
Flowers goldening our earth of red desire.
All the high gods who hid their visages
From the soiled passionate ritual of our hopes,
Reveal their names and their undying powers.
A fiery stillness wakes the slumbering cells,
A passion of the flesh becoming spirit,
And marvellously is fulfilled at last
The miracle for which our life was made.
A flame in a white voiceless cupola
Is seen and faces of immortal light,
The radiant limbs that know not birth and death,
The breasts that suckle the first-born of the Sun,
The wings that crowd thought's ardent silences,
The eyes that look into spiritual Space.
Our hidden centres of celestial force
Open like flowers to a heavenly atmosphere;
Mind pauses thrilled with the supernal Ray,
And even this transient body then can feel
Ideal love and flawless happiness

And laughter of the heart's sweetness and delight
Freed from the rude and tragic hold of Time,
And beauty and the rhythmic feet of the hours.
This in high realms touches immortal kind;
What here is in the bud has blossomed there.
There is the secrecy of the House of Flame,
The blaze of godlike thought and golden bliss,
The rapt idealism of heavenly sense;
There are the wonderful voices, the sun-laugh,
A gurgling eddy in rivers of God's joy,
And the mysteried vineyards of the gold moon-wine,
All the fire and sweetness of which hardly here
A brilliant shadow visits mortal life.
Although are witnessed there the joys of Time,
Pressed on the bosom the Immortal's touch is felt,
Heard are the flutings of the Infinite.
Here upon earth are early awakenings,
Moments that tremble in an air divine,
And grown upon the yearning of her soil
Time's sun-flowers' gaze at gold Eternity:
There are the imperishable beatitudes.
A million lotuses swaying on one stem,
World after coloured and ecstatic world
Climbs towards some far unseen epiphany.
　　On the other side of the eternal stairs
The mighty kingdoms of the deathless Flame
Aspired to reach the Being's absolutes.
Out of the sorrow and darkness of the world,
Out of the depths where life and thought are tombed,
Lonely mounts up to heaven the deathless Flame.
In a veiled Nature's hallowed secrecies
It burns for ever on the altar Mind,
Its priests the souls of dedicated gods,
Humanity its house of sacrifice.
Once kindled, never can its flamings cease.
A fire along the mystic paths of earth,

It rises through the mortal's hemisphere,
Till borne by runners of the Day and Dusk
It enters the occult eternal Light
And clambers whitening to the invisible Throne.
Its worlds are steps of an ascending Force:
A dream of giant contours, titan lines,
Homes of unfallen and illumined Might,
Heavens of unchanging Good pure and unborn,
Heights of the grandeur of Truth's ageless ray,
As in a symbol sky they start to view
And call our souls into a vaster air.
On their summits they bear up the sleepless Flame;
Dreaming of a mysterious Beyond,
Transcendent of the paths of Fate and Time,
They point above themselves with index peaks
Through a pale-sapphire ether of god-mind
Towards some gold Infinite's apocalypse.
A thunder rolling mid the hills of God,
Tireless, severe is their tremendous Voice:
Exceeding us, to exceed ourselves they call
And bid us rise incessantly above.
Far from our eager reach those summits live,
Too lofty for our mortal strength and height,
Hardly in a dire ecstasy of toil
Climbed by the spirit's naked athlete will.
Austere, intolerant they claim from us
Efforts too lasting for our mortal nerve
Our hearts cannot cleave to nor our flesh support;
Only the Eternal's strength in us can dare
To attempt the immense adventure of that climb
And the sacrifice of all we cherish here.
Our human knowledge is a candle burnt
On a dim altar to a sun-vast Truth;
Man's virtue, a coarse-spun ill-fitting dress,
Apparels wooden images of Good;
Passionate and blinded, bleeding, stained with mire

His energy stumbles towards a deathless Force.
An imperfection dogs our highest strength;
Portions and pale reflections are our share.
Happy the worlds that have not felt our fall,
Where Will is one with Truth and Good with Power;
Impoverished not by earth-mind's indigence,
They keep God's natural breath of mightiness,
His bare spontaneous swift intensities;
There is his great transparent mirror, Self,
And there his sovereign autarchy of bliss
In which immortal natures have their part,
Heirs and cosharers of divinity.
   He through the Ideal's kingdoms moved at will,
Accepted their beauty and their greatness bore,
Partook of the glories of their wonder fields,
But passed nor stayed beneath their splendour's rule.
All there was an intense but partial light.
In each a seraph-winged high-browed Idea
United all knowledge by one master thought,
Persuaded all action to one golden sense,
All powers subjected to a single power
And made a world where it could reign alone,
An absolute ideal's perfect home.
Insignia of their victory and their faith,
They offered to the Traveller at their gates
A quenchless flame or an unfading flower,
Emblem of a high kingdom's privilege.
A glorious shining Angel of the Way
Presented to the seeking of the soul
The sweetness and the might of an idea,
Each deemed Truth's intimate fount and summit force,
The heart of the meaning of the universe,
Perfection's key, passport to Paradise.
Yet were there regions where these absolutes met
And made a circle of bliss with married hands;
Light stood embraced by light, fire wedded fire,

But none in the other would his body lose
To find his soul in the world's single Soul,
A multiplied rapture of infinity.
Onward he passed to a diviner sphere:
There, joined in a common greatness, light and bliss,
All high and beautiful and desirable powers
Forgetting their difference and their separate reign
Become a single multitudinous whole.
Above the parting of the roads of Time,
Above the Silence and its thousandfold Word,
In the immutable and inviolate Truth
For ever united and inseparable,
The radiant children of Eternity dwell
On the wide spirit height where all are one.

END OF CANTO TWELVE

Canto Thirteen

In the Self of Mind

AT LAST there came a bare indifferent sky
Where Silence listened to the cosmic Voice,
But answered nothing to a million calls;
The soul's endless question met with no response.
An abrupt conclusion ended eager hopes,
A deep cessation in a mighty calm,
A finis-line on the last page of thought
And a margin and a blank of wordless peace.
There paused the climbing hierarchy of worlds.
He stood on a wide arc of summit Space
Alone with an enormous Self of Mind
Which held all life in a corner of its vasts.
Omnipotent, immobile and aloof,
In the world which sprang from it, it took no part:
It gave no heed to the paeans of victory,
It was indifferent to its own defeats,
It heard the cry of grief and made no sign;
Impartial fell its gaze on evil and good,
It saw destruction come and did not move.
An equal Cause of things, a lonely Seer
And Master of its multitude of forms,
It acted not but bore all thoughts and deeds,
The witness Lord of Nature's myriad acts
Consenting to the movements of her Force.
His mind reflected this vast quietism.
This witness hush is the Thinker's secret base:
Hidden in silent depths the word is formed,
From hidden silences the act is born
Into the voiceful mind, the labouring world;
In secrecy wraps the seed the Eternal sows
Silence, the mystic birthplace of the soul.

In God's supreme withdrawn and timeless hush
A seeing Self and potent Energy met;
The Silence knew itself and thought took form:
Self-made from the dual power creation rose.
In the still self he lived and it in him;
Its mute immemorable listening depths,
Its vastness and its stillness were his own;
One being with it he grew wide, powerful, free.
Apart, unbound, he looked on all things done.
As one who builds his own imagined scenes
And loses not himself in what he sees,
Spectator of a drama self-conceived,
He looked on the world and watched its motive thoughts
With the burden of luminous prophecy in their eyes,
Its forces with their feet of wind and fire
Arisen from the dumbness in his soul.
All now he seemed to understand and know;
Desire came not nor any gust of will,
The great perturbed inquirer lost his task;
Nothing was asked nor wanted any more.
There he could stay, the Self, the Silence won:
His soul had peace, it knew the cosmic Whole.
Then suddenly a luminous finger fell
On all things seen or touched or heard or felt
And showed his mind that nothing could be known;
That must be reached from which all knowledge comes.
The sceptic Ray disrupted all that seems
And smote at the very roots of thought and sense.
In a universe of Nescience they have grown,
Aspiring towards a superconscient Sun,
Playing in shine and rain from heavenlier skies
They never can win however high their reach
Or overpass however keen their probe.
A doubt corroded even the means to think,
Distrust was thrown upon Mind's instruments;
All that it takes for reality's shining coin,

Proved fact, fixed inference, deduction clear,
Firm theory, assured significance,
Appeared as frauds upon Time's credit bank
Or assets valueless in Truth's treasury.
An Ignorance on an uneasy throne
Travestied with a fortuitous sovereignty
A figure of knowledge garbed in dubious words
And tinsel thought-forms brightly inadequate.
A labourer in the dark dazzled by half-light,
What it knew was an image in a broken glass,
What it saw was real but its sight untrue.
All the ideas in its vast repertory
Were like the mutterings of a transient cloud
That spent itself in sound and left no trace.
A frail house hanging in uncertain air,
The thin ingenious web round which it moves,
Put out awhile on the tree of the universe,
And gathered up into itself again,
Was only a trap to catch life's insect food,
Winged thoughts that flutter fragile in brief light
But dead, once captured in fixed forms of mind,
Aims puny but looming large in man's small scale,
Flickers of imagination's brilliant gauze
And cobweb-wrapped beliefs alive no more.
The magic hut of built-up certitudes
Made out of glittering dust and bright moonshine
In which it shrines its image of the Real,
Collapsed into the Nescience whence it rose.
Only a gleam was there of symbol facts
That shroud the mystery lurking in their glow,
And falsehoods based on hidden realities
By which they live until they fall from Time.
Our mind is a house haunted by the slain past,
Ideas soon mummified, ghosts of old truths,
God's spontaneities tied with formal strings
And packed into drawers of reason's trim bureau,

A grave of great lost opportunities,
Or an office for misuse of soul and life
And all the waste man makes of heaven's gifts
And all his squanderings of Nature's store,
A stage for the comedy of Ignorance.
The world seemed a long aeonic failure's scene:
All sterile grew, no base was left secure.
Assailed by the edge of the convicting beam
The builder Reason lost her confidence
In the successful sleight and turn of thought
That makes the soul the prisoner of a phrase.
Its highest wisdom was a brilliant guess,
Its mighty structured science of the worlds
A passing light on being's surfaces.
There was nothing there but a schema drawn by sense,
A substitute for eternal mysteries,
A scrawl figure of reality, a plan
And elevation by the architect Word
Imposed upon the semblances of Time.
Existence' self was shadowed by a doubt;
Almost it seemed a lotus-leaf afloat
On a nude pool of cosmic Nothingness.
This great spectator and creator Mind
Was only some half-seeing's delegate,
A veil that hung between the soul and Light,
An idol, not the living body of God.
Even the still spirit that looks upon its works
Was some pale front of the Unknowable;
A shadow seemed the wide and witness Self,
Its liberation and immobile calm
A void recoil of being from Time-made things,
Not the self-vision of Eternity.
Deep peace was there, but not the nameless Force:
Our sweet and mighty Mother was not there
Who gathers to her bosom her children's lives,
Her clasp that takes the world into her arms

In the fathomless rapture of the Infinite,
The Bliss that is creation's splendid grain
Or the white passion of God-ecstasy
That laughs in the blaze of the boundless heart of Love.
A greater Spirit than the Self of Mind
Must answer to the questioning of his soul.
For here was no firm clue and no sure road;
High-climbing pathways ceased in the unknown;
An artist Sight constructed the Beyond
In contrary patterns and conflicting hues;
A part-experience fragmented the Whole.
He looked above, but all was blank and still:
A sapphire firmament of abstract Thought
Escaped into a formless Vacancy.
He looked below, but all was dark and mute.
A noise was heard, between, of thought and prayer,
A strife, a labour without end or pause;
A vain and ignorant seeking raised its voice.
A rumour and a movement and a call,
A foaming mass, a cry innumerable
Rolled ever upon the ocean surge of Life
Along the coasts of mortal Ignorance.
On its unstable and enormous breast
Beings and forces, forms, ideas like waves
Jostled for figure and supremacy,
And rose and sank and rose again in Time;
And at the bottom of the sleepless stir,
A Nothingness parent of the struggling worlds,
A huge creator Death, a mystic Void,
For ever sustaining the irrational cry,
For ever excluding the supernal Word,
Motionless, refusing question and response,
Reposed beneath the voices and the march
The dim Inconscient's dumb incertitude.
Two firmaments of darkness and of light
Opposed their limits to the spirit's walk;

It moved veiled in from Self's infinity
In a world of beings and momentary events
Where all must die to live and live to die.
Immortal by renewed mortality,
It wandered in the spiral of its acts
Or ran around the cycles of its thought,
Yet was no more than its original self
And knew no more than when it first began.
To be was a prison, extinction the escape.

END OF CANTO THIRTEEN

The World-Soul

A COVERT answer to his seeking came.
In a far shimmering background of Mind-Space
A glowing mouth was seen, a luminous shaft;
A recluse gate it seemed, musing on joy,
A veiled retreat and escape to mystery.
Away from the unsatisfied surface world
It fled into the bosom of the unknown,
A well, a tunnel of the depths of God.
It plunged as if a mystic groove of hope
Through many layers of formless voiceless self
To reach the last profound of the world's heart,
And from that heart there surged a wordless call
Pleading with some still impenetrable Mind,
Voicing some passionate unseen desire.
As if a beckoning finger of secrecy
Outstretched into a crystal mood of air,
Pointing at him from some near hidden depth,
As if a message from the world's deep soul,
An intimation of a lurking joy
That flowed out from a cup of brooding bliss,
There shimmered stealing out into the Mind
A mute and quivering ecstasy of light,
A passion and delicacy of roseate fire.
As one drawn to his lost spiritual home
Feels now the closeness of a waiting love,
Into a passage dim and tremulous
That clasped him in from day and night's pursuit,
He travelled led by a mysterious sound.
A murmur multitudinous and lone,
All sounds it was in turn, yet still the same.
A hidden call to unforeseen delight

In the summoning voice of one long-known, well-loved,
But nameless to the unremembering mind,
It led to rapture back the truant heart.
The immortal cry ravished the captive ear.
Then, lowering its imperious mystery,
It sank to a whisper circling round the soul.
It seemed the yearning of a lonely flute
That roamed along the shores of memory
And filled the eyes with tears of longing joy.
A cricket's rash and fiery single note,
It marked with shrill melody night's moonless hush
And beat upon a nerve of mystic sleep
Its high insistent magical reveille.
A jingling silver laugh of anklet bells
Travelled the roads of a solitary heart;
Its dance solaced an eternal loneliness:
An old forgotten sweetness sobbing came.
Or from a far harmonious distance heard
The tinkling pace of a long caravan
It seemed at times, or a vast forest's hymn,
The solemn reminder of a temple gong,
A bee-croon honey-drunk in summer isles
Ardent with ecstasy in a slumbrous noon,
Or the far anthem of a pilgrim sea.
An incense floated in the quivering air,
A mystic happiness trembled in the breast
As if the invisible Beloved had come
Assuming the sudden loveliness of a face
And close glad hands could seize his fugitive feet
And the world change with the beauty of a smile.
Into a wonderful bodiless realm he came,
The home of a passion without name or voice,
A depth he felt answering to every height,
A nook was found that could embrace all worlds,
A point that was the conscious knot of Space,
An hour eternal in the heart of Time.

The silent Soul of all the world was there:
A Being lived, a Presence and a Power,
A single Person who was himself and all
And cherished Nature's sweet and dangerous throbs
Transfigured into beats divine and pure.
One who could love without return for love,
Meeting and turning to the best the worst,
It healed the bitter cruelties of earth,
Transforming all experience to delight;
Intervening in the sorrowful paths of birth
It rocked the cradle of the cosmic Child
And stilled all weeping with its hand of joy;
It led things evil towards their secret good,
It turned racked falsehood into happy truth;
Its power was to reveal divinity.
Infinite, coeval with the mind of God,
It bore within itself a seed, a flame,
A seed from which the Eternal is new-born,
A flame that cancels death in mortal things.
All grew to all kindred and self and near;
The intimacy of God was everywhere,
No veil was felt, no brute barrier inert,
Distance could not divide, Time could not change.
A fire of passion burned in spirit-depths,
A constant touch of sweetness linked all hearts,
The throb of one adoration's single bliss
In a rapt ether of undying love.
An inner happiness abode in all,
A sense of universal harmonies,
A measureless secure eternity
Of truth and beauty and good and joy made one.
Here was the welling core of finite life;
A formless spirit became the soul of form.

     All there was soul or made of sheer soul-stuff;
A sky of soul covered a deep soul-ground.

All here was known by a spiritual sense:
Thought was not there but a knowledge near and one
Seized on all things by a moved identity,
A sympathy of self with other selves,
The touch of consciousness on consciousness
And being's look on being with inmost gaze
And heart laid bare to heart without walls of speech
And the unanimity of seeing minds
In myriad forms luminous with the one God.
Life was not there, but an impassioned force,
Finer than fineness, deeper than the deeps,
Felt as a subtle and spiritual power,
A quivering out from soul to answering soul,
A mystic movement, a close influence,
A free and happy and intense approach
Of being to being with no screen or check,
Without which life and love could never have been.
Body was not there, for bodies were needed not,
The soul itself was its own deathless form
And met at once the touch of other souls
Close, blissful, concrete, wonderfully true.
As when one walks in sleep through luminous dreams
And, conscious, knows the truth their figures mean,
Here where reality was its own dream,
He knew things by their soul and not their shape:
As those who have lived long made one in love
Need word nor sign for heart's reply to heart,
He met and communed without bar of speech
With beings unveiled by a material frame.
There was a strange spiritual scenery,
A loveliness of lakes and streams and hills,
A flow, a fixity in a soul-space,
And plains and valleys, stretches of soul-joy,
And gardens that were flower-tracts of the spirit,
Its meditations of tinged reverie.
Air was the breath of a pure infinite.

A fragrance wandered in a coloured haze
As if the scent and hue of all sweet flowers
Had mingled to copy heaven's atmosphere.
Appealing to the soul and not the eye
Beauty lived there at home in her own house,
There all was beautiful by its own right
And needed not the splendour of a robe.
All objects were like bodies of the Gods,
A spirit symbol environing a soul,
For world and self were one reality.

   Immersed in voiceless internatal trance
The beings that once wore forms on earth sat there
In shining chambers of spiritual sleep.
Passed were the pillar-posts of birth and death,
Passed was their little scene of symbol deeds,
Passed were the heavens and hells of their long road;
They had returned into the world's deep soul.
All now was gathered into pregnant rest:
Person and nature suffered a slumber change.
In trance they gathered back their bygone selves,
In a background memory's foreseeing muse
Prophetic of new personality
Arranged the map of their coming destiny's course:
Heirs of their past, their future's discoverers,
Electors of their own self-chosen lot,
They waited for the adventure of new life.
A Person persistent through the lapse of worlds,
Although the same for ever in many shapes
By the outward mind unrecognisable,
Assuming names unknown in unknown climes
Imprints through Time upon the earth's worn page
A growing figure of its secret self,
And learns by experience what the spirit knew,
Till it can see its truth alive and God.
Once more they must face the problem-game of birth,

The soul's experiment of joy and grief
And thought and impulse lighting the blind act,
And venture on the roads of circumstance,
Through inner movements and external scenes
Travelling to self across the forms of things.
Into creation's centre he had come.
The spirit wandering from state to state
Finds here the silence of its starting-point
In the formless force and the still fixity
And brooding passion of the world of Soul.
All that is made and once again unmade,
The calm persistent vision of the One
Inevitably re-makes, it lives anew:
Forces and lives and beings and ideas
Are taken into the stillness for a while;
There they remould their purpose and their drift,
Recast their nature and re-form their shape.
Ever they change and changing ever grow,
And passing through a fruitful stage of death
And after long reconstituting sleep
Resume their place in the process of the Gods
Until their work in cosmic Time is done.
    Here was the fashioning chamber of the worlds.
An interval was left twixt act and act,
Twixt birth and birth, twixt dream and waking dream,
A pause that gave new strength to do and be.
Beyond were regions of delight and peace,
Mute birthplaces of light and hope and love,
And cradles of heavenly rapture and repose.
In a slumber of the voices of the world
He of the eternal moment grew aware;
His knowledge stripped bare of the garbs of sense
Knew by identity without thought or word;
His being saw itself without its veils,
Life's line fell from the spirit's infinity.
Along a road of pure interior light,

Alone between tremendous Presences,
Under the watching eyes of nameless Gods,
His soul passed on, a single conscious power,
Towards the end which ever begins again,
Approaching through a stillness dumb and calm
To the source of all things human and divine.
There he beheld in their mighty union's poise
The figure of the deathless Two-in-One,
A single being in two bodies clasped,
A diarchy of two united souls,
Seated absorbed in deep creative joy;
Their trance of bliss sustained the mobile world.
Behind them in a morning dusk One stood
Who brought them forth from the Unknowable.
Ever disguised she awaits the seeking spirit;
Watcher on the supreme unreachable peaks,
Guide of the traveller of the unseen paths,
She guards the austere approach to the Alone.
At the beginning of each far-spread plane
Pervading with her power the cosmic suns
She reigns, inspirer of its multiple works
And thinker of the symbol of its scene.
Above them all she stands supporting all,
The sole omnipotent Goddess ever-veiled
Of whom the world is the inscrutable mask;
The ages are the footfalls of her tread,
Their happenings the figure of her thoughts,
And all creation is her endless act.
His spirit was made a vessel of her force;
Mute in the fathomless passion of his will
He outstretched to her his folded hands of prayer.
Then in a sovereign answer to his heart
A gesture came as of worlds thrown away,
And from her raiment's lustrous mystery raised
One arm half-parted the eternal veil.
A light appeared still and imperishable.

Attracted to the large and luminous depths
Of the ravishing enigma of her eyes,
He saw the mystic outline of a face.
Overwhelmed by her implacable light and bliss,
An atom of her illimitable self
Mastered by the honey and lightning of her power,
Tossed towards the shores of her ocean-ecstasy,
Drunk with a deep golden spiritual wine,
He cast from the rent stillness of his soul
A cry of adoration and desire
And the surrender of his boundless mind
And the self-giving of his silent heart.
He fell down at her feet unconscious, prone.

END OF CANTO FOURTEEN

Canto Fifteen

The Kingdoms of the Greater Knowledge

AFTER a measureless moment of the soul
Again returning to these surface fields
Out of the timeless depths where he had sunk,
He heard once more the slow tread of the hours.
All once perceived and lived was far away;
Himself was to himself his only scene.
Above the Witness and his universe
He stood in a realm of boundless silences
Awaiting the Voice that spoke and built the worlds.
A light was round him wide and absolute,
A diamond purity of eternal sight;
A consciousness lay still, devoid of forms,
Free, wordless, uncoerced by sign or rule,
For ever content with only being and bliss;
A sheer existence lived in its own peace
On the single spirit's bare and infinite ground.
Out of the sphere of Mind he had arisen,
He had left the reign of Nature's hues and shades;
He dwelt in his self's colourless purity.
It was a plane of undetermined spirit
That could be a zero or round sum of things,
A state in which all ceased and all began.
All it became that figures the absolute,
A high vast peak whence Spirit could see the worlds,
Calm's wide epiphany, wisdom's mute home,
A lonely station of Omniscience,
A diving-board of the Eternal's power,
A white floor in the house of All-Delight.
Here came the thought that passes beyond Thought,
Here the still Voice which our listening cannot hear,
The Knowledge by which the knower is the known,

The Love in which beloved and lover are one.
All stood in an original plenitude,
Hushed and fulfilled before they could create
The glorious dream of their universal acts;
Here was engendered the spiritual birth,
Here closed the finite's crawl to the Infinite.
A thousand roads leaped into Eternity
Or singing ran to meet God's veilless face.
The Known released him from its limiting chain;
He knocked at the doors of the Unknowable.
Thence gazing with an immeasurable outlook
One with self's inlook into its own pure vasts,
He saw the splendour of the spirit's realms,
The greatness and wonder of its boundless works,
The power and passion leaping from its calm,
The rapture of its movement and its rest,
And its fire-sweet miracle of transcendent life,
The million-pointing undivided grasp
Of its vision of one same stupendous All,
Its inexhaustible acts in a timeless Time,
A space that is its own infinity.
A glorious multiple of one radiant Self,
Answering to joy with joy, to love with love,
All there were moving mansions of God-bliss;
Eternal and unique they lived the One.
There forces are great outbursts of God's truth
And objects are its pure spiritual shapes;
Spirit no more is hid from its own view,
All sentience is a sea of happiness
And all creation is an act of light.
Out of the neutral silence of his soul
He passed to its fields of puissance and of calm
And saw the Powers that stand above the world,
Traversed the realms of the supreme Idea
And sought the summit of created things
And the almighty source of cosmic change.

There Knowledge called him to her mystic peaks
Where thought is held in a vast internal sense
And feeling swims across a sea of peace
And vision climbs beyond the reach of Time.
An equal of the first creator seers,
Accompanied by an all-revealing light
He moved through regions of transcendent Truth
Inward, immense, innumerably one.
There distance was his own huge spirit's extent;
Delivered from the fictions of the mind
Time's triple dividing step baffled no more;
Its inevitable and continuous stream,
The long flow of its manifesting course,
Was held in spirit's single wide regard.
A universal beauty showed its face:
The invisible deep-fraught significances,
Here sheltered behind form's insensible screen,
Uncovered to him their deathless harmony
And the key to the wonder-book of common things.
In their uniting law stood up revealed
The multiple measures of the upbuilding force,
The lines of the World-Geometer's technique,
The enchantments that uphold the cosmic web
And the magic underlying simple shapes.
On peaks where Silence listens with still heart
To the rhythmic metres of the rolling worlds,
He served the sessions of the triple Fire.
On the rim of two continents of slumber and trance
He heard the ever unspoken Reality's voice
Awaken revelation's mystic cry,
The birthplace found of the sudden infallible Word
And lived in the rays of an intuitive Sun.
Absolved from the ligaments of death and sleep
He rode the lightning seas of cosmic Mind
And crossed the ocean of original sound;
On the last step to the supernal birth

He trod along extinction's narrow edge
Near the high verges of eternity,
And mounted the gold ridge of the world-dream
Between the slayer and the saviour fires;
The belt he reached of the unchanging Truth,
Met borders of the inexpressible Light
And thrilled with the presence of the Ineffable.
Above him he saw the flaming Hierarchies,
The wings that fold around created Space,
The sun-eyed Guardians and the golden Sphinx
And the tiered planes and the immutable Lords.
A wisdom waiting on Omniscience
Sat voiceless in a vast passivity;
It judged not, measured not, nor strove to know,
But listened for the veiled all-seeing Thought
And the burden of a calm transcendent Voice.
He had reached the top of all that can be known:
His sight surpassed creation's head and base;
Ablaze the triple heavens revealed their suns,
The obscure Abyss exposed its monstrous rule.
All but the ultimate Mystery was his field,
Almost the Unknowable disclosed its rim.
His self's infinities began to emerge,
The hidden universes cried to him;
Eternities called to eternities
Sending their speechless message still remote.
Arisen from the marvel of the depths
And burning from the superconscious heights
And sweeping in great horizontal gyres
A million energies joined and were the One.
All flowed immeasurably to one sea:
All living forms became its atom homes.
A Panergy that harmonised all life
Held now existence in its vast control;
A portion of that majesty he was made.
At will he lived in the unoblivious Ray.

In that high realm where no untruth can come,
Where all are different and all is one,
In the Impersonal's ocean without shore
The Person in the World-Spirit anchored rode;
It thrilled with the mighty marchings of World-Force,
Its acts were the comrades of God's infinite peace.
An adjunct glory and a symbol self,
The body was delivered to the soul, —
An immortal point of power, a block of poise
In a cosmicity's wide formless surge,
A conscious edge of the Transcendent's might
Carving perfection from a bright world-stuff,
It figured in it a universe's sense.
There consciousness was a close and single weft;
The far and near were one in spirit-space,
The moments there were pregnant with all time.
The superconscient's screen was ripped by thought,
Idea rotated symphonies of sight,
Sight was a flame-throw from identity;
Life was a marvellous journey of the spirit,
Feeling a wave from the universal Bliss.
In the kingdom of the Spirit's power and light,
As if one who arrived out of infinity's womb
He came new-born, infant and limitless
And grew in the wisdom of the timeless Child;
He was a vast that soon became a Sun.
A great luminous silence whispered to his heart;
His knowledge an inview caught unfathomable,
An outview by no brief horizons cut:
He thought and felt in all, his gaze had power.
He communed with the Incommunicable;
Beings of a wider consciousness were his friends,
Forms of a larger subtler make drew near;
The Gods conversed with him behind Life's veil.
Neighbour his being grew to Nature's crests.
The primal Energy took him in its arms;

His brain was wrapped in overwhelming light,
An all-embracing knowledge seized his heart:
Thoughts rose in him no earthly mind can hold,
Mights played that never coursed through mortal nerves:
He scanned the secrets of the Overmind,
He bore the rapture of the Oversoul.
A borderer of the empire of the Sun,
Attuned to the supernal harmonies,
He linked creation to the Eternal's sphere.
His finite parts approached their absolutes,
His actions framed the movements of the Gods,
His will took up the reins of cosmic Force.

END OF CANTO FIFTEEN
End of Book Two

BOOK THREE

The Book of the Divine Mother

Canto One

The Pursuit of the Unknowable

ALL is too little that the world can give:
Its power and knowledge are the gifts of Time
And cannot fill the spirit's sacred thirst.
Although of One these forms of greatness are
And by its breath of grace our lives abide,
Although more near to us than nearness' self,
It is some utter truth of what we are;
Hidden by its own works, it seemed far-off,
Impenetrable, occult, voiceless, obscure.
The Presence was lost by which all things have charm,
The Glory lacked of which they are dim signs.
The world lived on made empty of its Cause,
Like love when the beloved's face is gone.
The labour to know seemed a vain strife of Mind;
All knowledge ended in the Unknowable:
The effort to rule seemed a vain pride of Will;
A trivial achievement scorned by Time,
All power retired into the Omnipotent.
A cave of darkness guards the eternal Light.
A silence settled on his striving heart;
Absolved from the voices of the world's desire,
He turned to the Ineffable's timeless call.
A Being intimate and unnameable,
A wide compelling ecstasy and peace
Felt in himself and all and yet ungrasped,
Approached and faded from his soul's pursuit
As if for ever luring him beyond.
Near, it retreated; far, it called him still.
Nothing could satisfy but its delight:
Its absence left the greatest actions dull,
Its presence made the smallest seem divine.

When it was there, the heart's abyss was filled;
But when the uplifting Deity withdrew,
Existence lost its aim in the Inane.
The order of the immemorial planes,
The godlike fullness of the instruments
Were turned to props for an impermanent scene.
But who that mightiness was he knew not yet.
Impalpable, yet filling all that is,
It made and blotted out a million worlds
And took and lost a thousand shapes and names.
It wore the guise of an indiscernible Vast,
Or was a subtle kernel in the soul:
A distant greatness left it huge and dim,
A mystic closeness shut it sweetly in:
It seemed sometimes a figment or a robe
And seemed sometimes his own colossal shade.
A giant doubt overshadowed his advance.
Across a neutral all-supporting Void
Whose blankness nursed his lone immortal spirit,
Allured towards some recondite Supreme,
Aided, coerced by enigmatic Powers,
Aspiring and half-sinking and upborne,
Invincibly he ascended without pause.
Always a signless vague Immensity
Brooded, without approach, beyond response,
Condemning finite things to nothingness,
Fronting him with the incommensurable.
Then to the ascent there came a mighty term.
A height was reached where nothing made could live,
A line where every hope and search must cease
Neared some intolerant bare Reality,
A zero formed pregnant with boundless change.
On a dizzy verge where all disguises fail
And human mind must abdicate in Light
Or die like a moth in the naked blaze of Truth,
He stood compelled to a tremendous choice.

All he had been and all towards which he grew
Must now be left behind or else transform
Into a self of That which has no name.
Alone and fronting an intangible Force
Which offered nothing to the grasp of Thought,
His spirit faced the adventure of the Inane.
Abandoned by the worlds of Form he strove.
A fruitful world-wide Ignorance foundered here;
Thought's long far-circling journey touched its close
And ineffective paused the actor Will.
The symbol modes of being helped no more,
The structures Nescience builds collapsing failed,
And even the spirit that holds the universe
Fainted in luminous insufficiency.
In an abysmal lapse of all things built
Transcending every perishable support
And joining at last its mighty origin,
The separate self must melt or be reborn
Into a Truth beyond the mind's appeal.
All glory of outline, sweetness of harmony,
Rejected like a grace of trivial notes,
Expunged from Being's silence nude, austere,
Died into a fine and blissful Nothingness.
The Demiurges lost their names and forms,
The great schemed worlds that they had planned and wrought
Passed, taken and abolished one by one.
The universe removed its coloured veil,
And at the unimaginable end
Of the huge riddle of created things
Appeared the far-seen Godhead of the whole,
His feet firm-based on Life's stupendous wings,
Omnipotent, a lonely seer of Time,
Inward, inscrutable, with diamond gaze.
Attracted by the unfathomable regard
The unsolved slow cycles to their fount returned
To rise again from that invisible sea.

All from his puissance born was now undone;
Nothing remained the cosmic Mind conceives.
Eternity prepared to fade and seemed
A hue and imposition on the Void,
Space was the fluttering of a dream that sank
Before its ending into Nothing's deeps.
The spirit that dies not and the Godhead's self
Seemed myths projected from the Unknowable;
From It all sprang, in It is called to cease.
But what That was, no thought nor sight could tell.
Only a formless Form of self was left,
A tenuous ghost of something that had been,
The last experience of a lapsing wave
Before it sinks into a bourneless sea, —
As if it kept even on the brink of Nought
Its bare feeling of the ocean whence it came.
A Vastness brooded free from sense of Space,
An Everlastingness cut off from Time;
A strange sublime inalterable Peace
Silent rejected from it world and soul.
A stark companionless Reality
Answered at last to his soul's passionate search:
Passionless, wordless, absorbed in its fathomless hush,
Keeping the mystery none would ever pierce,
It brooded inscrutable and intangible
Facing him with its dumb tremendous calm.
It had no kinship with the universe:
There was no act, no movement in its Vast:
Life's question met by its silence died on her lips,
The world's effort ceased convicted of ignorance
Finding no sanction of supernal Light:
There was no mind there with its need to know,
There was no heart there with its need to love.
All person perished in its namelessness.
There was no second, it had no partner or peer;
Only itself was real to itself.

A pure existence safe from thought and mood,
A consciousness of unshared immortal bliss,
It dwelt aloof in its bare infinite,
One and unique, unutterably sole.
A Being formless, featureless and mute
That knew itself by its own timeless self,
Aware for ever in its motionless depths,
Uncreating, uncreated and unborn,
The One by whom all live, who lives by none,
An immeasurable luminous secrecy
Guarded by the veils of the Unmanifest,
Above the changing cosmic interlude
Abode supreme, immutably the same,
A silent Cause occult, impenetrable, —
Infinite, eternal, unthinkable, alone.

END OF CANTO ONE

Canto Two

The Adoration of the Divine Mother

A STILLNESS absolute, incommunicable,
Meets the sheer self-discovery of the soul;
A wall of stillness shuts it from the world,
A gulf of stillness swallows up the sense
And makes unreal all that mind has known,
All that the labouring senses still would weave
Prolonging an imaged unreality.
Self's vast spiritual silence occupies Space;
Only the Inconceivable is left,
Only the Nameless without space and time:
Abolished is the burdening need of life:
Thought falls from us, we cease from joy and grief;
The ego is dead; we are freed from being and care,
We have done with birth and death and work and fate.
O soul, it is too early to rejoice!
Thou hast reached the boundless silence of the Self,
Thou hast leaped into a glad divine abyss;
But where hast thou thrown Self's mission and Self's power?
On what dead bank on the Eternal's road?
One was within thee who was self and world,
What hast thou done for his purpose in the stars?
Escape brings not the victory and the crown!
Something thou cam'st to do from the Unknown,
But nothing is finished and the world goes on
Because only half God's cosmic work is done.
Only the everlasting No has neared
And stared into thy eyes and killed thy heart:
But where is the Lover's everlasting Yes,
And immortality in the secret heart,
The voice that chants to the creator Fire,
The symbolled OM, the great assenting Word,

The bridge between the rapture and the calm,
The passion and the beauty of the Bride,
The chamber where the glorious enemies kiss,
The smile that saves, the golden peak of things?
This too is Truth at the mystic fount of Life.
A black veil has been lifted; we have seen
The mighty shadow of the omniscient Lord;
But who has lifted up the veil of light
And who has seen the body of the King?
The mystery of God's birth and acts remains
Leaving unbroken the last chapter's seal,
Unsolved the riddle of the unfinished Play;
The cosmic Player laughs within his mask,
And still the last inviolate secret hides
Behind the human glory of a Form,
Behind the gold eidolon of a Name.
A large white line has figured as a goal,
But far beyond the ineffable suntracks blaze:
What seemed the source and end was a wide gate,
A last bare step into eternity.
An eye has opened upon timelessness,
Infinity takes back the forms it gave,
And through God's darkness or his naked light
His million rays return into the Sun.
There is a zero sign of the Supreme;
Nature left nude and still uncovers God.
But in her grandiose nothingness all is there:
When her strong garbs are torn away from us,
The soul's ignorance is slain but not the soul:
The zero covers an immortal face.
A high and blank negation is not all,
A huge extinction is not God's last word,
Life's ultimate sense, the close of being's course,
The meaning of this great mysterious world.
In absolute silence sleeps an absolute Power.
Awaking, it can wake the trance-bound soul

And in the ray reveal the parent sun:
It can make the world a vessel of Spirit's force,
It can fashion in the clay God's perfect shape.
To free the self is but one radiant pace;
Here to fulfil himself was God's desire.

        Even while he stood on being's naked edge
And all the passion and seeking of his soul
Faced their extinction in some featureless Vast,
The Presence he yearned for suddenly drew close.
Across the silence of the ultimate Calm,
Out of a marvellous Transcendence' core,
A body of wonder and translucency
As if a sweet mystic summary of her self
Escaping into the original Bliss
Had come enlarged out of eternity,
Someone came infinite and absolute.
A being of wisdom, power and delight,
Even as a mother draws her child to her arms,
Took to her breast Nature and world and soul.
Abolishing the signless emptiness,
Breaking the vacancy and voiceless hush,
Piercing the limitless Unknowable,
Into the liberty of the motionless depths
A beautiful and felicitous lustre stole.
The Power, the Light, the Bliss no word can speak
Imaged itself in a surprising beam
And built a golden passage to his heart
Touching through him all longing sentient things.
A moment's sweetness of the All-Beautiful
Cancelled the vanity of the cosmic whirl.
A Nature throbbing with a Heart divine
Was felt in the unconscious universe;
It made the breath a happy mystery.
A love that bore the cross of pain with joy
Eudaemonised the sorrow of the world,

Made happy the weight of long unending Time,
The secret caught of God's felicity.
Affirming in life a hidden ecstasy
It held the spirit to its miraculous course;
Carrying immortal values to the hours
It justified the labour of the suns.
For one was there supreme behind the God.
A Mother Might brooded upon the world;
A Consciousness revealed its marvellous front
Transcending all that is, denying none:
Imperishable above our fallen heads
He felt a rapturous and unstumbling Force.
The undying Truth appeared, the enduring Power
Of all that here is made and then destroyed,
The Mother of all godheads and all strengths
Who, mediatrix, binds earth to the Supreme.
The Enigma ceased that rules our nature's night,
The covering Nescience was unmasked and slain;
Its mind of error was stripped off from things
And the dull moods of its perverting will.
Illumined by her all-seeing identity
Knowledge and Ignorance could strive no more;
No longer could the titan Opposites,
Antagonist poles of the world's artifice,
Impose the illusion of their twofold screen
Throwing their figures between us and her.
The Wisdom was near, disguised by its own works,
Of which the darkened universe is the robe.
No more existence seemed an aimless fall,
Extinction was no more the sole release.
The hidden Word was found, the long-sought clue,
Revealed was the meaning of our spirit's birth,
Condemned to an imperfect body and mind,
In the inconscience of material things
And the indignity of mortal life.
A Heart was felt in the spaces wide and bare,

A burning Love from white spiritual founts
Annulled the sorrow of the ignorant depths;
Suffering was lost in her immortal smile.
A Life from beyond grew conqueror here of death;
To err no more was natural to mind;
Wrong could not come where all was light and love.
The Formless and the Formed were joined in her:
Immensity was exceeded by a look,
A Face revealed the crowded Infinite.
Incarnating inexpressibly in her limbs
The boundless joy the blind world-forces seek,
Her body of beauty mooned the seas of bliss.
At the head she stands of birth and toil and fate,
In their slow round the cycles turn to her call;
Alone her hands can change Time's dragon base.
Hers is the mystery the Night conceals;
The spirit's alchemist energy is hers;
She is the golden bridge, the wonderful fire.
The luminous heart of the Unknown is she,
A power of silence in the depths of God;
She is the Force, the inevitable Word,
The magnet of our difficult ascent,
The Sun from which we kindle all our suns,
The Light that leans from the unrealised Vasts,
The joy that beckons from the impossible,
The Might of all that never yet came down.
All Nature dumbly calls to her alone
To heal with her feet the aching throb of life
And break the seals on the dim soul of man
And kindle her fire in the closed heart of things.
All here shall be one day her sweetness' home,
All contraries prepare her harmony;
Towards her our knowledge climbs, our passion gropes;
In her miraculous rapture we shall dwell,
Her clasp shall turn to ecstasy our pain.
Our self shall be one self with all through her.

In her confirmed because transformed in her,
Our life shall find in its fulfilled response
Above, the boundless hushed beatitudes,
Below, the wonder of the embrace divine.
This known as in a thunder-flash of God,
The rapture of things eternal filled his limbs;
Amazement fell upon his ravished sense;
His spirit was caught in her intolerant flame.
Once seen, his heart acknowledged only her.
Only a hunger of infinite bliss was left.
All aims in her were lost, then found in her;
His base was gathered to one pointing spire.

This was a seed cast into endless Time.
A Word is spoken or a Light is shown,
A moment sees, the ages toil to express.
So flashing out of the Timeless leaped the worlds;
An eternal instant is the cause of the years.
All he had done was to prepare a field;
His small beginnings asked for a mighty end:
For all that he had been must now new-shape
In him her joy to embody, to enshrine
Her beauty and greatness in his house of life.
But now his being was too wide for self;
His heart's demand had grown immeasurable:
His single freedom could not satisfy,
Her light, her bliss he asked for earth and men.
But vain are human power and human love
To break earth's seal of ignorance and death;
His nature's might seemed now an infant's grasp;
Heaven is too high for outstretched hands to seize.
This Light comes not by struggle or by thought;
In the mind's silence the Transcendent acts
And the hushed heart hears the unuttered Word.
A vast surrender was his only strength.
A Power that lives upon the heights must act,

Bring into life's closed room the Immortal's air
And fill the finite with,the Infinite.
All that denies must be torn out and slain
And crushed the many longings for whose sake
We lose the One for whom our lives were made.
Now other claims had hushed in him their cry:
Only he longed to draw her presence and power
Into his heart and mind and breathing frame;
Only he yearned to call for ever down
Her healing touch of love and truth and joy
Into the darkness of the suffering world.
His soul was freed and given to her alone.

END OF CANTO TWO

Canto Three

The House of the Spirit and the New Creation

A MIGHTIER task remained than all he had done.
To That he turned from which all being comes,
A sign attending from the Secrecy
Which knows the Truth ungrasped behind our thoughts
And guards the world with its all-seeing gaze.
In the unapproachable stillness of his soul,
Intense, one-pointed, monumental, lone,
Patient he sat like an incarnate hope
Motionless on a pedestal of prayer.
A strength he sought that was not yet on earth,
Help from a Power too great for mortal will,
The light of a Truth now only seen afar,
A sanction from his high omnipotent Source.
But from the appalling heights there stooped no voice;
The timeless lids were closed; no opening came.
A neutral helpless void oppressed the years.
In the texture of our bound humanity
He felt the stark resistance huge and dumb
Of our inconscient and unseeing base,
The stubborn mute rejection in life's depths,
The ignorant No in the origin of things.
A veiled collaboration with the Night
Even in himself survived and hid from his view:
Still something in his earthly being kept
Its kinship with the Inconscient whence it came.
A shadowy unity with a vanished past
Treasured in an old-world frame was lurking there,
Secret, unnoted by the illumined mind,
And in subconscious whispers and in dream
Still murmured at the mind's and spirit's choice.
Its treacherous elements spread like slippery grains

Hoping the incoming Truth might stumble and fall,
And old ideal voices wandering moaned
And pleaded for a heavenly leniency
To the gracious imperfections of our earth
And the sweet weaknesses of our mortal state.
This now he willed to discover and exile,
The element in him betraying God.
All Nature's recondite spaces were stripped bare,
All her dim crypts and corners searched with fire
Where refugee instincts and unshaped revolts
Could shelter find in darkness' sanctuary
Against the white purity of heaven's cleansing flame.
All seemed to have perished that was undivine:
Yet some minutest dissident might escape
And still a centre lurk of the blind force.
For the Inconscient too is infinite;
The more its abysses we insist to sound,
The more it stretches, stretches endlessly.
Then lest a human cry should spoil the Truth
He tore desire up from its bleeding roots
And offered to the gods the vacant place.
Thus could he bear the touch immaculate.
A last and mightiest transformation came.
His soul was all in front like a great sea
Flooding the mind and body with its waves;
His being, spread to embrace the universe,
United the within and the without
To make of life a cosmic harmony,
An empire of the immanent Divine.
In this tremendous universality
Not only his soul-nature and mind-sense
Included every soul and mind in his,
But even the life of flesh and nerve was changed
And grew one flesh and nerve with all that lives;
He felt the joy of others as his joy,
He bore the grief of others as his grief;

His universal sympathy upbore,
Immense like ocean, the creation's load
As earth upbears all beings' sacrifice,
Thrilled with the hidden Transcendent's joy and peace.
There was no more division's endless scroll;
One grew the Spirit's secret unity,
All Nature felt again the single bliss.
There was no cleavage between soul and soul,
There was no barrier between world and God.
Overpowered were form and memory's limiting line;
The covering mind was seized and torn apart;
It was dissolved and now no more could be,
The one Consciousness that made the world was seen;
All now was luminosity and force.
Abolished in its last thin fainting trace
The circle of the little self was gone;
The separate being could no more be felt;
It disappeared and knew itself no more,
Lost in the spirit's wide identity.
His nature grew a movement of the All,
Exploring itself to find that all was He,
His soul was a delegation of the All
That turned from itself to join the one Supreme.
Transcended was the human formula;
Man's heart that had obscured the Inviolable
Assumed the mighty beating of a god's;
His seeking mind ceased in the Truth that knows;
His life was a flow of the universal life.
He stood fulfilled on the world's highest line
Awaiting the ascent beyond the world,
Awaiting the descent the world to save.
A Splendour and a Symbol wrapped the earth,
Serene epiphanies looked and hallowed vasts
Surrounded, wise infinitudes were close
And bright remotenesses leaned near and kin.
Sense failed in that tremendous lucency;

Ephemeral voices from his hearing fell
And Thought potent no more sank large and pale
Like a tired god into mysterious seas.
The robes of mortal thinking were cast down
Leaving his knowledge bare to absolute sight;
Fate's driving ceased and Nature's sleepless spur:
The athlete heavings of the will were stilled
In the Omnipotent's unmoving peace.
Life in his members lay down vast and mute;
Naked, unwalled, unterrified it bore
The immense regard of Immortality.
The last movement died and all at once grew still.
A weight that was the unseen Transcendent's hand
Laid on his limbs the Spirit's measureless seal,
Infinity swallowed him into shoreless trance.

As one who sets his sail towards mysteried shores
Driven through huge oceans by the breath of God,
The fathomless below, the unknown around,
His soul abandoned the blind star-field, Space.
Afar from all that makes the measured world,
Plunging to hidden eternities it withdrew
Back from mind's foaming surface to the Vasts
Voiceless within us in omniscient sleep.
Above the imperfect reach of word and thought,
Beyond the sight that seeks support of form,
Lost in deep tracts of superconscient Light,
Or voyaging in blank featureless Nothingness,
Sole in the trackless Incommensurable,
Or past not-self and self and selflessness,
Transgressing the dream-shores of conscious mind
He reached at last his sempiternal base.
On sorrowless heights no winging cry disturbs,
Pure and untouched above this mortal play
Is spread the spirit's hushed immobile air.
There no beginning is and there no end;

There is the stable force of all that moves;
There the aeonic labourer is at rest.
There turns no keyed creation in the void,
No giant mechanism watched by a soul;
There creaks no fate-turned huge machinery;
The marriage of evil with good within one breast,
The clash of strife in the very clasp of love,
The dangerous pain of life's experiment
In the values of Inconsequence and Chance,
The peril of mind's gamble, throwing our lives
As stake in a wager of indifferent gods
And the shifting lights and shadows of the idea
Falling upon the surface consciousness,
And in the dream of a mute witness soul
Creating the error of a half-seen world
Where knowledge is a seeking ignorance,
Life's steps a stumbling series without suit,
Its aspect of fortuitous design,
Its equal measure of the true and false
In that immobile and immutable realm
Find no access, no cause, no right to live:
There only reigns the spirit's motionless power
Poised in itself through still eternity
And its omniscient and omnipotent peace.
Thought clashes not with thought and truth with truth,
There is no war of right with rival right;
There are no stumbling and half-seeing lives
Passing from chance to unexpected chance,
No suffering of hearts compelled to beat
In bodies of the inert Inconscient's make.
Armed with the immune occult unsinking Fire
The guardians of Eternity keep its law
For ever fixed upon Truth's giant base
In her magnificent and termless home.
There Nature on her dumb spiritual couch
Immutably transcendent knows her source

And to the stir of multitudinous worlds
Assents unmoved in a perpetual calm.
All-causing, all-sustaining and aloof,
The Witness looks from his unshaken poise,
An Eye immense regarding all things done.
Apart, at peace above creation's stir,
Immersed in the eternal altitudes,
He abode defended in his shoreless self,
Companioned only by the all-seeing One.
A Mind too mighty to be bound by Thought,
A Life too boundless for the play in Space,
A Soul without borders unconvinced of Time,
He felt the extinction of the world's long pain,
He became the unborn Self that never dies,
He joined the sessions of Infinity.
On the cosmic murmur primal loneliness fell,
Annulled was the contact formed with time-born things,
Empty grew Nature's wide community.
All things were brought back to their formless seed,
The world was silent for a cyclic hour.
Although the afflicted Nature he had left
Maintained beneath him her broad numberless fields,
Her enormous act, receding, failed remote
As if a soulless dream at last had ceased.
No voice came down from the high Silences,
None answered from her desolate solitudes.
A stillness of cessation reigned, the wide
Immortal hush before the gods are born;
A universal Force awaited, mute,
The veiled Transcendent's ultimate decree.

Then suddenly there came a downward look.
As if a sea exploring its own depths,
A living Oneness widened at its core
And joined him to unnumbered multitudes.
A Bliss, a Light, a Power, a flame-white Love

Caught all into a sole immense embrace;
Existence found its truth on Oneness' breast
And each became the self and space of all.
The great world-rhythms were heart-beats of one Soul,
To feel was a flame-discovery of God,
All mind was a single harp of many strings,
All life a song of many meeting lives;
For worlds were many, but the Self was one.
This knowledge now was made a cosmos' seed:
This seed was cased in the safety of the Light,
It needed not a sheath of Ignorance.
Then from the trance of that tremendous clasp
And from the throbbings of that single Heart
And from the naked Spirit's victory
A new and marvellous creation rose.
Incalculable outflowing infinitudes
Laughing out an unmeasured happiness
Lived their innumerable unity;
Worlds where the being is unbound and wide
Bodied unthinkably the egoless Self;
Rapture of beatific energies
Joined Time to the Timeless, poles of a single joy;
White vasts were seen where all is wrapped in all.
There were no contraries, no sundered parts,
All by spiritual links were joined to all
And bound indissolubly to the One:
Each was unique, but took all lives as his own,
And, following out these tones of the Infinite,
Recognised in himself the universe.
A splendid centre of infinity's whirl
Pushed to its zenith's height, its last expanse,
Felt the divinity of its own self-bliss
Repeated in its numberless other selves:
It took up tirelessly into its scope
Persons and figures of the Impersonal,
As if prolonging in a ceaseless count,

In a rapturous multiplication's sum,
The recurring decimals of eternity.
None was apart, none lived for himself alone,
Each lived for God in him and God in all,
Each soleness inexpressibly held the whole.
There Oneness was not tied to monotone;
It showed a thousand aspects of itself,
Its calm immutable stability
Upbore on a changeless ground for ever safe,
Compelled to a spontaneous servitude,
The ever-changing incalculable steps,
The seeming-reckless dance's subtle plan
Of immense world-forces in their perfect play.
Appearance looked back to its hidden truth
And made of difference oneness' smiling play;
It made all persons fractions of the Unique,
Yet all were being's secret integers.
All struggle was turned to a sweet strife of love
In the harmonised circle of a sure embrace.
Identity's reconciling happiness gave
A rich security to difference.
On a meeting line of hazardous extremes
The game of games was played to its breaking-point,
Where through self-finding by divine self-loss
There leaps out unity's supreme delight
Whose blissful undivided sweetness feels
A communality of the Absolute.
There was no sob of suffering anywhere;
Experience ran from point to point of joy:
Bliss was the pure undying truth of things.
All Nature was a conscious front of God:
A wisdom worked in all, self-moved, self-sure,
A plenitude of illimitable Light,
An authenticity of intuitive Truth,
A glory and passion of creative Force.
Infallible, leaping from eternity,

The moment's thought inspired the passing act.
A word, a laughter, sprang from Silence' breast,
A rhythm of Beauty in the calm of Space,
A knowledge in the fathomless heart of Time.
All turned to all without reserve's recoil:
A single ecstasy without a break,
Love was a close and thrilled identity
In the throbbing heart of all that luminous life.
A universal vision that unites,
A sympathy of nerve replying to nerve,
Hearing that listens to thought's inner sound
And follows the rhythmic meanings of the heart,
A touch that needs not hands to feel, to clasp,
Were there the native means of consciousness
And heightened the intimacy of soul with soul.
A grand orchestra of spiritual powers,
A diapason of soul-interchange
Harmonised a Oneness deep, immeasurable.
In these new worlds projected he became
A portion of the universal gaze,
A station of the all-inhabiting light,
A ripple on a single sea of peace.
His mind answered to countless communing minds,
His words were syllables of the cosmos' speech,
His life a field of the vast cosmic stir.
He felt the footsteps of a million wills
Moving in unison to a single goal.
A stream ever new-born that never dies,
Caught in its thousandfold current's ravishing flow,
With eddies of immortal sweetness thrilled,
He bore coiling through his members as they passed
Calm movements of interminable delight,
The bliss of a myriad myriads who are one.

    In this vast outbreak of perfection's law
Imposing its fixity on the flux of things

He saw a hierarchy of lucent planes
Enfeoffed to this highest kingdom of God-state.
Attuning to one Truth their own right rule
Each housed the gladness of a bright degree,
Alone in beauty, perfect in self-kind,
An image cast by one deep truth's absolute,
Married to all in happy difference.
Each gave its powers to help its neighbours' parts,
But suffered no diminution by the gift;
Profiteers of a mystic interchange,
They grew by what they took and what they gave,
All others they felt as their own complements,
One in the might and joy of multitude.
Even in the poise where Oneness draws apart
To feel the rapture of its separate selves,
The Sole in its solitude yearned towards the All
And the Many turned to look back at the One.
An all-revealing all-creating Bliss,
Seeking for forms to manifest truths divine,
Aligned in their significant mystery
The gleams of the symbols of the Ineffable
Blazoned like hues upon a colourless air
On the white purity of the Witness Soul.
These hues were the very prism of the Supreme,
His beauty, power, delight creation's cause.
A vast Truth-Consciousness took up these signs
To pass them on to some divine child Heart
That looked on them with laughter and delight
And joyed in these transcendent images
Living and real as the truths they house.
The Spirit's white neutrality became
A playground of miracles, a rendezvous
For the secret powers of a mystic Timelessness:
It made of Space a marvel house of God,
It poured through Time its works of ageless might,
Unveiled seen as a luring rapturous face

The wonder and beauty of its Love and Force.
The eternal Goddess moved in her cosmic house
Sporting with God as a Mother with her child:
To him the universe was her bosom of love,
His toys were the immortal verities.
All here self-lost had there its divine place.
The Powers that here betray our hearts and err,
Were there sovereign in truth, perfect in joy,
Masters in a creation without flaw,
Possessors of their own infinitude.
There Mind, a splendid sun of vision's rays,
Shaped substance by the glory of its thoughts
And moved amidst the grandeur of its dreams.
Imagination's great ensorcelling rod
Summoned the unknown and gave to it a home,
Outspread luxuriantly in golden air
Truth's iris-coloured wings of fantasy,
Or sang to the intuitive heart of joy
Wonder's dream-notes that bring the Real close.
Its power that makes the unknowable near and true,
In the temple of the ideal shrined the One:
It peopled thought and mind and happy sense
Filled with bright aspects of the might of God
And living persons of the one Supreme,
The speech that voices the ineffable,
The ray revealing unseen Presences,
The virgin forms through which the Formless shines,
The Word that ushers divine experience
And the Ideas that crowd the Infinite.
There was no gulf between the thought and fact,
Ever they replied like bird to calling bird;
The will obeyed the thought, the act the will.
There was a harmony woven twixt soul and soul.
A marriage with eternity divinised Time.
There Life pursued, unwearied of her sport,
Joy in her heart and laughter on her lips,

The bright adventure of God's game of chance.
In her ingenious ardour of caprice,
In her transfiguring mirth she mapped on Time
A fascinating puzzle of events,
Lured at each turn by new vicissitudes
To self-discovery that could never cease.
Ever she framed stark bonds for the will to break,
Brought new creations for the thought's surprise
And passionate ventures for the heart to dare,
Where Truth recurred with an unexpected face
Or else repeated old familiar joy
Like the return of a delightful rhyme.
At hide-and-seek on a Mother-Wisdom's breast,
An artist teeming with her world-idea,
She never could exhaust its numberless thoughts
And vast adventure into thinking shapes
And trial and lure of a new living's dreams.
Untired of sameness and untired of change,
Endlessly she unrolled her moving act,
A mystery drama of divine delight,
A living poem of world-ecstasy,
A kakemono of significant forms,
A coiled perspective of developing scenes,
A brilliant chase of self-revealing shapes,
An ardent hunt of soul looking for soul,
A seeking and a finding as of gods.
There Matter is the Spirit's firm density,
An artistry of glad outwardness of self,
A treasure-house of lasting images
Where sense can build a world of pure delight:
The home of a perpetual happiness,
It lodged the hours as in a pleasant inn.
The senses there were outlets of the soul;
Even the youngest child-thought of the mind
Incarnated some touch of highest things.
There substance was a resonant harp of self,

A net for the constant lightnings of the spirit,
A magnet power of love's intensity
Whose yearning throb and adoration's cry
Drew God's approaches close, sweet, wonderful.
Its solidity was a mass of heavenly make;
Its fixity and sweet permanence of charm
Made a bright pedestal for felicity.
Its bodies woven by a divine sense
Prolonged the nearness of soul's clasp with soul;
Its warm play of external sight and touch
Reflected the glow and thrill of the heart's joy,
Mind's climbing brilliant thoughts, the spirit's bliss;
Life's rapture kept for ever its flame and cry.
All that now passes lived immortal there
In the proud beauty and fine harmony
Of Matter plastic to spiritual light.
Its ordered hours proclaimed the eternal Law;
Vision reposed on a safety of deathless forms;
Time was Eternity's transparent robe.
An architect hewing out self's living rock,
Phenomenon built Reality's summer-house
On the beaches of the sea of Infinity.

   Against this glory of spiritual states,
Their parallels and yet their opposites,
Floated and swayed, eclipsed and shadowlike
As if a doubt made substance, flickering, pale,
This other scheme two vast negations found.
A world that knows not its inhabiting Self
Labours to find its cause and need to be;
A spirit ignorant of the world it made,
Obscured by Matter, travestied by Life,
Struggles to emerge, to be free, to know and reign;
These were close-tied in one disharmony,
Yet the divergent lines met not at all.
Three Powers governed its irrational course,

In the beginning an unknowing Force,
In the middle an embodied striving soul,
In its end a silent spirit denying life.
A dull and infelicitous interlude
Unrolls its dubious truth to a questioning Mind
Compelled by the ignorant Power to play its part
And to record her inconclusive tale,
The mystery of her inconscient plan
And the riddle of a being born from Night
By a marriage of Necessity with Chance.
This darkness hides our nobler destiny.
A chrysalis of a great and glorious truth,
It stifles the winged marvel in its sheath
Lest from the prison of Matter it escape
And, wasting its beauty on the formless Vast,
Merged into the Unknowable's mystery,
Leave unfulfilled the world's miraculous fate.
As yet thought only some high spirit's dream
Or a vexed illusion in man's toiling mind,
A new creation from the old shall rise,
A Knowledge inarticulate find speech,
Beauty suppressed burst into paradise bloom,
Pleasure and pain dive into absolute bliss.
A tongueless oracle shall speak at last,
The Superconscient conscious grow on earth,
The Eternal's wonders join the dance of Time.
But now all seemed a vainly teeming vast
Upheld by a deluded Energy
To a spectator self-absorbed and mute,
Careless of the unmeaning show he watched,
Regarding the bizarre procession pass
Like one who waits for an expected end.
He saw a world that is from a world to be.
There he divined rather than saw or felt,
Far off upon the rim of consciousness,
Transient and frail this little whirling globe

And on it left like a lost dream's vain mould,
A fragile copy of the spirit's shell,
His body gathered into mystic sleep.
A foreign shape it seemed, a mythic shade.

Alien now seemed that dim far universe,
Self and eternity alone were true.
Then memory climbed to him from the striving planes
Bringing a cry from once-loved cherished things,
And to the cry as to its own lost call
A ray replied from the occult Supreme.
For even there the boundless Oneness dwells.
To its own sight unrecognisable,
It lived still sunk in its own tenebrous seas,
Upholding the world's inconscient unity
Hidden in Matter's insentient multitude.
This seed-self sown in the Indeterminate
Forfeits its glory of divinity,
Concealing the omnipotence of its Force,
Concealing the omniscience of its Soul;
An agent of its own transcendent Will,
It merges knowledge in the inconscient deep;
Accepting error, sorrow, death and pain,
It pays the ransom of the ignorant Night,
Redeeming by its substance Nature's fall.
Himself he knew and why his soul had gone
Into earth's passionate obscurity
To share the labour of an errant Power
Which by division hopes to find the One.
Two beings he was, one wide and free above,
One struggling, bound, intense, its portion here.
A tie between them still could bridge two worlds;
There was a dim response, a distant breath;
All had not ceased in the unbounded hush.
His heart lay somewhere conscious and alone
Far down below him like a lamp in night;

Abandoned it lay, alone, imperishable,
Immobile with excess of passionate will,
His living, sacrificed and offered heart
Absorbed in adoration mystical,
Turned to its far-off fount of light and love.
In the luminous stillness of its mute appeal
It looked up to the heights it could not see;
It yearned from the longing depths it could not leave.
In the centre of his vast and fateful trance
Half-way between his free and fallen selves,
Interceding twixt God's day and the mortal's night,
Accepting worship as its single law,
Accepting bliss as the sole cause of things,
Refusing the austere joy which none can share,
Refusing the calm that lives for calm alone,
To her it turned for whom it willed to be.
In the passion of its solitary dream
It lay like a closed soundless oratory
Where sleeps a consecrated argent floor
Lit by a single and untrembling ray
And an invisible Presence kneels in prayer.
On some deep breast of liberating peace
All else was satisfied with quietude;
This only knew there was a truth beyond.
All other parts were dumb in centred sleep
Consenting to the slow deliberate Power
Which tolerates the world's error and its grief,
Consenting to the cosmic long delay,
Timelessly waiting through the patient years
Her coming they had asked for earth and men;
This was the fiery point that called her now.
Extinction could not quench that lonely fire;
Its seeing filled the blank of mind and will;
Thought dead, its changeless force abode and grew.
Armed with the intuition of a bliss
To which some moved tranquillity was the key,

It persevered through life's huge emptiness
Amid the blank denials of the world.
It sent its voiceless prayer to the Unknown;
It listened for the footsteps of its hopes
Returning through the void immensities,
It waited for the fiat of the Word
That comes through the still self from the Supreme.

END OF CANTO THREE

The Vision and the Boon

THEN suddenly there rose a sacred stir.
Amid the lifeless silence of the Void
In a solitude and an immensity
A sound came quivering like a loved footfall
Heard in the listening spaces of the soul;
A touch perturbed his fibres with delight.
An Influence had approached the mortal range,
A boundless Heart was near his longing heart,
A mystic Form enveloped his earthly shape.
All at her contact broke from silence' seal;
Spirit and body thrilled identified,
Linked in the grasp of an unspoken joy;
Mind, members, life were merged in ecstasy.
Intoxicated as with nectarous rain
His nature's passioning stretches flowed to her,
Flashing with lightnings, mad with luminous wine.
All was a limitless sea that heaved to the moon.
A divinising stream possessed his veins,
His body's cells awoke to spirit sense,
Each nerve became a burning thread of joy:
Tissue and flesh partook beatitude.
Alight, the dun unplumbed subconscient caves
Thrilled with the prescience of her longed-for tread
And filled with flickering crests and praying tongues.
Even lost in slumber, mute, inanimate
His very body answered to her power.
The One he worshipped was within him now:
Flame-pure, ethereal-tressed, a mighty Face
Appeared and lips moved by immortal words;
Lids, Wisdom's leaves, drooped over rapture's orbs.
A marble monument of ponderings, shone

A forehead, sight's crypt, and large like ocean's gaze
Towards Heaven, two tranquil eyes of boundless thought
Looked into man's and saw the god to come.
A Shape was seen on threshold Mind, a Voice
Absolute and wise in the heart's chambers spoke:
"O Son of Strength who climbst creation's peaks,
No soul is thy companion in the light;
Alone thou standest at the eternal doors.
What thou hast won is thine, but ask no more.
O Spirit aspiring in an ignorant frame,
O Voice arisen from the Inconscient's world,
How shalt thou speak for men whose hearts are dumb,
Make purblind earth the soul's seer-vision's home
Or lighten the burden of the senseless globe?
I am the Mystery beyond reach of mind,
I am the goal of the travail of the suns;
My fire and sweetness are the cause of life.
But too immense my danger and my joy.
Awake not the immeasurable descent,
Speak not my secret name to hostile Time;
Man is too weak to bear the Infinite's weight.
Truth born too soon might break the imperfect earth.
Leave the all-seeing Power to hew its way:
In thy single vast achievement reign apart
Helping the world with thy great lonely days.
I ask thee not to merge thy heart of flame
In the Immobile's wide uncaring bliss,
Turned from the fruitless motion of the years,
Deserting the fierce labour of the worlds,
Aloof from beings, lost in the Alone.
How shall thy mighty spirit brook repose
While Death is still unconquered on the earth
And Time a field of suffering and pain?
Thy soul was born to share the laden Force;
Obey thy nature and fulfil thy fate:
Accept the difficulty and godlike toil,

For the slow-paced omniscient purpose live.
The Enigma's knot is tied in humankind.
A lightning from the heights that think and plan,
Ploughing the air of life with vanishing trails,
Man, sole awake in an unconscious world,
Aspires in vain to change the cosmic dream.
Arrived from some half-luminous Beyond
He is a stranger in the mindless vasts;
A traveller in his oft-shifting home
Amid the tread of many infinities,
He has pitched a tent of life in desert Space.
Heaven's fixed regard beholds him from above,
In the house of Nature a perturbing guest,
A voyager twixt Thought's inconstant shores,
A hunter of unknown and beautiful Powers,
A nomad of the far mysterious Light,
In the wide ways a little spark of God.
Against his spirit all is in dire league,
A Titan influence stops his Godward gaze.
Around him hungers the unpitying Void,
The eternal Darkness seeks him with her hands,
Inscrutable Energies drive him and deceive,
Immense implacable deities oppose.
An inert Soul and a somnambulist Force
Have made a world estranged from life and thought;
The Dragon of the dark foundations keeps
Unalterable the law of Chance and Death;
On his long way through Time and Circumstance
The grey-hued riddling nether shadow-Sphinx,
Her dreadful paws upon the swallowing sands,
Awaits him armed with the soul-slaying word:
Across his path sits the dim camp of Night.
His day is a moment in perpetual Time;
He is the prey of the minutes and the hours.
Assailed on earth and unassured of heaven,
Descended here unhappy and sublime,

A link between the demigod and the beast,
He knows not his own greatness nor his aim;
He has forgotten why he has come and whence.
His spirit and his members are at war;
His heights break off too low to reach the skies,
His mass is buried in the animal mire.
A strange antinomy is his nature's rule.
A riddle of opposites is made his field:
Freedom he asks but needs to live in bonds,
He has need of darkness to perceive some light
And need of grief to feel a little bliss;
He has need of death to find a greater life.
All sides he sees and turns to every call;
He has no certain light by which to walk;
His life is a blind-man's-buff, a hide-and-seek;
He seeks himself and from himself he runs;
Meeting himself, he thinks it other than he.
Always he builds, but finds no constant ground,
Always he journeys, but nowhere arrives;
He would guide the world, himself he cannot guide;
He would save his soul, his life he cannot save.
The light his soul had brought his mind has lost;
All he has learned is soon again in doubt;
A sun to him seems the shadow of his thoughts,
Then all is shadow again and nothing true:
Unknowing what he does or whither he tends
He fabricates signs of the Real in Ignorance.
He has hitched his mortal error to Truth's star.
Wisdom attracts him with her luminous masks,
But never has he seen the face behind:
A giant Ignorance surrounds his lore.
Assigned to meet the cosmic mystery
In the dumb figure of a material world,
His passport of entry false and his personage,
He is compelled to be what he is not;
He obeys the Inconscience he had come to rule

And sinks in Matter to fulfil his soul.
Awakened from her lower driven forms
The Earth-Mother gave her forces to his hands
And painfully he guards the heavy trust;
His mind is a lost torch-bearer on her roads.
Illumining breath to think and plasm to feel,
He labours with his slow and sceptic brain
Helped by the reason's vacillating fires,
To make his thought and will a magic door
For knowledge to enter the darkness of the world
And love to rule a realm of strife and hate.
A mind impotent to reconcile heaven and earth
And tied to Matter with a thousand bonds,
He lifts himself to be a conscious god.
Even when a glory of wisdom crowns his brow,
When mind and spirit shed a grandiose ray
To exalt this product of the sperm and gene,
This alchemist's miracle from plasm and gas,
And he who shared the animal's run and crawl
Lifts his thought-stature to the Immortal's heights,
His life still keeps the human middle way;
His body he resigns to death and pain,
Abandoning Matter, his too heavy charge.
A thaumaturge sceptic of miracles,
A spirit left sterile of its occult power
By an unbelieving brain and credulous heart,
He leaves the world to end where it began:
His work unfinished he claims a heavenly prize.
Thus has he missed creation's absolute.
Half-way he stops his star of destiny:
A vast and vain long-tried experiment,
An ill-served high conception doubtfully done,
The world's life falters on not seeing its goal, —
A zigzag towards unknown dangerous ground
Ever repeating its habitual walk,
Ever retreating after marches long

And hardiest victories without sure result,
Drawn endlessly an inconclusive game.
In an ill-fitting and voluminous robe
A radiant purpose still conceals its face,
A mighty blindness stumbles hoping on,
Feeding its strength on gifts of luminous Chance.
Because the human instrument has failed,
The Godhead frustrate sleeps within its seed,
A spirit entangled in the forms it made.
His failure is not failure whom God leads;
Through all the slow mysterious march goes on:
An immutable Power has made this mutable world;
A self-fulfilling transcendence treads man's road;
The driver of the soul upon its path,
It knows its steps, its way is inevitable,
And how shall the end be vain when God is guide?
However man's mind may tire or fail his flesh,
A will prevails cancelling his conscious choice:
The goal recedes, a bourneless vastness calls
Retreating into an immense Unknown;
There is no end to the world's stupendous march,
There is no rest for the embodied soul.
It must live on, describe all Time's huge curve.
An Influx presses from the closed Beyond
Forbidding to him rest and earthly ease,
Till he has found himself he cannot pause.
A Light there is that leads, a Power that aids;
Unmarked, unfelt it sees in him and acts:
Ignorant, he forms the All-Conscient in his depths,
Human, looks up to superhuman peaks:
A borrower of Supernature's gold,
He paves his road to Immortality.
The high gods look on man and watch and choose
Today's impossibles for the future's base.
His transience trembles with the Eternal's touch,
His barriers cede beneath the Infinite's tread;

The Immortals have their entries in his life:
The Ambassadors of the Unseen draw near.
A splendour sullied by the mortal air,
Love passes through his heart, a wandering guest.
Beauty surrounds him for a magic hour,
He has visits of a large revealing joy,
Brief widenesses release him from himself,
Enticing towards a glory ever in front
Hopes of a deathless sweetness lure and leave.
His mind is crossed by strange discovering fires,
Rare intimations lift his stumbling speech
To a moment's kinship with the eternal Word;
A masque of Wisdom circles through his brain
Perturbing him with glimpses half divine.
He lays his hands sometimes on the Unknown;
He communes sometimes with Eternity.
A strange and grandiose symbol was his birth
And immortality and spirit-room
And pure perfection and a shadowless bliss
Are this afflicted creature's mighty fate.
In him the Earth-Mother sees draw near the change
Foreshadowed in her dumb and fiery depths,
A godhead drawn from her transmuted limbs,
An alchemy of Heaven on Nature's base.
Adept of the self-born unfailing line,
Leave not the light to die the ages bore,
Help still humanity's blind and suffering life:
Obey thy spirit's wide omnipotent urge.
A witness to God's parley with the Night,
It leaned compassionate from immortal calm
And housed desire, the troubled seed of things.
Assent to thy high self, create, endure.
Cease not from knowledge, let thy toil be vast.
No more can earthly limits pen thy force;
Equal thy work with long unending Time's.
Traveller upon the bare eternal heights,

Tread still the difficult and dateless path
Joining the cycles with its austere curve
Measured for man by the initiate Gods.
My light shall be in thee, my strength thy force.
Let not the impatient Titan drive thy heart,
Ask not the imperfect fruit, the partial prize.
Only one boon, to greaten thy spirit, demand;
Only one joy, to raise thy kind, desire.
Above blind fate and the antagonist powers
Moveless there stands a high unchanging Will;
To its omnipotence leave thy work's result.
All things shall change in God's transfiguring hour."

August and sweet sank hushed that mighty Voice.
Nothing now moved in the vast brooding space:
A stillness came upon the listening world,
A mute immensity of the Eternal's peace.
But Aswapati's heart replied to her,
A cry amid the silence of the Vasts:
"How shall I rest content with mortal days
And the dull measure of terrestrial things,
I who have seen behind the cosmic mask
The glory and the beauty of thy face?
Hard is the doom to which thou bindst thy sons!
How long shall our spirits battle with the Night
And bear defeat and the brute yoke of Death,
We who are vessels of a deathless Force
And builders of the godhead of the race?
Or if it is thy work I do below
Amid the error and waste of human life
In the vague light of man's half-conscious mind,
Why breaks not in some distant gleam of thee?
Ever the centuries and millenniums pass.
Where in the greyness is thy coming's ray?
Where is the thunder of thy victory's wings?
Only we hear the feet of passing gods.

A plan in the occult eternal Mind
Mapped out to backward and prophetic sight,
The aeons ever repeat their changeless round,
The cycles all rebuild and ever aspire.
All we have done is ever still to do.
All breaks and all renews and is the same.
Huge revolutions of life's fruitless gyre,
The new-born ages perish like the old,
As if the sad Enigma kept its right
Till all is done for which this scene was made.
Too little the strength that now with us is born,
Too faint the light that steals through Nature's lids,
Too scant the joy with which she buys our pain.
In a brute world that knows not its own sense,
Thought-racked upon the wheel of birth we live,
The instruments of an impulse not our own
Moved to achieve with our heart's blood for price
Half-knowledge, half-creations that soon tire.
A foiled immortal soul in perishing limbs,
Baffled and beaten back we labour still;
Annulled, frustrated, spent, we still survive.
In anguish we labour that from us may rise
A larger-seeing man with nobler heart,
A golden vessel of the incarnate Truth,
The executor of the divine attempt
Equipped to wear the earthly body of God,
Communicant and prophet and lover and king.
I know that thy creation cannot fail:
For even through the mists of mortal thought
Infallible are thy mysterious steps,
And, though Necessity dons the garb of Chance,
Hidden in the blind shifts of Fate she keeps
The slow calm logic of Infinity's pace
And the inviolate sequence of its will.
All life is fixed in an ascending scale
And adamantine is the evolving Law;

In the beginning is prepared the close.
This strange irrational product of the mire,
This compromise between the beast and god,
Is not the crown of thy miraculous world.
I know there shall inform the inconscient cells,
At one with Nature and at height with heaven,
A spirit vast as the containing sky
And swept with ecstasy from invisible founts,
A god come down and greater by the fall.
A Power arose out of my slumber's cell.
Abandoning the tardy limp of the hours
And the inconstant blink of mortal sight,
There where the Thinker sleeps in too much light
And intolerant flames the lone all-witnessing Eye
Hearing the word of Fate from Silence' heart
In the endless moment of Eternity,
It saw from timelessness the works of Time.
Overpassed were the leaden formulas of the Mind,
Overpowered the obstacle of mortal Space:
The unfolding Image showed the things to come.
A giant dance of Shiva tore the past;
There was a thunder as of worlds that fall;
Earth was o'errun with fire and the roar of Death
Clamouring to slay a world his hunger had made;
There was a clangour of Destruction's wings:
The Titan's battle-cry was in my ears,
Alarm and rumour shook the armoured Night.
I saw the Omnipotent's flaming pioneers
Over the heavenly verge which turns towards life
Come crowding down the amber stairs of birth;
Forerunners of a divine multitude,
Out of the paths of the morning star they came
Into the little room of mortal life.
I saw them cross the twilight of an age,
The sun-eyed children of a marvellous dawn,
The great creators with wide brows of calm,

The massive barrier-breakers of the world
And wrestlers with destiny in her lists of will,
The labourers in the quarries of the gods,
The messengers of the Incommunicable,
The architects of immortality.
Into the fallen human sphere they came,
Faces that wore the Immortal's glory still,
Voices that communed still with the thoughts of God,
Bodies made beautiful by the spirit's light,
Carrying the magic word, the mystic fire,
Carrying the Dionysian cup of joy,
Approaching eyes of a diviner man,
Lips chanting an unknown anthem of the soul,
Feet echoing in the corridors of Time.
High priests of wisdom, sweetness, might and bliss,
Discoverers of beauty's sunlit ways
And swimmers of Love's laughing fiery floods
And dancers within rapture's golden doors,
Their tread one day shall change the suffering earth
And justify the light on Nature's face.
Although Fate lingers in the high Beyond
And the work seems vain on which our heart's force was spent,
All shall be done for which our pain was borne.
Even as of old man came behind the beast
This high divine successor surely shall come
Behind man's inefficient mortal pace,
Behind his vain labour, sweat and blood and tears:
He shall know what mortal mind barely durst think,
He shall do what the heart of the mortal could not dare.
Inheritor of the toil of human time,
He shall take on him the burden of the gods;
All heavenly light shall visit the earth's thoughts,
The might of heaven shall fortify earthly hearts;
Earth's deeds shall touch the superhuman's height,
Earth's seeing widen into the infinite.
Heavy unchanged weighs still the imperfect world;

The splendid youth of Time has passed and failed;
Heavy and long are the years our labour counts
And still the seals are firm upon man's soul
And weary is the ancient Mother's heart.
O Truth defended in thy secret sun,
Voice of her mighty musings in shut heavens
On things withdrawn within her luminous depths,
O Wisdom-Splendour, Mother of the universe,
Creatrix, the Eternal's artist Bride,
Linger not long with thy transmuting hand
Pressed vainly on one golden bar of Time,
As if Time dare not open its heart to God.
O radiant fountain of the world's delight
World-free and unattainable above,
O Bliss who ever dwellst deep-hid within
While men seek thee outside and never find,
Mystery and Muse with hieratic tongue,
Incarnate the white passion of thy force,
Mission to earth some living form of thee.
One moment fill with thy eternity,
Let thy infinity in one body live,
All-Knowledge wrap one mind in seas of light,
All-Love throb single in one human heart.
Immortal, treading the earth with mortal feet
All heaven's beauty crowd in earthly limbs!
Omnipotence, girdle with the power of God
Movements and moments of a mortal will,
Pack with the eternal might one human hour
And with one gesture change all future time.
Let a great word be spoken from the heights
And one great act unlock the doors of Fate."

His prayer sank down in the resisting Night
Oppressed by the thousand forces that deny,
As if too weak to climb to the Supreme.
But there arose a wide consenting Voice;

The spirit of beauty was revealed in sound:
Light floated round the marvellous Vision's brow
And on her lips the Immortal's joy took shape.
"O strong forerunner, I have heard thy cry.
One shall descend and break the iron Law,
Change Nature's doom by the lone spirit's power.
A limitless Mind that can contain the world,
A sweet and violent heart of ardent calms
Moved by the passions of the gods shall come.
All mights and greatnesses shall join in her;
Beauty shall walk celestial on the earth,
Delight shall sleep in the cloud-net of her hair,
And in her body as on his homing tree
Immortal Love shall beat his glorious wings.
A music of griefless things shall weave her charm;
The harps of the Perfect shall attune her voice,
The streams of Heaven shall murmur in her laugh,
Her lips shall be the honeycombs of God,
Her limbs his golden jars of ecstasy,
Her breasts the rapture-flowers of Paradise.
She shall bear Wisdom in her voiceless bosom,
Strength shall be with her like a conqueror's sword
And from her eyes the Eternal's bliss shall gaze.
A seed shall be sown in Death's tremendous hour,
A branch of heaven transplant to human soil;
Nature shall overleap her mortal step;
Fate shall be changed by an unchanging will."

    As a flame disappears in endless Light
Immortally extinguished in its source,
Vanished the splendour and was stilled the word.
An echo of delight that once was close,
The harmony journeyed towards some distant hush,
A music failing in the ear of trance,
A cadence called by distant cadences,
A voice that trembled into strains withdrawn.

Her form retreated from the longing earth
Forsaking nearness to the abandoned sense,
Ascending to her unattainable home.
Lone, brilliant, vacant lay the inner fields;
All was unfilled inordinate spirit space,
Indifferent, waste, a desert of bright peace.
Then a line moved on the far edge of calm:
The warm-lipped sentient soft terrestrial wave,
A quick and many-murmured moan and laugh,
Came gliding in upon white feet of sound.
Unlocked was the deep glory of Silence' heart;
The absolute unmoving stillnesses
Surrendered to the breath of mortal air,
Dissolving boundlessly the heavens of trance
Collapsed to waking mind. Eternity
Cast down its incommunicable lids
Over its solitudes remote from ken
Behind the voiceless mystery of sleep.
The grandiose respite failed, the wide release.
Across the light of fast-receding planes
That fled from him as from a falling star,
Compelled to fill its human house in Time
His soul drew back into the speed and noise
Of the vast business of created things.
A chariot of the marvels of the heavens
Broad-based to bear the gods on fiery wheels,
Flaming he swept through the spiritual gates.
The mortal stir received him in its midst.
Once more he moved amid material scenes,
Lifted by intimations from the heights
And in the pauses of the building brain
Touched by the thoughts that skim the fathomless surge
Of Nature and wing back to hidden shores.
The eternal seeker in the aeonic field
Besieged by the intolerant press of hours
Again was strong for great swift-footed deeds.

Awake beneath the ignorant vault of Night,
He saw the unnumbered people of the stars
And heard the questioning of the unsatisfied flood
And toiled with the form-maker, measuring Mind.
A wanderer from the occult invisible suns
Accomplishing the fate of transient things,
A god in the figure of the arisen beast,
He raised his brow of conquest to the heavens
Establishing the empire of the soul
On Matter and its bounded universe
As on a solid rock in infinite seas.
The Lord of Life resumed his mighty rounds
In the scant field of the ambiguous globe.

END OF BOOK THREE, CANTO FOUR
End of Part One

PART TWO

BOOKS IV – VIII

BOOK FOUR

The Book of Birth and Quest

Canto One

The Birth and Childhood of the Flame

A MAENAD of the cycles of desire
Around a Light she must not dare to touch,
Hastening towards a far-off unknown goal
Earth followed the endless journey of the Sun.
A mind but half-awake in the swing of the void
On the bosom of Inconscience dreamed out life
And bore this finite world of thought and deed
Across the immobile trance of the Infinite.
A vast immutable silence with her ran:
Prisoner of speed upon a jewelled wheel,
She communed with the mystic heart in Space.
Amid the ambiguous stillness of the stars
She moved towards some undisclosed event
And her rhythm measured the long whirl of Time.
In ceaseless motion round the purple rim
Day after day sped by like coloured spokes,
And through a glamour of shifting hues of air
The seasons drew in linked significant dance
The symbol pageant of the changing year.
Across the burning languor of the soil
Paced Summer with his pomp of violent noons
And stamped his tyranny of torrid light
And the blue seal of a great burnished sky.
Next through its fiery swoon or clotted knot
Rain-tide burst in upon torn wings of heat,
Startled with lightnings air's unquiet drowse,
Lashed with life-giving streams the torpid soil,
Overcast with flare and sound and storm-winged dark
The star-defended doors of heaven's dim sleep,
Or from the gold eye of her paramour
Covered with packed cloud-veils the earth's brown face.

Armies of revolution crossed the time-field,
The clouds' unending march besieged the world,
Tempests' pronunciamentos claimed the sky
And thunder drums announced the embattled gods.
A traveller from unquiet neighbouring seas,
The dense-maned monsoon rode neighing through earth's hours:
Thick now the emissary javelins:
Enormous lightnings split the horizon's rim
And, hurled from the quarters as from contending camps,
Married heaven's edges steep and bare and blind:
A surge and hiss and onset of huge rain,
The long straight sleet-drift, clamours of winged storm-charge,
Throngs of wind-faces, rushing of wind-feet
Hurrying swept through the prone afflicted plains:
Heaven's waters trailed and dribbled through the drowned land.
Then all was a swift stride, a sibilant race,
Or all was tempest's shout and water's fall.
A dimness sagged on the grey floor of day,
Its dingy sprawling length joined morn to eve,
Wallowing in sludge and shower it reached black dark.
Day a half darkness wore as its dull dress.
Light looked into dawn's tarnished glass and met
Its own face there, twin to a half-lit night's:
Downpour and drip and seeping mist swayed all
And turned dry soil to bog and reeking mud:
Earth was a quagmire, heaven a dismal block.
None saw through dank drenched weeks the dungeon sun.
Even when no turmoil vexed air's sombre rest,
Or a faint ray glimmered through weeping clouds
As a sad smile gleams veiled by returning tears,
All promised brightness failed at once denied
Or, soon condemned, died like a brief-lived hope.
Then a last massive deluge thrashed dead mire
And a subsiding mutter left all still,
Or only the muddy creep of sinking floods
Or only a whisper and green toss of trees.

Earth's mood now changed; she lay in lulled repose,
The hours went by with slow contented tread:
A wide and tranquil air remembered peace,
Earth was the comrade of a happy sun.
A calmness neared as of the approach of God,
A light of musing trance lit soil and sky
And an identity and ecstasy
Filled meditation's solitary heart.
A dream loitered in the dumb mind of Space,
Time opened its chambers of felicity,
An exaltation entered and a hope:
An inmost self looked up to a heavenlier height,
An inmost thought kindled a hidden flame
And the inner sight adored an unseen sun.
Three thoughtful seasons passed with shining tread
And scanning one by one the pregnant hours
Watched for a flame that lurked in luminous depths,
The vigil of some mighty birth to come.
Autumn led in the glory of her moons
And dreamed in the splendour of her lotus pools
And Winter and Dew-time laid their calm cool hands
On Nature's bosom still in a half sleep
And deepened with hues of lax and mellow ease
The tranquil beauty of the waning year.
Then Spring, an ardent lover, leaped through leaves
And caught the earth-bride in his eager clasp;
His advent was a fire of irised hues,
His arms were a circle of the arrival of joy.
His voice was a call to the Transcendent's sphere
Whose secret touch upon our mortal lives
Keeps ever new the thrill that made the world,
Remoulds an ancient sweetness to new shapes
And guards intact unchanged by death and Time
The answer of our hearts to Nature's charm
And keeps for ever new, yet still the same,
The throb that ever wakes to the old delight

And beauty and rapture and the joy to live.
His coming brought the magic and the spell;
At his touch life's tired heart grew glad and young;
He made joy a willing prisoner in her breast.
His grasp was a young god's upon earth's limbs:
Changed by the passion of his divine outbreak
He made her body beautiful with his kiss.
Impatient for felicity he came,
High-fluting with the coïl's happy voice,
His peacock turban trailing on the trees;
His breath was a warm summons to delight,
The dense voluptuous azure was his gaze.
A soft celestial urge surprised the blood
Rich with the instinct of God's sensuous joys;
Revealed in beauty, a cadence was abroad
Insistent on the rapture-thrill in life:
Immortal movements touched the fleeting hours.
A godlike packed intensity of sense
Made it a passionate pleasure even to breathe;
All sights and voices wove a single charm.
The life of the enchanted globe became
A storm of sweetness and of light and song,
A revel of colour and of ecstasy,
A hymn of rays, a litany of cries:
A strain of choral priestly music sang
And, swung on the swaying censer of the trees,
A sacrifice of perfume filled the hours.
Asocas burned in crimson spots of flame,
Pure like the breath of an unstained desire
White jasmines haunted the enamoured air,
Pale mango-blossoms fed the liquid voice
Of the love-maddened coïl, and the brown bee
Muttered in fragrance mid the honey-buds.
The sunlight was a great god's golden smile.
All Nature was at beauty's festival.

In this high signal moment of the gods
Answering earth's yearning and her cry for bliss,
A greatness from our other countries came.
A silence in the noise of earthly things
Immutably revealed the secret Word,
A mightier influx filled the oblivious clay:
A lamp was lit, a sacred image made.
A mediating ray had touched the earth
Bridging the gulf between man's mind and God's;
Its brightness linked our transience to the Unknown.
A spirit of its celestial source aware
Translating heaven into a human shape
Descended into earth's imperfect mould
And wept not fallen to mortality,
But looked on all with large and tranquil eyes.
One had returned from the transcendent planes
And bore anew the load of mortal breath,
Who had striven of old with our darkness and our pain;
She took again her divine unfinished task:
Survivor of death and the aeonic years,
Once more with her fathomless heart she fronted Time.
Again there was renewed, again revealed
The ancient closeness by earth-vision veiled,
The secret contact broken off in Time,
A consanguinity of earth and heaven,
Between the human portion toiling here
And an as yet unborn and limitless Force.
Again the mystic deep attempt began,
The daring wager of the cosmic game.
For since upon this blind and whirling globe
Earth-plasm first quivered with the illumining mind
And life invaded the material sheath
Afflicting Inconscience with the need to feel,
Since in Infinity's silence woke a word,
A Mother-wisdom works in Nature's breast
To pour delight on the heart of toil and want

And press perfection on life's stumbling powers,
Impose heaven-sentience on the obscure abyss
And make dumb Matter conscious of its God.
Although our fallen minds forget to climb,
Although our human stuff resists or breaks,
She keeps her will that hopes to divinise clay;
Failure cannot repress, defeat o'erthrow;
Time cannot weary her nor the Void subdue,
The ages have not made her passion less;
No victory she admits of Death or Fate.
Always she drives the soul to new attempt;
Always her magical infinitude
Forces to aspire the inert brute elements;
As one who has all infinity to waste,
She scatters the seed of the Eternal's strength
On a half-animate and crumbling mould,
Plants heaven's delight in the heart's passionate mire,
Pours godhead's seekings into a bare beast frame,
Hides immortality in a mask of death.
Once more that Will put on an earthly shape.
A Mind empowered from Truth's immutable seat
Was framed for vision and interpreting act
And instruments were sovereignly designed
To express divinity in terrestrial signs.
Outlined by the pressure of this new descent
A lovelier body formed than earth had known.
As yet a prophecy only and a hint,
The glowing arc of a charmed unseen whole,
It came into the sky of mortal life
Bright like the crescent horn of a gold moon
Returning in a faint illumined eve.
At first glimmering like an unshaped idea
Passive she lay sheltered in wordless sleep,
Involved and drowned in Matter's giant trance,
An infant heart of the deep-caved world-plan
In cradle of divine inconscience rocked

By the universal ecstasy of the suns.
Some missioned Power in the half-wakened frame
Nursed a transcendent birth's dumb glorious seed
For which this vivid tenement was made.
But soon the link of soul with form grew sure;
Flooded was the dim cave with slow conscient light,
The seed grew into a delicate marvellous bud,
The bud disclosed a great and heavenly bloom.
At once she seemed to found a mightier race.
Arrived upon the strange and dubious globe
The child remembering inly a far home
Lived guarded in her spirit's luminous cell,
Alone mid men in her diviner kind.
Even in her childish movements could be felt
The nearness of a light still kept from earth,
Feelings that only eternity could share,
Thoughts natural and native to the gods.
As needing nothing but its own rapt flight
Her nature dwelt in a strong separate air
Like a strange bird with large rich-coloured breast
That sojourns on a secret fruited bough,
Lost in the emerald glory of the woods
Or flies above divine unreachable tops.
Harmoniously she impressed the earth with heaven.
Aligned to a swift rhythm of sheer delight
And singing to themselves her days went by;
Each minute was a throb of beauty's heart;
The hours were tuned to a sweet-toned content
Which asked for nothing, but took all life gave
Sovereignly as her nature's inborn right.
Near was her spirit to its parent Sun,
The Breath within to the eternal joy.
The first fair life that breaks from Nature's swoon,
Mounts in a line of rapture to the skies;
Absorbed in its own happy urge it lives,
Sufficient to itself, yet turned to all:

It has no seen communion with its world,
No open converse with surrounding things.
There is a oneness native and occult
That needs no instruments and erects no form;
In unison it grows with all that is.
All contacts it assumes into its trance,
Laugh-tossed consents to the wind's kiss and takes
Transmutingly the shocks of sun and breeze:
A blissful yearning riots in its leaves,
A magic passion trembles in its blooms,
Its boughs aspire in hushed felicity.
An occult godhead of this beauty is cause,
The spirit and intimate guest of all this charm,
This sweetness's priestess and this reverie's muse.
Invisibly protected from our sense
The Dryad lives drenched in a deeper ray
And feels another air of storms and calms
And quivers inwardly with mystic rain.
This at a heavenlier height was shown in her.
Even when she bent to meet earth's intimacies
Her spirit kept the stature of the gods;
It stooped but was not lost in Matter's reign.
A world translated was her gleaming mind,
And marvel-mooned bright crowding fantasies
Fed with spiritual sustenance of dreams
The ideal goddess in her house of gold.
Aware of forms to which our eyes are closed,
Conscious of nearnesses we cannot feel,
The Power within her shaped her moulding sense
In deeper figures than our surface types.
An invisible sunlight ran within her veins
And flooded her brain with heavenly brilliances
That woke a wider sight than earth could know.
Outlined in the sincerity of that ray
Her springing childlike thoughts were richly turned
Into luminous patterns of her soul's deep truth,

And from her eyes she cast another look
On all around her than man's ignorant view.
All objects were to her shapes of living selves
And she perceived a message from her kin
In each awakening touch of outward things.
Each was a symbol power, a vivid flash
In the circuit of infinities half-known;
Nothing was alien or inanimate,
Nothing without its meaning or its call.
For with a greater Nature she was one.
As from the soil sprang glory of branch and flower,
As from the animal's life rose thinking man,
A new epiphany appeared in her.
A mind of light, a life of rhythmic force,
A body instinct with hidden divinity
Prepared an image of the coming god;
And when the slow rhyme of the expanding years
And the rich murmurous swarm-work of the days
Had honey-packed her sense and filled her limbs,
Accomplishing the moon-orb of her grace,
Self-guarded in the silence of her strength
Her solitary greatness was not less.
Nearer the godhead to the surface pressed,
A sun replacing childhood's nebula
Sovereign in a blue and lonely sky.
Upward it rose to grasp the human scene:
The strong Inhabitant turned to watch her field.
A lovelier light assumed her spirit brow
And sweet and solemn grew her musing gaze;
Celestial-human deep warm slumbrous fires
Woke in the long fringed glory of her eyes
Like altar-burnings in a mysteried shrine.
Out of those crystal windows gleamed a will
That brought a large significance to life.
Holding her forehead's candid stainless space
Behind the student arch a noble power

Of wisdom looked from light on transient things.
A scout of victory in a vigil tower,
Her aspiration called high destiny down;
A silent warrior paced in her city of strength
Inviolate, guarding Truth's diamond throne.
A nectarous haloed moon her passionate heart
Loved all and spoke no word and made no sign,
But kept her bosom's rapturous secrecy
A blissful ardent moved and voiceless world.
Proud, swift and joyful ran the wave of life
Within her like a stream in Paradise.
Many high gods dwelt in one beautiful home;
Yet was her nature's orb a perfect whole,
Harmonious like a chant with many tones,
Immense and various like a universe.
The body that held this greatness seemed almost
An image made of heaven's transparent light.
Its charm recalled things seen in vision's hours,
A golden bridge spanning a faery flood,
A moon-touched palm-tree single by a lake
Companion of the wide and glimmering peace,
A murmur as of leaves in Paradise
Moving when feet of the Immortals pass,
A fiery halo over sleeping hills,
A strange and starry head alone in Night.

END OF CANTO ONE

Canto Two

The Growth of the Flame

A LAND of mountains and wide sun-beat plains
And giant rivers pacing to vast seas,
A field of creation and spiritual hush,
Silence swallowing life's acts into the deeps,
Of thought's transcendent climb and heavenward leap,
A brooding world of reverie and trance,
Filled with the mightiest works of God and man,
Where Nature seemed a dream of the Divine
And beauty and grace and grandeur had their home,
Harboured the childhood of the incarnate Flame.
Over her watched millennial influences
And the deep godheads of a grandiose past
Looked on her and saw the future's godheads come
As if this magnet drew their powers unseen.
Earth's brooding wisdom spoke to her still breast;
Mounting from mind's last peaks to mate with gods,
Making earth's brilliant thoughts a springing-board
To dive into the cosmic vastnesses,
The knowledge of the thinker and the seer
Saw the unseen and thought the unthinkable,
Opened the enormous doors of the unknown,
Rent man's horizons into infinity.
A shoreless sweep was lent to the mortal's acts,
And art and beauty sprang from the human depths;
Nature and soul vied in nobility.
Ethics the human keyed to imitate heaven;
The harmony of a rich culture's tones
Refined the sense and magnified its reach
To hear the unheard and glimpse the invisible
And taught the soul to soar beyond things known,
Inspiring life to greaten and break its bounds,

Aspiring to the Immortals' unseen world.
Leaving earth's safety daring wings of Mind
Bore her above the trodden fields of thought
Crossing the mystic seas of the Beyond
To live on eagle heights near to the Sun.
There Wisdom sits on her eternal throne.
All her life's turns led her to symbol doors
Admitting to secret Powers that were her kin;
Adept of truth, initiate of bliss,
A mystic acolyte trained in Nature's school,
Aware of the marvel of created things
She laid the secrecies of her heart's deep muse
Upon the altar of the Wonderful;
Her hours were a ritual in a timeless fane;
Her acts became gestures of sacrifice.
Invested with a rhythm of higher spheres
The word was used as a hieratic means
For the release of the imprisoned spirit
Into communion with its comrade gods.
Or it helped to beat out new expressive forms
Of that which labours in the heart of life,
Some immemorial Soul in men and things,
Seeker of the unknown and the unborn
Carrying a light from the Ineffable
To rend the veil of the last mysteries.
Intense philosophies pointed earth to heaven
Or on foundations broad as cosmic Space
Upraised the earth-mind to superhuman heights.
Overpassing lines that please the outward eyes
But hide the sight of that which lives within
Sculpture and painting concentrated sense
Upon an inner vision's motionless verge,
Revealed a figure of the invisible,
Unveiled all Nature's meaning in a form,
Or caught into a body the Divine.
The architecture of the Infinite

Discovered here its inward-musing shapes
Captured into wide breadths of soaring stone:
Music brought down celestial yearnings, song
Held the merged heart absorbed in rapturous depths,
Linking the human with the cosmic cry;
The world-interpreting movements of the dance
Moulded idea and mood to a rhythmic sway
And posture; crafts minute in subtle lines
Eternised a swift moment's memory
Or showed in a carving's sweep, a cup's design
The underlying patterns of the unseen:
Poems in largeness cast like moving worlds
And metres surging with the ocean's voice
Translated by grandeurs locked in Nature's heart
But thrown now into a crowded glory of speech
The beauty and sublimity of her forms,
The passion of her moments and her moods
Lifting the human word nearer to the god's.
Man's eyes could look into the inner realms;
His scrutiny discovered number's law
And organised the motions of the stars,
Mapped out the visible fashioning of the world,
Questioned the process of his thoughts or made
A theorised diagram of mind and life.
These things she took in as her nature's food,
But these alone could fill not her wide Self:
A human seeking limited by its gains,
To her they seemed the great and early steps
Hazardous of a young discovering spirit
Which saw not yet by its own native light;
It tapped the universe with testing knocks
Or stretched to find truth mind's divining rod;
There was a growing out to numberless sides,
But not the widest seeing of the soul,
Not yet the vast direct immediate touch,
Nor yet the art and wisdom of the Gods.

A boundless knowledge greater than man's thought,
A happiness too high for heart and sense
Locked in the world and yearning for release
She felt in her; waiting as yet for form,
It asked for objects around which to grow
And natures strong to bear without recoil
The splendour of her native royalty,
Her greatness and her sweetness and her bliss,
Her might to possess and her vast power to love:
Earth made a stepping-stone to conquer heaven,
The soul saw beyond heaven's limiting boundaries,
Met a great light from the Unknowable
And dreamed of a transcendent action's sphere.
Aware of the universal Self in all
She turned to living hearts and human forms,
Her soul's reflections, complements, counterparts,
The close outlying portions of her being
Divided from her by walls of body and mind
Yet to her spirit bound by ties divine.
Overcoming invisible hedge and masked defence
And the loneliness that separates soul from soul,
She wished to make all one immense embrace
That she might house in it all living things
Raised into a splendid point of seeing light
Out of division's dense inconscient cleft,
And make them one with God and world and her.
Only a few responded to her call:
Still fewer felt the screened divinity
And strove to mate its godhead with their own,
Approaching with some kinship to her heights.
Uplifted towards luminous secrecies
Or conscious of some splendour hidden above
They leaped to find her in a moment's flash,
Glimpsing a light in a celestial vast,
But could not keep the vision and the power
And fell back to life's dull ordinary tone.

A mind daring heavenly experiment,
Growing towards some largeness they felt near,
Testing the unknown's bound with eager touch
They still were prisoned by their human grain:
They could not keep up with her tireless step;
Too small and eager for her large-paced will,
Too narrow to look with the unborn Infinite's gaze
Their nature weary grew of things too great.
For even the close partners of her thoughts
Who could have walked the nearest to her ray,
Worshipped the power and light they felt in her
But could not match the measure of her soul.
A friend and yet too great wholly to know,
She walked in their front towards a greater light,
Their leader and queen over their hearts and souls,
One close to their bosoms, yet divine and far.
Admiring and amazed they saw her stride
Attempting with a godlike rush and leap
Heights for their human stature too remote
Or with a slow great many-sided toil
Pushing towards aims they hardly could conceive;
Yet forced to be the satellites of her sun
They moved unable to forego her light,
Desiring they clutched at her with outstretched hands
Or followed stumbling in the paths she made.
Or longing with their self of life and flesh
They clung to her for heart's nourishment and support:
The rest they could not see in visible light;
Vaguely they bore her inner mightiness.
Or bound by the senses and the longing heart,
Adoring with a turbid human love,
They could not grasp the mighty spirit she was
Or change by closeness to be even as she.
Some felt her with their souls and thrilled with her,
A greatness felt near yet beyond mind's grasp;
To see her was a summons to adore,

To be near her drew a high communion's force.
So men worship a god too great to know,
Too high, too vast to wear a limiting shape;
They feel a Presence and obey a might,
Adore a love whose rapture invades their breasts;
To a divine ardour quickening the heart-beats,
A law they follow greatening heart and life.
Opened to the breath is a new diviner air,
Opened to man is a freer, happier world:
He sees high steps climbing to Self and Light.
Her divine parts the soul's allegiance called:
It saw, it felt, it knew the deity.
Her will was puissant on their nature's acts,
Her heart's inexhaustible sweetness lured their hearts,
A being they loved whose bounds exceeded theirs;
Her measure they could not reach but bore her touch,
Answering with the flower's answer to the sun
They gave themselves to her and asked no more.
One greater than themselves, too wide for their ken,
Their minds could not understand nor wholly know,
Their lives replied to hers, moved at her words:
They felt a godhead and obeyed a call,
Answered to her lead and did her work in the world;
Their lives, their natures moved compelled by hers
As if the truth of their own larger selves
Put on an aspect of divinity
To exalt them to a pitch beyond their earth's.
They felt a larger future meet their walk;
She held their hands, she chose for them their paths:
They were moved by her towards great unknown things,
Faith drew them and the joy to feel themselves hers;
They lived in her, they saw the world with her eyes.
Some turned to her against their nature's bent;
Divided between wonder and revolt,
Drawn by her charm and mastered by her will,
Possessed by her, her striving to possess,

Impatient subjects, their tied longing hearts
Hugging the bonds close of which they most complained,
Murmured at a yoke they would have wept to lose,
The splendid yoke of her beauty and her love:
Others pursued her with life's blind desires
And claiming all of her as their lonely own,
Hastened to engross her sweetness meant for all.
As earth claims light for its lone separate need
Demanding her for their sole jealous clasp,
They asked from her movements bounded like their own
And to their smallness craved a like response.
Or they repined that she surpassed their grip,
And hoped to bind her close with longing's cords.
Or finding her touch desired too strong to bear
They blamed her for a tyranny they loved,
Shrank into themselves as from too bright a sun,
Yet hankered for the splendour they refused.
Angrily enamoured of her sweet passionate ray
The weakness of their earth could hardly bear,
They longed but cried out at the touch desired
Inapt to meet divinity so close,
Intolerant of a Force they could not house.
Some drawn unwillingly by her divine sway
Endured it like a sweet but alien spell;
Unable to mount to levels too sublime,
They yearned to draw her down to their own earth.
Or forced to centre round her their passionate lives,
They hoped to bind to their heart's human needs
Her glory and grace that had enslaved their souls.

But mid this world, these hearts that answered her call,
None could stand up her equal and her mate.
In vain she stooped to equal them with her heights,
Too pure that air was for small souls to breathe.
These comrade selves to raise to her own wide breadths
Her heart desired and fill with her own power

That a diviner Force might enter life,
A breath of Godhead greaten human time.
Although she leaned down to their littleness
Covering their lives with her strong passionate hands
And knew by sympathy their needs and wants
And dived in the shallow wave-depths of their lives
And met and shared their heart-beats of grief and joy
And bent to heal their sorrow and their pride,
Lavishing the might that was hers on her lone peak
To lift to it their aspiration's cry,
And though she drew their souls into her vast
And surrounded with the silence of her deeps
And held as the great Mother holds her own,
Only her earthly surface bore their charge
And mixed its fire with their mortality:
Her greater self lived sole, unclaimed, within.
Oftener in dumb Nature's stir and peace
A nearness she could feel serenely one;
The Force in her drew earth's subhuman broods;
And to her spirit's large and free delight
She joined the ardent-hued magnificent lives
Of animal and bird and flower and tree.
They answered to her with the simple heart.
In man a dim disturbing somewhat lives;
It knows but turns away from divine Light
Preferring the dark ignorance of the fall.
Among the many who came drawn to her
Nowhere she found her partner of high tasks,
The comrade of her soul, her other self
Who was made with her, like God and Nature, one.
Some near approached, were touched, caught fire, then failed,
Too great was her demand, too pure her force.
Thus lighting earth around her like a sun,
Yet in her inmost sky an orb aloof,
A distance severed her from those most close.
Puissant, apart her soul as the gods live.

As yet unlinked with the broad human scene,
In a small circle of young eager hearts,
Her being's early school and closed domain,
Apprentice in the business of earth-life,
She schooled her heavenly strain to bear its touch,
Content in her little garden of the gods
As blooms a flower in an unvisited place.
Earth nursed, unconscious still, the inhabiting flame,
Yet something deeply stirred and dimly knew;
There was a movement and a passionate call,
A rainbow dream, a hope of golden change;
Some secret wing of expectation beat,
A growing sense of something new and rare
And beautiful stole across the heart of Time.
Then a faint whisper of her touched the soil,
Breathed like a hidden need the soul divines;
The eye of the great world discovered her
And wonder lifted up its bardic voice.
A key to a Light still kept in being's cave,
The sun-word of an ancient mystery's sense,
Her name ran murmuring on the lips of men
Exalted and sweet like an inspired verse
Struck from the epic lyre of rumour's winds
Or sung like a chanted thought by the poet Fame.
But like a sacred symbol's was that cult.
Admired, unsought, intangible to the grasp
Her beauty and flaming strength were seen afar
Like lightning playing with the fallen day,
A glory unapproachably divine.
No equal heart came close to join her heart,
No transient earthly love assailed her calm,
No hero passion had the strength to seize;
No eyes demanded her replying eyes.
A Power within her awed the imperfect flesh;
The self-protecting genius in our clay
Divined the goddess in the woman's shape

And drew back from a touch beyond its kind
The earth-nature bound in sense-life's narrow make.
The hearts of men are amorous of clay-kin
And bear not spirits lone and high who bring
Fire-intimations from the deathless planes
Too vast for souls not born to mate with heaven.
Whoever is too great must lonely live.
Adored he walks in mighty solitude;
Vain is his labour to create his kind,
His only comrade is the Strength within.
Thus was it for a while with Savitri.
All worshipped marvellingly, none dared to claim.
Her mind sat high pouring its golden beams,
Her heart was a crowded temple of delight.
A single lamp lit in perfection's house,
A bright pure image in a priestless shrine,
Midst those encircling lives her spirit dwelt,
Apart in herself until her hour of fate.

END OF CANTO TWO

The Call to the Quest

A MORN that seemed a new creation's front,
Bringing a greater sunlight, happier skies,
Came burdened with a beauty moved and strange
Out of the changeless origin of things.
An ancient longing struck again new roots:
The air drank deep of unfulfilled desire;
The high trees trembled with a wandering wind
Like souls that quiver at the approach of joy,
And in a bosom of green secrecy
For ever of its one love-note untired
A lyric coïl cried among the leaves.
Away from the terrestrial murmur turned
Where transient calls and answers mix their flood,
King Aswapati listened through the ray
To other sounds than meet the sense-formed ear.
On a subtle interspace which rings our life,
Unlocked were the inner spirit's trance-closed doors:
The inaudible strain in Nature could be caught;
Across this cyclic tramp of eager lives,
Across the deep urgency of present cares,
Earth's wordless hymn to the Ineffable
Arose from the silent heart of the cosmic Void;
He heard the voice repressed of unborn Powers
Murmuring behind the luminous bars of Time.
Again the mighty yearning raised its flame
That asks a perfect life on earth for men
And prays for certainty in the uncertain mind
And shadowless bliss for suffering human hearts
And Truth embodied in an ignorant world
And godhead divinising mortal forms.
A word that leaped from some far sky of thought,

Admitted by the cowled receiving scribe
Traversed the echoing passages of his brain
And left its stamp on the recording cells.
"O Force-compelled, Fate-driven earth-born race,
O petty adventurers in an infinite world
And prisoners of a dwarf humanity,
How long will you tread the circling tracks of mind
Around your little self and petty things?
But not for a changeless littleness were you meant,
Not for vain repetition were you built;
Out of the Immortal's substance you were made;
Your actions can be swift revealing steps,
Your life a changeful mould for growing gods.
A Seer, a strong Creator, is within,
The immaculate Grandeur broods upon your days,
Almighty powers are shut in Nature's cells.
A greater destiny waits you in your front:
This transient earthly being if he wills
Can fit his acts to a transcendent scheme.
He who now stares at the world with ignorant eyes
Hardly from the Inconscient's night aroused,
That look at images and not at Truth,
Can fill those orbs with an immortal's sight.
Yet shall the godhead grow within your hearts,
You shall awake into the spirit's air
And feel the breaking walls of mortal mind
And hear the message which left life's heart dumb
And look through Nature with sun-gazing lids
And blow your conch-shells at the Eternal's gate.
Authors of earth's high change, to you it is given
To cross the dangerous spaces of the soul
And touch the mighty Mother stark awake
And meet the Omnipotent in this house of flesh
And make of life the million-bodied One.
The earth you tread is a border screened from heaven;
The life you lead conceals the light you are.

Immortal Powers sweep flaming past your doors;
Far-off upon your tops the god-chant sounds
While to exceed yourselves thought's trumpets call,
Heard by a few, but fewer dare aspire,
The nympholepts of the ecstasy and the blaze.
An epic of hope and failure breaks earth's heart;
Her force and will exceed her form and fate.
A goddess in a net of transience caught,
Self-bound in the pastures of death she dreams of life,
Self-racked with the pains of hell aspires to joy,
And builds to hope her altars of despair,
Knows that one high step might enfranchise all
And, suffering, looks for greatness in her sons.
But dim in human hearts the ascending fire,
The invisible Grandeur sits unworshipped there;
Man sees the Highest in a limiting form
Or looks upon a Person, hears a Name.
He turns for little gains to ignorant Powers
Or kindles his altar lights to a demon face.
He loves the Ignorance fathering his pain.
A spell is laid upon his glorious strengths;
He has lost the inner Voice that led his thoughts,
And masking the oracular tripod seat
A specious Idol fills the marvel shrine.
The great Illusion wraps him in its veils,
The soul's deep intimations come in vain,
In vain is the unending line of seers,
The sages ponder in unsubstantial light,
The poets lend their voice to outward dreams,
A homeless fire inspires the prophet tongues.
Heaven's flaming lights descend and back return,
The luminous Eye approaches and retires;
Eternity speaks, none understands its word;
Fate is unwilling and the Abyss denies;
The Inconscient's mindless waters block all done.
Only a little lifted is Mind's screen;

The Wise who know see but one half of Truth,
The strong climb hardly to a low-peaked height,
The hearts that yearn are given one hour to love.
His tale half told, falters the secret Bard;
The gods are still too few in mortal forms."
The Voice withdrew into its hidden skies.
But like a shining answer from the gods
Approached through sun-bright spaces Savitri.
Advancing amid tall heaven-pillaring trees,
Apparelled in her flickering-coloured robe
She seemed, burning towards the eternal realms,
A bright moved torch of incense and of flame
That from the sky-roofed temple-soil of earth
A pilgrim hand lifts in an invisible shrine.
There came the gift of a revealing hour:
He saw through depths that reinterpret all,
Limited not now by the dull body's eyes,
New-found through an arch of clear discovery,
This intimation of the world's delight,
This wonder of the divine Artist's make
Carved like a nectar-cup for thirsty gods,
This breathing Scripture of the Eternal's joy,
This net of sweetness woven of aureate fire.
Transformed the delicate image-face became
A deeper Nature's self-revealing sign,
A gold-leaf palimpsest of sacred births,
A grave world-symbol chiselled out of life.
Her brow, a copy of clear unstained heavens,
Was meditation's pedestal and defence,
The very room and smile of musing Space,
Its brooding line infinity's symbol curve.
Amid her tresses' cloudy multitude
Her long eyes shadowed as by wings of Night
Under that moon-gold forehead's dreaming breadth
Were seas of love and thought that held the world;
Marvelling at life and earth they saw truths far.

A deathless meaning filled her mortal limbs;
As in a golden vase's poignant line
They seemed to carry the rhythmic sob of bliss
Of earth's mute adoration towards heaven
Released in beauty's cry of living form
Towards the perfection of eternal things.
Transparent grown the ephemeral living dress
Bared the expressive deity to his view.
Escaped from surface sight and mortal sense
The seizing harmony of its shapes became
The strange significant icon of a Power
Renewing its inscrutable descent
Into a human figure of its works
That stood out in life's bold abrupt relief
On the soil of the evolving universe,
A godhead sculptured on a wall of thought,
Mirrored in the flowing hours and dimly shrined
In Matter as in a cathedral cave.
Annulled were the transient values of the mind,
The body's sense renounced its earthly look;
Immortal met immortal in their gaze.
Awaked from the close spell of daily use
That hides soul-truth with the outward form's disguise,
He saw through the familiar cherished limbs
The great and unknown spirit born his child.
An impromptu from the deeper sight within,
Thoughts rose in him that knew not their own scope.
Then to those large and brooding depths whence Love
Regarded him across the straits of mind,
He spoke in sentences from the unseen Heights.
For the hidden prompters of our speech sometimes
Can use the formulas of a moment's mood
To weigh unconscious lips with words from Fate:
A casual passing phrase can change our life.
"O spirit, traveller of eternity,
Who cam'st from the immortal spaces here

Armed for the splendid hazard of thy life
To set thy conquering foot on Chance and Time,
The moon shut in her halo dreams like thee.
A mighty Presence still defends thy frame.
Perhaps the heavens guard thee for some great soul,
Thy fate, thy work are kept somewhere afar.
Thy spirit came not down a star alone.
O living inscription of the beauty of love
Missalled in aureate virginity,
What message of heavenly strength and bliss in thee
Is written with the Eternal's sun-white script,
One shall discover and greaten with it his life
To whom thou loosenest thy heart's jewelled strings.
O rubies of silence, lips from which there stole
Low laughter, music of tranquillity,
Star-lustrous eyes awake in sweet large night
And limbs like fine-linked poems made of gold
Stanzaed to glimmering curves by artist gods,
Depart where love and destiny call your charm.
Venture through the deep world to find thy mate.
For somewhere on the longing breast of earth,
Thy unknown lover waits for thee the unknown.
Thy soul has strength and needs no other guide
Than One who burns within thy bosom's powers.
There shall draw near to meet thy approaching steps
The second self for whom thy nature asks,
He who shall walk until thy body's end
A close-bound traveller pacing with thy pace,
The lyrist of thy soul's most intimate chords
Who shall give voice to what in thee is mute.
Then shall you grow like vibrant kindred harps,
One in the beats of difference and delight,
Responsive in divine and equal strains,
Discovering new notes of the eternal theme.
One force shall be your mover and your guide,
One light shall be around you and within;

Hand in strong hand confront Heaven's question, life:
Challenge the ordeal of the immense disguise.
Ascend from Nature to divinity's heights;
Face the high gods, crowned with felicity,
Then meet a greater god, thy self beyond Time."
This word was seed of all the thing to be:
A hand from some Greatness opened her heart's locked doors
And showed the work for which her strength was born.
As when the mantra sinks in Yoga's ear,
Its message enters stirring the blind brain
And keeps in the dim ignorant cells its sound;
The hearer understands a form of words
And, musing on the index thought it holds,
He strives to read it with the labouring mind,
But finds bright hints, not the embodied truth:
Then, falling silent in himself to know
He meets the deeper listening of his soul:
The Word repeats itself in rhythmic strains:
Thought, vision, feeling, sense, the body's self
Are seized unutterably and he endures
An ecstasy and an immortal change;
He feels a Wideness and becomes a Power,
All knowledge rushes on him like a sea:
Transmuted by the white spiritual ray
He walks in naked heavens of joy and calm,
Sees the God-face and hears transcendent speech:
An equal greatness in her life was sown.
Accustomed scenes were now an ended play:
Moving in muse amid familiar powers,
Touched by new magnitudes and fiery signs,
She turned to vastnesses not yet her own;
Allured her heart throbbed to unknown sweetnesses;
The secrets of an unseen world were close.
The morn went up into a smiling sky;
Cast from its sapphire pinnacle of trance
Day sank into the burning gold of eve;

The moon floated, a luminous waif through heaven
And sank below the oblivious edge of dream;
Night lit the watch-fires of eternity.
Then all went back into mind's secret caves;
A darkness stooping on the heaven-bird's wings
Sealed in her senses from external sight
And opened the stupendous depths of sleep.
When the pale dawn slipped through Night's shadowy guard,
Vainly the new-born light desired her face;
The palace woke to its own emptiness;
The sovereign of its daily joys was far;
Her moonbeam feet tinged not the lucent floors:
The beauty and divinity were gone.
Delight had fled to search the spacious world.

END OF CANTO THREE

Canto Four

The Quest

THE world-ways opened before Savitri.
At first a strangeness of new brilliant scenes
Peopled her mind and kept her body's gaze.
But as she moved across the changing earth
A deeper consciousness welled up in her:
A citizen of many scenes and climes,
Each soil and country it had made its home;
It took all clans and peoples for her own,
Till the whole destiny of mankind was hers.
These unfamiliar spaces on her way
Were known and neighbours to a sense within,
Landscapes recurred like lost forgotten fields,
Cities and rivers and plains her vision claimed
Like slow-recurring memories in front,
The stars at night were her past's brilliant friends,
The winds murmured to her of ancient things
And she met nameless comrades loved by her once.
All was a part of old forgotten selves:
Vaguely or with a flash of sudden hints
Her acts recalled a line of bygone power,
Even her motion's purpose was not new:
Traveller to a prefigured high event,
She seemed to her remembering witness soul
To trace again a journey often made.
A guidance turned the dumb revolving wheels
And in the eager body of their speed
The dim-masked hooded godheads rode who move
Assigned to man immutably from his birth,
Receivers of the inner and outer law,
At once the agents of his spirit's will
And witnesses and executors of his fate.

Inexorably faithful to their task,
They hold his nature's sequence in their guard
Carrying the unbroken thread old lives have spun.
Attendants on his destiny's measured walk
Leading to joys he has won and pains he has called,
Even in his casual steps they intervene.
Nothing we think or do is void or vain;
Each is an energy loosed and holds its course.
The shadowy keepers of our deathless past
Have made our fate the child of our own acts,
And from the furrows laboured by our will
We reap the fruit of our forgotten deeds.
But since unseen the tree that bore this fruit
And we live in a present born from an unknown past,
They seem but parts of a mechanic Force
To a mechanic mind tied by earth's laws;
Yet are they instruments of a Will supreme,
Watched by a still all-seeing Eye above.
A prescient architect of Fate and Chance
Who builds our lives on a foreseen design
The meaning knows and consequence of each step
And watches the inferior stumbling powers.
Upon her silent heights she was aware
Of a calm Presence throned above her brows
Who saw the goal and chose each fateful curve;
It used the body for its pedestal;
The eyes that wandered were its searchlight fires,
The hands that held the reins its living tools;
All was the working of an ancient plan,
A way proposed by an unerring Guide.
Across wide noons and glowing afternoons,
She met with Nature and with human forms
And listened to the voices of the world;
Driven from within she followed her long road,
Mute in the luminous cavern of her heart,
Like a bright cloud through the resplendent day.

At first her path ran far through peopled tracts:
Admitted to the lion eye of States
And theatres of the loud act of man,
Her carven chariot with its fretted wheels
Threaded through clamorous marts and sentinel towers
Past figured gates and high dream-sculptured fronts
And gardens hung in the sapphire of the skies,
Pillared assembly halls with armoured guards,
Small fanes where one calm Image watched man's life
And temples hewn as if by exiled gods
To imitate their lost eternity.
Often from gilded dusk to argent dawn,
Where jewel-lamps flickered on frescoed walls
And the stone lattice stared at moonlit boughs,
Half-conscious of the tardy listening night
Dimly she glided between banks of sleep
At rest in the slumbering palaces of kings.
Hamlet and village saw the fate-wain pass,
Homes of a life bent to the soil it ploughs
For sustenance of its short and passing days
That, transient, keep their old repeated course,
Unchanging in the circle of a sky
Which alters not above our mortal toil.
Away from this thinking creature's burdened hours
To free and griefless spaces now she turned
Not yet perturbed by human joys and fears.
Here was the childhood of primaeval earth,
Here timeless musings large and glad and still,
Men had forborne as yet to fill with cares,
Imperial acres of the eternal sower
And wind-stirred grass-lands winking in the sun:
Or mid green musing of woods and rough-browed hills,
In the grove's murmurous bee-air humming wild
Or past the long lapsing voice of silver floods
Like a swift hope journeying among its dreams
Hastened the chariot of the golden bride.

Out of the world's immense unhuman past
Tract-memories and ageless remnants came,
Domains of light enfeoffed to antique calm
Listened to the unaccustomed sound of hooves
And large immune entangled silences
Absorbed her into emerald secrecy
And slow hushed wizard nets of fiery bloom
Environed with their coloured snare her wheels.
The strong importunate feet of Time fell soft
Along these lonely ways, his titan pace
Forgotten and his stark and ruinous rounds.
The inner ear that listens to solitude,
Leaning self-rapt unboundedly could hear
The rhythm of the intenser wordless Thought
That gathers in the silence behind life,
And the low sweet inarticulate voice of earth
In the great passion of her sun-kissed trance
Ascended with its yearning undertone.
Afar from the brute noise of clamorous needs
The quieted all-seeking mind could feel,
At rest from its blind outwardness of will,
The unwearied clasp of her mute patient love
And know for a soul the mother of our forms.
This spirit stumbling in the fields of sense,
This creature bruised in the mortar of the days
Could find in her broad spaces of release.
Not yet was a world all occupied by care.
The bosom of our mother kept for us still
Her austere regions and her musing depths,
Her impersonal reaches lonely and inspired
And the mightinesses of her rapture haunts.
Muse-lipped she nursed her symbol mysteries
And guarded for her pure-eyed sacraments
The valley clefts between her breasts of joy,
Her mountain altars for the fires of dawn
And nuptial beaches where the ocean couched

And the huge chanting of her prophet woods.
Fields had she of her solitary mirth,
Plains hushed and happy in the embrace of light,
Alone with the cry of birds and hue of flowers,
And wildernesses of wonder lit by her moons
And grey seer-evenings kindling with the stars
And dim movement in the night's infinitude.
August, exulting in her Maker's eye,
She felt her nearness to him in earth's breast,
Conversed still with a Light behind the veil,
Still communed with Eternity beyond.
A few and fit inhabitants she called
To share the glad communion of her peace;
The breadth, the summit were their natural home.
The strong king-sages from their labour done,
Freed from the warrior tension of their task,
Came to her serene sessions in these wilds;
The strife was over, the respite lay in front.
Happy they lived with birds and beasts and flowers
And sunlight and the rustle of the leaves,
And heard the wild winds wandering in the night,
Mused with the stars in their mute constant ranks,
And lodged in the mornings as in azure tents,
And with the glory of the noons were one.
Some deeper plunged; from life's external clasp
Beckoned into a fiery privacy
In the soul's unprofaned star-white recess
They sojourned with an everliving Bliss;
A Voice profound in the ecstasy and the hush
They heard, beheld an all-revealing Light.
All time-made difference they overcame;
The world was fibred with their own heart-strings;
Close drawn to the heart that beats in every breast,
They reached the one self in all through boundless love.
Attuned to Silence and to the world-rhyme,
They loosened the knot of the imprisoning mind;

Achieved was the wide untroubled witness gaze,
Unsealed was Nature's great spiritual eye;
To the height of heights rose now their daily climb:
Truth leaned to them from her supernal realm;
Above them blazed eternity's mystic suns.
Nameless the austere ascetics without home
Abandoning speech and motion and desire
Aloof from creatures sat absorbed, alone,
Immaculate in tranquil heights of self
On concentration's luminous voiceless peaks,
World-naked hermits with their matted hair
Immobile as the passionless great hills
Around them grouped like thoughts of some vast mood
Awaiting the Infinite's behest to end.
The seers attuned to the universal Will,
Content in Him who smiles behind earth's forms,
Abode ungrieved by the insistent days.
About them like green trees girdling a hill
Young grave disciples fashioned by their touch,
Trained to the simple act and conscious word,
Greatened within and grew to meet their heights.
Far-wandering seekers on the Eternal's path
Brought to these quiet founts their spirit's thirst
And spent the treasure of a silent hour
Bathed in the purity of the mild gaze
That, uninsistent, ruled them from its peace,
And by its influence found the ways of calm.
The Infants of the monarchy of the worlds,
The heroic leaders of a coming time,
King-children nurtured in that spacious air
Like lions gambolling in sky and sun
Received half-consciously their godlike stamp:
Formed in the type of the high thoughts they sang
They learned the wide magnificence of mood
That makes us comrades of the cosmic urge,
No longer chained to their small separate selves,

Plastic and firm beneath the eternal hand,
Met Nature with a bold and friendly clasp
And served in her the Power that shapes her works.
One-souled to all and free from narrowing bonds,
Large like a continent of warm sunshine
In wide equality's impartial joy,
These sages breathed for God's delight in things.
Assisting the slow entries of the gods,
Sowing in young minds immortal thoughts they lived,
Taught the great Truth to which man's race must rise
Or opened the gates of freedom to a few.
Imparting to our struggling world the Light
They breathed like spirits from Time's dull yoke released,
Comrades and vessels of the cosmic Force,
Using a natural mastery like the sun's:
Their speech, their silence was a help to earth.
A magic happiness flowed from their touch;
Oneness was sovereign in that sylvan peace,
The wild beast joined in friendship with its prey;
Persuading the hatred and the strife to cease
The love that flows from the one Mother's breast
Healed with their hearts the hard and wounded world.
Others escaped from the confines of thought
To where Mind motionless sleeps waiting Light's birth,
And came back quivering with a nameless Force,
Drunk with a wine of lightning in their cells;
Intuitive knowledge leaping into speech,
Seized, vibrant, kindling with the inspired word,
Hearing the subtle voice that clothes the heavens,
Carrying the splendour that has lit the suns,
They sang Infinity's names and deathless powers
In metres that reflect the moving worlds,
Sight's sound-waves breaking from the soul's great deeps.
Some lost to the person and his strip of thought
In a motionless ocean of impersonal Power,
Sat mighty, visioned with the Infinite's light,

Or, comrades of the everlasting Will,
Surveyed the plan of past and future Time.
Some winged like birds out of the cosmic sea
And vanished into a bright and featureless Vast:
Some silent watched the universal dance,
Or helped the world by world-indifference.
Some watched no more merged in a lonely Self,
Absorbed in the trance from which no soul returns,
All the occult world-lines for ever closed,
The chains of birth and person cast away:
Some uncompanioned reached the Ineffable.

As floats a sunbeam through a shady place,
The golden virgin in her carven car
Came gliding among meditation's seats.
Often in twilight mid returning troops
Of cattle thickening with their dust the shades
When the loud day had slipped below the verge,
Arriving in a peaceful hermit grove
She rested drawing round her like a cloak
Its spirit of patient muse and potent prayer.
Or near to a lion river's tawny mane
And trees that worshipped on a praying shore,
A domed and templed air's serene repose
Beckoned to her hurrying wheels to stay their speed.
In the solemnity of a space that seemed
A mind remembering ancient silences,
Where to the heart great bygone voices called
And the large liberty of brooding seers
Had left the long impress of their soul's scene,
Awake in candid dawn or darkness mooned,
To the still touch inclined the daughter of Flame
Drank in hushed splendour between tranquil lids
And felt the kinship of eternal calm.
But morn broke in reminding her of her quest
And from low rustic couch or mat she rose

And went impelled on her unfinished way
And followed the fateful orbit of her life
Like a desire that questions silent gods
Then passes starlike to some bright Beyond.
Thence to great solitary tracts she came,
Where man was a passer-by towards human scenes
Or sole in Nature's vastness strove to live
And called for help to ensouled invisible Powers,
Overwhelmed by the immensity of his world
And unaware of his own infinity.
The earth multiplied to her a changing brow
And called her with a far and nameless voice.
The mountains in their anchorite solitude,
The forests with their multitudinous chant
Disclosed to her the masked divinity's doors.
On dreaming plains, an indolent expanse,
The death-bed of a pale enchanted eve
Under the glamour of a sunken sky,
Impassive she lay as at an age's end,
Or crossed an eager pack of huddled hills
Lifting their heads to hunt a lairlike sky,
Or travelled in a strange and empty land
Where desolate summits camped in a weird heaven,
Mute sentinels beneath a drifting moon,
Or wandered in some lone tremendous wood
Ringing for ever with the crickets' cry
Or followed a long glistening serpent road
Through fields and pastures lapped in moveless light
Or reached the wild beauty of a desert space
Where never plough was driven nor herd had grazed
And slumbered upon stripped and thirsty sands
Amid the savage wild-beast night's appeal.
Still unaccomplished was the fateful quest;
Still she found not the one predestined face
For which she sought amid the sons of men.
A grandiose silence wrapped the regal day:

The months had fed the passion of the sun
And now his burning breath assailed the soil.
The tiger heats prowled through the fainting earth;
All was licked up as by a lolling tongue.
The spring winds failed; the sky was set like bronze.

End of Canto Four
End of Book Four

BOOK FIVE

The Book of Love

Canto One

The Destined Meeting-Place

BUT now the destined spot and hour were close;
Unknowing she had neared her nameless goal.
For though a dress of blind and devious chance
Is laid upon the work of all-wise Fate,
Our acts interpret an omniscient Force
That dwells in the compelling stuff of things,
And nothing happens in the cosmic play
But at its time and in its foreseen place.
To a space she came of soft and delicate air
That seemed a sanctuary of youth and joy,
A highland world of free and green delight
Where spring and summer lay together and strove
In indolent and amicable debate,
Inarmed, disputing with laughter who should rule.
There expectation beat wide sudden wings
As if a soul had looked out from earth's face,
And all that was in her felt a coming change
And forgetting obvious joys and common dreams,
Obedient to Time's call, to the spirit's fate,
Was lifted to a beauty calm and pure
That lived under the eyes of Eternity.
A crowd of mountainous heads assailed the sky
Pushing towards rival shoulders nearer heaven,
The armoured leaders of an iron line;
Earth prostrate lay beneath their feet of stone.
Below them crouched a dream of emerald woods
And gleaming borders solitary as sleep:
Pale waters ran like glimmering threads of pearl.
A sigh was straying among happy leaves;
Cool-perfumed with slow pleasure-burdened feet
Faint stumbling breezes faltered among flowers.

The white crane stood, a vivid motionless streak,
Peacock and parrot jewelled soil and tree,
The dove's soft moan enriched the enamoured air
And fire-winged wild-drakes swam in silvery pools.
Earth couched alone with her great lover Heaven,
Uncovered to her consort's azure eye.
In a luxurious ecstasy of joy
She squandered the love-music of her notes,
Wasting the passionate pattern of her blooms
And festival riot of her scents and hues.
A cry and leap and hurry was around,
The stealthy footfalls of her chasing things,
The shaggy emerald of her centaur mane,
The gold and sapphire of her warmth and blaze.
Magician of her rapt felicities,
Blithe, sensuous-hearted, careless and divine,
Life ran or hid in her delightful rooms;
Behind all brooded Nature's grandiose calm.
Primaeval peace was there and in its bosom
Held undisturbed the strife of bird and beast.
Man the deep-browed artificer had not come
To lay his hand on happy inconscient things,
Thought was not there nor the measurer, strong-eyed toil,
Life had not learned its discord with its aim.
The Mighty Mother lay outstretched at ease.
All was in line with her first satisfied plan;
Moved by a universal will of joy
The trees bloomed in their green felicity
And the wild children brooded not on pain.
At the end reclined a stern and giant tract
Of tangled depths and solemn questioning hills,
Peaks like a bare austerity of the soul,
Armoured, remote and desolately grand
Like the thought-screened infinities that lie
Behind the rapt smile of the Almighty's dance.
A matted forest-head invaded heaven

As if a blue-throated ascetic peered
From the stone fastness of his mountain cell
Regarding the brief gladness of the days;
His vast extended spirit couched behind.
A mighty murmur of immense retreat
Besieged the ear, a sad and limitless call
As of a soul retiring from the world.
This was the scene which the ambiguous Mother
Had chosen for her brief felicitous hour;
Here in this solitude far from the world
Her part she began in the world's joy and strife.
Here were disclosed to her the mystic courts,
The lurking doors of beauty and surprise,
The wings that murmur in the golden house,
The temple of sweetness and the fiery aisle.
A stranger on the sorrowful roads of Time,
Immortal under the yoke of death and fate,
A sacrificant of the bliss and pain of the spheres,
Love in the wilderness met Savitri.

END OF CANTO ONE

Canto Two

Satyavan

ALL she remembered on this day of Fate,
The road that hazarded not the solemn depths
But turned away to flee to human homes,
The wilderness with its mighty monotone,
The morning like a lustrous seer above,
The passion of the summits lost in heaven,
The titan murmur of the endless woods.
As if a wicket gate to joy were there
Ringed in with voiceless hint and magic sign,
Upon the margin of an unknown world
Reclined the curve of a sun-held recess;
Groves with strange flowers like eyes of gazing nymphs
Peered from their secrecy into open space,
Boughs whispering to a constancy of light
Sheltered a dim and screened felicity,
And slowly a supine inconstant breeze
Ran like a fleeting sigh of happiness
Over slumbrous grasses pranked with green and gold.
Hidden in the forest's bosom of loneliness
Amid the leaves the inmate voices called,
Sweet like desires enamoured and unseen,
Cry answering to low insistent cry.
Behind slept emerald dumb remotenesses,
Haunt of a Nature passionate, veiled, denied
To all but her own vision lost and wild.
Earth in this beautiful refuge free from cares
Murmured to the soul a song of strength and peace.
Only one sign was there of a human tread:
A single path, shot thin and arrowlike
Into this bosom of vast and secret life,
Pierced its enormous dream of solitude.

Here first she met on the uncertain earth
The one for whom her heart had come so far.
As might a soul on Nature's background limned
Stand out for a moment in a house of dream
Created by the ardent breath of life,
So he appeared against the forest verge
Inset twixt green relief and golden ray.
As if a weapon of the living Light,
Erect and lofty like a spear of God
His figure led the splendour of the morn.
Noble and clear as the broad peaceful heavens
A tablet of young wisdom was his brow;
Freedom's imperious beauty curved his limbs,
The joy of life was on his open face.
His look was a wide daybreak of the gods,
His head was a youthful Rishi's touched with light,
His body was a lover's and a king's.
In the magnificent dawning of his force
Built like a moving statue of delight
He illumined the border of the forest page.
Out of the ignorant eager toil of the years
Abandoning man's loud drama he had come
Led by the wisdom of an adverse Fate
To meet the ancient Mother in her groves.
In her divine communion he had grown
A foster-child of beauty and solitude,
Heir to the centuries of the lonely wise,
A brother of the sunshine and the sky,
A wanderer communing with depth and marge.
A Veda-knower of the unwritten book
Perusing the mystic scripture of her forms,
He had caught her hierophant significances,
Her sphered immense imaginations learned,
Taught by sublimities of stream and wood
And voices of the sun and star and flame
And chant of the magic singers on the boughs

And the dumb teaching of four-footed things.
Helping with confident steps her slow great hands
He leaned to her influence like a flower to rain
And, like the flower and tree a natural growth,
Widened with the touches of her shaping hours.
The mastery free natures have was his
And their assent to joy and spacious calm;
One with the single Spirit inhabiting all,
He laid experience at the Godhead's feet;
His mind was open to her infinite mind,
His acts were rhythmic with her primal force;
He had subdued his mortal thought to hers.
That day he had turned from his accustomed paths;
For One who, knowing every moment's load,
Can move in all our studied or careless steps,
Had laid the spell of destiny on his feet
And drawn him to the forest's flowering verge.
　　At first her glance that took life's million shapes
Impartially to people its treasure-house
Along with sky and flower and hill and star,
Dwelt rather on the bright harmonious scene.
It saw the green-gold of the slumbrous sward,
The grasses quivering with the slow wind's tread,
The branches haunted by the wild bird's call.
Awake to Nature, vague as yet to life,
The eager prisoner from the Infinite,
The immortal wrestler in its mortal house,
Its pride, power, passion of a striving God,
It saw this image of veiled deity,
This thinking master creature of the earth,
This last result of the beauty of the stars,
But only saw like fair and common forms
The artist spirit needs not for its work
And puts aside in memory's shadowy rooms.
A look, a turn decides our ill-poised fate.
Thus in the hour that most concerned her all,

Wandering unwarned by the slow surface mind,
The heedless scout beneath her tenting lids
Admired indifferent beauty and cared not
To wake her body's spirit to its king.
So might she have passed by on chance ignorant roads
Missing the call of Heaven, losing life's aim,
But the god touched in time her conscious soul.
Her vision settled, caught and all was changed.
Her mind at first dwelt in ideal dreams,
Those intimate transmuters of earth's signs
That make known things a hint of unseen spheres,
And saw in him the genius of the spot,
A symbol figure standing mid earth's scenes,
A king of life outlined in delicate air.
Yet this was but a moment's reverie;
For suddenly her heart looked out at him,
The passionate seeing used thought cannot match,
And knew one nearer than its own close strings.
All in a moment was surprised and seized,
All in inconscient ecstasy lain wrapped
Or under imagination's coloured lids
Held up in a large mirror-air of dream,
Broke forth in flame to recreate the world,
And in that flame to new things she was born.
A mystic tumult from her depths arose;
Haled, smitten erect like one who dreamed at ease,
Life ran to gaze from every gate of sense:
Thoughts indistinct and glad in moon-mist heavens,
Feelings as when a universe takes birth,
Swept through the turmoil of her bosom's space
Invaded by a swarm of golden gods:
Arising to a hymn of wonder's priests
Her soul flung wide its doors to this new sun.
An alchemy worked, the transmutation came;
The missioned face had wrought the Master's spell.
In the nameless light of two approaching eyes

A swift and fated turning of her days
Appeared and stretched to a gleam of unknown worlds.
Then trembling with the mystic shock her heart
Moved in her breast and cried out like a bird
Who hears his mate upon a neighbouring bough.
Hooves trampling fast, wheels largely stumbling ceased;
The chariot stood like an arrested wind.
And Satyavan looked out from his soul's doors
And felt the enchantment of her liquid voice
Fill his youth's purple ambience and endured
The haunting miracle of a perfect face.
Mastered by the honey of a strange flower-mouth,
Drawn to soul-spaces opening round a brow,
He turned to the vision like a sea to the moon
And suffered a dream of beauty and of change,
Discovered the aureole round a mortal's head,
Adored a new divinity in things.
His self-bound nature foundered as in fire;
His life was taken into another's life.
The splendid lonely idols of his brain
Fell prostrate from their bright sufficiencies,
As at the touch of a new infinite,
To worship a godhead greater than their own.
An unknown imperious force drew him to her.
Marvelling he came across the golden sward:
Gaze met close gaze and clung in sight's embrace.
A visage was there, noble and great and calm,
As if encircled by a halo of thought,
A span, an arch of meditating light,
As though some secret nimbus half was seen;
Her inner vision still remembering knew
A forehead that wore the crown of all her past,
Two eyes her constant and eternal stars,
Comrade and sovereign eyes that claimed her soul,
Lids known through many lives, large frames of love.
He met in her regard his future's gaze,

A promise and a presence and a fire,
Saw an embodiment of aeonic dreams,
A mystery of the rapture for which all
Yearns in this world of brief mortality
Made in material shape his very own.
This golden figure given to his grasp
Hid in its breast the key of all his aims,
A spell to bring the Immortal's bliss on earth,
To mate with heaven's truth our mortal thought,
To lift earth-hearts nearer the Eternal's sun.
In these great spirits now incarnate here
Love brought down power out of eternity
To make of life his new undying base.
His passion surged a wave from fathomless deeps;
It leaped to earth from far forgotten heights,
But kept its nature of infinity.
On the dumb bosom of this oblivious globe
Although as unknown beings we seem to meet,
Our lives are not aliens nor as strangers join,
Moved to each other by a causeless force.
The soul can recognise its answering soul
Across dividing Time and, on life's roads
Absorbed wrapped traveller, turning it recovers
Familiar splendours in an unknown face
And touched by the warning finger of swift love
It thrills again to an immortal joy
Wearing a mortal body for delight.
There is a Power within that knows beyond
Our knowings; we are greater than our thoughts,
And sometimes earth unveils that vision here.
To live, to love are signs of infinite things,
Love is a glory from eternity's spheres.
Abased, disfigured, mocked by baser mights
That steal his name and shape and ecstasy,
He is still the godhead by which all can change.
A mystery wakes in our inconscient stuff,

A bliss is born that can remake our life.
Love dwells in us like an unopened flower
Awaiting a rapid moment of the soul,
Or he roams in his charmed sleep mid thoughts and things;
The child-god is at play, he seeks himself
In many hearts and minds and living forms:
He lingers for a sign that he can know
And, when it comes, wakes blindly to a voice,
A look, a touch, the meaning of a face.
His instrument the dim corporeal mind,
Of celestial insight now forgetful grown,
He seizes on some sign of outward charm
To guide him mid the throng of Nature's hints,
Reads heavenly truths into earth's semblances,
Desires the image for the godhead's sake,
Divines the immortalities of form
And takes the body for the sculptured soul.
Love's adoration like a mystic seer
Through vision looks at the invisible,
In earth's alphabet finds a godlike sense;
But the mind only thinks, "Behold the one
For whom my life has waited long unfilled,
Behold the sudden sovereign of my days."
Heart feels for heart, limb cries for answering limb;
All strives to enforce the unity all is.
Too far from the Divine, Love seeks his truth
And Life is blind and the instruments deceive
And Powers are there that labour to debase.
Still can the vision come, the joy arrive.
Rare is the cup fit for love's nectar wine,
As rare the vessel that can hold God's birth;
A soul made ready through a thousand years
Is the living mould of a supreme Descent.
These knew each other though in forms thus strange.
Although to sight unknown, though life and mind
Had altered to hold a new significance,

These bodies summed the drift of numberless births,
And the spirit to the spirit was the same.
Amazed by a joy for which they had waited long,
The lovers met upon their different paths,
Travellers across the limitless plains of Time
Together drawn from fate-led journeyings
In the self-closed solitude of their human past,
To a swift rapturous dream of future joy
And the unexpected present of these eyes.
By the revealing greatness of a look,
Form-smitten the spirit's memory woke in sense.
The mist was torn that lay between two lives;
Her heart unveiled and his to find her turned;
Attracted as in heaven star by star,
They wondered at each other and rejoiced
And wove affinity in a silent gaze.
A moment passed that was eternity's ray,
An hour began, the matrix of new Time.

END OF CANTO TWO

Canto Three

Satyavan and Savitri

OUT of the voiceless mystery of the past
In a present ignorant of forgotten bonds
These spirits met upon the roads of Time.
Yet in the heart their secret conscious selves
At once aware grew of each other warned
By the first call of a delightful voice
And a first vision of the destined face.
As when being cries to being from its depths
Behind the screen of the external sense
And strives to find the heart-disclosing word,
The passionate speech revealing the soul's need,
But the mind's ignorance veils the inner sight,
Only a little breaks through our earth-made bounds,
So now they met in that momentous hour,
So utter the recognition in the deeps,
The remembrance lost, the oneness felt and missed.
Thus Satyavan spoke first to Savitri:
"O thou who com'st to me out of Time's silences,
Yet thy voice has wakened my heart to an unknown bliss,
Immortal or mortal only in thy frame,
For more than earth speaks to me from thy soul
And more than earth surrounds me in thy gaze,
How art thou named among the sons of men?
Whence hast thou dawned filling my spirit's days,
Brighter than summer, brighter than my flowers,
Into the lonely borders of my life,
O sunlight moulded like a golden maid?
I know that mighty gods are friends of earth.
Amid the pageantries of day and dusk,
Long have I travelled with my pilgrim soul
Moved by the marvel of familiar things.

Earth could not hide from me the powers she veils:
Even though moving mid an earthly scene
And the common surfaces of terrestrial things,
My vision saw unblinded by her forms;
The Godhead looked at me from familiar scenes.
I witnessed the virgin bridals of the dawn
Behind the glowing curtains of the sky
Or vying in joy with the bright morning's steps
I paced along the slumbrous coasts of noon,
Or the gold desert of the sunlight crossed
Traversing great wastes of splendour and of fire,
Or met the moon gliding amazed through heaven
In the uncertain wideness of the night,
Or the stars marched on their long sentinel routes
Pointing their spears through the infinitudes:
The day and dusk revealed to me hidden shapes;
Figures have come to me from secret shores
And happy faces looked from ray and flame.
I have heard strange voices cross the ether's waves,
The Centaur's wizard song has thrilled my ear;
I have glimpsed the Apsaras bathing in the pools,
I have seen the wood-nymphs peering through the leaves;
The winds have shown to me their trampling lords,
I have beheld the princes of the Sun
Burning in thousand-pillared homes of light.
So now my mind could dream and my heart fear
That from some wonder-couch beyond our air
Risen in a wide morning of the gods
Thou drov'st thy horses from the Thunderer's worlds.
Although to heaven thy beauty seems allied,
Much rather would my thoughts rejoice to know
That mortal sweetness smiles between thy lids
And thy heart can beat beneath a human gaze
And thy aureate bosom quiver with a look
And its tumult answer to an earth-born voice.
If our time-vexed affections thou canst feel,

Earth's ease of simple things can satisfy,
If thy glance can dwell content on earthly soil,
And this celestial summary of delight,
Thy golden body, dally with fatigue
Oppressing with its grace our terrain, while
The frail sweet passing taste of earthly food
Delays thee and the torrent's leaping wine,
Descend. Let thy journey cease, come down to us.
Close is my father's creepered hermitage
Screened by the tall ranks of these silent kings,
Sung to by voices of the hue-robed choirs
Whose chants repeat transcribed in music's notes
The passionate coloured lettering of the boughs
And fill the hours with their melodious cry.
Amid the welcome-hum of many bees
Invade our honied kingdom of the woods;
There let me lead thee into an opulent life.
Bare, simple is the sylvan hermit-life;
Yet is it clad with the jewelry of earth.
Wild winds run — visitors midst the swaying tops,
Through the calm days heaven's sentinels of peace
Couched on a purple robe of sky above
Look down on a rich secrecy and hush
And the chambered nuptial waters chant within.
Enormous, whispering, many-formed around
High forest gods have taken in their arms
The human hour, a guest of their centuried pomps.
Apparelled are the morns in gold and green,
Sunlight and shadow tapestry the walls
To make a resting chamber fit for thee."
Awhile she paused as if hearing still his voice,
Unwilling to break the charm, then slowly spoke.
Musing she answered, "I am Savitri,
Princess of Madra. Who art thou? What name
Musical on earth expresses thee to men?
What trunk of kings watered by fortunate streams

Has flowered at last upon one happy branch?
Why is thy dwelling in the pathless wood
Far from the deeds thy glorious youth demands,
Haunt of the anchorites and earth's wilder broods,
Where only with thy witness self thou roamst
In Nature's green unhuman loneliness
Surrounded by enormous silences
And the blind murmur of primaeval calms?"
And Satyavan replied to Savitri:
"In days when yet his sight looked clear on life,
King Dyumatsena once, the Shalwa, reigned
Through all the tract which from behind these tops
Passing its days of emerald delight
In trusting converse with the traveller winds
Turns, looking back towards the southern heavens,
And leans its flank upon the musing hills.
But equal Fate removed her covering hand.
A living night enclosed the strong man's paths,
Heaven's brilliant gods recalled their careless gifts,
Took from blank eyes their glad and helping ray
And led the uncertain goddess from his side.
Outcast from empire of the outer light,
Lost to the comradeship of seeing men,
He sojourns in two solitudes, within
And in the solemn rustle of the woods.
Son of that king, I, Satyavan, have lived
Contented, for not yet of thee aware,
In my high-peopled loneliness of spirit
And this huge vital murmur kin to me,
Nursed by the vastness, pupil of solitude.
Great Nature came to her recovered child;
I reigned in a kingdom of a nobler kind
Than men can build upon dull Matter's soil;
I met the frankness of the primal earth,
I enjoyed the intimacy of infant God.
In the great tapestried chambers of her state,

Free in her boundless palace I have dwelt
Indulged by the warm mother of us all,
Reared with my natural brothers in her house.
I lay in the wide bare embrace of heaven,
The sunlight's radiant blessing clasped my brow,
The moonbeams' silver ecstasy at night
Kissed my dim lids to sleep. Earth's morns were mine;
Lured by faint murmurings with the green-robed hours
I wandered lost in woods, prone to the voice
Of winds and waters, partner of the sun's joy,
A listener to the universal speech:
My spirit satisfied within me knew
Godlike our birthright, luxuried our life
Whose close belongings are the earth and skies.
Before Fate led me into this emerald world,
Aroused by some foreshadowing touch within,
An early prescience in my mind approached
The great dumb animal consciousness of earth
Now grown so close to me who have left old pomps
To live in this grandiose murmur dim and vast.
Already I met her in my spirit's dream.
As if to a deeper country of the soul
Transposing the vivid imagery of earth,
Through an inner seeing and sense a wakening came.
A visioned spell pursued my boyhood's hours,
All things the eye had caught in coloured lines
Were seen anew through the interpreting mind
And in the shape it sought to seize the soul.
An early child-god took my hand that held,
Moved, guided by the seeking of his touch,
Bright forms and hues which fled across his sight;
Limned upon page and stone they spoke to men.
High beauty's visitants my intimates were.
The neighing pride of rapid life that roams
Wind-maned through our pastures, on my seeing mood
Cast shapes of swiftness; trooping spotted deer

Against the vesper sky became a song
Of evening to the silence of my soul.
I caught for some eternal eye the sudden
King-fisher flashing to a darkling pool;
A slow swan silvering the azure lake,
A shape of magic whiteness, sailed through dream;
Leaves trembling with the passion of the wind,
Pranked butterflies, the conscious flowers of air,
And wandering wings in blue infinity
Lived on the tablets of my inner sight;
Mountains and trees stood there like thoughts from God.
The brilliant long-bills in their vivid dress,
The peacock scattering on the breeze his moons
Painted my memory like a frescoed wall.
I carved my vision out of wood and stone;
I caught the echoes of a word supreme
And metred the rhythm-beats of infinity
And listened through music for the eternal Voice.
I felt a covert touch, I heard a call,
But could not clasp the body of my God
Or hold between my hands the World-Mother's feet.
In men I met strange portions of a Self
That sought for fragments and in fragments lived:
Each lived in himself and for himself alone
And with the rest joined only fleeting ties;
Each passioned over his surface joy and grief,
Nor saw the Eternal in his secret house.
I conversed with Nature, mused with the changeless stars,
God's watch-fires burning in the ignorant Night,
And saw upon her mighty visage fall
A ray prophetic of the Eternal's sun.
I sat with the forest sages in their trance:
There poured awakening streams of diamond light,
I glimpsed the presence of the One in all.
But still there lacked the last transcendent power
And Matter still slept empty of its Lord.

The Spirit was saved, the body lost and mute
Lived still with Death and ancient Ignorance;
The Inconscient was its base, the Void its fate.
But thou hast come and all will surely change:
I shall feel the World-Mother in thy golden limbs
And hear her wisdom in thy sacred voice.
The child of the Void shall be reborn in God,
My Matter shall evade the Inconscient's trance.
My body like my spirit shall be free.
It shall escape from Death and Ignorance."
And Savitri, musing still, replied to him:
"Speak more to me, speak more, O Satyavan,
Speak of thyself and all thou art within;
I would know thee as if we had ever lived
Together in the chamber of our souls.
Speak till a light shall come into my heart
And my moved mortal mind shall understand
What all the deathless being in me feels.
It knows that thou art he my spirit has sought
Amidst earth's thronging visages and forms
Across the golden spaces of my life."
And Satyavan like a replying harp
To the insistent calling of a flute
Answered her questioning and let stream to her
His heart in many-coloured waves of speech:
"O golden princess, perfect Savitri,
More I would tell than failing words can speak,
Of all that thou hast meant to me, unknown,
All that the lightning-flash of love reveals
In one great hour of the unveiling gods.
Even a brief nearness has reshaped my life.
For now I know that all I lived and was
Moved towards this moment of my heart's rebirth;
I look back on the meaning of myself,
A soul made ready on earth's soil for thee.
Once were my days like days of other men:

To think and act was all, to enjoy and breathe;
This was the width and height of mortal hope:
Yet there came glimpses of a deeper self
That lives behind Life and makes her act its scene.
A truth was felt that screened its shape from mind,
A Greatness working towards a hidden end,
And vaguely through the forms of earth there looked
Something that life is not and yet must be.
I groped for the Mystery with the lantern, Thought.
Its glimmerings lighted with the abstract word
A half-visible ground and travelling yard by yard
It mapped a system of the Self and God.
I could not live the truth it spoke and thought.
I turned to seize its form in visible things,
Hoping to fix its rule by mortal mind,
Imposed a narrow structure of world-law
Upon the freedom of the Infinite,
A hard firm skeleton of outward Truth,
A mental scheme of a mechanic Power.
This light showed more the darknesses unsearched;
It made the original Secrecy more occult;
It could not analyse its cosmic Veil
Or glimpse the Wonder-worker's hidden hand
And trace the pattern of his magic plans.
I plunged into an inner seeing Mind
And knew the secret laws and sorceries
That make of Matter mind's bewildered slave:
The mystery was not solved but deepened more.
I strove to find its hints through Beauty and Art,
But Form cannot unveil the indwelling Power;
Only it throws its symbols at our hearts.
It evoked a mood of self, invoked a sign
Of all the brooding glory hidden in sense:
I lived in the ray but faced not to the sun.
I looked upon the world and missed the Self,
And when I found the Self, I lost the world,

My other selves I lost and the body of God,
The link of the finite with the Infinite,
The bridge between the appearance and the Truth,
The mystic aim for which the world was made,
The human sense of Immortality.
But now the gold link comes to me with thy feet
And His gold sun has shone on me from thy face.
For now another realm draws near with thee
And now diviner voices fill my ear,
A strange new world swims to me in thy gaze
Approaching like a star from unknown heavens;
A cry of spheres comes with thee and a song
Of flaming gods. I draw a wealthier breath
And in a fierier march of moments move.
My mind transfigures to a rapturous seer.
A foam-leap travelling from the waves of bliss
Has changed my heart and changed the earth around:
All with thy coming fills. Air, soil and stream
Wear bridal raiment to be fit for thee
And sunlight grows a shadow of thy hue
Because of change within me by thy look.
Come nearer to me from thy car of light
On this green sward disdaining not our soil.
For here are secret spaces made for thee
Whose caves of emerald long to screen thy form.
Wilt thou not make this mortal bliss thy sphere?
Descend, O happiness, with thy moon-gold feet
Enrich earth's floors upon whose sleep we lie.
O my bright beauty's princess Savitri,
By my delight and thy own joy compelled
Enter my life, thy chamber and thy shrine.
In the great quietness where spirits meet,
Led by my hushed desire into my woods
Let the dim rustling arches over thee lean;
One with the breath of things eternal live,
Thy heart-beats near to mine, till there shall leap

Enchanted from the fragrance of the flowers
A moment which all murmurs shall recall
And every bird remember in its cry."

    Allured to her lashes by his passionate words
Her fathomless soul looked out at him from her eyes;
Passing her lips in liquid sounds it spoke.
This word alone she uttered and said all:
"O Satyavan, I have heard thee and I know;
I know that thou and only thou art he."
Then down she came from her high carven car
Descending with a soft and faltering haste;
Her many-hued raiment glistening in the light
Hovered a moment over the wind-stirred grass,
Mixed with a glimmer of her body's ray
Like lovely plumage of a settling bird.
Her gleaming feet upon the green-gold sward
Scattered a memory of wandering beams
And lightly pressed the unspoken desire of earth
Cherished in her too brief passing by the soil.
Then flitting like pale-brilliant moths her hands
Took from the sylvan verge's sunlit arms
A load of their jewel-faces' clustering swarms,
Companions of the spring-time and the breeze.
A candid garland set with simple forms
Her rapid fingers taught a flower song,
The stanzaed movement of a marriage hymn.
Profound in perfume and immersed in hue
They mixed their yearning's coloured signs and made
The bloom of their purity and passion one.
A sacrament of joy in treasuring palms
She brought, flower-symbol of her offered life,
Then with raised hands that trembled a little now
At the very closeness that her soul desired,
This bond of sweetness, their bright union's sign,
She laid on the bosom coveted by her love.

As if inclined before some gracious god
Who has out of his mist of greatness shone
To fill with beauty his adorer's hours,
She bowed and touched his feet with worshipping hands;
She made her life his world for him to tread
And made her body the room of his delight,
Her beating heart a remembrancer of bliss.
He bent to her and took into his own
Their married yearning joined like folded hopes;
As if a whole rich world suddenly possessed,
Wedded to all he had been, became himself,
An inexhaustible joy made his alone,
He gathered all Savitri into his clasp.
Around her his embrace became the sign
Of a locked closeness through slow intimate years,
A first sweet summary of delight to come,
One brevity intense of all long life.
In a wide moment of two souls that meet
She felt her being flow into him as in waves
A river pours into a mighty sea.
As when a soul is merging into God
To live in Him for ever and know His joy,
Her consciousness grew aware of him alone
And all her separate self was lost in his.
As a starry heaven encircles happy earth,
He shut her into himself in a circle of bliss
And shut the world into himself and her.
A boundless isolation made them one;
He was aware of her enveloping him
And let her penetrate his very soul
As is a world by the world's spirit filled,
As the mortal wakes into Eternity,
As the finite opens to the Infinite.
Thus were they in each other lost awhile,
Then drawing back from their long ecstasy's trance
Came into a new self and a new world.

Each now was a part of the other's unity,
The world was but their twin self-finding's scene
Or their own wedded being's vaster frame.
On the high glowing cupola of the day
Fate tied a knot with morning's halo threads
While by the ministry of an auspice-hour
Heart-bound before the sun, their marriage fire,
The wedding of the eternal Lord and Spouse
Took place again on earth in human forms:
In a new act of the drama of the world
The united Two began a greater age.
In the silence and murmur of that emerald world
And the mutter of the priest-wind's sacred verse,
Amid the choral whispering of the leaves
Love's twain had joined together and grew one.
The natural miracle was wrought once more:
In the immutable ideal world
One human moment was eternal made.

   Then down the narrow path where their lives had met
He led and showed to her her future world,
Love's refuge and corner of happy solitude.
At the path's end through a green cleft in the trees
She saw a clustering line of hermit-roofs
And looked now first on her heart's future home,
The thatch that covered the life of Satyavan.
Adorned with creepers and red climbing flowers
It seemed a sylvan beauty in her dreams
Slumbering with brown body and tumbled hair
In her chamber inviolate of emerald peace.
Around it stretched the forest's anchorite mood
Lost in the depths of its own solitude.
Then moved by the deep joy she could not speak,
A little depth of it quivering in her words,
Her happy voice cried out to Satyavan:
"My heart will stay here on this forest verge

And close to this thatched roof while I am far:
Now of more wandering it has no need.
But I must haste back to my father's house
Which soon will lose one loved accustomed tread
And listen in vain for a once cherished voice.
For soon I shall return nor ever again
Oneness must sever its recovered bliss
Or fate sunder our lives while life is ours."
Once more she mounted on the carven car
And under the ardour of a fiery noon
Less bright than the splendour of her thoughts and dreams
She sped swift-reined, swift-hearted but still saw
In still lucidities of sight's inner world
Through the cool-scented wood's luxurious gloom
On shadowy paths between great rugged trunks
Pace towards a tranquil clearing Satyavan.
A nave of trees enshrined the hermit thatch,
The new deep covert of her felicity,
Preferred to heaven her soul's temple and home.
This now remained with her, her heart's constant scene.

END OF CANTO THREE
End of Book Five

BOOK SIX

The Book of Fate

BOOK SIX

The Book of Fate

Canto One

The Word of Fate

IN SILENT bounds bordering the mortal's plane
Crossing a wide expanse of brilliant peace
Narad the heavenly sage from Paradise
Came chanting through the large and lustrous air.
Attracted by the golden summer-earth
That lay beneath him like a glowing bowl
Tilted upon a table of the Gods,
Turning as if moved round by an unseen hand
To catch the warmth and blaze of a small sun,
He passed from the immortals' happy paths
To a world of toil and quest and grief and hope,
To these rooms of the see-saw game of death with life.
Across an intangible border of soul-space
He passed from Mind into material things
Amid the inventions of the inconscient Self
And the workings of a blind somnambulist Force.
Below him circling burned the myriad suns:
He bore the ripples of the etheric sea;
A primal Air brought the first joy of touch;
A secret Spirit drew its mighty breath
Contracting and expanding this huge world
In its formidable circuit through the Void;
The secret might of the creative Fire
Displayed its triple power to build and form,
Its infinitesimal wave-sparks' weaving dance,
Its nebulous units grounding shape and mass,
Magic foundation and pattern of a world,
Its radiance bursting into the light of stars;
He felt a sap of life, a sap of death;
Into solid Matter's dense communion
Plunging and its obscure oneness of forms

He shared with a dumb Spirit identity.
He beheld the cosmic Being at his task,
His eyes measured the spaces, gauged the depths,
His inner gaze the movements of the soul,
He saw the eternal labour of the Gods,
And looked upon the life of beasts and men.
A change now fell upon the singer's mood,
A rapture and a pathos moved his voice;
He sang no more of Light that never wanes,
And oneness and pure everlasting bliss,
He sang no more the deathless heart of Love,
His chant was a hymn of Ignorance and Fate.
He sang the name of Vishnu and the birth
And joy and passion of the mystic world,
And how the stars were made and life began
And the mute regions stirred with the throb of a Soul.
He sang the Inconscient and its secret self,
Its power omnipotent knowing not what it does,
All-shaping without will or thought or sense,
Its blind unerring occult mystery,
And darkness yearning towards the eternal Light,
And Love that broods within the dim abyss
And waits the answer of the human heart,
And death that climbs to immortality.
He sang of the Truth that cries from Night's blind deeps,
And the Mother-Wisdom hid in Nature's breast
And the Idea that through her dumbness works
And the miracle of her transforming hands,
Of life that slumbers in the stone and sun
And Mind subliminal in mindless life,
And the Consciousness that wakes in beasts and men.
He sang of the glory and marvel still to be born,
Of Godhead throwing off at last its veil,
Of bodies made divine and life made bliss,
Immortal sweetness clasping immortal might,
Heart sensing heart, thought looking straight at thought,

And the delight when every barrier falls,
And the transfiguration and the ecstasy.
And as he sang the demons wept with joy
Foreseeing the end of their long dreadful task
And the defeat for which they hoped in vain,
And glad release from their self-chosen doom
And return into the One from whom they came.
He who has conquered the Immortals' seats,
Came down to men on earth the Man divine.
As darts a lightning streak, a glory fell
Nearing until the rapt eyes of the sage
Looked out from luminous cloud and, strangely limned,
His face, a beautiful mask of antique joy,
Appearing in light descended where arose
King Aswapati's palace to the winds
In Madra, flowering up in delicate stone.
There welcomed him the sage and thoughtful king,
At his side a creature beautiful, passionate, wise,
Aspiring like a sacrificial flame
Skyward from its earth-seat through luminous air,
Queen-browed, the human mother of Savitri.
There for an hour untouched by the earth's siege
They ceased from common life and care and sat
Inclining to the high and rhythmic voice,
While in his measured chant the heavenly seer
Spoke of the toils of men and what the gods
Strive for on earth, and joy that throbs behind
The marvel and the mystery of pain.
He sang to them of the lotus-heart of love
With all its thousand luminous buds of truth,
Which quivering sleeps veiled by apparent things.
It trembles at each touch, it strives to wake
And one day it shall hear a blissful voice
And in the garden of the Spouse shall bloom
When she is seized by her discovered lord.
A mighty shuddering coil of ecstasy

Crept through the deep heart of the universe.
Out of her Matter's stupor, her mind's dreams,
She woke, she looked upon God's unveiled face.

   Even as he sang and rapture stole through earth-time
And caught the heavens, came with a call of hooves,
As of her swift heart hastening, Savitri;
Her radiant tread glimmered across the floor.
A happy wonder in her fathomless gaze,
Changed by the halo of her love she came;
Her eyes rich with a shining mist of joy
As one who comes from a heavenly embassy
Discharging the proud mission of her heart,
One carrying the sanction of the gods
To her love and its luminous eternity,
She stood before her mighty father's throne
And, eager for beauty on discovered earth
Transformed and new in her heart's miracle-light,
Saw like a rose of marvel, worshipping,
The fire-tinged sweetness of the son of Heaven.
He flung on her his vast immortal look;
His inner gaze surrounded her with its light
And reining back knowledge from his immortal lips
He cried to her, "Who is this that comes, the bride,
The flame-born, and round her illumined head
Pouring their lights her hymeneal pomps
Move flashing about her? From what green glimmer of glades
Retreating into dewy silences
Or half-seen verge of waters moon-betrayed
Bringst thou this glory of enchanted eyes?
Earth has gold-hued expanses, shadowy hills
That cowl their dreaming phantom heads in night,
And, guarded in a cloistral joy of woods,
Screened banks sink down into felicity
Seized by the curved incessant yearning hands
And ripple-passion of the upgazing stream:

Amid cool-lipped murmurs of its pure embrace
They lose their souls on beds of trembling reeds.
And all these are mysterious presences
In which some spirit's immortal bliss is felt,
And they betray the earth-born heart to joy.
There hast thou paused, and marvelling borne eyes
Unknown, or heard a voice that forced thy life
To strain its rapture through thy listening soul?
Or, if my thought could trust this shimmering gaze,
It would say thou hast not drunk from an earthly cup,
But stepping through azure curtains of the noon
Thou wast surrounded on a magic verge
In brighter countries than man's eyes can bear.
Assailed by trooping voices of delight
And seized mid a sunlit glamour of the boughs
In faery woods, led down the gleaming slopes
Of Gandhamadan where the Apsaras roam,
Thy limbs have shared the sports which none has seen,
And in god-haunts thy human footsteps strayed,
Thy mortal bosom quivered with god-speech
And thy soul answered to a Word unknown.
What feet of gods, what ravishing flutes of heaven
Have thrilled high melodies round, from near and far
Approaching through the soft and revelling air,
Which still surprised thou hearest? They have fed
Thy silence on some red strange-ecstasied fruit
And thou hast trod the dim moon-peaks of bliss.
Reveal, O winged with light, whence thou hast flown
Hastening bright-hued through the green tangled earth,
Thy body rhythmical with the spring-bird's call.
The empty roses of thy hands are filled
Only with their own beauty and the thrill
Of a remembered clasp, and in thee glows
A heavenly jar, thy firm deep-honied heart,
New-brimming with a sweet and nectarous wine.
Thou hast not spoken with the kings of pain.

Life's perilous music rings yet to thy ear
Far-melodied, rapid and grand, a Centaur's song,
Or soft as water plashing mid the hills,
Or mighty as a great chant of many winds.
Moon-bright thou livest in thy inner bliss.
Thou comest like a silver deer through groves
Of coral flowers and buds of glowing dreams,
Or fleest like a wind-goddess through leaves,
Or roamst, O ruby-eyed and snow-winged dove,
Flitting through thickets of thy pure desires
In the unwounded beauty of thy soul.
These things are only images to thy earth,
But truest truth of that which in thee sleeps.
For such is thy spirit, a sister of the gods,
Thy earthly body lovely to the eyes
And thou art kin in joy to heaven's sons.
O thou who hast come to this great perilous world
Now only seen through the splendour of thy dreams,
Where hardly love and beauty can live safe,
Thyself a being dangerously great,
A soul alone in a golden house of thought
Has lived walled in by the safety of thy dreams.
On heights of happiness leaving doom asleep
Who hunts unseen the unconscious lives of men,
If thy heart could live locked in the ideal's gold,
As high, as happy might thy waking be!
If for all time doom could be left to sleep!"
   He spoke but held his knowledge back from words.
As a cloud plays with lightnings' vivid laugh,
But still holds back the thunder in its heart,
Only he let bright images escape.
His speech like glimmering music veiled his thoughts;
As a wind flatters the bright summer air,
Pitiful to mortals, only to them it spoke
Of living beauty and of present bliss:
He hid in his all-knowing mind the rest.

To those who hearkened to his celestial voice,
The veil heaven's pity throws on future pain
The Immortals' sanction seemed of endless joy.
But Aswapati answered to the seer; —
His listening mind had marked the dubious close,
An ominous shadow felt behind the words,
But calm like one who ever sits facing Fate
Here mid the dangerous contours of earth's life,
He answered covert thought with guarded speech:
"O deathless sage who knowest all things here,
If I could read by the ray of my own wish
Through the carved shield of symbol images
Which thou hast thrown before thy heavenly mind
I might see the steps of a young godlike life
Happily beginning luminous-eyed on earth;
Between the Unknowable and the Unseen
Born on the borders of two wonder-worlds,
It flames out symbols of the infinite
And lives in a great light of inner suns.
For it has read and broken the wizard seals;
It has drunk of the Immortal's wells of joy,
It has looked across the jewel bars of heaven,
It has entered the aspiring Secrecy,
It sees beyond terrestrial common things
And communes with the Powers that build the worlds,
Till through the shining gates and mystic streets
Of the city of lapis lazuli and pearl
Proud deeds step forth, a rank and march of gods.
Although in pauses of our human lives
Earth keeps for man some short and perfect hours
When the inconstant tread of Time can seem
The eternal moment which the deathless live,
Yet rare that touch upon the mortal's world:
Hardly a soul and body here are born
In the fierce difficult movement of the stars,
Whose life can keep the paradisal note,

Its rhythm repeat the many-toned melody
Tirelessly throbbing through the rapturous air
Caught in the song that sways the Apsara's limbs
When she floats gleaming like a cloud of light,
A wave of joy on heaven's moonstone floor.
Behold this image cast by light and love,
A stanza of the ardour of the gods
Perfectly rhymed, a pillared ripple of gold!
Her body like a brimmed pitcher of delight
Shaped in a splendour of gold-coloured bronze
As if to seize earth's truth of hidden bliss.
Dream-made illumined mirrors are her eyes
Draped subtly in a slumbrous fringe of jet,
Retaining heaven's reflections in their depths.
Even as her body, such is she within.
Heaven's lustrous mornings gloriously recur,
Like drops of fire upon a silver page,
In her young spirit yet untouched with tears.
All beautiful things eternal seem and new
To virgin wonder in her crystal soul.
The unchanging blue reveals its spacious thought;
Marvellous the moon floats on through wondering skies;
Earth's flowers spring up and laugh at time and death;
The charmed mutations of the enchanter life
Race like bright children past the smiling hours.
If but this joy of life could last, nor pain
Throw its bronze note into her rhythmed days!
Behold her, singer with the prescient gaze,
And let thy blessing chant that this fair child
Shall pour the nectar of a sorrowless life
Around her from her lucid heart of love,
Heal with her bliss the tired breast of earth
And cast like a happy snare felicity.
As grows the great and golden bounteous tree
Flowering by Alacananda's murmuring waves,
Where with enamoured speed the waters run

Lisping and babbling to the splendour of morn
And cling with lyric laughter round the knees
Of heaven's daughters dripping magic rain
Pearl-bright from moon-gold limbs and cloudy hair,
So are her dawns like jewelled leaves of light,
So casts she her felicity on men.
A flame of radiant happiness she was born
And surely will that flame set earth alight:
Doom surely will see her pass and say no word!
But too often here the careless Mother leaves
Her chosen in the envious hands of Fate:
The harp of God falls mute, its call to bliss
Discouraged fails mid earth's unhappy sounds;
The strings of the siren Ecstasy cry not here
Or soon are silenced in the human heart.
Of sorrow's songs we have enough: bid once
Her glad and griefless days bring heaven here.
Or must fire always test the great of soul?
Along the dreadful causeway of the Gods,
Armoured with love and faith and sacred joy,
A traveller to the Eternal's house,
Once let unwounded pass a mortal life."
But Narad answered not; silent he sat,
Knowing that words are vain and Fate is lord.
He looked into the unseen with seeing eyes,
Then, dallying with the mortal's ignorance
Like one who knows not, questioning, he cried:
"On what high mission went her hastening wheels?
Whence came she with this glory in her heart
And Paradise made visible in her eyes?
What sudden God has met, what face supreme?"
To whom the king, "The red asoca watched
Her going forth which now sees her return.
Arisen into an air of flaming dawn
Like a bright bird tired of her lonely branch,
To find her own lord, since to her on earth

He came not yet, this sweetness wandered forth
Cleaving her way with the beat of her rapid wings.
Led by a distant call her vague swift flight
Threaded the summer morns and sunlit lands.
The happy rest her burdened lashes keep
And these charmed guardian lips hold treasured still.
Virgin who comest perfected by joy,
Reveal the name thy sudden heart-beats learned.
Whom hast thou chosen, kingliest among men?"
And Savitri answered with her still calm voice
As one who speaks beneath the eyes of Fate:
"Father and king, I have carried out thy will.
One whom I sought I found in distant lands;
I have obeyed my heart, I have heard its call.
On the borders of a dreaming wilderness
Mid Shalwa's giant hills and brooding woods
In his thatched hermitage Dyumatsena dwells,
Blind, exiled, outcast, once a mighty king.
The son of Dyumatsena, Satyavan,
I have met on the wild forest's lonely verge.
My father, I have chosen. This is done."
Astonished, all sat silent for a space.
Then Aswapati looked within and saw
A heavy shadow float above the name
Chased by a sudden and stupendous light;
He looked into his daughter's eyes and spoke:
"Well hast thou done and I approve thy choice.
If this is all, then all is surely well;
If there is more, then all can still be well.
Whether it seem good or evil to men's eyes,
Only for good the secret Will can work.
Our destiny is written in double terms:
Through Nature's contraries we draw nearer God;
Out of the darkness we still grow to light.
Death is our road to immortality.
'Cry woe, cry woe,' the world's lost voices wail,

Yet conquers the eternal Good at last."
Then might the sage have spoken, but the king
In haste broke out and stayed the dangerous word:
"O singer of the ultimate ecstasy,
Lend not a dangerous vision to the blind
Because by native right thou hast seen clear.
Impose not on the mortal's tremulous breast
The dire ordeal that foreknowledge brings;
Demand not now the Godhead in our acts.
Here are not happy peaks the heaven-nymphs roam
Or Coilas or Vaicountha's starry stair:
Abrupt, jagged hills only the mighty climb
Are here where few dare even think to rise;
Far voices call down from the dizzy rocks,
Chill, slippery, precipitous are the paths.
Too hard the gods are with man's fragile race;
In their large heavens they dwell exempt from Fate
And they forget the wounded feet of man,
His limbs that faint beneath the whips of grief,
His heart that hears the tread of time and death.
The future's road is hid from mortal sight:
He moves towards a veiled and secret face.
To light one step in front is all his hope
And only for a little strength he asks
To meet the riddle of his shrouded fate.
Awaited by a vague and half-seen force,
Aware of danger to his uncertain hours
He guards his flickering yearnings from her breath;
He feels not when the dreadful fingers close
Around him with the grasp none can elude.
If thou canst loose her grip, then only speak.
Perhaps from the iron snare there is escape:
Our mind perhaps deceives us with its words
And gives the name of doom to our own choice;
Perhaps the blindness of our will is Fate."
He said and Narad answered not the king.

But now the queen alarmed lifted her voice:
"O seer, thy bright arrival has been timed
To this high moment of a happy life;
Then let the speech benign of griefless spheres
Confirm this blithe conjunction of two stars
And sanction joy with thy celestial voice.
Here drag not in the peril of our thoughts,
Let not our words create the doom they fear.
Here is no cause for dread, no chance for grief
To raise her ominous head and stare at love.
A single spirit in a multitude,
Happy is Satyavan mid earthly men
Whom Savitri has chosen for her mate,
And fortunate the forest hermitage
Where leaving her palace and riches and a throne
My Savitri will dwell and bring in heaven.
Then let thy blessing put the immortals' seal
On these bright lives' unstained felicity
Pushing the ominous Shadow from their days.
Too heavy falls a Shadow on man's heart;
It dares not be too happy upon earth.
It dreads the blow dogging too vivid joys,
A lash unseen in Fate's extended hand,
The danger lurking in fortune's proud extremes,
An irony in life's indulgent smile,
And trembles at the laughter of the gods.
Or if crouches unseen a panther doom,
If wings of Evil brood above that house,
Then also speak, that we may turn aside
And rescue our lives from hazard of wayside doom
And chance entanglement of an alien fate."
And Narad slowly answered to the queen:
"What help is in prevision to the driven?
Safe doors cry opening near, the doomed pass on.
A future knowledge is an added pain,
A torturing burden and a fruitless light

On the enormous scene that Fate has built.
The eternal poet, universal Mind,
Has paged each line of his imperial act;
Invisible the giant actors tread
And man lives like some secret player's mask.
He knows not even what his lips shall speak.
For a mysterious Power compels his steps
And life is stronger than his trembling soul.
None can refuse what the stark Force demands:
Her eyes are fixed upon her mighty aim;
No cry or prayer can turn her from her path.
She has leaped an arrow from the bow of God."
His words were theirs who live unforced to grieve
And help by calm the swaying wheels of life
And the long restlessness of transient things
And the trouble and passion of the unquiet world.
As though her own bosom were pierced the mother saw
The ancient human sentence strike her child,
Her sweetness that deserved another fate
Only a larger measure given of tears.
Aspiring to the nature of the gods,
A mind proof-armoured mailed in mighty thoughts,
A will entire couchant behind wisdom's shield,
Though to still heavens of knowledge she had risen,
Though calm and wise and Aswapati's queen,
Human was she still and opened her doors to grief;
The stony-eyed injustice she accused
Of the marble godhead of inflexible Law,
Nor sought the strength extreme adversity brings
To lives that stand erect and front the World-Power:
Her heart appealed against the impartial judge,
Taxed with perversity the impersonal One.
Her tranquil spirit she called not to her aid,
But as a common man beneath his load
Grows faint and breathes his pain in ignorant words,
So now she arraigned the world's impassive will:

"What stealthy doom has crept across her path
Emerging from the dark forest's sullen heart,
What evil thing stood smiling by the way
And wore the beauty of the Shalwa boy?
Perhaps he came an enemy from her past
Armed with a hidden force of ancient wrongs,
Himself unknowing, and seized her unknown.
Here dreadfully entangled love and hate
Meet us blind wanderers mid the perils of Time.
Our days are links of a disastrous chain,
Necessity avenges casual steps;
Old cruelties come back unrecognised,
The gods make use of our forgotten deeds.
Yet all in vain the bitter law was made.
Our own minds are the justicers of doom.
For nothing have we learned, but still repeat
Our stark misuse of self and others' souls.
There are dire alchemies of the human heart
And fallen from his ethereal element
Love darkens to the spirit of nether gods.
The dreadful angel, angry with his joys
Woundingly sweet he cannot yet forego,
Is pitiless to the soul his gaze disarmed,
He visits with his own pangs his quivering prey
Forcing us to cling enamoured to his grip
As if in love with our own agony.
This is one poignant misery in the world,
And grief has other lassoes for our life.
Our sympathies become our torturers.
Strength have I my own punishment to bear,
Knowing it just, but on this earth perplexed,
Smitten in the sorrow of scourged and helpless things,
Often it faints to meet other suffering eyes.
We are not as the gods who know not grief
And look impassive on a suffering world,
Calm they gaze down on the little human scene

And the short-lived passion crossing mortal hearts.
An ancient tale of woe can move us still,
We keep the ache of breasts that breathe no more,
We are shaken by the sight of human pain,
And share the miseries that others feel.
Ours not the passionless lids that cannot age.
Too hard for us is heaven's indifference:
Our own tragedies are not enough for us,
All pathos and all sufferings we make ours;
We have sorrow for a greatness passed away
And feel the touch of tears in mortal things.
Even a stranger's anguish rends my heart,
And this, O Narad, is my well-loved child.
Hide not from us our doom, if doom is ours.
This is the worst, an unknown face of Fate,
A terror ominous, mute, felt more than seen
Behind our seat by day, our couch by night,
A Fate lurking in the shadow of our hearts,
The anguish of the unseen that waits to strike.
To know is best, however hard to bear."
Then cried the sage piercing the mother's heart,
Forcing to steel the will of Savitri,
His words set free the spring of cosmic Fate.
The great Gods use the pain of human hearts
As a sharp axe to hew their cosmic road:
They squander lavishly men's blood and tears
For a moment's purpose in their fateful work.
This cosmic Nature's balance is not ours
Nor the mystic measure of her need and use.
A single word lets loose vast agencies;
A casual act determines the world's fate.
So now he set free destiny in that hour.
"The truth thou hast claimed; I give to thee the truth.
A marvel of the meeting earth and heavens
Is he whom Savitri has chosen mid men,
His figure is the front of Nature's march,

His single being excels the works of Time.
A sapphire cutting from the sleep of heaven,
Delightful is the soul of Satyavan,
A ray out of the rapturous Infinite,
A silence waking to a hymn of joy.
A divinity and kingliness gird his brow;
His eyes keep a memory from a world of bliss.
As brilliant as a lonely moon in heaven,
Gentle like the sweet bud that spring desires,
Pure like a stream that kisses silent banks,
He takes with bright surprise spirit and sense.
A living knot of golden Paradise,
A blue Immense he leans to the longing world,
Time's joy borrowed out of eternity,
A star of splendour or a rose of bliss.
In him soul and Nature, equal Presences,
Balance and fuse in a wide harmony.
The Happy in their bright ether have not hearts
More sweet and true than this of mortal make
That takes all joy as the world's native gift
And to all gives joy as the world's natural right.
His speech carries a light of inner truth,
And a large-eyed communion with the Power
In common things has made veilless his mind,
A seer in earth-shapes of garbless deity.
A tranquil breadth of sky windless and still
Watching the world like a mind of unplumbed thought,
A silent space musing and luminous
Uncovered by the morning to delight,
A green tangle of trees upon a happy hill
Made into a murmuring nest by southern winds,
These are his images and parallels,
His kin in beauty and in depth his peers.
A will to climb lifts a delight to live,
Heaven's height companion of earth-beauty's charm,
An aspiration to the immortals' air

Lain on the lap of mortal ecstasy.
His sweetness and his joy attract all hearts
To live with his own in a glad tenancy,
His strength is like a tower built to reach heaven,
A godhead quarried from the stones of life.
O loss, if death into its elements
Of which his gracious envelope was built,
Shatter this vase before it breathes its sweets,
As if earth could not keep too long from heaven
A treasure thus unique loaned by the gods,
A being so rare, of so divine a make!
In one brief year when this bright hour flies back
And perches careless on a branch of Time,
This sovereign glory ends heaven lent to earth,
This splendour vanishes from the mortal's sky:
Heaven's greatness came, but was too great to stay.
Twelve swift-winged months are given to him and her;
This day returning Satyavan must die."
A lightning bright and nude the sentence fell.
But the queen cried: "Vain then can be heaven's grace!
Heaven mocks us with the brilliance of its gifts,
For Death is a cupbearer of the wine
Of too brief joy held up to mortal lips
For a passionate moment by the careless gods.
But I reject the grace and the mockery.
Mounting thy car go forth, O Savitri,
And travel once more through the peopled lands.
Alas, in the green gladness of the woods
Thy heart has stooped to a misleading call.
Choose once again and leave this fated head,
Death is the gardener of this wonder-tree;
Love's sweetness sleeps in his pale marble hand.
Advancing in a honeyed line but closed,
A little joy would buy too bitter an end.
Plead not thy choice, for death has made it vain.
Thy youth and radiance were not born to lie

A casket void dropped on a careless soil;
A choice less rare may call a happier fate."
But Savitri answered from her violent heart, —
Her voice was calm, her face was fixed like steel:
"Once my heart chose and chooses not again.
The word I have spoken can never be erased,
It is written in the record book of God.
The truth once uttered, from the earth's air effaced,
By mind forgotten, sounds immortally
For ever in the memory of Time.
Once the dice fall thrown by the hand of Fate
In an eternal moment of the gods.
My heart has sealed its troth to Satyavan:
Its signature adverse Fate cannot efface,
Its seal not Fate nor Death nor Time dissolve.
Those who shall part who have grown one being within?
Death's grip can break our bodies, not our souls;
If death take him, I too know how to die.
Let Fate do with me what she will or can;
I am stronger than death and greater than my fate;
My love shall outlast the world, doom falls from me
Helpless against my immortality.
Fate's law may change, but not my spirit's will."
An adamant will, she cast her speech like bronze.
But in the queen's mind listening her words
Rang like the voice of a self-chosen Doom
Denying every issue of escape.
To her own despair answer the mother made;
As one she cried who in her heavy heart
Labours amid the sobbing of her hopes
To wake a note of help from sadder strings:
"O child, in the magnificence of thy soul
Dwelling on the border of a greater world
And dazzled by thy superhuman thoughts,
Thou lendst eternity to a mortal hope.
Here on this mutable and ignorant earth

Who is the lover and who is the friend?
All passes here, nothing remains the same.
None is for any on this transient globe.
He whom thou lovest now, a stranger came
And into a far strangeness shall depart:
His moment's part once done upon life's stage
Which for a time was given him from within,
To other scenes he moves and other players
And laughs and weeps mid faces new, unknown.
The body thou hast loved is cast away
Amidst the brute unchanging stuff of worlds
To indifferent mighty Nature and becomes
Crude matter for the joy of others' lives.
But for our souls, upon the wheel of God
For ever turning, they arrive and go,
Married and sundered in the magic round
Of the great Dancer of the boundless dance.
Our emotions are but high and dying notes
Of his wild music changed compellingly
By the passionate movements of a seeking Heart
In the inconstant links of hour with hour.
To call down heaven's distant answering song,
To cry to an unseized bliss is all we dare;
Once seized, we lose the heavenly music's sense;
Too near, the rhythmic cry has fled or failed;
All sweetnesses are baffling symbols here.
Love dies before the lover in our breast:
Our joys are perfumes in a brittle vase.
O then what wreck is this upon Time's sea
To spread life's sails to the hurricane desire
And call for pilot the unseeing heart!
O child, wilt thou proclaim, wilt thou then follow
Against the Law that is the eternal will
The autarchy of the rash Titan's mood
To whom his own fierce will is the one law
In a world where Truth is not, nor Light nor God?

Only the gods can speak what now thou speakst.
Thou who art human, think not like a god.
For man, below the god, above the brute,
Is given the calm reason as his guide;
He is not driven by an unthinking will
As are the actions of the bird and beast;
He is not moved by stark Necessity
Like the senseless motion of inconscient things.
The giant's and the Titan's furious march
Climbs to usurp the kingdom of the gods
Or skirts the demon magnitudes of Hell;
In the unreflecting passion of their hearts
They dash their lives against the eternal Law
And fall and break by their own violent mass:
The middle path is made for thinking man.
To choose his steps by reason's vigilant light,
To choose his path among the many paths
Is given him, for each his difficult goal
Hewn out of infinite possibility.
Leave not thy goal to follow a beautiful face.
Only when thou hast climbed above thy mind
And liv'st in the calm vastness of the One
Can love be eternal in the eternal Bliss
And love divine replace the human tie.
There is a shrouded law, an austere force:
It bids thee strengthen thy undying spirit;
It offers its severe benignancies
Of work and thought and measured grave delight
As steps to climb to God's far secret heights.
Then is our life a tranquil pilgrimage,
Each year a mile upon the heavenly Way,
Each dawn opens into a larger Light.
Thy acts are thy helpers, all events are signs,
Waking and sleep are opportunities
Given to thee by an immortal Power.
So canst thou raise thy pure unvanquished spirit,

Till spread to heaven in a wide vesper calm,
Indifferent and gentle as the sky,
It greatens slowly into timeless peace."
But Savitri replied with steadfast eyes:
"My will is part of the eternal Will,
My fate is what my spirit's strength can make,
My fate is what my spirit's strength can bear;
My strength is not the Titan's; it is God's.
I have discovered my glad reality
Beyond my body in another's being:
I have found the deep unchanging soul of love.
Then how shall I desire a lonely good,
Or slay, aspiring to white vacant peace,
The endless hope that made my soul spring forth
Out of its infinite solitude and sleep?
My spirit has glimpsed the glory for which it came,
The beating of one vast heart in the flame of things,
My eternity clasped by his eternity
And, tireless of the sweet abysms of Time,
Deep possibility always to love.
This, this is first, last joy and to its throb
The riches of a thousand fortunate years
Are poverty. Nothing to me are death and grief
Or ordinary lives and happy days.
And what to me are common souls of men
Or eyes and lips that are not Satyavan's?
I have no need to draw back from his arms
And the discovered paradise of his love
And journey into a still infinity.
Only now for my soul in Satyavan
I treasure the rich occasion of my birth:
In sunlight and a dream of emerald ways
I shall walk with him like gods in Paradise.
If for a year, that year is all my life.
And yet I know this is not all my fate
Only to live and love awhile and die.

For I know now why my spirit came on earth
And who I am and who he is I love.
I have looked at him from my immortal Self,
I have seen God smile at me in Satyavan;
I have seen the Eternal in a human face."
Then none could answer to her words. Silent
They sat and looked into the eyes of Fate.

END OF CANTO ONE

Canto Two

The Way of Fate and the Problem of Pain

A SILENCE sealed the irrevocable decree,
The word of Fate that fell from heavenly lips
Fixing a doom no power could ever reverse
Unless heaven's will itself could change its course.
Or so it seemed: yet from the silence rose
One voice that questioned changeless destiny,
A will that strove against the immutable Will.
A mother's heart had heard the fateful speech
That rang like a sanction to the call of death
And came like a chill close to life and hope.
Yet hope sank down like an extinguished fire.
She felt the leaden inevitable hand
Invade the secrecy of her guarded soul
And smite with sudden pain its still content
And the empire of her hard-won quietude.
Awhile she fell to the level of human mind,
A field of mortal grief and Nature's law;
She shared, she bore the common lot of men
And felt what common hearts endure in Time.
Voicing earth's question to the inscrutable power
The queen now turned to the still immobile seer:
Assailed by the discontent in Nature's depths,
Partner in the agony of dumb driven things
And all the misery, all the ignorant cry,
Passionate like sorrow questioning heaven she spoke.
Lending her speech to the surface soul on earth
She uttered the suffering in the world's dumb heart
And man's revolt against his ignorant fate.
"O seer, in the earth's strange twi-natured life
By what pitiless adverse Necessity
Or what cold freak of a Creator's will,

By what random accident or governed Chance
That shaped a rule out of fortuitous steps,
Made destiny from an hour's emotion, came
Into the unreadable mystery of Time
The direr mystery of grief and pain?
Is it thy God who made this cruel law?
Or some disastrous Power has marred his work
And he stands helpless to defend or save?
A fatal seed was sown in life's false start
When evil twinned with good on earthly soil.
Then first appeared the malady of mind,
Its pang of thought, its quest for the aim of life.
It twisted into forms of good and ill
The frank simplicity of the animal's acts;
It turned the straight path hewn by the body's gods,
Followed the zigzag of the uncertain course
Of life that wanders seeking for its aim
In the pale starlight falling from thought's skies,
Its guides the unsure idea, the wavering will.
Lost was the instinct's safe identity
With the arrow-point of being's inmost sight,
Marred the sure steps of Nature's simple walk
And truth and freedom in the growing soul.
Out of some ageless innocence and peace,
Privilege of souls not yet betrayed to birth,
Cast down to suffer on this hard dangerous earth
Our life was born in pain and with a cry.
Although earth-nature welcomes heaven's breath
Inspiring Matter with the will to live,
A thousand ills assail the mortal's hours
And wear away the natural joy of life;
Our bodies are an engine cunningly made,
But for all its parts as cunningly are planned,
Contrived ingeniously with demon skill,
Its apt inevitable heritage
Of mortal danger and peculiar pain,

Its payment of the tax of Time and Fate,
Its way to suffer and its way to die.
This is the ransom of our high estate,
The sign and stamp of our humanity.
A grisly company of maladies
Come, licensed lodgers, into man's bodily house,
Purveyors of death and torturers of life.
In the malignant hollows of the world,
In its subconscient cavern-passages
Ambushed they lie waiting their hour to leap,
Surrounding with danger the sieged city of life:
Admitted into the citadel of man's days
They mine his force and maim or suddenly kill.
Ourselves within us lethal forces nurse;
We make of our own enemies our guests:
Out of their holes like beasts they creep and gnaw
The chords of the divine musician's lyre
Till frayed and thin the music dies away
Or crashing snaps with a last tragic note.
All that we are is like a fort beset:
All that we strive to be alters like a dream
In the grey sleep of Matter's ignorance.
Mind suffers lamed by the world's disharmony
And the unloveliness of human things.
A treasure misspent or cheaply, fruitlessly sold
In the bazaar of a blind destiny,
A gift of priceless value from Time's gods
Lost or mislaid in an uncaring world,
Life is a marvel missed, an art gone wry;
A seeker in a dark and obscure place,
An ill-armed warrior facing dreadful odds,
An imperfect worker given a baffling task,
An ignorant judge of problems Ignorance made,
Its heavenward flights reach closed and keyless gates,
Its glorious outbursts peter out in mire.
On Nature's gifts to man a curse was laid:

All walks inarmed by its own opposites,
Error is the comrade of our mortal thought
And falsehood lurks in the deep bosom of truth,
Sin poisons with its vivid flowers of joy
Or leaves a red scar burnt across the soul;
Virtue is a grey bondage and a gaol.
At every step is laid for us a snare.
Alien to reason and the spirit's light,
Our fount of action from a darkness wells;
In ignorance and nescience are our roots.
A growing register of calamities
Is the past's account, the future's book of Fate:
The centuries pile man's follies and man's crimes
Upon the countless crowd of Nature's ills;
As if the world's stone load was not enough,
A crop of miseries obstinately is sown
By his own hand in the furrows of the gods,
The vast increasing tragic harvest reaped
From old misdeeds buried by oblivious Time.
He walks by his own choice into Hell's trap;
This mortal creature is his own worst foe.
His science is an artificer of doom;
He ransacks earth for means to harm his kind;
He slays his happiness and others' good.
Nothing has he learned from Time and its history;
Even as of old in the raw youth of Time,
When Earth ignorant ran on the highways of Fate,
Old forms of evil cling to the world's soul:
War making nought the sweet smiling calm of life,
Battle and rapine, ruin and massacre
Are still the fierce pastimes of man's warring tribes;
An idiot hour destroys what centuries made,
His wanton rage or frenzied hate lays low
The beauty and greatness by his genius wrought
And the mighty output of a nation's toil.
All he has achieved he drags to the precipice.

His grandeur he turns to an epic of doom and fall;
His littleness crawls content through squalor and mud,
He calls heaven's retribution on his head
And wallows in his self-made misery.
A part author of the cosmic tragedy,
His will conspires with death and time and fate.
His brief appearance on the enigmaed earth
Ever recurs but brings no high result
To this wanderer through the aeon-rings of God
That shut his life in their vast longevity.
His soul's wide search and ever returning hopes
Pursue the useless orbit of their course
In a vain repetition of lost toils
Across a track of soon forgotten lives.
All is an episode in a meaningless tale.
Why is it all and wherefore are we here?
If to some being of eternal bliss
It is our spirit's destiny to return
Or some still impersonal height of endless calm,
Since That we are and out of That we came,
Whence rose the strange and sterile interlude
Lasting in vain through interminable Time?
Who willed to form or feign a universe
In the cold and endless emptiness of Space?
Or if these beings must be and their brief lives,
What need had the soul of ignorance and tears?
Whence rose the call for sorrow and for pain?
Or all came helplessly without a cause?
What power forced the immortal spirit to birth?
The eternal witness once of eternity,
A deathless sojourner mid transient scenes,
He camps in life's half-lit obscurity
Amid the debris of his thoughts and dreams.
Or who persuaded it to fall from bliss
And forfeit its immortal privilege?
Who laid on it the ceaseless will to live

A wanderer in this beautiful, sorrowful world,
And bear its load of joy and grief and love?
Or if no being watches the works of Time,
What hard impersonal Necessity
Compels the vain toil of brief living things?
A great Illusion then has built the stars.
But where then is the soul's security,
Its poise in this circling of unreal suns?
Or else it is a wanderer from its home
Who strayed into a blind alley of Time and chance
And finds no issue from a meaningless world.
Or where begins and ends Illusion's reign?
Perhaps the soul we feel is only a dream,
Eternal self a fiction sensed in trance."

    Then after a silence Narad made reply:
Tuning his lips to earthly sound he spoke,
And something now of the deep sense of fate
Weighted the fragile hints of mortal speech.
His forehead shone with vision solemnised,
Turned to a tablet of supernal thoughts
As if characters of an unwritten tongue
Had left in its breadth the inscriptions of the gods.
Bare in that light Time toiled, his unseen works
Detected; the broad-flung far-seeing schemes
Unfinished which his aeoned flight unrolls
Were mapped already in that world-wide look.
"Was then the sun a dream because there is night?
Hidden in the mortal's heart the Eternal lives:
He lives secret in the chamber of thy soul,
A Light shines there nor pain nor grief can cross.
A darkness stands between thyself and him,
Thou canst not hear or feel the marvellous Guest,
Thou canst not see the beatific sun.
O queen, thy thought is a light of the Ignorance,
Its brilliant curtain hides from thee God's face.

It illumes a world born from the Inconscience
But hides the Immortal's meaning in the world.
Thy mind's light hides from thee the Eternal's thought,
Thy heart's hopes hide from thee the Eternal's will,
Earth's joys shut from thee the Immortal's bliss.
Thence rose the need of a dark intruding god,
The world's dread teacher, the creator, pain.
Where Ignorance is, there suffering too must come;
Thy grief is a cry of darkness to the Light;
Pain was the first-born of the Inconscience
Which was thy body's dumb original base;
Already slept there pain's subconscient shape:
A shadow in a shadowy tenebrous womb,
Till life shall move, it waits to wake and be.
In one caul with joy came forth the dreadful Power.
In life's breast it was born hiding its twin;
But pain came first, then only joy could be.
Pain ploughed the first hard ground of the world-drowse.
By pain a spirit started from the clod,
By pain Life stirred in the subliminal deep.
Interned, submerged, hidden in Matter's trance
Awoke to itself the dreamer, sleeping Mind;
It made a visible realm out of its dreams,
It drew its shapes from the subconscient depths,
Then turned to look upon the world it had made.
By pain and joy, the bright and tenebrous twins,
The inanimate world perceived its sentient soul,
Else had the Inconscient never suffered change.
Pain is the hammer of the Gods to break
A dead resistance in the mortal's heart,
His slow inertia as of living stone.
If the heart were not forced to want and weep,
His soul would have lain down content, at ease,
And never thought to exceed the human start
And never learned to climb towards the Sun.
This earth is full of labour, packed with pain;

Throes of an endless birth coerce her still;
The centuries end, the ages vainly pass
And yet the Godhead in her is not born.
The ancient Mother faces all with joy,
Calls for the ardent pang, the grandiose thrill;
For with pain and labour all creation comes.
This earth is full of the anguish of the gods;
Ever they travail driven by Time's goad,
And strive to work out the eternal Will
And shape the life divine in mortal forms.
His will must be worked out in human breasts
Against the Evil that rises from the gulfs,
Against the world's Ignorance and its obstinate strength,
Against the stumblings of man's pervert will,
Against the deep folly of his human mind,
Against the blind reluctance of his heart.
The spirit is doomed to pain till man is free.
There is a clamour of battle, a tramp, a march:
A cry arises like a moaning sea,
A desperate laughter under the blows of death,
A doom of blood and sweat and toil and tears.
Men die that man may live and God be born.
An awful Silence watches tragic Time.
Pain is the hand of Nature sculpturing men
To greatness: an inspired labour chisels
With heavenly cruelty an unwilling mould.
Implacable in the passion of their will,
Lifting the hammers of titanic toil
The demiurges of the universe work;
They shape with giant strokes their own; their sons
Are marked with their enormous stamp of fire.
Although the shaping god's tremendous touch
Is torture unbearable to mortal nerves,
The fiery spirit grows in strength within
And feels a joy in every titan pang.
He who would save himself lives bare and calm;

He who would save the race must share its pain:
This he shall know who obeys that grandiose urge.
The Great who came to save this suffering world
And rescue out of Time's shadow and the Law,
Must pass beneath the yoke of grief and pain;
They are caught by the Wheel that they had hoped to break,
On their shoulders they must bear man's load of fate.
Heaven's riches they bring, their sufferings count the price
Or they pay the gift of knowledge with their lives.
The Son of God born as the Son of man
Has drunk the bitter cup, owned Godhead's debt,
The debt the Eternal owes to the fallen kind
His will has bound to death and struggling life
That yearns in vain for rest and endless peace.
Now is the debt paid, wiped off the original score.
The Eternal suffers in a human form,
He has signed salvation's testament with his blood:
He has opened the doors of his undying peace.
The Deity compensates the creature's claim,
The Creator bears the law of pain and death;
A retribution smites the incarnate God.
His love has paved the mortal's road to Heaven:
He has given his life and light to balance here
The dark account of mortal ignorance.
It is finished, the dread mysterious sacrifice,
Offered by God's martyred body for the world;
Gethsemane and Calvary are his lot,
He carries the cross on which man's soul is nailed;
His escort is the curses of the crowd;
Insult and jeer are his right's acknowledgment;
Two thieves slain with him mock his mighty death.
He has trod with bleeding brow the Saviour's way.
He who has found his identity with God
Pays with the body's death his soul's vast light.
His knowledge immortal triumphs by his death.
Hewn, quartered on the scaffold as he falls,

His crucified voice proclaims, 'I, I am God;'
'Yes, all is God,' peals back Heaven's deathless call.
The seed of Godhead sleeps in mortal hearts,
The flower of Godhead grows on the world-tree:
All shall discover God in self and things.
But when God's messenger comes to help the world
And lead the soul of earth to higher things,
He too must carry the yoke he came to unloose;
He too must bear the pang that he would heal:
Exempt and unafflicted by earth's fate,
How shall he cure the ills he never felt?
He covers the world's agony with his calm;
But though to the outward eye no sign appears
And peace is given to our torn human hearts,
The struggle is there and paid the unseen price;
The fire, the strife, the wrestle are within.
He carries the suffering world in his own breast;
Its sins weigh on his thoughts, its grief is his:
Earth's ancient load lies heavy on his soul;
Night and its powers beleaguer his tardy steps,
The Titan adversary's clutch he bears;
His march is a battle and a pilgrimage.
Life's evil smites, he is stricken with the world's pain:
A million wounds gape in his secret heart.
He journeys sleepless through an unending night;
Antagonist forces crowd across his path;
A siege, a combat is his inner life.
Even worse may be the cost, direr the pain:
His large identity and all-harbouring love
Shall bring the cosmic anguish into his depths,
The sorrow of all living things shall come
And knock at his doors and live within his house;
A dreadful cord of sympathy can tie
All suffering into his single grief and make
All agony in all the worlds his own.
He meets an ancient adversary Force,

He is lashed with the whips that tear the world's worn heart;
The weeping of the centuries visits his eyes:
He wears the blood-glued fiery Centaur shirt,
The poison of the world has stained his throat.
In the market-place of Matter's capital
Amidst the chafferings of the affair called life
He is tied to the stake of a perennial Fire;
He burns on an unseen original verge
That Matter may be turned to spirit stuff:
He is the victim in his own sacrifice.
The Immortal bound to earth's mortality
Appearing and perishing on the roads of Time
Creates God's moment by eternity's beats.
He dies that the world may be new-born and live.
Even if he escapes the fiercest fires,
Even if the world breaks not in, a drowning sea,
Only by hard sacrifice is high heaven earned:
He must face the fight, the pang who would conquer Hell.
A dark concealed hostility is lodged
In the human depths, in the hidden heart of Time
That claims the right to change and mar God's work.
A secret enmity ambushes the world's march;
It leaves a mark on thought and speech and act:
It stamps stain and defect on all things done;
Till it is slain peace is forbidden on earth.
There is no visible foe, but the unseen
Is round us, forces intangible besiege,
Touches from alien realms, thoughts not our own
Overtake us and compel the erring heart;
Our lives are caught in an ambiguous net.
An adversary Force was born of old:
Invader of the life of mortal man,
It hides from him the straight immortal path.
A power came in to veil the eternal Light,
A power opposed to the eternal will
Diverts the messages of the infallible Word,

Contorts the contours of the cosmic plan:
A whisper lures to evil the human heart,
It seals up wisdom's eyes, the soul's regard,
It is the origin of our suffering here,
It binds earth to calamity and pain.
This all must conquer who would bring down God's peace.
This hidden foe lodged in the human breast
Man must overcome or miss his higher fate.
This is the inner war without escape.

"Hard is the world-redeemer's heavy task;
The world itself becomes his adversary,
Those he would save are his antagonists:
This world is in love with its own ignorance,
Its darkness turns away from the saviour light,
It gives the cross in payment for the crown.
His work is a trickle of splendour in a long night;
He sees the long march of Time, the little won;
A few are saved, the rest strive on and fail:
A Sun has passed, on earth Night's shadow falls.
Yes, there are happy ways near to God's sun;
But few are they who tread the sunlit path;
Only the pure in soul can walk in light.
An exit is shown, a road of hard escape
From the sorrow and the darkness and the chain;
But how shall a few escaped release the world?
The human mass lingers beneath the yoke.
Escape, however high, redeems not life,
Life that is left behind on a fallen earth.
Escape cannot uplift the abandoned race
Or bring to it victory and the reign of God.
A greater power must come, a larger light.
Although Light grows on earth and Night recedes,
Yet till the evil is slain in its own home
And Light invades the world's inconscient base
And perished has the adversary Force,

He still must labour on, his work half done.
One yet may come armoured, invincible;
His will immobile meets the mobile hour;
The world's blows cannot bend that victor head;
Calm and sure are his steps in the growing Night;
The goal recedes, he hurries not his pace,
He turns not to high voices in the night;
He asks no aid from the inferior gods;
His eyes are fixed on his immutable aim.
Man turns aside or chooses easier paths;
He keeps to the one high and difficult road
That sole can climb to the Eternal's peaks;
The ineffable planes already have felt his tread;
He has made heaven and earth his instruments,
But the limits fall from him of earth and heaven;
Their law he transcends but uses as his means.
He has seized life's hands, he has mastered his own heart.
The feints of Nature mislead not his sight,
Inflexible his look towards Truth's far end;
Fate's deaf resistance cannot break his will.
In the dreadful passages, the fatal paths,
Invulnerable his soul, his heart unslain,
He lives through the opposition of earth's Powers
And Nature's ambushes and the world's attacks.
His spirit's stature transcending pain and bliss,
He fronts evil and good with calm and equal eyes.
He too must grapple with the riddling Sphinx
And plunge into her long obscurity.
He has broken into the Inconscient's depths
That veil themselves even from their own regard:
He has seen God's slumber shape these magic worlds.
He has watched the dumb God fashioning Matter's frame,
Dreaming the dreams of its unknowing sleep,
And watched the unconscious Force that built the stars.
He has learned the Inconscient's workings and its law,
Its incoherent thoughts and rigid acts,

Its hazard wastes of impulse and idea,
The chaos of its mechanic frequencies,
Its random calls, its whispers falsely true,
Misleaders of the hooded listening soul.
All things come to its ear but nothing abides;
All rose from the silence, all goes back to its hush.
Its somnolence founded the universe,
Its obscure waking makes the world seem vain.
Arisen from Nothingness and towards Nothingness turned,
Its dark and potent nescience was earth's start;
It is the waste stuff from which all was made;
Into its deeps creation can collapse.
Its opposition clogs the march of the soul,
It is the mother of our ignorance.
He must call light into its dark abysms,
Else never can Truth conquer Matter's sleep
And all earth look into the eyes of God.
All things obscure his knowledge must relume,
All things perverse his power must unknot:
He must pass to the other shore of falsehood's sea,
He must enter the world's dark to bring there light.
The heart of evil must be bared to his eyes,
He must learn its cosmic dark necessity,
Its right and its dire roots in Nature's soil.
He must know the thought that moves the demon act
And justifies the Titan's erring pride
And the falsehood lurking in earth's crooked dreams:
He must enter the eternity of Night
And know God's darkness as he knows his Sun.
For this he must go down into the pit,
For this he must invade the dolorous Vasts.
Imperishable and wise and infinite,
He still must travel Hell the world to save.
Into the eternal Light he shall emerge
On borders of the meeting of all worlds;
There on the verge of Nature's summit steps

The secret Law of each thing is fulfilled,
All contraries heal their long dissidence.
There meet and clasp the eternal opposites,
There pain becomes a violent fiery joy;
Evil turns back to its original good,
And sorrow lies upon the breasts of Bliss:
She has learned to weep glad tears of happiness;
Her gaze is charged with a wistful ecstasy.
Then shall be ended here the Law of Pain.
Earth shall be made a home of Heaven's light,
A seer heaven-born shall lodge in human breasts;
The superconscient beam shall touch men's eyes
And the truth-conscious world come down to earth
Invading Matter with the Spirit's ray,
Awaking its silence to immortal thoughts,
Awaking the dumb heart to the living Word.
This mortal life shall house Eternity's bliss,
The body's self taste immortality.
Then shall the world-redeemer's task be done.

"Till then must life carry its seed of death
And sorrow's plaint be heard in the slow Night.
O mortal, bear this great world's law of pain,
In thy hard passage through a suffering world
Lean for thy soul's support on Heaven's strength,
Turn towards high Truth, aspire to love and peace.
A little bliss is lent thee from above,
A touch divine upon thy human days.
Make of thy daily way a pilgrimage,
For through small joys and griefs thou mov'st towards God.
Haste not towards Godhead on a dangerous road,
Open not thy doorways to a nameless Power,
Climb not to Godhead by the Titan's road.
Against the Law he pits his single will,
Across its way he throws his pride of might.
Heavenward he clambers on a stair of storms

Aspiring to live near the deathless sun.
He strives with a giant strength to wrest by force
From life and Nature the immortals' right;
He takes by storm the world and fate and heaven.
He comes not to the high World-maker's seat,
He waits not for the outstretched hand of God
To raise him out of his mortality.
All he would make his own, leave nothing free,
Stretching his small self to cope with the infinite.
Obstructing the gods' open ways he makes
His own estate of the earth's air and light;
A monopolist of the world-energy,
He dominates the life of common men.
His pain and others' pain he makes his means:
On death and suffering he builds his throne.
In the hurry and clangour of his acts of might,
In a riot and excess of fame and shame,
By his magnitudes of hate and violence,
By the quaking of the world beneath his tread
He matches himself against the Eternal's calm
And feels in himself the greatness of a god:
Power is his image of celestial self.
The Titan's heart is a sea of fire and force;
He exults in the death of things and ruin and fall,
He feeds his strength with his own and others' pain;
In the world's pathos and passion he takes delight,
His pride, his might call for the struggle and pang.
He glories in the sufferings of the flesh
And covers the stigmata with the Stoic's name.
His eyes blinded and visionless stare at the sun,
The seeker's Sight receding from his heart
Can find no more the light of eternity;
He sees the beyond as an emptiness void of soul
And takes his night for a dark infinite.
His nature magnifies the unreal's blank
And sees in Nought the sole reality:

He would stamp his single figure on the world,
Obsess the world's rumours with his single name.
His moments centre the vast universe.
He sees his little self as very God.
His little 'I' has swallowed the whole world,
His ego has stretched into infinity.
His mind, a beat in original Nothingness,
Ciphers his thought on a slate of hourless Time.
He builds on a mighty vacancy of soul
A huge philosophy of Nothingness.
In him Nirvana lives and speaks and acts
Impossibly creating a universe.
An eternal zero is his formless self,
His spirit the void impersonal absolute.
Take not that stride, O growing soul of man;
Cast not thy self into that night of God.
The soul suffering is not eternity's key,
Or ransom by sorrow heaven's demand on life.
O mortal, bear, but ask not for the stroke,
Too soon will grief and anguish find thee out.
Too enormous is that venture for thy will;
Only in limits can man's strength be safe;
Yet is infinity thy spirit's goal;
Its bliss is there behind the world's face of tears.
A power is in thee that thou knowest not;
Thou art a vessel of the imprisoned spark.
It seeks relief from Time's envelopment,
And while thou shutst it in, the seal is pain:
Bliss is the Godhead's crown, eternal, free,
Unburdened by life's blind mystery of pain:
Pain is the signature of the Ignorance
Attesting the secret god denied by life:
Until life finds him pain can never end.
Calm is self's victory overcoming fate.
Bear; thou shalt find at last thy road to bliss.
Bliss is the secret stuff of all that lives,

Even pain and grief are garbs of world-delight,
It hides behind thy sorrow and thy cry.
Because thy strength is a part and not God's whole,
Because afflicted by the little self
Thy consciousness forgets to be divine
As it walks in the vague penumbra of the flesh
And cannot bear the world's tremendous touch,
Thou criest out and sayst that there is pain.
Indifference, pain and joy, a triple disguise,
Attire of the rapturous Dancer in the ways,
Withhold from thee the body of God's bliss.
Thy spirit's strength shall make thee one with God,
Thy agony shall change to ecstasy,
Indifference deepen into infinity's calm
And joy laugh nude on the peaks of the Absolute.

"O mortal who complainst of death and fate,
Accuse none of the harms thyself hast called;
This troubled world thou hast chosen for thy home,
Thou art thyself the author of thy pain.
Once in the immortal boundlessness of Self,
In a vast of Truth and Consciousness and Light
The soul looked out from its felicity.
It felt the Spirit's interminable bliss,
It knew itself deathless, timeless, spaceless, one,
It saw the Eternal, lived in the Infinite.
Then, curious of a shadow thrown by Truth,
It strained towards some otherness of self,
It was drawn to an unknown Face peering through night.
It sensed a negative infinity,
A void supernal whose immense excess
Imitating God and everlasting Time
Offered a ground for Nature's adverse birth
And Matter's rigid hard unconsciousness
Harbouring the brilliance of a transient soul
That lights up birth and death and ignorant life.

A Mind arose that stared at Nothingness
Till figures formed of what could never be;
It housed the contrary of all that is.
A Nought appeared as Being's huge sealed cause,
Its dumb support in a blank infinite,
In whose abysm spirit must disappear:
A darkened Nature lived and held the seed
Of Spirit hidden and feigning not to be.
Eternal Consciousness became a freak
Of an unsouled almighty Inconscient
And, breathed no more as spirit's native air,
Bliss was an incident of a mortal hour,
A stranger in the insentient universe.
As one drawn by the grandeur of the Void
The soul attracted leaned to the Abyss:
It longed for the adventure of Ignorance
And the marvel and surprise of the Unknown
And the endless possibility that lurked
In the womb of Chaos and in Nothing's gulf
Or looked from the unfathomed eyes of Chance.
It tired of its unchanging happiness,
It turned away from immortality:
It was drawn to hazard's call and danger's charm,
It yearned to the pathos of grief, the drama of pain,
Perdition's peril, the wounded bare escape,
The music of ruin and its glamour and crash,
The savour of pity and the gamble of love
And passion and the ambiguous face of Fate.
A world of hard endeavour and difficult toil,
And battle on extinction's perilous verge,
A clash of forces, a vast incertitude,
The joy of creation out of Nothingness,
Strange meetings on the roads of Ignorance
And the companionship of half-known souls
Or the solitary greatness and lonely force
Of a separate being conquering its world,

Called it from its too safe eternity.
A huge descent began, a giant fall:
For what the spirit sees, creates a truth
And what the soul imagines is made a world.
A Thought that leaped from the Timeless can become,
Indicator of cosmic consequence
And the itinerary of the gods,
A cyclic movement in eternal Time.
Thus came, born from a blind tremendous choice,
This great perplexed and discontented world,
This haunt of Ignorance, this home of Pain:
There are pitched desire's tents, grief's headquarters.
A vast disguise conceals the Eternal's bliss."

    Then Aswapati answered to the seer:
"Is then the spirit ruled by an outward world?
O seer, is there no remedy within?
But what is Fate if not the spirit's will
After long time fulfilled by cosmic Force?
I deemed a mighty Power had come with her;
Is not that Power the high compeer of Fate?"
But Narad answered covering truth with truth:
"O Aswapati, random seem the ways
Along whose banks your footsteps stray or run
In casual hours or moments of the gods,
Yet your least stumblings are foreseen above.
Infallibly the curves of life are drawn
Following the stream of Time through the unknown;
They are led by a clue the calm immortals keep.
This blazoned hieroglyph of prophet morns
A meaning more sublime in symbols writes
Than sealed Thought wakes to, but of this high script
How shall my voice convince the mind of earth?
Heaven's wiser love rejects the mortal's prayer;
Unblinded by the breath of his desire,
Unclouded by the mists of fear and hope,

It bends above the strife of love with death;
It keeps for her her privilege of pain.
A greatness in thy daughter's soul resides
That can transform herself and all around
But must cross on stones of suffering to its goal.
Although designed like a nectar cup of heaven,
Of heavenly ether made she sought this air,
She too must share the human need of grief
And all her cause of joy transmute to pain.
The mind of mortal man is led by words,
His sight retires behind the walls of Thought
And looks out only through half-opened doors.
He cuts the boundless Truth into sky-strips
And every strip he takes for all the heavens.
He stares at infinite possibility
And gives to the plastic Vast the name of Chance;
He sees the long results of an all-wise Force
Planning a sequence of steps in endless Time
But in its links imagines a senseless chain
Or the dead hand of cold Necessity;
He answers not to the mystic Mother's heart,
Misses the ardent heavings of her breast
And feels cold rigid limbs of lifeless Law.
The will of the Timeless working out in Time
In the free absolute steps of cosmic Truth
He thinks a dead machine or unconscious Fate.
A Magician's formulas have made Matter's laws
And while they last, all things by them are bound;
But the spirit's consent is needed for each act
And Freedom walks in the same pace with Law.
All here can change if the Magician choose.
If human will could be made one with God's,
If human thought could echo the thoughts of God,
Man might be all-knowing and omnipotent;
But now he walks in Nature's doubtful ray.
Yet can the mind of man receive God's light,

The force of man can be driven by God's force,
Then is he a miracle doing miracles.
For only so can he be Nature's king.
It is decreed and Satyavan must die;
The hour is fixed, chosen the fatal stroke.
What else shall be is written in her soul
But till the hour reveals the fateful script,
The writing waits illegible and mute.
Fate is Truth working out in Ignorance.
O King, thy fate is a transaction done
At every hour between Nature and thy soul
With God for its foreseeing arbiter.
Fate is a balance drawn in Destiny's book.
Man can accept his fate, he can refuse.
Even if the One maintains the unseen decree
He writes thy refusal in thy credit page:
For doom is not a close, a mystic seal.
Arisen from the tragic crash of life,
Arisen from the body's torture and death,
The spirit rises mightier by defeat;
Its godlike wings grow wider with each fall.
Its splendid failures sum to victory.
O man, the events that meet thee on thy road,
Though they smite thy body and soul with joy and grief,
Are not thy fate,—they touch thee awhile and pass;
Even death can cut not short thy spirit's walk:
Thy goal, the road thou choosest are thy fate.
On the altar throwing thy thoughts, thy heart, thy works,
Thy fate is a long sacrifice to the gods
Till they have opened to thee thy secret self
And made thee one with the indwelling God.
O soul, intruder in Nature's ignorance,
Armed traveller to the unseen supernal heights,
Thy spirit's fate is a battle and ceaseless march
Against invisible opponent Powers,
A passage from Matter into timeless self.

Adventurer through blind unforeseeing Time,
A forced advance through a long line of lives,
It pushes its spearhead through the centuries.
Across the dust and mire of the earthly plain,
On many guarded lines and dangerous fronts,
In dire assaults, in wounded slow retreats,
Holding the ideal's ringed and battered fort
Or fighting against odds in lonely posts,
Or camped in night around the bivouac's fires
Awaiting the tardy trumpets of the dawn,
In hunger and in plenty and in pain,
Through peril and through triumph and through fall,
Through life's green lanes and over her desert sands,
Up the bald moor, along the sunlit ridge,
In serried columns with a straggling rear
Led by its nomad vanguard's signal fires,
Marches the army of the waylost god.
Then late the joy ineffable is felt,
Then he remembers his forgotten self;
He has refound the skies from which he fell.
At length his front's indomitable line
Forces the last passes of the Ignorance:
Advancing beyond Nature's last known bounds,
Reconnoitring the formidable unknown,
Beyond the landmarks of things visible,
It mounts through a miraculous upper air
Till climbing the mute summit of the world
He stands upon the splendour-peaks of God.
In vain thou mournst that Satyavan must die;
His death is a beginning of greater life,
Death is the spirit's opportunity.
A vast intention has brought two souls close
And love and death conspire towards one great end.
For out of danger and pain heaven-bliss shall come,
Time's unforeseen event, God's secret plan.
This world was not built with random bricks of Chance,

A blind god is not destiny's architect;
A conscious power has drawn the plan of life,
There is a meaning in each curve and line.
It is an architecture high and grand
By many named and nameless masons built
In which unseeing hands obey the Unseen,
And of its master-builders she is one.
    "Queen, strive no more to change the secret will;
Time's accidents are steps in its vast scheme.
Bring not thy brief and helpless human tears
Across the fathomless moments of a heart
That knows its single will and God's as one:
It can embrace its hostile destiny;
It sits apart with grief and facing death,
Affronting adverse fate armed and alone.
In this enormous world standing apart
In the mightiness of her silent spirit's will,
In the passion of her soul of sacrifice
Her lonely strength facing the universe,
Affronting fate, asks not man's help nor god's:
Sometimes one life is charged with earth's destiny,
It cries not for succour from the time-bound powers.
Alone she is equal to her mighty task.
Intervene not in a strife too great for thee,
A struggle too deep for mortal thought to sound,
Its question to this Nature's rigid bounds
When the soul fronts nude of garbs the infinite,
Its too vast theme of a lonely mortal will
Pacing the silence of eternity.
As a star, uncompanioned, moves in heaven
Unastonished by the immensities of Space,
Travelling infinity by its own light,
The great are strongest when they stand alone.
A God-given might of being is their force,
A ray from self's solitude of light the guide;
The soul that can live alone with itself meets God;

Its lonely universe is their rendezvous.
A day may come when she must stand unhelped
On a dangerous brink of the world's doom and hers,
Carrying the world's future on her lonely breast,
Carrying the human hope in a heart left sole
To conquer or fail on a last desperate verge,
Alone with death and close to extinction's edge.
Her single greatness in that last dire scene
Must cross alone a perilous bridge in Time
And reach an apex of world-destiny
Where all is won or all is lost for man.
In that tremendous silence lone and lost
Of a deciding hour in the world's fate,
In her soul's climbing beyond mortal time
When she stands sole with Death or sole with God
Apart upon a silent desperate brink,
Alone with her self and death and destiny
As on some verge between Time and Timelessness
When being must end or life rebuild its base,
Alone she must conquer or alone must fall.
No human aid can reach her in that hour,
No armoured god stand shining at her side.
Cry not to heaven, for she alone can save.
For this the silent Force came missioned down;
In her the conscious Will took human shape:
She only can save herself and save the world.
O queen, stand back from that stupendous scene,
Come not between her and her hour of Fate.
Her hour must come and none can intervene:
Think not to turn her from her heaven-sent task,
Strive not to save her from her own high will.
Thou hast no place in that tremendous strife;
Thy love and longing are not arbiters there;
Leave the world's fate and her to God's sole guard.
Even if he seems to leave her to her lone strength,
Even though all falters and falls and sees an end

And the heart fails and only are death and night,
God-given her strength can battle against doom
Even on a brink where Death alone seems close
And no human strength can hinder or can help.
Think not to intercede with the hidden Will,
Intrude not twixt her spirit and its force
But leave her to her mighty self and Fate."

He spoke and ceased and left the earthly scene.
Away from the strife and suffering on our globe,
He turned towards his far-off blissful home.
A brilliant arrow pointing straight to heaven,
The luminous body of the ethereal seer
Assailed the purple glory of the noon
And disappeared like a receding star
Vanishing into the light of the Unseen.
But still a cry was heard in the infinite,
And still to the listening soul on mortal earth
A high and far imperishable voice
Chanted the anthem of eternal love.

END OF CANTO TWO
End of Book Six

BOOK SEVEN

The Book of Yoga

Canto One

The Joy of Union; the Ordeal of the Foreknowledge of Death and the Heart's Grief and Pain

FATE followed her foreseen immutable road.
Man's hopes and longings build the journeying wheels
That bear the body of his destiny
And lead his blind will towards an unknown goal.
His fate within him shapes his acts and rules;
Its face and form already are born in him,
Its parentage is in his secret soul:
Here Matter seems to mould the body's life
And the soul follows where its nature drives.
Nature and Fate compel his free-will's choice.
But greater spirits this balance can reverse
And make the soul the artist of its fate.
This is the mystic truth our ignorance hides:
Doom is a passage for our inborn force,
Our ordeal is the hidden spirit's choice,
Ananke is our being's own decree.
All was fulfilled the heart of Savitri
Flower-sweet and adamant, passionate and calm,
Had chosen and on her strength's unbending road
Forced to its issue the long cosmic curve.
Once more she sat behind loud hastening hooves;
A speed of armoured squadrons and a voice
Far-heard of chariots bore her from her home.
A couchant earth wakened in its dumb muse
Looked up at her from a vast indolence:
Hills wallowing in a bright haze, large lands
That lolled at ease beneath the summer heavens,
Region on region spacious in the sun,
Cities like chrysolites in the wide blaze
And yellow rivers pacing lion-maned

Led to the Shalwa marches' emerald line,
A happy front to iron vastnesses
And austere peaks and titan solitudes.
Once more was near the fair and fated place,
The borders gleaming with the groves' delight
Where first she met the face of Satyavan
And he saw like one waking into a dream
Some timeless beauty and reality,
The moon-gold sweetness of heaven's earth-born child.
The past receded and the future neared:
Far now behind lay Madra's spacious halls,
The white carved pillars, the cool dim alcoves,
The tinged mosaic of the crystal floors,
The towered pavilions, the wind-rippled pools
And gardens humming with the murmur of bees,
Forgotten soon or a pale memory
The fountain's plash in the white stone-bound pool,
The thoughtful noontide's brooding solemn trance,
The colonnade's dream grey in the quiet eve,
The slow moonrise gliding in front of Night.
Left far behind were now the faces known,
The happy silken babble on laughter's lips
And the close-clinging clasp of intimate hands
And adoration's light in cherished eyes
Offered to the one sovereign of their life.
Nature's primaeval loneliness was here:
Here only was the voice of bird and beast, —
The ascetic's exile in the dim-souled huge
Inhuman forest far from cheerful sound
Of man's blithe converse and his crowded days.
In a broad eve with one red eye of cloud,
Through a narrow opening, a green flowered cleft,
Out of the stare of sky and soil they came
Into a mighty home of emerald dusk.
There onward led by a faint brooding path
Which toiled through the shadow of enormous trunks

And under arches misers of sunshine,
They saw low thatched roofs of a hermitage
Huddled beneath a patch of azure hue
In a sunlit clearing that seemed the outbreak
Of a glad smile in the forest's monstrous heart,
A rude refuge of the thought and will of man
Watched by the crowding giants of the wood.
Arrived in that rough-hewn homestead they gave,
Questioning no more the strangeness of her fate,
Their pride and loved one to the great blind king,
A regal pillar of fallen mightiness
And the stately care-worn woman once a queen
Who now hoped nothing for herself from life,
But all things only hoped for her one child,
Calling on that single head from partial Fate
All joy of earth, all heaven's beatitude.
Adoring wisdom and beauty like a young god's,
She saw him loved by heaven as by herself,
She rejoiced in his brightness and believed in his fate
And knew not of the evil drawing near.
Lingering some days upon the forest verge
Like men who lengthen out departure's pain,
Unwilling to separate sorrowful clinging hands,
Unwilling to see for the last time a face,
Heavy with the sorrow of a coming day
And wondering at the carelessness of Fate
Who breaks with idle hands her supreme works,
They parted from her with pain-fraught burdened hearts
As forced by inescapable fate we part
From one whom we shall never see again;
Driven by the singularity of her fate,
Helpless against the choice of Savitri's heart
They left her to her rapture and her doom
In the tremendous forest's savage charge.
All put behind her that was once her life,
All welcomed that henceforth was his and hers,

She abode with Satyavan in the wild woods:
Priceless she deemed her joy so close to death;
Apart with love she lived for love alone.
As if self-poised above the march of days,
Her immobile spirit watched the haste of Time,
A statue of passion and invincible force,
An absolutism of sweet imperious will,
A tranquillity and a violence of the gods
Indomitable and immutable.

At first to her beneath the sapphire heavens
The sylvan solitude was a gorgeous dream,
An altar of the summer's splendour and fire,
A sky-topped flower-hung palace of the gods
And all its scenes a smile on rapture's lips
And all its voices bards of happiness.
There was a chanting in the casual wind,
There was a glory in the least sunbeam;
Night was a chrysoprase on velvet cloth,
A nestling darkness or a moonlit deep;
Day was a purple pageant and a hymn,
A wave of the laughter of light from morn to eve.
His absence was a dream of memory,
His presence was the empire of a god.
A fusing of the joys of earth and heaven,
A tremulous blaze of nuptial rapture passed,
A rushing of two spirits to be one,
A burning of two bodies in one flame.
Opened were gates of unforgettable bliss:
Two lives were locked within an earthly heaven
And fate and grief fled from that fiery hour.
But soon now failed the summer's ardent breath
And throngs of blue-black clouds crept through the sky
And rain fled sobbing over the dripping leaves
And storm became the forest's titan voice.
Then listening to the thunder's fatal crash

And the fugitive pattering footsteps of the showers
And the long unsatisfied panting of the wind
And sorrow muttering in the sound-vexed night,
The grief of all the world came near to her.
Night's darkness seemed her future's ominous face.
The shadow of her lover's doom arose
And fear laid hands upon her mortal heart.
The moments swift and ruthless raced; alarmed
Her thoughts, her mind remembered Narad's date.
A trembling moved accountant of her riches,
She reckoned the insufficient days between:
A dire expectancy knocked at her breast;
Dreadful to her were the footsteps of the hours:
Grief came, a passionate stranger to her gate:
Banished when in his arms, out of her sleep
It rose at morn to look into her face.
Vainly she fled into abysms of bliss
From her pursuing foresight of the end.
The more she plunged into love that anguish grew;
Her deepest grief from sweetest gulfs arose.
Remembrance was a poignant pang, she felt
Each day a golden leaf torn cruelly out
From her too slender book of love and joy.
Thus swaying in strong gusts of happiness
And swimming in foreboding's sombre waves
And feeding sorrow and terror with her heart, —
For now they sat among her bosom's guests
Or in her inner chamber paced apart, —
Her eyes stared blind into the future's night.
Out of her separate self she looked and saw,
Moving amid the unconscious faces loved,
In mind a stranger though in heart so near,
The ignorant smiling world go happily by
Upon its way towards an unknown doom
And wondered at the careless lives of men.
As if in different worlds they walked, though close,

They confident of the returning sun,
They wrapped in little hourly hopes and tasks,—
She in her dreadful knowledge was alone.
The rich and happy secrecy that once
Enshrined her as if in a silver bower
Apart in a bright nest of thoughts and dreams
Made room for tragic hours of solitude
And lonely grief that none could share or know,
A body seeing the end too soon of joy
And the fragile happiness of its mortal love.
Her quiet visage still and sweet and calm,
Her graceful daily acts were now a mask;
In vain she looked upon her depths to find
A ground of stillness and the spirit's peace.
Still veiled from her was the silent Being within
Who sees life's drama pass with unmoved eyes,
Supports the sorrow of the mind and heart
And bears in human breasts the world and fate.
A glimpse or flashes came, the Presence was hid.
Only her violent heart and passionate will
Were pushed in front to meet the immutable doom;
Defenceless, nude, bound to her human lot
They had no means to act, no way to save.
These she controlled, nothing was shown outside:
She was still to them the child they knew and loved;
The sorrowing woman they saw not within.
No change was in her beautiful motions seen:
A worshipped empress all once vied to serve,
She made herself the diligent serf of all,
Nor spared the labour of broom and jar and well,
Or close gentle tending or to heap the fire
Of altar and kitchen, no slight task allowed
To others that her woman's strength might do.
In all her acts a strange divinity shone:
Into a simplest movement she could bring
A oneness with earth's glowing robe of light,
A lifting up of common acts by love.

All-love was hers and its one heavenly cord
Bound all to all with her as golden tie.
But when her grief to the surface pressed too close,
These things, once gracious adjuncts of her joy,
Seemed meaningless to her, a gleaming shell,
Or were a round mechanical and void,
Her body's actions shared not by her will.
Always behind this strange divided life
Her spirit like a sea of living fire
Possessed her lover and to his body clung,
One locked embrace to guard its threatened mate.
At night she woke through the slow silent hours
Brooding on the treasure of his bosom and face,
Hung o'er the sleep-bound beauty of his brow
Or laid her burning cheek upon his feet.
Waking at morn her lips endlessly clung to his,
Unwilling ever to separate again
Or lose that honeyed drain of lingering joy,
Unwilling to loose his body from her breast,
The warm inadequate signs that love must use.
Intolerant of the poverty of Time
Her passion catching at the fugitive hours
Willed the expense of centuries in one day
Of prodigal love and the surf of ecstasy;
Or else she strove even in mortal time
To build a little room for timelessness
By the deep union of two human lives,
Her soul secluded shut into his soul.
After all was given she demanded still;
Even by his strong embrace unsatisfied,
She longed to cry, "O tender Satyavan,
O lover of my soul, give more, give more
Of love while yet thou canst, to her thou lov'st.
Imprint thyself for every nerve to keep
That thrills to thee the message of my heart.
For soon we part and who shall know how long
Before the great wheel in its monstrous round

Restore us to each other and our love?"
Too well she loved to speak a fateful word
And lay her burden on his happy head;
She pressed the outsurging grief back into her breast
To dwell within silent, unhelped, alone.
But Satyavan sometimes half understood,
Or felt at least with the uncertain answer
Of our thought-blinded hearts the unuttered need,
The unplumbed abyss of her deep passionate want.
All of his speeding days that he could spare
From labour in the forest hewing wood
And hunting food in the wild sylvan glades
And service to his father's sightless life
He gave to her and helped to increase the hours
By the nearness of his presence and his clasp,
And lavish softness of heart-seeking words
And the close beating felt of heart on heart.
All was too little for her bottomless need.
If in his presence she forgot awhile,
Grief filled his absence with its aching touch;
She saw the desert of her coming days
Imaged in every solitary hour.
Although with a vain imaginary bliss
Of fiery union through death's door of escape
She dreamed of her body robed in funeral flame,
She knew she must not clutch that happiness
To die with him and follow, seizing his robe
Across our other countries, travellers glad
Into the sweet or terrible Beyond.
For those sad parents still would need her here
To help the empty remnant of their day.
Often it seemed to her the ages' pain
Had pressed their quintessence into her single woe,
Concentrating in her a tortured world.
Thus in the silent chamber of her soul
Cloistering her love to live with secret grief
She dwelt like a dumb priest with hidden gods

Unappeased by the wordless offering of her days,
Lifting to them her sorrow like frankincense,
Her life the altar, herself the sacrifice.
Yet ever they grew into each other more
Until it seemed no power could rend apart,
Since even the body's walls could not divide.
For when he wandered in the forest, oft
Her conscious spirit walked with him and knew
His actions as if in herself he moved;
He, less aware, thrilled with her from afar.
Always the stature of her passion grew;
Grief, fear became the food of mighty love.
Increased by its torment it filled the whole world;
It was all her life, became her whole earth and heaven.
Although life-born, an infant of the hours,
Immortal it walked unslayable as the gods:
Her spirit stretched measureless in strength divine,
An anvil for the blows of Fate and Time:
Or tired of sorrow's passionate luxury,
Grief's self became calm, dull-eyed, resolute,
Awaiting some issue of its fiery struggle,
Some deed in which it might for ever cease,
Victorious over itself and death and tears.
    The year now paused upon the brink of change.
No more the storms sailed with stupendous wings
And thunder strode in wrath across the world,
But still was heard a muttering in the sky
And rain dripped wearily through the mournful air
And grey slow-drifting clouds shut in the earth.
So her grief's heavy sky shut in her heart.
A still self hid behind but gave no light:
No voice came down from the forgotten heights;
Only in the privacy of its brooding pain
Her human heart spoke to the body's fate.

END OF CANTO ONE

Canto Two

The Parable of the Search for the Soul

As IN the vigilance of the sleepless night
Through the slow heavy-footed silent hours,
Repressing in her bosom its load of grief,
She sat staring at the dumb tread of Time
And the approach of ever-nearing Fate,
A summons from her being's summit came,
A sound, a call that broke the seals of Night.
Above her brows where will and knowledge meet
A mighty Voice invaded mortal space.
It seemed to come from inaccessible heights
And yet was intimate with all the world
And knew the meaning of the steps of Time
And saw eternal destiny's changeless scene
Filling the far prospect of the cosmic gaze.
As the Voice touched, her body became a stark
And rigid golden statue of motionless trance,
A stone of God lit by an amethyst soul.
Around her body's stillness all grew still:
Her heart listened to its slow measured beats,
Her mind renouncing thought heard and was mute:
"Why camest thou to this dumb deathbound earth,
This ignorant life beneath indifferent skies
Tied like a sacrifice on the altar of Time,
O spirit, O immortal energy,
If 'twas to nurse grief in a helpless heart
Or with hard tearless eyes await thy doom?
Arise, O soul, and vanquish Time and Death."
But Savitri's heart replied in the dim night:
"My strength is taken from me and given to Death.
Why should I lift my hands to the shut heavens
Or struggle with mute inevitable Fate

Or hope in vain to uplift an ignorant race
Who hug their lot and mock the saviour Light
And see in Mind wisdom's sole tabernacle,
In its harsh peak and its inconscient base
A rock of safety and an anchor of sleep?
Is there a God whom any cry can move?
He sits in peace and leaves the mortal's strength
Impotent against his calm omnipotent Law
And Inconscience and the almighty hands of Death.
What need have I, what need has Satyavan
To avoid the black-meshed net, the dismal door,
Or call a mightier Light into life's closed room,
A greater Law into man's little world?
Why should I strive with earth's unyielding laws
Or stave off death's inevitable hour?
This surely is best to pactise with my fate
And follow close behind my lover's steps
And pass through night from twilight to the sun
Across the tenebrous river that divides
The adjoining parishes of earth and heaven.
Then could we lie inarmed breast upon breast,
Untroubled by thought, untroubled by our hearts,
Forgetting man and life and time and its hours,
Forgetting eternity's call, forgetting God."
The Voice replied: "Is this enough, O spirit?
And what shall thy soul say when it wakes and knows
The work was left undone for which it came?
Or is this all for thy being born on earth
Charged with a mandate from eternity,
A listener to the voices of the years,
A follower of the footprints of the gods,
To pass and leave unchanged the old dusty laws?
Shall there be no new tables, no new Word,
No greater light come down upon the earth
Delivering her from her unconsciousness,
Man's spirit from unalterable Fate?

Cam'st thou not down to open the doors of Fate,
The iron doors that seemed for ever closed,
And lead man to Truth's wide and golden road
That runs through finite things to eternity?
Is this then the report that I must make,
My head bowed with shame before the Eternal's seat, —
His power he kindled in thy body has failed,
His labourer returns, her task undone?"
Then Savitri's heart fell mute, it spoke no word.
But holding back her troubled rebel heart,
Abrupt, erect and strong, calm like a hill,
Surmounting the seas of mortal ignorance,
Its peak immutable above mind's air,
A Power within her answered the still Voice:
"I am thy portion here charged with thy work,
As thou myself seated for ever above,
Speak to my depths, O great and deathless Voice,
Command, for I am here to do thy will."
The Voice replied: "Remember why thou cam'st:
Find out thy soul, recover thy hid self,
In silence seek God's meaning in thy depths,
Then mortal nature change to the divine.
Open God's door, enter into his trance.
Cast Thought from thee, that nimble ape of Light:
In his tremendous hush stilling thy brain
His vast Truth wake within and know and see.
Cast from thee sense that veils thy spirit's sight:
In the enormous emptiness of thy mind
Thou shalt see the Eternal's body in the world,
Know him in every voice heard by thy soul,
In the world's contacts meet his single touch;
All things shall fold thee into his embrace.
Conquer thy heart's throbs, let thy heart beat in God:
Thy nature shall be the engine of his works,
Thy voice shall house the mightiness of his Word:
Then shalt thou harbour my force and conquer Death."

Then Savitri by her doomed husband sat,
Still rigid in her golden motionless pose,
A statue of the fire of the inner sun.
In the black night the wrath of storm swept by,
The thunder crashed above her, the rain hissed,
Its million footsteps pattered on the roof.
Impassive mid the movement and the cry,
Witness of the thoughts of mind, the moods of life,
She looked into herself and sought for her soul.

A dream disclosed to her the cosmic past,
The crypt-seed and the mystic origins,
The shadowy beginnings of world-fate:
A lamp of symbol lighting hidden truth
Imaged to her the world's significance.
In the indeterminate formlessness of Self
Creation took its first mysterious steps,
It made the body's shape a house of soul
And Matter learned to think and person grew;
She saw Space peopled with the seeds of life
And saw the human creature born in Time.
At first appeared a dim half-neutral tide
Of being emerging out of infinite Nought:
A consciousness looked at the inconscient Vast
And pleasure and pain stirred in the insensible Void.
All was the deed of a blind World-Energy:
Unconscious of her own exploits she worked,
Shaping a universe out of the Inane.
In fragmentary beings she grew aware:
A chaos of little sensibilities
Gathered round a small ego's pin-point head;
In it a sentient creature found its poise,
It moved and lived a breathing, thinking whole.
On a dim ocean of subconscient life
A formless surface consciousness awoke:
A stream of thoughts and feelings came and went,

A foam of memories hardened and became
A bright crust of habitual sense and thought,
A seat of living personality
And recurrent habits mimicked permanence.
Mind nascent laboured out a mutable form,
It built a mobile house on shifting sands,
A floating isle upon a bottomless sea.
A conscious being was by this labour made;
It looked around it on its difficult field
In the green wonderful and perilous earth;
It hoped in a brief body to survive,
Relying on Matter's false eternity.
It felt a godhead in its fragile house;
It saw blue heavens, dreamed immortality.
    A conscious soul in the Inconscient's world,
Hidden behind our thoughts and hopes and dreams,
An indifferent Master signing Nature's acts
Leaves the vicegerent mind a seeming king.
In his floating house upon the sea of Time
The regent sits at work and never rests:
He is a puppet of the dance of Time;
He is driven by the hours, the moment's call
Compels him with the thronging of life's need
And the babel of the voices of the world.
This mind no silence knows nor dreamless sleep,
In the incessant circling of its steps
Thoughts tread for ever through the listening brain;
It toils like a machine and cannot stop.
Into the body's many-storeyed rooms
Endless crowd down the dream-god's messages.
All is a hundred-toned murmur and babble and stir,
There is a tireless running to and fro,
A haste of movement and a ceaseless cry.
The hurried servant senses answer apace
To every knock upon the outer doors,
Bring in time's visitors, report each call,

Admit the thousand queries and the calls
And the messages of communicating minds
And the heavy business of unnumbered lives
And all the thousandfold commerce of the world.
Even in the tracts of sleep is scant repose;
He mocks life's steps in strange subconscient dreams,
He strays in a subtle realm of symbol scenes,
His night with thin-air visions and dim forms
He packs or peoples with slight drifting shapes
And only a moment spends in silent Self.
Adventuring into infinite mind-space
He unfolds his wings of thought in inner air,
Or travelling in imagination's car
Crosses the globe, journeys beneath the stars,
To subtle worlds takes his ethereal course,
Visits the Gods on Life's miraculous peaks,
Communicates with Heaven, tampers with Hell.
This is the little surface of man's life.
He is this and he is all the universe;
He scales the Unseen, his depths dare the Abyss;
A whole mysterious world is locked within.
Unknown to himself he lives a hidden king
Behind rich tapestries in great secret rooms;
An epicure of the spirit's unseen joys,
He lives on the sweet honey of solitude:
A nameless god in an unapproachable fane,
In the secret adytum of his inmost soul
He guards the being's covered mysteries
Beneath the threshold, behind shadowy gates
Or shut in vast cellars of inconscient sleep.
The immaculate Divine All-Wonderful
Casts into the argent purity of his soul
His splendour and his greatness and the light
Of self-creation in Time's infinity
As into a sublimely mirroring glass.
Man in the world's life works out the dreams of God.

But all is there, even God's opposites;
He is a little front of Nature's works,
A thinking outline of a cryptic Force.
All she reveals in him that is in her,
Her glories walk in him and her darknesses.
Man's house of life holds not the gods alone:
There are occult Shadows, there are tenebrous Powers,
Inhabitants of life's ominous nether rooms,
A shadowy world's stupendous denizens.
A careless guardian of his nature's powers,
Man harbours dangerous forces in his house.
The Titan and the Fury and the Djinn
Lie bound in the subconscient's cavern pit
And the Beast grovels in his antre den:
Dire mutterings rise and murmur in their drowse.
Insurgent sometimes raises its huge head
A monstrous mystery lurking in life's deeps,
The mystery of dark and fallen worlds,
The dread visages of the adversary Kings.
The dreadful powers held down within his depths
Become his masters or his ministers;
Enormous they invade his bodily house,
Can act in his acts, infest his thought and life.
Inferno surges into the human air
And touches all with a perverting breath.
Grey forces like a thin miasma creep,
Stealing through chinks in his closed mansion's doors,
Discolouring the walls of upper mind
In which he lives his fair and specious life,
And leave behind a stench of sin and death:
Not only rise in him perverse drifts of thought
And formidable formless influences,
But there come presences and awful shapes:
Tremendous forms and faces mount dim steps
And stare at times into his living-rooms,
Or called up for a moment's passionate work

Lay a dire custom's claim upon his heart:
Aroused from sleep, they can be bound no more.
Afflicting the daylight and alarming night,
Invading at will his outer tenement,
The stark gloom's grisly dire inhabitants
Mounting into God's light all light perturb.
All they have touched or seen they make their own,
In Nature's basement lodge, mind's passages fill,
Disrupt thought's links and musing sequences,
Break through the soul's stillness with a noise and cry
Or they call the inhabitants of the abyss,
Invite the instincts to forbidden joys,
A laughter wake of dread demoniac mirth
And with nether riot and revel shake life's floor.
Impotent to quell his terrible prisoners,
Appalled the householder helpless sits above,
Taken from him his house is his no more.
He is bound and forced, a victim of the play,
Or, allured, joys in the mad and mighty din.
His nature's dangerous forces have arisen
And hold at will a rebel's holiday.
Aroused from the darkness where they crouched in the depths,
Prisoned from the sight, they can be held no more;
His nature's impulses are now his lords.
Once quelled or wearing specious names and vests
Infernal elements, demon powers are there.
Man's lower nature hides these awful guests.
Their vast contagion grips sometimes man's world.
An awful insurgence overpowers man's soul.
In house and house the huge uprising grows:
Hell's companies are loosed to do their work,
Into the earth-ways they break out from all doors,
Invade with blood-lust and the will to slay
And fill with horror and carnage God's fair world.
Death and his hunters stalk a victim earth;
The terrible Angel smites at every door:

An awful laughter mocks at the world's pain
And massacre and torture grin at Heaven:
All is the prey of the destroying force;
Creation rocks and tremble top and base.
This evil Nature housed in human hearts,
A foreign inhabitant, a dangerous guest:
The soul that harbours it it can dislodge,
Expel the householder, possess the house.
An opposite potency contradicting God,
A momentary Evil's almightiness
Has straddled the straight path of Nature's acts.
It imitates the Godhead it denies,
Puts on his figure and assumes his face.
A Manichean creator and destroyer,
This can abolish man, annul his world.
But there is a guardian power, there are Hands that save,
Calm eyes divine regard the human scene.

All the world's possibilities in man
Are waiting as the tree waits in its seed:
His past lives in him; it drives his future's pace;
His present's acts fashion his coming fate.
The unborn gods hide in his house of Life.
The daemons of the unknown overshadow his mind
Casting their dreams into live moulds of thought,
The moulds in which his mind builds out its world.
His mind creates around him its universe.
All that has been renews in him its birth;
All that can be is figured in his soul.
Issuing in deeds it scores on the roads of the world,
Obscure to the interpreting reason's guess,
Lines of the secret purpose of the gods.
In strange directions runs the intricate plan;
Held back from human foresight is their end
And the far intention of some ordering Will
Or the order of life's arbitrary Chance

Finds out its settled poise and fated hour.
Our surface watched in vain by reason's gaze,
Invaded by the impromptus of the unseen,
Helpless records the accidents of Time,
The involuntary turns and leaps of life.
Only a little of us foresees its steps,
Only a little has will and purposed pace.
A vast subliminal is man's measureless part.
The dim subconscient is his cavern base.
Abolished vainly in the walks of Time
Our past lives still in our unconscious selves
And by the weight of its hidden influences
Is shaped our future's self-discovery.
Thus all is an inevitable chain
And yet a series seems of accidents.
The unremembering hours repeat the old acts,
Our dead past round our future's ankles clings
And drags back the new nature's glorious stride,
Or from its buried corpse old ghosts arise,
Old thoughts, old longings, dead passions live again,
Recur in sleep or move the waking man
To words that force the barrier of the lips,
To deeds that suddenly start and o'erleap
His head of reason and his guardian will.
An old self lurks in the new self we are;
Hardly we escape from what we once had been:
In the dim gleam of habit's passages,
In the subconscient's darkling corridors
All things are carried by the porter nerves
And nothing checked by subterranean mind,
Unstudied by the guardians of the doors
And passed by a blind instinctive memory,
The old gang dismissed, old cancelled passports serve.
Nothing is wholly dead that once had lived;
In dim tunnels of the world's being and in ours
The old rejected nature still survives;

The corpses of its slain thoughts raise their heads
And visit mind's nocturnal walks in sleep,
Its stifled impulses breathe and move and rise;
All keeps a phantom immortality.
Irresistible are Nature's sequences:
The seeds of sins renounced sprout from hid soil;
The evil cast from our hearts once more we face;
Our dead selves come to slay our living soul.
A portion of us lives in present Time,
A secret mass in dim inconscience gropes;
Out of the inconscient and subliminal
Arisen, we live in mind's uncertain light
And strive to know and master a dubious world
Whose purpose and meaning are hidden from our sight.
Above us dwells a superconscient God
Hidden in the mystery of his own light:
Around us is a vast of ignorance
Lit by the uncertain ray of human mind,
Below us sleeps the Inconscient dark and mute.
    But this is only Matter's first self-view,
A scale and series in the Ignorance.
This is not all we are or all our world.
Our greater self of knowledge waits for us,
A supreme light in the truth-conscious Vast:
It sees from summits beyond thinking mind,
It moves in a splendid air transcending life.
It shall descend and make earth's life divine.
Truth made the world, not a blind Nature-Force.
For here are not our large diviner heights;
Our summits in the superconscient's blaze
Are glorious with the very face of God:
There is our aspect of eternity,
There is the figure of the god we are,
His young unaging look on deathless things,
His joy in our escape from death and Time,
His immortality and light and bliss.

Our larger being sits behind cryptic walls:
There are greatnesses hidden in our unseen parts
That wait their hour to step into life's front:
We feel an aid from deep indwelling Gods;
One speaks within, Light comes to us from above.
Our soul from its mysterious chamber acts;
Its influence pressing on our heart and mind
Pushes them to exceed their mortal selves.
It seeks for Good and Beauty and for God;
We see beyond self's walls our limitless self,
We gaze through our world's glass at half-seen vasts,
We hunt for the Truth behind apparent things.
Our inner Mind dwells in a larger light,
Its brightness looks at us through hidden doors;
Our members luminous grow and Wisdom's face
Appears in the doorway of the mystic ward:
When she enters into our house of outward sense,
Then we look up and see, above, her sun.
A mighty life-self with its inner powers
Supports the dwarfish modicum we call life;
It can graft upon our crawl two puissant wings.
Our body's subtle self is throned within
In its viewless palace of veridical dreams
That are bright shadows of the thoughts of God.
In the prone obscure beginnings of the race
The human grew in the bowed apelike man.
He stood erect, a godlike form and force,
And a soul's thoughts looked out from earth-born eyes;
Man stood erect, he wore the thinker's brow:
He looked at heaven and saw his comrade stars;
A vision came of beauty and greater birth
Slowly emerging from the heart's chapel of light
And moved in a white lucent air of dreams.
He saw his being's unrealised vastnesses,
He aspired and housed the nascent demigod.
Out of the dim recesses of the self

The occult seeker into the open came:
He heard the far and touched the intangible,
He gazed into the future and the unseen;
He used the powers earth-instruments cannot use,
A pastime made of the impossible;
He caught up fragments of the Omniscient's thought,
He scattered formulas of omnipotence.
Thus man in his little house made of earth's dust
Grew towards an unseen heaven of thought and dream
Looking into the vast vistas of his mind
On a small globe dotting infinity.
At last climbing a long and narrow stair
He stood alone on the high roof of things
And saw the light of a spiritual sun.
Aspiring he transcends his earthly self;
He stands in the largeness of his soul new-born,
Redeemed from encirclement by mortal things
And moves in a pure free spiritual realm
As in the rare breath of a stratosphere;
A last end of far lines of divinity,
He mounts by a frail thread to his high source;
He reaches his fount of immortality,
He calls the Godhead into his mortal life.
All this the spirit concealed had done in her:
A portion of the mighty Mother came
Into her as into its own human part:
Amid the cosmic workings of the Gods
It marked her the centre of a wide-drawn scheme,
Dreamed in the passion of her far-seeing spirit
To mould humanity into God's own shape
And lead this great blind struggling world to light
Or a new world discover or create.
Earth must transform herself and equal Heaven
Or Heaven descend into earth's mortal state.
But for such vast spiritual change to be,
Out of the mystic cavern in man's heart

The heavenly Psyche must put off her veil
And step into common nature's crowded rooms
And stand uncovered in that nature's front
And rule its thoughts and fill the body and life.
Obedient to a high command she sat:
Time, life and death were passing incidents
Obstructing with their transient view her sight,
Her sight that must break through and liberate the god
Imprisoned in the visionless mortal man.
The inferior nature born into ignorance
Still took too large a place, it veiled her self
And must be pushed aside to find her soul.

END OF CANTO TWO

Canto Three

The Entry into the Inner Countries

AT FIRST out of the busy hum of mind
As if from a loud thronged market into a cave
By an inward moment's magic she had come.
A stark hushed emptiness became her self:
Her mind unvisited by the voice of thought
Stared at a void deep's dumb infinity.
Her heights receded, her depths behind her closed;
All fled away from her and left her blank.
But when she came back to her self of thought,
Once more she was a human thing on earth,
A lump of Matter, a house of closed sight,
A mind compelled to think out ignorance,
A life-force pressed into a camp of works
And the material world her limiting field.
Amazed like one unknowing she sought her way
Out of the tangle of man's ignorant past
That took the surface person for the soul.
Then a Voice spoke that dwelt on secret heights:
"For man thou seekst, not for thyself alone.
Only if God assumes the human mind
And puts on mortal ignorance for his cloak
And makes himself the Dwarf with triple stride,
Can he help man to grow into the God.
As man disguised the cosmic Greatness works
And finds the mystic inaccessible gate
And opens the Immortal's golden door.
Man, human, follows in God's human steps.
Accepting his darkness thou must bring to him light,
Accepting his sorrow thou must bring to him bliss.
In Matter's body find thy heaven-born soul."
Then Savitri surged out of her body's wall

And stood a little span outside herself
And looked into her subtle being's depths
And in its heart as a lotus-bud
Divined her secret and mysterious soul.
At the dim portal of the inner life
That bars out from our depths the body's mind
And all that lives but by the body's breath,
She knocked and pressed against the ebony gate.
The living portal groaned with sullen hinge:
Heavily reluctant it complained inert
Against the tyranny of the spirit's touch.
A formidable voice cried from within:
"Back, creature of earth, lest tortured and torn thou die."
A dreadful murmur rose like a dim sea;
The Serpent of the threshold hissing rose,
A fatal guardian hood with monstrous coils,
The hounds of darkness growled with jaws agape,
And trolls and gnomes and goblins scowled and stared
And wild beast roarings thrilled the blood with fear
And menace muttered in a dangerous tongue.
Unshaken her will pressed on the rigid bars:
The gate swung wide with a protesting jar,
The opponent Powers withdrew their dreadful guard;
Her being entered into the inner worlds.
In a narrow passage, the subconscient's gate,
She breathed with difficulty and pain and strove
To find the inner self concealed in sense.
Into a dense of subtle Matter packed,
A cavity filled with a blind mass of power,
An opposition of misleading gleams,
A heavy barrier of unseeing sight,
She forced her way through body to the soul.
Across a perilous border line she passed
Where Life dips into the subconscient dusk
Or struggles from Matter into chaos of mind,
Aswarm with elemental entities

And fluttering shapes of vague half-bodied thought
And crude beginnings of incontinent force.
At first a difficult narrowness was there,
A press of uncertain powers and drifting wills;
For all was there but nothing in its place.
At times an opening came, a door was forced;
She crossed through spaces of a secret self
And trod in passages of inner Time.
At last she broke into a form of things,
A start of finiteness, a world of sense:
But all was still confused, nothing self-found.
Soul was not there but only cries of life.
A thronged and clamorous air environed her.
A horde of sounds defied significance,
A dissonant clash of cries and contrary calls;
A mob of visions broke across the sight,
A jostled sequence lacking sense and suite,
Feelings pushed through a packed and burdened heart,
Each forced its separate inconsequent way
But cared for nothing but its ego's drive.
A rally without key of common will,
Thought stared at thought and pulled at the taut brain
As if to pluck the reason from its seat
And cast its corpse into life's wayside drain;
So might forgotten lie in Nature's mud
Abandoned the slain sentinel of the soul.
So could life's power shake from it mind's rule,
Nature renounce the spirit's government
And the bare elemental energies
Make of the sense a glory of boundless joy,
A splendour of ecstatic anarchy,
A revel mighty and mad of utter bliss.
This was the sense's instinct void of soul
Or when the soul sleeps hidden void of power,
But now the vital godhead wakes within
And lifts the life with the Supernal's touch.

But how shall come the glory and the flame
If mind is cast away into the abyss?
For body without mind has not the light,
The rapture of spirit sense, the joy of life;
All then becomes subconscient, tenebrous,
Inconscience puts its seal on Nature's page
Or else a mad disorder whirls the brain
Posting along a ravaged nature's roads,
A chaos of disordered impulses
In which no light can come, no joy, no peace.
This state now threatened, this she pushed from her.
As if in a long endless tossing street
One driven mid a trampling hurrying crowd
Hour after hour she trod without release
Holding by her will the senseless meute at bay;
Out of the dreadful press she dragged her will
And fixed her thought upon the saviour Name;
Then all grew still and empty; she was free.
A large deliverance came, a vast calm space.
Awhile she moved through a blank tranquillity
Of naked Light from an invisible sun,
A void that was a bodiless happiness,
A blissful vacuum of nameless peace.
But now a mightier danger's front drew near:
The press of bodily mind, the Inconscient's brood
Of aimless thought and will had fallen from her.
Approaching loomed a giant head of Life
Ungoverned by mind or soul, subconscient, vast.
It tossed all power into a single drive,
It made its power a might of dangerous seas.
Into the stillness of her silent self,
Into the whiteness of its muse of Space
A spate, a torrent of the speed of Life
Broke like a wind-lashed driven mob of waves
Racing on a pale floor of summer sand;
It drowned its banks, a mountain of climbing waves.

Enormous was its vast and passionate voice.
It cried to her listening spirit as it ran,
Demanding God's submission to chainless Force.
A deaf force calling to a status dumb,
A thousand voices in a muted Vast,
It claimed the heart's support for its clutch at joy,
For its need to act the witness Soul's consent,
For its lust of power her neutral being's seal.
Into the wideness of her watching self
It brought a grandiose gust of the Breath of Life;
Its torrent carried the world's hopes and fears,
All life's, all Nature's dissatisfied hungry cry,
And the longing all eternity cannot fill.
It called to the mountain secrecies of the soul
And the miracle of the never-dying fire,
It spoke to some first inexpressible ecstasy
Hidden in the creative beat of Life;
Out of the nether unseen deeps it tore
Its lure and magic of disordered bliss,
Into earth-light poured its maze of tangled charm
And heady draught of Nature's primitive joy
And the fire and mystery of forbidden delight
Drunk from the world-libido's bottomless well,
And the honey-sweet poison-wine of lust and death,
But dreamed a vintage of glory of life's gods,
And felt as celestial rapture's golden sting.
The cycles of the infinity of desire
And the mystique that made an unrealised world
Wider than the known and closer than the unknown
In which hunt for ever the hounds of mind and life,
Tempted a deep dissatisfied urge within
To long for the unfulfilled and ever far
And make this life upon a limiting earth
A climb towards summits vanishing in the void,
A search for the glory of the impossible.
It dreamed of that which never has been known,

It grasped at that which never has been won,
It chased into an Elysian memory
The charms that flee from the heart's soon lost delight;
It dared the force that slays, the joys that hurt,
The imaged shape of unaccomplished things
And the summons to a Circean transmuting dance
And passion's tenancy of the courts of love
And the wild Beast's ramp and romp with Beauty and Life.
It brought its cry and surge of opposite powers,
Its moments of the touch of luminous planes,
Its flame-ascensions and sky-pitched vast attempts,
Its fiery towers of dream built on the winds,
Its sinkings towards the darkness and the abyss,
Its honey of tenderness, its sharp wine of hate,
Its changes of sun and cloud, of laughter and tears,
Its bottomless danger-pits and swallowing gulfs,
Its fear and joy and ecstasy and despair,
Its occult wizardries, its simple lines
And great communions and uplifting moves,
Its faith in heaven, its intercourse with hell.
These powers were not blunt with the dead weight of earth,
They gave ambrosia's taste and poison's sting.
There was an ardour in the gaze of Life
That saw heaven blue in the grey air of Night:
The impulses godward soared on passion's wings.
Mind's quick-paced thoughts floated from their high necks,
A glowing splendour as of an irised mane,
A parure of pure intuition's light;
Its flame-foot gallop they could imitate:
Mind's voices mimicked inspiration's stress,
Its ictus of infallibility,
Its speed and lightning heaven-leap of the Gods.
A trenchant blade that shore the nets of doubt,
Its sword of discernment seemed almost divine.
Yet all that knowledge was a borrowed sun's;
The forms that came were not heaven's native births:

An inner voice could speak the unreal's Word;
Its puissance dangerous and absolute
Could mingle poison with the wine of God.
On these high shining backs falsehood could ride;
Truth lay with delight in error's passionate arms
Gliding downstream in a blithe gilded barge:
She edged her ray with a magnificent lie.
Here in Life's nether realms all contraries meet;
Truth stares and does her works with bandaged eyes
And Ignorance is Wisdom's patron here:
Those galloping hooves in their enthusiast speed
Could bear to a dangerous intermediate zone
Where Death walks wearing a robe of deathless Life.
Or they enter the valley of the wandering Gleam
Whence, captives or victims of the specious Ray,
Souls trapped in that region never can escape.
Agents, not masters, they serve Life's desires
Toiling for ever in the snare of Time.
Their bodies born out of some Nihil's womb
Ensnare the spirit in the moment's dreams,
Then perish vomiting the immortal soul
Out of Matter's belly into the sink of Nought.
Yet some uncaught, unslain, can warily pass
Carrying Truth's image in the sheltered heart,
Pluck Knowledge out of error's screening grip,
Break paths through the blind walls of little self,
Then travel on to reach a greater life.
All this streamed past her and seemed to her vision's sight
As if around a high and voiceless isle
A clamour of waters from far unknown hills
Swallowed its narrow banks in crowding waves
And made a hungry world of white wild foam:
Hastening, a dragon with a million feet,
Its foam and cry a drunken giant's din,
Tossing a mane of Darkness into God's sky,
It ebbed receding into a distant roar.

Then smiled again a large and tranquil air:
Blue heaven, green earth, partners of Beauty's reign,
Lived as of old, companions in happiness;
And in the world's heart laughed the joy of life.
All now was still, the soil shone dry and pure.
Through it all she moved not, plunged not in the vain waves.
Out of the vastness of the silent self
Life's clamour fled; her spirit was mute and free.

   Then journeying forward through the self's wide hush
She came into a brilliant ordered Space.
There Life dwelt parked in an armed tranquillity;
A chain was on her strong insurgent heart.
Tamed to the modesty of a measured pace,
She kept no more her vehement stride and rush;
She had lost the careless majesty of her muse
And the ample grandeur of her regal force;
Curbed were her mighty pomps, her splendid waste,
Sobered the revels of her bacchant play,
Cut down were her squanderings in desire's bazaar,
Coerced her despot will, her fancy's dance,
A cold stolidity bound the riot of sense.
A royalty without freedom was her lot;
The sovereign throned obeyed her ministers:
Her servants mind and sense governed her house:
Her spirit's bounds they cast in rigid lines
And guarding with a phalanx of armoured rules
The reason's balanced reign, kept order and peace.
Her will lived closed in adamant walls of law,
Coerced was her force by chains that feigned to adorn,
Imagination was prisoned in a fort,
Her wanton and licentious favourite;
Reality's poise and reason's symmetry
Were set in its place sentinelled by marshalled facts,
They gave to the soul for throne a bench of Law,
For kingdom a small world of rule and line:

The ages' wisdom, shrivelled to scholiast lines,
Shrank patterned into a copy-book device.
The Spirit's almighty freedom was not here:
A schoolman mind had captured life's large space,
But chose to live in bare and paltry rooms
Parked off from the too vast dangerous universe,
Fearing to lose its soul in the infinite.
Even the Idea's ample sweep was cut
Into a system, chained to fixed pillars of thought
Or rivetted to Matter's solid ground:
Or else the soul was lost in its own heights:
Obeying the Ideal's high-browed law
Thought based a throne on unsubstantial air
Disdaining earth's flat triviality:
It barred reality out to live in its dreams.
Or all stepped into a systemed universe:
Life's empire was a managed continent,
Its thoughts an army ranked and disciplined;
Uniformed they kept the logic of their fixed place
At the bidding of the trained centurion mind.
Or each stepped into its station like a star
Or marched through fixed and constellated heavens
Or kept its feudal rank among its peers
In the sky's unchanging cosmic hierarchy.
Or like a high-bred maiden with chaste eyes
Forbidden to walk unveiled the public ways,
She must in close secluded chambers move,
Her feeling in cloisters live or gardened paths.
Life was consigned to a safe level path,
It dared not tempt the great and difficult heights
Or climb to be neighbour to a lonely star
Or skirt the danger of the precipice
Or tempt the foam-curled breakers' perilous laugh,
Adventure's lyrist, danger's amateur,
Or into her chamber call some flaming god,
Or leave the world's bounds and where no limits are

Meet with the heart's passion the Adorable
Or set the world ablaze with the inner Fire.
A chastened epithet in the prose of life,
She must fill with colour just her sanctioned space,
Not break out of the cabin of the idea
Nor trespass into rhythms too high or vast.
Even when it soared into ideal air,
Thought's flight lost not itself in heaven's blue:
It drew upon the skies a patterned flower
Of disciplined beauty and harmonic light.
A temperate vigilant spirit governed life:
Its acts were tools of the considering thought,
Too cold to take fire and set the world ablaze,
Or the careful reason's diplomatic moves
Testing the means to a prefigured end,
Or at the highest pitch some calm Will's plan
Or a strategy of some High Command within
To conquer the secret treasures of the gods
Or win for a masked king some glorious world,
Not a reflex of the spontaneous self,
An index of the being and its moods,
A winging of conscious spirit, a sacrament
Of life's communion with the still Supreme
Or its pure movement on the Eternal's road.
Or else for the body of some high Idea
A house was built with too close-fitting bricks;
Action and thought cemented made a wall
Of small ideals limiting the soul.
Even meditation mused on a narrow seat;
And worship turned to an exclusive God,
To the Universal in a chapel prayed
Whose doors were shut against the universe;
Or kneeled to the bodiless Impersonal
A mind shut to the cry and fire of love:
A rational religion dried the heart.
It planned a smooth life's acts with ethics' rule

Or offered a cold and flameless sacrifice.
The sacred Book lay on its sanctified desk
Wrapped in interpretation's silken strings:
A credo sealed up its spiritual sense.

Here was a quiet country of fixed mind,
Here life no more was all nor passion's voice;
The cry of sense had sunk into a hush.
Soul was not there nor spirit but mind alone;
Mind claimed to be the spirit and the soul.
The spirit saw itself as form of mind,
Lost itself in the glory of the thought,
A light that made invisible the sun.
Into a firm and settled space she came
Where all was still and all things kept their place.
Each found what it had sought and knew its aim.
All had a final last stability.
There one stood forth who bore authority
On an important brow and held a rod;
Command was incarnate in his gesture and tone;
Tradition's petrified wisdom carved his speech,
His sentences savoured the oracle.
"Traveller or pilgrim of the inner world,
Fortunate art thou to reach our brilliant air
Flaming with thought's supreme finality.
O aspirant to the perfect way of life,
Here find it; rest from search and live at peace.
Ours is the home of cosmic certainty.
Here is the truth, God's harmony is here.
Register thy name in the book of the elite,
Admitted by the sanction of the few,
Adopt thy station of knowledge, thy post in mind,
Thy ticket of order draw in Life's bureau
And praise thy fate that made thee one of ours.
All here, docketed and tied, the mind can know,
All schemed by law that God permits to life.

This is the end and there is no beyond.
Here is the safety of the ultimate wall,
Here is the clarity of the sword of Light,
Here is the victory of a single Truth,
Here burns the diamond of flawless bliss.
A favourite of Heaven and Nature live."
But to the too satisfied and confident sage
Savitri replied casting into his world
Sight's deep release, the heart's questioning inner voice:
For here the heart spoke not, only clear daylight
Of intellect reigned here, limiting, cold, precise.
"Happy are they who in this chaos of things,
This coming and going of the feet of Time,
Can find the single Truth, the eternal Law:
Untouched they live by hope and doubt and fear.
Happy are men anchored on fixed belief
In this uncertain and ambiguous world,
Or who have planted in the heart's rich soil
One small grain of spiritual certitude.
Happiest who stand on faith as on a rock.
But I must pass leaving the ended search,
Truth's rounded outcome firm, immutable
And this harmonic building of world-fact,
This ordered knowledge of apparent things.
Here I can stay not, for I seek my soul."
None answered in that bright contented world,
Or only turned on their accustomed way
Astonished to hear questioning in that air
Or thoughts that could still turn to the Beyond.
But some murmured, passers-by from kindred spheres:
Each by his credo judged the thought she spoke.
"Who then is this who knows not that the soul
Is a least gland or a secretion's fault
Disquieting the sane government of the mind,
Disordering the function of the brain,
Or a yearning lodged in Nature's mortal house

Or dream whispered in man's cave of hollow thought
Who would prolong his brief unhappy term
Or cling to living in a sea of death?"
But others, "Nay, it is her spirit she seeks.
A splendid shadow of the name of God,
A formless lustre from the Ideal's realm,
The Spirit is the Holy Ghost of Mind;
But none has touched its limbs or seen its face.
Each soul is the great Father's crucified Son,
Mind is that soul's one parent, its conscious cause,
The ground on which trembles a brief passing light,
Mind, sole creator of the apparent world.
All that is here is part of our own self;
Our minds have made the world in which we live."
Another with mystic and unsatisfied eyes
Who loved his slain belief and mourned its death,
"Is there one left who seeks for a Beyond?
Can still the path be found, opened the gate?"

So she fared on across her silent self.
To a road she came thronged with an ardent crowd
Who sped brilliant, fire-footed, sunlight-eyed,
Pressing to reach the world's mysterious wall,
And pass through masked doorways into outer mind
Where the Light comes not nor the mystic voice,
Messengers from our subliminal greatnesses,
Guests from the cavern of the secret soul.
Into dim spiritual somnolence they break
Or shed wide wonder on our waking self,
Ideas that haunt us with their radiant tread,
Dreams that are hints of unborn Reality,
Strange goddesses with deep-pooled magical eyes,
Strong wind-haired gods carrying the harps of hope,
Great moon-hued visions gliding through gold air,
Aspiration's sun-dream head and star-carved limbs,
Emotions making common hearts sublime.

And Savitri mingling in that glorious crowd,
Yearning to the spiritual light they bore,
Longed once to hasten like them to save God's world;
But she reined back the high passion in her heart;
She knew that first she must discover her soul.
Only who save themselves can others save.
In contrary sense she faced life's riddling truth:
They carrying the light to suffering men
Hurried with eager feet to the outer world;
Her eyes were turned towards the eternal source.
Outstretching her hands to stay the throng she cried:
"O happy company of luminous gods,
Reveal, who know, the road that I must tread, —
For surely that bright quarter is your home, —
To find the birthplace of the occult Fire
And the deep mansion of my secret soul."
One answered pointing to a silence dim
On a remote extremity of sleep
In some far background of the inner world.
"O Savitri, from thy hidden soul we come.
We are the messengers, the occult gods
Who help men's drab and heavy ignorant lives
To wake to beauty and the wonder of things
Touching them with glory and divinity;
In evil we light the deathless flame of good
And hold the torch of knowledge on ignorant roads;
We are thy will and all men's will towards Light.
O human copy and disguise of God
Who seekst the deity thou keepest hid
And livest by the Truth thou hast not known,
Follow the world's winding highway to its source.
There in the silence few have ever reached,
Thou shalt see the Fire burning on the bare stone
And the deep cavern of thy secret soul."
Then Savitri following the great winding road
Came where it dwindled into a narrow path

Trod only by rare wounded pilgrim feet.
A few bright forms emerged from unknown depths
And looked at her with calm immortal eyes.
There was no sound to break the brooding hush;
One felt the silent nearness of the soul.

END OF CANTO THREE

Canto Four

The Triple Soul-Forces

HERE from a low and prone and listless ground
The passion of the first ascent began;
A moon-bright face in a sombre cloud of hair,
A Woman sat in a pale lustrous robe.
A rugged and ragged soil was her bare seat,
Beneath her feet a sharp and wounding stone.
A divine pity on the peaks of the world,
A spirit touched by the grief of all that lives,
She looked out far and saw from inner mind
This questionable world of outward things,
Of false appearances and plausible shapes,
This dubious cosmos stretched in the ignorant Void,
The pangs of earth, the toil and speed of the stars
And the difficult birth and dolorous end of life.
Accepting the universe as her body of woe,
The Mother of the seven sorrows bore
The seven stabs that pierced her bleeding heart:
The beauty of sadness lingered on her face,
Her eyes were dim with the ancient stain of tears.
Her heart was riven with the world's agony
And burdened with the sorrow and struggle in Time,
An anguished music trailed in her rapt voice.
Absorbed in a deep compassion's ecstasy,
Lifting the mild ray of her patient gaze,
In soft sweet training words slowly she spoke:
"O Savitri, I am thy secret soul.
To share the suffering of the world I came,
I draw my children's pangs into my breast.
I am the nurse of the dolour beneath the stars;
I am the soul of all who wailing writhe
Under the ruthless harrow of the Gods.

I am woman, nurse and slave and beaten beast;
I tend the hands that gave me cruel blows.
The hearts that spurned my love and zeal I serve;
I am the courted queen, the pampered doll,
I am the giver of the bowl of rice,
I am the worshipped Angel of the House.
I am in all that suffers and that cries.
Mine is the prayer that climbs in vain from earth,
I am traversed by my creatures' agonies,
I am the spirit in a world of pain.
The scream of tortured flesh and tortured hearts
Fall'n back on heart and flesh unheard by Heaven
Has rent with helpless grief and wrath my soul.
I have seen the peasant burning in his hut,
I have seen the slashed corpse of the slaughtered child,
Heard woman's cry ravished and stripped and haled
Amid the bayings of the hell-hound mob,
I have looked on, I had no power to save.
I have brought no arm of strength to aid or slay;
God gave me love, he gave me not his force.
I have shared the toil of the yoked animal drudge
Pushed by the goad, encouraged by the whip;
I have shared the fear-filled life of bird and beast,
Its long hunt for the day's precarious food,
Its covert slink and crouch and hungry prowl,
Its pain and terror seized by beak and claw.
I have shared the daily life of common men,
Its petty pleasures and its petty cares,
Its press of troubles and haggard horde of ills,
Earth's trail of sorrow hopeless of relief,
The unwanted tedious labour without joy,
And the burden of misery and the strokes of fate.
I have been pity, leaning over pain
And the tender smile that heals the wounded heart
And sympathy making life less hard to bear.
Man has felt near my unseen face and hands;

I have become the sufferer and his moan,
I have lain down with the mangled and the slain,
I have lived with the prisoner in his dungeon cell.
Heavy on my shoulders weighs the yoke of Time:
Nothing refusing of creation's load,
I have borne all and know I still must bear:
Perhaps when the world sinks into a last sleep,
I too may sleep in dumb eternal peace.
I have borne the calm indifference of Heaven,
Watched Nature's cruelty to suffering things
While God passed silent by nor turned to help.
Yet have I cried not out against his will,
Yet have I not accused his cosmic Law.
Only to change this great hard world of pain
A patient prayer has risen from my breast;
A pallid resignation lights my brow,
Within me a blind faith and mercy dwell;
I carry the fire that never can be quenched
And the compassion that supports the suns.
I am the hope that looks towards my God,
My God who never came to me till now;
His voice I hear that ever says 'I come':
I know that one day he shall come at last."
She ceased, and like an echo from below
Answering her pathos of divine complaint
A voice of wrath took up the dire refrain,
A growl of thunder or roar of angry beast,
The beast that crouching growls within man's depths,—
Voice of a tortured Titan once a God.
"I am the Man of Sorrows, I am he
Who is nailed on the wide cross of the universe;
To enjoy my agony God built the earth,
My passion he has made his drama's theme.
He has sent me naked into his bitter world
And beaten me with his rods of grief and pain
That I might cry and grovel at his feet

And offer him worship with my blood and tears.
I am Prometheus under the vulture's beak,
Man the discoverer of the undying fire,
In the flame he kindled burning like a moth;
I am the seeker who can never find,
I am the fighter who can never win,
I am the runner who never touched his goal:
Hell tortures me with the edges of my thought,
Heaven tortures me with the splendour of my dreams.
What profit have I of my animal birth;
What profit have I of my human soul?
I toil like the animal, like the animal die.
I am man the rebel, man the helpless serf;
Fate and my fellows cheat me of my wage.
I loosen with my blood my servitude's seal
And shake from my aching neck the oppressor's knees
Only to seat new tyrants on my back:
My teachers lesson me in slavery,
I am shown God's stamp and my own signature
Upon the sorry contract of my fate.
I have loved, but none has loved me since my birth;
My fruit of works is given to other hands.
All that is left me is my evil thoughts,
My sordid quarrel against God and man,
Envy of the riches that I cannot share,
Hate of a happiness that is not mine.
I know my fate will ever be the same,
It is my nature's work that cannot change:
I have loved for mine, not for the beloved's sake,
I have lived for myself and not for others' lives.
Each in himself is sole by Nature's law.
So God has made his harsh and dreadful world,
So has he built the petty heart of man.
Only by force and ruse can man survive:
For pity is a weakness in his breast,
His goodness is a laxity in the nerves,

His kindness an investment for return,
His altruism is ego's other face:
He serves the world that him the world may serve.
If once the Titan's strength could wake in me,
If Enceladus from Etna could arise,
I then would reign the master of the world
And like a god enjoy man's bliss and pain.
But God has taken from me the ancient Force.
There is a dull consent in my sluggish heart,
A fierce satisfaction with my special pangs
As if they made me taller than my kind;
Only by suffering can I excel.
I am the victim of titanic ills,
I am the doer of demoniac deeds;
I was made for evil, evil is my lot;
Evil I must be and by evil live;
Nought other can I do but be myself;
What Nature made me, that I must remain.
I suffer and toil and weep; I moan and hate."
And Savitri heard the voice, the echo heard
And turning to her being of pity spoke:
"Madonna of suffering, Mother of grief divine,
Thou art a portion of my soul put forth
To bear the unbearable sorrow of the world.
Because thou art, men yield not to their doom,
But ask for happiness and strive with fate;
Because thou art, the wretched still can hope.
But thine is the power to solace, not to save.
One day I will return, a bringer of strength,
And make thee drink from the Eternal's cup;
His streams of force shall triumph in thy limbs
And Wisdom's calm control thy passionate heart.
Thy love shall be the bond of humankind,
Compassion the bright key of Nature's acts:
Misery shall pass abolished from the earth;
The world shall be freed from the anger of the Beast,

From the cruelty of the Titan and his pain.
There shall be peace and joy for ever more."

On passed she in her spirit's upward route.
An ardent grandeur climbed mid ferns and rocks,
A quiet wind flattered the heart to warmth,
A finer perfume breathed from slender trees.
All beautiful grew, subtle and high and strange.
Here on a boulder carved like a huge throne
A Woman sat in gold and purple sheen,
Armed with the trident and the thunderbolt,
Her feet upon a couchant lion's back.
A formidable smile curved round her lips,
Heaven-fire laughed in the corners of her eyes;
Her body a mass of courage and heavenly strength,
She menaced the triumph of the nether gods.
A halo of lightnings flamed around her head
And sovereignty, a great cestus, zoned her robe
And majesty and victory sat with her
Guarding in the wide cosmic battlefield
Against the flat equality of Death
And the all-levelling insurgent Night
The hierarchy of the ordered Powers,
The high changeless values, the peaked eminences,
The privileged aristocracy of Truth,
And in the governing Ideal's sun
The triumvirate of wisdom, love and bliss
And the sole autocracy of the absolute Light.
August on her seat in the inner world of Mind,
The Mother of Might looked down on passing things,
Listened to the advancing tread of Time,
Saw the irresistible wheeling of the suns
And heard the thunder of the march of God.
Amid the swaying Forces in their strife
Sovereign was her word of luminous command,
Her speech like a war-cry rang or a pilgrim chant.

A charm restoring hope in failing hearts
Aspired the harmony of her puissant voice:
"O Savitri, I am thy secret soul.
I have come down into the human world
And the movement watched by an unsleeping Eye
And the dark contrariety of earth's fate
And the battle of the bright and sombre Powers.
I stand upon earth's paths of danger and grief
And help the unfortunate and save the doomed.
To the strong I bring the guerdon of their strength,
To the weak I bring the armour of my force;
To men who long I carry their coveted joy:
I am fortune justifying the great and wise
By the sanction of the plaudits of the crowd,
Then trampling them with the armed heel of fate.
My ear is leaned to the cry of the oppressed,
I topple down the thrones of tyrant kings:
A cry comes from proscribed and hunted lives
Appealing to me against a pitiless world,
A voice of the forsaken and desolate
And the lone prisoner in his dungeon cell.
Men hail in my coming the Almighty's force
Or praise with thankful tears his saviour Grace.
I smite the Titan who bestrides the world
And slay the ogre in his blood-stained den.
I am Durga, goddess of the proud and strong,
And Lakshmi, queen of the fair and fortunate;
I wear the face of Kali when I kill,
I trample the corpses of the demon hordes.
I am charged by God to do his mighty work,
Uncaring I serve his will who sent me forth,
Reckless of peril and earthly consequence.
I reason not of virtue and of sin
But do the deed he has put into my heart.
I fear not for the angry frown of Heaven,
I flinch not from the red assault of Hell;

I crush the opposition of the gods,
Tread down a million goblin obstacles.
I guide man to the path of the Divine
And guard him from the red Wolf and the Snake.
I set in his mortal hand my heavenly sword
And put on him the breastplate of the gods.
I break the ignorant pride of human mind
And lead the thought to the wideness of the Truth;
I rend man's narrow and successful life
And force his sorrowful eyes to gaze at the sun
That he may die to earth and live in his soul.
I know the goal, I know the secret route;
I have studied the map of the invisible worlds;
I am the battle's head, the journey's star.
But the great obstinate world resists my Word,
And the crookedness and evil in man's heart
Is stronger than Reason, profounder than the Pit,
And the malignancy of hostile Powers
Puts craftily back the clock of destiny
And mightier seems than the eternal Will.
The cosmic evil is too deep to unroot,
The cosmic suffering is too vast to heal.
A few I guide who pass me towards the Light;
A few I save, the mass falls back unsaved;
A few I help, the many strive and fail.
But my heart I have hardened and I do my work:
Slowly the light grows greater in the East,
Slowly the world progresses on God's road.
His seal is on my task, it cannot fail:
I shall hear the silver swing of heaven's gates
When God comes out to meet the soul of the world."
She spoke and from the lower human world
An answer, a warped echo met her speech;
The voice came through the spaces of the mind
Of the dwarf-Titan, the deformed chained god
Who strives to master his nature's rebel stuff

And make the universe his instrument.
The Ego of this great world of desire
Claimed earth and the wide heavens for the use
Of man, head of the life it shapes on earth,
Its representative and conscious soul,
And symbol of evolving light and force
And vessel of the godhead that must be.
A thinking animal, Nature's struggling lord,
Has made of her his nurse and tool and slave
And pays to her as wage and emolument
Inescapably by a deep law in things
His heart's grief and his body's death and pain:
His pains are her means to grow, to see and feel;
His death assists her immortality.
A tool and slave of his own slave and tool,
He praises his free will and his master mind
And is pushed by her upon her chosen paths;
Possessor he is possessed and, ruler, ruled,
Her conscious automaton, her desire's dupe.
His soul is her guest, a sovereign mute, inert,
His body her robot, his life her way to live,
His conscious mind her strong revolted serf.
The voice rose up and smote some inner sun.
"I am the heir of the forces of the earth,
Slowly I make good my right to my estate;
A growing godhead in her divinised mud,
I climb, a claimant to the throne of heaven.
The last-born of the earth I stand the first;
Her slow millenniums waited for my birth.
Although I live in Time besieged by Death,
Precarious owner of my body and soul
Housed on a little speck amid the stars,
For me and my use the universe was made.
Immortal spirit in the perishing clay,
I am God still unevolved in human form;
Even if he is not, he becomes in me.

The sun and moon are lights upon my path;
Air was invented for my lungs to breathe,
Conditioned as a wide and wall-less space
For my winged chariot's wheels to cleave a road,
The sea was made for me to swim and sail
And bear my golden commerce on its back:
It laughs cloven by my pleasure's gliding keel,
I laugh at its black stare of fate and death.
The earth is my floor, the sky my living's roof.
All was prepared through many a silent age,
God made experiments with animal shapes,
Then only when all was ready I was born.
I was born weak and small and ignorant,
A helpless creature in a difficult world
Travelling through my brief years with death at my side;
I have grown greater than Nature, wiser than God.
I have made real what she never dreamed,
I have seized her powers and harnessed for my work,
I have shaped her metals and new metals made;
I will make glass and raiment out of milk,
Make iron velvet, water unbreakable stone,
Like God in his astuce of artist skill,
Mould from one primal plasm protean forms,
In single Nature multitudinous lives,
All that imagination can conceive
In mind intangible, remould anew
In Matter's plastic solid and concrete.
No magic can surpass my magic's skill.
There is no miracle I shall not achieve.
What God imperfect left, I will complete,
Out of a tangled mind and half-made soul
His sin and error I will eliminate;
What he invented not, I shall invent:
He was the first creator, I am the last.
I have found the atoms from which he built the worlds:
The first tremendous cosmic energy

Missioned shall leap to slay my enemy kin,
Expunge a nation or abolish a race,
Death's silence leave where there was laughter and joy.
Or the fissured invisible shall spend God's force
To extend my comforts and expand my wealth,
To speed my car which now the lightnings drive
And turn the engines of my miracles.
I will take his means of sorcery from his hands
And do with them greater wonders than his best.
Yet through it all I have kept my balanced thought;
I have studied my being, I have examined the world,
I have grown a master of the arts of life.
I have tamed the wild beast, trained to be my friend;
He guards my house, looks up waiting my will.
I have taught my kind to serve and to obey.
I have used the mystery of the cosmic waves
To see far distance and to hear far words;
I have conquered Space and knitted close all earth.
Soon I shall know the secrets of the Mind;
I play with knowledge and with ignorance
And sin and virtue my inventions are
I can transcend or sovereignly use.
I shall know mystic truths, seize occult powers.
I shall slay my enemies with a look or thought,
I shall sense the unspoken feelings of all hearts
And see and hear the hidden thoughts of men.
When earth is mastered, I shall conquer heaven;
The gods shall be my aides or menial folk,
No wish I harbour unfulfilled shall die:
Omnipotence and omniscience shall be mine."
And Savitri heard the voice, the warped echo heard
And turning to her being of power she spoke:
"Madonna of might, Mother of works and force,
Thou art a portion of my soul put forth
To help mankind and help the travail of Time.
Because thou art in him, man hopes and dares;

Because thou art, men's souls can climb the heavens
And walk like gods in the presence of the Supreme.
But without wisdom power is like a wind,
It can breathe upon the heights and kiss the sky,
It cannot build the extreme eternal things.
Thou hast given men strength, wisdom thou couldst not give.
One day I will return, a bringer of light;
Then will I give to thee the mirror of God;
Thou shalt see self and world as by him they are seen
Reflected in the bright pool of thy soul.
Thy wisdom shall be vast as vast thy power.
Then hate shall dwell no more in human hearts,
And fear and weakness shall desert men's lives,
The cry of the ego shall be hushed within,
Its lion roar that claims the world as food,
All shall be might and bliss and happy force."

    Ascending still her spirit's upward route
She came into a high and happy space,
A wide tower of vision whence all could be seen
And all was centred in a single view
As when by distance separate scenes grow one
And a harmony is made of hues at war.
The wind was still and fragrance packed the air.
There was a carol of birds and murmur of bees,
And all that is common and natural and sweet,
Yet intimately divine to heart and soul.
A nearness thrilled of the spirit to its source
And deepest things seemed obvious, close and true.
Here, living centre of that vision of peace,
A Woman sat in clear and crystal light:
Heaven had unveiled its lustre in her eyes,
Her feet were moonbeams, her face was a bright sun,
Her smile could persuade a dead lacerated heart
To live again and feel the hands of calm.
A low music heard became her floating voice:

"O Savitri, I am thy secret soul.
I have come down to the wounded desolate earth
To heal her pangs and lull her heart to rest
And lay her head upon the Mother's lap
That she may dream of God and know his peace
And draw the harmony of higher spheres
Into the rhythm of earth's rude troubled days.
I show to her the figures of bright gods
And bring strength and solace to her struggling life;
High things that now are only words and forms
I reveal to her in the body of their power.
I am peace that steals into man's war-worn breast,
Amid the reign of Hell his acts create
A hostel where Heaven's messengers can lodge;
I am charity with the kindly hands that bless,
I am silence mid the noisy tramp of life;
I am Knowledge poring on her cosmic map.
In the anomalies of the human heart
Where Good and Evil are close bedfellows
And Light is by Darkness dogged at every step,
Where his largest knowledge is an ignorance,
I am the Power that labours towards the best
And works for God and looks up towards the heights.
I make even sin and error stepping-stones
And all experience a long march towards Light.
Out of the Inconscient I build consciousness,
And lead through death to reach immortal Life.
Many are God's forms by which he grows in man;
They stamp his thoughts and deeds with divinity,
Uplift the stature of the human clay
Or slowly transmute it into heaven's gold.
He is the Good for which men fight and die,
He is the war of Right with Titan wrong;
He is Freedom rising deathless from her pyre;
He is Valour guarding still the desperate pass
Or lone and erect on the shattered barricade

Or a sentinel in the dangerous echoing Night.
He is the crown of the martyr burned in flame
And the glad resignation of the saint
And courage indifferent to the wounds of Time
And the hero's might wrestling with death and fate.
He is Wisdom incarnate on a glorious throne
And the calm autocracy of the sage's rule.
He is the high and solitary Thought
Aloof above the ignorant multitude:
He is the prophet's voice, the sight of the seer.
He is Beauty, nectar of the passionate soul,
He is the Truth by which the spirit lives.
He is the riches of the spiritual Vast
Poured out in healing streams on indigent Life;
He is Eternity lured from hour to hour,
He is infinity in a little space:
He is immortality in the arms of death.
These powers I am and at my call they come.
Thus slowly I lift man's soul nearer the Light.
But human mind clings to its ignorance
And to its littleness the human heart
And to its right to grief the earthly life.
Only when Eternity takes Time by the hand,
Only when infinity weds the finite's thought,
Can man be free from himself and live with God.
I bring meanwhile the gods upon the earth;
I bring back hope to the despairing heart;
I give peace to the humble and the great,
And shed my grace on the foolish and the wise.
I shall save earth, if earth consents to be saved.
Then Love shall at last unwounded tread earth's soil;
Man's mind shall admit the sovereignty of Truth
And body bear the immense descent of God."
She spoke and from the ignorant nether plane
A cry, a warped echo naked and shuddering came.
A voice of the sense-shackled human mind

Carried its proud complaint of godlike power
Hedged by the limits of a mortal's thoughts,
Bound in the chains of earthly ignorance.
Imprisoned in his body and his brain
The mortal cannot see God's mighty whole,
Or share in his vast and deep identity
Who stands unguessed within our ignorant hearts
And knows all things because he is one with all.
Man only sees the cosmic surfaces.
Then wondering what may lie hid from the sense
A little way he delves to depths below:
But soon he stops, he cannot reach life's core
Or commune with the throbbing heart of things.
He sees the naked body of the Truth
Though often baffled by her endless garbs,
But cannot look upon her soul within.
Then, furious for a knowledge absolute,
He tears all details out and stabs and digs:
Only the shape's contents he holds for use;
The spirit escapes or dies beneath his knife.
He sees as a blank stretch, a giant waste
The crowding riches of infinity.
The finite he has made his central field,
Its plan dissects, masters its processes,
That which moves all is hidden from his gaze,
His poring eyes miss the unseen behind.
He has the blind man's subtle unerring touch
Or the slow traveller's sight of distant scenes;
The soul's revealing contacts are not his.
Yet is he visited by intuitive light
And inspiration comes from the Unknown;
But only reason and sense he feels as sure,
They only are his trusted witnesses.
Thus is he baulked, his splendid effort vain;
His knowledge scans bright pebbles on the shore
Of the huge ocean of his ignorance.

Yet grandiose were the accents of that cry,
A cosmic pathos trembled in its tone.
"I am the mind of God's great ignorant world
Ascending to knowledge by the steps he made;
I am the all-discovering Thought of man.
I am a god fettered by Matter and sense,
An animal prisoned in a fence of thorns,
A beast of labour asking for his food,
A smith tied to his anvil and his forge.
Yet have I loosened the cord, enlarged my room.
I have mapped the heavens and analysed the stars,
Described their orbits through the grooves of Space,
Measured the miles that separate the suns,
Computed their longevity in Time.
I have delved into earth's bowels and torn out
The riches guarded by her dull brown soil.
I have classed the changes of her stony crust
And of her biography discovered the dates,
Rescued the pages of all Nature's plan.
The tree of evolution I have sketched,
Each branch and twig and leaf in its own place,
In the embryo tracked the history of forms,
And the genealogy framed of all that lives.
I have detected plasm and cell and gene,
The protozoa traced, man's ancestors,
The humble originals from whom he rose;
I know how he was born and how he dies:
Only what end he serves I know not yet
Or if there is aim at all or any end
Or push of rich creative purposeful joy
In the wide works of the terrestrial power.
I have caught her intricate processes, none is left:
Her huge machinery is in my hands;
I have seized the cosmic energies for my use.
I have pored on her infinitesimal elements
And her invisible atoms have unmasked:

All Matter is a book I have perused;
Only some pages now are left to read.
I have seen the ways of life, the paths of mind;
I have studied the methods of the ant and ape
And the behaviour learned of man and worm.
If God is at work, his secrets I have found.
But still the Cause of things is left in doubt,
Their truth flees from pursuit into a void;
When all has been explained nothing is known.
What chose the process, whence the Power sprang
I know not and perhaps shall never know.
A mystery is this mighty Nature's birth;
A mystery is the elusive stream of mind,
A mystery the protean freak of life.
What I have learned, Chance leaps to contradict;
What I have built is seized and torn by Fate.
I can foresee the acts of Matter's force,
But not the march of the destiny of man:
He is driven upon paths he did not choose,
He falls trampled underneath the rolling wheels.
My great philosophies are a reasoned guess;
The mystic heavens that claim the human soul
Are a charlatanism of the imagining brain:
All is a speculation or a dream.
In the end the world itself becomes a doubt:
The infinitesimal's jest mocks mass and shape,
A laugh peals from the infinite's finite mask.
Perhaps the world is an error of our sight,
A trick repeated in each flash of sense,
An unreal mind hallucinates the soul
With a stress-vision of false reality,
Or a dance of Maya veils the void Unborn.
Even if a greater consciousness I could reach,
What profit is it then for Thought to win
A Real which is for ever ineffable
Or hunt to its lair the bodiless Self or make

The Unknowable the target of the soul?
Nay, let me work within my mortal bounds,
Not live beyond life nor think beyond the mind;
Our smallness saves us from the Infinite.
In a frozen grandeur lone and desolate
Call me not to die the great eternal death,
Left naked of my own humanity
In the chill vast of the spirit's boundlessness.
Each creature by its nature's limits lives,
And how can one evade his native fate?
Human I am, human let me remain
Till in the Inconscient I fall dumb and sleep.
A high insanity, a chimaera is this,
To think that God lives hidden in the clay
And that eternal Truth can dwell in Time,
And call to her to save our self and world.
How can man grow immortal and divine
Transmuting the very stuff of which he is made?
This wizard gods may dream, not thinking men."
    And Savitri heard the voice, the warped answer heard
And turning to her being of light she spoke:
"Madonna of light, Mother of joy and peace,
Thou art a portion of my self put forth
To raise the spirit to its forgotten heights
And wake the soul by touches of the heavens.
Because thou art, the soul draws near to God;
Because thou art, love grows in spite of hate
And knowledge walks unslain in the pit of Night.
But not by showering heaven's golden rain
Upon the intellect's hard and rocky soil
Can the tree of Paradise flower on earthly ground
And the Bird of Paradise sit upon life's boughs
And the winds of Paradise visit mortal air.
Even if thou rain down intuition's rays,
The mind of man will think it earth's own gleam,
His spirit by spiritual ego sink,

Or his soul dream shut in sainthood's brilliant cell
Where only a bright shadow of God can come.
His hunger for the eternal thou must nurse
And fill his yearning heart with heaven's fire
And bring God down into his body and life.
One day I will return, His hand in mine,
And thou shalt see the face of the Absolute.
Then shall the holy marriage be achieved,
Then shall the divine family be born.
There shall be light and peace in all the worlds."

END OF CANTO FOUR

Canto Five

The Finding of the Soul

ONWARD she passed seeking the soul's mystic cave.
At first she stepped into a night of God.
The light was quenched that helps the labouring world,
The power that struggles and stumbles in our life;
This inefficient mind gave up its thoughts,
The striving heart its unavailing hopes.
All knowledge failed and the Idea's forms
And Wisdom screened in awe her lowly head
Feeling a Truth too great for thought or speech,
Formless, ineffable, for ever the same.
An innocent and holy Ignorance
Adored like one who worships formless God
The unseen Light she could not claim nor own.
In a simple purity of emptiness
Her mind knelt down before the unknowable.
All was abolished save her naked self
And the prostrate yearning of her surrendered heart:
There was no strength in her, no pride of force;
The lofty burning of desire had sunk
Ashamed, a vanity of separate self,
The hope of spiritual greatness fled,
Salvation she asked not nor a heavenly crown:
Humility seemed now too proud a state.
Her self was nothing, God alone was all,
Yet God she knew not but only knew he was.
A sacred darkness brooded now within,
The world was a deep darkness great and nude.
This void held more than all the teeming worlds,
This blank felt more than all that Time has borne,
This dark knew dumbly, immensely the Unknown.
But all was formless, voiceless, infinite.

As might a shadow walk in a shadowy scene,
A small nought passing through a mightier Nought,
A night of person in a bare outline
Crossing a fathomless impersonal Night,
Silent she moved, empty and absolute.
In endless Time her soul reached a wide end,
The spaceless Vast became her spirit's place.
At last a change approached, the emptiness broke;
A wave rippled within, the world had stirred;
Once more her inner self became her space.
There was felt a blissful nearness to the goal;
Heaven leaned low to kiss the sacred hill,
The air trembled with passion and delight.
A rose of splendour on a tree of dreams,
The face of Dawn out of mooned twilight grew.
Day came, priest of a sacrifice of joy
Into the worshipping silence of her world;
He carried immortal lustre as his robe,
Trailed heaven like a purple scarf and wore
As his vermilion caste-mark a red sun.
As if an old remembered dream come true,
She recognised in her prophetic mind
The imperishable lustre of that sky,
The tremulous sweetness of that happy air
And, covered from mind's view and life's approach,
The mystic cavern in the sacred hill
And knew the dwelling of her secret soul.
As if in some Elysian occult depth,
Truth's last retreat from thought's profaning touch,
As if in a rock-temple's solitude hid,
God's refuge from an ignorant worshipping world,
It lay withdrawn even from life's inner sense,
Receding from the entangled heart's desire.
A marvellous brooding twilight met the eyes
And a holy stillness held that voiceless space.
An awful dimness wrapped the great rock-doors

Carved in the massive stone of Matter's trance.
Two golden serpents round the lintel curled,
Enveloping it with their pure and dreadful strength,
Looked out with wisdom's deep and luminous eyes.
An eagle covered it with wide conquering wings:
Flames of self-lost immobile reverie,
Doves crowded the grey musing cornices
Like sculptured postures of white-bosomed peace.
Across the threshold's sleep she entered in
And found herself amid great figures of gods
Conscious in stone and living without breath,
Watching with fixed regard the soul of man,
Executive figures of the cosmic self,
World-symbols of immutable potency.
On the walls covered with significant shapes
Looked at her the life-scene of man and beast
And the high meaning of the life of gods,
The power and necessity of these numberless worlds,
And faces of beings and stretches of world-space
Spoke the succinct and inexhaustible
Hieratic message of the climbing planes.
In their immensitude signing infinity
They were the extension of the self of God
And housed, impassively receiving all,
His figures and his small and mighty acts
And his passion and his birth and life and death
And his return to immortality.
To the abiding and eternal is their climb,
To the pure existence everywhere the same,
To the sheer consciousness and the absolute force
And the unimaginable and formless bliss,
To the mirth in Time and the timeless mystery
Of the triune being who is all and one
And yet is no one but himself apart.
There was no step of breathing men, no sound,
Only the living nearness of the soul.

Yet all the worlds and God himself were there,
For every symbol was a reality
And brought the presence which had given it life.
All this she saw and inly felt and knew
Not by some thought of mind but by the self.
A light not born of sun or moon or fire,
A light that dwelt within and saw within
Shedding an intimate visibility
Made secrecy more revealing than the word:
Our sight and sense are a fallible gaze and touch
And only the spirit's vision is wholly true.
As thus she passed in that mysterious place
Through room and room, through door and rock-hewn door,
She felt herself made one with all she saw.
A sealed identity within her woke;
She knew herself the Beloved of the Supreme:
These Gods and Goddesses were he and she:
The Mother was she of Beauty and Delight,
The Word in Brahma's vast creating clasp,
The World-Puissance on almighty Shiva's lap, —
The Master and the Mother of all lives
Watching the worlds their twin regard had made,
And Krishna and Radha for ever entwined in bliss,
The Adorer and Adored self-lost and one.
In the last chamber on a golden seat
One sat whose shape no vision could define;
Only one felt the world's unattainable fount,
A Power of which she was a straying Force,
An invisible Beauty, goal of the world's desire,
A Sun of which all knowledge is a beam,
A Greatness without whom no life could be.
Thence all departed into silent self,
And all became formless and pure and bare.
Then through a tunnel dug in the last rock
She came out where there shone a deathless sun.
A house was there all made of flame and light

And crossing a wall of doorless living fire
There suddenly she met her secret soul.

A being stood immortal in transience,
Deathless dallying with momentary things,
In whose wide eyes of tranquil happiness
Which pity and sorrow could not abrogate
Infinity turned its gaze on finite shapes:
Observer of the silent steps of the hours,
Eternity upheld the minute's acts
And the passing scenes of the Everlasting's play.
In the mystery of its selecting will,
In the Divine Comedy a participant,
The Spirit's conscious representative,
God's delegate in our humanity,
Comrade of the universe, the Transcendent's ray,
She had come into the mortal body's room
To play at ball with Time and Circumstance.
A joy in the world her master movement here,
The passion of the game lighted her eyes:
A smile on her lips welcomed earth's bliss and grief,
A laugh was her return to pleasure and pain.
All things she saw as a masquerade of Truth
Disguised in the costumes of Ignorance,
Crossing the years to immortality;
All she could front with the strong spirit's peace.
But since she knows the toil of mind and life
As a mother feels and shares her children's lives,
She puts forth a small portion of herself,
A being no bigger than the thumb of man
Into a hidden region of the heart
To face the pang and to forget the bliss,
To share the suffering and endure earth's wounds
And labour mid the labour of the stars.
This in us laughs and weeps, suffers the stroke,
Exults in victory, struggles for the crown;

Identified with the mind and body and life,
It takes on itself their anguish and defeat,
Bleeds with Fate's whips and hangs upon the cross,
Yet is the unwounded and immortal self
Supporting the actor in the human scene.
Through this she sends us her glory and her powers,
Pushes to wisdom's heights, through misery's gulfs;
She gives us strength to do our daily task
And sympathy that partakes of others' grief
And the little strength we have to help our race,
We who must fill the role of the universe
Acting itself out in a slight human shape
And on our shoulders carry the struggling world.
This is in us the godhead small and marred;
In this human portion of divinity
She seats the greatness of the Soul in Time
To uplift from light to light, from power to power,
Till on a heavenly peak it stands, a king.
In body weak, in its heart an invincible might,
It climbs stumbling, held up by an unseen hand,
A toiling spirit in a mortal shape.
Here in this chamber of flame and light they met;
They looked upon each other, knew themselves,
The secret deity and its human part,
The calm immortal and the struggling soul.
Then with a magic transformation's speed
They rushed into each other and grew one.

Once more she was human upon earthly soil
In the muttering night amid the rain-swept woods
And the rude cottage where she sat in trance:
That subtle world withdrew deeply within
Behind the sun-veil of the inner sight.
But now the half-opened lotus bud of her heart
Had bloomed and stood disclosed to the earthly ray;
In an image shone revealed her secret soul.

There was no wall severing the soul and mind,
No mystic fence guarding from the claims of life.
In its deep lotus home her being sat
As if on concentration's marble seat,
Calling the mighty Mother of the worlds
To make this earthly tenement her house.
As in a flash from a supernal light,
A living image of the original Power,
A face, a form came down into her heart
And made of it its temple and pure abode.
But when its feet had touched the quivering bloom,
A mighty movement rocked the inner space
As if a world were shaken and found its soul:
Out of the Inconscient's soulless mindless night
A flaming Serpent rose released from sleep.
It rose billowing its coils and stood erect
And climbing mightily, stormily on its way
It touched her centres with its flaming mouth;
As if a fiery kiss had broken their sleep,
They bloomed and laughed surcharged with light and bliss.
Then at the crown it joined the Eternal's space.
In the flower of the head, in the flower of Matter's base,
In each divine stronghold and Nature-knot
It held together the mystic stream which joins
The viewless summits with the unseen depths,
The string of forts that make the frail defence
Safeguarding us against the enormous world,
Our lines of self-expression in its Vast.
An image sat of the original Power
Wearing the mighty Mother's form and face.
Armed, bearer of the weapon and the sign
Whose occult might no magic can imitate,
Manifold yet one she sat, a guardian force:
A saviour gesture stretched her lifted arm,
And symbol of some native cosmic strength,
A sacred beast lay prone below her feet,

A silent flame-eyed mass of living force.
All underwent a high celestial change:
Breaking the black Inconscient's blind mute wall,
Effacing the circles of the Ignorance,
Powers and divinities burst flaming forth;
Each part of the being trembling with delight
Lay overwhelmed with tides of happiness
And saw her hand in every circumstance
And felt her touch in every limb and cell.
In the country of the lotus of the head
Which thinking mind has made its busy space,
In the castle of the lotus twixt the brows
Whence it shoots the arrows of its sight and will,
In the passage of the lotus of the throat
Where speech must rise and the expressing mind
And the heart's impulse run towards word and act,
A glad uplift and a new working came.
The immortal's thoughts displaced our bounded view,
The immortal's thoughts earth's drab idea and sense;
All things now bore a deeper heavenlier sense.
A glad clear harmony marked their truth's outline,
Reset the balance and measures of the world.
Each shape showed its occult design, unveiled
God's meaning in it for which it was made
And the vivid splendour of his artist thought.
A channel of the mighty Mother's choice,
The immortal's will took into its calm control
Our blind or erring government of life;
A loose republic once of wants and needs,
Then bowed to the uncertain sovereign mind,
Life now obeyed to a diviner rule
And every act became an act of God.
In the kingdom of the lotus of the heart
Love chanting its pure hymeneal hymn
Made life and body mirrors of sacred joy
And all the emotions gave themselves to God.

In the navel lotus' broad imperial range
Its proud ambitions and its master lusts
Were tamed into instruments of a great calm sway
To do a work of God on earthly soil.
In the narrow nether centre's petty parts
Its childish game of daily dwarf desires
Was changed into a sweet and boisterous play,
A romp of little gods with life in Time.
In the deep place where once the Serpent slept,
There came a grip on Matter's giant powers
For large utilities in life's little space;
A firm ground was made for Heaven's descending might.
Behind all reigned her sovereign deathless soul:
Casting aside its veil of Ignorance,
Allied to gods and cosmic beings and powers
It built the harmony of its human state;
Surrendered into the great World-Mother's hands
Only she obeyed her sole supreme behest
In the enigma of the Inconscient's world.
A secret soul behind supporting all
Is master and witness of our ignorant life,
Admits the Person's look and Nature's role.
But once the hidden doors are flung apart
Then the veiled king steps out in Nature's front;
A Light comes down into the Ignorance,
Its heavy painful knot loosens its grasp:
The mind becomes a mastered instrument
And life a hue and figure of the soul.
All happily grows towards knowledge and towards bliss.
A divine Puissance then takes Nature's place
And pushes the movements of our body and mind;
Possessor of our passionate hopes and dreams,
The beloved despot of our thoughts and acts,
She streams into us with her unbound force,
Into mortal limbs the Immortal's rapture and power.
An inner law of beauty shapes our lives;

Our words become the natural speech of Truth,
Each thought is a ripple on a sea of Light.
Then sin and virtue leave the cosmic lists;
They struggle no more in our delivered hearts:
Our acts chime with God's simple natural good
Or serve the rule of a supernal Right.
All moods unlovely, evil and untrue
Forsake their stations in fierce disarray
And hide their shame in the subconscient's dusk.
Then lifts the mind a cry of victory:
"O soul, my soul, we have created Heaven,
Within we have found the kingdom here of God,
His fortress built in a loud ignorant world.
Our life is entrenched between two rivers of Light,
We have turned space into a gulf of peace
And made the body a Capitol of bliss.
What more, what more, if more must still be done?"
In the slow process of the evolving spirit,
In the brief stade between a death and birth
A first perfection's stage is reached at last;
Out of the wood and stone of our nature's stuff
A temple is shaped where the high gods could live.
Even if the struggling world is left outside
One man's perfection still can save the world.
There is won a new proximity to the skies,
A first betrothal of the Earth to Heaven,
A deep concordat between Truth and Life:
A camp of God is pitched in human time.

END OF CANTO FIVE

Canto Six

Nirvana and the Discovery of the All-Negating Absolute

A CALM slow sun looked down from tranquil heavens.
A routed sullen rearguard of retreat,
The last rains had fled murmuring across the woods
Or failed, a sibilant whisper mid the leaves,
And the great blue enchantment of the sky
Recovered the deep rapture of its smile.
Its mellow splendour unstressed by storm-licked heats
Found room for a luxury of warm mild days,
The night's gold treasure of autumnal moons
Came floating shipped through ripples of faery air.
And Savitri's life was glad, fulfilled like earth's;
She had found herself, she knew her being's aim.
Although her kingdom of marvellous change within
Remained unspoken in her secret breast,
All that lived round her felt its magic's charm:
The trees' rustling voices told it to the winds,
Flowers spoke in ardent hues an unknown joy,
The birds' carolling became a canticle,
The beasts forgot their strife and lived at ease.
Absorbed in wide communion with the Unseen
The mild ascetics of the wood received
A sudden greatening of their lonely muse.
This bright perfection of her inner state
Poured overflowing into her outward scene,
Made beautiful dull common natural things
And action wonderful and time divine.
Even the smallest meanest work became
A sweet or glad and glorious sacrament,
An offering to the self of the great world
Or a service to the One in each and all.

A light invaded all from her being's light;
Her heart-beats' dance communicated bliss:
Happiness grew happier, shared with her, by her touch
And grief some solace found when she drew near.
Above the cherished head of Satyavan
She saw not now Fate's dark and lethal orb;
A golden circle round a mystic sun
Disclosed to her new-born predicting sight
The cyclic rondure of a sovereign life.
In her visions and deep-etched veridical dreams,
In brief shiftings of the future's heavy screen,
He lay not by a dolorous decree
A victim in the dismal antre of death
Or borne to blissful regions far from her
Forgetting the sweetness of earth's warm delight,
Forgetting the passionate oneness of love's clasp,
Absolved in the self-rapt immortal's bliss.
Always he was with her, a living soul
That met her eyes with close enamoured eyes,
A living body near to her body's joy.
But now no longer in these great wild woods
In kinship with the days of bird and beast
And levelled to the bareness of earth's brown breast,
But mid the thinking high-built lives of men
In tapestried chambers and on crystal floors,
In armoured town or gardened pleasure-walks,
Even in distance closer than her thoughts,
Body to body near, soul near to soul,
Moving as if by a common breath and will
They were tied in the single circling of their days
Together by love's unseen atmosphere,
Inseparable like the earth and sky.
Thus for a while she trod the Golden Path;
This was the sun before abysmal Night.
    Once as she sat in deep felicitous muse,
Still quivering from her lover's strong embrace,

And made her joy a bridge twixt earth and heaven,
An abyss yawned suddenly beneath her heart.
A vast and nameless fear dragged at her nerves
As drags a wild beast its half-slaughtered prey;
It seemed to have no den from which it sprang:
It was not hers, but hid its unseen cause.
Then rushing came its vast and fearful Fount.
A formless Dread with shapeless endless wings
Filling the universe with its dangerous breath,
A denser darkness than the Night could bear,
Enveloped the heavens and possessed the earth.
A rolling surge of silent death, it came
Curving round the far edge of the quaking globe;
Effacing heaven with its enormous stride
It willed to expunge the choked and anguished air
And end the fable of the joy of life.
It seemed her very being to forbid,
Abolishing all by which her nature lived,
And laboured to blot out her body and soul,
A clutch of some half-seen Invisible,
An ocean of terror and of sovereign might,
A person and a black infinity.
It seemed to cry to her without thought or word
The message of its dark eternity
And the awful meaning of its silences:
Out of some sullen monstrous vast arisen,
Out of an abysmal deep of grief and fear
Imagined by some blind regardless self,
A consciousness of being without its joy,
Empty of thought, incapable of bliss,
That felt life blank and nowhere found a soul,
A voice to the dumb anguish of the heart
Conveyed a stark sense of unspoken words;
In her own depths she heard the unuttered thought
That made unreal the world and all life meant.
"Who art thou who claimst thy crown of separate birth,

The illusion of thy soul's reality
And personal godhead on an ignorant globe
In the animal body of imperfect man?
Hope not to be happy in a world of pain
And dream not, listening to the unspoken Word
And dazzled by the inexpressible Ray,
Transcending the mute Superconscient's realm,
To give a body to the Unknowable,
Or for a sanction to thy heart's delight
To burden with bliss the silent still Supreme
Profaning its bare and formless sanctity,
Or call into thy chamber the Divine
And sit with God tasting a human joy.
I have created all, all I devour;
I am Death and the dark terrible Mother of life,
I am Kali black and naked in the world,
I am Maya and the universe is my cheat.
I lay waste human happiness with my breath
And slay the will to live, the joy to be
That all may pass back into nothingness
And only abide the eternal and absolute.
For only the blank Eternal can be true.
All else is shadow and flash in Mind's bright glass,
Mind, hollow mirror in which Ignorance sees
A splendid figure of its own false self
And dreams it sees a glorious solid world.
O soul, inventor of man's thoughts and hopes,
Thyself the invention of the moments' stream,
Illusion's centre or subtle apex point,
At last know thyself, from vain existence cease."
A shadow of the negating Absolute,
The intolerant Darkness travelled surging past
And ebbed in her the formidable Voice.
It left behind her inner world laid waste:
A barren silence weighed upon her heart,
Her kingdom of delight was there no more;

Only her soul remained, its emptied stage,
Awaiting the unknown eternal Will.
Then from the heights a greater Voice came down,
The Word that touches the heart and finds the soul,
The voice of Light after the voice of Night:
The cry of the Abyss drew Heaven's reply,
A might of storm chased by the might of the Sun.
"O soul, bare not thy kingdom to the foe;
Consent to hide thy royalty of bliss
Lest Time and Fate find out its avenues
And beat with thunderous knock upon thy gates.
Hide whilst thou canst thy treasure of separate self
Behind the luminous rampart of thy depths
Till of a vaster empire it grows part.
But not for self alone the Self is won:
Content abide not with one conquered realm;
Adventure all to make the whole world thine,
To break into greater kingdoms turn thy force.
Fear not to be nothing that thou mayst be all;
Assent to the emptiness of the Supreme
That all in thee may reach its absolute.
Accept to be small and human on the earth,
Interrupting thy new-born divinity,
That man may find his utter self in God.
If for thy own sake only thou hast come,
An immortal spirit into the mortal's world,
To found thy luminous kingdom in God's dark,
In the Inconscient's realm one shining star,
One door in the Ignorance opened upon light,
Why hadst thou any need to come at all?
Thou hast come down into a struggling world
To aid a blind and suffering mortal race,
To open to Light the eyes that could not see,
To bring down bliss into the heart of grief,
To make thy life a bridge twixt earth and heaven;
If thou wouldst save the toiling universe,

The vast universal suffering feel as thine:
Thou must bear the sorrow that thou claimst to heal;
The day-bringer must walk in darkest night.
He who would save the world must share its pain.
If he knows not grief, how shall he find grief's cure?
If far he walks above mortality's head,
How shall the mortal reach that too high path?
If one of theirs they see scale heaven's peaks,
Men then can hope to learn that titan climb.
God must be born on earth and be as man
That man being human may grow even as God.
He who would save the world must be one with the world,
All suffering things contain in his heart's space
And bear the grief and joy of all that lives.
His soul must be wider than the universe
And feel eternity as its very stuff,
Rejecting the moment's personality
Know itself older than the birth of Time,
Creation an incident in its consciousness,
Arcturus and Belphegor grains of fire
Circling in a corner of its boundless self,
The world's destruction a small transient storm
In the calm infinity it has become.
If thou wouldst a little loosen the vast chain,
Draw back from the world that the Idea has made,
Thy mind's selection from the Infinite,
Thy senses' gloss on the Infinitesimal's dance,
Then shalt thou know how the great bondage came.
Banish all thought from thee and be God's void.
Then shalt thou uncover the Unknowable
And the Superconscient conscious grow on thy tops;
Infinity's vision through thy gaze shall pierce;
Thou shalt look into the eyes of the Unknown,
Find the hid Truth in things seen null and false,
Behind things known discover Mystery's rear.
Thou shalt be one with God's bare reality

And the miraculous world he has become
And the diviner miracle still to be
When Nature who is now unconscious God
Translucent grows to the Eternal's light,
Her seeing his sight, her walk his steps of power
And life is filled with a spiritual joy
And Matter is the Spirit's willing bride.
Consent to be nothing and none, dissolve Time's work,
Cast off thy mind, step back from form and name.
Annul thyself that only God may be."

Thus spoke the mighty and uplifting Voice,
And Savitri heard; she bowed her head and mused
Plunging her deep regard into herself
In her soul's privacy in the silent Night.
Aloof and standing back detached and calm,
A witness of the drama of herself,
A student of her own interior scene,
She watched the passion and the toil of life
And heard in the crowded thoroughfares of mind
The unceasing tread and passage of her thoughts.
All she allowed to rise that chose to stir;
Calling, compelling nought, forbidding nought,
She left all to the process formed in Time
And the free initiative of Nature's will.
Thus following the complex human play
She heard the prompter's voice behind the scenes,
Perceived the original libretto's set
And the organ theme of the composer Force.
All she beheld that surges from man's depths,
The animal instincts prowling mid life's trees,
The impulses that whisper to the heart
And passion's thunder-chase sweeping the nerves;
She saw the Powers that stare from the Abyss
And the wordless Light that liberates the soul.
But most her gaze pursued the birth of thought.

Affranchised from the look of surface mind
She paused not to survey the official case,
The issue of forms from the office of the brain,
Its factory of thought-sounds and soundless words
And voices stored within unheard by men,
Its mint and treasury of shining coin.
These were but counters in mind's symbol game,
A gramophone's discs, a reproduction's film,
A list of signs, a cipher and a code.
In our unseen subtle body thought is born
Or there it enters from the cosmic field.
Oft from her soul stepped out a naked thought
Luminous with mysteried lips and wonderful eyes;
Or from her heart emerged some burning face
And looked for life and love and passionate truth,
Aspired to heaven or embraced the world
Or led the fancy like a fleeting moon
Across the dull sky of man's common days,
Amidst the doubtful certitudes of earth's lore,
To the celestial beauty of faith gave form,
As if at flower-prints in a dingy room
Laughed in a golden vase one living rose.
A thaumaturgist sat in her heart's deep,
Compelled the forward stride, the upward look,
Till wonder leaped into the illumined breast
And life grew marvellous with transfiguring hope.
A seeing will pondered between the brows;
Thoughts, glistening Angels, stood behind the brain
In flashing armour, folding hands of prayer,
And poured heaven's rays into the earthly form.
Imaginations flamed up from her breast,
Unearthly beauty, touches of surpassing joy
And plans of miracle, dreams of delight:
Around her navel lotus clustering close
Her large sensations of the teeming worlds
Streamed their dumb movements of the unformed Idea;

Invading the small sensitive flower of the throat
They brought their mute unuttered resonances
To kindle the figures of a heavenly speech.
Below, desires formed their wordless wish,
And longings of physical sweetness and ecstasy
Translated into the accents of a cry
Their grasp on objects and their clasp on souls.
Her body's thoughts climbed from her conscious limbs
And carried their yearnings to its mystic crown
Where Nature's murmurs meet the Ineffable.
But for the mortal prisoned in outward mind
All must present their passports at its door;
Disguised they must don the official cap and mask
Or pass as manufactures of the brain,
Unknown their secret truth and hidden source.
Only to the inner mind they speak direct,
Put on a body and assume a voice,
Their passage seen, their message heard and known,
Their birthplace and their natal mark revealed,
And stand confessed to an immortal's sight,
Our nature's messengers to the witness soul.
Impenetrable, withheld from mortal sense,
The inner chambers of the spirit's house
Disclosed to her their happenings and their guests;
Eyes looked through crevices in the invisible wall
And through the secrecy of unseen doors
There came into mind's little frontal room
Thoughts that enlarged our limited human range,
Lifted the ideal's half-quenched or sinking torch
Or peered through the finite at the infinite.
A sight opened upon the invisible
And sensed the shapes that mortal eyes see not,
The sounds that mortal listening cannot hear,
The blissful sweetness of the intangible's touch;
The objects that to us are empty air,
Are there the stuff of daily experience

And the common pabulum of sense and thought.
The beings of the subtle realms appeared
And scenes concealed behind our earthly scene;
She saw the life of remote continents
And distance deafened not to voices far;
She felt the movements crossing unknown minds;
The past's events occurred before her eyes.
The great world's thoughts were part of her own thought,
The feelings dumb for ever and unshared,
The ideas that never found an utterance.
The dim subconscient's incoherent hints
Laid bare a meaning twisted, deep and strange,
The bizarre secret of their fumbling speech,
Their links with underlying reality.
The unseen grew visible and audible:
Thoughts leaped down from a superconscient field
Like eagles swooping from a viewless peak,
Thoughts gleamed up from the screened subliminal depths
Like golden fishes from a hidden sea.
This world is a vast unbroken totality,
A deep solidarity joins its contrary powers;
God's summits look back on the mute Abyss.
So man evolving to divinest heights
Colloques still with the animal and the Djinn;
The human godhead with star-gazer eyes
Lives still in one house with the primal beast.
The high meets the low, all is a single plan.
So she beheld the many births of thought,
If births can be of what eternal is;
For the Eternal's powers are like himself,
Timeless in the Timeless, in Time ever born.
This too she saw that all in outer mind
Is made, not born, a product perishable,
Forged in the body's factory by earth-force.
This mind is a dynamic small machine
Producing ceaselessly, till it wears out,

With raw material drawn from the outside world,
The patterns sketched out by an artist God.
Often our thoughts are finished cosmic wares
Admitted by a silent office gate
And passed through the subconscient's galleries,
Then issued in Time's mart as private make.
For now they bear the living person's stamp;
A trick, a special hue claims them his own.
All else is Nature's craft and this too hers.
Our tasks are given, we are but instruments;
Nothing is all our own that we create:
The Power that acts in us is not our force.
The genius too receives from some high fount
Concealed in a supernal secrecy
The work that gives him an immortal name.
The word, the form, the charm, the glory and grace
Are missioned sparks from a stupendous Fire;
A sample from the laboratory of God
Of which he holds the patent upon earth,
Comes to him wrapped in golden coverings;
He listens for Inspiration's postman knock
And takes delivery of the priceless gift
A little spoilt by the receiver mind
Or mixed with the manufacture of his brain;
When least defaced, then is it most divine.
Although his ego claims the world for its use,
Man is a dynamo for the cosmic work;
Nature does most in him, God the high rest:
Only his soul's acceptance is his own.
This independent, once a power supreme,
Self-born before the universe was made,
Accepting cosmos, binds himself Nature's serf
Till he becomes her freedman — or God's slave.
This is the appearance in our mortal front;
Our greater truth of being lies behind:
Our consciousness is cosmic and immense,

But only when we break through Matter's wall
In that spiritual vastness can we stand
Where we can live the masters of our world
And mind is only a means and body a tool.
For above the birth of body and of thought
Our spirit's truth lives in the naked self
And from that height, unbound, surveys the world.
Out of the mind she rose to escape its law
That it might sleep in some deep shadow of self
Or fall silent in the silence of the Unseen.
High she attained and stood from Nature free
And saw creation's life from far above,
Thence upon all she laid her sovereign will
To dedicate it to God's timeless calm:
Then all grew tranquil in her being's space,
Only sometimes small thoughts arose and fell
Like quiet waves upon a silent sea
Or ripples passing over a lonely pool
When a stray stone disturbs its dreaming rest.
Yet the mind's factory had ceased to work,
There was no sound of the dynamo's throb,
There came no call from the still fields of life.
Then even those stirrings rose in her no more;
Her mind now seemed like a vast empty room
Or like a peaceful landscape without sound.
This men call quietude and prize as peace.
But to her deeper sight all yet was there,
Effervescing like a chaos under a lid;
Feelings and thoughts cried out for word and act
But found no response in the silenced brain:
All was suppressed but nothing yet expunged;
At every moment might explosion come.
Then this too paused; the body seemed a stone.
All now was a wide mighty vacancy,
But still excluded from eternity's hush;
For still was far the repose of the Absolute

And the ocean silence of Infinity.
Even now some thoughts could cross her solitude;
These surged not from the depths or from within
Cast up from formlessness to seek a form,
Spoke not the body's need nor voiced life's call.
These seemed not born nor made in human Time:
Children of cosmic Nature from a far world,
Idea's shapes in complete armour of words
Posted like travellers in an alien space.
Out of some far expanse they seemed to come
As if carried on vast wings like large white sails,
And with easy access reached the inner ear
As though they used a natural privileged right
To the high royal entries of the soul.
As yet their path lay deep-concealed in light.
Then looking to know whence the intruders came
She saw a spiritual immensity
Pervading and encompassing the world-space
As ether our transparent tangible air,
And through it sailing tranquilly a thought.
As smoothly glides a ship nearing its port,
Ignorant of embargo and blockade,
Confident of entrance and the visa's seal,
It came to the silent city of the brain
Towards its accustomed and expectant quay,
But met a barring will, a blow of Force
And sank vanishing in the immensity.
After a long vacant pause another appeared
And others one by one suddenly emerged,
Mind's unexpected visitors from the Unseen
Like far-off sails upon a lonely sea.
But soon that commerce failed, none reached mind's coast.
Then all grew still, nothing moved any more:
Immobile, self-rapt, timeless, solitary
A silent spirit pervaded silent Space.

In that absolute stillness bare and formidable
There was glimpsed an all-negating Void Supreme
That claimed its mystic Nihil's sovereign right
To cancel Nature and deny the soul.
Even the nude sense of self grew pale and thin:
Impersonal, signless, featureless, void of forms
A blank pure consciousness had replaced the mind.
Her spirit seemed the substance of a name,
The world a pictured symbol drawn on self,
A dream of images, a dream of sounds
Built up the semblance of a universe
Or lent to spirit the appearance of a world.
This was self-seeing; in that intolerant hush
No notion and no concept could take shape,
There was no sense to frame the figure of things,
A sheer self-sight was there, no thought arose.
Emotion slept deep down in the still heart
Or lay buried in a cemetery of peace:
All feelings seemed quiescent, calm or dead,
As if the heart-strings rent could work no more
And joy and grief could never rise again.
The heart beat on with an unconscious rhythm
But no response came from it and no cry.
Vain was the provocation of events;
Nothing within answered an outside touch,
No nerve was stirred and no reaction rose.
Yet still her body saw and moved and spoke;
It understood without the aid of thought,
It said whatever needed to be said,
It did whatever needed to be done.
There was no person there behind the act,
No mind that chose or passed the fitting word:
All wrought like an unerring apt machine.
As if continuing old habitual turns,
And pushed by an old unexhausted force
The engine did the work for which it was made:

Her consciousness looked on and took no part;
All it upheld, in nothing had a share.
There was no strong initiator will;
An incoherence crossing a firm void
Slipped into an order of related chance.
A pure perception was the only power
That stood behind her action and her sight.
If that retired, all objects would be extinct,
Her private universe would cease to be,
The house she had built with bricks of thought and sense
In the beginning after the birth of Space.
This seeing was identical with the seen;
It knew without knowledge all that could be known,
It saw impartially the world go by,
But in the same supine unmoving glance
Saw too its abysmal unreality.
It watched the figure of the cosmic game,
But the thought and inner life in forms seemed dead,
Abolished by her own collapse of thought:
A hollow physical shell persisted still.
All seemed a brilliant shadow of itself,
A cosmic film of scenes and images:
The enduring mass and outline of the hills
Was a design sketched on a silent mind
And held to a tremulous false solidity
By constant beats of visionary sight.
The forest with its emerald multitudes
Clothed with its show of hues vague empty Space,
A painting's colours hiding a surface void
That flickered upon dissolution's edge;
The blue heavens, an illusion of the eyes,
Roofed in the mind's illusion of a world.
The men who walked beneath an unreal sky
Seemed mobile puppets out of cardboard cut
And pushed by unseen hands across the soil
Or moving pictures upon Fancy's film:

There was no soul within, no power of life.
The brain's vibrations that appear like thought,
The nerve's brief answer to each contact's knock,
The heart's quiverings felt as joy and grief and love
Were twitchings of the body, their seeming self,
That body forged from atoms and from gas
A manufactured lie of Maya's make,
Its life a dream seen by the sleeping Void.
The animals lone or trooping through the glades
Fled like a passing vision of beauty and grace
Imagined by some all-creating Eye.
Yet something was there behind the fading scene;
Wherever she turned, at whatsoever she looked,
It was perceived, yet hid from mind and sight.
The One only real shut itself from Space
And stood aloof from the idea of Time.
Its truth escaped from shape and line and hue.
All else grew unsubstantial, self-annulled,
This only everlasting seemed and true,
Yet nowhere dwelt, it was outside the hours.
This only could justify the labour of sight,
But sight could not define for it a form;
This only could appease the unsatisfied ear
But hearing listened in vain for a missing sound;
This answered not the sense, called not to Mind.
It met her as the uncaught inaudible Voice
That speaks for ever from the Unknowable.
It met her like an omnipresent point
Pure of dimensions, unfixed, invisible,
The single oneness of its multiplied beat
Accentuating its sole eternity.
It faced her as some vast Nought's immensity,
An endless No to all that seems to be,
An endless Yes to things ever unconceived
And all that is unimagined and unthought,
An eternal zero or untotalled Aught,

A spaceless and a placeless Infinite.
Yet eternity and infinity seemed but words
Vainly affixed by mind's incompetence
To its stupendous lone reality.
The world is but a spark-burst from its light,
All moments flashes from its Timelessness,
All objects glimmerings of the Bodiless
That disappear from Mind when That is seen.
It held, as if a shield before its face,
A consciousness that saw without a seer,
The Truth where knowledge is not nor knower nor known,
The Love enamoured of its own delight
In which the Lover is not nor the Beloved
Bringing their personal passion into the Vast,
The Force omnipotent in quietude,
The Bliss that none can ever hope to taste.
It cancelled the convincing cheat of self;
A truth in nothingness was its mighty clue.
If all existence could renounce to be
And Being take refuge in Non-being's arms
And Non-being could strike out its ciphered round,
Some lustre of that Reality might appear.
A formless liberation came on her.
Once sepulchred alive in brain and flesh
She had risen up from body, mind and life;
She was no more a Person in a world,
She had escaped into infinity.
What once had been herself had disappeared;
There was no frame of things, no figure of soul.
A refugee from the domain of sense,
Evading the necessity of thought,
Delivered from Knowledge and from Ignorance
And rescued from the true and the untrue,
She shared the Superconscient's high retreat
Beyond the self-born Word, the nude Idea,
The first bare solid ground of consciousness;

Beings were not there, existence had no place,
There was no temptation of the joy to be.
Unutterably effaced, no one and null,
A vanishing vestige like a violet trace,
A faint record merely of a self now past,
She was a point in the unknowable.
Only some last annulment now remained,
Annihilation's vague indefinable step:
A memory of being still was there
And kept her separate from nothingness:
She was in That but still became not That.
This shadow of herself so close to nought
Could be again self's point d'appui to live,
Return out of the Inconceivable
And be what some mysterious vast might choose.
Even as the Unknowable decreed,
She might be nought or new-become the All,
Or if the omnipotent Nihil took a shape
Emerge as someone and redeem the world.
Even, she might learn what the mystic cipher held,
This seeming exit or closed end of all
Could be a blind tenebrous passage screened from sight,
Her state the eclipsing shell of a darkened sun
On its secret way to the Ineffable.
Even now her splendid being might flame back
Out of the silence and the nullity,
A gleaming portion of the All-Wonderful,
A power of some all-affirming Absolute,
A shining mirror of the eternal Truth
To show to the One-in-all its manifest face,
To the souls of men their deep identity.
Or she might wake into God's quietude
Beyond the cosmic day and cosmic night
And rest appeased in his white eternity.
But this was now unreal or remote
Or covered in the mystic fathomless blank.

In infinite Nothingness was the ultimate sign
Or else the Real was the Unknowable.
A lonely Absolute negated all:
It effaced the ignorant world from its solitude
And drowned the soul in its everlasting peace.

END OF CANTO SIX

Canto Seven

The Discovery of the Cosmic Spirit
and the Cosmic Consciousness

In the little hermitage in the forest's heart,
In the sunlight and the moonlight and the dark
The daily human life went plodding on
Even as before with its small unchanging works
And its spare outward body of routine
And happy quiet of ascetic peace.
The old beauty smiled of the terrestrial scene;
She too was her old gracious self to men.
The Ancient Mother clutched her child to her breast
Pressing her close in her environing arms,
As if earth ever the same could for ever keep
The living spirit and body in her clasp,
As if death were not there nor end nor change.
Accustomed only to read outward signs
None saw aught new in her, none divined her state;
They saw a person where was only God's vast,
A still being or a mighty nothingness.
To all she was the same perfect Savitri:
A greatness and a sweetness and a light
Poured out from her upon her little world.
Life showed to all the same familiar face,
Her acts followed the old unaltered round,
She spoke the words that she was wont to speak
And did the things that she had always done.
Her eyes looked out on earth's unchanging face,
Around her soul's muteness all moved as of old;
A vacant consciousness watched from within,
Empty of all but bare Reality.
There was no will behind the word and act,
No thought formed in her brain to guide the speech:

An impersonal emptiness walked and spoke in her,
Something perhaps unfelt, unseen, unknown
Guarded the body for its future work,
Or Nature moved in her old stream of force.
Perhaps she bore made conscious in her breast
The miraculous Nihil, origin of our souls
And source and sum of the vast world's events,
The womb and grave of thought, a cipher of God,
A zero circle of being's totality.
It used her speech and acted in her acts,
It was beauty in her limbs, life in her breath;
The original Mystery wore her human face.
Thus was she lost within to separate self;
Her mortal ego perished in God's night.
Only a body was left, the ego's shell
Afloat mid drift and foam of the world-sea,
A sea of dream watched by a motionless sense
In a figure of unreal reality.
An impersonal foresight could already see, —
In the unthinking knowledge of the spirit
Even now it seemed nigh done, inevitable, —
The individual die, the cosmos pass;
These gone, the transcendental grew a myth,
The Holy Ghost without the Father and Son,
Or, a substratum of what once had been,
Being that never willed to bear a world
Restored to its original loneliness,
Impassive, sole, silent, intangible.
Yet all was not extinct in this deep loss;
The being travelled not towards nothingness.
There was some high surpassing Secrecy,
And when she sat alone with Satyavan,
Her moveless mind with his that searched and strove,
In the hush of the profound and intimate night
She turned to the face of a veiled voiceless Truth
Hid in the dumb recesses of the heart

Or waiting beyond the last peak climbed by Thought, —
Unseen itself it sees the struggling world
And prompts our quest, but cares not to be found, —
Out of that distant Vast came a reply.
Something unknown, unreached, inscrutable
Sent down the messages of its bodiless Light,
Cast lightning flashes of a thought not ours
Crossing the immobile silence of her mind:
In its might of irresponsible sovereignty
It seized on speech to give those flamings shape,
Made beat the heart of wisdom in a word
And spoke immortal things through mortal lips.
Or, listening to the sages of the woods,
In question and in answer broke from her
High strange revealings impossible to men,
Something or someone secret and remote
Took hold of her body for his mystic use,
Her mouth was seized to channel ineffable truths,
Knowledge unthinkable found an utterance.
Astonished by a new enlightenment,
Invaded by a streak of the Absolute,
They marvelled at her, for she seemed to know
What they had only glimpsed at times afar.
These thoughts were formed not in her listening brain,
Her vacant heart was like a stringless harp;
Impassive the body claimed not its own voice,
But let the luminous greatness through it pass.
A dual Power at being's occult poles
Still acted, nameless and invisible:
Her divine emptiness was their instrument.
Inconscient Nature dealt with the world it had made,
And using still the body's instruments
Slipped through the conscious void she had become;
The superconscient Mystery through that Void
Missioned its word to touch the thoughts of men.
As yet this great impersonal speech was rare.

But now the unmoving wide spiritual space
In which her mind survived tranquil and bare,
Admitted a traveller from the cosmic breadths:
A thought came through draped as an outer voice.
It called not for the witness of the mind,
It spoke not to the hushed receiving heart;
It came direct to the pure perception's seat,
An only centre now of consciousness,
If centre could be where all seemed only space;
No more shut in by body's walls and gates
Her being, a circle without circumference,
Already now surpassed all cosmic bounds
And more and more spread into infinity.
This being was its own unbounded world,
A world without form or feature or circumstance;
It had no ground, no wall, no roof of thought,
Yet saw itself and looked on all around
In a silence motionless and illimitable.
There was no person there, no centred mind,
No seat of feeling on which beat events
Or objects wrought and shaped reaction's stress.
There was no motion in this inner world,
All was a still and even infinity.
In her the Unseen, the Unknown waited his hour.

But now she sat by sleeping Satyavan,
Awake within, and the enormous Night
Surrounded her with the Unknowable's vast.
A voice began to speak from her own heart
That was not hers, yet mastered thought and sense.
As it spoke all changed within her and without;
All was, all lived; she felt all being one;
The world of unreality ceased to be:
There was no more a universe built by mind,
Convicted as a structure or a sign;
A spirit, a being saw created things

And cast itself into unnumbered forms
And was what it saw and made; all now became
An evidence of one stupendous truth,
A Truth in which negation had no place,
A being and a living consciousness,
A stark and absolute Reality.
There the unreal could not find a place,
The sense of unreality was slain:
There all was conscious, made of the Infinite,
All had a substance of Eternity.
Yet this was the same Indecipherable;
It seemed to cast from it universe like a dream
Vanishing for ever into an original Void.
But this was no more some vague ubiquitous point
Or a cipher of vastness in unreal Nought.
It was the same but now no more seemed far
To the living clasp of her recovered soul.
It was her self, it was the self of all,
It was the reality of existing things,
It was the consciousness of all that lived
And felt and saw; it was Timelessness and Time,
It was the Bliss of formlessness and form.
It was all Love and the one Beloved's arms,
It was sight and thought in one all-seeing Mind,
It was joy of Being on the peaks of God.
She passed beyond Time into eternity,
Slipped out of space and became the Infinite;
Her being rose into unreachable heights
And found no end of its journey in the Self.
It plunged into the unfathomable deeps
And found no end to the silent mystery
That held all world within one lonely breast,
Yet harboured all creation's multitudes.
She was all vastness and one measureless point,
She was a height beyond heights, a depth beyond depths,
She lived in the everlasting and was all

That harbours death and bears the wheeling hours.
All contraries were true in one huge spirit
Surpassing measure, change and circumstance.
An individual, one with cosmic self
In the heart of the Transcendent's miracle
And the secret of World-personality
Was the creator and the lord of all.
Mind was a single innumerable look
Upon himself and all that he became.
Life was his drama and the Vast a stage,
The universe was his body, God its soul.
All was one single immense reality,
All its innumerable phenomenon.
   Her spirit saw the world as living God;
It saw the One and knew that all was He.
She knew him as the Absolute's self-space,
One with her self and ground of all things here
In which the world wanders seeking for the Truth
Guarded behind its face of ignorance:
She followed him through the march of endless Time.
All Nature's happenings were events in her,
The heart-beats of the cosmos were her own,
All beings thought and felt and moved in her;
She inhabited the vastness of the world,
Its distances were her nature's boundaries,
Its closenesses her own life's intimacies.
Her mind became familiar with its mind,
Its body was her body's larger frame
In which she lived and knew herself in it
One, multitudinous in its multitudes.
She was a single being, yet all things;
The world was her spirit's wide circumference,
The thoughts of others were her intimates,
Their feelings close to her universal heart,
Their bodies her many bodies kin to her;
She was no more herself but all the world.

Out of the infinitudes all came to her,
Into the infinitudes sentient she spread,
Infinity was her own natural home.
Nowhere she dwelt, her spirit was everywhere,
The distant constellations wheeled round her;
Earth saw her born, all worlds were her colonies,
The greater worlds of life and mind were hers;
All Nature reproduced her in its lines,
Its movements were large copies of her own.
She was the single self of all these selves,
She was in them and they were all in her.
This first was an immense identity
In which her own identity was lost:
What seemed herself was an image of the Whole.
She was a subconscient life of tree and flower,
The outbreak of the honied buds of spring;
She burned in the passion and splendour of the rose,
She was the red heart of the passion-flower,
The dream-white of the lotus in its pool.
Out of subconscient life she climbed to mind,
She was thought and the passion of the world's heart,
She was the godhead hid in the heart of man,
She was the climbing of his soul to God.
The cosmos flowered in her, she was its bed.
She was Time and the dreams of God in Time;
She was Space and the wideness of his days.
From this she rose where Time and Space were not;
The superconscient was her native air,
Infinity was her movement's natural space;
Eternity looked out from her on Time.

END OF CANTO SEVEN
End of Book Seven

BOOK EIGHT

The Book of Death

Canto Three*

Death in the Forest

Now it was here in this great golden dawn.
By her still sleeping husband lain she gazed
Into her past as one about to die
Looks back upon the sunlit fields of life
Where he too ran and sported with the rest,
Lifting his head above the huge dark stream
Into whose depths he must for ever plunge.
All she had been and done she lived again.
The whole year in a swift and eddying race
Of memories swept through her and fled away
Into the irrecoverable past.
Then silently she rose and, service done,
Bowed down to the great goddess simply carved
By Satyavan upon a forest stone.
What prayer she breathed her soul and Durga knew.
Perhaps she felt in the dim forest huge
The infinite Mother watching over her child,
Perhaps the shrouded Voice spoke some still word.
At last she came to the pale mother queen.
She spoke but with guarded lips and tranquil face
Lest some stray word or some betraying look
Should let pass into the mother's unknowing breast,
Slaying all happiness and need to live,
A dire foreknowledge of the grief to come.
Only the needed utterance passage found:
All else she pressed back into her anguished heart
And forced upon her speech an outward peace.

---

* The Book of Death was taken from Canto Three of an early version of *Savitri* which had only six cantos and an epilogue. It was slightly revised at a late stage and a number of new lines were added, but it was never fully worked into the final version of the poem. Its original designation, "Canto Three", has been retained as a reminder of this.

"One year that I have lived with Satyavan
Here on the emerald edge of the vast woods
In the iron ring of the enormous peaks
Under the blue rifts of the forest sky,
I have not gone into the silences
Of this great woodland that enringed my thoughts
With mystery, nor in its green miracles
Wandered, but this small clearing was my world.
Now has a strong desire seized all my heart
To go with Satyavan holding his hand
Into the life that he has loved and touch
Herbs he has trod and know the forest flowers
And hear at ease the birds and the scurrying life
That starts and ceases, rich far rustle of boughs
And all the mystic whispering of the woods.
Release me now and let my heart have rest."
She answered: "Do as thy wise mind desires,
O calm child-sovereign with the eyes that rule.
I hold thee for a strong goddess who has come
Pitying our barren days; so dost thou serve
Even as a slave might, yet art thou beyond
All that thou doest, all our minds conceive,
Like the strong sun that serves earth from above."
Then the doomed husband and the woman who knew
Went with linked hands into that solemn world
Where beauty and grandeur and unspoken dream,
Where Nature's mystic silence could be felt
Communing with the secrecy of God.
Beside her Satyavan walked full of joy
Because she moved with him through his green haunts:
He showed her all the forest's riches, flowers
Innumerable of every odour and hue
And soft thick clinging creepers red and green
And strange rich-plumaged birds, to every cry
That haunted sweetly distant boughs replied
With the shrill singer's name more sweetly called.

He spoke of all the things he loved: they were
His boyhood's comrades and his playfellows,
Coevals and companions of his life
Here in this world whose every mood he knew:
Their thoughts which to the common mind are blank,
He shared, to every wild emotion felt
An answer. Deeply she listened, but to hear
The voice that soon would cease from tender words
And treasure its sweet cadences beloved
For lonely memory when none by her walked
And the beloved voice could speak no more.
But little dwelt her mind upon their sense;
Of death, not life she thought or life's lone end.
Love in her bosom hurt with the jagged edges
Of anguish moaned at every step with pain
Crying, "Now, now perhaps his voice will cease
For ever." Even by some vague touch oppressed
Sometimes her eyes looked round as if their orbs
Might see the dim and dreadful god's approach.
But Satyavan had paused. He meant to finish
His labour here that happy, linked, uncaring
They two might wander free in the green deep
Primaeval mystery of the forest's heart.
A tree that raised its tranquil head to heaven
Luxuriating in verdure, summoning
The breeze with amorous wideness of its boughs,
He chose and with his steel assailed the arm
Brown, rough and strong hidden in its emerald dress.
Wordless but near she watched, no turn to lose
Of the bright face and body which she loved.
Her life was now in seconds, not in hours,
And every moment she economised
Like a pale merchant leaned above his store,
The miser of his poor remaining gold.
But Satyavan wielded a joyous axe.
He sang high snatches of a sage's chant

That pealed of conquered death and demons slain,
And sometimes paused to cry to her sweet speech
Of love and mockery tenderer than love:
She like a pantheress leaped upon his words
And carried them into her cavern heart.
But as he worked, his doom upon him came.
The violent and hungry hounds of pain
Travelled through his body biting as they passed
Silently, and all his suffering breath besieged
Strove to rend life's strong heart-cords and be free.
Then helped, as if a beast had left its prey,
A moment in a wave of rich relief
Reborn to strength and happy ease he stood
Rejoicing and resumed his confident toil
But with less seeing strokes. Now the great woodsman
Hewed at him and his labour ceased: lifting
His arm he flung away the poignant axe
Far from him like an instrument of pain.
She came to him in silent anguish and clasped,
And he cried to her, "Savitri, a pang
Cleaves through my head and breast as if the axe
Were piercing it and not the living branch.
Such agony rends me as the tree must feel
When it is sundered and must lose its life.
Awhile let me lay my head upon thy lap
And guard me with thy hands from evil fate:
Perhaps because thou touchest, death may pass."
Then Savitri sat under branches wide,
Cool, green against the sun, not the hurt tree
Which his keen axe had cloven,—that she shunned;
But leaned beneath a fortunate kingly trunk
She guarded him in her bosom and strove to soothe
His anguished brow and body with her hands.
All grief and fear were dead within her now
And a great calm had fallen. The wish to lessen
His suffering, the impulse that opposes pain

Were the one mortal feeling left. It passed:
Griefless and strong she waited like the gods.
But now his sweet familiar hue was changed
Into a tarnished greyness and his eyes
Dimmed over, forsaken of the clear light she loved.
Only the dull and physical mind was left,
Vacant of the bright spirit's luminous gaze.
But once before it faded wholly back,
He cried out in a clinging last despair,
"Savitri, Savitri, O Savitri,
Lean down, my soul, and kiss me while I die."
And even as her pallid lips pressed his,
His failed, losing last sweetness of response;
His cheek pressed down her golden arm. She sought
His mouth still with her living mouth, as if
She could persuade his soul back with her kiss;
Then grew aware they were no more alone.
Something had come there conscious, vast and dire.
Near her she felt a silent shade immense
Chilling the noon with darkness for its back.
An awful hush had fallen upon the place:
There was no cry of birds, no voice of beasts.
A terror and an anguish filled the world,
As if annihilation's mystery
Had taken a sensible form. A cosmic mind
Looked out on all from formidable eyes
Contemning all with its unbearable gaze
And with immortal lids and a vast brow
It saw in its immense destroying thought
All things and beings as a pitiful dream,
Rejecting with calm disdain Nature's delight,
The wordless meaning of its deep regard
Voicing the unreality of things
And life that would be for ever but never was
And its brief and vain recurrence without cease,
As if from a Silence without form or name

The Shadow of a remote uncaring god
Doomed to his Nought the illusory universe,
Cancelling its show of idea and act in Time
And its imitation of eternity.
She knew that visible Death was standing there
And Satyavan had passed from her embrace.

END OF BOOK EIGHT, "CANTO THREE"
End of Part Two

PART THREE

BOOKS IX – XII

PART THREE.

BOOK NINE

The Book of Eternal Night

Canto One

Towards the Black Void

SO WAS she left alone in the huge wood,
Surrounded by a dim unthinking world,
Her husband's corpse on her forsaken breast.
In her vast silent spirit motionless
She measured not her loss with helpless thoughts,
Nor rent with tears the marble seals of pain:
She rose not yet to face the dreadful god.
Over the body she loved her soul leaned out
In a great stillness without stir or voice,
As if her mind had died with Satyavan.
But still the human heart in her beat on.
Aware still of his being near to hers,
Closely she clasped to her the mute lifeless form
As though to guard the oneness they had been
And keep the spirit still within its frame.
Then suddenly there came on her the change
Which in tremendous moments of our lives
Can overtake sometimes the human soul
And hold it up towards its luminous source.
The veil is torn, the thinker is no more:
Only the spirit sees and all is known.
Then a calm Power seated above our brows
Is seen, unshaken by our thoughts and deeds,
Its stillness bears the voices of the world:
Immobile, it moves Nature, looks on life.
It shapes immutably its far-seen ends;
Untouched and tranquil amid error and tears
And measureless above our striving wills,
Its gaze controls the turbulent whirl of things.
To mate with the Glory it sees, the spirit grows:
The voice of life is tuned to infinite sounds,

The moments on great wings of lightning come
And godlike thoughts surprise the mind of earth.
Into the soul's splendour and intensity
A crescent of miraculous birth is tossed,
Whose horn of mystery floats in a bright void.
As into a heaven of strength and silence thought
Is ravished, all this living mortal clay
Is seized and in a swift and fiery flood
Of touches shaped by a Harmonist unseen.
A new sight comes, new voices in us form
A body of the music of the Gods.
Immortal yearnings without name leap down,
Large quiverings of godhead seeking run
And weave upon a puissant field of calm
A high and lonely ecstasy of will.
This in a moment's depths was born in her.
Now to the limitless gaze disclosed that sees
Things barred from human thinking's earthly lids,
The Spirit who had hidden in Nature soared
Out of his luminous nest within the worlds:
Like a vast fire it climbed the skies of night.
Thus were the cords of self-oblivion torn:
Like one who looks up to far heights she saw,
Ancient and strong as on a windless summit
Above her where she had worked in her lone mind
Labouring apart in a sole tower of self,
The source of all which she had seemed or wrought,
A power projected into cosmic space,
A slow embodiment of the aeonic will,
A starry fragment of the eternal Truth,
The passionate instrument of an unmoved Power.
A Presence was there that filled the listening world;
A central All assumed her boundless life.
A sovereignty, a silence and a swiftness,
One brooded over abysses who was she.
As in a choric robe of unheard sounds

A Force descended trailing endless lights;
Linking Time's seconds to infinity,
Illimitably it girt the earth and her:
It sank into her soul and she was changed.
Then like a thought fulfilled by some great word
That mightiness assumed a symbol form:
Her being's spaces quivered with its touch,
It covered her as with immortal wings;
On its lips the curve of the unuttered Truth,
A halo of Wisdom's lightnings for its crown,
It entered the mystic lotus in her head,
A thousand-petalled home of power and light.
Immortal leader of her mortality,
Doer of her works and fountain of her words,
Invulnerable by Time, omnipotent,
It stood above her calm, immobile, mute.

All in her mated with that mighty hour,
As if the last remnant had been slain by Death
Of the humanity that once was hers.
Assuming a spiritual wide control,
Making life's sea a mirror of heaven's sky,
The young divinity in her earthly limbs
Filled with celestial strength her mortal part.
Over was the haunted pain, the rending fear:
Her grief had passed away, her mind was still,
Her heart beat quietly with a sovereign force.
There came a freedom from the heart-strings' clutch,
Now all her acts sprang from a godhead's calm.
Calmly she laid upon the forest soil
The dead who still reposed upon her breast
And bore to turn away from the dead form:
Sole now she rose to meet the dreadful god.
That mightier spirit turned its mastering gaze
On life and things, inheritor of a work
Left to it unfinished from her halting past,

When yet the mind, a passionate learner, toiled
And ill-shaped instruments were crudely moved.
Transcended now was the poor human rule;
A sovereign power was there, a godlike will.
A moment yet she lingered motionless
And looked down on the dead man at her feet;
Then like a tree recovering from a wind
She raised her noble head; fronting her gaze
Something stood there, unearthly, sombre, grand,
A limitless denial of all being
That wore the terror and wonder of a shape.
In its appalling eyes the tenebrous Form
Bore the deep pity of destroying gods;
A sorrowful irony curved the dreadful lips
That speak the word of doom. Eternal Night
In the dire beauty of an immortal face
Pitying arose, receiving all that lives
For ever into its fathomless heart, refuge
Of creatures from their anguish and world-pain.
His shape was nothingness made real, his limbs
Were monuments of transience and beneath
Brows of unwearying calm large godlike lids
Silent beheld the writhing serpent, life.
Unmoved their timeless wide unchanging gaze
Had seen the unprofitable cycles pass,
Survived the passing of unnumbered stars
And sheltered still the same immutable orbs.
The two opposed each other with their eyes,
Woman and universal god: around her,
Piling their void unbearable loneliness
Upon her mighty uncompanioned soul,
Many inhuman solitudes came close.
Vacant eternities forbidding hope
Laid upon her their huge and lifeless look,
And to her ears, silencing earthly sounds,
A sad and formidable voice arose

Which seemed the whole adverse world's. "Unclasp", it cried,
"Thy passionate influence and relax, O slave
Of Nature, changing tool of changeless Law,
Who vainly writh'st rebellion to my yoke,
Thy elemental grasp; weep and forget.
Entomb thy passion in its living grave.
Leave now the once-loved spirit's abandoned robe:
Pass lonely back to thy vain life on earth."
It ceased, she moved not, and it spoke again,
Lowering its mighty key to human chords, —
Yet a dread cry behind the uttered sounds,
Echoing all sadness and immortal scorn,
Moaned like a hunger of far wandering waves.
"Wilt thou for ever keep thy passionate hold,
Thyself a creature doomed like him to pass,
Denying his soul death's calm and silent rest?
Relax thy grasp; this body is earth's and thine,
His spirit now belongs to a greater power.
Woman, thy husband suffers." Savitri
Drew back her heart's force that clasped his body still
Where from her lap renounced on the smooth grass
Softly it lay, as often before in sleep
When from their couch she rose in the white dawn
Called by her daily tasks: now too, as if called,
She rose and stood gathered in lonely strength,
Like one who drops his mantle for a race
And waits the signal, motionlessly swift.
She knew not to what course: her spirit above
On the crypt-summit of her secret form
Like one left sentinel on a mountain crest,
A fiery-footed splendour puissant-winged,
Watched flaming-silent, with her voiceless soul
Like a still sail upon a windless sea.
White passionless it rode, an anchored might,
Waiting what far-ridged impulse should arise
Out of the eternal depths and cast its surge.

Then Death the king leaned boundless down, as leans
Night over tired lands, when evening pales
And fading gleams break down the horizon's walls,
Nor yet the dusk grows mystic with the moon.
The dim and awful godhead rose erect
From his brief stooping to his touch on earth,
And, like a dream that wakes out of a dream,
Forsaking the poor mould of that dead clay,
Another luminous Satyavan arose,
Starting upright from the recumbent earth
As if someone over viewless borders stepped
Emerging on the edge of unseen worlds.
In the earth's day the silent marvel stood
Between the mortal woman and the god.
Such seemed he as if one departed came
Wearing the light of a celestial shape
Splendidly alien to the mortal air.
The mind sought things long loved and fell back foiled
From unfamiliar hues, beheld yet longed,
By the sweet radiant form unsatisfied,
Incredulous of its too bright hints of heaven;
Too strange the brilliant phantasm to life's clasp
Desiring the warm creations of the earth
Reared in the ardour of material suns,
The senses seized in vain a glorious shade:
Only the spirit knew the spirit still,
And the heart divined the old loved heart, though changed.
Between two realms he stood, not wavering,
But fixed in quiet strong expectancy,
Like one who, sightless, listens for a command.
So were they immobile on that earthly field,
Powers not of earth, though one in human clay.
On either side of one two spirits strove;
Silence battled with silence, vast with vast.
But now the impulse of the Path was felt
Moving from the Silence that supports the stars

To touch the confines of the visible world.
Luminous he moved away; behind him Death
Went slowly with his noiseless tread, as seen
In dream-built fields a shadowy herdsman glides
Behind some wanderer from his voiceless herds,
And Savitri moved behind eternal Death,
Her mortal pace was equalled with the god's.
Wordless she travelled in her lover's steps,
Planting her human feet where his had trod,
Into the perilous silences beyond.

At first in a blind stress of woods she moved
With strange inhuman paces on the soil,
Journeying as if upon an unseen road.
Around her on the green and imaged earth
The flickering screen of forests ringed her steps;
Its thick luxurious obstacle of boughs
Besieged her body pressing dimly through
In a rich realm of whispers palpable,
And all the murmurous beauty of the leaves
Rippled around her like an emerald robe.
But more and more this grew an alien sound,
And her old intimate body seemed to her
A burden which her being remotely bore.
Herself lived far in some uplifted scene
Where to the trance-claimed vision of pursuit,
Sole presences in a high spaceless dream,
The luminous spirit glided stilly on
And the great shadow travelled vague behind.
Still with an amorous crowd of seeking hands
Softly entreated by their old desires
Her senses felt earth's close and gentle air
Cling round them and in troubled branches knew
Uncertain treadings of a faint-foot wind:
She bore dim fragrances, far callings touched;
The wild bird's voice and its winged rustle came

As if a sigh from some forgotten world.
Earth stood aloof, yet near: round her it wove
Its sweetness and its greenness and delight,
Its brilliance suave of well-loved vivid hues,
Sunlight arriving to its golden noon,
And the blue heavens and the caressing soil.
The ancient mother offered to her child
Her simple world of kind familiar things.
But now, as if the body's sensuous hold
Curbing the godhead of her infinite walk
Had freed those spirits to their grander road
Across some boundary's intangible bar,
The silent god grew mighty and remote
In other spaces, and the soul she loved
Lost its consenting nearness to her life.
Into a deep and unfamiliar air
Enormous, windless, without stir or sound
They seemed to enlarge away, drawn by some wide
Pale distance, from the warm control of earth
And her grown far: now, now they would escape.
Then flaming from her body's nest alarmed
Her violent spirit soared at Satyavan.
Out mid the plunge of heaven-surrounded rocks
So in a terror and a wrath divine
From her eyrie streams against the ascending death,
Indignant at its crouching point of steel,
A fierce she-eagle threatened in her brood,
Borne on a rush of puissance and a cry,
Outwinging like a mass of golden fire.
So on a spirit's flaming outrush borne
She crossed the borders of dividing sense;
Like pale discarded sheaths dropped dully down
Her mortal members fell back from her soul.
A moment of a secret body's sleep,
Her trance knew not of sun or earth or world;
Thought, time and death were absent from her grasp:

She knew not self, forgotten was Savitri.
All was the violent ocean of a will
Where lived captive to an immense caress,
Possessed in a supreme identity,
Her aim, joy, origin, Satyavan alone.
Her sovereign prisoned in her being's core,
He beat there like a rhythmic heart, — herself
But different still, one loved, enveloped, clasped,
A treasure saved from the collapse of space.
Around him nameless, infinite she surged,
Her spirit fulfilled in his spirit, rich with all Time,
As if Love's deathless moment had been found,
A pearl within eternity's white shell.
Then out of the engulfing sea of trance
Her mind rose drenched to light streaming with hues
Of vision and, awake once more to Time,
Returned to shape the lineaments of things
And live in borders of the seen and known.
Onward the three still moved in her soul-scene.
As if pacing through fragments of a dream,
She seemed to travel on, a visioned shape
Imagining other musers like herself,
By them imagined in their lonely sleep.
Ungrasped, unreal, yet familiar, old,
Like clefts of unsubstantial memory,
Scenes often traversed, never lived in, fled
Past her unheeding to forgotten goals.
In voiceless regions they were travellers
Alone in a new world where souls were not,
But only living moods: a strange hushed weird
Country was round them, strange far skies above,
A doubting space where dreaming objects lived
Within themselves their one unchanged idea.
Weird were the grasses, weird the treeless plains;
Weird ran the road which like fear hastening
Towards that of which it has most terror, passed

Phantasmal between pillared conscious rocks
Sombre and high, gates brooding, whose stone thoughts
Lost their huge sense beyond in giant night.
Enigma of the Inconscient's sculptural sleep,
Symbols of the approach to darkness old
And monuments of her titanic reign,
Opening to depths like dumb appalling jaws
That wait a traveller down a haunted path
Attracted to a mystery that slays,
They watched across her road, cruel and still;
Sentinels they stood of dumb Necessity,
Mute heads of vigilant and sullen gloom,
Carved muzzle of a dim enormous world.
Then, to that chill sere heavy line arrived
Where his feet touched the shadowy marches' brink,
Turning arrested luminous Satyavan
Looked back with his wonderful eyes at Savitri.
But Death pealed forth his vast abysmal cry:
"O mortal, turn back to thy transient kind;
Aspire not to accompany Death to his home,
As if thy breath could live where Time must die.
Think not thy mind-born passion strength from heaven
To uplift thy spirit from its earthly base
And, breaking out from the material cage,
To upbuoy thy feet of dream in groundless Nought
And bear thee through the pathless infinite.
Only in human limits man lives safe.
Trust not in the unreal Lords of Time,
Immortal deeming this image of thyself
Which they have built on a Dream's floating ground.
Let not the dreadful goddess move thy soul
To enlarge thy vehement trespass into worlds
Where it shall perish like a helpless thought.
Know the cold term-stones of thy hopes in life.
Armed vainly with the Ideal's borrowed might,
Dare not to outstep man's bound and measured force:

Ignorant and stumbling, in brief boundaries pent,
He crowns himself the world's mock suzerain,
Tormenting Nature with the works of Mind.
O sleeper, dreaming of divinity,
Wake trembling mid the indifferent silences
In which thy few weak chords of being die.
Impermanent creatures, sorrowful foam of Time,
Your transient loves bind not the eternal gods."
The dread voice ebbed in the consenting hush
Which seemed to close upon it, wide, intense,
A wordless sanction from the jaws of Night.
The Woman answered not. Her high nude soul,
Stripped of the girdle of mortality,
Against fixed destiny and the grooves of law
Stood up in its sheer will a primal force.
Still like a statue on its pedestal,
Lone in the silence and to vastness bared,
Against midnight's dumb abysses piled in front
A columned shaft of fire and light she rose.

END OF CANTO ONE

Canto Two

The Journey in Eternal Night
and the Voice of the Darkness

AWHILE on the chill dreadful edge of Night
All stood as if a world were doomed to die
And waited on the eternal silence' brink.
Heaven leaned towards them like a cloudy brow
Of menace through the dim and voiceless hush.
As thoughts stand mute on a despairing verge
Where the last depths plunge into nothingness
And the last dreams must end, they paused; in their front
Were glooms like shadowy wings, behind them, pale,
The lifeless evening was a dead man's gaze.
Hungry beyond, the night desired her soul.
But still in its lone niche of templed strength
Motionless, her flame-bright spirit, mute, erect,
Burned like a torch-fire from a windowed room
Pointing against the darkness' sombre breast.
The Woman first affronted the Abyss
Daring to journey through the eternal Night.
Armoured with light she advanced her foot to plunge
Into the dread and hueless vacancy;
Immortal, unappalled, her spirit faced
The danger of the ruthless eyeless waste.
Against night's inky ground they stirred, moulding
Mysterious motion on her human tread,
A swimming action and a drifting march
Like figures moving before eyelids closed:
All as in dreams went slipping, gliding on.
The rock-gate's heavy walls were left behind;
As if through passages of receding time
Present and past into the Timeless lapsed;
Arrested upon dim adventure's brink,

The future ended drowned in nothingness.
Amid collapsing shapes they wound obscure;
The fading vestibules of a tenebrous world
Received them, where they seemed to move and yet
Be still, nowhere advancing yet to pass,
A dumb procession a dim picture bounds,
Not conscious forms threading a real scene.
A mystery of terror's boundlessness,
Gathering its hungry strength the huge pitiless void
Surrounded slowly with its soundless depths,
And monstrous, cavernous, a shapeless throat
Devoured her into its shadowy strangling mass,
The fierce spiritual agony of a dream.
A curtain of impenetrable dread,
The darkness hung around her cage of sense
As, when the trees have turned to blotted shades
And the last friendly glimmer fades away,
Around a bullock in the forest tied
By hunters closes in no empty night.
The thought that strives in the world was here unmade;
Its effort it renounced to live and know,
Convinced at last that it had never been;
It perished, all its dream of action done:
This clotted cypher was its dark result.
In the smothering stress of this stupendous Nought
Mind could not think, breath could not breathe, the soul
Could not remember or feel itself; it seemed
A hollow gulf of sterile emptiness,
A zero oblivious of the sum it closed,
An abnegation of the Maker's joy
Saved by no wide repose, no depth of peace.
On all that claims here to be Truth and God
And conscious self and the revealing Word
And the creative rapture of the Mind
And Love and Knowledge and heart's delight, there fell
The immense refusal of the eternal No.

As disappears a golden lamp in gloom
Borne into distance from the eyes' desire,
Into the shadows vanished Savitri.
There was no course, no path, no end or goal:
Visionless she moved amid insensible gulfs,
Or drove through some great black unknowing waste,
Or whirled in a dumb eddy of meeting winds
Assembled by the titan hands of Chance.
There was none with her in the dreadful Vast:
She saw no more the vague tremendous god,
Her eyes had lost their luminous Satyavan.
Yet not for this her spirit failed, but held
More deeply than the bounded senses can
Which grasp externally and find to lose,
Its object loved. So when on earth they lived
She had felt him straying through the glades, the glades
A scene in her, its clefts her being's vistas
Opening their secrets to his search and joy,
Because to jealous sweetness in her heart
Whatever happy space his cherished feet
Preferred, must be at once her soul embracing
His body, passioning dumbly to his tread.
But now a silent gulf between them came
And to abysmal loneliness she fell,
Even from herself cast out, from love remote.
Long hours, since long it seems when sluggish time
Is measured by the throbs of the soul's pain,
In an unreal darkness empty and drear
She travelled treading on the corpse of life,
Lost in a blindness of extinguished souls.
Solitary in the anguish of the void
She lived in spite of death, she conquered still;
In vain her puissant being was oppressed:
Her heavy long monotony of pain
Tardily of its fierce self-torture tired.
At first a faint inextinguishable gleam,

Pale but immortal, flickered in the gloom
As if a memory came to spirits dead,
A memory that wished to live again,
Dissolved from mind in Nature's natal sleep.
It wandered like a lost ray of the moon
Revealing to the night her soul of dread;
Serpentine in the gleam the darkness lolled,
Its black hoods jewelled with the mystic glow;
Its dull sleek folds shrank back and coiled and slid,
As though they felt all light a cruel pain
And suffered from the pale approach of hope.
Night felt assailed her heavy sombre reign;
The splendour of some bright eternity
Threatened with this faint beam of wandering Truth
Her empire of the everlasting Nought.
Implacable in her intolerant strength
And confident that she alone was true,
She strove to stifle the frail dangerous ray;
Aware of an all-negating immensity
She reared her giant head of Nothingness,
Her mouth of darkness swallowing all that is;
She saw in herself the tenebrous Absolute.
But still the light prevailed and still it grew,
And Savitri to her lost self awoke;
Her limbs refused the cold embrace of death,
Her heart-beats triumphed in the grasp of pain;
Her soul persisted claiming for its joy
The soul of the beloved now seen no more.
Before her in the stillness of the world
Once more she heard the treading of a god,
And out of the dumb darkness Satyavan,
Her husband, grew into a luminous shade.
Then a sound pealed through that dead monstrous realm:
Vast like the surge in a tired swimmer's ears,
Clamouring, a fatal iron-hearted roar,
Death missioned to the night his lethal call.

"This is my silent dark immensity,
This is the home of everlasting Night,
This is the secrecy of Nothingness
Entombing the vanity of life's desires.
Hast thou beheld thy source, O transient heart,
And known from what the dream thou art was made?
In this stark sincerity of nude emptiness
Hopest thou still always to last and love?"
The Woman answered not. Her spirit refused
The voice of Night that knew and Death that thought.
In her beginningless infinity
Through her soul's reaches unconfined she gazed;
She saw the undying fountains of her life,
She knew herself eternal without birth.
But still opposing her with endless night
Death, the dire god, inflicted on her eyes
The immortal calm of his tremendous gaze:
"Although thou hast survived the unborn void
Which never shall forgive, while Time endures,
The primal violence that fashioned thought,
Forcing the immobile vast to suffer and live,
This sorrowful victory only hast thou won
To live for a little without Satyavan.
What shall the ancient goddess give to thee
Who helps thy heart-beats? Only she prolongs
The nothing dreamed existence and delays
With the labour of living thy eternal sleep.
A fragile miracle of thinking clay,
Armed with illusions walks the child of Time.
To fill the void around he feels and dreads,
The void he came from and to which he goes,
He magnifies his self and names it God.
He calls the heavens to help his suffering hopes.
He sees above him with a longing heart
Bare spaces more unconscious than himself
That have not even his privilege of mind,

And empty of all but their unreal blue,
And peoples them with bright and merciful powers.
For the sea roars around him and earth quakes
Beneath his steps, and fire is at his doors,
And death prowls baying through the woods of life.
Moved by the Presences with which he yearns,
He offers in implacable shrines his soul
And clothes all with the beauty of his dreams.
The gods who watch the earth with sleepless eyes
And guide its giant stumblings through the void,
Have given to man the burden of his mind;
In his unwilling heart they have lit their fires
And sown in it incurable unrest.
His mind is a hunter upon tracks unknown;
Amusing Time with vain discovery,
He deepens with thought the mystery of his fate
And turns to song his laughter and his tears.
His mortality vexing with the immortal's dreams,
Troubling his transience with the infinite's breath,
They gave him hungers which no food can fill;
He is the cattle of the shepherd gods.
His body the tether with which he is tied,
They cast for fodder grief and hope and joy:
His pasture ground they have fenced with Ignorance.
Into his fragile undefended breast
They have breathed a courage that is met by death,
They have given a wisdom that is mocked by night,
They have traced a journey that foresees no goal.
Aimless man toils in an uncertain world,
Lulled by inconstant pauses of his pain,
Scourged like a beast by the infinite desire,
Bound to the chariot of the dreadful gods.
But if thou still canst hope and still wouldst love,
Return to thy body's shell, thy tie to earth,
And with thy heart's little remnants try to live.
Hope not to win back to thee Satyavan.

Yet since thy strength deserves no trivial crown,
Gifts I can give to soothe thy wounded life.
The pacts which transient beings make with fate,
And the wayside sweetness earth-bound hearts would pluck,
These if thy will accepts make freely thine.
Choose a life's hopes for thy deceiving prize."
As ceased the ruthless and tremendous Voice,
Unendingly there rose in Savitri,
Like moonlit ridges on a shuddering flood,
A stir of thoughts out of some silence born
Across the sea of her dumb fathomless heart.
At last she spoke; her voice was heard by Night:
"I bow not to thee, O huge mask of death,
Black lie of night to the cowed soul of man,
Unreal, inescapable end of things,
Thou grim jest played with the immortal spirit.
Conscious of immortality I walk.
A victor spirit conscious of my force,
Not as a suppliant to thy gates I came:
Unslain I have survived the clutch of Night.
My first strong grief moves not my seated mind;
My unwept tears have turned to pearls of strength:
I have transformed my ill-shaped brittle clay
Into the hardness of a statued soul.
Now in the wrestling of the splendid gods
My spirit shall be obstinate and strong
Against the vast refusal of the world.
I stoop not with the subject mob of minds
Who run to glean with eager satisfied hands
And pick from its mire mid many trampling feet
Its scornful small concessions to the weak.
Mine is the labour of the battling gods:
Imposing on the slow reluctant years
The flaming will that reigns beyond the stars,
They lay the law of Mind on Matter's works
And win the soul's wish from earth's inconscient Force.

First I demand whatever Satyavan,
My husband, waking in the forest's charm
Out of his long pure childhood's lonely dreams,
Desired and had not for his beautiful life.
Give, if thou must, or, if thou canst, refuse."
Death bowed his head in scornful cold assent,
The builder of this dreamlike earth for man
Who has mocked with vanity all gifts he gave.
Uplifting his disastrous voice he spoke:
"Indulgent to the dreams my touch shall break,
I yield to his blind father's longing heart
Kingdom and power and friends and greatness lost
And royal trappings for his peaceful age,
The pallid pomps of man's declining days,
The silvered decadent glories of life's fall.
To one who wiser grew by adverse Fate,
Goods I restore the deluded soul prefers
To impersonal nothingness's bare sublime.
The sensuous solace of the light I give
To eyes which could have found a larger realm,
A deeper vision in their fathomless night.
For that this man desired and asked in vain
While still he lived on earth and cherished hope.
Back from the grandeur of my perilous realms
Go, mortal, to thy small permitted sphere!
Hasten swift-footed, lest to slay thy life
The great laws thou hast violated, moved,
Open at last on thee their marble eyes."
But Savitri answered the disdainful Shade:
"World-spirit, I was thy equal spirit born.
My will too is a law, my strength a god.
I am immortal in my mortality.
I tremble not before the immobile gaze
Of the unchanging marble hierarchies
That look with the stone eyes of Law and Fate.
My soul can meet them with its living fire.

Out of thy shadow give me back again
Into earth's flowering spaces Satyavan
In the sweet transiency of human limbs
To do with him my spirit's burning will.
I will bear with him the ancient Mother's load,
I will follow with him earth's path that leads to God.
Else shall the eternal spaces open to me,
While round us strange horizons far recede,
Travelling together the immense unknown.
For I who have trod with him the tracts of Time,
Can meet behind his steps whatever night
Or unimaginable stupendous dawn
Breaks on our spirits in the untrod Beyond.
Wherever thou leadst his soul I shall pursue."
But to her claim opposed, implacable,
Insisting on the immutable Decree,
Insisting on the immitigable Law
And the insignificance of created things,
Out of the rolling wastes of night there came
Born from the enigma of the unknowable depths
A voice of majesty and appalling scorn.
As when the storm-haired Titan-striding sea
Throws on a swimmer its tremendous laugh
Remembering all the joy its waves have drowned,
So from the darkness of the sovereign night
Against the Woman's boundless heart arose
The almighty cry of universal Death.
"Hast thou god-wings or feet that tread my stars,
Frail creature with the courage that aspires,
Forgetting thy bounds of thought, thy mortal role?
Their orbs were coiled before thy soul was formed.
I, Death, created them out of my void;
All things I have built in them and I destroy.
I made the worlds my net, each joy a mesh.
A Hunger amorous of its suffering prey,
Life that devours, my image see in things.

Mortal, whose spirit is my wandering breath,
Whose transience was imagined by my smile,
Flee clutching thy poor gains to thy trembling breast
Pierced by my pangs Time shall not soon appease.
Blind slave of my deaf force whom I compel
To sin that I may punish, to desire
That I may scourge thee with despair and grief
And thou come bleeding to me at the last,
Thy nothingness recognised, my greatness known,
Turn nor attempt forbidden happy fields
Meant for the souls that can obey my law,
Lest in their sombre shrines thy tread awake
From their uneasy iron-hearted sleep
The Furies who avenge fulfilled desire.
Dread lest in skies where passion hoped to live,
The Unknown's lightnings start and, terrified,
Lone, sobbing, hunted by the hounds of heaven,
A wounded and forsaken soul thou flee
Through the long torture of the centuries,
Nor many lives exhaust the tireless Wrath
Hell cannot slake nor Heaven's mercy assuage.
I will take from thee the black eternal grip:
Clasping in thy heart thy fate's exiguous dole
Depart in peace, if peace for man is just."
But Savitri answered meeting scorn with scorn,
The mortal woman to the dreadful Lord:
"Who is this God imagined by thy night,
Contemptuously creating worlds disdained,
Who made for vanity the brilliant stars?
Not he who has reared his temple in my thoughts
And made his sacred floor my human heart.
My God is will and triumphs in his paths,
My God is love and sweetly suffers all.
To him I have offered hope for sacrifice
And gave my longings as a sacrament.
Who shall prohibit or hedge in his course,

The wonderful, the charioteer, the swift?
A traveller of the million roads of life,
His steps familiar with the lights of heaven
Tread without pain the sword-paved courts of hell;
There he descends to edge eternal joy.
Love's golden wings have power to fan thy void:
The eyes of love gaze starlike through death's night,
The feet of love tread naked hardest worlds.
He labours in the depths, exults on the heights;
He shall remake thy universe, O Death."
She spoke and for a while no voice replied,
While still they travelled through the trackless night
And still that gleam was like a pallid eye
Troubling the darkness with its doubtful gaze.
Then once more came a deep and perilous pause
In that unreal journey through blind Nought;
Once more a Thought, a Word in the void arose
And Death made answer to the human soul:
"What is thy hope? to what dost thou aspire?
This is thy body's sweetest lure of bliss,
Assailed by pain, a frail precarious form,
To please for a few years thy faltering sense
With honey of physical longings and the heart's fire
And, a vain oneness seeking, to embrace
The brilliant idol of a fugitive hour.
And thou, what art thou, soul, thou glorious dream
Of brief emotions made and glittering thoughts,
A thin dance of fireflies speeding through the night,
A sparkling ferment in life's sunlit mire?
Wilt thou claim immortality, O heart,
Crying against the eternal witnesses
That thou and he are endless powers and last?
Death only lasts and the inconscient Void.
I only am eternal and endure.
I am the shapeless formidable Vast,
I am the emptiness that men call Space,

I am a timeless Nothingness carrying all,
I am the Illimitable, the mute Alone.
I, Death, am He; there is no other God.
All from my depths are born, they live by death;
All to my depths return and are no more.
I have made a world by my inconscient Force.
My Force is Nature that creates and slays
The hearts that hope, the limbs that long to live.
I have made man her instrument and slave,
His body I made my banquet, his life my food.
Man has no other help but only Death;
He comes to me at his end for rest and peace.
I, Death, am the one refuge of thy soul.
The Gods to whom man prays can help not man;
They are my imaginations and my moods
Reflected in him by illusion's power.
That which thou seest as thy immortal self
Is a shadowy icon of my infinite,
Is Death in thee dreaming of eternity.
I am the Immobile in which all things move,
I am the nude Inane in which they cease:
I have no body and no tongue to speak,
I commune not with human eye and ear;
Only thy thought gave a figure to my void.
Because, O aspirant to divinity,
Thou calledst me to wrestle with thy soul,
I have assumed a face, a form, a voice.
But if there were a Being witnessing all,
How should he help thy passionate desire?
Aloof he watches sole and absolute,
Indifferent to thy cry in nameless calm.
His being is pure, unwounded, motionless, one.
One endless watches the inconscient scene
Where all things perish, as the foam the stars.
The One lives for ever. There no Satyavan
Changing was born and there no Savitri

Claims from brief life her bribe of joy. There love
Came never with his fretful eyes of tears,
Nor Time is there nor the vain vasts of Space.
It wears no living face, it has no name,
No gaze, no heart that throbs; it asks no second
To aid its being or to share its joys.
It is delight immortally alone.
If thou desirest immortality,
Be then alone sufficient to thy soul:
Live in thyself; forget the man thou lov'st.
My last grand death shall rescue thee from life;
Then shalt thou rise into thy unmoved source."
But Savitri replied to the dread Voice:
"O Death, who reasonest, I reason not,
Reason that scans and breaks, but cannot build
Or builds in vain because she doubts her work.
I am, I love, I see, I act, I will."
Death answered her, one deep surrounding cry:
"Know also. Knowing, thou shalt cease to love
And cease to will, delivered from thy heart.
So shalt thou rest for ever and be still,
Consenting to the impermanence of things."
But Savitri replied for man to Death:
"When I have loved for ever, I shall know.
Love in me knows the truth all changings mask.
I know that knowledge is a vast embrace:
I know that every being is myself,
In every heart is hidden the myriad One.
I know the calm Transcendent bears the world,
The veiled Inhabitant, the silent Lord:
I feel his secret act, his intimate fire;
I hear the murmur of the cosmic Voice.
I know my coming was a wave from God.
For all his suns were conscient in my birth,
And one who loves in us came veiled by death.
Then was man born among the monstrous stars

Dowered with a mind and heart to conquer thee."
In the eternity of his ruthless will
Sure of his empire and his armoured might,
Like one disdaining violent helpless words
From victim lips Death answered not again.
He stood in silence and in darkness wrapped,
A figure motionless, a shadow vague,
Girt with the terrors of his secret sword.
Half-seen in clouds appeared a sombre face;
Night's dusk tiara was his matted hair,
The ashes of the pyre his forehead's sign.
Once more a wanderer in the unending Night,
Blindly forbidden by dead vacant eyes,
She travelled through the dumb unhoping vasts.
Around her rolled the shuddering waste of gloom,
Its swallowing emptiness and joyless death
Resentful of her thought and life and love.
Through the long fading night by her compelled,
Gliding half-seen on their unearthly path,
Phantasmal in the dimness moved the three.

END OF CANTO TWO
End of Book Nine

BOOK TEN

The Book of the Double Twilight

Canto One

The Dream Twilight of the Ideal

ALL still was darkness dread and desolate;
There was no change nor any hope of change.
In this black dream which was a house of Void,
A walk to Nowhere in a land of Nought,
Ever they drifted without aim or goal;
Gloom led to worse gloom, depth to an emptier depth,
In some positive Non-being's purposeless Vast
Through formless wastes dumb and unknowable.
An ineffectual beam of suffering light
Through the despairing darkness dogged their steps
Like the remembrance of a glory lost;
Even while it grew, it seemed unreal there,
Yet haunted Nihil's chill stupendous realm,
Unquenchable, perpetual, lonely, null,
A pallid ghost of some dead eternity.
It was as if she must pay now her debt,
Her vain presumption to exist and think,
To some brilliant Maya that conceived her soul.
This most she must absolve with endless pangs,
Her deep original sin, the will to be
And the sin last, greatest, the spiritual pride,
That, made of dust, equalled itself with heaven,
Its scorn of the worm writhing in the mud,
Condemned ephemeral, born from Nature's dream,
Refusal of the transient creature's role,
The claim to be a living fire of God,
The will to be immortal and divine.
In that tremendous darkness heavy and bare
She atoned for all since the first act whence sprang
The error of the consciousness of Time,
The rending of the Inconscient's seal of sleep,

The primal and unpardoned revolt that broke
The peace and silence of the Nothingness
Which was before a seeming universe
Appeared in a vanity of imagined Space
And life arose engendering grief and pain:
A great Negation was the Real's face
Prohibiting the vain process of Time:
And when there is no world, no creature more,
When Time's intrusion has been blotted out,
It shall last, unbodied, saved from thought, at peace.
Accursed in what had been her godhead source,
Condemned to live for ever empty of bliss,
Her immortality her chastisement,
Her spirit, guilty of being, wandered doomed,
Moving for ever through eternal Night.
But Maya is a veil of the Absolute;
A Truth occult has made this mighty world:
The Eternal's wisdom and self-knowledge act
In ignorant Mind and in the body's steps.
The Inconscient is the Superconscient's sleep.
An unintelligible Intelligence
Invents creation's paradox profound;
Spiritual thought is crammed in Matter's forms,
Unseen it throws out a dumb energy
And works a miracle by a machine.
All here is a mystery of contraries:
Darkness a magic of self-hidden Light,
Suffering some secret rapture's tragic mask
And death an instrument of perpetual life.
Although Death walks beside us on Life's road,
A dim bystander at the body's start
And a last judgment on man's futile works,
Other is the riddle of its ambiguous face:
Death is a stair, a door, a stumbling stride
The soul must take to cross from birth to birth,
A grey defeat pregnant with victory,

A whip to lash us towards our deathless state.
The inconscient world is the spirit's self-made room,
Eternal Night shadow of eternal Day.
Night is not our beginning nor our end;
She is the dark Mother in whose womb we have hid
Safe from too swift a waking to world-pain.
We came to her from a supernal Light,
By Light we live and to the Light we go.
Here in this seat of Darkness mute and lone,
In the heart of everlasting Nothingness
Light conquered now even by that feeble beam:
Its faint infiltration drilled the blind deaf mass;
Almost it changed into a glimmering sight
That housed the phantom of an aureate Sun
Whose orb pupilled the eye of Nothingness.
A golden fire came in and burned Night's heart;
Her dusky mindlessness began to dream;
The Inconscient conscious grew, Night felt and thought.
Assailed in the sovereign emptiness of its reign
The intolerant Darkness paled and drew apart
Till only a few black remnants stained that Ray.
But on a failing edge of dumb lost space
Still a great dragon body sullenly loomed;
Adversary of the slow struggling Dawn
Defending its ground of tortured mystery,
It trailed its coils through the dead martyred air
And curving fled down a grey slope of Time.

There is a morning twilight of the gods;
Miraculous from sleep their forms arise
And God's long nights are justified by dawn.
There breaks a passion and splendour of new birth
And hue-winged visions stray across the lids,
Heaven's chanting heralds waken dim-eyed Space.
The dreaming deities look beyond the seen
And fashion in their thoughts the ideal worlds

Sprung from a limitless moment of desire
That once had lodged in some abysmal heart.
Passed was the heaviness of the eyeless dark
And all the sorrow of the night was dead:
Surprised by a blind joy with groping hands
Like one who wakes to find his dreams were true,
Into a happy misty twilit world
Where all ran after light and joy and love
She slipped; there far-off raptures drew more close
And deep anticipations of delight,
For ever eager to be grasped and held,
Were never grasped, yet breathed strange ecstasy.
A pearl-winged indistinctness fleeting swam,
An air that dared not suffer too much light.
Vague fields were there, vague pastures gleamed, vague trees,
Vague scenes dim-hearted in a drifting haze;
Vague cattle white roamed glimmering through the mist;
Vague spirits wandered with a bodiless cry,
Vague melodies touched the soul and fled pursued
Into harmonious distances unseized;
Forms subtly elusive and half-luminous powers
Wishing no goal for their unearthly course
Strayed happily through vague ideal lands,
Or floated without footing or their walk
Left steps of reverie on sweet memory's ground;
Or they paced to the mighty measure of their thoughts
Led by a low far chanting of the gods.
A ripple of gleaming wings crossed the far sky;
Birds like pale-bosomed imaginations flew
With low disturbing voices of desire,
And half-heard lowings drew the listening ear,
As if the Sun-god's brilliant kine were there
Hidden in mist and passing towards the sun.
These fugitive beings, these elusive shapes
Were all that claimed the eye and met the soul,
The natural inhabitants of that world.

But nothing there was fixed or stayed for long;
No mortal feet could rest upon that soil,
No breath of life lingered embodied there.
In that fine chaos joy fled dancing past
And beauty evaded settled line and form
And hid its sense in mysteries of hue;
Yet gladness ever repeated the same notes
And gave the sense of an enduring world;
There was a strange consistency of shapes,
And the same thoughts were constant passers-by
And all renewed unendingly its charm
Alluring ever the expectant heart
Like music that one always waits to hear,
Like the recurrence of a haunting rhyme.
One touched incessantly things never seized,
A skirt of worlds invisibly divine.
As if a trail of disappearing stars
There showered upon the floating atmosphere
Colours and lights and evanescent gleams
That called to follow into a magic heaven,
And in each cry that fainted on the ear
There was the voice of an unrealised bliss.
An adoration reigned in the yearning heart,
A spirit of purity, an elusive presence
Of faery beauty and ungrasped delight
Whose momentary and escaping thrill,
However unsubstantial to our flesh,
And brief even in imperishableness,
Much sweeter seemed than any rapture known
Earth or all-conquering heaven can ever give.
Heaven ever young and earth too firm and old
Delay the heart by immobility:
Their raptures of creation last too long,
Their bold formations are too absolute;
Carved by an anguish of divine endeavour
They stand up sculptured on the eternal hills,

Or quarried from the living rocks of God
Win immortality by perfect form.
They are too intimate with eternal things:
Vessels of infinite significances,
They are too clear, too great, too meaningful;
No mist or shadow soothes the vanquished sight,
No soft penumbra of incertitude.
These only touched a golden hem of bliss,
The gleaming shoulder of some godlike hope,
The flying feet of exquisite desires.
On a slow trembling brink between night and day
They shone like visitants from the morning star,
Satisfied beginnings of perfection, first
Tremulous imaginings of a heavenly world:
They mingle in a passion of pursuit,
Thrilled with a spray of joy too slight to tire.
All in this world was shadowed forth, not limned,
Like faces leaping on a fan of fire
Or shapes of wonder in a tinted blur,
Like fugitive landscapes painting silver mists.
Here vision fled back from the sight alarmed,
And sound sought refuge from the ear's surprise,
And all experience was a hasty joy.
The joys here snatched were half-forbidden things,
Timorous soul-bridals delicately veiled
As when a goddess' bosom dimly moves
To first desire and her white soul transfigured,
A glimmering Eden crossed by faery gleams,
Trembles to expectation's fiery wand,
But nothing is familiar yet with bliss.
All things in this fair realm were heavenly strange
In a fleeting gladness of untired delight,
In an insistency of magic change.
Past vanishing hedges, hurrying hints of fields,
Mid swift escaping lanes that fled her feet
Journeying she wished no end: as one through clouds

Travels upon a mountain ridge and hears
Arising to him out of hidden depths
Sound of invisible streams, she walked besieged
By the illusion of a mystic space,
A charm of bodiless touches felt and heard
A sweetness as of voices high and dim
Calling like travellers upon seeking winds
Melodiously with an alluring cry.
As if a music old yet ever new,
Moving suggestions on her heart-strings dwelt,
Thoughts that no habitation found, yet clung
With passionate repetition to her mind,
Desires that hurt not, happy only to live
Always the same and always unfulfilled
Sang in the breast like a celestial lyre.
Thus all could last yet nothing ever be.
In this beauty as of mind made visible,
Dressed in its rays of wonder Satyavan
Before her seemed the centre of its charm,
Head of her loveliness of longing dreams
And captain of the fancies of her soul.
Even the dreadful majesty of Death's face
And its sombre sadness could not darken nor slay
The intangible lustre of those fleeting skies.
The sombre Shadow sullen, implacable
Made beauty and laughter more imperative;
Enhanced by his grey, joy grew more bright and dear;
His dark contrast edging ideal sight
Deepened unuttered meanings to the heart;
Pain grew a trembling undertone of bliss
And transience immortality's floating hem,
A moment's robe in which she looked more fair,
Its antithesis sharpening her divinity.
A comrade of the Ray and Mist and Flame,
By a moon-bright face a brilliant moment drawn,
Almost she seemed a thought mid floating thoughts,

Seen hardly by a visionary mind
Amid the white inward musings of the soul.
Half-vanquished by the dream-happiness around,
Awhile she moved on an enchantment's soil,
But still remained possessor of her soul.
Above, her spirit in its mighty trance
Saw all, but lived for its transcendent task,
Immutable like a fixed eternal star.

END OF CANTO ONE

The Gospel of Death and Vanity of the Ideal

THEN pealed the calm inexorable voice:
Abolishing hope, cancelling life's golden truths,
Fatal its accents smote the trembling air.
That lovely world swam thin and frail, most like
Some pearly evanescent farewell gleam
On the faint verge of dusk in moonless eves.
"Prisoner of Nature, many-visioned spirit,
Thought's creature in the ideal's realm enjoying
Thy unsubstantial immortality
The subtle marvellous mind of man has feigned,
This is the world from which thy yearnings came.
When it would build eternity from the dust,
Man's thought paints images illusion rounds;
Prophesying glories it shall never see,
It labours delicately among its dreams.
Behold this fleeing of light-tasselled shapes,
Aerial raiment of unbodied gods;
A rapture of things that never can be born,
Hope chants to hope a bright immortal choir;
Cloud satisfies cloud, phantom to longing phantom
Leans sweetly, sweetly is clasped or sweetly chased.
This is the stuff from which the ideal is formed:
Its builder is thought, its base the heart's desire,
But nothing real answers to their call.
The ideal dwells not in heaven, nor on the earth,
A bright delirium of man's ardour of hope
Drunk with the wine of its own fantasy.
It is a brilliant shadow's dreamy trail.
Thy vision's error builds the azure skies,
Thy vision's error drew the rainbow's arch;

Thy mortal longing made for thee a soul.
This angel in thy body thou callst love,
Who shapes his wings from thy emotion's hues,
In a ferment of thy body has been born
And with the body that housed it it must die.
It is a passion of thy yearning cells,
It is flesh that calls to flesh to serve its lust;
It is thy mind that seeks an answering mind
And dreams awhile that it has found its mate;
It is thy life that asks a human prop
To uphold its weakness lonely in the world
Or feeds its hunger on another's life.
A beast of prey that pauses in its prowl,
It crouches under a bush in splendid flower
To seize a heart and body for its food:
This beast thou dreamst immortal and a god.
O human mind, vainly thou torturest
An hour's delight to stretch through infinity's
Long void and fill its formless, passionless gulfs,
Persuading the insensible Abyss
To lend eternity to perishing things,
And trickst the fragile movements of thy heart
With thy spirit's feint of immortality.
All here emerges born from Nothingness;
Encircled it lasts by the emptiness of Space,
Awhile upheld by an unknowing Force,
Then crumbles back into its parent Nought:
Only the mute Alone can for ever be.
In the Alone there is no room for love.
In vain to clothe love's perishable mud
Thou hast woven on the Immortals' borrowed loom
The ideal's gorgeous and unfading robe.
The ideal never yet was real made.
Imprisoned in form that glory cannot live;
Into a body shut it breathes no more.
Intangible, remote, for ever pure,

A sovereign of its own brilliant void,
Unwillingly it descends to earthly air
To inhabit a white temple in man's heart:
In his heart it shines rejected by his life.
Immutable, bodiless, beautiful, grand and dumb,
Immobile on its shining throne it sits;
Dumb it receives his offering and his prayer.
It has no voice to answer to his call,
No feet that move, no hands to take his gifts:
Aerial statue of the nude Idea,
Virgin conception of a bodiless god,
Its light stirs man the thinker to create
An earthly semblance of diviner things.
Its hued reflection falls upon man's acts;
His institutions are its cenotaphs,
He signs his dead conventions with its name;
His virtues don the Ideal's skiey robe
And a nimbus of the outline of its face:
He hides their littleness with the divine Name.
Yet insufficient is the bright pretence
To screen their indigent and earthy make:
Earth only is there and not some heavenly source.
If heavens there are they are veiled in their own light,
If a Truth eternal somewhere reigns unknown,
It burns in a tremendous void of God;
For truth shines far from the falsehoods of the world;
How can the heavens come down to unhappy earth
Or the eternal lodge in drifting time?
How shall the Ideal tread earth's dolorous soil
Where life is only a labour and a hope,
A child of Matter and by Matter fed,
A fire flaming low in Nature's grate,
A wave that breaks upon a shore in Time,
A journey's toilsome trudge with death for goal?
The Avatars have lived and died in vain,
Vain was the sage's thought, the prophet's voice;

In vain is seen the shining upward Way.
Earth lies unchanged beneath the circling sun;
She loves her fall and no omnipotence
Her mortal imperfections can erase,
Force on man's crooked ignorance Heaven's straight line
Or colonise a world of death with gods.
O traveller in the chariot of the Sun,
High priestess in thy holy fancy's shrine
Who with a magic ritual in earth's house
Worshippest ideal and eternal love,
What is this love thy thought has deified,
This sacred legend and immortal myth?
It is a conscious yearning of thy flesh,
It is a glorious burning of thy nerves,
A rose of dream-splendour petalling thy mind,
A great red rapture and torture of thy heart.
A sudden transfiguration of thy days,
It passes and the world is as before.
A ravishing edge of sweetness and of pain,
A thrill in its yearning makes it seem divine,
A golden bridge across the roar of the years,
A cord tying thee to eternity.
And yet how brief and frail! how soon is spent
This treasure wasted by the gods on man,
This happy closeness as of soul to soul,
This honey of the body's companionship,
This heightened joy, this ecstasy in the veins,
This strange illumination of the sense!
If Satyavan had lived, love would have died;
But Satyavan is dead and love shall live
A little while in thy sad breast, until
His face and body fade on memory's wall
Where other bodies, other faces come.
When love breaks suddenly into the life
At first man steps into a world of the sun;
In his passion he feels his heavenly element:

But only a fine sunlit patch of earth
The marvellous aspect took of heaven's outburst;
The snake is there and the worm in the heart of the rose.
A word, a moment's act can slay the god;
Precarious is his immortality,
He has a thousand ways to suffer and die.
Love cannot live by heavenly food alone,
Only on sap of earth can it survive.
For thy passion was a sensual want refined,
A hunger of the body and the heart;
Thy want can tire and cease or turn elsewhere.
Or love may meet a dire and pitiless end
By bitter treason, or wrath with cruel wounds
Separate, or thy unsatisfied will to others
Depart when first love's joy lies stripped and slain:
A dull indifference replaces fire
Or an endearing habit imitates love:
An outward and uneasy union lasts
Or the routine of a life's compromise:
Where once the seed of oneness had been cast
Into a semblance of spiritual ground
By a divine adventure of heavenly powers
Two strive, constant associates without joy,
Two egos straining in a single leash,
Two minds divided by their jarring thoughts,
Two spirits disjoined, for ever separate.
Thus is the ideal falsified in man's world;
Trivial or sombre, disillusion comes,
Life's harsh reality stares at the soul:
Heaven's hour adjourned flees into bodiless Time.
Death saves thee from this and saves Satyavan:
He now is safe, delivered from himself;
He travels to silence and felicity.
Call him not back to the treacheries of earth
And the poor petty life of animal Man.
In my vast tranquil spaces let him sleep

In harmony with the mighty hush of death
Where love lies slumbering on the breast of peace.
And thou, go back alone to thy frail world:
Chastise thy heart with knowledge, unhood to see,
Thy nature raised into clear living heights,
The heaven-bird's view from unimagined peaks.
For when thou givest thy spirit to a dream
Soon hard necessity will smite thee awake:
Purest delight began and it must end.
Thou too shalt know, thy heart no anchor swinging,
Thy cradled soul moored in eternal seas.
Vain are the cycles of thy brilliant mind.
Renounce, forgetting joy and hope and tears,
Thy passionate nature in the bosom profound
Of a happy Nothingness and worldless Calm,
Delivered into my mysterious rest.
One with my fathomless Nihil all forget.
Forget thy fruitless spirit's waste of force,
Forget the weary circle of thy birth,
Forget the joy and the struggle and the pain,
The vague spiritual quest which first began
When worlds broke forth like clusters of fire-flowers,
And great burning thoughts voyaged through the sky of mind
And Time and its aeons crawled across the vasts
And souls emerged into mortality."
      But Savitri replied to the dark Power:
"A dangerous music now thou findst, O Death,
Melting thy speech into harmonious pain,
And flut'st alluringly to tired hopes
Thy falsehoods mingled with sad strains of truth.
But I forbid thy voice to slay my soul.
My love is not a hunger of the heart,
My love is not a craving of the flesh;
It came to me from God, to God returns.
Even in all that life and man have marred,
A whisper of divinity still is heard,

A breath is felt from the eternal spheres.
Allowed by Heaven and wonderful to man
A sweet fire-rhythm of passion chants to love.
There is a hope in its wild infinite cry;
It rings with callings from forgotten heights,
And when its strains are hushed to high-winged souls
In their empyrean, its burning breath
Survives beyond, the rapturous core of suns
That flame for ever pure in skies unseen,
A voice of the eternal Ecstasy.
One day I shall behold my great sweet world
Put off the dire disguises of the gods,
Unveil from terror and disrobe from sin.
Appeased we shall draw near our mother's face,
We shall cast our candid souls upon her lap;
Then shall we clasp the ecstasy we chase,
Then shall we shudder with the long-sought god,
Then shall we find Heaven's unexpected strain.
Not only is there hope for godheads pure;
The violent and darkened deities
Leaped down from the one breast in rage to find
What the white gods had missed: they too are safe;
A mother's eyes are on them and her arms
Stretched out in love desire her rebel sons.
One who came love and lover and beloved
Eternal, built himself a wondrous field
And wove the measures of a marvellous dance.
There in its circles and its magic turns
Attracted he arrives, repelled he flees.
In the wild devious promptings of his mind
He tastes the honey of tears and puts off joy
Repenting, and has laughter and has wrath,
And both are a broken music of the soul
Which seeks out reconciled its heavenly rhyme.
Ever he comes to us across the years
Bearing a new sweet face that is the old.

His bliss laughs to us or it calls concealed
Like a far-heard unseen entrancing flute
From moonlit branches in the throbbing woods,
Tempting our angry search and passionate pain.
Disguised the Lover seeks and draws our souls.
He named himself for me, grew Satyavan.
For we were man and woman from the first,
The twin souls born from one undying fire.
Did he not dawn on me in other stars?
How has he through the thickets of the world
Pursued me like a lion in the night
And come upon me suddenly in the ways
And seized me with his glorious golden leap!
Unsatisfied he yearned for me through time,
Sometimes with wrath and sometimes with sweet peace
Desiring me since first the world began.
He rose like a wild wave out of the floods
And dragged me helpless into seas of bliss.
Out of my curtained past his arms arrive;
They have touched me like the soft persuading wind,
They have plucked me like a glad and trembling flower,
And clasped me happily burned in ruthless flame.
I too have found him charmed in lovely forms
And run delighted to his distant voice
And pressed to him past many dreadful bars.
If there is a yet happier greater god,
Let him first wear the face of Satyavan
And let his soul be one with him I love;
So let him seek me that I may desire.
For only one heart beats within my breast
And one god sits there throned. Advance, O Death,
Beyond the phantom beauty of this world;
For of its citizens I am not one.
I cherish God the Fire, not God the Dream."
But Death once more inflicted on her heart
The majesty of his calm and dreadful voice:

"A bright hallucination are thy thoughts.
A prisoner haled by a spiritual cord,
Of thy own sensuous will the ardent slave,
Thou sendest eagle-poised to meet the sun
Words winged with the red splendour of thy heart.
But knowledge dwells not in the passionate heart;
The heart's words fall back unheard from Wisdom's throne.
Vain is thy longing to build heaven on earth.
Artificer of Ideal and Idea,
Mind, child of Matter in the womb of Life,
To higher levels persuades his parents' steps:
Inapt, they follow ill the daring guide.
But Mind, a glorious traveller in the sky,
Walks lamely on the earth with footsteps slow;
Hardly he can mould the life's rebellious stuff,
Hardly can he hold the galloping hooves of sense:
His thoughts look straight into the very heavens;
They draw their gold from a celestial mine,
His acts work painfully a common ore.
All thy high dreams were made by Matter's mind
To solace its dull work in Matter's jail,
Its only house where it alone seems true.
A solid image of reality
Carved out of being to prop the works of Time,
Matter on the firm earth sits strong and sure.
It is the first-born of created things,
It stands the last when mind and life are slain,
And if it ended all would cease to be.
All else is only its outcome or its phase:
Thy soul is a brief flower by the gardener Mind
Created in thy matter's terrain plot;
It perishes with the plant on which it grows,
For from earth's sap it draws its heavenly hue:
Thy thoughts are gleams that pass on Matter's verge,
Thy life a lapsing wave on Matter's sea.
A careful steward of Truth's limited means,

Treasuring her founded facts from the squandering Power,
It tethers mind to the tent-posts of sense,
To a leaden grey routine clamps Life's caprice
And ties all creatures with the cords of Law.
A vessel of transmuting alchemies,
A glue that sticks together mind and life,
If Matter fails, all crumbling cracks and falls.
All upon Matter stands as on a rock.
Yet this security and guarantor
Pressed for credentials an impostor proves:
A cheat of substance where no substance is,
An appearance and a symbol and a nought,
Its forms have no original right to birth:
Its aspect of a fixed stability
Is the cover of a captive motion's swirl,
An order of the steps of Energy's dance
Whose footmarks leave for ever the same signs,
A concrete face of unsubstantial Time,
A trickle dotting the emptiness of Space:
A stable-seeming movement without change,
Yet change arrives and the last change is death.
What seemed most real once, is Nihil's show.
Its figures are snares that trap and prison the sense;
The beginningless Void was its artificer:
Nothing is there but aspects limned by Chance
And seeming shapes of seeming Energy.
All by Death's mercy breathe and live awhile,
All think and act by the Inconscient's grace.
Addict of the roseate luxury of thy thoughts,
Turn not thy gaze within thyself to look
At visions in the gleaming crystal, Mind,
Close not thy lids to dream the forms of Gods.
At last to open thy eyes consent and see
The stuff of which thou and the world are made.
Inconscient in the dumb inconscient Void
Inexplicably a moving world sprang forth:

Awhile secure, happily insensible,
It could not rest content with its own truth.
For something on its nescient breast was born
Condemned to see and know, to feel and love,
It watched its acts, imagined a soul within;
It groped for truth and dreamed of Self and God.
When all unconscious was, then all was well.
I, Death, was king and kept my regal state,
Designing my unwilled, unerring plan,
Creating with a calm insentient heart.
In my sovereign power of unreality
Obliging nothingness to take a form,
Infallibly my blind unthinking force
Making by chance a fixity like fate's,
By whim the formulas of Necessity,
Founded on the hollow ground of the Inane
The sure bizarrerie of Nature's scheme.
I curved the vacant ether into Space;
A huge expanding and contracting Breath
Harboured the fires of the universe:
I struck out the supreme original spark
And spread its sparse ranked armies through the Inane,
Manufactured the stars from the occult radiances,
Marshalled the platoons of the invisible dance;
I formed earth's beauty out of atom and gas,
And built from chemic plasm the living man.
Then Thought came in and spoiled the harmonious world:
Matter began to hope and think and feel,
Tissue and nerve bore joy and agony.
The inconscient cosmos strove to learn its task;
An ignorant personal God was born in Mind
And to understand invented reason's law,
The impersonal Vast throbbed back to man's desire,
A trouble rocked the great world's blind still heart
And Nature lost her wide immortal calm.
Thus came this warped incomprehensible scene

Of souls emmeshed in life's delight and pain
And Matter's sleep and Mind's mortality,
Of beings in Nature's prison waiting death
And consciousness left in seeking ignorance
And evolution's slow arrested plan.
This is the world in which thou mov'st, astray
In the tangled pathways of the human mind,
In the issueless circling of thy human life,
Searching for thy soul and thinking God is here.
But where is room for soul or place for God
In the brute immensity of a machine?
A transient Breath thou takest for thy soul,
Born from a gas, a plasm, a sperm, a gene,
A magnified image of man's mind for God,
A shadow of thyself thrown upon Space.
Interposed between the upper and nether Void,
Thy consciousness reflects the world around
In the distorting mirror of Ignorance
Or upwards turns to catch imagined stars.
Or if a half-Truth is playing with the earth
Throwing its light on a dark shadowy ground,
It touches only and leaves a luminous smudge.
Immortality thou claimest for thy spirit,
But immortality for imperfect man,
A god who hurts himself at every step,
Would be a cycle of eternal pain.
Wisdom and love thou claimest as thy right;
But knowledge in this world is error's mate,
A brilliant procuress of Nescience,
And human love a posturer on earth-stage
Who imitates with verve a faery dance.
An extract pressed from hard experience,
Man's knowledge casked in the barrels of Memory
Has the harsh savour of a mortal draught:
A sweet secretion from the erotic glands
Flattering and torturing the burning nerves,

Love is a honey and poison in the breast
Drunk by it as the nectar of the gods.
Earth's human wisdom is no great-browed power,
And love no gleaming angel from the skies;
If they aspire beyond earth's dullard air,
Arriving sunwards with frail waxen wings,
How high could reach that forced unnatural flight?
But not on earth can divine wisdom reign
And not on earth can divine love be found;
Heaven-born, only in heaven can they live;
Or else there too perhaps they are shining dreams.
Nay, is not all thou art and doest a dream?
Thy mind and life are tricks of Matter's force.
If thy mind seems to thee a radiant sun,
If thy life runs a swift and glorious stream,
This is the illusion of thy mortal heart
Dazzled by a ray of happiness or light.
Impotent to live by their own right divine,
Convinced of their brilliant unreality,
When their supporting ground is cut away,
These children of Matter into Matter die.
Even Matter vanishes into Energy's vague
And Energy is a motion of old Nought.
How shall the Ideal's unsubstantial hues
Be painted stiff on earth's vermilion blur,
A dream within a dream come doubly true?
How shall the will-o'-the-wisp become a star?
The Ideal is a malady of thy mind,
A bright delirium of thy speech and thought,
A strange wine of beauty lifting thee to false sight.
A noble fiction of thy yearnings made,
Thy human imperfection it must share:
Its forms in Nature disappoint the heart,
And never shall it find its heavenly shape
And never can it be fulfilled in Time.
O soul misled by the splendour of thy thoughts,

O earthly creature with thy dream of heaven,
Obey, resigned and still, the earthly law.
Accept the brief light that falls upon thy days;
Take what thou canst of Life's permitted joy;
Submitting to the ordeal of fate's scourge
Suffer what thou must of toil and grief and care.
There shall approach silencing thy passionate heart
My long calm night of everlasting sleep:
There into the hush from which thou cam'st retire."

END OF CANTO TWO

Canto Three

The Debate of Love and Death

A SAD destroying cadence the voice sank;
It seemed to lead the advancing march of Life
Into some still original Inane.
But Savitri answered to almighty Death:
"O dark-browed sophist of the universe
Who veilst the Real with its own Idea,
Hiding with brute objects Nature's living face,
Masking eternity with thy dance of death,
Thou hast woven the ignorant mind into a screen
And made of Thought error's purveyor and scribe,
And a false witness of mind's servant sense.
An aesthete of the sorrow of the world,
Champion of a harsh and sad philosophy
Thou hast used words to shutter out the Light
And called in Truth to vindicate a lie.
A lying reality is falsehood's crown
And a perverted truth her richest gem.
O Death, thou speakest truth but truth that slays,
I answer to thee with the Truth that saves.
A traveller new-discovering himself,
One made of Matter's world his starting-point,
He made of Nothingness his living-room
And Night a process of the eternal light
And death a spur towards immortality.
God wrapped his head from sight in Matter's cowl,
His consciousness dived into inconscient depths,
All-Knowledge seemed a huge dark Nescience;
Infinity wore a boundless zero's form.
His abysms of bliss became insensible deeps,
Eternity a blank spiritual Vast.
Annulling an original nullity

The Timeless took its ground in emptiness
And drew the figure of a universe,
That the spirit might adventure into Time
And wrestle with adamant Necessity
And the soul pursue a cosmic pilgrimage.
A spirit moved in black immensities
And built a Thought in ancient Nothingness;
A soul was lit in God's tremendous Void,
A secret labouring glow of nascent fire.
In Nihil's gulf his mighty Puissance wrought;
She swung her formless motion into shapes,
Made Matter the body of the Bodiless.
Infant and dim the eternal Mights awoke.
In inert Matter breathed a slumbering Life,
In a subconscient Life Mind lay asleep;
In waking Life it stretched its giant limbs
To shake from it the torpor of its drowse;
A senseless substance quivered into sense,
The world's heart commenced to beat, its eyes to see,
In the crowded dumb vibrations of a brain
Thought fumbled in a ring to find itself,
Discovered speech and fed the new-born Word
That bridged with spans of light the world's ignorance.
In waking Mind, the Thinker built his house.
A reasoning animal willed and planned and sought;
He stood erect among his brute compeers,
He built life new, measured the universe,
Opposed his fate and wrestled with unseen Powers,
Conquered and used the laws that rule the world,
And hoped to ride the heavens and reach the stars,
A master of his huge environment.
Now through Mind's windows stares the demigod
Hidden behind the curtains of man's soul:
He has seen the Unknown, looked on Truth's veilless face;
A ray has touched him from the eternal sun;
Motionless, voiceless in foreseeing depths,

He stands awake in Supernature's light
And sees a glory of arisen wings
And sees the vast descending might of God.
      "O Death, thou lookst on an unfinished world
Assailed by thee and of its road unsure,
Peopled by imperfect minds and ignorant lives,
And sayest God is not and all is vain.
How shall the child already be the man?
Because he is infant, shall he never grow?
Because he is ignorant, shall he never learn?
In a small fragile seed a great tree lurks,
In a tiny gene a thinking being is shut;
A little element in a little sperm,
It grows and is a conqueror and a sage.
Then wilt thou spew out, Death, God's mystic truth,
Deny the occult spiritual miracle?
Still wilt thou say there is no spirit, no God?
A mute material Nature wakes and sees;
She has invented speech, unveiled a will.
Something there waits beyond towards which she strives,
Something surrounds her into which she grows:
To uncover the spirit, to change back into God,
To exceed herself is her transcendent task.
In God concealed the world began to be,
Tardily it travels towards manifest God:
Our imperfection towards perfection toils,
The body is the chrysalis of a soul:
The infinite holds the finite in its arms,
Time travels towards revealed eternity.
A miracle structure of the eternal Mage,
Matter its mystery hides from its own eyes,
A scripture written out in cryptic signs,
An occult document of the All-Wonderful's art.
All here bears witness to his secret might,
In all we feel his presence and his power.
A blaze of his sovereign glory is the sun,

A glory is the gold and glimmering moon,
A glory is his dream of purple sky.
A march of his greatness are the wheeling stars.
His laughter of beauty breaks out in green trees,
His moments of beauty triumph in a flower;
The blue sea's chant, the rivulet's wandering voice
Are murmurs falling from the Eternal's harp.
This world is God fulfilled in outwardness.
His ways challenge our reason and our sense;
By blind brute movements of an ignorant Force,
By means we slight as small, obscure or base,
A greatness founded upon little things,
He has built a world in the unknowing Void.
His forms he has massed from infinitesimal dust;
His marvels are built from insignificant things.
If mind is crippled, life untaught and crude,
If brutal masks are there and evil acts,
They are incidents of his vast and varied plot,
His great and dangerous drama's needed steps;
He makes with these and all his passion-play,
A play and yet no play but the deep scheme
Of a transcendent Wisdom finding ways
To meet her Lord in the shadow and the Night:
Above her is the vigil of the stars;
Watched by a solitary Infinitude
She embodies in dumb Matter the Divine,
In symbol minds and lives the Absolute.
A miracle-monger her mechanical craft;
Matter's machine worked out the laws of thought,
Life's engines served the labour of a soul:
The Mighty Mother her creation wrought,
A huge caprice self-bound by iron laws,
And shut God into an enigmatic world:
She lulled the Omniscient into nescient sleep,
Omnipotence on Inertia's back she drove,
Trod perfectly with divine unconscious steps

The enormous circle of her wonder-works.
Immortality assured itself by death;
The Eternal's face was seen through drifts of Time.
His knowledge he disguised as Ignorance,
His Good he sowed in Evil's monstrous bed,
Made error a door by which Truth could enter in,
His plant of bliss watered with Sorrow's tears.
A thousand aspects point back to the One;
A dual Nature covered the Unique.
In this meeting of the Eternal's mingling masques,
This tangle-dance of passionate contraries
Locking like lovers in a forbidden embrace
The quarrel of their lost identity,
Through this wrestle and wrangle of the extremes of Power
Earth's million roads struggled towards deity.
All stumbled on behind a stumbling Guide,
Yet every stumble is a needed pace
On unknown routes to an unknowable goal.
All blundered and straggled towards the One Divine.
As if transmuted by a titan spell
The eternal Powers assumed a dubious face:
Idols of an oblique divinity,
They wore the heads of animal or troll,
Assumed ears of the faun, the satyr's hoof,
Or harboured the demoniac in their gaze:
A crooked maze they made of thinking mind,
They suffered a metamorphosis of the heart,
Admitting bacchant revellers from the Night
Into its sanctuary of delights,
As in a Dionysian masquerade.
On the highways, in the gardens of the world
They wallowed oblivious of their divine parts,
As drunkards of a dire Circean wine
Or a child who sprawls and sports in Nature's mire.
Even wisdom, hewer of the roads of God,
Is a partner in the deep disastrous game:

Lost is the pilgrim's wallet and the scrip,
She fails to read the map and watch the star.
A poor self-righteous virtue is her stock
And reason's pragmatic grope or abstract sight,
Or the technique of a brief hour's success
She teaches, an usher in utility's school.
On the ocean surface of vast Consciousness
Small thoughts in shoals are fished up into a net
But the great truths escape her narrow cast;
Guarded from vision by creation's depths,
Obscure they swim in blind enormous gulfs
Safe from the little sounding leads of mind,
Too far for the puny diver's shallow plunge.
Our mortal vision peers with ignorant eyes;
It has no gaze on the deep heart of things.
Our knowledge walks leaning on Error's staff,
A worshipper of false dogmas and false gods,
Or fanatic of a fierce intolerant creed
Or a seeker doubting every truth he finds,
A sceptic facing Light with adamant No
Or chilling the heart with dry ironic smile,
A cynic stamping out the god in man;
A darkness wallows in the paths of Time
Or lifts its giant head to blot the stars;
It makes a cloud of the interpreting mind
And intercepts the oracles of the Sun.
Yet Light is there; it stands at Nature's doors:
It holds a torch to lead the traveller in.
It waits to be kindled in our secret cells;
It is a star lighting an ignorant sea,
A lamp upon our poop piercing the night.
As knowledge grows Light flames up from within:
It is a shining warrior in the mind,
An eagle of dreams in the divining heart,
An armour in the fight, a bow of God.
Then larger dawns arrive and Wisdom's pomps

Cross through the being's dim half-lighted fields;
Philosophy climbs up Thought's cloud-bank peaks
And Science tears out Nature's occult powers,
Enormous djinns who serve a dwarf's small needs,
Exposes the sealed minutiae of her art
And conquers her by her own captive force.
On heights unreached by mind's most daring soar,
Upon a dangerous edge of failing Time
The soul draws back into its deathless Self;
Man's knowledge becomes God's supernal Ray.
There is the mystic realm whence leaps the power
Whose fire burns in the eyes of seer and sage;
A lightning flash of visionary sight,
It plays upon an inward verge of mind:
Thought silenced gazes into a brilliant Void.
A voice comes down from mystic unseen peaks:
A cry of splendour from a mouth of storm,
It is the voice that speaks to night's profound,
It is the thunder and the flaming call.
Above the planes that climb from nescient earth,
A hand is lifted towards the Invisible's realm,
Beyond the superconscient's blinding line
And plucks away the screens of the Unknown;
A spirit within looks into the Eternal's eyes.
It hears the Word to which our hearts were deaf,
It sees through the blaze in which our thoughts grew blind;
It drinks from the naked breasts of glorious Truth,
It learns the secrets of eternity.
Thus all was plunged into the riddling Night,
Thus all is raised to meet a dazzling Sun.
O Death, this is the mystery of thy reign.
In earth's anomalous and magic field
Carried in its aimless journey by the sun
Mid the forced marches of the great dumb stars,
A darkness occupied the fields of God,
And Matter's world was governed by thy shape.

Thy mask has covered the Eternal's face,
The Bliss that made the world has fallen asleep.
Abandoned in the Vast she slumbered on:
An evil transmutation overtook
Her members till she knew herself no more.
Only through her creative slumber flit
Frail memories of the joy and beauty meant
Under the sky's blue laugh mid green-scarfed trees
And happy squanderings of scents and hues,
In the field of the golden promenade of the sun
And the vigil of the dream-light of the stars,
Amid high meditating heads of hills,
On the bosom of voluptuous rain-kissed earth
And by the sapphire tumblings of the sea.
But now the primal innocence is lost
And Death and Ignorance govern the mortal world
And Nature's visage wears a greyer hue.
Earth still has kept her early charm and grace,
The grandeur and the beauty still are hers,
But veiled is the divine Inhabitant.
The souls of men have wandered from the Light
And the great Mother turns away her face.
The eyes of the creatrix Bliss are closed
And sorrow's touch has found her in her dreams.
As she turns and tosses on her bed of Void,
Because she cannot wake and find herself
And cannot build again her perfect shape,
Oblivious of her nature and her state,
Forgetting her instinct of felicity,
Forgetting to create a world of joy,
She weeps and makes her creatures' eyes to weep;
Testing with sorrow's edge her children's breasts,
She spends on life's vain waste of hope and toil
The poignant luxury of grief and tears.
In the nightmare change of her half-conscious dream,
Tortured herself and torturing by her touch,

She comes to our hearts and bodies and our lives
Wearing a hard and cruel mask of pain.
Our nature twisted by the abortive birth
Returns wry answers to life's questioning shocks,
An acrid relish finds in the world's pangs,
Drinks the sharp wine of grief's perversity.
A curse is laid on the pure joy of life:
Delight, God's sweetest sign and Beauty's twin,
Dreaded by aspiring saint and austere sage,
Is shunned, a dangerous and ambiguous cheat,
A specious trick of an infernal Power
It tempts the soul to its self-hurt and fall.
A puritan God made pleasure a poisonous fruit,
Or red drug in the market-place of Death,
And sin the child of Nature's ecstasy.
Yet every creature hunts for happiness,
Buys with harsh pangs or tears by violence
From the dull breast of the inanimate globe
Some fragment or some broken shard of bliss.
Even joy itself becomes a poisonous draught;
Its hunger is made a dreadful hook of Fate.
All means are held good to catch a single beam,
Eternity sacrificed for a moment's bliss:
Yet for joy and not for sorrow earth was made
And not as a dream in endless suffering Time.
Although God made the world for his delight,
An ignorant Power took charge and seemed his Will
And Death's deep falsity has mastered Life.
All grew a play of Chance simulating Fate.

  "A secret air of pure felicity
Deep like a sapphire heaven our spirits breathe;
Our hearts and bodies feel its obscure call,
Our senses grope for it and touch and lose.
If this withdrew, the world would sink in the Void;
If this were not, nothing could move or live.

A hidden Bliss is at the root of things.
A mute Delight regards Time's countless works:
To house God's joy in things Space gave wide room,
To house God's joy in self our souls were born.
This universe an old enchantment guards;
Its objects are carved cups of World-Delight
Whose charmed wine is some deep soul's rapture-drink:
The All-Wonderful has packed heaven with his dreams,
He has made blank ancient Space his marvel-house;
He spilled his spirit into Matter's signs:
His fires of grandeur burn in the great sun,
He glides through heaven shimmering in the moon;
He is beauty carolling in the fields of sound;
He chants the stanzas of the odes of Wind;
He is silence watching in the stars at night;
He wakes at dawn and calls from every bough,
Lies stunned in the stone and dreams in flower and tree.
Even in this labour and dolour of Ignorance,
On the hard perilous ground of difficult earth,
In spite of death and evil circumstance
A will to live persists, a joy to be.
There is a joy in all that meets the sense,
A joy in all experience of the soul,
A joy in evil and a joy in good,
A joy in virtue and a joy in sin:
Indifferent to the threat of Karmic law,
Joy dares to grow upon forbidden soil,
Its sap runs through the plant and flowers of Pain:
It thrills with the drama of fate and tragic doom,
It tears its food from sorrow and ecstasy,
On danger and difficulty whets its strength;
It wallows with the reptile and the worm
And lifts its head, an equal of the stars;
It shares the faeries' dance, dines with the gnome:
It basks in the light and heat of many suns,
The sun of Beauty and the sun of Power

Flatter and foster it with golden beams;
It grows towards the Titan and the God.
On earth it lingers drinking its deep fill,
Through the symbol of her pleasure and her pain,
Of the grapes of Heaven and the flowers of the Abyss,
Of the flame-stabs and the torment-craft of Hell
And dim fragments of the glory of Paradise.
In the small paltry pleasures of man's life,
In his petty passions and joys it finds a taste,
A taste in tears and torture of broken hearts,
In the crown of gold and in the crown of thorns,
In life's nectar of sweetness and its bitter wine.
All being it explores for unknown bliss,
Sounds all experience for things new and strange.
Life brings into the earthly creature's days
A tongue of glory from a brighter sphere:
It deepens in his musings and his Art,
It leaps at the splendour of some perfect word,
It exults in his high resolves and noble deeds,
Wanders in his errors, dares the abyss's brink,
It climbs in his climbings, wallows in his fall.
Angel and demon brides his chamber share,
Possessors or competitors for life's heart.
To the enjoyer of the cosmic scene
His greatness and his littleness equal are,
His magnanimity and meanness hues
Cast on some neutral background of the gods:
The Artist's skill he admires who planned it all.
But not for ever endures this danger game:
Beyond the earth, but meant for delivered earth,
Wisdom and joy prepare their perfect crown;
Truth superhuman calls to thinking man.
At last the soul turns to eternal things,
In every shrine it cries for the clasp of God.
Then is there played the crowning Mystery,
Then is achieved the longed-for miracle.

Immortal Bliss her wide celestial eyes
Opens on the stars, she stirs her mighty limbs;
Time thrills to the sapphics of her amour-song
And Space fills with a white beatitude.
Then leaving to its grief the human heart,
Abandoning speech and the name-determined realms,
Through a gleaming far-seen sky of wordless thought,
Through naked thought-free heavens of absolute sight,
She climbs to the summits where the unborn Idea
Remembering the future that must be
Looks down upon the works of labouring Force,
Immutable above the world it made.
In the vast golden laughter of Truth's sun
Like a great heaven-bird on a motionless sea
Is poised her winged ardour of creative joy
On the still deep of the Eternal's peace.
This was the aim, this the supernal Law,
Nature's allotted task when beauty-drenched
In dim mist-waters of inconscient sleep,
Out of the Void this grand creation rose,—
For this the Spirit came into the Abyss
And charged with its power Matter's unknowing force,
In Night's bare session to cathedral Light,
In Death's realm repatriate immortality.
A mystic slow transfiguration works.
All our earth starts from mud and ends in sky,
And Love that was once an animal's desire,
Then a sweet madness in the rapturous heart,
An ardent comradeship in the happy mind,
Becomes a wide spiritual yearning's space.
A lonely soul passions for the Alone,
The heart that loved man thrills to the love of God,
A body is his chamber and his shrine.
Then is our being rescued from separateness;
All is itself, all is new-felt in God:
A Lover leaning from his cloister's door

Gathers the whole world into his single breast.
Then shall the business fail of Night and Death:
When unity is won, when strife is lost
And all is known and all is clasped by Love
Who would turn back to ignorance and pain?
    "O Death, I have triumphed over thee within;
I quiver no more with the assault of grief;
A mighty calmness seated deep within
Has occupied my body and my sense:
It takes the world's grief and transmutes to strength,
It makes the world's joy one with the joy of God.
My love eternal sits throned on God's calm;
For Love must soar beyond the very heavens
And find its secret sense ineffable;
It must change its human ways to ways divine,
Yet keep its sovereignty of earthly bliss.
O Death, not for my heart's sweet poignancy
Nor for my happy body's bliss alone
I have claimed from thee the living Satyavan,
But for his work and mine, our sacred charge.
Our lives are God's messengers beneath the stars;
To dwell under death's shadow they have come
Tempting God's light to earth for the ignorant race,
His love to fill the hollow in men's hearts,
His bliss to heal the unhappiness of the world.
For I, the woman, am the force of God,
He the Eternal's delegate soul in man.
My will is greater than thy law, O Death;
My love is stronger than the bonds of Fate:
Our love is the heavenly seal of the Supreme.
I guard that seal against thy rending hands.
Love must not cease to live upon the earth;
For Love is the bright link twixt earth and heaven,
Love is the far Transcendent's angel here;
Love is man's lien on the Absolute."
But to the woman Death the god replied,

With the ironic laughter of his voice
Discouraging the labour of the stars:
"Even so men cheat the Truth with splendid thoughts.
Thus wilt thou hire the glorious charlatan, Mind,
To weave from his Ideal's gossamer air
A fine raiment for thy body's nude desires
And thy heart's clutching greedy passion clothe?
Daub not the web of life with magic hues:
Make rather thy thought a plain and faithful glass
Reflecting Matter and mortality,
And know thy soul a product of the flesh,
A made-up self in a constructed world.
Thy words are large murmurs in a mystic dream.
For how in the soiled heart of man could dwell
The immaculate grandeur of thy dream-built God,
Or who can see a face and form divine
In the naked two-legged worm thou callest man?
O human face, put off mind-painted masks:
The animal be, the worm that Nature meant;
Accept thy futile birth, thy narrow life.
For truth is bare like stone and hard like death;
Bare in the bareness, hard with truth's hardness live."
But Savitri replied to the dire God:
"Yes, I am human. Yet shall man by me,
Since in humanity waits his hour the God,
Trample thee down to reach the immortal heights,
Transcending grief and pain and fate and death.
Yes, my humanity is a mask of God:
He dwells in me, the mover of my acts,
Turning the great wheel of his cosmic work.
I am the living body of his light,
I am the thinking instrument of his power,
I incarnate Wisdom in an earthly breast,
I am his conquering and unslayable will.
The formless Spirit drew in me its shape;
In me are the Nameless and the secret Name."

Death from the incredulous Darkness sent its cry:
"O priestess in Imagination's house,
Persuade first Nature's fixed immutable laws
And make the impossible thy daily work.
How canst thou force to wed two eternal foes?
Irreconcilable in their embrace
They cancel the glory of their pure extremes:
An unhappy wedlock maims their stunted force.
How shall thy will make one the true and false?
Where Matter is all, there Spirit is a dream:
If all are the Spirit, Matter is a lie,
And who was the liar who forged the universe?
The Real with the unreal cannot mate.
He who would turn to God, must leave the world;
He who would live in the Spirit, must give up life;
He who has met the Self, renounces self.
The voyagers of the million routes of mind
Who have travelled through Existence to its end,
Sages exploring the world-ocean's vasts,
Have found extinction the sole harbour safe.
Two only are the doors of man's escape,
Death of his body Matter's gate to peace,
Death of his soul his last felicity.
In me all take refuge, for I, Death, am God."
But Savitri replied to mighty Death:
"My heart is wiser than the Reason's thoughts,
My heart is stronger than thy bonds, O Death.
It sees and feels the one Heart beat in all,
It feels the high Transcendent's sunlike hands,
It sees the cosmic Spirit at its work;
In the dim Night it lies alone with God.
My heart's strength can carry the grief of the universe
And never falter from its luminous track,
Its white tremendous orbit through God's peace.
It can drink up the sea of All-Delight
And never lose the white spiritual touch,

The calm that broods in the deep Infinite."
He said, "Art thou indeed so strong, O heart,
O soul, so free? And canst thou gather then
Bright pleasure from my wayside flowering boughs,
Yet falter not from thy hard journey's goal,
Meet the world's dangerous touch and never fall?
Show me thy strength and freedom from my laws."
But Savitri answered, "Surely I shall find
Among the green and whispering woods of Life
Close-bosomed pleasures, only mine since his,
Or mine for him, because our joys are one.
And if I linger, Time is ours and God's,
And if I fall, is not his hand near mine?
All is a single plan; each wayside act
Deepens the soul's response, brings nearer the goal."
Death the contemptuous Nihil answered her:
"So prove thy absolute force to the wise gods,
By choosing earthly joy! For self demand
And yet from self and its gross masks live free.
Then will I give thee all thy soul desires,
All the brief joys earth keeps for mortal hearts.
Only the one dearest wish that outweighs all,
Hard laws forbid and thy ironic fate.
My will once wrought remains unchanged through Time,
And Satyavan can never again be thine."
But Savitri replied to the vague Power:
"If the eyes of Darkness can look straight at Truth,
Look in my heart and, knowing what I am,
Give what thou wilt or what thou must, O Death.
Nothing I claim but Satyavan alone."
There was a hush as if of doubtful fates.
As one disdainful still who yields a point
Death bowed his sovereign head in cold assent:
"I give to thee, saved from death and poignant fate
Whatever once the living Satyavan
Desired in his heart for Savitri.

Bright noons I give thee and unwounded dawns,
Daughters of thy own shape in heart and mind,
Fair hero sons and sweetness undisturbed
Of union with thy husband dear and true.
And thou shalt harvest in thy joyful house
Felicity of thy surrounded eves.
Love shall bind by thee many gathered hearts.
The opposite sweetness in thy days shall meet
Of tender service to thy life's desired
And loving empire over all thy loved,
Two poles of bliss made one, O Savitri.
Return, O child, to thy forsaken earth."
But Savitri replied, "Thy gifts resist.
Earth cannot flower if lonely I return."
Then Death sent forth once more his angry cry,
As chides a lion his escaping prey:
"What knowst thou of earth's rich and changing life
Who thinkst that one man dead all joy must cease?
Hope not to be unhappy till the end:
For grief dies soon in the tired human heart;
Soon other guests the empty chambers fill.
A transient painting on a holiday's floor
Traced for a moment's beauty love was made.
Or if a voyager on the eternal trail,
Its objects fluent change in its embrace
Like waves to a swimmer upon infinite seas."
But Savitri replied to the vague god,
"Give me back Satyavan, my only lord.
Thy thoughts are vacant to my soul that feels
The deep eternal truth in transient things."
Death answered her, "Return and try thy soul!
Soon shalt thou find appeased that other men
On lavish earth have beauty, strength and truth,
And when thou hast half forgotten, one of these
Shall wind himself around thy heart that needs
Some human answering heart against thy breast;

For who, being mortal, can dwell glad alone?
Then Satyavan shall glide into the past,
A gentle memory pushed away from thee
By new love and thy children's tender hands,
Till thou shalt wonder if thou lov'dst at all.
Such is the life earth's travail has conceived,
A constant stream that never is the same."
But Savitri replied to mighty Death:
"O dark ironic critic of God's work,
Thou mockst the mind and body's faltering search
For what the heart holds in a prophet hour
And the immortal spirit shall make its own.
Mine is a heart that worshipped, though forsaken,
The image of the god its love adored;
I have burned in flame to travel in his steps.
Are we not they who bore vast solitude
Seated upon the hills alone with God?
Why dost thou vainly strive with me, O Death,
A mind delivered from all twilight thoughts,
To whom the secrets of the gods are plain?
For now at last I know beyond all doubt,
The great stars burn with my unceasing fire
And life and death are both its fuel made.
Life only was my blind attempt to love:
Earth saw my struggle, heaven my victory;
All shall be seized, transcended; there shall kiss
Casting their veils before the marriage fire
The eternal bridegroom and eternal bride.
The heavens accept our broken flights at last.
On our life's prow that breaks the waves of Time
No signal light of hope has gleamed in vain."
She spoke; the boundless members of the god
As if by secret ecstasy assailed,
Shuddered in silence as obscurely stir
Ocean's dim fields delivered to the moon.
Then lifted up as by a sudden wind

Around her in that vague and glimmering world
The twilight trembled like a bursting veil.
　　Thus with armed speech the great opponents strove.
Around those spirits in the glittering mist
A deepening half-light fled with pearly wings
As if to reach some far ideal Morn.
Outlined her thoughts flew through the gleaming haze
Mingling bright-pinioned with its lights and veils
And all her words like dazzling jewels were caught
Into the glow of a mysterious world,
Or tricked in the rainbow shifting of its hues
Like echoes swam fainting into far sound.
All utterance, all mood must there become
An unenduring tissue sewn by mind
To make a gossamer robe of beautiful change.
Intent upon her silent will she walked
On the dim grass of vague unreal plains,
A floating veil of visions in her front,
A trailing robe of dreams behind her feet.
But now her spirit's flame of conscient force
Retiring from a sweetness without fruit
Called back her thoughts from speech to sit within
In a deep room in meditation's house.
For only there could dwell the soul's firm truth:
Imperishable, a tongue of sacrifice,
It flamed unquenched upon the central hearth
Where burns for the high houselord and his mate
The homestead's sentinel and witness fire
From which the altars of the gods are lit.
All still compelled went gliding on unchanged,
Still was the order of these worlds reversed:
The mortal led, the god and spirit obeyed
And she behind was leader of their march
And they in front were followers of her will.
Onward they journeyed through the drifting ways
Vaguely companioned by the glimmering mists.

But faster now all fled as if perturbed
Escaping from the clearness of her soul.
A heaven-bird upon jewelled wings of wind
Borne like a coloured and embosomed fire,
By spirits carried in a pearl-hued cave,
On through the enchanted dimness moved her soul.
Death walked in front of her and Satyavan,
In the dark front of Death, a failing star.
Above was the unseen balance of his fate.

END OF CANTO THREE

Canto Four

The Dream Twilight of the Earthly Real

THERE came a slope that slowly downward sank;
It slipped towards a stumbling grey descent.
The dim-heart marvel of the ideal was lost;
Its crowding wonder of bright delicate dreams
And vague half-limned sublimities she had left:
Thought fell towards lower levels; hard and tense
It passioned for some crude reality.
The twilight floated still but changed its hues
And heavily swathed a less delightful dream;
It settled in tired masses on the air;
Its symbol colours tuned with duller reds
And almost seemed a lurid mist of day.
A straining taut and dire besieged her heart;
Heavy her sense grew with a dangerous load,
And sadder, greater sounds were in her ears,
And through stern breakings of the lambent glare
Her vision caught a hurry of driving plains
And cloudy mountains and wide tawny streams,
And cities climbed in minarets and towers
Towards an unavailing changeless sky:
Long quays and ghauts and harbours white with sails
Challenged her sight awhile and then were gone.
Amidst them travailed toiling multitudes
In ever shifting perishable groups,
A foiled cinema of lit shadowy shapes
Enveloped in the grey mantle of a dream.
Imagining meanings in life's heavy drift,
They trusted in the uncertain environment
And waited for death to change their spirit's scene.
A savage din of labour and a tramp
Of armoured life and the monotonous hum

Of thoughts and acts that ever were the same,
As if the dull reiterated drone
Of a great brute machine, beset her soul,—
A grey dissatisfied rumour like a ghost
Of the moaning of a loud unquiet sea.
A huge inhuman cyclopean voice,
A Babel-builders' song towering to heaven,
A throb of engines and the clang of tools
Brought the deep undertone of labour's pain.
As when pale lightnings tear a tortured sky,
High overhead a cloud-rimmed series flared
Chasing like smoke from a red funnel driven,
The forced creations of an ignorant Mind:
Drifting she saw like pictured fragments flee
Phantoms of human thought and baffled hopes,
The shapes of Nature and the arts of man,
Philosophies and disciplines and laws,
And the dead spirit of old societies,
Constructions of the Titan and the worm.
As if lost remnants of forgotten light,
Before her mind there fled with trailing wings
Dimmed revelations and delivering words,
Emptied of their mission and their strength to save,
The messages of the evangelist gods,
Voices of prophets, scripts of vanishing creeds.
Each in its hour eternal claimed went by:
Ideals, systems, sciences, poems, crafts
Tireless there perished and again recurred,
Sought restlessly by some creative Power;
But all were dreams crossing an empty vast.
Ascetic voices called of lonely seers
On mountain summits or by river banks
Or from the desolate heart of forest glades
Seeking heaven's rest or the spirit's worldless peace,
Or in bodies motionless like statues, fixed
In tranced cessations of their sleepless thought

Sat sleeping souls, and this too was a dream.
All things the past has made and slain were there,
Its lost forgotten forms that once had lived,
And all the present loves as new-revealed
And all the hopes the future brings had failed
Already, caught and spent in efforts vain,
Repeated fruitlessly age after age.
Unwearied all returned insisting still
Because of joy in the anguish of pursuit
And joy to labour and to win and lose
And joy to create and keep and joy to kill.
The rolling cycles passed and came again,
Brought the same toils and the same barren end,
Forms ever new and ever old, the long
Appalling revolutions of the world.

Once more arose the great destroying Voice:
Across the fruitless labour of the worlds
His huge denial's all-defeating might
Pursued the ignorant march of dolorous Time.
"Behold the figures of this symbol realm,
Its solid outlines of creative dream
Inspiring the great concrete tasks of earth.
In its motion-parable of human life
Here thou canst trace the outcome Nature gives
To the sin of being and the error in things
And the desire that compels to live
And man's incurable malady of hope.
In an immutable order's hierarchy
Where Nature changes not, man cannot change:
Ever he obeys her fixed mutation's law;
In a new version of her oft-told tale
In ever-wheeling cycles turns the race.
His mind is pent in circling boundaries:
For mind is man, beyond thought he cannot soar.
If he could leave his limits he would be safe:

He sees but cannot mount to his greater heavens;
Even winged, he sinks back to his native soil.
He is a captive in his net of mind
And beats soul-wings against the walls of life.
In vain his heart lifts up its yearning prayer,
Peopling with brilliant Gods the formless Void;
Then disappointed to the Void he turns
And in its happy nothingness asks release,
The calm Nirvana of his dream of self:
The Word in silence ends, in Nought the name.
Apart amid the mortal multitudes,
He calls the Godhead incommunicable
To be the lover of his lonely soul
Or casts his spirit into its void embrace.
Or he finds his copy in the impartial All;
He imparts to the Immobile his own will,
Attributes to the Eternal wrath and love
And to the Ineffable lends a thousand names.
Hope not to call God down into his life.
How shalt thou bring the Everlasting here?
There is no house for him in hurrying Time.
Vainly thou seekst in Matter's world an aim;
No aim is there, only a will to be.
All walk by Nature bound for ever the same.
Look on these forms that stay awhile and pass,
These lives that long and strive, then are no more,
These structures that have no abiding truth,
The saviour creeds that cannot save themselves,
But perish in the strangling hands of the years,
Discarded from man's thought, proved false by Time,
Philosophies that strip all problems bare
But nothing ever have solved since earth began,
And sciences omnipotent in vain
By which men learn of what the suns are made,
Transform all forms to serve their outward needs,
Ride through the sky and sail beneath the sea,

But learn not what they are or why they came;
These polities, architectures of man's brain,
That, bricked with evil and good, wall in man's spirit
And, fissured houses, palace at once and jail,
Rot while they reign and crumble before they crash;
These revolutions, demon or drunken god,
Convulsing the wounded body of mankind
Only to paint in new colours an old face;
These wars, carnage triumphant, ruin gone mad,
The work of centuries vanishing in an hour,
The blood of the vanquished and the victor's crown
Which men to be born must pay for with their pain,
The hero's face divine on satyr's limbs,
The demon's grandeur mixed with the demigod's,
The glory and the beasthood and the shame;
Why is it all, the labour and the din,
The transient joys, the timeless sea of tears,
The longing and the hoping and the cry,
The battle and the victory and the fall,
The aimless journey that can never pause,
The waking toil, the incoherent sleep,
Song, shouts and weeping, wisdom and idle words,
The laughter of men, the irony of the gods?
Where leads the march, whither the pilgrimage?
Who keeps the map of the route or planned each stage?
Or else self-moved the world walks its own way,
Or nothing is there but only a Mind that dreams:
The world is a myth that happened to come true,
A legend told to itself by conscious Mind,
Imaged and played on a feigned Matter's ground
On which it stands in an unsubstantial Vast.
Mind is the author, spectator, actor, stage:
Mind only is and what it thinks is seen.
If Mind is all, renounce the hope of bliss;
If Mind is all, renounce the hope of Truth.
For Mind can never touch the body of Truth

And Mind can never see the soul of God;
Only his shadow it grasps nor hears his laugh
As it turns from him to the vain seeming of things.
Mind is a tissue woven of light and shade
Where right and wrong have sewn their mingled parts;
Or Mind is Nature's marriage of convenance
Between truth and falsehood, between joy and pain:
This struggling pair no court can separate.
Each thought is a gold coin with bright alloy
And error and truth are its obverse and reverse:
This is the imperial mintage of the brain
And of this kind is all its currency.
Think not to plant on earth the living Truth
Or make of Matter's world the home of God;
Truth comes not there but only the thought of Truth,
God is not there but only the name of God.
If Self there is it is bodiless and unborn;
It is no one and it is possessed by none.
On what shalt thou then build thy happy world?
Cast off thy life and mind, then art thou Self,
An all-seeing omnipresence stark, alone.
If God there is he cares not for the world;
All things he sees with calm indifferent gaze,
He has doomed all hearts to sorrow and desire,
He has bound all life with his implacable laws;
He answers not the ignorant voice of prayer.
Eternal while the ages toil beneath,
Unmoved, untouched by aught that he has made,
He sees as minute details mid the stars
The animal's agony and the fate of man:
Immeasurably wise, he exceeds thy thought;
His solitary joy needs not thy love.
His truth in human thinking cannot dwell:
If thou desirest Truth, then still thy mind
For ever, slain by the dumb unseen Light.
Immortal bliss lives not in human air:

How shall the mighty Mother her calm delight
Keep fragrant in this narrow fragile vase,
Or lodge her sweet unbroken ecstasy
In hearts which earthly sorrow can assail
And bodies careless Death can slay at will?
Dream not to change the world that God has planned,
Strive not to alter his eternal law.
If heavens there are whose gates are shut to grief,
There seek the joy thou couldst not find on earth;
Or in the imperishable hemisphere
Where Light is native and Delight is king
And Spirit is the deathless ground of things,
Choose thy high station, child of Eternity.
If thou art Spirit and Nature is thy robe,
Cast off thy garb and be thy naked self
Immutable in its undying truth,
Alone for ever in the mute Alone.
Turn then to God, for him leave all behind;
Forgetting love, forgetting Satyavan,
Annul thyself in his immobile peace.
O soul, drown in his still beatitude.
For thou must die to thyself to reach God's height:
I, Death, am the gate of immortality."
But Savitri answered to the sophist God:
"Once more wilt thou call Light to blind Truth's eyes,
Make Knowledge a catch of the snare of Ignorance
And the Word a dart to slay my living soul?
Offer, O King, thy boons to tired spirits
And hearts that could not bear the wounds of Time,
Let those who were tied to body and to mind,
Tear off those bonds and flee into white calm
Crying for a refuge from the play of God.
Surely thy boons are great since thou art He!
But how shall I seek rest in endless peace
Who house the mighty Mother's violent force,
Her vision turned to read the enigmaed world,

Her will tempered in the blaze of Wisdom's sun
And the flaming silence of her heart of love?
The world is a spiritual paradox
Invented by a need in the Unseen,
A poor translation to the creature's sense
Of That which for ever exceeds idea and speech,
A symbol of what can never be symbolised,
A language mispronounced, misspelt, yet true.
Its powers have come from the eternal heights
And plunged into the inconscient dim Abyss
And risen from it to do their marvellous work.
The soul is a figure of the Unmanifest,
The mind labours to think the Unthinkable,
The life to call the Immortal into birth,
The body to enshrine the Illimitable.
The world is not cut off from Truth and God.
In vain thou hast dug the dark unbridgeable gulf,
In vain thou hast built the blind and doorless wall:
Man's soul crosses through thee to Paradise,
Heaven's sun forces its way through death and night;
Its light is seen upon our being's verge.
My mind is a torch lit from the eternal sun,
My life a breath drawn by the immortal Guest,
My mortal body is the Eternal's house.
Already the torch becomes the undying ray,
Already the life is the Immortal's force,
The house grows of the householder part and one.
How sayst thou Truth can never light the human mind
And Bliss can never invade the mortal's heart
Or God descend into the world he made?
If in the meaningless Void creation rose,
If from a bodiless Force Matter was born,
If Life could climb in the unconscious tree,
Its green delight break into emerald leaves
And its laughter of beauty blossom in the flower,
If sense could wake in tissue, nerve and cell

And Thought seize the grey matter of the brain,
And soul peep from its secrecy through the flesh,
How shall the nameless Light not leap on men,
And unknown powers emerge from Nature's sleep?
Even now hints of a luminous Truth like stars
Arise in the mind-mooned splendour of Ignorance;
Even now the deathless Lover's touch we feel:
If the chamber's door is even a little ajar,
What then can hinder God from stealing in
Or who forbid his kiss on the sleeping soul?
Already God is near, the Truth is close:
Because the dark atheist body knows him not,
Must the sage deny the Light, the seer his soul?
I am not bound by thought or sense or shape;
I live in the glory of the Infinite,
I am near to the Nameless and Unknowable,
The Ineffable is now my household mate.
But standing on Eternity's luminous brink
I have discovered that the world was He;
I have met Spirit with spirit, Self with self,
But I have loved too the body of my God.
I have pursued him in his earthly form.
A lonely freedom cannot satisfy
A heart that has grown one with every heart:
I am a deputy of the aspiring world,
My spirit's liberty I ask for all."

Then rang again a deeper cry of Death.
As if beneath its weight of sterile law
Oppressed by its own obstinate meaningless will,
Disdainful, weary and compassionate,
It kept no more its old intolerant sound,
But seemed like life's in her unnumbered paths
Toiling for ever and achieving nought
Because of birth and change, her mortal powers
By which she lasts, around the term-posts fixed

Turning of a wide circling aimless race
Whose course for ever speeds and is the same.
In its long play with Fate and Chance and Time
Assured of the game's vanity lost or won,
Crushed by its load of ignorance and doubt
Which knowledge seems to increase and growth to enlarge,
The earth-mind sinks and it despairs and looks
Old, weary and discouraged on its work.
Yet was all nothing then or vainly achieved?
Some great thing has been done, some light, some power
Delivered from the huge Inconscient's grasp:
It has emerged from night; it sees its dawns
Circling for ever though no dawn can stay.
This change was in the godhead's far-flung voice;
His form of dread was altered and admitted
Our transient effort at eternity,
Yet flung vast doubts of what might else have been
On grandiose hints of an impossible day.
The great voice surging cried to Savitri:
"Because thou knowst the wisdom that transcends
Both veil of forms and the contempt of forms,
Arise delivered by the seeing gods.
If free thou hadst kept thy mind from life's fierce stress,
Thou mightst have been like them omniscient, calm.
But the violent and passionate heart forbids.
It is the storm bird of an anarch Power
That would upheave the world and tear from it
The indecipherable scroll of Fate,
Death's rule and Law and the unknowable Will.
Hasteners to action, violators of God
Are these great spirits who have too much love,
And they who formed like thee, for both art thou,
Have come into the narrow bounds of life
With too large natures overleaping time.
Worshippers of force who know not her recoil,
Their giant wills compel the troubled years.

The wise are tranquil; silent the great hills
Rise ceaselessly towards their unreached sky,
Seated on their unchanging base, their heads
Dreamless in heaven's immutable domain.
On their aspiring tops, sublime and still,
Lifting half-way to heaven the climbing soul
The mighty mediators stand content
To watch the revolutions of the stars:
Motionlessly moving with the might of earth,
They see the ages pass and are the same.
The wise think with the cycles, they hear the tread
Of far-off things; patient, unmoved they keep
Their dangerous wisdom in their depths restrained,
Lest man's frail days into the unknown should sink
Dragged like a ship by bound leviathan
Into the abyss of his stupendous seas.
Lo, how all shakes when the gods tread too near!
All moves, is in peril, anguished, torn, upheaved.
The hurrying aeons would stumble on too swift
If strength from heaven surprised the imperfect earth
And veilless knowledge smote these unfit souls.
The deities have screened their dreadful power:
God hides his thought and, even, he seems to err.
Be still and tardy in the slow wise world.
Mighty art thou with the dread goddess filled,
To whom thou criedst at dawn in the dim woods.
Use not thy strength like the wild Titan souls!
Touch not the seated lines, the ancient laws,
Respect the calm of great established things."
But Savitri replied to the huge god:
"What is the calm thou vauntst, O Law, O Death?
Is it not the dull-visioned tread inert
Of monstrous energies chained in a stark round
Soulless and stone-eyed with mechanic dreams?
Vain the soul's hope if changeless Law is all:
Ever to the new and the unknown press on

The speeding aeons justifying God.
What were earth's ages if the grey restraint
Were never broken and glories sprang not forth
Bursting their obscure seed, while man's slow life
Leaped hurried into sudden splendid paths
By divine words and human gods revealed?
Impose not upon sentient minds and hearts
The dull fixity that binds inanimate things.
Well is the unconscious rule for the animal breeds
Content to live beneath the immutable yoke;
Man turns to a nobler walk, a master path.
I trample on thy law with living feet;
For to arise in freedom I was born.
If I am mighty let my force be unveiled
Equal companion of the dateless powers,
Or else let my frustrated soul sink down
Unworthy of Godhead in the original sleep.
I claim from Time my will's eternity,
God from his moments." Death replied to her,
"Why should the noble and immortal will
Stoop to the petty works of transient earth,
Freedom forgotten and the Eternal's path?
Or is this the high use of strength and thought,
To struggle with the bonds of death and time
And spend the labour that might earn the gods
And battle and bear agony of wounds
To grasp the trivial joys that earth can guard
In her small treasure-chest of passing things?
Child, hast thou trodden the gods beneath thy feet
Only to win poor shreds of earthly life
For him thou lov'st cancelling the grand release,
Keeping from early rapture of the heavens
His soul the lenient deities have called?
Are thy arms sweeter than the courts of God?"
She answered, "Straight I trample on the road
The strong hand hewed for me which planned our paths.

I run where his sweet dreadful voice commands
And I am driven by the reins of God.
Why drew he wide his scheme of mighty worlds
Or filled infinity with his passionate breath?
Or wherefore did he build my mortal form
And sow in me his bright and proud desires,
If not to achieve, to flower in me, to love,
Carving his human image richly shaped
In thoughts and largenesses and golden powers?
Far Heaven can wait our coming in its calm.
Easy the heavens were to build for God.
Earth was his difficult matter, earth the glory
Gave of the problem and the race and strife.
There are the ominous masks, the terrible powers;
There it is greatness to create the gods.
Is not the spirit immortal and absolved
Always, delivered from the grasp of Time?
Why came it down into the mortal's Space?
A charge he gave to his high spirit in man
And wrote a hidden decree on Nature's tops.
Freedom is this with ever seated soul,
Large in life's limits, strong in Matter's knots,
Building great stuff of action from the worlds
To make fine wisdom from coarse, scattered strands
And love and beauty out of war and night,
The wager wonderful, the game divine.
What liberty has the soul which feels not free
Unless stripped bare and cannot kiss the bonds
The Lover winds around his playmate's limbs,
Choosing his tyranny, crushed in his embrace?
To seize him better with her boundless heart
She accepts the limiting circle of his arms,
Bows full of bliss beneath his mastering hands
And laughs in his rich constraints, most bound, most free.
This is my answer to thy lures, O Death."

Immutable, Death's denial met her cry:
"However mighty, whatever thy secret name
Uttered in hidden conclaves of the gods,
Thy heart's ephemeral passion cannot break
The iron rampart of accomplished things
With which the great Gods fence their camp in Space.
Whoever thou art behind thy human mask,
Even if thou art the Mother of the worlds
And pegst thy claim upon the realms of Chance,
The cosmic Law is greater than thy will.
Even God himself obeys the Laws he made:
The Law abides and never can it change,
The Person is a bubble on Time's sea.
A forerunner of a greater Truth to come,
Thy soul creator of its freer Law,
Vaunting a Force behind on which it leans,
A Light above which none but thou hast seen,
Thou claimst the first fruits of Truth's victory.
But what is Truth and who can find her form
Amid the specious images of sense,
Amid the crowding guesses of the mind
And the dark ambiguities of a world
Peopled with the incertitudes of Thought?
For where is Truth and when was her footfall heard
Amid the endless clamour of Time's mart
And which is her voice amid the thousand cries
That cross the listening brain and cheat the soul?
Or is Truth aught but a high starry name
Or a vague and splendid word by which man's thought
Sanctions and consecrates his nature's choice,
The heart's wish donning knowledge as its robe,
The cherished idea elect among the elect,
Thought's favourite mid the children of half-light
Who high-voiced crowd the playgrounds of the mind
Or people its dormitories in infant sleep?
All things hang here between God's yes and no,

Two Powers real but to each other untrue,
Two consort stars in the mooned night of mind
That towards two opposite horizons gaze,
The white head and black tail of the mystic drake,
The swift and the lame foot, wing strong, wing broken
Sustaining the body of the uncertain world,
A great surreal dragon in the skies.
Too dangerously thy high proud truth must live
Entangled in Matter's mortal littleness.
All in this world is true, yet all is false:
Its thoughts into an eternal cipher run,
Its deeds swell to Time's rounded zero sum.
Thus man at once is animal and god,
A disparate enigma of God's make
Unable to free the Godhead's form within,
A being less than himself, yet something more,
The aspiring animal, the frustrate god
Yet neither beast nor deity but man,
But man tied to the kind earth's labour strives to exceed
Climbing the stairs of God to higher things.
Objects are seemings and none knows their truth,
Ideas are guesses of an ignorant god.
Truth has no home in earth's irrational breast:
Yet without reason life is a tangle of dreams,
But reason is poised above a dim abyss
And stands at last upon a plank of doubt.
Eternal truth lives not with mortal men.
Or if she dwells within thy mortal heart,
Show me the body of the living Truth
Or draw for me the outline of her face
That I too may obey and worship her.
Then will I give thee back thy Satyavan.
But here are only facts and steel-bound Law.
This truth I know that Satyavan is dead
And even thy sweetness cannot lure him back.
No magic Truth can bring the dead to life,

No power of earth cancel the thing once done,
No joy of the heart can last surviving death,
No bliss persuade the past to live again.
But Life alone can solace the mute Void
And fill with thought the emptiness of Time.
Leave then thy dead, O Savitri, and live."
The Woman answered to the mighty Shade,
And as she spoke, mortality disappeared;
Her Goddess self grew visible in her eyes,
Light came, a dream of heaven, into her face.
"O Death, thou too art God and yet not He,
But only his own black shadow on his path
As leaving the Night he takes the upward Way
And drags with him its clinging inconscient Force.
Of God unconscious thou art the dark head,
Of his Ignorance thou art the impenitent sign,
Of its vast tenebrous womb the natural child,
On his immortality the sinister bar.
All contraries are aspects of God's face.
The Many are the innumerable One,
The One carries the multitude in his breast;
He is the Impersonal, inscrutable, sole,
He is the one infinite Person seeing his world;
The Silence bears the Eternal's great dumb seal,
His light inspires the eternal Word;
He is the Immobile's deep and deathless hush,
Its white and signless blank negating calm,
Yet stands the creator Self, the almighty Lord
And watches his will done by the forms of Gods
And the desire that goads half-conscious man
And the reluctant and unseeing Night.
These wide divine extremes, these inverse powers
Are the right and left side of the body of God;
Existence balanced twixt two mighty arms
Confronts the mind with unsolved abysms of Thought.
Darkness below, a fathomless Light above,

In Light are joined, but sundered by severing Mind
Stand face to face, opposite, inseparable,
Two contraries needed for his great World-task,
Two poles whose currents wake the immense World-Force.
In the stupendous secrecy of his Self,
Above the world brooding with equal wings,
He is both in one, beginningless, without end:
Transcending both, he enters the Absolute.
His being is a mystery beyond mind,
His ways bewilder mortal ignorance;
The finite in its little sections parked,
Amazed, credits not God's audacity
Who dares to be the unimagined All
And see and act as might one Infinite.
Against human reason this is his offence,
Being known to be for ever unknowable,
To be all and yet transcend the mystic whole,
Absolute, to lodge in a relative world of Time,
Eternal and all-knowing, to suffer birth,
Omnipotent, to sport with Chance and Fate,
Spirit, yet to be Matter and the Void,
Illimitable, beyond form or name,
To dwell within a body, one and supreme
To be animal and human and divine:
A still deep sea, he laughs in rolling waves;
Universal, he is all, — transcendent, none.
To man's righteousness this is his cosmic crime,
Almighty beyond good and evil to dwell
Leaving the good to their fate in a wicked world
And evil to reign in this enormous scene.
All opposition seems and strife and chance,
An aimless labour with but scanty sense,
To eyes that see a part and miss the whole;
The surface men scan, the depths refuse their search:
A hybrid mystery challenges the view,
Or a discouraging sordid miracle.

Yet in the exact Inconscient's stark conceit,
In the casual error of the world's ignorance
A plan, a hidden Intelligence is glimpsed.
There is a purpose in each stumble and fall;
Nature's most careless lolling is a pose
Preparing some forward step, some deep result.
Ingenious notes plugged into a motived score,
These million discords dot the harmonious theme
Of the evolution's huge orchestral dance.
A Truth supreme has forced the world to be;
It has wrapped itself in Matter as in a shroud,
A shroud of Death, a shroud of Ignorance.
It compelled the suns to burn through silent Space,
Flame-signs of its uncomprehended Thought
In a wide brooding ether's formless muse:
It made of Knowledge a veiled and struggling light,
Of Being a substance nescient, dense and dumb,
Of Bliss the beauty of an insentient world.
In finite things the conscious Infinite dwells:
Involved it sleeps in Matter's helpless trance,
It rules the world from its sleeping senseless Void;
Dreaming it throws out mind and heart and soul
To labour crippled, bound, on the hard earth;
A broken whole it works through scattered points;
Its gleaming shards are Wisdom's diamond thoughts,
Its shadowy reflex our ignorance.
It starts from the mute mass in countless jets,
It fashions a being out of brain and nerve,
A sentient creature from its pleasures and pangs.
A pack of feelings obscure, a dot of sense
Survives awhile answering the shocks of life,
Then, crushed or its force spent, leaves the dead form,
Leaves the huge universe in which it lived
An insignificant unconsidered guest.
But the soul grows concealed within its house;
It gives to the body its strength and magnificence;

It follows aims in an ignorant aimless world,
It lends significance to earth's meaningless life.
A demigod animal, came thinking man;
He wallows in mud, yet heavenward soars in thought;
He plays and ponders, laughs and weeps and dreams,
Satisfies his little longings like the beast;
He pores upon life's book with student eyes.
Out of this tangle of intellect and sense,
Out of the narrow scope of finite thought
At last he wakes into spiritual mind;
A high liberty begins and luminous room:
He glimpses eternity, touches the infinite,
He meets the gods in great and sudden hours,
He feels the universe as his larger self,
Makes Space and Time his opportunity
To join the heights and depths of being in light,
In the heart's cave speaks secretly with God.
But these are touches and high moments lived;
Fragments of Truth supreme have lit his soul,
Reflections of the sun in waters still.
A few have dared the last supreme ascent
And break through borders of blinding light above,
And feel a breath around of mightier air,
Receive a vaster being's messages
And bathe in its immense intuitive Ray.
On summit Mind are radiant altitudes
Exposed to the lustre of Infinity,
Outskirts and dependencies of the house of Truth,
Upraised estates of Mind and measureless.
There man can visit but there he cannot live.
A cosmic Thought spreads out its vastitudes;
Its smallest parts are here philosophies
Challenging with their detailed immensity,
Each figuring an omniscient scheme of things.
But higher still can climb the ascending light;
There are vasts of vision and eternal suns,

Oceans of an immortal luminousness,
Flame-hills assaulting heaven with their peaks,
There dwelling all becomes a blaze of sight;
A burning head of vision leads the mind,
Thought trails behind it its long comet tail;
The heart glows, an illuminate and seer,
And sense is kindled into identity.
A highest flight climbs to a deepest view:
In a wide opening of its native sky
Intuition's lightnings range in a bright pack
Hunting all hidden truths out of their lairs,
Its fiery edge of seeing absolute
Cleaves into locked unknown retreats of self,
Rummages the sky-recesses of the brain,
Lights up the occult chambers of the heart;
Its spear-point ictus of discovery
Pressed on the cover of name, the screen of form,
Strips bare the secret soul of all that is.
Thought there has revelation's sun-bright eyes;
The Word, a mighty and inspiring Voice,
Enters Truth's inmost cabin of privacy
And tears away the veil from God and life.
Then stretches the boundless finite's last expanse,
The cosmic empire of the Overmind,
Time's buffer state bordering Eternity,
Too vast for the experience of man's soul:
All here gathers beneath one golden sky:
The Powers that build the cosmos station take
In its house of infinite possibility;
Each god from there builds his own nature's world;
Ideas are phalanxed like a group of suns,
Each marshalling his company of rays.
Thought crowds in masses seized by one regard;
All Time is one body, Space a single look:
There is the Godhead's universal gaze
And there the boundaries of immortal Mind:

The line that parts and joins the hemispheres
Closes in on the labour of the Gods
Fencing eternity from the toil of Time.
In her glorious kingdom of eternal light
All-ruler, ruled by none, the Truth supreme,
Omnipotent, omniscient and alone,
In a golden country keeps her measureless house;
In its corridor she hears the tread that comes
Out of the Unmanifest never to return
Till the Unknown is known and seen by men.
Above the stretch and blaze of cosmic Sight,
Above the silence of the wordless Thought,
Formless creator of immortal forms,
Nameless, investitured with the name divine,
Transcending Time's hours, transcending Timelessness,
The Mighty Mother sits in lucent calm
And holds the eternal Child upon her knees
Attending the day when he shall speak to Fate.
There is the image of our future's hope;
There is the sun for which all darkness waits,
There is the imperishable harmony;
The world's contradictions climb to her and are one:
There is the Truth of which the world's truths are shreds,
The Light of which the world's ignorance is the shade
Till Truth draws back the shade that it has cast,
The Love our hearts call down to heal all strife,
The Bliss for which the world's derelict sorrows yearn:
Thence comes the glory sometimes seen on earth,
The visits of Godhead to the human soul,
The Beauty and the dream on Nature's face.
There the perfection born from eternity
Calls to it the perfection born in Time,
The truth of God surprising human life,
The image of God overtaking finite shapes.
There in a world of everlasting Light,
In the realms of the immortal Supermind

Truth who hides here her head in mystery,
Her riddle deemed by reason impossible
In the stark structure of material form,
Unenigmaed lives, unmasked her face and there
Is Nature and the common law of things.
There in a body made of spirit stuff,
The hearth-stone of the everliving Fire,
Action translates the movements of the soul,
Thought steps infallible and absolute
And life is a continual worship's rite,
A sacrifice of rapture to the One.
A cosmic vision, a spiritual sense
Feels all the Infinite lodged in finite form
And seen through a quivering ecstasy of light
Discovers the bright face of the Bodiless,
In the truth of a moment, in the moment's soul
Can sip the honey-wine of Eternity.
A Spirit who is no one and innumerable,
The one mystic infinite Person of his world
Multiplies his myriad personality,
On all his bodies seals his divinity's stamp
And sits in each immortal and unique.
The Immobile stands behind each daily act,
A background of the movement and the scene,
Upholding creation on its might and calm
And change on the Immutable's deathless poise.
The Timeless looks out from the travelling hours;
The Ineffable puts on a robe of speech
Where all its words are woven like magic threads
Moving with beauty, inspiring with their gleam,
And every thought takes up its destined place
Recorded in the memory of the world.
The Truth supreme, vast and impersonal
Fits faultlessly the hour and circumstance,
Its substance a pure gold ever the same
But shaped into vessels for the spirit's use,

Its gold becomes the wine jar and the vase.
All there is a supreme epiphany:
The All-Wonderful makes a marvel of each event,
The All-Beautiful is a miracle in each shape;
The All-Blissful smites with rapture the heart's throbs,
A pure celestial joy is the use of sense.
Each being there is a member of the Self,
A portion of the million-thoughted All,
A claimant to the timeless Unity,
The many's sweetness, the joy of difference
Edged with the intimacy of the One.
  "But who can show to thee Truth's glorious face?
Our human words can only shadow her.
To thought she is an unthinkable rapture of light,
To speech a marvel inexpressible.
O Death, if thou couldst touch the Truth supreme
Thou wouldst grow suddenly wise and cease to be.
If our souls could see and love and clasp God's Truth,
Its infinite radiance would seize our hearts,
Our being in God's image be remade
And earthly life become the life divine."
Then Death the last time answered Savitri:
"If Truth supreme transcends her shadow here
Severed by Knowledge and the climbing vasts,
What bridge can cross the gulf that she has left
Between her and the dream-world she has made?
Or who could hope to bring her down to men
And persuade to tread the harsh globe with wounded feet
Leaving her unapproachable glory and bliss,
Wasting her splendour on pale earthly air?
Is thine that strength, O beauty of mortal limbs,
O soul who flutterest to escape my net?
Who then art thou hiding in human guise?
Thy voice carries the sound of infinity,
Knowledge is with thee, Truth speaks through thy words;
The light of things beyond shines in thy eyes.

But where is thy strength to conquer Time and Death?
Hast thou God's force to build heaven's values here?
For truth and knowledge are an idle gleam
If Knowledge brings not power to change the world,
If Might comes not to give to Truth her right.
A blind Force, not Truth has made this ignorant world,
A blind Force, not Truth orders the lives of men:
By Power, not Light, the great Gods rule the world;
Power is the arm of God, the seal of Fate.
O human claimant to immortality,
Reveal thy power, lay bare thy spirit's force,
Then will I give back to thee Satyavan.
Or if the Mighty Mother is with thee,
Show me her face that I may worship her;
Let deathless eyes look into the eyes of Death,
An imperishable Force touching brute things
Transform earth's death into immortal life.
Then can thy dead return to thee and live.
The prostrate earth perhaps shall lift her gaze
And feel near her the secret body of God
And love and joy overtake fleeing Time."

And Savitri looked on Death and answered not.
Almost it seemed as if in his symbol shape
The world's darkness had consented to Heaven-light
And God needed no more the Inconscient's screen.
A mighty transformation came on her.
A halo of the indwelling Deity,
The Immortal's lustre that had lit her face
And tented its radiance in her body's house,
Overflowing made the air a luminous sea.
In a flaming moment of apocalypse
The Incarnation thrust aside its veil.
A little figure in infinity
Yet stood and seemed the Eternal's very house,
As if the world's centre was her very soul

And all wide space was but its outer robe.
A curve of the calm hauteur of far heaven
Descending into earth's humility,
Her forehead's span vaulted the Omniscient's gaze,
Her eyes were two stars that watched the universe.
The Power that from her being's summit reigned,
The Presence chambered in lotus secrecy,
Came down and held the centre in her brow
Where the mind's Lord in his control-room sits;
There throned on concentration's native seat
He opens that third mysterious eye in man,
The Unseen's eye that looks at the unseen,
When Light with a golden ecstasy fills his brain
And the Eternal's wisdom drives his choice
And eternal Will seizes the mortal's will.
It stirred in the lotus of her throat of song,
And in her speech throbbed the immortal Word,
Her life sounded with the steps of the world-soul
Moving in harmony with the cosmic Thought.
As glides God's sun into the mystic cave
Where hides his light from the pursuing gods,
It glided into the lotus of her heart
And woke in it the Force that alters Fate.
It poured into her navel's lotus depth,
Lodged in the little life-nature's narrow home,
On the body's longings grew heaven-rapture's flower
And made desire a pure celestial flame,
Broke into the cave where coiled World-Energy sleeps
And smote the thousand-hooded serpent Force
That blazing towered and clasped the World-Self above,
Joined Matter's dumbness to the Spirit's hush
And filled earth's acts with the Spirit's silent power.
Thus changed she waited for the Word to speak.
Eternity looked into the eyes of Death
And Darkness saw God's living Reality.
Then a Voice was heard that seemed the stillness' self

Or the low calm utterance of infinity
When it speaks to the silence in the heart of sleep.
"I hail thee, almighty and victorious Death,
Thou grandiose Darkness of the Infinite.
O Void that makest room for all to be,
Hunger that gnawest at the universe
Consuming the cold remnants of the suns
And eatst the whole world with thy jaws of fire,
Waster of the energy that has made the stars,
Inconscience, carrier of the seeds of thought,
Nescience in which All-Knowledge sleeps entombed
And slowly emerges in its hollow breast
Wearing the mind's mask of bright Ignorance.
Thou art my shadow and my instrument.
I have given thee thy awful shape of dread
And thy sharp sword of terror and grief and pain
To force the soul of man to struggle for light
On the brevity of his half-conscious days.
Thou art his spur to greatness in his works,
The whip to his yearning for eternal bliss,
His poignant need of immortality.
Live, Death, awhile, be still my instrument.
One day man too shall know thy fathomless heart
Of silence and the brooding peace of Night
And grave obedience to eternal Law
And the calm inflexible pity in thy gaze.
But now, O timeless Mightiness, stand aside
And leave the path of my incarnate Force.
Relieve the radiant God from thy black mask:
Release the soul of the world called Satyavan
Freed from thy clutch of pain and ignorance
That he may stand master of life and fate,
Man's representative in the house of God,
The mate of Wisdom and the spouse of Light,
The eternal bridegroom of the eternal bride."
She spoke; Death unconvinced resisted still,

Although he knew refusing still to know,
Although he saw refusing still to see.
Unshakable he stood claiming his right.
His spirit bowed; his will obeyed the law
Of its own nature binding even on Gods.
The Two opposed each other face to face.
His being like a huge fort of darkness towered;
Around it her light grew, an ocean's siege.
Awhile the Shade survived defying heaven:
Assailing in front, oppressing from above,
A concrete mass of conscious power, he bore
The tyranny of her divine desire.
A pressure of intolerable force
Weighed on his unbowed head and stubborn breast;
Light like a burning tongue licked up his thoughts,
Light was a luminous torture in his heart,
Light coursed, a splendid agony, through his nerves;
His darkness muttered perishing in her blaze.
Her mastering Word commanded every limb
And left no room for his enormous will
That seemed pushed out into some helpless space
And could no more re-enter but left him void.
He called to Night but she fell shuddering back,
He called to Hell but sullenly it retired:
He turned to the Inconscient for support,
From which he was born, his vast sustaining self;
It drew him back towards boundless vacancy
As if by himself to swallow up himself:
He called to his strength, but it refused his call.
His body was eaten by light, his spirit devoured.
At last he knew defeat inevitable
And left crumbling the shape that he had worn,
Abandoning hope to make man's soul his prey
And force to be mortal the immortal spirit.
Afar he fled shunning her dreaded touch
And refuge took in the retreating Night.

In the dream twilight of that symbol world
The dire universal Shadow disappeared
Vanishing into the Void from which it came.
As if deprived of its original cause,
The twilight realm passed fading from their souls,
And Satyavan and Savitri were alone.
But neither stirred: between those figures rose
A mute invisible and translucent wall.
In the long blank moment's pause nothing could move:
All waited on the unknown inscrutable Will.

END OF CANTO FOUR
End of Book Ten

BOOK ELEVEN

The Book of Everlasting Day

The Eternal Day: The Soul's Choice
and the Supreme Consummation

A MARVELLOUS sun looked down from ecstasy's skies
On worlds of deathless bliss, perfection's home,
Magical unfoldings of the Eternal's smile
Capturing his secret heart-beats of delight.
God's everlasting day surrounded her,
Domains appeared of sempiternal light
Invading all Nature with the Absolute's joy.
Her body quivered with eternity's touch,
Her soul stood close to the founts of the infinite.
Infinity's finite fronts she lived in, new
For ever to an everliving sight.
Eternity multiplied its vast self-look
Translating its endless mightiness and joy
Into delight souls playing with Time could share
In grandeurs ever new-born from the unknown depths,
In powers that leaped immortal from unknown heights,
In passionate heart-beats of an undying love,
In scenes of a sweetness that can never fade.
Immortal to the rapturous heart and eyes,
In serene arches of translucent calm
From Wonder's dream-vasts cloudless skies slid down
An abyss of sapphire; sunlight visited eyes
Which suffered without pain the absolute ray
And saw immortal clarities of form.
Twilight and mist were exiles from that air,
Night was impossible to such radiant heavens.
Firm in the bosom of immensity
Spiritual breadths were seen, sublimely born
From a still beauty of creative joy;
Embodied thoughts to sweet dimensions held

To please some carelessness of divine peace,
Answered the deep demand of an infinite sense
And its need of forms to house its bodiless thrill.
A march of universal powers in Time,
The harmonic order of self's vastitudes
In cyclic symmetries and metric planes
Harboured a cosmic rapture's revelry,
An endless figuring of the spirit in things
Planned by the artist who has dreamed the worlds;
Of all the beauty and the marvel here,
Of all Time's intricate variety
Eternity was the substance and the source;
Not from a plastic mist of Matter made,
They offered the suggestion of their depths
And opened the great series of their powers.
Arisen beneath a triple mystic heaven
The seven immortal earths were seen, sublime:
Homes of the blest released from death and sleep
Where grief can never come nor any pang
Arriving from self-lost and seeking worlds
Alter Heaven-nature's changeless quietude
And mighty posture of eternal calm,
Its pose of ecstasy immutable.
Plains lay that seemed the expanse of God's wide sleep,
Thought's wings climbed up towards heaven's vast repose
Lost in blue deeps of immortality.
A changed earth-nature felt the breath of peace.
Air seemed an ocean of felicity
Or the couch of the unknown spiritual rest,
A vast quiescence swallowing up all sound
Into a voicelessness of utter bliss;
Even Matter brought a close spiritual touch,
All thrilled with the immanence of one divine.
The lowest of these earths was still a heaven
Translating into the splendour of things divine
The beauty and brightness of terrestrial scenes.

Eternal mountains ridge on gleaming ridge
Whose lines were graved as on a sapphire plate
And etched the borders of heaven's lustrous noon
Climbed like piled temple stairs and from their heads
Of topless meditation heard below
The approach of a blue pilgrim multitude
And listened to a great arriving voice
Of the wide travel hymn of timeless seas.
A chanting crowd from mountain bosoms slipped
Past branches fragrant with a sigh of flowers
Hurrying through sweetnesses with revel leaps;
The murmurous rivers of felicity
Divinely rippled honey-voiced desires,
Mingling their sister eddies of delight,
Then, widening to a pace of calm-lipped muse,
Down many-glimmered estuaries of dream
Went whispering into lakes of liquid peace.
On a brink held of senseless ecstasy
And guarding an eternal poise of thought
Sat sculptured souls dreaming by rivers of sound
In changeless attitudes of marble bliss.
Around her lived the children of God's day
In an unspeakable felicity,
A happiness never lost, the immortal's ease,
A glad eternity's blissful multitude.
Around, the deathless nations moved and spoke,
Souls of a luminous celestial joy,
Faces of stark beauty, limbs of the moulded Ray;
In cities cut like gems of conscious stone
And wonderful pastures and on gleaming coasts
Bright forms were seen, eternity's luminous tribes.
Above her rhythming godheads whirled the spheres,
Rapt mobile fixities here blindly sought
By the huge erring orbits of our stars.
Ecstatic voices smote at hearing's chords,
Each movement found a music all its own;

Songs thrilled of birds upon unfading boughs
The colours of whose plumage had been caught
From the rainbow of imagination's wings.
Immortal fragrance packed the quivering breeze.
In groves that seemed moved bosoms and trembling depths
The million children of the undying spring
Bloomed, pure unnumbered stars of hued delight
Nestling for shelter in their emerald sky:
Faery flower-masses looked with laughing eyes.
A dancing chaos, an iridescent sea
Eternised to Heaven's ever-wakeful sight
The crowding petal-glow of marvel's tints
Which float across the curtained lids of dream.
Immortal harmonies filled her listening ear;
A great spontaneous utterance of the heights
On Titan wings of rhythmic grandeur borne
Poured from some deep spiritual heart of sound,
Strains trembling with the secrets of the gods.
A spirit wandered happily in the wind,
A spirit brooded in the leaf and stone;
The voices of thought-conscious instruments
Along a living verge of silence strayed,
And from some deep, a wordless tongue of things
Unfathomed, inexpressible, chantings rose
Translating into a voice the Unknown.
A climber on the invisible stair of sound,
Music not with these few and striving steps
Aspired that wander upon transient strings,
But changed its ever new uncounted notes
In a passion of unforeseeing discovery,
And kept its old unforgotten ecstasies
A growing treasure in the mystic heart.
A consciousness that yearned through every cry
Of unexplored attraction and desire,
It found and searched again the unsatisfied deeps
Hunting as if in some deep secret heart

To find some lost or missed felicity.
In those far-lapsing symphonies she could hear,
Breaking through enchantments of the ravished sense,
The lyric voyage of a divine soul
Mid spume and laughter tempting with its prow
The charm of innocent Circean isles,
Adventures without danger beautiful
In lands where siren Wonder sings its lures
From rhythmic rocks in ever-foaming seas.
In the harmony of an original sight
Delivered from our limiting ray of thought,
And the reluctance of our blinded hearts
To embrace the Godhead in whatever guise,
She saw all Nature marvellous without fault.
Invaded by beauty's universal revel
Her being's fibre reached out vibrating
And claimed deep union with its outer selves,
And on the heart's chords made pure to seize all tones
Heaven's subtleties of touch unwearying forced
More vivid raptures than earth's life can bear.
What would be suffering here, was fiery bliss.
All here but passionate hint and mystic shade
Divined by the inner prophet who perceives
The spirit of delight in sensuous things,
Turned to more sweetness than can now be dreamed.
The mighty signs of which earth fears the stress,
Trembling because she cannot understand,
And must keep obscure in forms strange and sublime,
Were here the first lexicon of an infinite mind
Translating the language of eternal bliss.
Here rapture was a common incident;
The lovelinesses of whose captured thrill
Our human pleasure is a fallen thread,
Lay, symbol shapes, a careless ornament,
Sewn on the rich brocade of Godhead's dress.
Things fashioned were the imaged homes where mind

Arrived to fathom a deep physical joy;
The heart was a torch lit from infinity,
The limbs were trembling densities of soul.
These were the first domains, the outer courts
Immense but least in range and least in price,
The slightest ecstasies of the undying gods.
Higher her swing of vision swept and knew,
Admitted through large sapphire opening gates
Into the wideness of a light beyond,
These were but sumptuous decorated doors
To worlds nobler, more felicitously fair.
Endless aspired the climbing of those heavens;
Realm upon realm received her soaring view.
Then on what seemed one crown of the ascent
Where finite and the infinite are one,
Immune she beheld the strong immortals' seats
Who live for a celestial joy and rule,
The middle regions of the unfading Ray.
Great forms of deities sat in deathless tiers,
Eyes of an unborn gaze towards her leaned
Through a transparency of crystal fire.
In the beauty of bodies wrought from rapture's lines,
Shapes of entrancing sweetness spilling bliss,
Feet glimmering upon the sunstone courts of mind,
Heaven's cupbearers bore round the Eternal's wine.
A tangle of bright bodies, of moved souls
Tracing the close and intertwined delight,
The harmonious tread of lives for ever joined
In the passionate oneness of a mystic joy
As if sunbeams made living and divine,
The golden-bosomed Apsara goddesses,
In groves flooded from an argent disk of bliss
That floated through a luminous sapphire dream,
In a cloud of raiment lit with golden limbs
And gleaming footfalls treading faery swards,
Virgin motions of bacchant innocences

Who know their riot for a dance of God,
Whirled linked in moonlit revels of the heart.
Impeccable artists of unerring forms,
Magician builders of sound and rhythmic words,
Wind-haired Gandharvas chanted to the ear
The odes that shape the universal thought,
The lines that tear the veil from Deity's face,
The rhythms that bring the sounds of wisdom's sea.
Immortal figures and illumined brows,
Our great forefathers in those splendours moved;
Termless in power and satisfied of light,
They enjoyed the sense of all for which we strive.
High seers, moved poets saw the eternal thoughts
That, travellers from on high, arrive to us
Deformed by our search, tricked by costuming mind,
Like gods disfigured by the pangs of birth,
Seized the great words which now are frail sounds caught
By difficult rapture on a mortal tongue.
The strong who stumble and sin were calm proud gods.
There lightning-filled with glory and with flame,
Melting in waves of sympathy and sight,
Smitten like a lyre that throbs to others' bliss,
Drawn by the cords of ecstasies unknown,
Her human nature faint with heaven's delight,
She beheld the clasp to earth denied and bore
The imperishable eyes of veilless love.
More climbed above, level to level reached,
Beyond what tongue can utter or mind dream:
Worlds of an infinite reach crowned Nature's stir.
There was a greater tranquil sweetness there,
A subtler and profounder ether's field
And mightier scheme than heavenliest sense can give.
There breath carried a stream of seeing mind,
Form was a tenuous raiment of the soul:
Colour was a visible tone of ecstasy;
Shapes seen half immaterial by the gaze

And yet voluptuously palpable
Made sensible to touch the indwelling spirit.
The high perfected sense illumined lived
A happy vassal of the inner ray,
Each feeling was the Eternal's mighty child
And every thought was a sweet burning god.
Air was a luminous feeling, sound a voice,
Sunlight the soul's vision and moonlight its dream.
On a wide living base of wordless calm
All was a potent and a lucid joy.
Into those heights her spirit went floating up
Like an upsoaring bird who mounts unseen
Voicing to the ascent his throbbing heart
Of melody till a pause of closing wings
Comes quivering in his last contented cry
And he is silent with his soul discharged,
Delivered of his heart's burden of delight.
Experience mounted on joy's coloured breast
To inaccessible spheres in spiral flight.
There Time dwelt with eternity as one;
Immense felicity joined rapt repose.

As one drowned in a sea of splendour and bliss,
Mute in the maze of these surprising worlds,
Turning she saw their living knot and source,
Key to their charm and fount of their delight,
And knew him for the same who snares our lives
Captured in his terrifying pitiless net,
And makes the universe his prison camp
And makes in his immense and vacant vasts
The labour of the stars a circuit vain
And death the end of every human road
And grief and pain the wages of man's toil.
One whom her soul had faced as Death and Night
A sum of all sweetness gathered into his limbs
And blinded her heart to the beauty of the suns.

Transfigured was the formidable shape.
His darkness and his sad destroying might
Abolishing for ever and disclosing
The mystery of his high and violent deeds,
A secret splendour rose revealed to sight
Where once the vast embodied Void had stood.
Night the dim mask had grown a wonderful face.
The vague infinity was slain whose gloom
Had outlined from the terrible unknown
The obscure disastrous figure of a god,
Fled was the error that arms the hands of grief,
And lighted the ignorant gulf whose hollow deeps
Had given to nothingness a dreadful voice.
As when before the eye that wakes in sleep
Is opened the sombre binding of a book,
Illumined letterings are seen which kept
A golden blaze of thought inscribed within,
A marvellous form responded to her gaze
Whose sweetness justified life's blindest pain;
All Nature's struggle was its easy price,
The universe and its agony seemed worth while.
As if the choric calyx of a flower
Aerial, visible on music's waves,
A lotus of light-petalled ecstasy
Took shape out of the tremulous heart of things.
There was no more the torment under the stars,
The evil sheltered behind Nature's mask;
There was no more the dark pretence of hate,
The cruel rictus on Love's altered face.
Hate was the grip of a dreadful amour's strife;
A ruthless love intent only to possess
Has here replaced the sweet original god.
Forgetting the Will-to-love that gave it birth,
The passion to lock itself in and to unite,
It would swallow all into one lonely self,
Devouring the soul that it had made its own,

By suffering and annihilation's pain
Punishing the unwillingness to be one,
Angry with the refusals of the world,
Passionate to take but knowing not how to give.
Death's sombre cowl was cast from Nature's brow;
There lightened on her the godhead's lurking laugh.
All grace and glory and all divinity
Were here collected in a single form;
All worshipped eyes looked through his from one face;
He bore all godheads in his grandiose limbs.
An oceanic spirit dwelt within;
Intolerant and invincible in joy
A flood of freedom and transcendent bliss
Into immortal lines of beauty rose.
In him the fourfold Being bore its crown
That wears the mystery of a nameless Name,
The universe writing its tremendous sense
In the inexhaustible meaning of a word.
In him the architect of the visible world,
At once the art and artist of his works,
Spirit and seer and thinker of things seen,
Virat, who lights his camp-fires in the suns
And the star-entangled ether is his hold,
Expressed himself with Matter for his speech:
Objects are his letters, forces are his words,
Events are the crowded history of his life,
And sea and land are the pages for his tale.
Matter is his means and his spiritual sign;
He hangs the thought upon a lash's lift,
In the current of the blood makes flow the soul.
His is the dumb will of atom and of clod;
A Will that without sense or motive acts,
An Intelligence needing not to think or plan,
The world creates itself invincibly;
For its body is the body of the Lord
And in its heart stands Virat, King of Kings.

In him shadows his form the Golden Child
Who in the Sun-capped Vast cradles his birth:
Hiranyagarbha, author of thoughts and dreams,
Who sees the invisible and hears the sounds
That never visited a mortal ear,
Discoverer of unthought realities
Truer to Truth than all we have ever known,
He is the leader on the inner roads;
A seer, he has entered the forbidden realms;
A magician with the omnipotent wand of thought,
He builds the secret uncreated worlds.
Armed with the golden speech, the diamond eye,
His is the vision and the prophecy:
Imagist casting the formless into shape,
Traveller and hewer of the unseen paths,
He is the carrier of the hidden fire,
He is the voice of the Ineffable,
He is the invisible hunter of the light,
The Angel of mysterious ecstasies,
The conqueror of the kingdoms of the soul.
A third spirit stood behind, their hidden cause,
A mass of superconscience closed in light,
Creator of things in his all-knowing sleep.
All from his stillness came as grows a tree;
He is our seed and core, our head and base.
All light is but a flash from his closed eyes:
An all-wise Truth is mystic in his heart,
The omniscient Ray is shut behind his lids:
He is the Wisdom that comes not by thought,
His wordless silence brings the immortal word.
He sleeps in the atom and the burning star,
He sleeps in man and god and beast and stone:
Because he is there the Inconscient does its work,
Because he is there the world forgets to die.
He is the centre of the circle of God,
He the circumference of Nature's run.

His slumber is an Almightiness in things,
Awake, he is the Eternal and Supreme.
Above was the brooding bliss of the Infinite,
Its omniscient and omnipotent repose,
Its immobile silence absolute and alone.
All powers were woven in countless concords here.
The bliss that made the world in his body lived,
Love and delight were the head of the sweet form.
In the alluring meshes of their snare
Recaptured, the proud blissful members held
All joys outrunners of the panting heart
And fugitive from life's outstripped desire.
Whatever vision has escaped the eye,
Whatever happiness comes in dream and trance,
The nectar spilled by love with trembling hands,
The joy the cup of Nature cannot hold,
Had crowded to the beauty of his face,
Were waiting in the honey of his laugh.
Things hidden by the silence of the hours,
The ideas that find no voice on living lips,
The soul's pregnant meeting with infinity
Had come to birth in him and taken fire:
The secret whisper of the flower and star
Revealed its meaning in his fathomless look.
His lips curved eloquent like a rose of dawn;
His smile that played with the wonder of the mind
And stayed in the heart when it had left his mouth
Glimmered with the radiance of the morning star
Gemming the wide discovery of heaven.
His gaze was the regard of eternity;
The spirit of its sweet and calm intent
Was a wise home of gladness and divulged
The light of the ages in the mirth of the hours,
A sun of wisdom in a miracled grove.
In the orchestral largeness of his mind
All contrary seekings their close kinship knew,

Rich-hearted, wonderful to each other met
In the mutual marvelling of their myriad notes
And dwelt like brothers of one family
Who had found their common and mysterious home.
As from the harp of some ecstatic god
There springs a harmony of lyric bliss
Striving to leave no heavenly joy unsung,
Such was the life in that embodied Light.
He seemed the wideness of a boundless sky,
He seemed the passion of a sorrowless earth,
He seemed the burning of a world-wide sun.
Two looked upon each other, Soul saw Soul.

Then like an anthem from the heart's lucent cave
A voice soared up whose magic sound could turn
The poignant weeping of the earth to sobs
Of rapture and her cry to spirit song.
"O human image of the deathless word,
How hast thou seen beyond the topaz walls
The gleaming sisters of the divine gate,
Summoned the genii of their wakeful sleep,
And under revelation's arches forced
The carved thought-shrouded doors to swing apart,
Unlocked the avenues of spiritual sight
And taught the entries of a heavenlier state
To thy rapt soul that bore the golden key?
In thee the secret sight man's blindness missed
Has opened its view past Time, my chariot-course,
And death, my tunnel which I drive through life
To reach my unseen distances of bliss.
I am the hushed search of the jealous gods
Pursuing my wisdom's vast mysterious work
Seized in the thousand meeting ways of heaven.
I am the beauty of the unveiled ray
Drawing through the deep roads of the infinite night
The unconquerable pilgrim soul of earth

Beneath the flaring torches of the stars.
I am the inviolable Ecstasy;
They who have looked on me, shall grieve no more.
The eyes that live in night shall see my form.
On the pale shores of foaming steely straits
That flow beneath a grey tormented sky,
Two powers from one original ecstasy born
Pace near but parted in the life of man;
One leans to earth, the other yearns to the skies:
Heaven in its rapture dreams of perfect earth,
Earth in its sorrow dreams of perfect heaven.
The two longing to join, yet walk apart,
Idly divided by their vain conceits;
They are kept from their oneness by enchanted fears;
Sundered mysteriously by miles of thought,
They gaze across the silent gulfs of sleep.
Or side by side reclined upon my vasts
Like bride and bridegroom magically divorced
They wake to yearn, but never can they clasp
While thinly flickering hesitates uncrossed
Between the lovers on their nuptial couch
The shadowy eidolon of a sword.
But when the phantom flame-edge fails undone,
Then never more can space or time divide
The lover from the loved; Space shall draw back
Her great translucent curtain, Time shall be
The quivering of the spirit's endless bliss.
Attend that moment of celestial fate.
Meanwhile you two shall serve the dual law
Which only now the scouts of vision glimpse
Who pressing through the forest of their thoughts
Have found the narrow bridges of the gods.
Wait patient of the brittle bars of form
Making division your delightful means
Of happy oneness rapturously enhanced
By attraction in the throbbing air between.

Yet if thou wouldst abandon the vexed world,
Careless of the dark moan of things below,
Tread down the isthmus, overleap the flood,
Cancel thy contract with the labouring Force;
Renounce the tie that joins thee to earth-kind,
Cast off thy sympathy with mortal hearts.
Arise, vindicate thy spirit's conquered right:
Relinquishing thy charge of transient breath,
Under the cold gaze of the indifferent stars
Leaving thy borrowed body on the sod,
Ascend, O soul, into thy blissful home.
Here in the playground of the eternal Child
Or in domains the wise Immortals tread
Roam with thy comrade splendour under skies
Spiritual lit by an unsetting sun,
As godheads live who care not for the world
And share not in the toil of Nature's powers:
Absorbed in their self-ecstasy they dwell.
Cast off the ambiguous myth of earth's desire,
O immortal, to felicity arise."
    On Savitri listening in her tranquil heart
To the harmony of the ensnaring voice
A joy exceeding earth's and heaven's poured down,
The bliss of an unknown eternity,
A rapture from some waiting Infinite.
A smile came rippling out in her wide eyes,
Its confident felicity's messenger
As if the first beam of the morning sun
Rippled along two wakened lotus-pools.
"O besetter of man's soul with life and death
And the world's pleasure and pain and Day and Night,
Tempting his heart with the far lure of heaven,
Testing his strength with the close touch of hell,
I climb not to thy everlasting Day,
Even as I have shunned thy eternal Night.
To me who turn not from thy terrestrial Way,

Give back the other self my nature asks.
Thy spaces need him not to help their joy;
Earth needs his beautiful spirit made by thee
To fling delight down like a net of gold.
Earth is the chosen place of mightiest souls;
Earth is the heroic spirit's battlefield,
The forge where the Archmason shapes his works.
Thy servitudes on earth are greater, King,
Than all the glorious liberties of heaven.
The heavens were once to me my natural home,
I too have wandered in star-jewelled groves,
Paced sun-gold pastures and moon-silver swards
And heard the harping laughter of their streams
And lingered under branches dropping myrrh;
I too have revelled in the fields of light
Touched by the ethereal raiment of the winds,
Thy wonder-rounds of music I have trod,
Lived in the rhyme of bright unlabouring thoughts,
I have beat swift harmonies of rapture vast,
Danced in spontaneous measures of the soul
The great and easy dances of the gods.
O fragrant are the lanes thy children walk
And lovely is the memory of their feet
Amid the wonder-flowers of Paradise:
A heavier tread is mine, a mightier touch.
There where the gods and demons battle in night
Or wrestle on the borders of the Sun,
Taught by the sweetness and the pain of life
To bear the uneven strenuous beat that throbs
Against the edge of some divinest hope,
To dare the impossible with these pangs of search,
In me the spirit of immortal love
Stretches its arms out to embrace mankind.
Too far thy heavens for me from suffering men.
Imperfect is the joy not shared by all.
O to spread forth, O to encircle and seize

More hearts till love in us has filled thy world!
O life, the life beneath the wheeling stars!
For victory in the tournament with death,
For bending of the fierce and difficult bow,
For flashing of the splendid sword of God!
O thou who soundst the trumpet in the lists,
Part not the handle from the untried steel,
Take not the warrior with his blow unstruck.
Are there not still a million fights to wage?
O king-smith, clang on still thy toil begun,
Weld us to one in thy strong smithy of life.
Thy fine-curved jewelled hilt call Savitri,
Thy blade's exultant smile name Satyavan.
Fashion to beauty, point us through the world.
Break not the lyre before the song is found;
Are there not still unnumbered chants to weave?
O subtle-souled musician of the years,
Play out what thou hast fluted on my stops;
Arise from the strain their first wild plaint divined
And that discover which is yet unsung.
I know that I can lift man's soul to God,
I know that he can bring the Immortal down.
Our will labours permitted by thy will
And without thee an empty roar of storm,
A senseless whirlwind is the Titan's force
And without thee a snare the strength of gods.
Let not the inconscient gulf swallow man's race
That through earth's ignorance struggles towards thy Light.
O Thunderer with the lightnings of the soul,
Give not to darkness and to death thy sun,
Achieve thy wisdom's hidden firm decree
And the mandate of thy secret world-wide love."
Her words failed lost in thought's immensities
Which seized them at the limits of their cry
And hid their meaning in the distances
That stir to more than ever speech has won

From the Unthinkable, end of all our thought,
And the Ineffable from whom all words come.

Then with a smile august as noonday heavens
The godhead of the vision wonderful:
"How shall earth-nature and man's nature rise
To the celestial levels, yet earth abide?
Heaven and earth towards each other gaze
Across a gulf that few can cross, none touch,
Arriving through a vague ethereal mist
Out of which all things form that move in space,
The shore that all can see but never reach.
Heaven's light visits sometimes the mind of earth;
Its thoughts burn in her sky like lonely stars;
In her heart there move celestial seekings soft
And beautiful like fluttering wings of birds,
Visions of joy that she can never win
Traverse the fading mirror of her dreams.
Faint seeds of light and bliss bear sorrowful flowers,
Faint harmonies caught from a half-heard song
Fall swooning mid the wandering voices' jar,
Foam from the tossing luminous seas where dwells
The beautiful and far delight of gods,
Raptures unknown, a miracled happiness
Thrill her and pass half-shaped to mind and sense.
Above her little finite steps she feels,
Careless of knot or pause, worlds which weave out
A strange perfection beyond law and rule,
A universe of self-found felicity,
An inexpressible rhythm of timeless beats,
The many-movemented heart-beats of the One,
Magic of the boundless harmonies of self,
Order of the freedom of the infinite,
The wonder-plastics of the Absolute.
There is the All-Truth and there the timeless bliss.
But hers are fragments of a star-lost gleam,

Hers are but careless visits of the gods.
They are a Light that fails, a Word soon hushed
And nothing they mean can stay for long on earth.
There are high glimpses, not the lasting sight.
A few can climb to an unperishing sun,
Or live on the edges of the mystic moon
And channel to earth-mind the wizard ray.
The heroes and the demigods are few
To whom the close immortal voices speak
And to their acts the heavenly clan are near.
Few are the silences in which Truth is heard,
Unveiling the timeless utterance in her deeps;
Few are the splendid moments of the seers.
Heaven's call is rare, rarer the heart that heeds;
The doors of light are sealed to common mind
And earth's needs nail to earth the human mass,
Only in an uplifting hour of stress
Men answer to the touch of greater things:
Or, raised by some strong hand to breathe heaven-air,
They slide back to the mud from which they climbed;
In the mud of which they are made, whose law they know
They joy in safe return to a friendly base,
And, though something in them weeps for glory lost
And greatness murdered, they accept their fall.
To be the common man they think the best,
To live as others live is their delight.
For most are built on Nature's early plan
And owe small debt to a superior plane;
The human average is their level pitch,
A thinking animal's material range.
In the long ever-mounting hierarchy,
In the stark economy of cosmic life
Each creature to its appointed task and place
Is bound by his nature's form, his spirit's force.
If this were easily disturbed, it would break
The settled balance of created things;

The perpetual order of the universe
Would tremble, and a gap yawn in woven Fate.
If men were not and all were brilliant gods,
The mediating stair would then be lost
By which the spirit awake in Matter winds
Accepting the circuits of the middle Way,
By heavy toil and slow aeonic steps
Reaching the bright miraculous fringe of God,
Into the glory of the Oversoul.
My will, my call is there in men and things;
But the Inconscient lies at the world's grey back
And draws to its breast of Night and Death and Sleep.
Imprisoned in its dark and dumb abyss
A little consciousness it lets escape
But jealous of the growing light holds back
Close to the obscure edges of its cave
As if a fond ignorant mother kept her child
Tied to her apron strings of Nescience.
The Inconscient could not read without man's mind
The mystery of the world its sleep has made:
Man is its key to unlock a conscious door.
But still it holds him dangled in its grasp:
It draws its giant circle round his thoughts,
It shuts his heart to the supernal Light.
A high and dazzling limit shines above,
A black and blinding border rules below:
His mind is closed between two firmaments.
He seeks through words and images the Truth,
And, poring on surfaces and brute outsides
Or dipping cautious feet in shallow seas,
Even his Knowledge is an Ignorance.
He is barred out from his own inner depths;
He cannot look on the face of the Unknown.
How shall he see with the Omniscient's eyes,
How shall he will with the Omnipotent's force?
O too compassionate and eager Dawn,

Leave to the circling aeons' tardy pace
And to the working of the inconscient Will,
Leave to its imperfect light the earthly race:
All shall be done by the long act of Time.
Although the race is bound by its own kind,
The soul in man is greater than his fate:
Above the wash and surge of Time and Space,
Disengaging from the cosmic commonalty
By which all life is kin in grief and joy,
Delivered from the universal Law
The sunlike single and transcendent spirit
Can blaze its way through the mind's barrier wall
And burn alone in the eternal sky,
Inhabitant of a wide and endless calm.
O flame, withdraw into thy luminous self.
Or else return to thy original might
On a seer-summit above thought and world;
Partner of my unhoured eternity,
Be one with the infinity of my power:
For thou art the World-Mother and the Bride.
Out of the fruitless yearning of earth's life,
Out of her feeble unconvincing dream,
Recovering wings that cross infinity
Pass back into the Power from which thou cam'st.
To that thou canst uplift thy formless flight,
Thy heart can rise from its unsatisfied beats
And feel the immortal and spiritual joy
Of a soul that never lost felicity.
Lift up the fallen heart of love which flutters
Cast down desire's abyss into the gulfs.
For ever rescued out of Nature's shapes
Discover what the aimless cycles want,
There intertwined with all thy life has meant,
Here vainly sought in a terrestrial form.
Break into eternity thy mortal mould;
Melt, lightning, into thy invisible flame!

Clasp, Ocean, deep into thyself thy wave,
Happy for ever in the embosoming surge.
Grow one with the still passion of the depths.
Then shalt thou know the Lover and the Loved,
Leaving the limits dividing him and thee.
Receive him into boundless Savitri,
Lose thyself into infinite Satyavan.
O miracle, where thou beganst, there cease!"
    But Savitri answered to the radiant God:
"In vain thou temptst with solitary bliss
Two spirits saved out of a suffering world;
My soul and his indissolubly linked
In the one task for which our lives were born,
To raise the world to God in deathless Light,
To bring God down to the world on earth we came,
To change the earthly life to life divine.
I keep my will to save the world and man;
Even the charm of thy alluring voice,
O blissful Godhead, cannot seize and snare.
I sacrifice not earth to happier worlds.
Because there dwelt the Eternal's vast Idea
And his dynamic will in men and things,
So only could the enormous scene begin.
Whence came this profitless wilderness of stars,
This mighty barren wheeling of the suns?
Who made the soul of futile life in Time,
Planted a purpose and a hope in the heart,
Set Nature to a huge and meaningless task
Or planned her million-aeoned effort's waste?
What force condemned to birth and death and tears
These conscious creatures crawling on the globe?
If earth can look up to the light of heaven
And hear an answer to her lonely cry,
Not vain their meeting, nor heaven's touch a snare.
If thou and I are true, the world is true;
Although thou hide thyself behind thy works,

To be is not a senseless paradox;
Since God has made earth, earth must make in her God;
What hides within her breast she must reveal.
I claim thee for the world that thou hast made.
If man lives bound by his humanity,
If he is tied for ever to his pain,
Let a greater being then arise from man,
The superhuman with the Eternal mate
And the Immortal shine through earthly forms.
Else were creation vain and this great world
A nothing that in Time's moments seems to be.
But I have seen through the insentient mask;
I have felt a secret spirit stir in things
Carrying the body of the growing God:
It looks through veiling forms at veilless truth;
It pushes back the curtain of the gods;
It climbs towards its own eternity."
But the god answered to the woman's heart:
"O living power of the incarnate Word,
All that the Spirit has dreamed thou canst create:
Thou art the force by which I made the worlds,
Thou art my vision and my will and voice.
But knowledge too is thine, the world-plan thou knowest
And the tardy process of the pace of Time.
In the impetuous drive of thy heart of flame,
In thy passion to deliver man and earth,
Indignant at the impediments of Time
And the slow evolution's sluggard steps,
Lead not the spirit in an ignorant world
To dare too soon the adventure of the Light,
Pushing the bound and slumbering god in man
Awakened mid the ineffable silences
Into endless vistas of the unknown and unseen,
Across the last confines of the limiting Mind
And the Superconscient's perilous border line
Into the danger of the Infinite.

But if thou wilt not wait for Time and God,
Do then thy work and force thy will on Fate.
As I have taken from thee my load of night
And taken from thee my twilight's doubts and dreams,
So now I take my light of utter Day.
These are my symbol kingdoms but not here
Can the great choice be made that fixes fate
Or uttered the sanction of the Voice supreme.
Arise upon a ladder of greater worlds
To the infinity where no world can be.
But not in the wide air where a greater Life
Uplifts its mystery and its miracle,
And not on the luminous peaks of summit Mind,
Or in the hold where subtle Matter's spirit
Hides in its light of shimmering secrecies,
Can there be heard the Eternal's firm command
That joins the head of destiny to its base.
These only are the mediating links;
Not theirs is the originating sight
Nor the fulfilling act or last support
That bears perpetually the cosmic pile.
Two are the Powers that hold the ends of Time;
Spirit foresees, Matter unfolds its thought,
The dumb executor of God's decrees,
Omitting no iota and no dot,
Agent unquestioning, inconscient, stark,
Evolving inevitably a charged content,
Intention of his force in Time and Space,
In animate beings and inanimate things;
Immutably it fulfils its ordered task,
It cancels not a tittle of things done;
Unswerving from the oracular command
It alters not the steps of the Unseen.
If thou must indeed deliver man and earth
On the spiritual heights look down on life,
Discover the truth of God and man and world;

Then do thy task knowing and seeing all.
Ascend, O soul, into thy timeless self;
Choose destiny's curve and stamp thy will on Time."
He ended and upon the falling sound
A power went forth that shook the founded spheres
And loosed the stakes that hold the tents of form.
Absolved from vision's grip and the folds of thought,
Rapt from her sense like disappearing scenes
In the stupendous theatre of Space
The heaven-worlds vanished in spiritual light.
A movement was abroad, a cry, a word,
Beginningless in its vast discovery,
Momentless in its unthinkable return:
Choired in calm seas she heard the eternal Thought
Rhythming itself abroad unutterably
In spaceless orbits and on timeless roads.
In an ineffable world she lived fulfilled.
An energy of the triune Infinite,
In a measureless Reality she dwelt,
A rapture and a being and a force,
A linked and myriad-motioned plenitude,
A virgin unity, a luminous spouse,
Housing a multitudinous embrace
To marry all in God's immense delight,
Bearing the eternity of every spirit,
Bearing the burden of universal love,
A wonderful mother of unnumbered souls.
All things she knew, all things imagined or willed:
Her ear was opened to ideal sound,
Shape the convention bound no more her sight,
A thousand doors of oneness was her heart.
A crypt and sanctuary of brooding light
Appeared, the last recess of things beyond.
Then in its rounds the enormous fiat paused,
Silence gave back to the Unknowable
All it had given. Still was her listening thought.

The form of things had ceased within her soul.
Invisible that perfect godhead now.
Around her some tremendous spirit lived,
Mysterious flame around a melting pearl,
And in the phantom of abolished Space
There was a voice unheard by ears that cried:
"Choose, spirit, thy supreme choice not given again;
For now from my highest being looks at thee
The nameless formless peace where all things rest.
In a happy vast sublime cessation know, —
An immense extinction in eternity,
A point that disappears in the infinite, —
Felicity of the extinguished flame,
Last sinking of a wave in a boundless sea,
End of the trouble of thy wandering thoughts,
Close of the journeying of thy pilgrim soul.
Accept, O music, weariness of thy notes,
O stream, wide breaking of thy channel banks."
The moments fell into eternity.
But someone yearned within a bosom unknown
And silently the woman's heart replied:
"Thy peace, O Lord, a boon within to keep
Amid the roar and ruin of wild Time
For the magnificent soul of man on earth.
Thy calm, O Lord, that bears thy hands of joy."
Limitless like ocean round a lonely isle
A second time the eternal cry arose:
"Wide open are the ineffable gates in front.
My spirit leans down to break the knot of earth,
Amorous of oneness without thought or sign
To cast down wall and fence, to strip heaven bare,
See with the large eye of infinity,
Unweave the stars and into silence pass."
In an immense and world-destroying pause
She heard a million creatures cry to her.
Through the tremendous stillness of her thoughts

Immeasurably the woman's nature spoke:
"Thy oneness, Lord, in many approaching hearts,
My sweet infinity of thy numberless souls."
Mightily retreating like a sea in ebb
A third time swelled the great admonishing call:
"I spread abroad the refuge of my wings.
Out of its incommunicable deeps
My power looks forth of mightiest splendour, stilled
Into its majesty of sleep, withdrawn
Above the dreadful whirlings of the world."
A sob of things was answer to the voice,
And passionately the woman's heart replied:
"Thy energy, Lord, to seize on woman and man,
To take all things and creatures in their grief
And gather them into a mother's arms."
Solemn and distant like a seraph's lyre
A last great time the warning sound was heard:
"I open the wide eye of solitude
To uncover the voiceless rapture of my bliss,
Where in a pure and exquisite hush it lies
Motionless in its slumber of ecstasy,
Resting from the sweet madness of the dance
Out of whose beat the throb of hearts was born."
Breaking the Silence with appeal and cry
A hymn of adoration tireless climbed,
A music beat of winged uniting souls,
Then all the woman yearningly replied:
"Thy embrace which rends the living knot of pain,
Thy joy, O Lord, in which all creatures breathe,
Thy magic flowing waters of deep love,
Thy sweetness give to me for earth and men."

     Then after silence a still blissful cry
Began, such as arose from the Infinite
When the first whisperings of a strange delight
Imagined in its deep the joy to seek,

The passion to discover and to touch,
The enamoured laugh which rhymed the chanting worlds:
"O beautiful body of the incarnate Word,
Thy thoughts are mine, I have spoken with thy voice.
My will is thine, what thou hast chosen I choose:
All thou hast asked I give to earth and men.
All shall be written out in destiny's book
By my trustee of thought and plan and act,
The executor of my will, eternal Time.
But since thou hast refused my maimless Calm
And turned from my termless peace in which is expunged
The visage of Space and the shape of Time is lost,
And from happy extinction of thy separate self
In my uncompanioned lone eternity, —
For not for thee the nameless worldless Nought,
Annihilation of thy living soul
And the end of thought and hope and life and love
In the blank measureless Unknowable, —
I lay my hands upon thy soul of flame,
I lay my hands upon thy heart of love,
I yoke thee to my power of work in Time.
Because thou hast obeyed my timeless will,
Because thou hast chosen to share earth's struggle and fate
And leaned in pity over earth-bound men
And turned aside to help and yearned to save,
I bind by thy heart's passion thy heart to mine
And lay my splendid yoke upon thy soul.
Now will I do in thee my marvellous works.
I will fasten thy nature with my cords of strength,
Subdue to my delight thy spirit's limbs
And make thee a vivid knot of all my bliss
And build in thee my proud and crystal home.
Thy days shall be my shafts of power and light,
Thy nights my starry mysteries of joy
And all my clouds lie tangled in thy hair
And all my springtides marry in thy mouth.

O Sun-Word, thou shalt raise the earth-soul to Light
And bring down God into the lives of men;
Earth shall be my work-chamber and my house,
My garden of life to plant a seed divine.
When all thy work in human time is done
The mind of earth shall be a home of light,
The life of earth a tree growing towards heaven,
The body of earth a tabernacle of God.
Awakened from the mortal's ignorance
Men shall be lit with the Eternal's ray
And the glory of my sun-lift in their thoughts
And feel in their hearts the sweetness of my love
And in their acts my Power's miraculous drive.
My will shall be the meaning of their days;
Living for me, by me, in me they shall live.
In the heart of my creation's mystery
I will enact the drama of thy soul,
Inscribe the long romance of Thee and Me.
I will pursue thee across the centuries;
Thou shalt be hunted through the world by love,
Naked of ignorance' protecting veil
And without covert from my radiant gods.
No shape shall screen thee from my divine desire,
Nowhere shalt thou escape my living eyes.
In the nudity of thy discovered self,
In a bare identity with all that is,
Disrobed of thy covering of humanity,
Divested of the dense veil of human thought,
Made one with every mind and body and heart,
Made one with all Nature and with Self and God,
Summing in thy single soul my mystic world
I will possess in thee my universe,
The universe find all I am in thee.
Thou shalt bear all things that all things may change,
Thou shalt fill all with my splendour and my bliss,
Thou shalt meet all with thy transmuting soul.

Assailed by my infinitudes above,
And quivering in immensities below,
Pursued by me through my mind's wall-less vast,
Oceanic with the surges of my life,
A swimmer lost between two leaping seas
By my outer pains and inner sweetnesses
Finding my joy in my opposite mysteries
Thou shalt respond to me from every nerve.
A vision shall compel thy coursing breath,
Thy heart shall drive thee on the wheel of works,
Thy mind shall urge thee through the flames of thought,
To meet me in the abyss and on the heights,
To feel me in the tempest and the calm,
And love me in the noble and the vile,
In beautiful things and terrible desire.
The pains of hell shall be to thee my kiss,
The flowers of heaven persuade thee with my touch.
My fiercest masks shall my attractions bring.
Music shall find thee in the voice of swords,
Beauty pursue thee through the core of flame.
Thou shalt know me in the rolling of the spheres
And cross me in the atoms of the whirl.
The wheeling forces of my universe
Shall cry to thee the summons of my name.
Delight shall drop down from my nectarous moon,
My fragrance seize thee in the jasmine's snare,
My eye shall look upon thee from the sun.
Mirror of Nature's secret spirit made,
Thou shalt reflect my hidden heart of joy,
Thou shalt drink down my sweetness unalloyed
In my pure lotus-cup of starry brim.
My dreadful hands laid on thy bosom shall force
Thy being bathed in fiercest longing's streams.
Thou shalt discover the one and quivering note,
And cry, the harp of all my melodies,
And roll, my foaming wave in seas of love.

Even my disasters' clutch shall be to thee
The ordeal of my rapture's contrary shape:
In pain's self shall smile on thee my secret face:
Thou shalt bear my ruthless beauty unabridged
Amid the world's intolerable wrongs,
Trampled by the violent misdeeds of Time
Cry out to the ecstasy of my rapture's touch.
All beings shall be to thy life my emissaries;
Drawn to me on the bosom of thy friend,
Compelled to meet me in thy enemy's eyes,
My creatures shall demand me from thy heart.
Thou shalt not shrink from any brother soul.
Thou shalt be attracted helplessly to all.
Men seeing thee shall feel my hands of joy,
In sorrow's pangs feel steps of the world's delight,
Their life experience its tumultuous shock
In the mutual craving of two opposites.
Hearts touched by thy love shall answer to my call,
Discover the ancient music of the spheres
In the revealing accents of thy voice
And nearer draw to me because thou art:
Enamoured of thy spirit's loveliness
They shall embrace my body in thy soul,
Hear in thy life the beauty of my laugh,
Know the thrilled bliss with which I made the worlds.
All that thou hast, shall be for others' bliss,
All that thou art, shall to my hands belong.
I will pour delight from thee as from a jar,
I will whirl thee as my chariot through the ways,
I will use thee as my sword and as my lyre,
I will play on thee my minstrelsies of thought.
And when thou art vibrant with all ecstasy,
And when thou liv'st one spirit with all things,
Then will I spare thee not my living fires,
But make thee a channel for my timeless force.
My hidden presence led thee unknowing on

From thy beginning in earth's voiceless bosom
Through life and pain and time and will and death,
Through outer shocks and inner silences
Along the mystic roads of Space and Time
To the experience which all Nature hides.
Who hunts and seizes me, my captive grows:
This shalt thou henceforth learn from thy heart-beats.
For ever love, O beautiful slave of God!
O lasso of my rapture's widening noose,
Become my cord of universal love.
The spirit ensnared by thee force to delight
Of creation's oneness sweet and fathomless,
Compelled to embrace my myriad unities
And all my endless forms and divine souls.
O Mind, grow full of the eternal peace;
O Word, cry out the immortal litany:
Built is the golden tower, the flame-child born.
    "Descend to life with him thy heart desires.
O Satyavan, O luminous Savitri,
I sent you forth of old beneath the stars,
A dual power of God in an ignorant world,
In a hedged creation shut from limitless self,
Bringing down God to the insentient globe,
Lifting earth-beings to immortality.
In the world of my knowledge and my ignorance
Where God is unseen and only is heard a Name
And knowledge is trapped in the boundaries of mind
And life is hauled in the drag-net of desire
And Matter hides the soul from its own sight,
You are my Force at work to uplift earth's fate,
My self that moves up the immense incline
Between the extremes of the spirit's night and day.
He is my soul that climbs from nescient Night
Through life and mind and supernature's Vast
To the supernal light of Timelessness
And my eternity hid in moving Time

And my boundlessness cut by the curve of Space.
It climbs to the greatness it has left behind
And to the beauty and joy from which it fell,
To the closeness and sweetness of all things divine,
To light without bounds and life illimitable,
Taste of the depths of the Ineffable's bliss,
Touch of the immortal and the infinite.
He is my soul that gropes out of the beast
To reach humanity's heights of lucent thought
And the vicinity of Truth's sublime.
He is the godhead growing in human lives
And in the body of earth-being's forms:
He is the soul of man climbing to God
In Nature's surge out of earth's ignorance.
O Savitri, thou art my spirit's Power,
The revealing voice of my immortal Word,
The face of Truth upon the roads of Time
Pointing to the souls of men the routes to God.
While the dim light from the veiled Spirit's peak
Falls upon Matter's stark inconscient sleep
As if a pale moonbeam on a dense glade,
And Mind in a half-light moves amid half-truths
And the human heart knows only human love
And life is a stumbling and imperfect force
And the body counts out its precarious days,
You shall be born into man's dubious hours
In forms that hide the soul's divinity
And show through veils of the earth's doubting air
My glory breaking as through clouds a sun,
Or burning like a rare and inward fire,
And with my nameless influence fill men's lives.
Yet shall they look up as to peaks of God
And feel God like a circumambient air
And rest on God as on a motionless base.
Yet shall there glow on mind like a horned moon
The Spirit's crescent splendour in pale skies

And light man's life upon his Godward road.
But more there is concealed in God's Beyond
That shall one day reveal its hidden face.
Now mind is all and its uncertain ray,
Mind is the leader of the body and life,
Mind the thought-driven chariot of the soul
Carrying the luminous wanderer in the night
To vistas of a far uncertain dawn,
To the end of the Spirit's fathomless desire,
To its dream of absolute truth and utter bliss.
There are greater destinies mind cannot surmise
Fixed on the summit of the evolving Path
The Traveller now treads in the Ignorance,
Unaware of his next step, not knowing his goal.
Mind is not all his tireless climb can reach,
There is a fire on the apex of the worlds,
There is a house of the Eternal's light,
There is an infinite truth, an absolute power.
The Spirit's mightiness shall cast off its mask;
Its greatness shall be felt shaping the world's course:
It shall be seen in its own veilless beams,
A star rising from the Inconscient's night,
A sun climbing to Supernature's peak.
Abandoning the dubious middle Way,
A few shall glimpse the miraculous Origin
And some shall feel in you the secret Force
And they shall turn to meet a nameless tread,
Adventurers into a mightier Day.
Ascending out of the limiting breadths of mind,
They shall discover the world's huge design
And step into the Truth, the Right, the Vast.
You shall reveal to them the hidden eternities,
The breath of infinitudes not yet revealed,
Some rapture of the bliss that made the world,
Some rush of the force of God's omnipotence,
Some beam of the omniscient Mystery.

But when the hour of the Divine draws near
The Mighty Mother shall take birth in Time
And God be born into the human clay
In forms made ready by your human lives.
Then shall the Truth supreme be given to men:
There is a being beyond the being of mind,
An Immeasurable cast into many forms,
A miracle of the multitudinous One,
There is a consciousness mind cannot touch,
Its speech cannot utter nor its thought reveal.
It has no home on earth, no centre in man,
Yet is the source of all things thought and done,
The fount of the creation and its works,
It is the origin of all truth here,
The sun-orb of mind's fragmentary rays,
Infinity's heaven that spills the rain of God,
The Immense that calls to man to expand the Spirit,
The wide Aim that justifies his narrow attempts,
A channel for the little he tastes of bliss.
Some shall be made the glory's receptacles
And vehicles of the Eternal's luminous power.
These are the high forerunners, the heads of Time,
The great deliverers of earth-bound mind,
The high transfigurers of human clay,
The first-born of a new supernal race.
The incarnate dual Power shall open God's door,
Eternal supermind touch earthly Time.
The superman shall wake in mortal man
And manifest the hidden demigod
Or grow into the God-Light and God-Force
Revealing the secret deity in the cave.
Then shall the earth be touched by the Supreme,
His bright unveiled Transcendence shall illumine
The mind and heart and force the life and act
To interpret his inexpressible mystery
In a heavenly alphabet of Divinity's signs.

His living cosmic spirit shall enring,
Annulling the decree of death and pain,
Erasing the formulas of the Ignorance,
With the deep meaning of beauty and life's hid sense,
The being ready for immortality,
His regard crossing infinity's mystic waves
Bring back to Nature her early joy to live,
The metred heart-beats of a lost delight,
The cry of a forgotten ecstasy,
The dance of the first world-creating Bliss.
The Immanent shall be the witness God
Watching on his many-petalled lotus-throne
His actionless being and his silent might
Ruling earth-nature by eternity's law,
A thinker waking the Inconscient's world,
An immobile centre of many infinitudes
In his thousand-pillared temple by Time's sea.
Then shall the embodied being live as one
Who is a thought, a will of the Divine,
A mask or robe of his divinity,
An instrument and partner of his Force,
A point or line drawn in the infinite,
A manifest of the Imperishable.
The supermind shall be his nature's fount,
The Eternal's truth shall mould his thoughts and acts,
The Eternal's truth shall be his light and guide.
All then shall change, a magic order come
Overtopping this mechanical universe.
A mightier race shall inhabit the mortal's world.
On Nature's luminous tops, on the Spirit's ground,
The superman shall reign as king of life,
Make earth almost the mate and peer of heaven,
And lead towards God and truth man's ignorant heart
And lift towards godhead his mortality.
A power released from circumscribing bounds,
Its height pushed up beyond death's hungry reach,

Life's tops shall flame with the Immortal's thoughts,
Light shall invade the darkness of its base.
Then in the process of evolving Time
All shall be drawn into a single plan,
A divine harmony shall be earth's law,
Beauty and joy remould her way to live:
Even the body shall remember God,
Nature shall draw back from mortality
And Spirit's fires shall guide the earth's blind force;
Knowledge shall bring into the aspirant Thought
A high proximity to Truth and God.
The supermind shall claim the world for Light
And thrill with love of God the enamoured heart
And place Light's crown on Nature's lifted head
And found Light's reign on her unshaking base.
A greater truth than earth's shall roof-in earth
And shed its sunlight on the roads of mind;
A power infallible shall lead the thought,
A seeing Puissance govern life and act,
In earthly hearts kindle the Immortal's fire.
A soul shall wake in the Inconscient's house;
The mind shall be God-vision's tabernacle,
The body intuition's instrument,
And life a channel for God's visible power.
All earth shall be the Spirit's manifest home,
Hidden no more by the body and the life,
Hidden no more by the mind's ignorance;
An unerring Hand shall shape event and act.
The Spirit's eyes shall look through Nature's eyes,
The Spirit's force shall occupy Nature's force.
This world shall be God's visible garden-house,
The earth shall be a field and camp of God,
Man shall forget consent to mortality
And his embodied frail impermanence.
This universe shall unseal its occult sense,
Creation's process change its antique front,

An ignorant evolution's hierarchy
Release the Wisdom chained below its base.
The Spirit shall be the master of his world
Lurking no more in form's obscurity
And Nature shall reverse her action's rule,
The outward world disclose the Truth it veils;
All things shall manifest the covert God,
All shall reveal the Spirit's light and might
And move to its destiny of felicity.
Even should a hostile force cling to its reign
And claim its right's perpetual sovereignty
And man refuse his high spiritual fate,
Yet shall the secret Truth in things prevail.
For in the march of all-fulfilling Time
The hour must come of the Transcendent's will:
All turns and winds towards his predestined ends
In Nature's fixed inevitable course
Decreed since the beginning of the worlds
In the deep essence of created things:
Even there shall come as a high crown of all
The end of Death, the death of Ignorance.
But first high Truth must set her feet on earth
And man aspire to the Eternal's light
And all his members feel the Spirit's touch
And all his life obey an inner Force.
This too shall be; for a new life shall come,
A body of the Superconscient's truth,
A native field of Supernature's mights:
It shall make earth's nescient ground Truth's colony,
Make even the Ignorance a transparent robe
Through which shall shine the brilliant limbs of Truth
And Truth shall be a sun on Nature's head
And Truth shall be the guide of Nature's steps
And Truth shall gaze out of her nether deeps.
When superman is born as Nature's king
His presence shall transfigure Matter's world:

He shall light up Truth's fire in Nature's night,
He shall lay upon the earth Truth's greater law;
Man too shall turn towards the Spirit's call.
Awake to his hidden possibility,
Awake to all that slept within his heart
And all that Nature meant when earth was formed
And the Spirit made this ignorant world his home,
He shall aspire to Truth and God and Bliss.
Interpreter of a diviner law
And instrument of a supreme design,
The higher kind shall lean to lift up man.
Man shall desire to climb to his own heights.
The truth above shall wake a nether truth,
Even the dumb earth become a sentient force.
The Spirit's tops and Nature's base shall draw
Near to the secret of their separate truth
And know each other as one deity.
The Spirit shall look out through Matter's gaze
And Matter shall reveal the Spirit's face.
Then man and superman shall be at one
And all the earth become a single life.
Even the multitude shall hear the Voice
And turn to commune with the Spirit within
And strive to obey the high spiritual law:
This earth shall stir with impulses sublime,
Humanity awake to deepest self,
Nature the hidden godhead recognise.
Even the many shall some answer make
And bear the splendour of the Divine's rush
And his impetuous knock at unseen doors.
A heavenlier passion shall upheave men's lives,
Their mind shall share in the ineffable gleam,
Their heart shall feel the ecstasy and the fire.
Earth's bodies shall be conscious of a soul;
Mortality's bondslaves shall unloose their bonds,
Mere men into spiritual beings grow

And see awake the dumb divinity.
Intuitive beams shall touch the nature's peaks,
A revelation stir the nature's depths;
The Truth shall be the leader of their lives,
Truth shall dictate their thought and speech and act,
They shall feel themselves lifted nearer to the sky,
As if a little lower than the gods.
For knowledge shall pour down in radiant streams
And even darkened mind quiver with new life
And kindle and burn with the Ideal's fire
And turn to escape from mortal ignorance.
The frontiers of the Ignorance shall recede,
More and more souls shall enter into light,
Minds lit, inspired, the occult summoner hear
And lives blaze with a sudden inner flame
And hearts grow enamoured of divine delight
And human wills tune to the divine will,
These separate selves the Spirit's oneness feel,
These senses of heavenly sense grow capable,
The flesh and nerves of a strange ethereal joy
And mortal bodies of immortality.
A divine force shall flow through tissue and cell
And take the charge of breath and speech and act
And all the thoughts shall be a glow of suns
And every feeling a celestial thrill.
Often a lustrous inner dawn shall come
Lighting the chambers of the slumbering mind;
A sudden bliss shall run through every limb
And Nature with a mightier Presence fill.
Thus shall the earth open to divinity
And common natures feel the wide uplift,
Illumine common acts with the Spirit's ray
And meet the deity in common things.
Nature shall live to manifest secret God,
The Spirit shall take up the human play,
This earthly life become the life divine."

The measure of that subtle music ceased.
Down with a hurried swimming floating lapse
Through unseen worlds and bottomless spaces forced
Sank like a star the soul of Savitri.
Amidst a laughter of unearthly lyres
She heard around her nameless voices cry
Triumphing, an innumerable sound.
A choir of rushing winds to meet her came.
She bore the burden of infinity
And felt the stir of all ethereal space.
Pursuing her in her fall, implacably sweet,
A face was over her which seemed a youth's,
Symbol of all the beauty eyes see not,
Crowned as with peacock plumes of gorgeous hue
Framing a sapphire, whose heart-disturbing smile
Insatiably attracted to delight,
Voluptuous to the embraces of her soul.
Changed in its shape, yet rapturously the same,
It grew a woman's dark and beautiful
Like a mooned night with drifting star-gemmed clouds,
A shadowy glory and a stormy depth,
Turbulent in will and terrible in love.
Eyes in which Nature's blind ecstatic life
Sprang from some spirit's passionate content,
Missioned her to the whirling dance of earth.
Amidst the headlong rapture of her fall
Held like a bird in a child's satisfied hands,
In an enamoured grasp her spirit strove
Admitting no release till Time should end,
And, as the fruit of the mysterious joy,
She kept within her strong embosoming soul
Like a flower hidden in the heart of spring
The soul of Satyavan drawn down by her
Inextricably in that mighty lapse.
Invisible heavens in a thronging flight
Soared past her as she fell. Then all the blind

And near attraction of the earth compelled
Fearful rapidities of downward bliss.
Lost in the giddy proneness of that speed,
Whirled, sinking, overcome she disappeared,
Like a leaf spinning from the tree of heaven,
In broad unconsciousness as in a pool;
A hospitable softness drew her in
Into a wonder of miraculous depths,
Above her closed a darkness of great wings
And she was buried in a mother's breast.
    Then from a timeless plane that watches Time,
A Spirit gazed out upon destiny,
In its endless moment saw the ages pass.
All still was in a silence of the gods.
The prophet moment covered limitless Space
And cast into the heart of hurrying Time
A diamond light of the Eternal's peace,
A crimson seed of God's felicity;
A glance from the gaze fell of undying Love.
A wonderful face looked out with deathless eyes;
A hand was seen drawing the golden bars
That guard the imperishable secrecies.
A key turned in a mystic lock of Time.
But where the silence of the gods had passed,
A greater harmony from the stillness born
Surprised with joy and sweetness yearning hearts,
An ecstasy and a laughter and a cry.
A power leaned down, a happiness found its home.
Over wide earth brooded the infinite bliss.

END OF CANTO ONE
End of Book Eleven

BOOK TWELVE

Epilogue

The Return to Earth

OUT of abysmal trance her spirit woke.
Lain on the earth-mother's calm inconscient breast
She saw the green-clad branches lean above
Guarding her sleep with their enchanted life,
And overhead a blue-winged ecstasy
Fluttered from bough to bough with high-pitched call.
Into the magic secrecy of the woods
Peering through an emerald lattice-window of leaves,
In indolent skies reclined, the thinning day
Turned to its slow fall into evening's peace.
She pressed the living body of Satyavan:
On her body's wordless joy to be and breathe
She bore the blissful burden of his head
Between her breasts' warm labour of delight,
The waking gladness of her members felt
The weight of heaven in his limbs, a touch
Summing the whole felicity of things,
And all her life was conscious of his life
And all her being rejoiced enfolding his.
The immense remoteness of her trance had passed;
Human she was once more, earth's Savitri,
Yet felt in her illimitable change.
A power dwelt in her soul too great for earth,
A bliss lived in her heart too large for heaven;
Light too intense for thought and love too boundless
For earth's emotions lit her skies of mind
And spread through her deep and happy seas of soul.
All that is sacred in the world drew near
To her divine passivity of mood.
A marvellous voice of silence breathed its thoughts.
All things in Time and Space she had taken for hers;

In her they moved, by her they lived and were,
The whole wide world clung to her for delight,
Created for her rapt embrace of love.
Now in her spaceless self released from bounds
Unnumbered years seemed moments long drawn out,
The brilliant time-flakes of eternity.
Outwingings of a bird from its bright home,
Her earthly morns were radiant flights of joy.
Boundless she was, a form of infinity.
Absorbed no longer by the moment's beat
Her spirit the unending future felt
And lived with all the unbeginning past.
Her life was a dawn's victorious opening,
The past and unborn days had joined their dreams,
Old vanished eves and far arriving noons
Hinted to her a vision of prescient hours.
Supine in musing bliss she lay awhile
Given to the wonder of a waking trance;
Half-risen then she sent her gaze around,
As if to recover old sweet trivial threads,
Old happy thoughts, small treasured memories,
And weave them into one immortal day.
Ever she held on the paradise of her breast
Her lover charmed into a fathomless sleep,
Lain like an infant spirit unaware
Lulled on the verge of two consenting worlds.
But soon she leaned down over her loved to call
His mind back to her with her travelling touch
On his closed eyelids; settled was her still look
Of strong delight, not yearning now, but large
With limitless joy or sovereign last content,
Pure, passionate with the passion of the gods.
Desire stirred not its wings; for all was made
An overarching of celestial rays
Like the absorbed control of sky on plain,
Heaven's leaning down to embrace from all sides earth,

A quiet rapture, a vast security.
Then sighing to her touch the soft-winged sleep
Rose hovering from his flowerlike lids and flew
Murmurous away. Awake, he found her eyes
Waiting for his, and felt her hands, and saw
The earth his home given back to him once more
And her made his again, his passion's all.
With his arms' encircling hold around her locked,
A living knot to make possession close,
He murmured with hesitating lips her name,
And vaguely recollecting wonder cried,
"Whence hast thou brought me captive back, love-chained,
To thee and sunlight's walls, O golden beam
And casket of all sweetness, Savitri,
Godhead and woman, moonlight of my soul?
For surely I have travelled in strange worlds
By thee companioned, a pursuing spirit,
Together we have disdained the gates of night.
I have turned away from the celestials' joy
And heaven's insufficient without thee.
Where now has passed that formidable Shape
Which rose against us, the Spirit of the Void,
Claiming the world for Death and Nothingness,
Denying God and soul? Or was all a dream
Or a vision seen in a spiritual sleep,
A symbol of the oppositions of Time
Or a mind-lit beacon of significance
In some stress of darkness lighting on the Way
Or guiding a swimmer through the straits of Death,
Or finding with the succour of its ray
In a gully mid the crowded streets of Chance
The soul that into the world-adventure came,
A scout and voyager from Eternity?"
But she replied, "Our parting was the dream;
We are together, we live, O Satyavan.
Look round thee and behold, glad and unchanged

Our home, this forest with its thousand cries
And the whisper of the wind among the leaves
And, through rifts in emerald scene, the evening sky,
God's canopy of blue sheltering our lives,
And the birds crying for heart's happiness,
Winged poets of our solitary reign,
Our friends on earth where we are king and queen.
Only our souls have left Death's night behind,
Changed by a mighty dream's reality,
Illumined by the light of symbol worlds
And the stupendous summit self of things,
And stood at Godhead's gates limitless, free."
   Then filled with the glory of their happiness
They rose and with safe clinging fingers locked
Hung on each other in a silent look.
But he with a new wonder in his heart
And a new flame of worship in his eyes:
"What high change is in thee, O Savitri? Bright
Ever thou wast, a goddess still and pure,
Yet dearer to me by thy sweet human parts
Earth gave thee making thee yet more divine.
My adoration mastered, my desire
Bent down to make its subject, my daring clasped,
Claiming by body and soul my life's estate,
Rapture's possession, love's sweet property,
A statue of silence in my templed spirit,
A yearning godhead and a golden bride.
But now thou seemst almost too high and great
For mortal worship; Time lies below thy feet
And the whole world seems only a part of thee,
Thy presence the hushed heaven I inhabit,
And thou lookst on me in the gaze of the stars,
Yet art the earthly keeper of my soul,
My life a whisper of thy dreaming thoughts,
My morns a gleaming of thy spirit's wings,
And day and night are of thy beauty part.

Hast thou not taken my heart to treasure it
In the secure environment of thy breast?
Awakened from the silence and the sleep,
I have consented for thy sake to be.
By thee I have greatened my mortal arc of life,
But now far heavens, unmapped infinitudes
Thou hast brought me, thy illimitable gift!
If to fill these thou lift thy sacred flight,
My human earth will still demand thy bliss.
Make still my life through thee a song of joy
And all my silence wide and deep with thee."
A heavenly queen consenting to his will,
She clasped his feet, by her enshrining hair
Enveloped in a velvet cloak of love,
And answered softly like a murmuring lute:
"All now is changed, yet all is still the same.
Lo, we have looked upon the face of God,
Our life has opened with divinity.
We have borne identity with the Supreme
And known his meaning in our mortal lives.
Our love has grown greater by that mighty touch
And learned its heavenly significance,
Yet nothing is lost of mortal love's delight.
Heaven's touch fulfils but cancels not our earth:
Our bodies need each other in the same last;
Still in our breasts repeat heavenly secret rhythm
Our human heart-beats passionately close.
Still am I she who came to thee mid the murmur
Of sunlit leaves upon this forest verge;
I am the Madran, I am Savitri.
All that I was before, I am to thee still,
Close comrade of thy thoughts and hopes and toils,
All happy contraries I would join for thee.
All sweet relations marry in our life;
I am thy kingdom even as thou art mine,
The sovereign and the slave of thy desire,

Thy prone possessor, sister of thy soul
And mother of thy wants; thou art my world,
The earth I need, the heaven my thoughts desire,
The world I inhabit and the god I adore.
Thy body is my body's counterpart
Whose every limb my answering limb desires,
Whose heart is key to all my heart-beats, — this
I am and thou to me, O Satyavan.
Our wedded walk through life begins anew,
No gladness lost, no depth of mortal joy.
Let us go through this new world that is the same,
For it is given back, but it is known,
A playing-ground and dwelling-house of God
Who hides himself in bird and beast and man
Sweetly to find himself again by love,
By oneness. His presence leads the rhythms of life
That seek for mutual joy in spite of pain.
We have each other found, O Satyavan,
In the great light of the discovered soul.
Let us go back, for eve is in the skies.
Now grief is dead and serene bliss remains
The heart of all our days for evermore.
Lo, all these beings in this wonderful world!
Let us give joy to all, for joy is ours.
For not for ourselves alone our spirits came
Out of the veil of the Unmanifest,
Out of the deep immense Unknowable
Upon the ignorant breast of dubious earth,
Into the ways of labouring, seeking men,
Two fires that burn towards that parent Sun,
Two rays that travel to the original Light.
To lead man's soul towards truth and God we are born,
To draw the chequered scheme of mortal life
Into some semblance of the Immortal's plan,
To shape it closer to an image of God,
A little nearer to the Idea divine."

She closed her arms about his breast and head
As if to keep him on her bosom worn
For ever through the journeying of the years.
So for a while they stood entwined, their kiss
And passion-tranced embrace a meeting-point
In their commingling spirits one for ever,
Two-souled, two-bodied for the joys of Time.
Then hand in hand they left that solemn place
Full now of mute unusual memories,
To the green distance of their sylvan home
Returning slowly through the forest's heart.
Round them the afternoon to evening changed;
Light slipped down to the brightly sleeping verge,
And the birds came back winging to their nests,
And day and night leaned to each other's arms.

   Now the dusk shadowy trees stood close around
Like dreaming spirits and, delaying night,
The grey-eyed pensive evening heard their steps,
And from all points the cries and movements came
Of the four-footed wanderers of the night
Approaching. Then a human rumour rose
Long alien to their solitary days,
Invading the charmed wilderness of leaves
Once sacred to secluded loneliness
With violent breaking of its virgin sleep.
Through the screened dusk it deepened still and there neared
Floating of many voices and the sound
Of many feet, till on their sight broke in
As if a coloured wave upon the eye
The brilliant strenuous crowded days of man.
Topped by a flaring multitude of lights
A great resplendent company arrived.
Life in its ordered tumult wavering came
Bringing its stream of unknown faces, thronged
With gold-fringed headdresses, gold-broidered robes,

Glittering of ornaments, fluttering of hems,
Hundreds of hands parted the forest-boughs,
Hundreds of eyes searched the entangled glades.
Calm white-clad priests their grave-eyed sweetness brought,
Strong warriors in their glorious armour shone,
The proud-hooved steeds came trampling through the wood.
In front King Dyumatsena walked, no more
Blind, faltering-limbed, but his far-questing eyes
Restored to all their confidence in light
Took seeingly this imaged outer world;
Firmly he trod with monarch step the soil.
By him that queen and mother's anxious face
Came changed from its habitual burdened look
Which in its drooping strength of tired toil
Had borne the fallen life of those she loved.
Her patient paleness wore a pensive glow
Like evening's subdued gaze of gathered light
Departing, which foresees sunrise her child.
Sinking in quiet splendours of her sky,
She lives awhile to muse upon that hope,
The brilliance of her rich receding gleam
A thoughtful prophecy of lyric dawn.
Her eyes were first to find her children's forms.
But at the vision of the beautiful twain
The air awoke perturbed with scaling cries,
And the swift parents hurrying to their child,—
Their cause of life now who had given him breath,—
Possessed him with their arms. Then tenderly
Cried Dyumatsena chiding Satyavan:
"The fortunate gods have looked on me today,
A kingdom seeking came and heaven's rays.
But where wast thou? Thou hast tormented gladness
With fear's dull shadow, O my child, my life.
What danger kept thee for the darkening woods?
Or how could pleasure in her ways forget
That useless orbs without thee are my eyes

Which only for thy sake rejoice at light?
Not like thyself was this done, Savitri,
Who ledst not back thy husband to our arms,
Knowing with him beside me only is taste
In food and for his touch evening and morn
I live content with my remaining days."
But Satyavan replied with smiling lips,
"Lay all on her; she is the cause of all.
With her enchantments she has twined me round.
Behold, at noon leaving this house of clay
I wandered in far-off eternities,
Yet still, a captive in her golden hands,
I tread your little hillock called green earth
And in the moments of your transient sun
Live glad among the busy works of men."
Then all eyes turned their wondering looks where stood,
A deepening redder gold upon her cheeks,
With lowered lids the noble lovely child,
And one consenting thought moved every breast.
"What gleaming marvel of the earth or skies
Stands silently by human Satyavan
To mark a brilliance in the dusk of eve?
If this is she of whom the world has heard,
Wonder no more at any happy change.
Each easy miracle of felicity
Of her transmuting heart the alchemy is."
Then one spoke there who seemed a priest and sage:
"O woman soul, what light, what power revealed,
Working the rapid marvels of this day,
Opens for us by thee a happier age?"
Her lashes fluttering upwards gathered in
To a vision which had scanned immortal things,
Rejoicing, human forms for their delight.
They claimed for their deep childlike motherhood
The life of all these souls to be her life,
Then falling veiled the light. Low she replied,

"Awakened to the meaning of my heart
That to feel love and oneness is to live
And this the magic of our golden change,
Is all the truth I know or seek, O sage."
Wondering at her and her too luminous words
Westward they turned in the fast-gathering night.

　From the entangling verges freed they came
Into a dimness of the sleeping earth
And travelled through her faint and slumbering plains.
Murmur and movement and the tread of men
Broke the night's solitude; the neigh of steeds
Rose from that indistinct and voiceful sea
Of life and all along its marchings swelled
The rhyme of hooves, the chariot's homeward voice.
Drawn by white manes upon a high-roofed car
In flare of the unsteady torches went
With linked hands Satyavan and Savitri,
Hearing a marriage march and nuptial hymn,
Where waited them the many-voiced human world.
Numberless the stars swam on their shadowy field
Describing in the gloom the ways of light.
Then while they skirted yet the southward verge,
Lost in the halo of her musing brows
Night, splendid with the moon dreaming in heaven
In silver peace, possessed her luminous reign.
She brooded through her stillness on a thought
Deep-guarded by her mystic folds of light,
And in her bosom nursed a greater dawn.

THE END

SRI AUROBINDO'S LETTERS

ON *SAVITRI*

LETTERS ON *SAVITRI*

1

There is a previous draft, the result of the many retouchings of which somebody told you; but in that form it would not have been a *"magnum opus"* at all. Besides, it would have been a legend and not a symbol. I therefore started recasting the whole thing; only the best passages and lines of the old draft will remain, altered so as to fit into the new frame.

No, I do not work at the poem once a week; I have other things to do. Once a month perhaps, I look at the new form of the first book and make such changes as inspiration points out to me — so that nothing shall fall below the minimum height which I have fixed for it.

— 1931

Savitri...is blank verse without enjambment (except rarely) — each line a thing by itself and arranged in paragraphs of one, two, three, four, five lines (rarely a longer series), in an attempt to catch something of the Upanishadic and Kalidasian movement, so far as that is a possibility in English. You can't take that as a model — it is too difficult a rhythm-structure to be a model. I shall myself know whether it is a success or not, only when I have finished two or three books. But where is the time now for such a work? When the supramental has finished coming down, then perhaps.

— 1932

Don't make prophecies. How do you know that *Savitri* is or is going to be supramental poetry? It is not, in fact — it is only an attempt to render into poetry a symbol of things occult and spiritual.

— 1933

Possibly[1] — but in this world certainties are few. Anyhow in the effort to quote I have succeeded in putting the first few hundred

---

[1] Sri Aurobindo was asked: "Will you be able after all to give quotations from *Savitri*? I really wish you could."

lines into something like a final form—which is a surprising progress and very gratifying to me even if it brings no immediate satisfaction to you.

—1933

What you write about your inspiration is very interesting. There is no invariable how—except that I receive from above my head and receive changes and corrections from above without any initiation by myself or labour of the brain. Even if I change a hundred times, the mind does not work at that, it only receives. Formerly it used not to be so, the mind was always labouring at the stuff of an unshaped formation.... The poems come as a stream beginning at the first line and ending at the last—only some remain with one or two changes, others have to be recast if the first inspiration was an inferior one. *Savitri* is a work by itself unlike all the others. I made some eight or ten recasts of it originally under the old insufficient inspiration. Afterwards I am altogether rewriting it, concentrating on the first book and working on it over and over again with the hope that every line may be of a perfect perfection—but I have hardly any time now for such work.

—1934

That is very simple.[1] I used *Savitri* as a means of ascension. I began with it on a certain mental level, each time I could reach a higher level I rewrote from that level. Moreover I was particular—if part seemed to me to come from any lower levels I was not satisfied to leave it because it was good poetry. All had to be as far as possible of the same mint. In fact *Savitri* has not been regarded by me as a poem to be written and finished, but as a field of experimentation to see how far poetry could be written from one's own yogic consciousness and how that could be made creative. I did not rewrite *Rose of God* or the sonnets except for two or three verbal alterations made at the moment.

—1936

---

[1] The question was: "We have been wondering why you should have to write and rewrite your poetry—for instance, *Savitri* ten or twelve times—when you have all the

Savitri was originally written many years ago before the Mother came, as a narrative poem in two parts, Part I Earth and Part II Beyond (these two parts are still extant in the scheme[1]) each of four books — or rather Part II consisted of three books and an epilogue. Twelve books to an epic is a classical superstition, but the new *Savitri* may extend to ten books — if much is added in the final version it may be even twelve.[2] The first book has been lengthening and lengthening out till it must be over 2000 lines, but I shall break up the original first four into five, I think — in fact I have already started doing so. These first five will be, as I conceive them now, the Book of Birth, the Book of Quest, the Book of Love, the Book of Fate, the Book of Death. As for the second Part, I have not touched it yet. There was no climbing of planes there in the first version — rather *Savitri* moved through the worlds of Night, of Twilight, of Day — all of course in a spiritual sense — and ended by calling down the power of the Highest Worlds of Sachchidananda. I had no idea of what the supramental World could be like at that time, so it could not enter into the scheme. As for expressing the supramental inspiration, that is a matter of the future.

—1936

Savitri is represented in the poem as an incarnation of the Divine Mother.... This incarnation is supposed to have taken place in far past times when the whole thing had to be opened, so as to "hew the ways of Immortality".

—1936

The poem was originally written from a lower level, a mixture perhaps of the inner mind, psychic, poetic intelligence, sublimised vital, afterwards with the Higher Mind, often illumined and intuitivised, intervening. Most of the stuff of the first book is new or else the old so altered as to be no more what it was; the best of the old has sometimes been kept almost intact because it had already

---

inspiration at your command and do not have to receive it with the difficulty that faces budding Yogis like us."

[1] In the present version, there are three parts.

[2] As is actually the case now.

the higher inspiration. Moreover, there have been made several
successive revisions each trying to lift the general level higher and
higher towards a possible Overmind poetry. As it now stands there
is a general Overmind influence, I believe, sometimes coming fully
through, sometimes colouring the poetry of the other higher planes
fused together, sometimes lifting any one of these higher planes to
its highest or the psychic, poetic intelligence or vital towards them.

—1936

I don't think about the technique because thinking is no longer in
my line. But I see and feel for it when the lines are coming through
and afterwards in revision of the work. I don't bother about details
while writing, because that would only hamper the inspiration. I
let it come through without interference; only pausing if there is an
obvious inadequacy felt, in which case I conclude that it is a wrong
inspiration or inferior level that has cut across the communication.
If the inspiration is the right one, then I have not to bother about the
technique then or afterwards, for there comes through the perfect
line with the perfect rhythm inextricably intertwined or rather
fused into an inseparable and single unity; if there is anything
wrong with the expression that carries with it an imperfection in
the rhythm, if there is a flaw in the rhythm, the expression also does
not carry its full weight, is not absolutely inevitable. If on the other
hand the inspiration is not throughout the right one, then there is
an after examination and recasting of part or whole. The things I lay
most stress on then are whether each line in itself is the inevitable
thing not only as a whole but in each word; whether there is the
right distribution of sentence lengths (an immensely important
thing in this kind of blank verse); whether the lines are in their right
place, for all the lines may be perfect, but they may not combine
perfectly together — bridges may be needed, alterations of position
so as to create the right development and perspective etc., etc.
Pauses hardly exist in this kind of blank verse; variations of rhythm
as between the lines, of caesura, of the distribution of long and
short, clipped and open syllables, manifold constructions of vowel
and consonant sounds, alliteration, assonances, etc., distribution
into one line, two line, three or four or five line, many line
sentences, care to make each line tell by itself in its own mass and
force and at the same time form a harmonious whole sentence —

these are the important things. But all that is usually taken care of by the inspiration itself, for as I know and have the habit of the technique, the inspiration provides what I want according to standing orders. If there is a defect I appeal to headquarters, till a proper version comes along or the defect is removed by a word or phrase substitute that flashes — with the necessary sound and sense. These things are not done by thinking or seeking for the right thing — the two agents are sight and call. Also feeling — the solar plexus has to be satisfied and, until it is, revision after revision has to continue. I may add that the technique does not go by any set mental rule — for the object is not perfect technical elegance according to precept but sound-significance filling out the word-significance. If that can be done by breaking rules, well, so much the worse for the rule.

— 1936

I can never be certain of newly written stuff (I mean in this *Savitri*) until I have looked at it again after an interval. Apart from the quality of new lines, there is the combination with others in the whole which I have modified more than anything else in my past revisions.

— 1936

Allow me to point out that whatever I did in a jiffy would not be any more than provisionally final. It is not a question of making a few changes in individual lines, that is a very minor problem; the real finality only comes when all is felt as a perfect whole, no line jarring with or falling away from the level of the whole though some may rise above it and also all the parts in their proper place making the right harmony. It is an inner feeling that has to decide that.... Unfortunately the mind can't arrange these things, one has to wait till the absolutely right thing comes in a sort of receptive self-opening and calling-down condition. Hence the months.

— 1936

I have done an enormous amount of work with *Savitri*. The third section has been recast — not rewritten — so as to give it a more consistent epic swing and amplitude and elevation of level. The fourth section, the Worlds, is undergoing transformation. The "Life" part is in a way finished, though I shall have to go over the ground perhaps some five or six times more to ensure perfection of detail. I am now starting a recasting of the "Mind" part of which I had only made a sort of basic rough draft. I hope that this time the work will stand as more final and definitive.

—1938

I have been kept too occupied with other things to make much headway with the poem — except that I have spoiled your beautiful neat copy of the "Worlds" under the oestrus of the restless urge for more and more perfection; but we are here for World-improvement, so I hope that is excusable.

—1938

I have not been able to make any headway with *Savitri* — owing to lack of time and also to an appalled perception of the disgraceful imperfection of all the sections after the first two. But I have tackled them again as I think I wrote to you and have pulled up the third section to a higher consistency of level; the "Worlds" have fallen into a state of manuscript chaos, corrections upon corrections, additions upon additions, rearrangements on rearrangements out of which perhaps some cosmic beauty will emerge!

—1938

You will see when you get the full typescript [of the first three books] that *Savitri* has grown to an enormous length so that it is no longer quite the same thing as the poem you saw then. There are now three books in the first part. The first, the Book of Beginnings, comprises five cantos which cover the same ground as what you typed but contains also much more that is new. The small passage about Aswapati and the other worlds has been replaced by a new book, the Book of the Traveller of the Worlds, in fourteen cantos with many thousand lines. There is also a third sufficiently long book, the Book of the Divine Mother. In the new plan of the poem there is a second part consisting of five books: two of these, the Book of Birth and Quest and the Book of Love, have been

completed and another, the Book of Fate, is almost complete. Two
others, the Book of Yoga and the Book of Death, have still to be
written, though a part needs only a thorough recasting. Finally,
there is the third part consisting of four books, the Book of Eternal
Night, the Book of the Dual Twilight, the Book of Everlasting Day
and the Return to Earth, which have to be entirely recast and the
third of them largely rewritten. So it will be a long time before
Savitri is complete.

In the new form it will be a sort of poetic philosophy of the
Spirit and of Life much profounder in its substance and vaster in its
scope than was intended in the original poem. I am trying of course
to keep it at a very high level of inspiration, but in so large a plan
covering most subjects of philosophical thought and vision and
many aspects of spiritual experience there is bound to be much
variation of tone: but that is, I think, necessary for the richness and
completeness of the treatment.

— 1946

I am not at all times impervious to criticism; I have accepted some
of yours and changed my lines accordingly; I have also though not
often accepted some adverse criticisms from outside and re-
moulded a line or a passage from the [poem] here and there. But
your criticisms are based upon an understanding appreciation of
the poem, its aim, meaning, method, the turn and quality of its lan-
guage and verse technique. In your friend's judgments I find an
entire absence of any such understanding and accordingly I find
his criticisms to be irrelevant and invalid. What one does not under-
stand or perceive its meaning and spirit, one cannot fruitfully
criticise.

— 1947

I am afraid I am too much preoccupied with the constant clashes
with the world and the devil to write anything at length even about
your new poems [*The Adventure of the Apocalypse*]: a few lines
must suffice. In fact as I had to explain the other day to Dilip, my
only other regular correspondent, my push to write letters or to
new literary production has dwindled almost to zero — this apart
from *Savitri* and even *Savitri* has very much slowed down and I am

only making the last revisions of the First Part already completed; the other two parts are just now in cold storage.

— 1948

2

As to the many criticisms[1] contained in your letter I have a good deal to say; some of them bring forward questions of the technique of mystic poetry about which I wanted to write in an introduction to *Savitri* when it is published, and I may as well say something about that here.

...Rapid transitions from one image to another are a constant feature in *Savitri* as in most mystic poetry. I am not here[2] building a long sustained single picture of the Dawn with a single continuous image or variations of the same image. I am describing a rapid series of transitions, piling one suggestion upon another. There is first a black quietude, then the persistent touch, then the first "beauty and wonder" leading to the magical gate and the "lucent corner". Then comes the failing of the darkness, the simile used ["a falling cloak"] suggesting the rapidity of the change. Then as a result the change of what was once a rift into a wide luminous gap, — if you want to be logically consistent you can look at the rift as a slit in the "cloak" which becomes a big tear. Then all changes into a "brief perpetual sign", the iridescence, then the blaze and the magnificent aura. In such a race of rapid transitions you cannot bind me down to a logical chain of figures or a classical monotone. The mystic Muse is more of an inspired Bacchante of the Dionysian wine than an orderly housewife.

...Again, do you seriously want me to give an accurate scientific description of the earth half in darkness and half in light so as

[1] The nature of these criticisms must not be misunderstood. Just as the merits of *Savitri* were appreciated to the utmost, whatever seemed a shortcoming no matter how slight and negligible in the midst of the abundant excellence was pointedly remarked upon so that Sri Aurobindo might not overlook anything in his work towards what he called "perfect perfection" before the poem came under the scrutiny of non-Aurobindonian critics at the time of publication. The commentator was anxious that there should be no spots on *Savitri's* sun. The purpose was also to get important issues cleared up in relation to the sort of poetry Sri Aurobindo was writing and some of his disciples aspired to write. Knowing the spirit and aim of the criticisms Sri Aurobindo welcomed them, even asked for them. On many occasions — and these provide most of the matter collected here — he vigorously defended himself, but on several he willingly agreed to introduce small changes. Once he is reported to have smiled and said: "Is he satisfied now?" Unfortunately, the opportunity to discuss every part of the poem did not arise and we have, therefore, only a limited number of psychological and technical elucidations by him of his art.

[2] Pp. 3–4.

to spoil my impressionist symbol [1] or else to revert to the conception of earth as a flat and immobile surface? I am not writing a scientific treatise, I am selecting certain ideas and impressions to form a symbol of a partial and temporary darkness of the soul and Nature which seems to a temporary feeling of that which is caught in the Night as if it were universal and eternal. One who is lost in that Night does not think of the other half of the earth as full of light; to him all is Night and the earth a forsaken wanderer in an enduring darkness. If I sacrifice this impressionism and abandon the image of the earth wheeling through dark space I might as well abandon the symbol altogether, for this is a necessary part of it. As a matter of fact in the passage itself earth in its wheeling does come into the dawn and pass from darkness into the light. You must take the idea as a whole and in all its transitions and not press one detail with too literal an insistence. In this poem I present constantly one partial view of life or another temporarily as if it were the whole in order to give full value to the experience of those who are bound by that view, as for instance, the materialist conception and experience of life, but if any one charges me with philosophical inconsistency, then it only means that he does not understand the technique of the Overmind interpretation of life.

... I come next to the passage which you so violently attack, about the Inconscient waking Ignorance. In the first place, the word "formless" is indeed defective, not so much because of any repetition but because it is not the right word or idea and I was not myself satisfied with it. I have changed the passage as follows:

> Then something in the inscrutable darkness stirred;
> A nameless movement, an unthought Idea
> Insistent, dissatisfied, without an aim,
> Something that wished but knew not how to be,
> Teased the Inconscient to wake Ignorance. [2]

But the teasing of the Inconscient remains and evidently you think that it is bad poetic taste to tease something so bodiless and unreal as the Inconscient. But here several fundamental issues arise. First of all, are words like Inconscient and Ignorance necessarily an abstract technical jargon? If so, do not words like consciousness, knowledge etc. undergo the same ban? Is it meant that they are

[1] P. 1.   [2] Pp. 1–2.

abstract philosophical terms and can have no real or concrete meaning, cannot represent things that one feels and senses or must often fight as one fights a visible foe? The Inconscient and the Ignorance may be mere empty abstractions and can be dismissed as irrelevant jargon if one has not come into collision with them or plunged into their dark and bottomless reality. But to me they are realities, concrete powers whose resistance is present everywhere and at all times in its tremendous and boundless mass. In fact, in writing this line I had no intention of teaching philosophy or forcing in an irrelevant metaphysical idea, although the idea may be there in implication. I was presenting a happening that was to me something sensible and, as one might say, psychologically and spiritually concrete. The Inconscient comes in persistently in the cantos of the First Book of *Savitri*: e.g.

> Opponent of that glory of escape,
> The black Inconscient swung its dragon tail
> Lashing a slumbrous Infinite by its force
> Into the deep obscurities of form.[1]

There too a metaphysical idea might be read into or behind the thing seen. But does that make it technical jargon or the whole thing an illegitimate mixture? It is not so to my poetic sense. But you might say, "It is so to the non-mystical reader and it is that reader whom you have to satisfy, as it is for the general reader that you are writing and not for yourself alone." But if I had to write for the general reader I could not have written *Savitri* at all. It is in fact for myself that I have written it and for those who can lend themselves to the subject-matter, images, technique of mystic poetry.

This is the real stumbling-block of mystic poetry and specially mystic poetry of this kind. The mystic feels real and present, even ever present to his experience, intimate to his being, truths which to the ordinary reader are intellectual abstractions or metaphysical speculations. He is writing of experiences that are foreign to the ordinary mentality. Either they are unintelligible to it and in meeting them it flounders about as if in an obscure abyss or it takes them as poetic fancies expressed in intellectually devised images. That was how a critic in the *Hindu* condemned such poems as *Nirvana* and *Transformation*. He said that they were mere intellectual

---

[1] P. 79.

conceptions and images and there was nothing of religious feeling or spiritual experience. Yet *Nirvana*[1] was as close a transcription of a major experience as could be given in language coined by the human mind of a realisation in which the mind was entirely silent and into which no intellectual conception could at all enter. One has to use words and images in order to convey to the mind some perception, some figure of that which is beyond thought. The critic's non-understanding was made worse by such a line as:

> Only the illimitable Permanent
>   Is here.

Evidently he took this as technical jargon, abstract philosophy. There was no such thing; I felt with an overpowering vividness the illimitability or at least something which could not be described by any other term and no other description except the "Permanent" could be made of That which alone existed. To the mystic there is no such thing as an abstraction. Everything which to the intellectual mind is abstract has a concreteness, substantiality which is more real than the sensible form of an object or of a physical event. To me, for instance, consciousness is the very stuff of existence and I can feel it everywhere enveloping and penetrating the stone as much as man or the animal. A movement, a flow of consciousness is not to me an image but a fact. If I wrote "His anger climbed against me in a stream", it would be to the general reader a mere image, not something that was felt by me in a sensible experience; yet I would only be describing in exact terms what actually happened once, a stream of anger, a sensible and violent current of it rising up

---

[1]   All is abolished but the mute Alone.
>   The mind from thought released, the heart from grief
>   Grow inexistent now beyond belief;
> There is no I, no Nature, known-unknown.
> The city, a shadow picture without tone,
>   Floats, quivers unreal; forms without relief
>   Flow, a cinema's vacant shapes; like a reef
> Foundering in shoreless gulfs the world is done.

> Only the illimitable Permanent
>   Is here. A Peace stupendous, featureless, still
>   Replaces all,— what once was I, in It
> A silent unnamed emptiness content
>   Either to fade in the Unknowable
>   Or thrill with the luminous seas of the Infinite.

from downstairs and rushing upon me as I sat in the veranda of the Guest-House, the truth of it being confirmed afterwards by the confession of the person who had the movement. This is only one instance, but all that is spiritual or psychological in Savitri is of that character. What is to be done under these circumstances? The mystical poet can only describe what he has felt, seen in himself or others or in the world just as he has felt or seen it or experienced through exact vision, close contact or identity and leave it to the general reader to understand or not understand or misunderstand according to his capacity. A new kind of poetry demands a new mentality in the recipient as well as in the writer.

Another question is the place of philosophy in poetry or whether it has any place at all. Some romanticists seem to believe that the poet has no right to think at all, only to see and feel. This accusation has been brought against me by many that I think too much and that when I try to write in verse, thought comes in and keeps out poetry. I hold, to the contrary, that philosophy has its place and can even take a leading place along with psychological experience as it does in the Gita.[1] All depends on how it is done, whether it is a dry or a living philosophy, an arid intellectual statement or the expression not only of the living truth of thought but of something of its beauty, its light or its power.

The theory which discourages the poet from thinking or at least from thinking for the sake of the thought proceeds from an extreme romanticist temper, it reaches its acme on one side in the question of the surrealist, "Why do you want poetry to mean anything?" and on the other in Housman's exaltation of pure poetry which he describes paradoxically as a sort of sublime nonsense which does not appeal at all to the mental intelligence but knocks at the solar plexus and awakes a vital and physical rather than intellectual sensation and response. It is of course not that really but a vividness of imagination and feeling which disregards the mind's positive view of things and its logical sequences; the centre or centres it knocks at are not the brain-mind, not even the

---

[1] This dictum about the role of thought should not be taken as contradicting any implication of the sentence in an earlier letter: "Thinking is no longer in my line." What comes from "overhead" through the mystic's silent mind, as in Sri Aurobindo's later poetry, can very well assume a philosophical form. It is the presence of thought-form in poetry that is spoken of here, not the source from which it ultimately derives or the process by which it enters a poem.

poetic intelligence but the subtle physical, the nervous, the vital or the psychic centre. The poem he quotes from Blake is certainly not nonsense, but it has no positive and exact meaning for the intellect or the surface mind; it expresses certain things that are true and real, not nonsense but a deeper sense which we feel powerfully with a great stirring of some inner emotion, but any attempt at exact intellectual statement of them sterilises their sense and spoils their appeal. This is not the method of *Savitri*. Its expression aims at a certain force, directness and spiritual clarity and reality. When it is not understood, it is because the truths it expresses are unfamiliar to the ordinary mind or belong to an untrodden domain or domains or enter into a field of occult experience: it is not because there is any attempt at a dark or vague profundity or at an escape from thought. The thinking is not intellectual but intuitive or more than intuitive, always expressing a vision, a spiritual contact or a knowledge which has come by entering into the thing itself, by identity.

It may be noted that the greater romantic poets did not shun thought; they thought abundantly, almost endlessly. They have their characteristic view of life, something that one might call their philosophy, their world-view, and they express it. Keats was the most romantic of poets, but he could write "To philosophise I dare not yet"; he did not write "I am too much of a poet to philosophise." To philosophise he regarded evidently as mounting on the admiral's flag-ship and flying an almost royal banner. The philosophy of *Savitri* is different but it is persistently there; it expresses or tries to express a total and many-sided vision and experience of all the planes of being and their action upon each other. Whatever language, whatever terms are necessary to convey this truth of vision and experience it uses without scruple or admitting any mental rule of what is or is not poetic. It does not hesitate to employ terms which might be considered as technical when these can be turned to express something direct, vivid and powerful. That need not be an introduction of technical jargon, that is to say, I suppose, special and artificial language, expressing in this case only abstract ideas and generalities without any living truth or reality in them. Such jargon cannot make good literature, much less good poetry. But there is a 'poeticism' which establishes a sanitary cordon against words and ideas which it considers as prosaic but which properly used can strengthen poetry and extend its range. That limitation I do not admit as legitimate.

I have been insisting on these points in view of certain criticisms that have been made by reviewers and others, some of them very capable, suggesting or flatly stating that there was too much thought in my poems or that I am even in my poetry a philosopher rather than a poet. I am justifying a poet's right to think as well as to see and feel, his right to "dare to philosophise". I agree with the modernists in their revolt against the romanticist's insistence on emotionalism and his objection to thinking and philosophical reflection in poetry. But the modernist went too far in his revolt. In trying to avoid what I may call poeticism he ceased to be poetic; wishing to escape from rhetorical writing, rhetorical pretension to greatness and beauty of style, he threw out true poetic greatness and beauty, turned from a deliberately poetic style to a colloquial tone and even to very flat writing; especially he turned away from poetic rhythm to a prose or half-prose rhythm or to no rhythm at all. Also he has weighed too much on thought and has lost the habit of intuitive sight; by turning emotion out of its intimate chamber in the house of Poetry, he has had to bring in to relieve the dryness of much of his thought too much exaggeration of the lower vital and sensational reactions untransformed or else transformed only by exaggeration. Nevertheless he has perhaps restored to the poet the freedom to think as well as to adopt a certain straightforwardness and directness of style.

Now I come to the law prohibiting repetition. This rule aims at a certain kind of intellectual elegance which comes into poetry when the poetic intelligence and the call for a refined and classical taste begin to predominate. It regards poetry as a cultural entertainment and amusement of the highly civilised mind; it interests by a faultless art of words, a constant and ingenious invention, a sustained novelty of ideas, incidents, word and phrase. An unfailing variety or the outward appearance of it is one of the elegances of this art. But all poetry is not of this kind; its rule does not apply to poets like Homer or Valmiki or other early writers. The Veda might almost be described as a mass of repetitions; so might the work of Vaishnava poets and the poetic literature of devotion generally in India. Arnold has noted this distinction when speaking of Homer; he mentioned especially that there is nothing objectionable in the close repetition of the same word in the Homeric way of writing. In many things Homer seems to make a point of repeating himself. He has stock descriptions, epithets always reiterated, lines

even which are constantly repeated again and again when the same
incident returns in his narrative: e.g. the line,

> Doupēsen de pesōn arabēse de teuche' ep' autōi.[1]
> "Down with a thud he fell and his armour clangoured upon
> him."

He does not hesitate also to repeat the bulk of a line with a variation
at the end, e.g.

> Bē de kat' Oulumpoio karēnōn chōomenos kēr.[2]

And again the

> Bē de kat' Oulumpoio karēnōn āïxāsa.[3]

"Down from the peaks of Olympus he came, wrath vexing his heart-
strings" and again, "Down from the peaks of Olympus she came
impetuously darting." He begins another line elsewhere with the
same word and a similar action and with the same nature of a
human movement physical and psychological in a scene of Nature,
here a man's silent sorrow listening to the roar of the ocean:

> Bē d'akeōn para thīna poluphloisboio thalassēs — [4]
> "Silent he walked by the shore of the many-rumoured ocean."

In mystic poetry also repetition is not objectionable; it is
resorted to by many poets, sometimes with insistence. I may cite as
an example the constant repetition of the word ṛtam, truth, some-
times eight or nine times in a short poem of nine or ten stanzas and
often in the same line. This does not weaken the poem, it gives it a
singular power and beauty. The repetition of the same key ideas,
key images and symbols, key words or phrases, key epithets, some-
times key lines or half lines is a constant feature. They give an
atmosphere, a significant structure, a sort of psychological frame,
an architecture. The object here is not to amuse or entertain but
the self-expression of an inner truth, a seeing of things and ideas
not familiar to the common mind, a bringing out of inner experi-
ence. It is the true more than the new that the poet is after. He uses

---

[1] *Iliad* IV.504, V.42, etc.   [2] *Ibid.* I.44.   [3] *Ibid.* IV.74.   [4] *Ibid.* I.34.

āvṛtti, repetition, as one of the most powerful means of carrying home what has been thought or seen and fixing it in the mind in an atmosphere of light and beauty. This kind of repetition I have used largely in *Savitri*. Moreover, the object is not only to present a secret truth in its true form and true vision but to drive it home by the finding of the true word, the true phrase, the *mot juste*, the true image or symbol, if possible the inevitable word; if that is there, nothing else, repetition included, matters much. This is natural when the repetition is intended, serves a purpose; but it can hold even when the repetition is not deliberate but comes in naturally in the stream of the inspiration. I see, therefore, no objection to the recurrence of the same or similar image such as sea and ocean, sky and heaven in one long passage provided each is the right thing and rightly worded in its place. The same rule applies to words, epithets, ideas. It is only if the repetition is clumsy or awkward, too burdensomely insistent, at once unneeded and inexpressive or amounts to a disagreeable and meaningless echo that it must be rejected.

. . . I think there is none of your objections that did not occur to me as possible from a certain kind of criticism when I wrote or I re-read what I had written; but I brushed them aside as invalid or as irrelevant to the kind of poem I was writing. So you must not be surprised at my disregard of them as too slight and unimperative.

— 1946

What you have written as the general theory of the matter seems to be correct and it does not differ substantially from what I wrote. But your phrase about unpurposive repetition might carry a suggestion which I would not be able to accept; it might seem to indicate that the poet must have a "purpose" in whatever he writes and must be able to give a logical account of it to the critical intellect. That is surely not the way in which the poet or at least the mystic poet has to do his work. He does not himself deliberately choose or arrange word and rhythm but only sees it as it comes in the very act of inspiration. If there is any purpose of any kind, it also comes by and in the process of inspiration. He can criticise himself and the work; he can see whether it was a wrong or an inferior movement, he does not set about correcting it by any intellectual method but waits for the true thing to come in its place.

He cannot always account to the logical intellect for what he has done: he feels or intuits, and the reader or critic has to do the same.

Thus I cannot tell you for what purpose I admitted the repetition of the word "great" in the line about the "great unsatisfied godhead",[1] I only felt that it was the one thing to write in that line as "her greatness" was the only right thing in a preceding line; I also felt that they did not and could not clash and that was enough for me. Again, it might be suggested that the "high" "warm" subtle ether of love was not only the right expression but that repetition of these epithets after they had been used in describing the atmosphere of Savitri's nature was justified and had a reason and purpose because it pointed and brought out the identity of the ether of love with Savitri's atmosphere. But as a matter of fact I have no such reason or purpose. It was the identity which brought spontaneously and inevitably the use of the same epithets and not any conscious intention which deliberately used the repetition for a purpose.

Your contention that in the lines which I found to be inferior to their original form and altered back to that form, the inferiority was due to a repetition is not valid. In the line about "a vastness like his own"[2] the word "wideness" which had accidentally replaced it would have been inferior even if there had been no "wide" or wideness" anywhere within a hundred miles and I would still have altered it back to the original word. So too with "sealed depths" and so many others.... These and other alterations were due to inadvertence and not intentional; repetition or non-repetition had nothing to do with the matter. It was the same with "Wisdom nursing Chance":[3] if "nursing" had been the right word and not a slip replacing the original phrase I would have kept it in spite of the word "nurse" occurring immediately afterwards: only perhaps I would have taken care to so arrange that the repetition of the figure would simply have constituted a two-headed instead of a one-headed evil. Yes, I have changed several places where you objected to repetitions but mostly for other reasons: I have kept many where there was a repetition and changed others where there was no repetition at all. I have indeed made modifications or changes where repetition came at a short distance at the end of a line; that was because the place made it too conspicuous. Of course where

[1] P. 15.   [2] P. 16.

[3] In an earlier version of p. 41, line 16:

Of Wisdom suckling the child-laughter of Chance.

the repetition amounts to a mistake, I would have no hesitation in making a change; for a mistake must always be acknowledged and corrected.

—1946

3

Obviously, the Overmind and aesthetics cannot be equated to-gether. Aesthetics is concerned mainly with beauty, but more generally with *rasa*, the response of the mind, the vital feeling and the sense to a certain "taste" in things which often may be but is not necessarily a spiritual feeling. Aesthetics belongs to the mental range and all that depends upon it; it may degenerate into aesthet-icism or may exaggerate or narrow itself into some version of the theory of "Art for Art's sake". The Overmind is essentially a spiritual power. Mind in it surpasses its ordinary self and rises and takes its stand on a spiritual foundation. It embraces beauty and sublimates it; it has an essential aesthesis which is not limited by rules and canons; it sees a universal and an eternal beauty while it takes up and transforms all that is limited and particular. It is besides concerned with things other than beauty or aesthetics. It is concerned especially with truth and knowledge or rather with a wisdom that exceeds what we call knowledge; its truth goes beyond truth of fact and truth of thought, even the higher thought which is the first spiritual range of the thinker. It has the truth of spiritual thought, spiritual feeling, spiritual sense and at its highest the truth that comes by the most intimate spiritual touch or by identity. Ultimately, truth and beauty come together and coincide, but in between there is a difference. Overmind in all its dealings puts truth first; it brings out the essential truth (and truths) in things and also its infinite possibilities; it brings out even the truth that lies behind falsehood and error; it brings out the truth of the Incon-scient and the truth of the Superconscient and all that lies in between. When it speaks through poetry, this remains its first essential quality; a limited aesthetical artistic aim is not its purpose. It can take up and uplift any or every style or at least put some stamp of itself upon it. More or less all that we have called Overhead poetry has something of this character whether it be from the Overmind or simply intuitive, illumined or strong with the strength of the higher revealing Thought; even when it is not intrinsically Overhead poetry, still some touch can come in. Even Overhead poetry itself does not always deal in what is new or striking or strange; it can take up the obvious, the common, the bare and even the bald, the old, even that which without it would seem stale and hackneyed and raise it to greatness. Take the lines:

I spoke as one who ne'er would speak again
And as a dying man to dying men.[1]

The writer is not a poet, not even a conspicuously talented versifier. The statement of the thought is bare and direct and the rhetorical device used is of the simplest, but the Overhead touch somehow got in through a passionate emotion and sincerity and is unmistakable. In all poetry a poetical aesthesis of some kind there must be in the writer and the recipient; but aesthetics is of many kinds and the ordinary kind is not sufficient for appreciating the Overhead element in poetry. A fundamental and universal aesthesis is needed, something also more intense that listens, sees and feels from deep within and answers to what is behind the surface. A greater, wider and deeper aesthesis then which can answer even to the transcendent and feel too whatever of the transcendent or spiritual enters into the things of life, mind and sense.

The business of the critical intellect is to appreciate and judge and here too it must judge; but it can judge and appreciate rightly here only if it first learns to see and sense inwardly and interpret. But it is dangerous for it to lay down its own laws or even laws and rules which it thinks it can deduce from some observed practice of the Overhead inspiration and use that to wall in the inspiration; for it runs the risk of seeing the Overhead inspiration step across its wall and pass on leaving it bewildered and at a loss. The mere critical intellect not touched by a rarer sight can do little here. We can take an extreme case, for in extreme cases certain incompatibilities come out more clearly. What might be called the Johnsonian critical method has obviously little or no place in this field, — the method which expects a precise logical order in thoughts and language and pecks at all that departs from a matter-of-fact or a strict and rational ideative coherence or a sober and restrained classical taste. Johnson himself is plainly out of his element when he deals crudely with one of Gray's delicate trifles and tramples and flounders about in the poet's basin of goldfish breaking it with his heavy and vicious kicks. But also this method is useless in dealing with any kind of romantic poetry. What would the Johnsonian critic say to Shakespeare's famous lines,

---

[1] Quoting from memory, Sri Aurobindo has modified and given a wider poignancy to Richard Baxter's first line which was in the original (*Love breathing thanks and praise*):

I preach'd as never sure to preach again!

> Or take up arms against a sea of troubles
> And by opposing end them?[1]

He would say, "What a mixture of metaphors and jumble of ideas! Only a lunatic could take up arms against a sea! A sea of troubles is too fanciful a metaphor and, in any case, one can't end the sea by opposing it, it is more likely to end you." Shakespeare knew very well what he was doing; he saw the mixture as well as any critic could and he accepted it because it brought home, with an inspired force which a neater language could not have had, the exact feeling and idea that he wanted to bring out. Still more scared would the Johnsonian be by any occult or mystic poetry. The Veda, for instance, uses with what seems like a deliberate recklessness the mixture, at least the association of disparate images, of things not associated together in the material world which in Shakespeare is only an occasional departure. What would the Johnsonian make of this Ṛk in the Veda: "That splendour of thee, O Fire, which is in heaven and in the earth and in the plants and in the waters and by which thou hast spread out the wide mid-air, is a vivid ocean of light which sees with a divine seeing"?[2] He would say, "What is this nonsense? How can there be a splendour of light in plants and in water and how can an ocean of light see divinely or otherwise? Anyhow, what meaning can there be in all this, it is a senseless mystical jargon." But, apart from these extremes, the mere critical intellect is likely to feel a distaste or an incomprehension with regard to mystical poetry even if that poetry is quite coherent in its ideas and well-appointed in its language. It is bound to stumble over all sorts of things that are contrary to its reason and offensive to its taste: association of contraries, excess or abruptness or crowding of images, disregard of intellectual limitations in the thought, concretisation of abstractions, the treating of things and forces as if there were a consciousness and a personality in them and a hundred other aberrations from the straight intellectual line. It is not likely either to tolerate departures in technique which disregard the canons of an established order. Fortunately here the modernists with all their errors have broken old bounds and the mystic poet may be

---

[1] The original lines (*Hamlet*, III.i) read:

> Or to take arms against a sea of troubles
> And by opposing end them?

[2] Ṛgveda III.22.2.

more free to invent his own technique.

Here is an instance in point. You refer to certain things I wrote and concessions I made when you were typing an earlier draft of the first books of *Savitri*. You instance my readiness to correct or do away with repetitions of words or clashes of sound such as "magnificent" in one line and "lucent" in the next. True, but I may observe that at that time I was passing through a transition from the habits of an old inspiration and technique to which I often deferred and the new inspiration that had begun to come. I would still alter this clash because it was a clash, but I would not as in the old days make a fixed rule of this avoidance. If lines like the following were to come to me now,

> His forehead was a dome magnificent,
> And there gazed forth two orbs of lucent truth
> That made the human air a world of light,

I would not reject them but accept "magnificent" and "lucent" as entirely in their place. But this would not be an undiscriminating acceptance; for if it had run

> His forehead was a wide magnificent dome
> And there gazed forth two orbs of lucent truth

I would not be so ready to accept it, for the repetition of sound here occurring in the same place in the line would lack the just rhythmical balance. I have accepted in the present version of *Savitri* several of the freedoms established by the modernists including internal rhyme, exact assonance of syllable, irregularities introduced into the iambic run of the metre and others which would have been equally painful to an earlier taste. But I have not taken this as a mechanical method or a mannerism, but only where I thought it rhythmically justified; for all freedom must have a truth in it and an order, either a rational or an instinctive and intuitive order.

— 1946

4

> ...the cosmic drowse of ignorant Force
> Whose moved creative slumber kindles the suns
> And carries our lives in its somnambulist whirl.[1]

I am not disposed to change "suns" to "stars" in the line about the
creative slumber of the ignorant Force; "stars" does not create the
same impression and brings in a different tone in the rhythm and
the sense. This line and that which follows it bring in a general
subordinate idea stressing the paradoxical nature of the creation
and the contrasts which it contains, the drowsed somnambulist as
the mother of the light of the suns and the activities of life. It is not
intended as a present feature in the darkness of the Night.

—1946

> As if a childlike finger laid on a cheek
> Reminding of the endless need in things
> The heedless Mother of the universe,
> An infant longing clutched the sombre Vast.[2]

Your objection to the "finger" and the "clutch" moves me only to
change "reminding" to "reminded" in the second line. It is not
intended that the two images "finger laid" and "clutch" should
correspond exactly to each other; for the "void"[3] and the "Mother
of the universe" are not the same thing. The "void" is only a mask
covering the Mother's cheek or face. What the "void" feels as a
clutch is felt by the Mother only as a reminding finger laid on her
cheek. It is one advantage of the expression "as if" that it leaves the
field open for such variation. It is intended to suggest without
saying it that behind the sombre void is the face of a mother. The
two other "as if"'s[4] have the same motive and I do not find them

---

[1] P. 1.

[2] An earlier version of p. 2, lines 19–22.

[3] Sri Aurobindo has somehow come to use "void" instead of the "Vast" that is
actually there in the line. It may be mentioned that, in the passage where this line and
the other three occur, the Vast is also called the void.

[4]   As if a soul long dead were moved to live...
         As if solicited in an alien world...

jarring upon me. The second is at a sufficient distance from the first and it is not obtrusive enough to prejudice the third which more nearly follows. . . . Your suggestion "as though" (for the third) does not appeal to me: it almost makes a suggestion of falsity and in any case it makes no real difference as the two expressions are too much kin to each other to repel the charge of reiteration.

—1946

As if solicited in an alien world
With timid and hazardous instinctive grace,
Orphaned and driven out to seek a home,
An errant marvel with no place to live,
Into a far-off nook of heaven there came
A slow miraculous gesture's dim appeal.[1]

You have made what seems to me a strange confusion as regards the passage about the "errant marvel" owing to the mistake in the punctuation which is now corrected. You took the word "solicited" as a past participle passive and this error seems to have remained fixed in your mind so as to distort the whole building and sense of the passage. The word "solicited" is the past tense and the subject of this verb is "an errant marvel" delayed to the fourth line by the parenthesis "Orphaned etc." This kind of inversion, though longer than usual, is common enough in poetical style and the object is to throw a strong emphasis and prominence upon the line, "An errant marvel with no place to live." That being explained, the rest about the gesture should be clear enough.

    I see no sufficient reason to alter the passage; certainly, I could not alter the line beginning "Orphaned . . ."; it is indispensable to the total idea and its omission would leave an unfilled gap. If I may not expect a complete alertness from the reader, — but how without it can he grasp the subtleties of a mystical and symbolic poem? — he surely ought to be alert enough when he reads the second line to see that it is somebody who is soliciting with a timid grace and it can't be somebody who is being gracefully solicited; also the line "Orphaned etc." ought to suggest to him at once that it is some orphan who is soliciting and not the other way round: the delusion of the past participle passive ought to be dissipated long before he

[1] P. 3.

reaches the subject of the verb in the fourth line. The obscurity throughout, if there is any, is in the mind of the hasty reader and not in the grammatical construction of the passage.

—1946

A slow miraculous gesture dimly came.

Man alive, your proposed emendations[1] are an admirable exposition of the art of bringing a line down the steps till my poor "slow miraculous" above-mind line meant to give or begin the concrete portrayal of an act of some hidden Godhead finally becomes a mere metaphor thrown out from its more facile mint by a brilliantly imaginative poetic intelligence. First of all, you shift my "dimly" out of the way and transfer it to something to which it does not inwardly belong, make it an epithet of the gesture or an adverb qualifying its epithet instead of something that qualifies the atmosphere in which the act of the Godhead takes place. That is a preliminary havoc which destroys what is very important to the action, its atmosphere. I never intended the gesture to be dim, it is a luminous gesture, but forcing its way through the black quietude it comes dimly. Then again the bald phrase "a gesture came" without anything to psychicise it becomes simply something that "happened", "came" being a poetic equivalent for "happened", instead of the expression of the slow coming of the gesture. The

---

[1] The suggested emendations of the original line which belonged to the 1936 version, but apropos of which Sri Aurobindo's comments are pertinent in general to his art, were:

> Miraculous and dim
> Miraculously dim   } a gesture came.
> Dimly miraculous
> Miraculous and slow

The emendations were not suggested as improvements in any way on the line which was splendid (though Sri Aurobindo himself subsequently altered it to

    A slow miraculous gesture's dim appeal

because of a new interrelation in the final expanded recast of his poem). They were only a hypothetical desperate resort in the interests of a point which is made clear in the footnote at the end of the next item. The object was to see if a certain change in the manner of adjective-use was possible so that a technical variety might be introduced in the passage of which the line in question was a part. The emendations unfortunately involved, among other things, the omission of one or another of the descriptive terms used by Sri Aurobindo. But variants not involving this were also offered for discussion, as the footnote already referred to will show.

words "slow" and "dimly" assure this sense of motion and this concreteness to the word's sense here. Remove one or both whether entirely or elsewhere and you ruin the vision and change altogether its character. That is at least what happens wholly in your penultimate version and as for the last its "came" gets another meaning and one feels that somebody very slowly decided to let out the gesture from himself and it was quite a miracle that it came out at all! "Dimly miraculous" means what precisely or what "miraculously dim" — it was miraculous that it managed to be so dim or there was something vaguely miraculous about it after all? No doubt they try to mean something else — but these interpretations come in their way and trip them over. The only thing that can stand is the first version which is no doubt fine poetry, but the trouble is that it does not give the effect I wanted to give, the effect which is necessary for the dawn's inner significance. Moreover, what becomes of the slow lingering rhythm of my line which is absolutely indispensable?

— 1936

Then a faint hesitating glimmer broke.
A slow miraculous gesture dimly came,
The persistent thrill of a transfiguring touch
Persuaded the inert black quietude
And beauty and wonder disturbed the fields of God.
A wandering hand of pale enchanted light
That glowed along a fading moment's brink
Fixed with gold panel and opalescent hinge
A gate of dreams ajar on mystery's verge.

Can't see the validity of any prohibition of double adjectives in abundance. If a slow wealth-burdened movement is the right thing, as it certainly is here[1] in my judgment, the necessary means have to

---

[1] The first two lines here are different from those that in the present version precede the rest of the passage (p. 3). The version on which Sri Aurobindo commented is that of 1936. But the comment which is concerned with the use of double adjectives does not lose its essential force when these lines are replaced by those of the final version:

> Into a far-off nook of heaven there came
> A slow miraculous gesture's dim appeal.

Only one pair of adjectives out of four closely occurring "doubles" drops out.

be used to bring it about — and the double adjective is admirably suited for the purpose.... Do not forget that *Savitri* is an experiment in mystic poetry, spiritual poetry cast into a symbolic figure. Done on this rule, it is really a new attempt and cannot be hampered by old ideas of technique except when they are assimilable. Least of all by a standard proper to a mere intellectual and abstract poetry which makes "reason and taste" the supreme arbiters, aims at a harmonised poetic intellectual balanced expression of the sense, elegance in language, a sober and subtle use of imaginative decoration, a restrained emotive element etc. The attempt at mystic spiritual poetry of the kind I am at demands above all a spiritual objectivity, an intense psychophysical concreteness. I do not know what you mean exactly here by "obvious" and "subtle". According to certain canons, epithets should be used sparingly, free use of them is rhetorical, an "obvious" device, a crowding of images is bad taste, there should be subtlety of art not displayed but severely concealed — *Summa ars est celare artem.* Very good for a certain standard of poetry, not so good or not good at all for others. Shakespeare kicks over these traces at every step, Aeschylus freely and frequently, Milton whenever he chooses. Such lines as

> With hideous ruin and combustion, down
> To bottomless perdition, there to dwell
> In adamantine chains and penal fire[1]

or

> Wilt thou upon the high and giddy mast
> Seal up the shipboy's eyes and rock his brains
> In cradle of the rude imperious surge[2]

(note two double adjectives in three lines in the last) — are not subtle or restrained, or careful to conceal their elements of powerful technique, they show rather a vivid richness or vehemence, forcing language to its utmost power of expression. That has to be done still more in this kind of mystic poetry. I cannot bring out the spiritual objectivity if I have to be miserly about epithets, images, or deny myself the use of all available resources of sound-significance. The double epithets are indispensable here and in the exact order

[1] Milton, *Paradise Lost*, I.46–48. [2] Shakespeare, *2 Henry IV*, III.i.

in which they are arranged by me. You say the rich burdened movement can be secured by other means, but a rich burdened movement of any kind is not my primary object, it is desirable only because it is needed to express the spirit of the action here; and the double epithets are wanted because they are the best, not only one way of securing it. The "gesture" must be "slow miraculous" — if it is merely miraculous or merely slow, that does not create a picture of the thing as it is, but of something quite abstract and ordinary or concrete but ordinary — it is the combination that renders the exact nature of the mystic movement, with the "dimly came" supporting it, so that "gesture" is not here a metaphor, but a thing actually done. Equally a pale light or an enchanted light may be very pretty, but it is only the combination that renders the luminosity which is that of the hand acting tentatively in the darkness. That darkness itself is described as a quietude, which gives it a subjective spiritual character and brings out the thing symbolised, but the double epithet "inert black" gives it the needed concreteness so that the quietude ceases to be something abstract and becomes something concrete, objective, but still spiritually subjective.... Every word must be the right word, with the right atmosphere, the right relation to all the other words, just as every sound in its place and the whole sound together must bring out the imponderable significance which is beyond verbal expression. One can't chop and change about on the principle that it is sufficient if the same mental sense or part of it is given with some poetical beauty or power. One can only change if the change brings out more perfectly the thing behind that is seeking for expression — brings out in full objectivity and also in the full mystic sense. If I can do that, well, other considerations have to take a back seat or seek their satisfaction elsewhere.[1]

                                                          — 1936

[1] The point discussed by Sri Aurobindo is a genuine and important one but it may be mentioned that the question which elicited the discussion gave rise to this precise point by some carelessness of phrasing. As Sri Aurobindo himself was informed later, the slight suspicion of "obviousness of method" referred not to the closely repeated use of double adjectives but to the manner in which two epithets had been thus used — that is, without any separation of one from the other and immediately before a noun. An alternative — "A gesture slow, miraculous, dimly came" — was suggested, but admittedly the revelatory suspense in Sri Aurobindo's line was spoiled by the "gesture" being

In the passage about Dawn your two suggestions I find unsatisfying. "Windowing hidden things"[1] presents a vivid image and suggests what I want to suggest and I must refuse to alter it; "vistaing" brings in a very common image and does not suggest anything except perhaps that there is a long line or wide range of hidden things. But that is quite unwanted and not a part of the thing seen. "Shroud" sounds to me too literary and artificial and besides it almost suggests that what it covers is a corpse which would not do at all; a slipping shroud sounds inapt while "slipped like a falling cloak"[2] gives a natural and true image. In any case, "shroud" would not be more naturally continuous in the succession of images than "cloak".

—1946

I am afraid I shall not be able to satisfy your demand for rejection and alteration of the lines about the Inconscient[3] and the cloak any more than I could do it with regard to the line about the silence and strength of the gods.[4] I looked at your suggestion about adding a line or two in the first case, but could get nothing that would either improve the passage or set your objection at rest. I am quite unable to agree that there is anything jargonish about the line any more than there is in the lines of Keats,

> Beauty is Truth, Truth Beauty—that is all
> Ye know on earth and all ye need to know.[5]

That amounts to a generalised philosophical statement or enunciation and the words "beauty" and "truth" are abstract metaphysical terms to which we give a concrete and emotional value because they are connected in our associations with true and beautiful things of which our senses or our minds are vividly aware. Men have not learnt yet to recognise the Inconscient on which the whole material world they see is built, or the Ignorance of which their

---

mentioned too soon. Also, "Miraculous, slow, a gesture dimly came" would blurt out things in its own way. "Yes, that is it," wrote Sri Aurobindo. And his general remark was: "The epithets are inseparable from the noun, they give a single impression which must not be broken up by giving a separate prominence to either noun or epithets."

[1] P. 3.   [2] *Ibid.*   [3] P. 2.   [4] P. 16.   [5] *Ode to a Grecian Urn.*

whole nature including their knowledge is built; they think that these words are only abstract metaphysical jargon flung about by the philosophers in their clouds or laboured out in long and wearisome books like *The Life Divine*. But it is not so with me and I take my stand on my own feeling and experience about them as Keats did on his about truth and beauty. My readers will have to do the same if they want to appreciate my poetry, which of course they are not bound to do.

Is it really a fact that even the ordinary reader would not be able to see any difference between the Inconscient and Ignorance unless the difference is expressly explained to him? This is not a matter of philosophical terminology but of common sense and the understood meaning of English words. One would say "even the inconscient stone" but one would not say, as one might of a child, "the ignorant stone". One must first be conscious before one can be ignorant. What is true is that the ordinary reader might not be familiar with the philosophical content of the word Inconscient and might not be familiar with the Vedantic idea of the Ignorance as the power behind the manifested world. But I don't see how I can acquaint him with these things in a single line, even with the most illuminating image or symbol. He might wonder, if he were Johnsonianly minded, how an Inconscient could be teased or how it could wake Ignorance. I am afraid, in the absence of a miracle of inspired poetical exegesis flashing through my mind, he will have to be left wondering. I am not set against adding a line if the miracle comes or if some vivid symbol occurs to me, but as yet none such is making its appearance.[1]

In the other case also, about the cloak, I maintain my position. Here, however, while I was looking at the passage an additional line occurred to me and I may keep it:

The darkness failed and slipped like a falling cloak
From the reclining body of a god.

But this additional line does not obviate your objection and it was

[1] What the commentator wished for was some symbolic suggestion as in other phrases of Sri Aurobindo's that made the Inconscient a black dragon or a black rock. As an alternative he desired a further touch of vividness to drive home the distinction between the Inconscient and Ignorance, as in another line in *Savitri*:

And the blind Void struggles to live and see.

not put in with that object. You have, by the way, made a curious misapplication of my image of the careful housewife; you attribute this line to her inspiration.[1] A careful housewife is meticulously and methodically careful to arrange everything in a perfect order, to put every object in its place and see that there is no disharmony anywhere; but according to you she has thrust a wrong object into a wrong place, something discordant with the surroundings and inferior in beauty to all that is near it; if so, she is not a careful housewife but a slattern. The Muse has a careful housewife, — there is Pope's, perfect in the classical or pseudo-classical style or Tennyson's, in the romantic or semi-romantic manner, while as a contrast there is Browning's with her energetic and rough-and-tumble dash and clatter.

You ask why in these and similar cases I could not convince you while I did in others. Well, there are several possible explanations. It may be that your first reaction to these lines was very vivid and left the mark of a *saṁskāra* which could not be obliterated. Or perhaps I was right in the other matters while your criticism may have been right in these, — my partiality for these lines may be due to an unjustified personal attachment founded on the vision which they gave me when I wrote them. Again, there are always differences of poetical appreciation due either to preconceived notions or to different temperamental reactions. Finally, it may be that my vision was true but for some reason you are not able to share it. For instance, you may have seen in the line about the cloak only the objective image in a detailed picture of the dawn where I felt a subjective suggestion in the failure of the darkness and the slipping of the cloak, not an image but an experience. It must be the same with the line,

The strength, the silence of the gods were hers.

You perhaps felt it to be an ordinary line with a superficial significance; perhaps it conveyed to you not much more than the stock phrase about the "strong silent man" admired by biographers, while to me it meant very much and expressed with a bare but

---

[1] The line meant is not the additional but the original single one, and the image Sri Aurobindo refers to is in his statement: "The mystic Muse is more of an inspired Bacchante of the Dionysian wine than an orderly housewife."

sufficient power what I always regarded as a great reality and a great experience.

— 1946

> Then through the pallid rift that seemed at first
> Hardly enough for a trickle from the suns,
> Outpoured the revelation and the flame.[1]

Your "barely enough", instead of the finer and more suggestive "hardly", falls flat upon my ear; one cannot substitute one word for another in this kind of poetry merely because it means intellectually the same thing; "hardly" is the *mot juste* in this context and, repetition or not, it must remain unless a word not only *juste* but inevitable comes to replace it.... On this point I may add that in certain contexts "barely" would be the right word, as for instance, "There is barely enough food left for two or three meals", where "hardly" would be adequate but much less forceful. It is the other way about in this line.

— 1946

> A lonely splendour from the invisible goal
> Almost was flung on the opaque Inane.[2]

No word will do except "invisible". I don't think there are too many "I's" — in fact such multiplications of a vowel or consonant assonance or several together as well as syllabic assonances in a single line or occasionally between line-endings (e.g. face-fate) are an accepted feature of the technique in *Savitri*. Purposeful repetitions also, or those which serve as echoes or key notes in the theme.

— 1936

> Air was a vibrant link between earth and heaven.[3]

---

[1] P. 3. [2] P. 4.

[3] P. 4. The question was: I notice that you have changed "twixt" to "between" when substituting "link" for "step" in the line, "Air was a vibrant step twixt earth and heaven." Is it merely because twelve lines earlier "twixt" has been used?

No, it is because "link twixt", two heavy syllables (heavy because ending with two consonants) with the same vowel, makes an awkward combination which can only be saved by good management of the whole line — but here the line was not written to suit such a combination, so it won't do.

—1936

*
**

I think you said in a letter that in the line

Our prostrate soil bore the awakening ray[1]

"soil" was an error for "soul". But "soil" is correct; for I am describing the revealing light falling upon the lower levels of the earth, not on the soul. No doubt, the whole thing is symbolic, but the symbol has to be kept in the front and the thing symbolised has to be concealed or only peep out from behind, it cannot come openly into the front and push aside the symbol.

—1946

*
**

The former pitch[2] continues, as far as I can see, up to Light, then it begins to come down to an intuitivised Higher Mind in order to suit the change of the subject, but it is only occasionally that it is pure Higher Mind — a mixture of the intuitive or illumined is usually there except when some truth has to be stated to the philosophic intelligence in as precise a manner as possible.

—1936

<hr>

[1] P. 5.

[2] The question referred to the whole shorter and somewhat different 1936 version of the opening of *Savitri* and sought to compare the planes of two passages concerned solely with the Dawn, in the first of which a direct luminosity was discerned and in the second a shift to the Higher Mind. Sri Aurobindo's answer is quoted because it seems applicable in general wherever in *Savitri* the Higher Mind comes into play.

["Its *passive* flower of love and doom it gave."] Good Heavens! how did Gandhi come in there? Passion-flower, sir—passion, *not* passive.[1]

—1936

Draped in the leaves' vivid emerald monotone.[2]

Five [feet], the first being taken as a dactyl. A little gambol like that must be occasionally allowed in an otherwise correct metrical performance.

—1936

Miltonism? Surely not. The Miltonic has a statelier more spreading rhythm and a less direct more loftily arranged language. Miltonically I should have written not

The Gods above and Nature sole below
Were the spectators of that mighty strife[3]

but

Only the Sons of Heaven and that executive She
Watched the arbitrament of the high dispute.

—1936

Never a rarer creature bore his shaft.[4]

Yes, like Shakespeare's

...rock his brains
In cradle of the rude imperious surge.

Mine has only three sonant r's, the others being inaudible—Shakespeare pours himself 5 in a close space.

—1936

[1] P. 7.   [2] P. 13.   [3] *Ibid.*
[4] P. 14. The question asked was: "Is the r-effect deliberate?"

All in her pointed to a nobler kind.[1]

It is a "connecting" line which prepares for what follows. It is
sometimes good technique, as I think, to intersperse lines like that
(provided they do not fall below standard), so as to give the
intellect the foothold of a clear unadorned statement of the gist of
what is coming, before taking a higher flight. This is of course a
technique for long poems and long descriptions, not for shorter
things or lyrical writing.

—1936

I refuse entirely to admit that that is poor poetry. It is not only just
the line that is needed to introduce what follows but it is very good
poetry with the strength and pointed directness, not intellectual-
ised like Pope's, but intuitive, which we often find in the
Elizabethans, for instance in Marlowe supporting adequately and
often more than adequately his "mighty lines". But the image must
be understood, as it was intended, in its concrete sense and not as a
vague rhetorical phrase substituted for a plainer wording,—it
shows Savitri as the forerunner or first creator of a new race. All
poets have lines which are bare and direct statements and meant to
be that in order to carry their full force; but to what category their
simplicity belongs or whether a line is only passable or more than
that depends on various circumstances. Shakespeare's

To be or not to be, that is the question[2]

introduces powerfully one of the most famous of all soliloquies and
it comes in with a great dramatic force, but in itself it is a bare
statement and some might say that it would not be otherwise
written in prose and is only saved by the metrical rhythm. The
same might be said of the well-known passage in Keats which I
have already quoted:

Beauty is Truth, Truth Beauty—that is all
Ye know on earth and all ye need to know.

The same might be said of Milton's famous line,

[1] P. 14.   [2] *Hamlet*, III.i.

Fall'n Cherub! to be weak is miserable.[1]

But obviously in all these lines there is not only a concentrated force, power or greatness of the thought, but also a concentration of intense poetic feeling which makes any criticism impossible. Then take Milton's lines,

Were it not better done, as others use,
To sport with Amaryllis in the shade
Or with the tangles of Neaera's hair?[2]

It might be said that the first line has nothing to distinguish it and is merely passable or only saved by the charm of what follows; but there is a beauty of rhythm and a *bhāva* or feeling brought in by the rhythm which makes the line beautiful in itself and not merely passable. If there is not some saving grace like that then the danger of laxity may become possible. I do not think there is much in *Savitri* which is of that kind. But I can perfectly understand your anxiety that all should be lifted to or towards at least the minimum Overhead level or so near as to be touched by its influence or at the very least a good substitute for it. I do not know whether that is always possible in so long a poem as *Savitri* dealing with so many various heights and degrees and so much varying substance of thought and feeling and descriptive matter and narrative. But that has been my general aim throughout and it is the reason why I have made so many successive drafts and continual alterations till I felt that I had got the thing intended by the higher inspiration in every line and passage. It is also why I keep myself open to every suggestion from a sympathetic and understanding quarter and weigh it well, rejecting only after due consideration and accepting when I see it to be well-founded. But for that the critic must be one who has seen and felt what is in the thing written, not like your friend who has not seen anything and understood only the word surface and not even always that; he must be open to this kind of poetry, able to see the spiritual vision it conveys, capable too of feeling the Overhead touch when it comes, — the fit reader.

— 1947

---

[1] *Paradise Lost*, I.157. [2] *Lycidas*, 67–69.

Near to earth's wideness, intimate with heaven,
Exalted and swift her young large-visioned spirit,
Winging through worlds of splendour and of calm,
O'erflew the ways of Thought to unborn things.
Ardent was her self-poised unstumbling will,
Her mind, a sea of white sincerity,
Passionate in flow, had not one turbid wave.
As in a mystic and dynamic dance
A priestess of immaculate ecstasies,
Inspired and ruled from Truth's revealing vault,
Moves in some prophet cavern of the Gods,
A heart of silence in the hands of joy
Inhabited with rich creative beats
A body like a parable of dawn
That seemed a niche for veiled divinity
Or golden temple-door to things beyond.
Immortal rhythms swayed in her time-born steps;
Her look, her smile awoke celestial sense
In this earth-stuff and their intense delight
Poured a supernal beauty on men's lives.
The great unsatisfied godhead here could dwell.
Vacant of the dwarf self's imprisoned air,
Her mood could harbour his sublimer breath
Spiritual that can make all things divine:
For even her gulfs were secrecies of light.
At once she was the stillness and the Word,
An ocean of untrembling virgin fire,
A continent of self-diffusing peace.
In her he met a vastness like his own;
His warm high subtle ether he refound
And moved in her as in his natural home.

This passage [1] is, I believe, what I might call the Overmind Intuition at work expressing itself in something like its own rhythm and language. It is difficult to say about one's own poetry, but I think I have succeeded here and in some passages later on in catching that

---

[1] This description of Savitri in whom the God of Love found "his perfect shrine" was subsequently expanded from its original 31 lines of the 1936 version to 51 (pp. 14–16).

very difficult note; in separate lines or briefer passages (i.e. a few lines at a time) I think it comes in not unoften.[1]

— 1936

I am unable to accept the alterations you suggest[2] because they are romantically decorative and do not convey any impression of directness and reality which is necessary in this style of writing. A "sapphire sky" is too obvious and common and has no significance in connection with the word "magnanimity" or its idea and "boundless" is somewhat meaningless and inapt when applied to sky. The same objections apply to both "opulence" and "amplitude"; but apart from that they have only a rhetorical value and are not the right word for what I want to say. Your "life's wounded wings of dream" and "the wounded wings of life" have also a very pronounced note of romanticism and do not agree with the strong reality of things stressed everywhere in this passage. In the poem I dwell often upon the idea of life as a dream, but here it would bring in a false note. It does not seem to me that magnanimity and greatness are the same thing or that this can be called a repetition. I myself see no objection to "heaven" and "haven"; it is not as if they were in successive lines; they are divided by two lines and it is surely an excessively meticulous ear that can take their similarity of sound at this distance as an offence. Most of your other objections

[1] The statement was in reply to the question: "Are not these lines which I regard as the *ne plus ultra* in world-poetry a snatch of the sheer Overmind?" Considering Sri Aurobindo's remark in 1946 about his attitude ten years earlier—"At that time I hesitated to assign anything like Overmind touch or inspiration to passages in English or other poetry and did not presume to claim any of my own writing as belonging to this order"—and considering also that several lines of other poets which he had hesitated about were later adjudged by him to be from the Overmind, it seems certain that this passage which he had ascribed to the Overmind Intuition, a plane defined by him as not Overmind itself but an intermediate level, would have been traced by him to the supreme source if he had been privately asked about it again.

[2] The alterations were suggested with reference to an additional passage between lines 20 and 21 in the description of Savitri as originally written in 1936. The passage was more or less the same as at present on p. 15, between lines 15 and 34 there, except that after line 21 and before line 28 stood the following:

> As to a sheltering bosom a stricken bird
> Escapes with tired wings from a world of storms,
> In a safe haven of splendid soft repose
> One could restore life's wounded happiness,
> Recover the lost habit of delight,...

hang upon your overscrupulous law against repetitions. . . . I consider that this law has no value in the technique of a mystic poem of this kind and that repetition of a certain kind can be even part of the technique; for instance, I see no objection to "sea" being repeated in a different context in the same passage or to the image of the ocean being resorted to in a third connection. I cannot see that the power and force or inevitability of these lines is at all diminished in their own context by their relative proximity or that that proximity makes each less inevitable in its place.

Then about the image about the bird and the bosom I understand what you mean, but it rests upon the idea that the whole passage must be kept at the same transcendental level. It is true that all the rest gives the transcendental values in the composition of Savitri's being, while here there is a departure to show how this transcendental greatness contacts the psychic demand of human nature in its weakness and responds to it and acts upon it. That was the purpose of the new passage and it is difficult to accomplish it without bringing in a normal psychic instead of a transcendental tone. The image of the bird and the bosom is obviously not new and original, it images a common demand of the human heart and does it by employing a physical and emotional figure so as to give it a vivid directness in its own kind. This passage was introduced because it brought in something in Savitri's relation with the human world which seemed to me a necessary part of a complete psychological description of her. If it had to be altered, — which would be only if the descent to the psychic level really spoils the consistent integrality of the description and lowers the height of the poetry, — I would have to find something equal and better, and just now I do not find any such satisfying alteration.

As for the line about the strength and silence of the Gods,

[The strength, the silence of the gods were hers] [1]

that has a similar motive of completeness. The line about the "stillness" and the "word"

[At once she was the stillness and the word,]

gives us the transcendental element in Savitri, for the Divine Savitri
[1] P. 16.

is the word that rises from the transcendental stillness; the next two
lines

> [A continent of self-diffusing peace,
> An ocean of untrembling virgin fire]

render that element into the poise of the spiritual consciousness;
this last line brings the same thing down to the outward character
and temperament in life. A union of strength and silence is insisted
upon in this poem as one of the most prominent characteristics of
Savitri and I have dwelt on it elsewhere, but it had to be brought in
here also if this description of her was to be complete. I do not find
that this line lacks poetry or power; if I did, I would alter it.

—1946

I doubt whether I shall have the courage to throw out again the
stricken and "too explicit" bird into the cold and storm outside; at
most I might change that one line, the first, and make it stronger. I
confess I fail to see what is so objectionable in its explicitness;
usually, according to my idea, it is only things that are in them-
selves vague that have to be kept vague. There is plenty of room for
the implicit and suggestive, but I do not see the necessity for that
where one has to bring home a physical image.

—1946

I have altered the bird passage and the repetition of "delight"[1] at the
end of a line; the new version runs —

> As might a soul fly like a hunted bird,
> Escaping with tired wings from a world of storms,
> And a quiet reach like a remembered breast,
> In a haven of safety and splendid soft repose
> One could drink life back in streams of honey-fire,
> Recover the lost habit of happiness,

---

[1] An earlier line, not far from the one ending with the word "delight" in the first
version of the Bird passage, had been pointed out as ending with the same word —

Even in earth-stuff, and their intense delight...

> Feel her bright nature's glorious ambience,
> And preen joy in her warmth and colour's rule.

—1946

The suggestion you make about the "soul" and the "bird" may have a slight justification, but I do not think it is fatal to the passage.[1] On the other hand there is a strong objection to the alteration you propose; it is that the image of the soul escaping from a world of storms would be impaired if it were only a physical bird that was escaping: a "world of storms" is too big an expression in relation to the smallness of the bird, it is only with the soul especially mentioned or else suggested and the "bird" subordinately there as a comparison that it fits perfectly well and gets its full value.

The word "one" which takes up the image of the "bird" has a more general application than the "soul" and is not quite identical with it; it means anyone who has lost happiness and is in need of spiritual comfort and revival. It is as if one said: "as might a soul like a hunted bird take refuge from the world in the peace of the Infinite and feel that as its own remembered home, so could one take refuge in her as in a haven of safety and like the tired bird reconstitute one's strength so as to face the world once more."

—1947

My remarks about the Bird passage are written from the point of view of the change made and the new character and atmosphere it gives: I think the old passage was right enough in its own atmosphere, but not so good as what has replaced it: the alteration you suggest may be as good as that, but the objections to it are valid from the new viewpoint.

—1947

---

[1] The suggestion was: "Although your new version carries a subtle multiform image more in tune, in my opinion, with the general vision of the rest of the description of Savitri, 'one' who is himself a soul is compared to 'a soul' acting like a bird taking shelter, as if to say: 'A soul who is doing so-and-so is like a soul doing something similar'—a comparison which perhaps brings in some loss of surprise and revelation."

As to the sixfold repetition of the indefinite article "a" in this passage, one should no doubt make it a general rule to avoid any such excessive repetition, but all rules have their exception and it might be phrased like this, "Except when some effect has to be produced which the repetition would serve or for which it is necessary." Here I feel that it does serve subtly such an effect; I have used the repetition of this "a" very frequently in the poem with a recurrence at the beginning of each successive line in order to produce an accumulative effect of multiple characteristics or a grouping of associated things or ideas or other similar massings.

—1947

> Almost they saw who lived within her light
> Her playmate in the sempiternal spheres
> Descended from its unattainable realms
> In her attracting advent's luminous wake,
> The white-fire dragon-bird of endless bliss
> Drifting with burning wings above her days.[1]

Yes; the purpose is to create a large luminous trailing repetitive movement like the flight of the Bird with its dragon tail of white fire.

—1936

All birds of that region are relatives.[2] But this is the bird of eternal Ananda, while the Hippogriff is the divinised Thought and the Bird of Fire is the Agni-bird, psychic and tapas. All that however is to mentalise too much and mentalising always takes most of the life out of spiritual things. That is why I say it can be seen but nothing said about it.

—1936

[1] P. 16. The question was: "Is an accumulating grandiose effect intended by the repetition of adjective-and-noun in four consecutive line-endings?"

[2] The question was: "In the mystical region, is the dragon bird any relation of your Bird of Fire with 'gold-white wings' or your Hippogriff with 'face lustred, pale-blue-lined'? And why do you write: 'What to say about him? One can only see'?"

> But joy cannot endure until the end:
> There is a darkness in terrestrial things
> That will not suffer long too glad a note.[1]

I do not think it is the poetic intelligence any more than Virgil's *Sunt lacrimae rerum et mentem mortalia tangunt,*[2] which I think to be the Higher Mind coming through to the psychic and blending with it. So also his *O passi graviora, dabit deus his quoque finem.*[3]

Here it may be the intuitive inner mind with the psychic fused together.

—1936

One dealt with her who meets the burdened great.[4]

Love? It is not Love who meets the burdened great and governs the fate of men! Nor is it Pain. Time also does not do these things — it only provides the field and movement of events. If I had wanted to give a name, I would have done it, but it has purposely to be left nameless because it is indefinable. He may use Love or Pain or Time or any of these powers but is not any of them. You can call him the Master of the Evolution, if you like.

—1936

[1] Pp. 16–17. The question was: "Are these lines the poetic intelligence at its deepest, say, like a mixture of Sophocles and Virgil? They may be the pure or the intuitivised higher mind."

[2] *Aeneid*, I.462. In 1946 Sri Aurobindo put the source of this line's inspiration much higher than he does here. See p. 810.

[3] *Aeneid*, I.199.

[4] The context of the line on p. 17 is:

> One dealt with her who meets the burdened great.
> Assigner of the ordeal and the path
> Who chooses in this holocaust of the soul
> Death, fall and sorrow as the spirit's goads,
> The dubious godhead with his torch of pain
> Lit up the chasm of the unfinished world
> And called her to fill with her vast self the abyss.

The question was: "Who is 'One' here? Is it Love, the godhead mentioned before? If not, does this 'dubious godhead with his torch of pain' correspond to 'the image white and high of godlike Pain' spoken of a little earlier? Or is it Time whose 'snare' occurs in the last line of the preceding passage?"

Her spirit refused struck from the starry list
To quench in dull despair the God-given light.

I omitted any punctuation[1] because it is a compressed construction meant to signify refused to be struck from the starry list and quenched in dull despair etc. — the quenching being the act of consent that would make effective the sentence of being struck from the starry list.

—1936

This truth broke in in a triumph of fire.[2]

The line you object to on account of forced rhythm "in a triumph of fire" has not been so arranged through negligence. It was very deliberately done and deliberately maintained. If it were altered the whole effect of rhythmic meaning and suggestion which I intended would be lost and the alterations you suggest would make a good line perhaps but with an ordinary and inexpressive rhythm. Obviously this is not a "natural rhythm", but there is no objection to its being forced when it is a forcible and violent action that has to be suggested. The rhythm cannot be called artificial, for that would mean something not true and genuine or significant but only patched up and insincere: the rhythm here is a turn of art and not a manufacture. The scansion is iamb, reversed spondee, pyrrhic, trochee, iamb. By reversed spondee I mean a foot with the first syllable long and highly stressed and the second stressed but short or with a less heavy ictus. In the ordinary spondee the greater ictus is on the second syllable while there are equal spondees with two heavy stresses, e.g. "vast space" or in such a line as

He has seized life in his resistless hands.

---

[1] A question was put to Sri Aurobindo: "Any punctuation missing? Perhaps a dash after 'refused' as well as after 'list'?" In the final version (p. 19) these lines have been expanded to:

> Her spirit refused to hug the common soil,
> Or, finding all life's golden meanings robbed,
> Compound with earth, struck from the starry list,
> Or quench with black despair the God-given light.

[2] P. 21.

In the first part of the line the rhythm is appropriate to the violent breaking in of the truth while in the second half it expresses a high exultation and exaltation in the inrush. This is brought out by the two long and highly stressed vowels in the first syllable of "triumph" and in the word "fire" (which in the elocution of the line have to be given their full force), coming after a pyrrhic with two short syllables between them. If one slurs over the slightly weighted short syllable in "triumph" where the concluding consonants exercise a certain check and delay in the voice, one could turn this half line into a very clumsy double anapaest, the first a glide and the second a stumble; this would be bad elocution and contrary to the natural movement of the words.

—1946

Certainly, Milton in the passages you quote[1] had a rhythmical effect in mind; he was much too careful and conscientious a metrist and much too consummate a master of rhythm to do anything carelessly or without good reason. If he found his inspiration stumbling or becoming slipshod in its rhythmical effects, he would have corrected it.

—1947

In the two passages ending with the same word "alone"[2] I think there is sufficient space between them and neither ear nor mind

---

[1]   And they bowed down to the Gods of their wives...
        Burned after them to the bottomless pit...

[2] P. 32.

        There knowing herself by her own termless self,
        Wisdom supernal, wordless, absolute
        Sat uncompanioned in the eternal Calm,
        All-seeing, motionless, sovereign and alone.

With a gap of 61 lines occurs the passage (pp. 33–34):

        The superconscient realms of motionless Peace
        Where judgment ceases and the word is mute
        And the Unconceived lies pathless and alone.

    The point raised was that, though "alone" was very fine in both cases, the occurrence of both in the context of a particular single whole of spiritual experience might slightly blunt for the reader the revelatory edge in the second case.

need be offended. The word "sole" would flatten the line [1] too much and the word "aloof" would here have no atmosphere and it would not express the idea. It is not distance and aloofness that has to be stressed but uncompanioned solitude.

— 1946

Beyond life's arc in spirit's immensities.[2]

"'Spirit' instead of 'spirit's'" might mean something else, the word "spirit" as an epithet is ambiguous — it might be spiritistic and not spiritual.

— 1936

The calm immensities of spirit space,
The golden plateaus of immortal Fire,
The moon-flame oceans of unfallen Bliss.

"Immensities" was the proper word because it helped to give the whole soul-scape of those worlds — the immensities of space, the plateaus of fire, the oceans of bliss. "Infinities" could just replace it, but now something has to be sacrificed. The only thing I can think of now is

The calm immunity of spirit space...[3]

"Immunities" in the plural is much feebler and philosophically abstract — one begins to think of things like "quantities" — naturally

---

[1]   All-seeing, motionless, sovereign and alone.

[2]   P. 44. It may be noted that Sri Aurobindo's comment here is related only to a certain type of context, as is evident from the line apropos of which the very next comment is made.

[3]   Owing to the close occurrence of the word "immensities" in another line, "immunity" was here used. At present the original word has been restored in a new context (p.47) and the line comes at the end instead of at the beginning of the sequence:

   Still regions of imperishable Light,
   All-seeing eagle-peaks of silent Power
   And moon-flame oceans of swift fathomless Bliss
   And calm immensities of spirit space.

it suggested itself to me as keeping up the plural sequence, but it grated on the sense of spiritual objective reality and I had to reject it at once. The calm immunity was a thing I could at once feel. With immunities the mind has to ask: "Well, what are they?"

— 1937

> And of the Timeless the still brooding face,
> And the creative eye of Eternity.[1]

As to the exact metrical identity in the first half of the two lines, it was certainly intentional, if by intention is meant not a manufacture by my personal mind but the spontaneous deliberateness of the inspiration which gave the lines to me and an acceptance in the receiving mind. The first halves of the two lines are metrically identical closely associating together the two things seen as of the same order, the still Timeless and the dynamic creative Eternity both of them together originating the manifest world: the latter halves of the lines diverge altogether, one into the slow massiveness of the "still brooding face", with its strong close, the other into the combination of two high and emphatic syllables with an indeterminate run of short syllables between and after, allowing the line to drop away into some unuttered endlessness rather than cease. In this rhythmical significance I can see no weakness.

— 1946

> As if the original Ukase still held back.

I have accented on the first syllable as I have done often with words like "occult", "divine". It is a Russian word and foreign words in English tend often to get their original accent shifted as far backward as possible. I have heard many do that with "ukase".[2]

— 1937

[1] P. 41.

[2] This note of Sri Aurobindo's has been entered here for its intrinsic interest. The line in question runs at present (p.75):

> He read the original ukase kept back.

Resiled from poor assent to Nature's terms.[1]

It ["resiled"] is a perfectly good English word, meaning originally to leap back, rebound (like an elastic) — so to draw back from, recoil, retreat (in military language it means to fall back from a position gained or to one's original position); but it is specially used for withdrawing from a contract, agreement, previous statement. It is therefore quite the just word here. Human nature has assented to Nature's terms and been kept by her to them, but now Aswapati resiles from the contract and the assent to it made by humanity to which he belonged. Resiled, resilient, resilience are all good words and in use.

— 1937

*
**

The incertitude of man's proud confident thought.[2]

"Uncertainty" would mean that the thought was confident but uncertain of itself, which would be a contradiction. "Incertitude" means that its truth is uncertain in spite of its proud confidence in itself.

— 1936

*
**

Aware of his occult omnipotent source,
Allured by the omniscient Ecstasy,
He felt the invasion and the nameless joy.[3]

I certainly won't have "attracted" [in place of "allured"] — there is

---

[1] P. 77. Sri Aurobindo's note apropos of this line was written when the line occurred in a context which contained no other phrase elaborating its sense. At present a further line follows:

   The harsh contract spurned and the diminished lease.

[2] P. 78.

[3] These lines, to a comment on which Sri Aurobindo has replied, are the 1937 version. At present (p. 79) the third line joins up with a passage immediately preceding the other two, thus:

   A Force came down into his mortal limbs,
   A current from eternal seas of Bliss;
   He felt the invasion and the nameless joy.

And the other two begin a new passage which continues after them:

an enormous difference between the force of the two words and merely "attracted by the Ecstasy" would take away all my ecstasy in the line—nothing so tepid can be admitted. Neither do I want "thrill" [in place of "joy"] which gives a false colour—precisely it would mean that the ecstasy was already touching him with its intensity which is far from my intention.

Your statement that "joy" is just another word for "ecstasy" is surprising. "Comfort", "pleasure", "joy", "bliss", "rapture", "ecstasy" would then be all equal and exactly synonymous terms and all distinction of shades and colours of words would disappear from literature. As well say that "flashlight" is just another word for "lightning"—or that glow, gleam, glitter, sheen, blaze are all equivalents which can be employed indifferently in the same place. One can feel allured to the supreme omniscient Ecstasy and feel a nameless joy touching one without that joy becoming itself the supreme Ecstasy. I see no loss of expressiveness by the joy coming in as a vague nameless hint of the immeasurable superior Ecstasy.

— 1937

That ["to blend and blur shades owing to technical exigencies"] might be all right for mental poetry—it won't do for what I am trying to create—in that, one word *won't* do for the other. Even in mental poetry I consider it an inferior method. "Gleam" and "glow" are two quite different things and the poet who uses them indifferently has constantly got his eye upon words rather than upon the object.

— 1937

And driven by a pointing hand of Light
Across his soul's unmapped immensitudes.[1]

A living centre of the Illimitable
Widened to equate with the world's circumference,
He turned to his immense spiritual fate.

But Sri Aurobindo's remarks do not lose their essential pertinence and force or their larger general implications.

[1] P. 80. The word "immensitude" occurs also on pp. 237 and 524:

A little gift comes from the Immensitudes...
In their immensitude signing infinity...

I take upon myself the right to coin new words. "Immensitudes" is not any more fantastic than "infinitudes" to pair "infinity".

["Would you also use 'eternitudes'?"] Not likely! I would think of the French *éternuer* and sneeze.

— 1936

The body and the life no more were all.

I still consider the line a very good one and it did perfectly express what I wanted to say. I don't see how I could have said it otherwise without diminishing or exaggerating the significance. As for "baldness", an occasionally bare and straightforward line without any trailing of luminous robes is not an improper element. E.g.

This was the day when Satyavan must die,[1]

which I would not remove from its position even if you were to give me the crown and income of the Kavi Samrat for doing it. If I have changed here, it is because the alterations all around it made the line no longer in harmony with its immediate environment.

Not at all ["bareness for bareness's sake"]. It was bareness for expression's sake, which is a different matter.... It was *juste* for expressing what I had to say then in a certain context. The context being entirely changed in its sense, bearing and atmosphere, it was no longer *juste* in that place. Its being an interloper in a new house does not show that it was an interloper in an old one. The colours and the spaces being heightened and widened this tint which was appropriate and needed in the old design could not remain in the new one. These things are a question of design; a line has to be seen not only in its own separate value but with a view to its just place in the whole.[2]

— 1937

---

[1] P. 10.

[2] The passage originally stood:

A cosmic vision looked at things through light:
Atomic now the shapes that loomed so large.
Illusion lost her aggrandising lens:
The body and the life no more were all,

As to the title of the three cantos about the Yoga of the King,[1] I intended the repetition of the word "Yoga" to bring out and emphasise the fact that this part of Aswapati's spiritual development consisted of two Yogic movements, one a psycho-spiritual transformation and the other a greater spiritual transformation with an ascent to a supreme power. The omission which you suggest would destroy this significance and leave only something more abstract. In the second of these three cantos there is a pause between the two movements and a description of the secret knowledge to which he is led and of which the results are described in the last canto, but there is no description of the Yoga itself or of the steps by which this knowledge came. That is only indicated, not narrated; so, to bring in "The Yoga of the King" as the title of this canto would not be very apposite. Aswapati's Yoga falls into three parts. First, he is achieving his own spiritual self-fulfilment as the individual and this is described as the Yoga of the King. Next, he makes the ascent as a typical representative of the race to win the possibility of discovery and possession of all the planes of consciousness and this is described in the Second Book: but this too is as yet only an individual victory. Finally, he aspires no longer for himself but for all, for a universal realisation and new creation. That is described in the Book of the Divine Mother.

— 1946

> The mind itself was only an outer court,
> His soul the tongue of an unmeasured fire.

The passage then became:

> A cosmic vision looked at things through light:
> Illusion lost her aggrandising lens,
> Atomic were her shapes that loomed so large
> And from her failing hand her measures fell:
> In the enormous spaces of the Self
> The living form seemed now a wandering shell;
> Earth was one room in his million-mansioned house,
> The mind a many-frescoed outer court,
> His soul the tongue of an unmeasured fire.

At present some of the lines have changed places in the poem and the passage as it stands on page 82 is not quite the same.

[1] Book I. Canto 3: The Yoga of the King: The Yoga of the Soul's Release.
  Canto 4: The Secret Knowledge.
  Canto 5: The Yoga of the King: The Yoga of the Spirit's Freedom and Greatness.

Largior hic campos aether et lumine vestit
Purpureo, solemque suum, sua sidera norunt.[1]

I don't know ["what plane is spoken of by Virgil"], but purple is a
light of the Vital. It may have been one of the vital heavens he was
thinking of. The ancients saw the vital heavens as the highest and
most of the religions also have done the same. I have used the
suggestion of Virgil to insert a needed line.

And griefless countries under purple suns.[2]

— 1936

Here too the gracious mighty Angel poured
Her splendour and her swiftness and her thrill,
Hoping to fill this new fair world with her joy.[3]

No, that ["pours" instead of "poured"] would take away all mean-
ing from "new fair world" — it is the attempted conquest of earth by
life when earth had been created — a past event though still
continuing in its sequel and result.

— 1936

The Mask is mentioned not twice but four times in this opening
passage[4] and it is purposely done to keep up the central connection
of the idea running through the whole. The ambassadors wear this
grey Mask, so your criticism cannot stand since there is no separate
mask coming as part of a new idea but a very pointed return to the
principal note indicating the identity of the influence throughout.
It is not a random recurrence but a purposeful touch carrying a
psychological meaning.

— 1948

---

[1] "Here an ampler ether spreads over the plains and clothes them in purple light,
and they have a sun of their own and their own stars."

[2] P. 120.

[3] An earlier version of p. 130, lines 4–6.

[4] Pp. 202–3.

> And overcast with error, grief and pain
> The soul's native will for truth and joy and light.[1]

The two trios are not intended to be exactly correspondent; "joy" answers to both "grief" and "pain" while "light" is an addition in the second trio indicating the conditions for "truth" and "joy".

—1948

> All evil starts from that ambiguous face.

Here again the same word "face" occurs a second time at the end of a line[2] but it belongs to a new section and a new turn of ideas. I am not attracted by your suggestion; the word "mien" here is an obvious literary substitution and not part of a straight and positive seeing: as such it sounds deplorably weak. The only thing would be to change the image, as for instance,

> All evil creeps from that ambiguous source.

But this is comparatively weak. I prefer to keep the "face" and insert a line before it so as to increase a little the distance between the two faces:

> Its breath is a subtle poison in men's hearts.

—1948

As to the two lines with "no man's land"[3] there can be no capital in the first line because there it is a description while the capital is needed in the other line, because the phrase has acquired there the force of a name or appellation. I am not sure about the hyphen; it could be put but the no hyphen might be better as it suggests that no one in particular has as yet got possession.

—1948

---

[1] P. 203.

[2] P. 205, line 21. The first occurrence is ten lines earlier:

> All beauty ended in an aging face.

[3] Pp. 206, 211.

The cliché you object to ... 'he quoted Scripture and Law' was put in there with fell purpose and was necessary for the effect I wanted to produce, the more direct its commonplace the better. However, I defer to your objection and have altered it to

He armed untruth with Scripture and the Law.[1]

I don't remember seeing the sentence about

Agreeing on the right to disagree

anywhere in a newspaper or in any book either; colloquial it is and perhaps for that reason only out of harmony in this passage. So I substitute

Only they agreed to differ in Evil's paths.[2]

— 1946

* * *

Often, a familiar visage studying ...
His vision warned by the spirit's inward eye
Discovered suddenly Hell's trademark there.[3]

It is a reference to the beings met in the vital world, that seem like human beings but, if one looks closely, they are seen to be Hostiles; often assuming the appearance of a familiar face they try to tempt or attack by surprise, and betray the stamp of their origin — there is also a hint that on earth too they take up human bodies or possess them for their own purpose.

— 1936

* * *

Bliss into black coma fallen, insensible.[4]

Neither of your scansions can stand. The best way will be to spell "fallen" "fall'n" as is occasionally done and treat "bliss into" as a dactyl.

— 1948

¹ P. 207.   ² P. 208.   ³ P. 215.   ⁴ P. 221.

> Bliss into black coma fallen, insensible,
> Coiled back to itself and God's eternal joy
> Through a false poignant figure of grief and pain
> Still dolorously nailed upon a cross
> Fixed in the soil of a dumb insentient world
> Where birth was a pang and death an agony,
> Lest all too soon should change again to bliss.

This has nothing to do with Christianity or Christ but only with the symbol of the cross used here to represent a seemingly eternal world-pain which appears falsely to replace the eternal bliss. It is not Christ but the world-soul which hangs here.

— 1948

> Performed the ritual of her Mysteries.[1]

It is "Mysteries" with capital M and means "mystic symbolic rites" as in the Orphic and Eleusinian "Mysteries". When written with capital M it does not mean secret mysterious things, but has this sense, e.g. a "Mystery play".

— 1936

An evolution from the Inconscient[2] need not be a painful one if there is no resistance; it can be a deliberately slow and beautiful efflorescence of the Divine. One ought to be able to see how beautiful outward Nature can be and usually is, although it is itself apparently "inconscient" — why should the growth of consciousness in inward Nature be attended by so much ugliness and evil

---

[1] P. 221.

[2] The question was in reference to a passage in the 1936 version which in the present one is much enlarged and runs from "It was the gate of a false Infinite" to "None can reach heaven who has not passed through hell" (pp. 221–27): "The passage suggests that there was an harmonious original plan of the Overmind Gods for earth's evolution, but that it was spoiled by the intrusion of the Rakshasic worlds. I should, however, have thought that an evolution, arising from the stark inconscient's sleep and the mute void, would hardly be an harmonious plan. The Rakshasas only shield themselves with the covering 'Ignorance', they don't create it. Do you mean that, if they had not interfered, there wouldn't have been resistance and conflict and suffering? How can they be called the artificers of Nature's fall and pain?"

spoiling the beauty of the outward creation? Because of a perversity born from the Ignorance, which came in with Life and increased in Mind — that is the Falsehood, the Evil that was born because of the starkness of the Inconscient's sleep separating its action from the secret luminous Conscience that is all the time within it. But it need not have been so except for the overriding Will of the Supreme which meant that the possibilities of Perversion by inconscience and ignorance should be manifested in order to be eliminated through being given their chance, since all possibility has to manifest somewhere: once it is eliminated the Divine Manifestation in Matter will be greater than it otherwise could be because it will combine all the possibilities involved in this difficult creation and not some of them as in an easier and less strenuous creation might naturally happen.

— 1937

"From beauty to greater beauty, from joy to intenser joy, by a special adjustment of the senses" — yes, that would be the normal course of a divine manifestation, however gradual, in Matter. "Discordant sound and offensive odour" are creations of a disharmony between consciousness and Nature and do not exist in themselves, they would not be present in a liberated and harmonised consciousness for they would be foreign to its being, nor would they afflict a rightly developing harmonised soul and Nature. Even the "belching volcano, crashing thunderstorm and whirling typhoon" are in themselves grandiose and beautiful things and only harmful or terrible to a consciousness unable to meet or deal with them or make a pact with the spirits of Wind and Fire. You are assuming that the manifestation from the Inconscient must be what it is now and here and that no other kind of world of Matter was possible, but the harmony of material Nature in itself shows that it need not necessarily be a discordant, evil, furiously perturbed and painful creation — the psychic being if allowed to manifest from the first in Life and Mind and lead the evolution instead of being relegated behind the veil would have been the principle of a harmony outflowing; everyone who has felt the psychic at work within him, free from the vital intervention, can at once see that this would be its effect because of its unerring perception, true choice, harmonic action. If it has not been so, it is because the dark Powers have made life a claimant instead of an instrument. The reality of the Hostiles and the nature of their role and trend of their endeavour cannot be doubted by any one who has had his inner vision unsealed and made their unpleasant acquaintance.

—1937

And the articles of the bound soul's contract.[1]

Liberty is very often taken with the last foot nowadays and usually it is just the liberty I have taken here. This liberty I took long ago in my earlier poetry.

—1948

They wouldn't be heavens if they were not immune[2]—a heaven with fear in it would be no heaven. The Life-Heavens have an influence on earth and so have the Life-Hells, but it does not follow that they influence each other in their own domain. Overmind can influence earth, so can the hostile Powers, but it does not follow that hostile Powers can penetrate the Overmind—they can't: they can only spoil what it sends to the earth. Each power of the Divine (life like mind and matter is a power of the Divine) has its own harmony inherent in the purity of its own principle—it is only if it is disturbed or perverted that it produces disorder. That is another reason why the evolution could have been a progressing harmony, not a series of discords through which harmony of a precarious and wounded kind has to be struggled for at each step; for the Divine Principle is there within. Each plane therefore has its heavens; there are the subtle physical heavens, the vital heavens, the mental

---

[1] P. 231.

[2] The question apropos of the canto called "The Paradise of the Life-Gods", pp. 233–37, ran: "Is the plane of the Life-Heavens perfectly immune? Is there no attack at times from the Life-Hells, no visitor from them thrusting in? The Life-Heavens do have an influence on earth, don't they? And as the Life-Hells too have, don't they ever clash in the subtle worlds?... And what exactly is the basis of the vital harmony? On the Overhead planes there is the consciousness of the One everywhere, but that can't happen here."

heavens. If Powers of disharmony got in, they would cease to be
heavens.

— 1937

There Love fulfilled her gold and roseate dreams
And Strength her crowned and mighty reveries.[1]

"Gold and roseate dreams" cannot be changed. "Muse" would
make it at once artificial. "Dreams" alone is the right word there.
"Reveries" also cannot be changed, especially as it is not any
particular "reverie" that is meant. Also, "dream" at the beginning
of a later line departs into another idea and is appropriate in its
place; I see no objection to this purposeful repetition. Anyway the
line cannot be altered. The only concession I can make to you is to
alter the first.[2]

— 1948

All reeled into a world of Kali's dance.[3]

It is "world", not "whirl". It means "all reeling in a clash and
confusion became a world of Kali's dance."

— 1948

Knowledge was rebuilt from cells of inference
Into a fixed body flasque and perishable.[4]

"Flasque" is a French word meaning "slack", "loose", "flaccid" etc.
I have more than once tried to thrust in a French word like this, for
instance, "A harlot empress in a bouge"— somewhat after the
manner of Eliot and Ezra Pound.

— 1946

**

---

[1] P. 235.

[2]   Adoring blue heaven with their happy dreams.

This line on page 234 ends now with the word "hymn".

[3] P. 255.   [4] P. 267.

For Truth is wider, greater than her forms.
A thousand icons they have made of her
And find her in the idols they adore;
But she remains herself and infinite.[1]

"They" means nobody in particular but corresponds to the French "On dit" meaning vaguely "people in general". This is a use permissible in English; for instance, "They say you are not so scrupulous as you should be."

—1948

"Depths" will not do,[2] since the meaning is not that it took no part in what came from the depths but did take part in what came from the shallows; the word would be merely a rhetorical flourish and take away the real sense. It would be easy in several ways to avoid the two "it"s coming together but the direct force would be lost. I think a comma at "it" and the slight pause it would bring in the reading would be sufficient. For instance, one could write "no part it took", instead of "it took no part", but the direct force I want would be lost.

—1948

**

Travestied with a fortuitous sovereignty.[3]

I am unable to follow your criticism. I find nothing pompous or bombastic in the line unless it is the resonance of the word "fortuitous" and the many closely packed "t"s that give you the impression. But "fortuitous" cannot be sacrificed as it exactly hits the meaning I want. Also I fail to see what is abstract and especially mental in it. Neither a travesty nor sovereignty are abstract things and the images here are all concrete, as they should be to express

---

[1] P. 276.

[2] P. 283. The reply is to: "Would it be an improvement if one of the two successive 'it's in

In the world which sprang from it it took no part

is avoided? Why not put something like 'its depths' for the first 'it'?"

[3] P. 285.

the inner vision's sense of concreteness of subtle things. The whole passage is of course about mental movements and mental powers, therefore about what the intellect sees as abstractions, but the inner vision does not feel them as that. To it mind has a substance and its energies and actions are very real and substantial things. Naturally there is a certain sense of scorn in this passage, for what the Ignorance regards as its sovereignty and positive truth has been exposed by the "sceptic ray" as fortuitous and unreal.

—1948

That clasped him in from day and night's pursuit.[1]

I do not realise what you mean by "stickiness", since there are only two hard labials and some nasals; is it that combination which makes you feel sticky, or does the addition of some hard dentals also help? Anyhow, sticky or not, I am unwilling to change anything.

I do not want to put "day's" and "night's"; I find it heavy and unnecessary. It ought to be clear enough to the reader that "day and night" are here one double entity or two hounds in a leash pursuing a common prey.

—1948

"Lulling" will never do. It is too ornamental and romantic and tender. I have put "slumber" in its place.[2]

[1] P. 289.

[2] P. 294. The suggestion offered to Sri Aurobindo was: "Your line,

In a stillness of the voices of the world,

is separated by twenty lines from

In the formless force and the still fixity.

So there is no fault here in 'stillness', but an added poetic quality might come if 'stillness' were avoided and some such word as 'lulling' used, especially as the line before runs:

And cradles of heavenly rapture and repose."

> A Panergy that harmonised all life.[1]

I do not think the word "Panergy" depends for its meaning on the word "energies" in a previous line. The "Panergy" suggested is a self-existent total power which may carry the cosmic energies in it and is their cause but is not constituted by them.

— 1948

I have wholly failed to feel the poetic flatness of which you accuse the line

> All he had been and all that now he was.

No doubt, the diction is extremely simple, direct and unadorned but that can be said of numberless good lines in poetry and even of some great lines. If there is style, if there is a balanced rhythm (rhyme is not necessary) and a balanced language and significance (for these two elements combined always create a good style), and if the line or the passage in which it occurs has some elevation or profundity or other poetic quality in the idea which it expresses, then there cannot be any flatness nor can any such line or passage be set aside as prosaic.

— 1946

Your new objection to the line,

> All he had been and all that now he was,

is somewhat self-contradictory. If a line has a rhythm and expressive turn which makes it poetic, then it must be good poetry; but I suppose what you mean is fine or elevated poetry. I would say that my line is good poetry and is further uplifted by rising towards its

---

[1] P. 300. The point raised was: "That 'Panergy' is a fine coinage, but, by following the word 'energies' in the third line before it, does it not become a little bit obvious, losing its mysterious suggestion? I dare say 'energies' helps to make it clear, but is it necessary to prepare it? Will not a better effect be produced by springing it suddenly upon the reader, preparing it only indirectly by using some synonym for 'energies' in the other line?"

subsequent context which gives it its full poetic meaning and suggestion, the evolution of the inner being and the abrupt end or failure of all that had been done unless it could suddenly transcend itself and become something greater. I do not think that this line in its context is merely passable, but I admit that it is less elevated and intense than what precedes or what follows. I do not see how that can be avoided without truncating the thought significance of the whole account by the omission of something necessary to its evolution or else overpitching the expression where it needs to be direct or clear and bare in its lucidity. In any case the emended version — "All he had been and all towards which he grew"[1] — cures any possibility of the line being merely passable as it raises both the idea and the expression through the vividness of image which makes us feel and not merely think the living evolution in Aswapati's inner being.

—1946

[1] P. 307.

5

You have asked me to comment on your friend X's comments on
my poetry and especially on Savitri.[1] But, first of all, it is not usual
for a poet to criticise the criticisms of his critics though a few
perhaps have done so; the poet writes for his own satisfaction, his
own delight in poetical creation or to express himself and he leaves
his work for the world, and rather for posterity than for the con-
temporary world, to recognise or to ignore, to judge and value
according to its perception or its pleasure. As for the contemporary
world he might be said rather to throw his poem in its face and
leave it to resent this treatment as an unpleasant slap, as a contem-
porary world treated the early poems of Wordsworth and Keats, or
to accept it as an abrupt but gratifying attention, which was ordi-
narily the good fortune of the great poets in ancient Athens and
Rome and of poets like Shakespeare and Tennyson in modern
times. Posterity does not always confirm the contemporary verdict,
very often it reverses it, forgets or depreciates the writer enthroned
by contemporary fame, or raises up to a great height work little
appreciated or quite ignored in its own time. The only safety for the
poet is to go his own way careless of the blows and caresses of the
critics; it is not his business to answer them. Then you ask me to
right the wrong turn your friend's critical mind has taken; but how
is it to be determined what is the right and what is the wrong turn,
since a critical judgment depends usually on a personal reaction
determined by the critic's temperament or the aesthetic trend in
him or by values, rules or canons which are settled for his intellect
and agree with the viewpoint from which his mind receives what-
ever comes to him for judgment; it is that which is right for him
though it may seem wrong to a different temperament, aesthetic
intellectuality or mental viewpoint. Your friend's judgments, ac-
cording to his own account of them, seem to be determined by a
sensitive temperament finely balanced in its own poise but limited
in its appreciations, clear and open to some kinds of poetic creation,

---

[1] The critic's comments were made apropos of the article "Sri Aurobindo — A New
Age of Mystical Poetry", by K. D. Sethna (Sri Aurobindo Circle, 1946). Passages from
Savitri appeared in print for the first time in this article, in which a few of Sri
Aurobindo's shorter poems were also discussed. The full text of Sri Aurobindo's letter,
from which relevant portions are quoted here, is to be found in On Himself, Sri
Aurobindo Birth Centenary Library, Vol. 26, pp. 238–63.

reserved towards others, against yet others closed and cold or excessively depreciative. This sufficiently explains his very different reactions to the two poems, *Descent* and *Flame-Wind*,[1] which he unreservedly admires and to *Savitri*. However, since you have asked me, I will answer, as between ourselves, in some detail and put forward my own comments on his comments and my own judgments on his judgments. It may be rather long; for if such things are done, they may as well be clearly and thoroughly done. I may also have something to say about the nature and intention of my poem and the technique necessitated by the novelty of the intention and nature.

Let me deal first with some of the details he stresses so as to get them out of the way. His detailed intellectual reasons for his judgments seem to me to be often arbitrary and fastidious, sometimes based on a misunderstanding and therefore invalid or else valid perhaps in other fields but here inapplicable. Take, for instance, his attack upon my use of the prepositional phrase. Here, it seems to me, he has fallen victim to a grammatical obsession and lumped together under the head of the prepositional twist a number of different turns some of which do not belong to that category at all. In the line,[2]

> Lone on my summits of calm I have brooded with voices around me,

there is no such twist; for I did not mean at all "on my calm summits", but intended straightforwardly to convey the natural, simple meaning of the word. If I write "the fields of beauty" or "walking on the paths of truth" I do not expect to be supposed to mean "in beautiful fields" or "in truthful paths"; it is the same with "summits of calm", I mean "summits of calm" and nothing else; it is a phrase like "He rose to high peaks of vision" or "He took his station on the highest summits of knowledge". The calm is the calm of the highest spiritual consciousness to which the soul has ascended, making those summits its own and looking down from their highest heights on all below: in spiritual experience, in the occult

---

[1] *Collected Poems*, Sri Aurobindo Birth Centenary Library, Vol. 5, pp. 563, 559. The poems and translations referred to in this letter were previously published in *Collected Poems and Plays* (1942), Vol. iI.

[2] Not in *Savitri* but in *Trance of Waiting* (*Collected Poems*, p. 558).

vision or feeling that accompanies it, this calm is not felt as an abstract quality or a mental condition but as something concrete and massive, a self-existent reality to which one reaches, so that the soul standing on its peak is rather a tangible fact of experience than a poetical image. Then there is the phrase "A face of rapturous calm":[1] he seems to think it is a mere trick of language, a substitution of a prepositional phrase for an epithet, as if I had intended to say "a rapturously calm face" and I said instead "a face of rapturous calm" in order to get an illegitimate and meaningless rhetorical effect. I meant nothing of the kind, nothing so tame and poor and scanty in sense: I meant a face which was an expression or rather a living image of the rapturous calm of the supreme and infinite consciousness, — it is indeed so that it can well be "Infinity's centre". The face of the liberated Buddha as presented to us by Indian art is such an expression or image of the calm of Nirvana and could, I think, be quite legitimately described as a face of Nirvanic calm, and that would be an apt and live phrase and not an ugly artifice or twist of rhetoric. It should be remembered that the calm of Nirvana or the calm of the supreme Consciousness is to spiritual experience something self-existent, impersonal and eternal and not dependent on the person — or the face — which manifests it. In these two passages I take then the liberty to regard X's criticism as erroneous at its base and therefore invalid and inadmissible.

Then there are the lines from the *Songs of the Sea*:

> The rains of deluge flee, a storm-tossed shade,
> Over thy breast of gloom...[2]

"Thy breast of gloom" is not used here as a mere rhetorical and meaningless variation of "thy gloomy breast"; it might have been more easily taken as that if it had been a human breast, though even then, it could have been entirely defensible in a fitting context; but it is the breast of the sea, an image for a vast expanse supporting and reflecting or subject to the moods or movements of the air and the sky. It is intended, in describing the passage of the rains of deluge over the breast of the sea, to present a picture of a

---

[1] *Savitri*, p. 4:

> Infinity's centre, a Face of rapturous calm
> Parted the eternal lids that open heaven.

[2] *Translations*, Sri Aurobindo Birth Centenary Library, Vol. 8, p. 366.

storm-tossed shade crossing a vast gloom: it is the gloom that has to be stressed and made the predominant idea and the breast or expanse is only its support and not the main thing: this could not have been suggested by merely writing "thy gloomy breast". A prepositional phrase need not be merely an artificial twist replacing an adjective; for instance, "a world of gloom and terror" means something more than "a gloomy and terrible world", it brings forward the gloom and terror as the very nature and constitution, the whole content of the world and not merely an attribute. So also if one wrote "Him too wilt thou throw to thy sword of sharpness" or "cast into thy pits of horror", would it merely mean "thy sharp sword" and "thy horrible pits"? and would not the sharpness and the horror rather indicate or represent formidable powers of which the sword is the instrument and the pits the habitation or lair? That would be rhetoric but it would be a rhetoric not meaningless but having in it meaning and power. Rhetoric is a word with which we can batter something we do not like; but rhetoric of one kind or another has been always a great part of the world's best literature; Demosthenes, Cicero, Bossuet and Burke are rhetoricians, but their work ranks with the greatest prose styles that have been left to us. In poetry the accusation of rhetoric might be brought against such lines as Keats'

> Thou wast not born for death, immortal Bird!
> No hungry generations tread thee down....[1]

To conclude, there is "the swords of sheen" in the translation of *Bande Mataram.*[2] That might be more open to the critic's stricture, for the expression can be used and perhaps has been used in verse as merely equivalent to "shining swords"; but for any one with an alert imagination it can mean in certain contexts something more than that, swords that emit brilliance and seem to be made of light. X says that to use this turn in any other than an adjectival sense is unidiomatic, but he admits that there need be no objection provided that it creates a sense of beauty, but he finds no beauty in any of these passages. But the beauty can be perceived only if the other sense is seen, and even then we come back to the question of personal reaction; you and other readers may feel beauty where he finds none. I do not myself share his sensitive abhorrence of this

---

[1] *Ode to a Nightingale.*   [2] *Translations,* p. 310.

prepositional phrase; it may be of course because there are coarser
rhetorical threads in my literary taste. I would not, for instance,
shrink from a sentence like this in a sort of free verse, "Where is thy
wall of safety? Where is thy arm of strength? Whither has fled thy
vanished face of glory?" Rhetoric of course, but it has in it an
element which can be attractive, and it seems to me to bring in a
more vivid note and mean more than "thy strong arm" or "thy
glorious face" or than "the strength of thy arm" and "the glory of thy
face".

I come next to the critic's trenchant attack on that passage in
my symbolic vision of Night and Dawn in which there is recorded
the conscious adoration of Nature when it feels the passage of the
omniscient Goddess of eternal Light. Trenchant, but with what
seems to me a false edge; or else if it is a sword of Damascus that
would cleave the strongest material mass of iron he is using it to cut
through subtle air, the air closes behind his passage and remains
unsevered. He finds here only poor and false poetry, unoriginal in
imagery and void of true wording and true vision, but that is again a
matter of personal reaction and everyone has a right to his own, you
to yours as he to his. I was not seeking for originality but for truth
and the effective poetical expression of my vision. He finds no
vision there, and that may be because I could not express myself
with any power; but it may also be because of his temperamental
failure to feel and see what I felt and saw. I can only answer to the
intellectual reasonings and judgments which turned up in him
when he tried to find the causes of his reaction. These seem to me to
be either fastidious and unsound or founded on a mistake of
comprehension and therefore invalid or else inapplicable to this
kind of poetry. His main charge is that there is a violent and
altogether illegitimate transference of epithet in the expression
"the wide-winged hymn of a great priestly wind".[1] A transference
of epithet is not necessarily illegitimate, especially if it expresses
something that is true or necessary to convey a sound feeling and
vision of things: for instance, if one writes in an Ovidian account of
the *dénouement* of a lovers' quarrel

In spite of a reluctant sullen heart
My willing feet were driven to thy door,

[1] *Savitri*, p. 4.

it might be said that it was something in the mind that was willing and the ascription of an emotion or state of mind to the feet is an illegitimate transfer of epithet; but the lines express a conflict of the members, the mind reluctant, the body obeying the force of the desire that moves it and the use of the epithet is therefore perfectly true and legitimate. But here no such defence is necessary because there is no transfer of epithets. The critic thinks that I imagined the wind as having a winged body and then took away the wings from its shoulders and clapped them on to its voice or hymn which could have no body. But I did nothing of the kind; I am not bound to give wings to the wind. In an occult vision the breath, sound, movement by which we physically know of a wind is not its real being but only the physical manifestation of the wind-god or the spirit of the air, as in the Veda the sacrificial fire is only a physical birth, temporary body or manifestation of the god of Fire, Agni. The gods of the Air and other godheads in the Indian tradition have no wings, the Maruts or storm-gods ride through the skies in their galloping chariots with their flashing golden lances, the beings of the middle world in the Ajanta frescoes are seen moving through the air not with wings but with a gliding natural motion proper to ethereal bodies. The epithet "wide-winged" then does not belong to the wind and is not transferred from it, but is proper to the voice of the wind which takes the form of a conscious hymn of aspiration and rises ascending from the bosom of the great priest, as might a great-winged bird released into the sky and sinks and rises again, aspires and fails and aspires again on the "altar hills". One can surely speak of a voice or a chant of aspiration rising on wide wings and I do not see how this can be taxed as a false or unpoetic image. Then the critic objects to the expression "altar hills" on the ground that this is superfluous as the imagination of the reader can very well supply this detail for itself from what has already been said: I do not think this is correct, a very alert reader might do so but most would not even think of it, and yet the detail is an essential and central feature of the thing seen and to omit it would be to leave a gap in the middle of the picture by dropping out something which is indispensable to its totality. Finally he finds that the line about the high boughs praying in the revealing sky does not help but attenuates, instead of more strongly etching the picture. I do not know why, unless he has failed to feel and to see. The picture is that of a conscious adoration offered by Nature and in that each element is conscious in its own way, the wind and its hymn, the hills, the trees. The wind is the great priest of this sacrifice of worship, his voice rises in a conscious hymn of aspiration, the hills offer themselves with the feeling of being an altar of the worship, the trees lift their high boughs towards heaven as the worshippers, silent figures of prayer, and the light of the sky into which their boughs rise reveals the Beyond towards which all aspires. At any rate this "picture" or rather this part of the vision is a complete rendering of what I saw in the light of the inspiration and the experience that came to me. I might indeed have elaborated more details, etched out at more length but that would have been superfluous and unnecessary; or I might have indulged in an ampler description but this would have been appropriate only if this part of the vision had been the whole. This last line[1] is an expression of an experience which I often had whether in the mountains or on the plains of Gujarat or looking from my window in Pondicherry not only in the dawn but at other times and I am unable to find any feebleness either in the experience or in the words that express it. If the critic or any reader does not feel or see what I so often felt and saw, that may be my fault, but that is not sure, for you and others have felt very differently about it; it may be a mental or a temperamental failure on their part and it will be then my or perhaps even the critic's or reader's misfortune.

I may refer here to X's disparaging characterisation of my epithets. He finds that their only merit is that they are good prose epithets, not otiose but right words in their right place and exactly descriptive but only descriptive without any suggestion of any poetic beauty or any kind of magic. Are there then prose epithets and poetic epithets and is the poet debarred from exact description using always the right word in the right place, the *mot juste*? I am under the impression that all poets, even the greatest, use as the bulk of their adjectives words that have that merit, and the difference from prose is that a certain turn in the use of them accompanied by the power of the rhythm in which they are carried lifts all to the poetic level. Take one of the passages I have quoted from Milton,[2]

On evil days though fall'n, and evil tongues...

---

[1] The high boughs prayed in a revealing sky.

[2] The reference is to the more general but earlier letter appearing here in the next section. See pp. 814–15.

> Blind Thamyris and blind Maeonides
> And Tiresias and Phineus, prophets old,

here the epithets are the same that would be used in prose, the right word in the right place, exact in statement, but all lies in the turn which makes them convey a powerful and moving emotion and the rhythm which gives them an uplifting passion and penetrating insistence. In more ordinary passages such as the beginning of *Paradise Lost* the epithets "forbidden tree" and "mortal taste" are of the same kind, but can we say that they are merely prose epithets, good descriptive adjectives and have no other merit? If you take the lines about Nature's worship in *Savitri*, I do not see how they can be described as prose epithets; at any rate I would never have dreamt of using in prose unless I wanted to write poetic prose such expressions as "wide-winged hymn" or "a great priestly wind" or "altar hills" or "revealing sky"; these epithets belong in their very nature to poetry alone whatever may be their other value or want of value. He says they are obvious and could have been supplied by any imaginative reader; well, so are Milton's in the passages quoted and perhaps there too the very remarkable imaginative reader whom X repeatedly brings in might have supplied them by his own unfailing poetic verve. Whether they or any of them prick a hidden beauty out of the picture is for each reader to feel or judge for himself; but perhaps he is thinking of such things as Keats' "magic casements" and "foam of perilous seas" and "fairy lands forlorn", but I do not think even in Keats the bulk of the epithets are of that unusual character.

I have said that his objections are sometimes inapplicable. I mean by this that they might have some force with regard to another kind of poetry but not to a poem like *Savitri*. He says, to start with, that if I had had a stronger imagination, I would have written a very different poem and a much shorter one. Obviously, and to say it is a truism; if I had had a different kind of imagination, whether stronger or weaker, I would have written a different poem and perhaps one more to his taste; but it would not have been *Savitri*. It would not have fulfilled the intention or had anything of the character, meaning, world-vision, description and expression of spiritual experience which was my object in writing this poem. Its length is an indispensable condition for carrying out its purpose and everywhere there is this length, critics may say an "unconscionable length" — I am quoting the *Times* reviewer's description[1] in his otherwise eulogistic criticism of *The Life Divine* — in every part, in every passage, in almost every canto or section of a canto. It has been planned not on the scale of *Lycidas* or *Comus* or some brief narrative poem, but of the longer epical narrative, almost a minor, though a very minor *Ramayana*; it aims not at a minimum but at an exhaustive exposition of its world-vision or world-interpretation. One artistic method is to select a limited subject and even on that to say only what is indispensable, what is centrally suggestive and leave the rest to the imagination or understanding of the reader. Another method which I hold to be equally artistic or, if you like, architectural is to give a large and even a vast, a complete inter-pretation, omitting nothing that is necessary, fundamental to the completeness: that is the method I have chosen in *Savitri*. But X has understood nothing of the significance or intention of the passages he is criticising, least of all, their inner sense — that is not his fault, but is partly due to the lack of the context and partly to his lack of equipment and you have there an unfair advantage over him which enables you to understand and see the poetic intention. He sees only an outward form of words and some kind of surface sense which is to him vacant and merely ornamental or rhetorical or something pretentious without any true meaning or true vision in it: inevitably he finds the whole thing false and empty, unjustifiably ambitious and pompous without deep meaning or, as he expresses it, pseudo and phoney. His objection of *longueur* would be per-fectly just if the description of the night and the dawn had been simply of physical night and physical dawn; but here the physical night and physical dawn are, as the title of the canto clearly sug-gests, a symbol, although what may be called a real symbol of an inner reality and the main purpose is to describe by suggestion the thing symbolised; here it is a relapse into Inconscience broken by a slow and difficult return of consciousness followed by a brief but splendid and prophetic outbreak of spiritual light leaving behind it the "day" of ordinary human consciousness in which the prophecy has to be worked out. The whole of *Savitri* is, according to the title of the poem, a legend that is a symbol and this opening canto is, it may be said, a key beginning and announcement. So understood there is nothing here otiose or unnecessary; all is needed to bring out by suggestion some aspect of the thing symbolised and so start

[1] *The Times Literary Supplement*, January 17, 1942.

adequately the working out of the significance of the whole poem. It will of course seem much too long to a reader who does not understand what is written or, understanding, takes no interest in the subject; but that is unavoidable.

To illustrate the inapplicability of some of his judgments one might take his objection to repetition of the cognates "sombre Vast", "unsounded Void", "opaque Inane", "vacant Vasts"[1] and his clinching condemnation of the inartistic inelegance of their occurrence in the same place at the end of the line. I take leave to doubt his statement that in each place his alert imaginative reader, still less any reader without that equipment, could have supplied these descriptions and epithets from the context, but let that pass. What was important for me was to keep constantly before the view of the reader, not imaginative but attentive to seize the whole truth of the vision in its totality, the ever-present sense of the Inconscience in which everything is occurring. It is the frame as well as the background without which all the details would either fall apart or stand out only as separate incidents. That necessity lasts until there is the full outburst of the dawn and then it disappears; each phrase gives a feature of this Inconscience proper to its place and context. It is the entrance of the "lonely splendour" into an otherwise inconscient obstructing and unreceptive world that has to be brought out and that cannot be done without the image of the "opaque Inane" of the Inconscience which is the scene and cause of the resistance. There is the same necessity for reminding the reader that the "tread" of the Divine Mother was an intrusion on the vacancy of the Inconscience and the herald of deliverance from it. The same reasoning applies to the other passages. As for the occurrence of the phrases in the same place each in its line, that is a rhythmic turn helpful, one might say necessary to bring out the intended effect, to emphasise this reiteration and make it not only understood but felt. It is not the result of negligence or an awkward and inartistic clumsiness, it is intentional and part of the technique. The structure of the pentameter blank verse in *Savitri* is of its own kind and different in plan from the blank verse that has come to be ordinarily used in English poetry. It dispenses with enjambment or uses it very sparingly and only when a special effect is intended; each line must be strong enough to stand by itself, while at the same time it fits harmoniously into the sentence or paragraph like stone

[1] Pp. 2–4.

added to stone; the sentence consists usually of one, two, three or four lines, more rarely five or six or seven: a strong close for the line and a strong close for the sentence are almost indispensable except when some kind of inconclusive cadence is desirable; there must be no laxity or diffusiveness in the rhythm or in the metrical flow anywhere, — there must be a flow but not a loose flux. This gives an added importance to what comes at the close of the line and this placing is used very often to give emphasis and prominence to a key phrase or a key idea, especially those which have to be often reiterated in the thought and vision of the poem so as to recall attention to things that are universal or fundamental or otherwise of the first consequence — whether for the immediate subject or in the total plan. It is this use that is served here by the reiteration at the end of the line.

I have not anywhere in *Savitri* written anything for the sake of mere picturesqueness or merely to produce a rhetorical effect; what I am trying to do everywhere in the poem is to express exactly something seen, something felt or experienced; if, for instance, I indulge in the wealth-burdened line or passage, it is not merely for the pleasure of the indulgence, but because there is that burden, or at least what I conceive to be that, in the vision or the experience. When the expression has been found, I have to judge, not by the intellect or by any set poetical rule, but by an intuitive feeling, whether it is entirely the right expression and, if it is not, I have to change and go on changing until I have received the absolutely right inspiration and the right transcription of it and must never be satisfied with any *à peu près* or imperfect transcription even if that makes good poetry of one kind or another. This is what I have tried to do. The critic or reader will judge for himself whether I have succeeded or failed; but if he has seen nothing and understood nothing, it does not follow that his adverse judgment is sure to be the right and true one, there is at least a chance that he may so conclude, not because there is nothing to see and nothing to understand, only poor pseudo-stuff or a rhetorical emptiness but because he was not equipped for the vision or the understanding. *Savitri* is the record of a seeing, of an experience which is not of the common kind and is often very far from what the general human mind sees and experiences. You must not expect appreciation or understanding from the general public or even from many at the first touch; as I have pointed out, there must be a new extension of consciousness and aesthesis to appreciate a new kind of mystic poetry. Moreover if it is really new in kind, it may employ a new technique, not perhaps absolutely new, but new in some or many of its elements: in that case old rules and canons and standards may be quite inapplicable; evidently, you cannot justly apply to the poetry of Whitman the principles of technique which are proper to the old metrical verse or the established laws of the old traditional poetry; so too when we deal with a modernist poet. We have to see whether what is essential to poetry is there and how far the new technique justifies itself by new beauty and perfection, and a certain freedom of mind from old conventions is necessary if our judgment is to be valid or rightly objective.

Your friend may say as he has said in another connection that all this is only special pleading or an apology rather than an apologia. But in that other connection he was mistaken and would be so here too, for in neither case have I the feeling that I had been guilty of some offence or some shortcoming and therefore there could be no place for an apology or special pleading such as is used to defend or cover up what one knows to be a false case. I have enough respect for truth not to try to cover up an imperfection; my endeavour would be rather to cure the recognised imperfection; if I have not poetical genius, at least I can claim a sufficient, if not an infinite capacity for painstaking: that I have sufficiently shown by my long labour on *Savitri*. Or rather, since it was not labour in the ordinary sense, not a labour of painstaking construction, I may describe it as an infinite capacity for waiting and listening for the true inspiration and rejecting all that fell short of it, however good it might seem from a lower standard until I got that which I felt to be absolutely right. X was evidently under a misconception with regard to my defence of the wealth-burdened line; he says that the principle enounced by me was sound but what mattered was my application of the principle, and he seems to think that I was trying to justify my application although I knew it to be bad and false by citing passages from Milton and Shakespeare as if my use of the wealth-burdened style were as good as theirs. But I was not defending the excellence of my practice, for the poetical value of my lines was not then in question; the question was whether it did not violate a valid law of a certain chaste economy by the use of too many epithets massed together: against this I was asserting the legitimacy of a massed richness, I was defending only its principle,

not my use of the principle. Even a very small poet can cite in aid of
his practice examples from greater poets without implying that his
poetry is on a par with theirs. But he further asserts that I showed
small judgment in choosing my citations, because Milton's passage [1]
is not at all an illustration of the principle and Shakespeare's [2] is
inferior in poetic value, lax and rhetorical in its richness and be-
longs to an early and inferior Shakespearean style. He says that
Milton's astounding effect is due only to the sound and not to the
words. That does not seem to me quite true: the sound, the rhyth-
mic resonance, the rhythmic significance is undoubtedly the pre-
dominant factor; it makes us hear and feel the crash and clamour
and clangour of the downfall of the rebel angels: but that is not all,
we do not merely hear as if one were listening to the roar of ruin of a
collapsing bomb-shattered house, but saw nothing, we have the
vision and the full psychological commotion of the "hideous" and
flaming ruin of the downfall, and it is the tremendous force of the
words that makes us see as well as hear. X's disparagement of the
Shakespearean passage on "sleep" and the line on the sea con-
sidered by the greatest critics and not by myself only as ranking
amongst the most admired and admirable things in Shakespeare is
surprising and it seems to me to illustrate a serious limitation in his
poetic perception and temperamental sympathies. Shakespeare's
later terse and packed style with its more powerful dramatic effects
can surely be admired without disparaging the beauty and opulence
of his earlier style; if he had never written in that style, it would
have been an unspeakable loss to the sum of the world's aesthetic
possessions. The lines I have quoted are neither lax nor merely
rhetorical, they have a terseness or at least a compactness of their
own, different in character from the lines, let us say, in the scene of
Antony's death or other memorable passages written in his great
tragic style but none the less at every step packed with pregnant
meanings and powerful significances which would not be possible
if it were merely a loose rhetoric. Anyone writing such lines would

[1]   With hideous ruin and combustion, down
        To bottomless perdition, there to dwell
        In adamantine chains and penal fire.

[2]   Wilt thou upon the high and giddy mast
        Seal up the shipboy's eyes and rock his brains
        In cradle of the rude imperious surge?

deserve to rank by them alone among the great and even the greatest poets....

As regards your friend's appraisal of the mystical poems, I need say little. I accept his reservation that there is much inequality as between the different poems: they were produced very rapidly — in the course of a week, I think — and they were not given the long reconsideration that I have usually given to my poetic work before publication; he has chosen the best, though there are others also that are good, though not so good; in others, the metre attempted and the idea and language have not been lifted to their highest possible value. I would like to say a word about his hesitation over some lines in *Thought the Paraclete*[1] which describe the spiritual planes. I can understand this hesitation; for these lines have not the vivid and forceful precision of the opening and the close and are less pressed home, they are general in description and therefore to one who has not the mystic experience may seem too large and vague. But they are not padding; a precise and exact description of these planes of experience would have made the poem too long, so only some large lines are given, but the description is true, the epithets hit the reality and even the colours mentioned in the poem, "gold-red feet" and "crimson-white mooned oceans", are faithful to experience. Significant colour, supposed by intellectual criticism to be symbolic but there is more than that, is a frequent element in mystic vision; I may mention the powerful and vivid vision in which Ramakrishna went up into the higher planes and saw the mystic truth behind the birth of Vivekananda. At least, the fact that these poems have appealed so strongly to your friend's mind may perhaps be taken by me as a sufficient proof that in this field my effort at interpretation of spiritual things has not been altogether a failure.

But how then are we to account for the same critic's condemnation or small appreciation of *Savitri* which is also a mystic and symbolic poem although cast into a different form and raised to a different pitch, and what value am I to attach to his criticism? Partly, perhaps, it is this very difference of form and pitch which accounts for his attitude and, having regard to his aesthetic temperament and its limitations, it was inevitable. He himself seems to suggest this reason when he compares this difference to the difference of his approach as between *Lycidas* and *Paradise Lost*. His

[1] *Collected Poems*, p. 582.

temperamental turn is shown by his special appreciation of Francis Thompson and Coventry Patmore and his response to *Descent* and *Flame-Wind* and the fineness of his judgment when speaking of the *Hound of Heaven* and the *Kingdom of God*, its limitation by his approach towards *Paradise Lost*. I think he would be naturally inclined to regard any very high-pitched poetry as rhetorical and unsound and declamatory, wherever he did not see in it something finely and subtly true coexisting with the high-pitched expression, — the combination we find in Thompson's later poem and it is this he seems to have missed in *Savitri*. For *Savitri* does contain or at least I intended it to contain what you and others have felt in it but he has not been able to feel because it is something which is outside his own experience and to which he has no access. One who has had the kind of experience which *Savitri* sets out to express or who, not having it, is prepared by his temperament, his mental turn, his previous intellectual knowledge or psychic training, to have some kind of access to it, the feeling of it if not the full understanding, can enter into the spirit and sense of the poem and respond to its poetic appeal; but without that it is difficult for an unprepared reader to respond, — all the more if this is, as you contend, a new poetry with a new law of expression and technique.

Lycidas is one of the finest poems in any literature, one of the most consistently perfect among works of an equal length and one can apply to it the epithet "exquisite" and it is to the exquisite that your friend's aesthetic temperament seems specially to respond. It would be possible to a reader with a depreciatory turn to find flaws in it, such as the pseudo-pastoral setting, the too powerful intrusion of St. Peter and puritan theological controversy into that incongruous setting and the image of the hungry sheep which someone not in sympathy with Christian feeling and traditional imagery might find even ludicrous or at least odd in its identification of pseudo-pastoral sheep and theological human sheep: but these would be hypercritical objections and are flooded out by the magnificence of the poetry. I am prepared to admit the very patent defects of *Paradise Lost*: Milton's heaven is indeed unconvincing and can be described as grotesque and so too is his gunpowder battle up there, and his God and angels are weak and unconvincing figures, even Adam and Eve, our first parents, do not effectively fill their part except in his outward description of them; and the later narrative falls far below the grandeur of the first four books but those four books stand for ever among the greatest things in the world's poetic literature. If *Lycidas* with its beauty and perfection had been the supreme thing done by Milton even with all the lyrical poetry and the sonnets added to it, Milton would still have been a great poet but he would not have ranked among the dozen greatest; it is *Paradise Lost* that gives him that place. There are deficiencies if not failures in almost all the great epics, the *Odyssey* and perhaps the *Divina Commedia* being the only exceptions, but still they are throughout in spite of them great epics. So too is *Paradise Lost*. The grandeur of his verse and language is constant and unsinking to the end and makes the presentation always sublime. We have to accept for the moment Milton's dry Puritan theology and his all too human picture of the celestial world and its denizens and then we can feel the full greatness of the epic. But the point is that this greatness in itself seems to have less appeal to X's aesthetic temperament; it is as if he felt less at home in its atmosphere, in an atmosphere of grandeur and sublimity than in the air of a less sublime but a fine and always perfect beauty. It is the difference between a magic hill-side woodland of wonder and a great soaring mountain climbing into a vast purple sky: to accept fully the greatness he needs to find in it a finer and subtler strain as in Thompson's *Kingdom of God*. On a lower scale this, his sentence about it seems to suggest, is the one fundamental reason for his complete pleasure in the mystical poems and his very different approach to *Savitri*. The pitch aimed at by *Savitri*, the greatness you attribute to it, would of itself have discouraged in him any abandonment to admiration and compelled from the beginning a cautious and dubious approach; that soon turned to lack of appreciation or a lowered appreciation even of the best that may be there and to depreciation and censure of the rest.

But there is the other reason which is more effective. He sees and feels nothing of the spiritual meaning and the spiritual appeal which you find in *Savitri*; it is for him empty of anything but an outward significance and that seems to him poor, as is natural since the outward meaning is only a part and a surface and the rest is to his eyes invisible. If there had been what he hoped or might have hoped to find in my poetry, a spiritual vision such as that of the Vedantin, arriving beyond the world towards the Ineffable, then he might have felt at home as he does with Thompson's poetry or might at least have found it sufficiently accessible. But this is not what *Savitri* has to say or rather it is only a small part of it and, even so, bound up with a cosmic vision and an acceptance of the world which in its kind is unfamiliar to his mind and psychic sense and foreign to his experience. The two passages with which he deals do not and cannot give any full presentation of this way of seeing things since one is an unfamiliar symbol and the other an incidental and, taken by itself apart from its context, an isolated circumstance. But even if he had had other more explicit and clearly revealing passages at his disposal, I do not think he would have been satisfied or much illuminated; his eyes would still have been fixed on the surface and caught only some intellectual meaning or outer sense. That at least is what we may suppose to have been the cause of his failure, if we maintain that there is anything at all in the poem; or else we must fall back on the explanation of a fundamental personal incompatibility and the rule *de gustibus non est disputandum*, or to put it in the Sanskrit form *nānārucirhi lokaḥ*. If you are right in maintaining that *Savitri* stands as a new mystical poetry with a new vision and expression of things, we should expect, at least at first, a widespread, perhaps, a general failure even in lovers of poetry to understand it or appreciate; even those who have some mystical turn or spiritual experience are likely to pass it by if it is a different turn from theirs or outside their range of experience. It took the world something like a hundred years to discover Blake; it would not be improbable that there might be a greater time-lag here, though naturally we hope for better things. For in India at least some understanding or feeling and an audience few and fit may be possible. Perhaps by some miracle there may be before long a larger appreciative audience.

At any rate this is the only thing one can do, especially when one is attempting a new creation, to go on with the work with such light and power as is given to one and leave the value of the work to be determined by the future. Contemporary judgments we know to be unreliable; there are only two judges whose joint verdict cannot easily be disputed, the World and Time. The Roman proverb says, *securus judicat orbis terrarum*; but the world's verdict is secure only when it is confirmed by Time. For it is not the opinion of the general mass of men that finally decides, the decision is really imposed by the judgment of a minority and *élite* which is finally accepted and settles down as the verdict of posterity; in Tagore's phrase it is the universal man, *Viśva Mānava*, or rather something universal using the general mind of man, we might say the Cosmic Self in the race that fixes the value of its own works. In regard to the great names in literature this final verdict seems to have in it something of the absolute, — so far as anything can be that in a temporal world of relativities in which the Absolute reserves itself hidden behind the veil of human ignorance. It is no use for some to contend that Virgil is a tame and elegant writer of a wearisome work in verse on agriculture and a tedious pseudo-epic written to imperial order and Lucretius the only really great poet in Latin literature or to depreciate Milton for his Latin English and inflated style and the largely uninteresting character of his two epics; the world either refuses to listen or there is a temporary effect, a brief fashion in literary criticism, but finally the world returns to its established verdict. Lesser reputations may fluctuate, but finally whatever has real value in its own kind settles itself and finds its just place in the durable judgment of the world. Work which was neglected and left aside like Blake's or at first admired with reservation and eclipsed like Donne's is singled out by a sudden glance of Time and its greatness recognised; or what seemed buried slowly emerges or re-emerges; all finally settles into its place. What was held as sovereign in its own time is rudely dethroned but afterwards recovers not its sovereign throne but its due position in the world's esteem; Pope is an example and Byron who at once burst into a supreme glory and was the one English poet, after Shakespeare, admired all over Europe but is now depreciated, may also recover his proper place. Encouraged by such examples, let us hope that these violently adverse judgments may not be final and absolute and decide that the waste paper basket is not the proper place for *Savitri*. There may still be a place for a poetry which seeks to enlarge the field of poetic creation and find for the inner spiritual life of man and his now occult or mystical knowledge and experience of the whole hidden range of his and the world's being, not a corner and a limited expression such as it had in the past, but a wide space and as manifold and integral an expression of the boundless and innumerable riches that lie hidden and unexplored as if kept apart under the direct gaze of the Infinite as has been found in the past for man's surface and finite view and experience of himself and the material world in which he has lived striving to know himself and it as best he can with a limited mind and senses. The door that has been shut to all but a few may open; the kingdom of the Spirit may be established not only in man's inner being but in his life and his works. Poetry also may have its share in that revolution and become part of the spiritual empire.

I had intended as the main subject of this letter to say something about technique and the inner working of the intuitive method by which *Savitri* was and is being created and of the intention and plan of the poem. X's idea of its way of creation, an intellectual construction by a deliberate choice of words and imagery, badly chosen at that, is the very opposite of the real way in which it was done. That was to be the body of the letter and the rest only a preface. But the preface has become so long that it has crowded out the body. I shall have to postpone it to a later occasion when I have more time.

— 1947

6

Something more might need to be said in regard to the Overhead note in poetry and the Overmind aesthesis; but these are exactly the subjects on which it is difficult to write with any precision or satisfy the intellect's demand for clear and positive statement.

I do not know that it is possible for me to say why I regard one line or passage as having the Overhead touch or the Overhead note while another misses it. When I said that in the lines about the dying man [1] the touch came in through some intense passion and sincerity in the writer, I was simply mentioning the psychological door through which the thing came. I did not mean to suggest that such passion and sincerity could of itself bring in the touch or that they constituted the Overhead note in the lines. I am afraid I have to say what Arnold said about the grand style; it has to be felt and cannot be explained or accounted for. One has an intuitive feeling, a recognition of something familiar to one's experience or one's deeper perception in the substance and the rhythm or in one or the other which rings out and cannot be gainsaid. One might put forward a theory or a description of what the Overhead character of the line consists in, but it is doubtful whether any such mentally constructed definition could be always applicable. You speak, for instance, of the sense of the Infinite and the One which is pervasive in the Overhead planes; that need not be explicitly there in the Overhead poetic expression or in the substance of any given line: it can be expressed indeed by Overhead poetry as no other can express it, but this poetry can deal with quite other things. I would certainly say that Shakespeare's lines

Absent thee from felicity awhile,
And in this harsh world draw thy breath in pain [2]

have the Overhead touch in the substance, the rhythm and the feeling; but Shakespeare is not giving us here the sense of the One and the Infinite. He is, as in the other lines of his which have this note, dealing as he always does with life, with vital emotions and reactions or the thoughts that spring out in the life-mind under the pressure of life. It is not any strict adhesion to a transcendental view of things that constitutes this kind of poetry, but something

[1] See p. 747. [2] *Hamlet*, V.ii.

behind not belonging to the mind or the vital and physical consciousness and with that a certain quality or power in the language and the rhythm which helps to bring out that deeper something. If I had to select the line in European poetry which most suggests an almost direct descent from the Overmind consciousness there might come first Virgil's line about "the touch of tears in mortal things":

Sunt lacrimae rerum et mentem mortalia tangunt.[1]

Another might be Shakespeare's

In the dark backward and abysm of Time[2]

or again Milton's

Those thoughts that wander through eternity.[3]

We might also add Wordsworth's line

The winds come to me from the fields of sleep.[4]

There are other lines ideative and more emotional or simply descriptive which might be added, such as Marlowe's

Was this the face that launched a thousand ships,
And burnt the topless towers of Ilium?[5]

If we could extract and describe the quality and the subtle something that mark the language and rhythm and feeling of these lines and underlie their substance we might attain hazardously to some mental understanding of the nature of Overhead poetry.

  The Overmind is not strictly a transcendental consciousness— that epithet would more accurately apply to the supramental and to the Sachchidananda consciousness—though it looks up to the transcendental and may receive something from it and though it does transcend the ordinary human mind and in its full and native self-power, when it does not lean down and become part of mind, is

---

[1] *Aeneid*, I.462. [2] *The Tempest*, I.ii. [3] *Paradise Lost*, II.148.
[4] *Ode on the Intimations of Immortality*, iii. [5] *Doctor Faustus*, V.i.

superconscient to us. It is more properly a cosmic consciousness, even the very base of the cosmic as we perceive, understand or feel it. It stands behind every particular in the cosmos and is the source of all our mental, vital or physical actualities and possibilities which are diminished and degraded derivations and variations from it and have not, except in certain formations and activities of genius and some intense self-exceeding, anything of the native Overmind quality and power. Nevertheless, because it stands behind as if covered by a veil, something of it can break through or shine through or even only dimly glimmer through and that brings the Overmind touch or note. We cannot get this touch frequently unless we have torn the veil, made a gap in it or rent it largely away and seen the very face of what is beyond, lived in the light of it or established some kind of constant intercourse. Or we can draw upon it from time to time without ever ascending into it if we have established a line of communication between the higher and the ordinary consciousness. What comes down may be very much diminished but it has something of that. The ordinary reader of poetry who has not that experience will usually not be able to distinguish but would at the most feel that here is something extraordinarily fine, profound, sublime or unusual, — or he might turn away from it as something too high-pitched and excessive; he might even speak depreciatingly of "purple passages", rhetoric, exaggeration or excess. One who had the line of communication open could on the other hand feel what is there and distinguish even if he could not adequately characterise or describe it. The essential character is perhaps that there is something behind of which I have already spoken and which comes not primarily from the mind or the vital emotion or the physical seeing but from the cosmic self and its consciousness standing behind them all and things then tend to be seen not as the mind or heart or body sees them but as this greater consciousness feels or sees or answers to them. In the direct Overmind transmission this something behind is usually forced to the front or close to the front by a combination of words which carries the suggestion of a deeper meaning or by the force of an image or, most of all, by an intonation and a rhythm which carry up the depths in their wide wash or long march or mounting surge. Sometimes it is left lurking behind and only suggested so that a subtle feeling of what is not actually expressed is needed if the reader is not to miss it. This is oftenest the case when there is just a touch or note pressed upon something that would be otherwise only of a mental, vital or physical poetic value and nothing of the body of the Overhead power shows itself through the veil, but at most a tremor and vibration, a gleam or a glimpse. In the lines I have chosen there is always an unusual quality in the rhythm, as prominently in Virgil's line, often in the very building and constantly in the intonation and the association of the sounds which meet in the line and find themselves linked together by a sort of inevitable felicity. There is also an inspired selection or an unusual bringing together of words which has the power to force a deeper sense on the mind as in Virgil's

Sunt lacrimae rerum.

One can note that this line if translated straight into English would sound awkward and clumsy as would many of the finest lines in Rig Veda; that is precisely because they are new and felicitous turns in the original language, discoveries of an unexpected and absolute phrase; they defy translation. If you note the combination of words and sounds in Shakespeare's line

And in this harsh world draw thy breath in pain

so arranged as to force on the mind and still more on the subtle nerves and sense the utter absoluteness of the difficulty and pain of living for the soul that has awakened to the misery of the world, you can see how this technique works. Here and elsewhere the very body and soul of the thing seen or felt come out into the open. The same dominant characteristic can be found in other lines which I have not cited, — in Leopardi's

L'insano indegno mistero delle cose[1]
(The insane and ignoble mystery of things)

or in Wordsworth's

_____
[1] *Le Ricordanze*, 71–72. Leopardi's original has one different word and is spread over parts of two lines:

l'acerbo indegno
Mistero delle cose...

Voyaging through strange seas of thought, alone.[1]

Milton's line lives by its choice of the word "wander" to collocate with "through eternity"; if he had chosen any other word, it would no longer have been an Overhead line, even if the surface sense had been exactly the same. On the other hand, take Shelley's stanza —

> We look before and after,
>   And pine for what is not:
> Our sincerest laughter
>   With some pain is fraught;
> Our sweetest songs are those that tell of saddest thought.[2]

This is perfect poetry with the most exquisite melody and beauty of wording and an unsurpassable poignancy of pathos, but there is no touch or note of the Overhead inspiration: it is the mind and the heart, the vital emotion, working at their highest pitch under the stress of a psychic inspiration. The rhythm is of the same character, a direct, straightforward, lucid and lucent movement welling out limpidly straight from the psychic source. The same characteristics are found in another short lyric of Shelley's which is perhaps the purest example of the psychic inspiration in English poetry:

> I can give not what men call love;
>   But wilt thou accept not
> The worship the heart lifts above
>   And the Heavens reject not, —
>
> The desire of the moth for the star,
>   Of the night for the morrow,
> The devotion to something afar
>   From the sphere of our sorrow?[3]

We have again extreme poetic beauty there, but nothing of the Overhead note.

In the other lines I have cited it is really the Overmind language and rhythm that have been to some extent transmitted; but of course all Overhead poetry is not from the Overmind, more

---

[1] *The Prelude*, III.63.   [2] *To a Skylark*.   [3] "One word is too often profaned".

often it comes from the Higher Thought, the Illumined Mind or the pure Intuition. This last is different from the mental intuition which is frequent enough in poetry that does not transcend the mental level. The language and rhythm from these other Overhead levels/ can be very different from that which is proper to the Overmind; for the Overmind thinks in a mass; its thought, feeling, vision is high or deep or wide or all these things together: to use the Vedic expression about fire, the divine messenger, it goes vast on its way to bring the divine riches, and it has a corresponding language and rhythm. The Higher Thought has a strong tread often with bare unsandalled feet and moves in a clear-cut light: a divine power, measure, dignity is its most frequent character. The outflow of the Illumined Mind comes in a flood brilliant with revealing words or a light of crowding images, sometimes surcharged with its burden of revelations, sometimes with a luminous sweep. The Intuition is usually a lightning flash showing up a single spot or plot of ground or scene with an entire and miraculous completeness of vision to the surprised ecstasy of the inner eye; its rhythm has a decisive inevitable sound which leaves nothing essential unheard, but very commonly is embodied in a single stroke. These, however, are only general or dominant characters; any number of variations is possible. There are besides mingled inspirations, several levels meeting and combining or modifying each other's notes, and an Overmind transmission can contain or bring with it all the rest, but how much of this description will be to the ordinary reader of poetry at all intelligible or clearly identifiable?

There are besides in mental poetry derivations or substitutes for all these styles. Milton's "grand style" is such a substitute for the manner of the Higher Thought. Take it anywhere at its ordinary level or in its higher elevation, there is always or almost always that echo there:

> Of man's first disobedience, and the fruit
> Of that forbidden tree [1]

or

> On evil days though fall'n, and evil tongues [2]

---

[1] *Paradise Lost*, I.1–2.   [2] *Ibid.*, VII.26.

or

> Blind Thamyris and blind Maeonides,
> And Tiresias and Phineus, prophets old.[1]

Shakespeare's poetry coruscates with a play of the hues of imagination which we may regard as a mental substitute for the inspiration of the Illumined Mind and sometimes by aiming at an exalted note he links on to the illumined Overhead inspiration itself as in the lines I have more than once quoted:

> Wilt thou upon the high and giddy mast
> Seal up the shipboy's eyes and rock his brains
> In cradle of the rude imperious surge?[2]

But the rest of that passage falls away in spite of its high-pitched language and resonant rhythm far below the Overhead strain. So it is easy for the mind to mistake and take the higher for the lower inspiration or *vice versa*. Thus Milton's lines might at first sight be taken because of a certain depth of emotion in their large lingering rhythm as having the Overhead complexion, but this rhythm loses something of its sovereign right because there are no depths of sense behind it. It conveys nothing but the noble and dignified pathos of the blindness and old age of a great personality fallen into evil days. Milton's architecture of thought and verse is high and powerful and massive, but there are usually no subtle echoes there, no deep chambers: the occult things in man's being are foreign to his intelligence, — for it is in the light of the poetic intelligence that he works. He does not stray into "the mystic cavern of the heart", does not follow the inner fire entering like a thief with the Cow of Light into the secrecy of secrecies. Shakespeare does sometimes get in as if by a splendid psychic accident in spite of his preoccupation with the colours and shows of life.

I do not know therefore whether I can speak with any certainty about the lines you quote; I would perhaps have to read them in their context first, but it seems to me that there is just a touch, as in the lines about the dying man. The thing that is described there may have happened often enough in times like those of the recent

---

[1] *Ibid.*, III.35–36.   [2] *2 Henry IV*, III.i.

wars and upheavals and in times of violent strife and persecution and catastrophe, but the greatness of the experience does not come out or not wholly, because men feel with the mind and heart and not with the soul; but here there is by some accident of wording and rhythm a suggestion of something behind, of the greatness of the soul's experience and its courageous acceptance of the tragic, the final, the fatal — and its resistance; it is only just a suggestion, but it is enough: the Overhead has touched and passed back to its heights. There is something very different but of the same essential calibre in the line you quote:

Sad eyes watch for feet that never come.

It is still more difficult to say anything very tangible about the Overmind aesthesis. When I wrote about it I was thinking of the static aesthesis that perceives and receives rather than of the dynamic aesthesis which creates; I was not thinking at all of superior or inferior grades of poetic greatness or beauty. If the complete Overmind power or even that of the lower Overhead planes could come down into the mind and entirely transform its action, then no doubt there might be greater poetry written than any that man has yet achieved, just as a greater superhuman life might be created if the Supermind could come down wholly into life and lift life wholly into itself and transform it. But what happens at present is that something comes down and accepts to work under the law of the mind and with a mixture of the mind and it must be judged by the laws and standards of the mind. It brings in new tones, new colours, new elements, but it does not change radically as yet the stuff of the consciousness with which we labour.

Whether it produces great poetry or not depends on the extent to which it manifests its power and overrides rather than serves the mentality which it is helping. At present it does not do that sufficiently to raise the work to the full greatness of the worker.

And then what do you mean exactly by greatness in poetry? One can say that Virgil is greater than Catullus and that many of Virgil's lines are greater than anything Catullus ever achieved. But poetical perfection is not the same thing as poetical greatness. Virgil is perfect at his best, but Catullus too is perfect at his best: even each has a certain exquisiteness of perfection, each in his own kind. Virgil's kind is large and deep, that of Catullus sweet and intense. Virgil's art reached or had from its beginning a greater and more constant ripeness than that of Catullus. We can say then that Virgil was a greater poet and artist of word and rhythm but we cannot say that his poetry, at his best, was more perfect poetry and that of Catullus less perfect. That renders futile many of the attempts at comparison like Arnold's comparison of Wordsworth's *Skylark* with Shelley's. You may say that Milton was a greater poet than Blake, but there can always be people, not aesthetically insensitive, who would prefer Blake's lyrical work to Milton's grander achievement, and there are certainly things in Blake which touch deeper chords than the massive hand of Milton could ever reach. So all poetic superiority is not summed up in the word greatness. Each kind has its own best which escapes from comparison and stands apart in its own value.

Let us then leave for the present the question of poetic greatness or superiority aside and come back to the Overmind aesthesis. By aesthesis is meant a reaction of the consciousness, mental and vital and even bodily, which receives a certain element in things, something that can be called their taste, Rasa, which, passing through the mind or sense or both, awakes a vital enjoyment of the taste, Bhoga, and this can again awaken us, awaken even the soul in us to something yet deeper and more fundamental than mere pleasure and enjoyment, to some form of the spirit's delight of existence, Ananda. Poetry, like all art, serves the seeking for these things, this aesthesis, this Rasa, Bhoga, Ananda; it brings us a Rasa of word and sound but also of the idea and, through the idea, of the things expressed by the word and sound and thought, a mental or vital or sometimes the spiritual image of their form, quality, impact upon us or even, if the poet is strong enough, of their world-essence, their cosmic reality, the very soul of them, the spirit that resides in them as it resides in all things. Poetry may do more than this, but this at least it must do to however small an extent or it is not poetry. Aesthesis therefore is of the very essence of poetry, as it is of all art. But it is not the sole element and aesthesis too is not confined to a reception of poetry and art; it extends to everything in the world: there is nothing we can sense, think or in any way experience to which there cannot be an aesthetic reaction of our conscious being. Ordinarily, we suppose that aesthesis is concerned with beauty, and that indeed is its most prominent concern: but it is concerned with many other things also. It is the universal Ananda that is the parent of aesthesis and the universal Ananda takes three major and original forms, beauty, love and delight, the delight of all existence, the delight in things, in all things. Universal Ananda is the artist and creator of the universe witnessing, experiencing and taking joy in its creation. In the lower consciousness it creates its opposites, the sense of ugliness as well as the sense of beauty, hate and repulsion and dislike as well as love and attraction and liking, grief and pain as well as joy and delight; and between these dualities or as a grey tint in the background there is a general tone of neutrality and indifference born from the universal insensibility into which the Ananda sinks in its dark negation in the Inconscient. All this is the sphere of aesthesis, its dullest reaction is indifference, its highest is ecstasy. Ecstasy is a sign of a return towards the original or supreme Ananda: that art or poetry is supreme which can bring us something of the supreme tone of ecstasy. For as the consciousness sinks from the supreme levels through various degrees towards the Inconscience the general sign of this descent is an always diminishing power of its intensity, intensity of being, intensity of consciousness, intensity of force, intensity of the delight in things and the delight of existence. So too as we ascend towards the supreme level, these intensities increase. As we climb beyond Mind, higher and wider values replace the values of our limited mind, life and bodily consciousness. Aesthesis shares in this intensification of capacity. The capacity for pleasure and pain, for liking and disliking is comparatively poor on the level of our mind and life; our capacity for ecstasy is brief and limited; these tones arise from a general ground of neutrality which is always dragging them back towards itself. As it enters the Overhead planes the ordinary aesthesis turns into a pure delight and becomes capable of a high, a large or a deep abiding ecstasy. The ground is no longer a general neutrality, but a pure spiritual ease and happiness upon which the special tones of the aesthetic consciousness come out or from which they arise. This is the first fundamental change.

Another change in this transition is a turn towards universality in place of the isolations, the conflicting generalities, the mutually opposing dualities of the lower consciousness. In the Overmind we have a first firm foundation of the experience of a universal beauty, a universal love, a universal delight. These things can come on the mental and vital plane even before those planes are directly touched or influenced by the spiritual consciousness; but they are there a temporary experience and not permanent or they are limited in their field and do not touch the whole being. They are a glimpse and not a change of vision or a change of nature. The artist for instance can look at things only plain or shabby or ugly or even repulsive to the ordinary sense and see in them and bring out of them beauty and the delight that goes with beauty. But this is a sort of special grace for the artistic consciousness and is limited within the field of his art. In the Overhead consciousness, especially in the Overmind, these things become more and more the law of the vision and the law of the nature. Wherever the Overmind spiritual man turns he sees a universal beauty touching and uplifting all things, expressing itself through them, moulding them into a field or objects of its divine aesthesis; a universal love goes out from him to all beings; he feels the Bliss which has created the worlds and upholds them and all that is expresses to him the universal delight, is made of it, is a manifestation of it and moulded into its image. This universal aesthesis of beauty and delight does not ignore or fail to understand the differences and oppositions, the gradations, the harmony and disharmony obvious to the ordinary consciousness; but, first of all, it draws a Rasa from them and with that comes the enjoyment, Bhoga, and the touch or the mass of the Ananda. It sees that all things have their meaning, their value, their deeper or total significance which the mind does not see, for the mind is only concerned with a surface vision, surface contacts and its own surface reactions. When something expresses perfectly what it was meant to express, the completeness brings with it a sense of harmony, a sense of artistic perfection; it gives even to what is discordant a place in a system of cosmic concordances and the discords become part of a vast harmony, and wherever there is harmony, there is a sense of beauty. Even in form itself, apart from the significance, the Overmind consciousness sees the object with a totality which changes its effect on the percipient even while it remains the same thing. It sees lines and masses and an underlying design which the physical eye does not see and which escapes even the keenest mental vision. Every form becomes beautiful to it in a deeper and larger sense of beauty than that commonly known to us. The Overmind looks also straight at and into the soul of each thing and not only at its form or its significance to the mind or to the life; this brings to it not only the true truth of the thing but the delight of it. It sees also the one spirit in all, the face of the Divine everywhere and there can be no greater Ananda than that; it feels oneness with all, sympathy, love, the bliss of the Brahman. In a highest, a most integral experience it sees all things as if made of existence, consciousness, power, bliss, every atom of them charged with and constituted of Sachchidananda. In all this the Overmind aesthesis takes its share and gives its response; for these things come not merely as an idea in the mind or a truth-seeing but as an experience of the whole being and a total response is not only possible but above a certain level imperative.

I have said that aesthesis responds not only to what we call beauty and beautiful things but to all things. We make a distinction between truth and beauty; but there can be an aesthetic response to truth also, a joy in its beauty, a love created by its charm, a rapture in the finding, a passion in the embrace, an aesthetic joy in its expression, a satisfaction of love in the giving of it to others. Truth is not merely a dry statement of facts or ideas to or by the intellect; it can be a splendid discovery, a rapturous revelation, a thing of beauty that is a joy for ever. The poet also can be a seeker and lover of truth as well as a seeker and lover of beauty. He can feel a poetic and aesthetic joy in the expression of the true as well as in the expression of the beautiful. He does not make a mere intellectual or philosophical statement of the truth; it is his vision of its beauty, its power, his thrilled reception of it, his joy in it that he tries to convey by an utmost perfection in word and rhythm. If he has the passion, then even a philosophical statement of it he can surcharge with this sense of power, force, light, beauty. On certain levels of the Overmind, where the mind element predominates over the element of gnosis, the distinction between truth and beauty is still valid. It is indeed one of the chief functions of the Overmind to separate the main powers of the consciousness and give to each its full separate development and satisfaction, bring out its utmost potency and meaning, its own soul and significant body and take it on its own way as far as it can go. It can take up each power of man and give it its full potentiality, its highest characteristic development. It can give to intellect its austerest intellectuality and to logic its most sheer unsparing logicality. It can give to beauty its most splendid passion of luminous form and the consciousness that receives it a supreme height and depth of ecstasy. It can create a sheer and pure poetry impossible for the intellect to sound to its depths or wholly grasp, much less to mentalise and analyse. It is the function of Overmind to give to every possibility its full potential, its own separate kingdom. But also there is another action of Overmind which sees and thinks and creates in masses, which reunites separated things, which reconciles opposites. On that level truth and beauty not only become constant companions but become one, involved in each other, inseparable: on that level the true is always beautiful and the beautiful is always true. Their highest fusion perhaps only takes place in the Supermind; but Overmind on its summits draws enough of the supramental light to see what the Supermind sees and do what the Supermind does though in a lower key and with a less absolute truth and power. On an inferior level Overmind may use the language of the intellect to convey as far as that language can do it its own greater meaning and message but on its summits Overmind uses its own native language and gives to its truths their own supreme utterance, and no intellectual speech, no mentalised poetry can equal or even come near to that power and beauty. Here your intellectual dictum that poetry lives by its aesthetic quality alone and has no need of truth or that truth must depend upon aesthetics to become poetic at all, has no longer any meaning. For there truth itself is highest poetry and has only to appear to be utterly beautiful to the vision, the hearing, the sensibility of the soul. There dwells and from there springs the mystery of the inevitable word, the supreme immortal rhythm, the absolute significance and the absolute utterance.

I hope you do not feel crushed under this avalanche of metaphysical psychology; you have called it upon yourself by your questioning about the Overmind's greater, larger and deeper aesthesis. What I have written is indeed very scanty and sketchy, only some of the few essential things that have to be said; but without it I could not try to give you any glimpse of the meaning of my phrase. This greater aesthesis is inseparable from the greater truth, it is deeper because of the depth of that truth, larger by all its immense largeness. I do not expect the reader of poetry to come anywhere near to all that, he could not without being a Yogi or at least a sadhak: but just as the Overhead poetry brings some touch of a deeper power of vision and creation into the mind without belonging itself wholly to the higher reaches, so also the full appreciation of all its burden needs at least some touch of a deeper response of the mind and some touch of a deeper aesthesis. Until that becomes general the Overhead or at least the Overmind is not going to do more than to touch here and there, as it did in the past, a few lines, a few passages, or perhaps as things advance, a little more, nor is it likely to pour into our utterance its own complete power and absolute value.

I have said that Overhead poetry is not necessarily greater or more perfect than any other kind of poetry. But perhaps a subtle qualification may be made to this statement. It is true that each kind of poetical writing can reach a highest or perfect perfection in its own line and in its own quality and what can be more perfect than a perfect perfection or can we say that one kind of absolute perfection is "greater" than another kind? What can be more absolute than the absolute? But then what do we mean by the perfection of poetry? There is the perfection of the language and there is the perfection of the word-music and the rhythm, beauty of speech and beauty of sound, but there is also the quality of the thing said which counts for something. If we consider only word and sound and what in themselves they evoke, we arrive at the application of the theory of art for art's sake to poetry. On that ground we might say that a lyric of Anacreon is as good poetry and as perfect poetry as anything in Aeschylus or Sophocles or Homer. The question of the elevation or depth or intrinsic beauty of the thing said cannot then enter into our consideration of poetry; and yet it does enter, with most of us at any rate, and is part of the aesthetic reaction even in the most "aesthetic" of critics and readers. From this point of view the elevation from which the inspiration comes may after all matter, provided the one who receives it is a fit and powerful instrument; for a great poet will do more with a lower level of the origin of inspiration than a smaller poet can do even when helped from the highest sources. In a certain sense all genius comes from Overhead; for genius is the entry or inrush of a greater consciousness into the mind or a possession of the mind by a greater power. Every operation of genius has at its back or infused within it an intuition, a revelation, an inspiration, an illumination or at the least a hint or touch or influx from some greater power or level of conscious being than those which men ordinarily possess or use. But this power has two ways of acting: in one it touches the ordinary modes of mind and deepens, heightens, intensifies or exquisitely refines their action but without changing its modes or transforming its normal character; in the other it brings down into these normal modes something of itself, something supernormal, something which one at once feels to be extraordinary and suggestive of a superhuman level. These two ways of action when working in poetry may produce things equally exquisite and beautiful, but the word "greater" may perhaps be applied, with the necessary qualifications, to the second way and its too rare poetic creation.

The great bulk of the highest poetry belongs to the first of these two orders. In the second order there are again two or perhaps three levels; sometimes a felicitous turn or an unusual force of language or a deeper note of feeling brings in the Overhead touch. More often it is the power of the rhythm that lifts up language that is simple and common or a feeling or idea that has often been expressed and awakes something which is not ordinarily there. If one listens with the mind only or from the vital centre only, one may have a wondering admiration for the skill and beauty of woven word and sound or be struck by the happy way or the power with which the feeling or idea is expressed. But there is something more in it than that; it is this that a deeper, more inward strand of the consciousness has seen and is speaking, and if we listen more profoundly we can get something more than the admiration and delight of the mind or Housman's thrill of the solar plexus. We can feel perhaps the Spirit of the universe lending its own depth to our mortal speech or listening from behind to some expression of itself, listening perhaps to its memories of

> Old, unhappy, far-off things
> And battles long ago[1]

or feeling and hearing, it may be said, the vast oceanic stillness and the cry of the cuckoo

> Breaking the silence of the seas
> Among the farthest Hebrides[2]

or it may enter again into Vyasa's

> "A void and dreadful forest ringing with the crickets' cry"

---

[1] Wordsworth, *The Solitary Reaper.*   [2] *Ibid.*

Vanaṁ pratibhayaṁ śūnyaṁ jhillikāgaṇanāditam.[1]

or remember its call to the soul of man,

Anityam asukhaṁ lokam imaṁ prāpya bhajasva mām[2]
"Thou who hast come to this transient and unhappy world,
love and worship Me."

There is a second level on which the poetry draws into itself a fuller
language of intuitive inspiration, illumination or the higher think-
ing and feeling. A very rich or great poetry may then emerge and
many of the most powerful passages in Shakespeare, Virgil or
Lucretius or the Mahabharata and Ramayana, not to speak of the
Gita, the Upanishads or the Rig Veda, have this inspiration. It is a
poetry "thick inlaid with patines of bright gold" or welling up in a
stream of passion, beauty and force. But sometimes there comes
down a supreme voice, the Overmind voice and the Overmind
music and it is to be observed that the lines and passages where that
happens rank among the greatest and most admired in all poetic
literature. It would be therefore too much to say that the Overhead
inspiration cannot bring in a greatness into poetry which could
surpass the other levels of inspiration, greater even from the purely
aesthetic point of view and certainly greater in the power of its
substance.

A conscious attempt to write Overhead poetry with a mind
aware of the planes from which this inspiration comes and seeking
always to ascend to those levels or bring down something from
them, would probably result in a partial success; at its lowest it
might attain to what I have called the first order, ordinarily it would
achieve the two lower levels of the second order and in its supreme
moments it might in lines and in sustained passages achieve the
supreme level, something of the highest summit of its potency. But
its greatest work will be to express adequately and constantly what
is now only occasionally and inadequately some kind of utterance
of the things above, the things beyond, the things behind the
apparent world and its external or superficial happenings and phe-
nomena. It would not only bring in the occult in its larger and
deeper ranges but the truths of the spiritual heights, the spiritual

---

[1] *Mahabharata*, Vana Parva, 64.1.   [2] *Bhagavadgita*, 9.33.

depths, the spiritual intimacies and vastnesses as also the truths of the inner mind, the inner life, an inner or subtle physical beauty and reality. It would bring in the concreteness, the authentic image, the inmost soul of identity and the heart of meaning of these things, so that it could never lack in beauty. If this could be achieved by one possessed, if not of a supreme, still of a sufficiently high and wide poetic genius, something new could be added to the domain of poetry and there would be no danger of the power of poetry beginning to fade, to fall into decadence, to fail us. It might even enter into the domain of the infinite and inexhaustible, catch some word of the Ineffable, show us revealing images which bring us near to the Reality that is secret in us and in all, of which the Upanishad speaks,

> *Anejad ekaṁ manaso javīyo nainad devā āpnuvan pūrvam arṣat....*
> *Tad ejati tan naijati tad dūre tad u antike.*[1]
> "The One unmoving is swifter than thought, the gods cannot overtake It, for It travels ever in front; It moves and It moves not, It is far away from us and It is very close."

The gods of the Overhead planes can do much to bridge that distance and to bring out that closeness, even if they cannot altogether overtake the Reality that exceeds and transcends them.

—1946

---

[1] *Isha Upanishad,* 5.

OTHER TITLES BY SRI AUROBINDO

Bases of Yoga (New U.S. Edition)	p	6.95
Dictionary of Sri Aurobindo's Yoga (compiled)	p	11.95
Essays on the Gita	p	16.50
Gems from Sri Aurobindo, 1st Series (compiled)	p	8.95
Gems from Sri Aurobindo, 2nd Series (compiled)	p	12.95
Growing Within	p	9.95
Hymns to the Mystic Fire	p	22.50
Integral Yoga: Sri Aurobindo's Teaching and Method of Practice (compiled)	p	14.95
The Life Divine	p	29.95
	hb	39.95
Lights on Yoga	p	2.95
Living Within (compiled)	p	8.95
The Mother	p	2.95
A Practical Guide to Integral Yoga (compiled)	p	7.95
The Psychic Being: Soul in Evolution (compiled)	p	8.95
Rebirth and Karma	p	9.95
Savitri: A Legend and a Symbol	p	24.95
The Secret of the Veda	p	15.00
The Synthesis of Yoga	p	29.95
	hb	34.95
The Upanishads	p	16.50
Vedic Symbolism (compiled)	p	6.95
Wisdom of the Gita, 2nd Series (compiled)	p	10.95
Wisdom of the Upanishads (compiled)	p	7.95

available from your local bookseller or
LOTUS LIGHT PUBLICATIONS
Box 325, Twin Lakes, WI 53181
USA
414/889-8561